SYSTEMS OUT OF BALANCE:

How Misinformation Hurts the Middle Class

To Ann,
A Fellow Norfolk native, wishing
you the best.

SYSTEMS OUT OF BALANCE:

How Misinformation Hurts the Middle Class

KIRK D. SINCLAIR, PhD

MILL CITY PRESS
MINNEAPOLIS, MINNESOTA

TABLE OF CONTENTS

ESSAY 1 – GREED OR MERIT

Overview

- Wealth is created through trade.
- Trade is enhanced through specialization, innovation, hype and control.
- Vanity, cynicism and apprehension cause desire for excessive wealth.
- Misinformation has linked happiness to greed.
- Good information meets standards of validity and reliability.
- A lack of want, known as affluence, contributes to happiness.
- The middle class benefits from free markets determining economic merit.
- *Laissez faire* economics, combined with business corporations, replaces free markets with an economic system devoted to greed.
- Faulty *laissez faire* logic and misinformation persuades the many to endorse a greed-based system that benefits the few.

Wealth And Trade

As defined by economists, the standard of living has more than doubled since my parents first came to this house on Emerson Street. Without such good fortune the middle class family currently in residence here would be in tough shape. The ratio of housing costs to median family income has skyrocketed, but who can complain as long as the stock market has increased tenfold over the past 30 years.[1] Tuition for college has gone through the roof over that same period of time, but that's a trivial concern given the dramatic increase in our Gross Domestic Product (GDP) that reflects the country's overall productivity of goods. Health care costs have become prohibitive for many, but the important thing is we remain the wealthiest nation on earth. Many economic indicators might concern middle class America—from the increasing amount of debt to the amount of work needed from a family unit to pay off that debt—but corporate media keeps things in proper perspective for the country. News regarding an increase of uninsured Americans may get one or two day's coverage tops, but we are provided the important stock market indicators daily.

      While the middle class may benefit psychologically by being spared the more depressing economic news affecting us, we run the risk of behaving like

---

1 To enhance the readability of these essays most of the number crunching is done only in "Essay 7 – An Economic Report Card."

1

"Hans in Luck," introduced to you in the prologue.[2] Hans works hard for seven years and earns a lump of gold which he intends to bring home to Mom. The lump gets heavy during his walk but "lucky" Hans is able to trade the gold for a horse to ride. The horse gives Hans a rough ride, but his continued "good fortune" allows him to trade a fine horse for a dried up cow. This trading continues, with Hans counting his blessings at every turn, until he is left with only a couple of stones. These fall into a well, relieving Hans of their burdensome weight. Hans arrives back at his mother's home with nothing to show for seven years of work, and still marveling on his good luck.

You may not think this fable relates to why our standard of living has doubled, but that is why we have economists. Trade creates wealth according to the economist. If you trade your gizmo for my gadget, presumably we both do so for personal gain. The value we place on our new possessions has increased, thus, so has our wealth. The man who took the huge lump of gold from Hans was better off, but so was Hans, as he considered the trade to have increased his good fortune. As Hans kept trading down he kept feeling fortunate about his trades, making him wealthier—by the definition used by economists—when he ended up with stones than when he had a bag of gold.

Now there's a lesson in positive thinking. Middle class America need not bemoan the increased difficulties of owning our own home, putting our kids through college, getting health insurance and attempting to save. As long as those extra hours worked by the average family contribute to increased wealth through trade our standard of living increases, indeed, doubles. The GDP be praised!

Still, given the choice between essential but expensive items being affordable on the one hand, and owning lots of mass-produced stuff on the other, many of us in the middle class would prefer the greater affordability of essential items. What we have been misinformed about is that there are choices to be made. Like the gullible Hans we have succumbed to the lure of persuasive forces that have figuratively caused us to "trade down," while thinking our situation has improved. The most fundamental of these choices is whether our market economy should be driven by greed or merit in the pursuit of happiness.

Increasing Wealth

If standards of living depend on wealth, and wealth depends on trade, then whatever boosts trade must also boost our standard of living. Good quality and large quantities of the things we need contribute to trade value, yet if the middle class only valued stuff we needed, particularly of fine quality, we would trade significantly less money for goods than we currently do. This would depress the

---

2 Few would conclude we have been spared depressing economic news of late. *Systems out of Balance* was a four year project, with the economic essays first crafted in 2006. As written they were a foretelling, not a reaction, to what was to come in the fall of 2008.

economy. The GDP increases dramatically when we value and obtain lots of stuff we want but don't need. Value and trade are enhanced by one or more of the following: specialization, innovation, hype and control.

Trade value starts with specialization. I specialize in growing lima beans, you in growing corn. We value each other's produce, make a trade and, voila, we both can eat succotash. Our society has taken specialization to an impressive level. One company makes aluminum foil, one company makes cardboard, one company makes ink, one company provides refrigerated transport, one company provides advertising, one company provides media access and one or two agribusinesses provide lima beans and corn. Now we can purchase succotash as a frozen TV dinner, creating wealth from many value-laden trades along the way.

Innovative goods or services enhance value and create incentives for continued trade. Some of these innovations may be substantive technological advancements, while others affect only style. Keeping a reliable car for ten years or more may provide a certain peace of mind for the owner, but dampens the economy. Trading in every three years contributes significantly more to our Gross Domestic Product (GDP) and the standard of living. The only thing innovative about the car may be a stylish new look, but this alone can enhance the value needed to warrant more trade and, consequently, more wealth.

Stylish innovations are much like another mechanism for increasing trade value, hype. When considering the role of hype in wealth-generating trade, we need to distinguish between value and necessity. Something has value simply from being wanted; necessity plays a limited role. For example, star athletes and entertainers are multimillionaires for labor that is not essential to anybody's needs. They attain huge value from all the hype given them in the media. On the other hand, air is absolutely necessary but has no value, since air is not a commodity that can be traded. Hyping air provides no economic return unless, in the future, a premium can be attached to clean air.

The control of goods and services also enhances value. The unique athleticism of star athletes allows them to control their market. Water once was as valueless as air; now clean water is controlled and delivered through a tap. The extra control involved in bottled water attaches even greater value, to the point where bottled water is more expensive than gasoline (at least at this current moment). A monopoly in the control of goods or services can increase value way out of proportion to actual worth; for this reason regulations are developed to prevent monopolies.

Since scarce resources can be controlled better than bountiful resources, they boost wealth more. If you obtained sufficient energy for your needs directly from an infinite resource like the sun, you would not need to continually trade much money for energy. Ah, but obtain your energy from a finite resource controlled by a few large corporations, like oil for example, and now you have something that can really stimulate an economy. The ability to dominate the extraction and production of an energy source means greater value for trade. Greater value in trade translates to a higher GDP and a higher standard of living. Why should investors concern themselves with making homes easier to afford for the middle class, by stimulating the development of local renewable energy sources with their investments, when their profit returns and our standard of living could be increased more by government commanded advantages for fossil fuels and nuclear power plants?

Materialism And Want

In addition to the basic methods for increasing value, we need to consider the basic motives behind increased want. The phrase "keeping up with the Joneses" comes to mind in describing the purchase of goods people otherwise would not want. Granted, perhaps only a few are obsessed with "keeping up with the Joneses." Yet virtually all of us with some disposable income, including the author, have succumbed at some point to this affliction, being "played" by a corporate culture. Let us explore what goes through the mind of Mr. Smith, a man who does not even like to swim, when Mr. Jones builds a new swimming pool.

Cynicism lays the foundation for Mr. Smith to covet Mr. Jones's new swimming pool. We will uncover the meaning of cynicism in our society more fully throughout these essays, but for now let us define cynicism as a lack of faith in anything that transcends the self. Materialism is the default value system for the cynical, though individualism ranks a close second. Mr. Smith gains insufficient happiness from merely having a good family in a supportive neighborhood. He covets the material possessions of others to fill a void created by cynicism. Mr. Smith seeks to keep up with Mr. Jones because he has no faith in any other guidepost for what might bring happiness besides indulging himself.

Vanity contributes to Mr. Smith's motivation to keep up with Mr. Jones. Unlike having a good family, material possessions confer status. Mr. Smith feels that his worldly success should be no less esteemed throughout the neighborhood than his neighbor Mr. Jones. Even though he doesn't even care for swimming that much, he wants to be at least on a par with that insufferable Mr. Jones in terms of material success.

Apprehension seals the deal in motivating Mr. Smith to keep up with Mr. Jones. When Mr. Smith witnesses the good times the Jones family seems to be having with their swimming pool, he is apprehensive that his family is missing out on the fun. Never mind that there are countless ways to have fun and he does not like to swim, Mr. Smith worries that his family cannot suitably adapt to those uncertain means without that swimming pool.

We associate "keeping up with the Joneses" with middle class consumers, but the same set of motivations can apply to all consumers at all levels. CEOs strive for a compensation package based not on their merits but on what other CEOs earn. Lobbyists at state and federal levels are not above using a little cynicism, vanity and apprehension to persuade governments to buy stuff they do not need.

This presents us with some interesting logic. When cynicism, vanity and apprehension motivate people to "keep up with the Joneses," these states of mind cause people to buy more stuff than they would otherwise. When cynicism, vanity and apprehension cause people to buy more stuff than they would otherwise, these states of mind contributed to our fast rising GDP over the past few decades. When cynicism, vanity and apprehension contributed to our fast rising GDP over the past few decades, these states of mind have enabled the doubling of our standard of living during that span. When cynicism, vanity and apprehension enabled the doubling of our standard of living during that span, these states of mind have enhanced our economic pursuit of happiness.

Cynicism, vanity and apprehension do not sound like ideal states of mind for producing happiness. But before we jump to conclusions let us take a look at a highly touted survey on happiness.

The Happiness Survey

A well-regarded survey on happiness, done in the fall of 2005 by the Pew Research Center, provides some insights regarding the economics of happiness.[3] The survey examined many factors related to happiness, with family income being the most prominently reported. The survey found that people with higher income tend to be happier and further comments that this appears to dispel the old saying that money can't buy you happiness. Maybe the cynicism, vanity and apprehension that contribute to insatiable want fulfill the pursuit of happiness after all. One needs to examine the details of the report to see that the empirical data actually points to a different conclusion. Let us start with the third paragraph that explains the overall findings of the study.

> " .... Just a third (34%) of adults in this country say they're very happy, according to the latest Pew Research Center survey. Another half say they are pretty happy and 15% consider themselves not too happy. These numbers have remained very stable for a very long time."

First, notice the emphasis on people who are "very happy," as opposed to people who report that they are at least "pretty happy." Whether this was the

---

3 The report is available at this web address: http://pewresearch.org/pubs/301/are-we-happy-yet.

intention of the researchers or not, this was wise for two reasons. People might report they are pretty happy because they think that is what they are expected to be in our wealthy society. People who report they are very happy are more likely to have happiness independent of what society (or a researcher) may expect of them. Additionally, should not "very happy," and not merely "pretty happy," be the goal of the wealthiest nation on earth?

Despite our wealth, power and prestige as a nation only a third of us claim to be very happy. This means one of two things. If happiness is indeed dependent on wealth, then we likely have reached the upper limit of how many people can be very happy in our society now and for ever more. That is a depressing thought. The other possibility, much more hopeful, is that happiness does not depend on our overall wealth.

The last statement in the paragraph refers to the trend in happiness that they tracked since 1972. "Very stable for a very long time" suggests the absence of a trend over the past thirty years. When you keep track of something for that long you have a pretty good dataset for making correlations. Since 1972 the stock market has increased tenfold, yet there has been no increase in happiness. Conclusion: the stock market and all that represents (investments, pensions, etc.) does not increase happiness. At best it has no impact. The per capita GDP and our standard of living have more than doubled since 1972, yet there has been no increase in happiness. Conclusion: a fast-rising GDP does not increase happiness.

Scientists know that a causal relationship can be dampened by the effects of unmeasured intervening variables. For example, maybe happiness has not increased with wealth because the disparity of wealth also has increased. This indeed may be a factor, but not one that consistently negates the relationship over a 30 year time span. As hard as this may be for some people to accept, our best longitudinal indicators of wealth show absolutely no correlation with happiness. Our major political parties have a better relationship than exists between these variables.

Empiricism Versus Scholasticism

The researchers concluded in the main body of their report that the relationship between family income and happiness was linear. Also in the main body, they lumped the original eight income categories they measured into four categories that seemed to support their conclusion. Yet the original eight categories of data revealed that a plateau was reached along three sequential middle income categories where 34%, 30%, and 34% reported they were very happy. The Pew researchers must interpret graphs differently than most scientists, because we would claim those three sequential income categories reveal no relationship at all between wealth and happiness. The two lowest income categories and the two highest income categories were much closer to each other than they were to these middle income categories, also refuting a simple linear relationship between wealth and happiness.

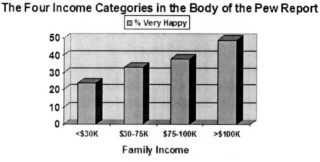

The Four Income Categories in the Body of the Pew Report

Family Income

The Eight Income Categories in the Pew Report's Appendix

Family Income

The title of the chart buried in the Pew report's Appendix is: "A Closer Look at Income and Happiness." This begs the question of why they did not consider this closer look worthy for the body of their report. One also wonders why they decided to lump the income categories in a way that makes less sense than the eight original. As income levels increases so does the natural spread between levels. Increasing income category ranges from $10,000 to $25,000 to $50,000 makes sense according to this principle. For the lumped categories of the survey one spread is $45,000 and the next higher one $25,000. That makes no sense at all ... unless you wanted to fit the data to your conclusion, rather than the other way around.

Science evolves around empirical data, which is information that can be experienced. Logical generalizations that we make about these experiences are coalesced into flexible beliefs known as theories. Additional experiences can change these flexible beliefs if they satisfy one or both of two important empirical criteria. Increasing the relevance of experiences, either through quantity or quality, increases the validity for either maintaining or changing a belief. Decreasing the

media, independent of experiencing real happiness in their lives, then finding a relationship between happiness and wealth has little meaning.

To avoid an inadvertent tautology, future surveys could include a definition of happiness based on counterexamples. Here are some suggestions that could be used for happiness. Happiness is the absence of cynicism. Cynicism creates a void that self-centered materialism might temporarily mask but cannot fill. Happiness is the absence of vanity. Vanity makes you desire to be indulged whether or not you already are rich. Happiness is the absence of apprehension. Being worried about where your next meal is coming from, how you will repay your debts or protecting your accumulated wealth detracts from your happiness. A skilled researcher would have to craft these definitions into more subtle and illustrative forms, while maintaining the use of counterexample.

One view of economic happiness was offered by John Galbraith, who coined the term *The Affluent Society*, in his book of that title (1958). Galbraith defined such a society as one with abundance and, therefore, without want. This view fits with the criteria of overcoming cynicism, vanity and apprehension in the pursuit of materialism.

Many cultural anthropologists accept a definition of affluence similar to Galbraith, as proposed by Marshall Sahlins in his book *Stone Age Economics* (1972). Sahlins suggested that an affluent society has abundant leisure while no member goes hungry. Does such a society even exist? Cultural anthropologists agree at least one did, the Dobe Ju/'hoansi of the Kalahari Desert in Africa.[4] As a foraging (hunting and gathering) culture these African bush men never lack food because they move around to where food is available. In contrast to the agrarian societies of Africa, or even Africa's industrial societies, the Dobe Ju/'hoansi have longer life spans that have reached 80 years. If that seems counterintuitive consider the impact of stress on health; the Ju/'hoansi have a much shorter work week by industrial standards, a little over twenty hours. Of course, with so much leisure time they are not being very productive. To make matters worse they share everything. You cannot generate much trade or wealth in a society like that but, in fairness to the Ju/'hoansi, without television they don't realize what they are missing.

The economics of happiness in this society must take a different form than donning a loin cloth and spear. My wife, Cindy, and I have backpacked for long periods in the wilderness, the longest trip being the 3000-mile Continental Divide Trail over a seven-month span. We were immensely happy during those journeys. Sure, we wanted to indulge ourselves with more showers and less bugs, but those wants could not be satisfied through market exchange. We had all the material

---

4 Richard Lee's *The Dobe Ju/'hoansi* (2002) is probably the most read work on their culture. In reality, the culture has been in the process of "modernization" since the 1970s, not due to their wishes and not entirely to their benefit. We will describe the culture in these essays mainly as they existed before 1970.

stuff we wanted, namely, the backpacking gear on our backs and the food in our bellies. Well, we always wanted more food in our bellies even after we stuffed ourselves like pigs, but let us overlook that one indulgence.

Unfortunately for us, long-distance backpacking is not a real option for long term happiness in our society. A second satisfactory period of my family's life would be more sustainable. For what became the best financial option for my family, a series of related events led me to accept a teaching assistantship and enroll in a doctoral program. We considered our kids too young for Cindy to work much during this era; I supported a family of five mostly with a graduate student's stipend. By society's standards we were below the poverty level.

We were happy because we curbed our wants in accordance with our means. We had no television, but enjoyed reading to our children for hours at a time. We had only one car, but I enjoyed the health and fitness I gained by walking to campus and back every day. We did not own a house, but rented an affordable apartment for the short term without regret, and with much less clutter than what we accumulated once we settled in to our own home.

Admittedly, we had help with our economic happiness. We were assisted by my father-in-law (who bought us a washer and dryer to save us the expense of going to Laundromats); our Church (who gave us $400 for a one-time financial emergency that occurred); and the government (who provided WIC support for the first six months as we adjusted to our poverty level income). My family benefited from affordable student health insurance purchased through Cornell University. Since the situation was temporary, settling for an apartment over having our own home caused no regrets or envy. With those basic needs satisfied our poverty-level existence was less stressful than many middle class people who struggle to own a home, have health insurance and otherwise attempt to make ends meet. I doubt we could convince a *laissez faire* economist like Milton Friedman of our happiness but Galbraith would have understood, as would cultural anthropologists.

In this society a more acceptable means of living beyond your means is to acquire debt. Now that we are back living on Emerson Street my family is much wealthier, thanks partly to the wonders of debt. We own a home, two entertainment centers, two cars and too many computers. While my father's only debt was a home mortgage, the two professional wage-earners now in residence enhance our wealth through a home mortgage (from buying the house from my four brothers), home equity (to cover education and home improvement costs), car payments, education loans and credit cards. In other words, we now are a typical middle class American family. Our middle class debt boosts our society's stock market, GDP and standard of living indicators, but our happiness has not increased along with our wealth.

Galbraith would have understood this paradox, but his economic philosophy is not prevalent in our current culture. Such noted economists as Milton

Friedman have led us in a return to *laissez faire* economics, formerly prevalent in the nineteenth century. *Laissez faire,* literally to "let do" or "let it be," means government should not impact a market economy. To understand what has gone wrong with this philosophy—and our economic system in general—we need a better understanding of market economies.

Our Market Economy

We consider our economic system to be based on free markets. As you read on you will understand that this is not true, but even Nobel Laureates refer to our market economy as free. *Laissez faire* economists focus on the "free" in free markets meaning a voluntary exchange of goods or services. They also focus on how government intervention impacts this free exchange either through disincentives such as taxes and regulations, or by commanding an advantage to some businesses over others with fiscal policy.

The focus on free exchange and government intervention is but a conveniently partial meaning of what "free" means in free markets. There needs to be a free flow of information about the goods and services being exchanged, to enable people to understand the costs and benefits of what they are exchanging. The labor that created the goods and services to be exchanged must be independently free as well. There are no truly free markets when slave or exploited labor is involved. For these reasons any complete definition of free markets stipulates that they cannot be impacted by either government intervention or private coercion.

A self-sufficient person would produce and consume goods based entirely on the merits of his/her own labor, like plants using photosynthesis to produce their own food. A free market is like the symbiotic relationship that occurs with organisms such as lichen. The algae in lichen produce food and the fungi provide protection; they exchange the natural merits of their independent labor to their mutual benefit. Private coercion of a market exchange reflects a parasitic relationship in nature, where two organisms are bound together yet one continually takes advantage of the other. Examples of private coercion would be false advertising that fooled people into exchanging their money for inferior goods, or corporate collusion to monopolize markets.

A free market enables people to specialize and exchange the merits of their independent labors, but does not objectively quantify the values in the exchange. The diversity of human nature means some folks would undersell themselves while others would overestimate their goods or services. As these tendencies balanced out in a trade network, the prices of goods and services would track towards the actual merit that produced them.[5] A free market economy thus preserves the merits

5 The chapter "Exchange Value and Primitive Trade," in Marshall Sahlin's *Stone Age Economics* (1972) provides a description of a simple Melanesian trade network that illustrates this balancing of social factors.

of what has been produced as the driving force in creating wealth through trade. Given the diversity of human nature and talents, a free market driven by merit would tend to diffuse wealth according to all the different specializations that occur. Some people work harder and better with inherently greater merit, and free market exchange would reward these merits accordingly. But the natural free market, absent of government intervention or private coercion, could not create such disparity as to value one person's labor one thousand times greater than another's. Large disparities in wealth reflect parasitism in the market system.

The parasitism evident in today's markets results from *laissez faire* economics and business corporations. The *laissez faire* creed derives from an interpretation of free market competition detailed by Herbert Spencer in his book, *Principles of Biology* (1864). The most important tenets of this creed are:

- Free market competition leads to survival of the fittest producers.
- Free market competition creates the greatest good for society.
- Free market competition requires government abstinence.

There are problems with all three assumptions about free market competition, but this basic *laissez faire* creed alone does not cause parasitism. Note that the additional abstinence of private coercion is not included in this creed. This opens the door for *laissez faire* economists to embrace the business corporation, whose mission is to expand markets to increase their "bottom line," or profits for shareholders. Because shareholders seldom are involved in the production specialty of the business corporation, wealth is concentrated independently of the labor that generated the wealth. Add the business corporation model to the *laissez faire* creed and you create an economic system that functions to reward greed.

The function of greed for our economic system has been adopted uncritically by economic textbooks, college courses, documentaries ("Greed," by ABC's *20/20*), and even pop movies (*Wall Street*, with the famous line "Greed is good"). *Laissez faire* economists envision that in free markets the survival of the fittest is survival of the greediest, in particular the greediest business corporations, with greed creating the greatest good for society. Government should not ameliorate negative consequences from greed, since this would interfere with the greatest good for society.

The ironies in this *laissez faire* position are delicious; I will come back to them repeatedly. The first irony is that apparently these economists have yet to figure out that only government can sanction greed in any type of economy. This is particularly true in a corporate society; corporations and commerce cannot even function, let alone prosper, without government intervention. Government's role in this will be explained more fully in other economic essays; for now let it suffice that corporations exist only through government charter, and that government is needed for the very existence of a capital market and how that market is structured to reward greed. The second irony is that once greed has been sanctioned through the necessary intervention of government and the coercion of corporations, a free market no longer exists. *Laissez faire* economists talk a good talk, but they neither want government abstinence nor a free market.

Governments could adopt one of two strategies to guide markets back towards the merit that characterizes free exchange under natural conditions. They could endorse the business corporation model, while using legislation to return some of the usurped wealth and benefits to the labors of production. Business corporations could survive under this scenario, but *laissez faire* economists would claim the government to be socialist. Such economists pretend or perhaps even believe that their own position adheres to the principles of a free market economy.

Government instead could refuse to provide the infrastructure that allows profits to be redistributed away from the labor of production and concentrated. Such a system would require profits siphoned away from market exchanges to be used more for enhancing the merits of future production, rather than maximizing the "bottom line" for those not involved with production. Proprietorships could thrive in this climate, but the business corporation would be eliminated or drastically altered. This better approximation of a free market would still have *laissez faire* economists howling "socialism" mind you. As you will learn, these folks never let the real meaning of experiences get in the way of their dogmatic beliefs.

Our fast rising GDP has been stimulated in part by our greed-based economic system contributing to insatiable want, using the techniques mentioned above. This is a form of private coercion where goods and services are exchanged according to culturally elevated demands rather than natural preferences. Instead of a natural free market driven by merit, we have a culturally biased market driven by greed. A biased market driven by greed concentrates wealth in those who best emulate that "attribute." Our economic system of greed creates greater parasitic wealth disparity than would otherwise occur through merit-based exchange in a free market void of private coercion. Greater wealth disparity means the ceiling for expensive goods such as housing gets inflated. This has little impact for upper income brackets but the majority of people, by definition, are not in an upper income bracket. A culturally biased market driven by greed, while great for stock markets and the GDP, disproportionately benefits a few at the expense of many. This begs the question of why the many would endorse such a system.

Laissez Faire Logic

Maybe during the 1950s and 60s, when low, middle and high income people all identified themselves as middle class, people would question a greed-based system. Now the middle class is shrinking, at least in perception. Another survey by the Pew Research Center reveals that only 53% of the public views themselves as middle class.[6] This underestimates the size of the middle class as predicted by a normal distribution (see the introductory essay "Losing Balance"). On the other hand, people now grossly overestimate their chances of becoming rich.[7] Such people endorse greed because they are fooling themselves.

A greed-based economic system would satisfy all if the wealthy get everything they want and the lower classes only want what they get. If the majority of Americans were simple-minded happiness could be achieved at a large scale. The wealthy present this logic when defending the increased disparity between the rich and all other economic classes. As long as the wealth for other classes increases a little bit, what does it matter if the wealth for the richest increases dramatically? One could nitpick that the wealth for the lowest economic quintile has actually decreased over the past thirty years, but maybe those folks could still be like our gullible friend Hans and feel wealthier even as they have less.

The problem with this strategy for the pursuit of happiness is the assumption that the wealthiest could ever have enough abundance to be satisfied. The greed of Enron, WorldCom and other corporations confirm that abundant wealth fuels abundant want. To be so indulged the wealthy ultimately must persuade middle class consumers to be greedy as well. On the one hand they want the middle class to think like Hans, to be satisfied with a decreasing percentage of the GDP, yet to be unsatisfied with what they have in order to fuel the GDP. That consequently leads to debt, not happiness.

Sometimes economic mobility is cited by *laissez faire* economists to deflect concerns over increasing disparity between rich and poor. What matters is the potential for the poor to become rich, and vice-versa, each according to their merits. Economic mobility in our society remains high; therefore our market system driven by greed must also be driven by merit.

This house on Emerson Street has witnessed upward mobility. The previous inhabitants, my parents, included only one wage earner, a specialty advertising salesmen. The current inhabitants include two professional wage earners. The merits of our labors, both in quantity and quality, surpass those of the previous inhabitants, and the substantial increase in our combined wages appears to reflect this. Unfortunately, the value of the house back then was twice my father's single income; now the value is three times our combined income. One semester's tuition at the state university was 4% of one salesman's income; now the value is 4% of the combined income of two professionals. The only debt my father incurred was the home mortgage; now we have home equity and other sources to extend our debt.

6 *From Inside the Middle Class: Bad Times Hit the Good Life* (April 2008), Pew Research Center.
7 Refer to Thomas A. Diprete's "Is This a Great Country? Upward Mobility and the Chances for Riches in Contemporary America." (2005)

One could question what upward mobility based on merit really means, if the upwardly mobile of the next generation pays a higher proportion of their income for essential items than did the previous generation, but let us leave that uncertainty aside for now. The upward mobility here on Emerson Street had little to do with a market system driven by greed and everything to do with education. Any *laissez faire* economist claiming that an economic system that increases the disparity of wealth also facilitates economic mobility is either incompetent or devious, as any statistician familiar with normal distributions would know. Our country still enjoys high economic mobility because we have, in terms of the production of graduates, the best system of higher education in the world. We can only pray that continues as long as possible, since the proportion of family income needed to pay for the tuition of our children in a biased market economy driven by greed rises even faster than our standard of living.[8]

Economic Paradigms

There are powerful forces preventing the middle class from endorsing merit over greed. Overcoming these forces will require what science calls a paradigm shift. A paradigm shift fundamentally changes the way people think about something. Academics consider heralding in a new paradigm to be the biggest plum of all. Scientists like Newton and Einstein stand out as giants precisely because they changed the way everybody thought about the physical universe.

Most paradigm shifts seek to make anomalies easier to explain. Einsteinian mechanics explained why large masses or negligible photons did not behave the same way as a falling apple. Keynesian economics, named after its champion John Maynard Keynes, could explain why the New Deal to stimulate economic demand did some good for the United States by getting people back to work, even though the actual depression would end later with World War II. For that matter, a corollary to Keynesian economics explains why foreign wars boost economies, though *laissez faire* economists tend to ignore this.

Laissez faire economists, unlike empirical scientists, apparently **prefer** their paradigms to increase anomalies. Championed by Milton Friedman, their paradigm shift in economic thinking leaves many scratching their **heads** as to whether the New Deal helped the country in a time of crisis or **amounted** to unnecessary government intervention in fiscal policy. In their view, **since** government programs putting people back to work interfered with free **markets** and constrained the money supply to halt inflation those programs did more **harm** than good. They say nothing about the government intervention that contributed to the Great Depression in the first place, such as the famous Supreme Court case *Lochner v. New York* (1905) that endorsed the corporate coercion of contracts.

---

8 Once again, the empirical numbers are being reserved for Essay 7.

The *laissez faire* paradigm uses the scholastic approach of fixed dogmatic beliefs determining the meaning of experience. They resolve the thorny little problem that business corporations, by strict definition, are an assault to free markets and economic freedom by changing what those concepts mean. Milton Friedman also *normatively* claimed that the *subjective* pursuits of utility and profit were *objective* standards for basing economic theory.[9] Profit numbers are indeed objects; but their definition, measurement and normative optimization are determined by economic scholars and/or scientists. If a little scholastic chicanery is all it takes to create a better paradigm we could all become Einsteins. Perhaps *laissez faire* economists need more grammatical training to help them distinguish between subject and object.

The *laissez faire* paradigm currently grips our society. The old version of *laissez faire* economics was popular during the heyday of the robber barons; that should alert you right there. Keynesian economics advocated a role for government in stimulating the demand for goods and labor at appropriate times. *Laissez faire* economics calls for biasing markets towards greed, and for government to both boost capital markets and to facilitate corporate expansion of markets. Both Keynesian and *laissez faire* paradigms depart from a free market in different respects, but the "new" paradigm has accompanied the most disparate distribution of wealth in our country, and the greatest departure from a merit-driven free market, since the days of the old *laissez faire* economics.

The new *laissez faire* economics have a variety of followers. The monetarists, with Friedman as their pioneer, focus on how monetary policy controls the flow of money. Supply-siders focus on how fiscal policy influences the distribution of money. These and other similar interests are lumped together under an umbrella of think tanks, public relation firms, lobbyists, media and even academics beholden to corporations. Together they form a powerful force with the following goals:

- Structure competition to favor business corporations over proprietorships;
- Maximize overall wealth overtly and wealth disparity covertly;
- Distort empirical evidence to fit their ideology; and
- Fool middle class people like Hans into endorsing greed over merit.

These themes will be explored throughout the remainder of these economic essays. This essay contrasted the function of an economic system as being a choice between either merit or greed. The next few essays will cover the structure of our economic system, exploring the demand for goods, supply of capital, self-interest of labor, market efficiency and corporate hypocrisy. I will then apply a systems analysis to evaluate our economic system, drawing upon important components

---

9 *Essays in Positive Economics* (1953), provides Friedman's normative criteria for judging positive economics.

of ecological systems. The economic part will conclude with a guide for how the homeostasis of our economic system has been disrupted through invalid and unreliable manipulation of misinformation.

ESSAY 2 – THE DEMAND FOR GOODS

Overview

- Our demand for goods favors large business corporations over proprietorships.
- The *laissez faire* approach to market demand is expanding demands and maximizing supply.
- The sustainable approach to market demand is moderating demand to stay within the limits of supply.
- Business corporations must hype the demand for goods to make their production efficiencies and economies of scale practical and profitable to shareholders.
- Business corporations thrive by creating renewable demands for products.
- Indulgence, waste and neglect negate savings from mass-produced goods.
- Large corporations have production costs that do not apply to proprietorships.
- Government commands the economy to compensate business corporations for their greater production costs.
- Proprietorships must compete mainly through the merits of production.
- Credit increases demand by artificially inflating the money supply.
- Colonialism increases demand by exploiting people and resources.

Business Demand

Small businesses have had a hard time succeeding in my rural town over the last 40 years. At one time we had three gas stations; now we have one. When I was growing up we had a grocery store, pharmacy and hardware store; now we have one convenience store. There are still a number of home businesses, ranging from the production of weather vanes to web sites, but gone are the days of the neighborhood candy store.

We have tried to attract small retail businesses back to town. We have created economic development committees, hosted charrettes and applied for grants to beautify the town center. Having had personal experience with grant applications, I was particularly impressed with the ISTEA grant our town obtained and the new facelift our main street received as a result. Barbara Kelley was not as impressed.

Mrs. Kelley was the matriarch of a blue collar family of Connecticut Yankees. You know the type: a person ruled by common sense and practical objectives. One fine summer day, as construction crews were busy at work making our town center look spiffy, I noticed Mrs. Kelley watching the progress. Thinking we must be of like mind regarding our good fortune, I went up to her and said: "Looking good."

"We could have used a new ambulance," was her dour reply.

Only recently have I understood the wisdom behind Mrs. Kelley's discontent. Our town center now looks terrific, the town was ranked the number one place to live in the state for small towns under 3500, and property values have increased sharply. None of this has enabled proprietorships like a hardware store to prosper. Instead, the town decreased in population through the last two decades of the twentieth century, with the exodus affecting mainly the middle class. Pastoral niceties such as spiffy town centers cater more to the upper classes. Middle class Yankees like Mrs. Kelley want things to be practical and need things to be affordable; giving the town center a facelift addressed neither concern.

National trends reflect the economics of this small town. The proportion of income that proprietorships receive from the GDP has shrunk over the past thirty years. The resulting economy provides many niceties for the middle class, but the cost of essentials like housing has skyrocketed. Both small businesses and the middle class have been foundations of this country's economy. Trends such as the decreasing proportion of GDP income to proprietorships and the increasing cost of essentials for the middle class deserve a hard look.[1] In particular, we need to consider how the demand for goods has been tilted in favor of business corporations at the expense of proprietorships, and whether this represents the best interests of the middle class.[2]

Supply and Demand

One compelling reason that has been offered in support of large business corporations is their ability to meet crucial demands through maximizing production. For example, many people in the world lack food. Some economists cite this as a self-evident justification for large agribusinesses, even to the extent of subsidizing them if need be. Creating dependency on large corporations for the absolute necessities of life decreases the importance of local friends, neighbors and businesses. We should take a closer look at how supply and demand works before accepting such a dubious tradeoff.

Economists and ecologists share a few things in common. Both fields boast their share of well-educated folks who like to prove a point with the use of graphs and models. Both fields feature curves related to supply and demand. The supply and demand curves in economics relate price to the quantity of goods or services. Basically, the more people that "demand" goods the more costly those goods will be. A large "supply" of those goods eases demand and brings down the cost. Economics 101 explains that the costs and benefits of both a supply

1 "Essay 7 – An Economic Report Card" will provide empirical data.
2 Throughout these essays small businesses imply sole proprietorships; large business corporations have shareholders. But not all corporations are large, nor are all proprietorships small.

curve and a demand curve intersect at a point called the equilibrium. This point theoretically determines the market costs that will induce the most willingness to trade by both sellers and buyers, and thus maximize wealth.

Supply and Demand Model

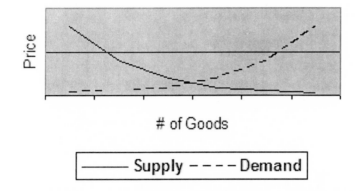

Population growth models in ecology feature a different type of supply and demand curve. A population growth curve reflects the increasing demand for resources in an environment, formed by a growing population. What is commonly known as the carrying capacity reflects the overall supply of resources that the environment can sustain. Ecology 101 explains that the growth of a population needs to taper off near the carrying capacity in order to be sustained. Beyond this level a population will decline. How severe the decline depends on how rapidly the population grew while nearing the carrying capacity.

Population Growth Model

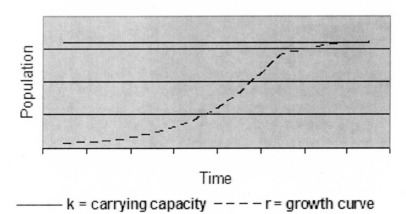

Despite their similar functions, these respective models provide a point of departure for how economists and ecologists think about systems of supply and demand. *Laissez faire* economists tend to focus on demand dictating supply, particularly in the case of necessities. A large demand necessitates creating a large supply to keep the cost of goods low at the theoretical equilibrium point that will maximize trade and wealth. The best suppliers to meet fast rising demand, in the eyes of *laissez faire* economists, are multinational business corporations. Have lots of people to feed? Let us maximize the supply from large agribusinesses to meet that demand at reasonable cost.

This makes sense according to the basic supply and demand curve of economics, but nothing in that basic model includes an assumption about the limits of the supply. The population growth curve implies that the important relationship between supply and demand works in the opposite direction. Carrying capacity limits on environmental supply ultimately dictate population demand. Ecologists focus on how the environment has limits in the supply of resources that can sustain growth, and one of those limits will inevitably curb the growth rate.

Air has not limited the growth rate of organisms. A population could grow exponentially and still have air to breathe. In contrast, the supply of food in an environment often limits the population growth. The demand of hungry humans would eventually be controlled by the supply of food the world provides regardless of whether the main sources of supply were large agribusinesses or family farms.

If possible, why not favor the production of agribusinesses to make food become effectively as limitless as air? What ecologists recognize is that even if the supply of food did not limit the demand from human population growth some other resource would. Other limiting factors to the human population could be water, energy or raw materials. Thus the objective is not to maximize the supply of any particular resource, since this will merely enable some other resource to limit demand, but to moderate the demand for all resources at a sustainable level. Such a strategy would never appeal to a large business corporation.

Hyped Demand

Large corporations have two production advantages over smaller businesses in meeting a demand for goods. A large corporation can borrow money, buy raw materials and pay blue-collar wages at bulk rates. These economies of scale enable large corporations to mass produce goods at cheaper costs to the consumer than offered by smaller businesses. Large corporations also can institute assembly line efficiencies. Henry Ford was a pioneer in this regards with his assembly line production of the Model T. Combined with cost savings from economies of scale, the assembly line production of cars turned a luxury item into a relatively inexpensive necessity for middle class America.

The advantages with large-scale production for business corporations come with a necessary burden. Corporations must turn a profit for shareholders and other investors not involved in the actual production of goods. Buying in bulk and employing the workers of a large assembly line turns a sufficient profit for shareholders only if a corporation can sell large volumes of goods. This is, in fact, the reason for business corporations to exist: to expand markets. Corporations were initially granted charters by government as a means of concentrating capital for the expansion of trade. The first stock was issued by the Dutch East India Company, a corporation set up for colonial trade expansion.[3]

Thus, large business corporations need to increase demand for their goods and services beyond what can be generated through local free market exchange. A large business corporation needs to convince many people over a large area to buy their product, or capture the business of large entities with concentrated purchasing power, such as governments or other large corporations. Expanding markets comes easily with a substantive innovation such as the affordable Model T, but not all the products of a large corporation are as innovative or useful. In order to survive business corporations often must use hype to create demand where none would exist based on people's normal needs and wants.

Let us modernize the Hans fable for an example of the cause and effects of hyped demand. The bachelor Hans has spent seven years working in a faraway place. He now has saved enough money for a sizable down payment on a house in his native town. One thing that helped Hans save money was his 2000 Toyota Echo, the first year of production for that particular model.[4] His car gets the best gas mileage of any four-cylinder, nonhybrid car made by a large auto manufacturer for the new millennium. He bought the car new at a relatively low $12,000, thanks in part to Toyota not including a lot of stylish options and advertising hype to increase the value of the car. The lack of hype generated for the Echo may explain why 2003 became the last year for the model, despite an affordable price tag, good performance, good reliability and the best gas mileage of all nonhybrid cars at the time.

The Echo has served Hans well, but marketing departments do not brand subcompacts as symbols of real freedom, churning back snow in the frozen tundra, conquering rutted roads as big as small canyons, and charging up the vertical walls of mesas. As a bachelor Hans needs no bigger car than his Echo, but his little car does not capture the "king of the road" feel portrayed in commercials. He would prefer driving the type of car that obstructs the line of sight from some punk-sized subcompact, rather than driving the car that was being obstructed. The Echo saved Hans a lot of money, but he cannot attract those gorgeous babes shown on the car commercials by being a penny-pincher.

---

3 See http://www.mondovisione.com/index.cfm?section=articles&action=detail&id=60613 for an overview and defense of stock exchanges-you won't find a defense of them here.
4 I drive a 2000 Toyota Echo, getting 43 mpg in summer, 40 mpg in winter.

Influenced by a marketing campaign of hype that entices people to "keep up with the Joneses," Hans trades in his Echo for a spanking new SUV. In addition to purchasing a new car Hans also upgrades his computer, cell phone, and entertainment system. A good number of commercials have assisted Hans with his attainment of a hyped, mass marketed image, with the unfortunate consequence of no longer being able to make a down payment for a house. He counts his blessings nevertheless because now he rents, avoiding completely the burden of being a home owner.

The lucky Hans has increased his own and society's standard of living through trade. By purchasing his SUV the lucky Hans contributed not only to the salaries of the blue-collar production line workers, whose salaries have not increased much since he first bought his 2000 Echo, but to white-collar managers and marketers as well, whose salaries have increased nicely indeed. If public relation experts, lobbyists and advertisers continue to do their job well the lucky Hans will continue to increase his standard of living, and theirs, by trading in the SUV three years down the road for an SUV hybrid, succumbing to the corporate objective of creating renewable demand.

Renewable Demand

Business corporations face an obstacle in that they can only increase demand so far with new customers. At some point they have to renew the demand from previous customers. Renewable demand has become a mainstay for the business corporation expanding markets for goods.

Virtual reality chambers, such as the holographic chamber used in *Star Trek*, may become available this century. This would be another generation of parlor room entertainment that has evolved from card games to radio to television to interactive video games. My best memories of parlor room entertainment come from playing cards with a great group of people, but I have been an enthusiastic consumer of the other options as well. Virtual reality chambers are not necessary for parlor room entertainment, in fact they would interfere with the ability of friends to enjoy each other's company in the parlor, but I will join with the millions contributing to the demand for such chambers if they become available in my lifetime.

If the production of virtual reality chambers never becomes feasible or practical, large corporations will not employ any of their tools to expand demand. There may be a large potential demand for such chambers, but there will never be a kinetic demand since nobody expects to own one. Without this expectation, the public will never consider virtual reality chambers a necessity, nor even lament their absence from the market. Perhaps virtual reality chambers can be produced in limited numbers. In this case the demand created among the public will be similar to the current demand for roller coaster rides. Once again, the public will not consider private ownership of these chambers a necessity.

If virtual reality chambers can be mass produced and distributed by a large business corporation, then everything changes. The VS Corporation will attempt to make every consumer covet a "VirtualStation." To the extent that they succeed, consumers will come to view the VirtualStation as a necessity, a "must have." By extension, they will consider the large VS Corporation to be crucial for a good economy. A product that consumers never would miss if it never existed contributes to the perception that large corporations are essential to meet our demands, that our pursuit of happiness and market economy would falter if not for the presence of large corporations mass producing stuff like VirtualStations.

The further irony in this is that the VS Corporation will shrewdly design and market their VirtualStations to create renewable demand. Large business corporations mass produce goods for the chance of mass profits, not for some intrinsic value of production or to provide a noble service to society. Large corporations often survive only by creating renewable demands that keep the customer coming back. VirtualStation 2 would come out after three years to be followed by VirtualStation 3 in a few years after that. Unlike the Model T that needed no advertising, millions of dollars would be spent creating hype for each new version of VirtualStation.

If the VS Corporation cannot accommodate the renewable demand they have created they just raise the cost and only the consumer loses. Yet even when consumers appear to be "winning" through the cheap goods available from mass production they may be, in fact, spending more than they need.

Indulgence, Waste and Neglect

The consumer costs grabbing my attention of late pertain to food, which had quadrupled for my family over the last fifteen years. Economists tell us that food costs have gone down in real dollars. However, many of these "real" dollars are being concentrated in upper income levels, and have not boosted either mine or most other middle class wages in the same proportion. At least, my salary has not quadrupled in fifteen years. Has yours? Rather than trusting in the pronouncements of *laissez faire* economists regarding the bargain price of food I took a hard look at how we could reduce our food bill.

Both Cindy and I are suckers for deals. In that regard we both fit the consumer profile large corporations love to cultivate. There are few places in America where you can be bombarded with so many great deals at once as at a large supermarket. Get one dollar off with your card. Buy ten for ten dollars. Buy one, get one free. Neither Cindy nor I could resist; we would buy in bulk now for consumption later.

What I finally began to notice was this greed based strategy did not work for us as planned. Sometimes we would buy now and eat now, a common affliction for former long-distance backpackers. Our family gets abundant exercise, yet most of us are slightly overweight. My teenage son stays thin, but I suspect the lad has a tapeworm. Sometimes we would buy now and throw away later, as some deals are indeed too good to be true. Sometimes we would buy now and just plain forget about it. In other words, falling prey to the great deals offered by large supermarkets led to indulgence, waste and neglect.

Indulgence, waste and neglect result at a larger scale than found at the supermarket, thanks to our market economy being driven by greed. Why buy only what you need when you can buy in excess cheaply and on credit? Take the purchase of a VirtualStation as an example. VirtualStation 2 comes out with the only enhancement being a feature to design your own holographic programs. You were completely satisfied with the original VirtualStation but you absolutely must indulge yourself with this new upgrade. The easiest thing for you to do with your old VirtualStation is put it out with the garbage. A good product goes to waste, but you can bet the VS Corporation has no regrets. You then find out you have no real interest in designing your own holographic programs and you neglect that new feature.

I volunteered to take over the food shopping for the family and endeavored to eliminate the indulgence, waste and neglect from our food bill. In other words, my consumption became driven by merit rather than greed. I bought only what I needed for the week ahead. I would take advantage of a deal if one met my need for the week, or if one applied to our basic staples, but otherwise I paid the regular price for those goods I needed and passed up the deals. Our food costs, without all the great deals, have gone down by about 20%. We also have a little less fat on us. I could have accomplished the same objective by buying all my food from the local grocery store and save money on gas as well .... Except that my town now has one convenience store rather than a true grocery store, hardware store and pharmacy.

Business Corporation Costs

People automatically conclude that proprietorships have a tough time competing with business corporations because of how production efficiencies affect the costs of goods. This is only part of the reason why business corporations compete so well in our economic system. In fact, if production efficiencies were all business corporations had going for them they likely would not be able to compete well with proprietorships at all. There are additional costs for business corporations that do not burden other businesses, costs that government has been persuaded to absorb.

Creating and meeting large demands necessitate costs that go beyond the actual production of goods. Large corporations must have a source for the money that grants them their production advantages. That is where shareholders, banks and other investors come in. These sources have to be repaid in interest, introducing a capital market that redistributes money away from the goods and labor markets. This latter point is important because enabling businesses to divert profits to shareholders and investors who do not contribute to the labor of production only happens through government charter and protection. The practice of using capital to profit from someone else's labor is essentially the same practice as loan-sharking, though government enforced contracts and regulations are less threatening than leg breakers.

Governments license this form of profiteering for the public good. The public good is served when corporations turn this means of profiteering into a vehicle for creating substantive innovations, such as the Model T. If corporations spend more money on expanding demand than creating substantive innovations they undermine the public good, the theoretical reason for government intervention to protect loan sharks, er, investors.

Management hierarchies bestow added costs to business corporations. Large corporations require hierarchical levels of management to accommodate geographical, operational and capital expansions. Each level increases the discrepancy between least and most compensated people responsible for producing the same goods. J. P. Morgan claimed that the chief executive of a corporation should make no more than twenty times as much as the blue collar worker in the same industry.[5] What this ratio has become now will be examined later, but for now we use Morgan's claim to further reveal that corporations with large volumes and market areas have extra costs not shared by smaller businesses.

Persuasion creates added costs for business corporations. The actual content of factual information costs little. Small businesses depend on comparatively inexpensive local advertising and word-of-mouth endorsements from customers. Word-of-mouth endorsements promote the actual merits of goods and services without hype or coercion, but cannot compete with the resources of a large business corporation for expanding markets through marketing and lobbying. Expanding markets through glitzy media, star power endorsements or golf outings in Scotland require the big bucks. Large corporations have large marketing/lobbying budgets that dwarf the costs of what local advertising would require. In fact, the marketing/lobbying budgets of large corporations can surpass their research and development budgets, a common occurrence even for corporations with ongoing research such as pharmaceuticals.

Let us review the ledger so far. When you purchase goods from a small proprietorship you pay a higher price for the production costs, but most of what you pay are for the direct merits of production. When you purchase goods from a

5 I could not track down the original source document for this claim. However, on the Internet even corporate board members were citing this ratio as having been made by Morgan.

large corporation you pay a lower price for the production costs, but you have to directly or indirectly cover the expenses of shareholders and investors, extended hierarchies and various methods of persuasion. In reviewing this ledger the demand for goods would seem to favor proprietorships. What, then, provides a competitive advantage to business corporations over proprietorships besides production efficiencies?

One thing to consider is that large business corporations compete for a different type of "customer" than proprietorships. Proprietorships compete best to satisfy consumers only. Business corporations compete with each other to best satisfy the greed of investors as well, if not mainly. There are exceptions, of course. Some corporations take pride in the quality rather than quantity of their goods; some sole proprietors of their own business are out to screw you. On balance, however, the success of business corporations depends as much on what they do to compete for investors as what they do to compete for consumers.

Every business seeks to bargain from a position of strength. The "strength" of large corporations allows them to "bargain" over supplies of capital and the self-interests of labor to gain an unfair advantage over smaller businesses. This advantage may be as benign as branding goods independently of merit through large marketing budgets, or as onerous as high-priced and well-connected lobbyists getting no-bid contracts passed by Congress. Both the benign and onerous expressions of corporate "strength" represent a form of market coercion altering the exchange that would have occurred otherwise due to natural merits and the free flow of information.

Both proprietorships and the middle class lose in a variety of ways with our economic system structured to favor business corporations. The higher costs of corporate lobbyists and lawyers pay for themselves when government is persuaded to command the economy in ways that favor large corporations. Subsidies for businesses in general tend to favor the large business corporation in particular. No-bid contracts with mucho government gravy and earmarks slipped into federal legislation favor the large business corporation over the proprietorship. Shifting the proportional tax burden away from capital gains to wages favors the large business corporation over both proprietorships and middle class laborers. In theory business corporations pass along these competitive favors in decreased costs of their goods and services for consumers. But the real cost of goods and services to the middle class are the cost to the middle class consumer plus the cost to the middle class taxpayer. Ultimately the middle class still shoulders the extra hidden costs of commanding the economy to benefit business corporations.

Economic data for the past thirty years reveals these costs (see Essay 7). The proportion of our gross domestic product generated by private enterprise has increased over the past thirty years. Net dividends have increased dramatically, more than double the rise in GDP, confirming with other data that much of this enterprise goes to business corporations at the expense of proprietorships. Yet despite all the cheaper goods we now supposedly buy our debt has increased dramatically over this time span, while our savings have decreased to virtually nothing. This begs the question of how we can consume so much when we appear to have increasingly less. The answer is credit.

Credit

Winston Churchill once said: "Play for more than you can afford to lose and you will learn the game." Indulgence, waste and neglect are byproducts of a mindset that we are never "playing for more than we can afford to lose," thanks to the wonders of credit. Yet there really is much being lost due to credit. Our society is absorbing costs in regards to greater trade deficits, wealth disparity, costs of essential goods, debt and rates of bankruptcies. On the other hand our stock markets and standard of living indicators have done well over the long term, so no worries mate.[6]

A limit on available spending serves to keep costs down in an economy. This is a guiding principle for monetary policy when addressing inflation. In contrast, extra wealth can be generated by expanding the supply of credit. Credit cards and other financial contrivances can make the limiting factor of money appear to not exist. That is why large corporations are eager to provide you with their own credit card. Take away the limit on available money through credit and the market can either bear higher prices for goods and services or corporations can entice you to purchase goods you otherwise might not want.

An expanded supply of credit trickles down to harm the middle class in another way. Large corporations have a greater discrepancy between the highest and lowest wage earners than small businesses, due to the extra managerial layers involved. Corporate executives and shareholders who receive much in income can spend much, in effect eliminating the supply of money as a limiting factor for purchasing expensive goods. For markets where demand approaches supply the price becomes artificially inflated, since there are still many buyers in our corporate society who can lift the ceiling price. The wonder of credit then inflates the money supply of those less well off who really cannot afford to keep pace. The interest collected from credit goes to financial institutions, from there into investments and from investments into the pockets of corporate executives and shareholders. The role of credit and debt in our society has corporate wealth singing: "May the Circle be Unbroken."

Some of the markets with the highest demand approaching available supply happen to be those that serve the most crucial needs: the housing market, for example. Everyone wants their own home—that is part of the American Dream.

---

6 I confess again that the bulk of the economic essays were written in 2006. The fact remains that stock markets and standard of living indicators track independently of the economic problems mentioned.

Here on Emerson Street I avoided some of the high cost of housing by purchasing our home from my four brothers during a downturn in the housing market. I have more housing debt than my father had, but less than the typical middle class family, who suffers from a form of trickle down economics.

The wealthy buyers from the corporate management class have enough available wealth to outbid each other for multiple homes, elevating the price beyond what would be the market equilibrium. When the purchasing power of the corporate elite inflates the costs of the most expensive homes, there is a trickle down effect on the costs of homes on Emerson Street and elsewhere in this country. Keep mortgage rates low enough, however, and you can entice enough borrowing to keep concentrating money in the hands of the few. Allow for home equity and credit cards and you can keep the borrowing and money flowing even faster. Unfortunately, where there is credit there is debt.

Our greed-based economic system of business corporations and credit provides the means for the middle class to accumulate many goods at less cost. This very same system also has inflated costs of essential goods in our society—those goods in high demand that we associate most with happiness—such as housing, education and health care. Accumulating mass produced goods and affording expensive but essential goods are not as compatible goals for the middle class as business corporations and *laissez faire* economists have trained us to believe. Our market economy over the past thirty years has shown that maximizing one comes at the expense of the other. Our economic system creates a boon of capital for business corporations but a bane of debt for consumers and proprietorships. Not even this ominous condition reveals the full problem with the demand for goods favoring business corporations.

Colonialism

Credit is a government backed system for increasing demand by artificially increasing the money supply. The flip side to this is a government backed system to artificially decrease the costs of goods. We have had such a system in place for hundreds of years, known as colonialism.

At around the same time that the concepts of stock and the business corporation were being constructed, western civilization embarked on a path of colonialism. These parallel paths were much more than coincidence. Colonialism expanded markets into foreign cultures, a practice that continues even to this day. Early on there were benign forms of colonialism, such as the Portuguese and Dutch setting up trade centers in foreign lands. There were also malignant forms, such as the Spanish and English empire approaches to conquest and exploitation.

We have grown more sophisticated in our colonial practices and objectives, from the scholastic justification of comparative advantages to forming the Washington Consensus network of trade organizations. The commonality for all approaches past and present is "to the victor go the spoils." The ultimate victors have been large business corporations, but the middle class of developed countries have benefited from a share of the spoils as well.

Like Pavlov's dogs the middle class has been conditioned to associate the multinational corporation with an elevated standard of living. We are not eager to hear that our elevated standard of living has been gained through benign and malignant forms of exploitation, and *laissez faire* economists oblige us with a deceptive and seductive siren's song about "free" trade. We hear the chant "buyer beware" as well, even when the effective "buyer" is a citizen of a military dictatorship whose leaders collude with American business corporations. Free market ideals are being butchered in this appeal to "free" trade, but the greatest travesty lies in our betrayal of ecology.

Let us refer back to the population growth curve. The tribulations of supply and demand that a population experiences depends not on whether the carrying capacity of resources provided by the environment (or an economy) is high or low, but on the rate of population demand. Populations with moderate growth and/or consumption reach the carrying capacity of an environment and hover around that level without much ado. Populations with extraordinarily high growth and/or consumption will shoot beyond the carrying capacity of their environment—unless they colonize another "environment" and transfer the hardships, such as happens with western colonialism.

The hardships of resource depletion may be transferable, but cannot be eliminated. An exploited country somewhere experiences hunger, famine or aggression when their resources are depleted by the demands of colonialism. Ecological studies confirm that populations become excessively aggressive with each other when they near their carrying capacity. Viewed from the dispassionate lens of ecology, wars can be a last resort to correct the problems of populations creating too much demand for their environments. An additional consequence of unrelenting demand is that the unsustainable depletion of resources lowers the carrying capacity of the environment in the future.

Thus an ecologist would view the *laissez faire* obsession with maximizing production through business corporations such as agribusinesses as bizarre. Organisms that rapidly colonize and exploit environments, such as bacteria, are called r-species by ecologists. In regards to their rapid expansion of supply and demand multinational corporations behave like bacteria, weeds and other similar vermin. Should agribusinesses facilitate a fast-growing population, such rapid growth could actually augment disease, famine and aggression in the future while reducing the future productivity of the land. Even if agribusinesses could prevent food from ever being the limiting factor to a fast growing population this simply enables dire consequences from other limiting factors to eventually occur. Moderated demand, not maximized supply, is the answer to satisfying economic needs throughout the world in a manner that avoids famine, disease and/ or aggression.

This ecological understanding of the supply and demand for resources partially rebukes those in developed countries ardently promoting the control of population growth elsewhere. First, under natural conditions our species moderates our own growth. In ecological terms this is known as k-species behavior, typical of many social mammals such as wolves. It provides some comfort to think we naturally evolved more like wolves than bacteria, though *laissez faire* economists would have us believe otherwise. As counterintuitive as this may sound to multinational corporations, the surest way to enable humans in foreign lands to moderate their behaviors in balance with their environment is to leave them alone. Instead, even our well-intentioned intervention in foreign lands invariably comes packaged with our consumptive demands on their culture and resources. For us to advocate the moderation of population growth in foreign countries, while dramatically increasing our own demand for resources world wide, is naïve at best and possibly diabolical.

Before the practice of colonialism and our cultural evolution to behave more like bacteria, widespread famine did not exist. Africa in particular has been a region victimized by both colonialism and famine. Ironically, the cultures least affected were the ones considered to have remained most primitive, such as the Ju/'hoansi.[7] Their population adjusted long ago to the carrying capacity limits of the Kalahari Desert, without the benefit of agribusinesses, colonialism or global economics. The only thing that might lead to widespread famine, disease or aggression among the Ju/'hoansi would be to subject them to the *laissez faire* economics that favors the expansion of markets by any means, which we currently seem determined to do.

---

7   The Ju/'hoansi, a foraging culture, were introduced in Essay 1.

ESSAY 3 – THE SUPPLY OF CAPITAL

Overview

- Economic pyramids redistribute and concentrate capital.
- Concentrating capital requires government intervention for commerce, capital markets and contracts.
- *Laissez faire* economics supports capital mainly serving capital.
- Supplying capital not backed by production inflates markets.
- Capital serving capital is a form of welfare that increases with the size of business corporations.
- Free market competition favors diffusion over the concentration of capital.
- Concentrated supplies of capital help maximize wealth.
- Concentrated supplies of capital do not maximize progress.
- Concentrated supplies of capital increase wealth disparity.
- Concentrated supplies of capital increase market vulnerability.
- Concentrated supplies of capital decrease market stability.
- "Rational" greed decreases economic efficiency.

Redistribution Pyramids

A close friend once persuaded me to attend an Amway meeting. I knew enough about Amway to know I probably would not be interested in their approach to making money; I attended mainly to oblige my friend. My friend and his Amway sponsor met with me and a couple others in a small room. The sponsor, a smartly dressed young man, presented from the front of the room with his poster board charts and other materials. He asked me point blank:

"Would you like to make a lot of money?"

"Not really," I replied.

The sponsor apparently had some experience or training with people not convinced that wealth is the answer to life. He adeptly switched to his next tactic.

"Wouldn't you like to have enough money to retire early and enjoy your golden years?"

"Not really," I again replied. The expression on his face revealed that my reply was unexpected. I explained my answer further: "I would rather enjoy my work throughout my golden years."

The Amway sponsor switched to one last tactic.

"What about your kids? Wouldn't you want to be able to provide for all their needs?"

"I don't want to give them whatever they want. I want to raise them to be able to get whatever they want. If I just hand them things they won't be able to get them on their own."

The Amway sponsor was unsettled by this last rebuff. Perhaps I was the first person he encountered who felt that removing all hardship from your children's lives was not the best thing you could do to prepare them for the real world. He grew angry and declared I was wasting his time.

Amway was an abbreviation for the American Way, so named because the founders believed their multilevel marketing approach embodied what was great about America's economic system.[1] In 1999 the founders responded to criticisms about their marketing system by changing the name of the corporation to Alticor. A subsidiary of Alticor named Quixtar was created to run the old Amway sales network. Whether known as Amway, Quixtar, or Alticor their multilevel marketing approach combines two objectives:

1. concentrate wealth by
2. redistributing money upwards.

These objectives are achieved through people known as distributors. A distributor enlists you into his/her network of product sales. By reselling these products both you and your distributor receive a commission. You eventually become a distributor and you, the salespeople in your network and your distributor all receive commissions from the sales in your network. The real money comes when you are far enough up the distribution pyramid to be receiving commissions from the labors of many salespeople at multiple levels below. This essay focuses on the problems inherent in different types of economic pyramids and the supply of capital.

Yes, Amway was essentially a pyramid scheme, though not as blatant as those chain letters in the mail asking you to give money and then "share this letter with six of your friends." Like any business corporation Amway wanted the market for their products to expand. Rather than spend large amounts of money on public relation firms or having celebrities sell their products in advertisements, Amway created new sales networks (new markets) by branching out from existing distributors, with the assistance of motivational tools. The pyramid scheme provided incentives for current distributors to enlist new distributors, as collaborators rather than competitors to their own wealth. This multilevel marketing pyramid had safeguards, such as distributors buying back unwanted product. Much of the

1 Two sources of information about Amway and Quixtar, both featuring former Amway insiders, are the book *Weapons of Deception* by Eric Sheibeler and the web site www.amquix.info.

criticism and investigation leveled at Amway really centered on the tight coupling of product sales with sales of motivational tools.

All pyramids, even ones with safeguards like Amway, have bottoms. The distributors at the bottom of the Amway pyramid may have had as much determination and talent as the ones at the top, but if they were in an area already saturated with Amway distributors they remained at the bottom. The distributors at the bottom of the pyramid do not receive commissions from other people's sales; in essence they marketed only to themselves. Hence, the potential wealth from the labor of their sales was redistributed to the higher marketing levels, while no wealth trickled down to them.

The concentration of wealth by redistributing money upwards may seem unfair, but happens all the time. Most economic systems redistribute money upwards. In fact, so does our very own system, which we call capitalism.

Market Economies and Capital

Capitalism involves a private means of producing goods that generates profit, or capital. From that empirical foundation beliefs about capitalism diverge. Just as the demand for goods can be tilted towards greed or merit, large business corporations or small proprietorships, so too can the supply of capital. Karl Marx believed that the supply of capital naturally empowered the exploitation of labor. Milton Friedman believed that capitalism naturally empowered the perfect expression of a free market. Let us start with an overview of capitalism that resists competing dogmas and is empirically grounded in the operational definitions of relevant terms. Warning: empiricism and scholarship do not always match. My limited qualifications as an economic scholar include a former career as a professional student, knowledge gleaned from a few economic courses and texts, research on the Internet and having slept at a Holiday Inn Express.[2]

Gizmos are produced in a free market economy without capitalism. All the sales income goes into further production of the same gizmos. The free exchange of money for gizmos, and wages for labor, are determined solely by supply and demand based on the merits of production. The company making gizmos receives no money from any source besides their sales, and there is no money left over after they pay for the labor and other costs of production. A problem occurs when the company decides they want to produce new and improved gizmos without the extra income that would be needed for research and/or retooling production.

Gadgets are produced in a capitalist economy without business corporations. The company receives income that transcends the costs of producing their gadgets. The extra income is known as profits, or capital. The profits are

---

2 As with much of the economic concepts and terminology used in these essays the most common sources were the book *Educational Finance* (1990) by David Monk and the lecture series *Economics* (1998), a course on CD by Timothy Taylor, offered through The Teaching Company.

invested into improving the future production of gadgets, as well as starting a new line of gizmos. The gadgets and gizmos are innovative and increase the value of the products. Consequently, the sales of the new and improved products continue to generate more income than needed to pay for the labor and materials used for production. By such means reinvesting capital sustains a business indefinitely. The problem comes when capital is desired not only to improve production, but to aggressively expand markets.

Contraptions are produced in a corporate economy without *laissez faire* economics. Contraptions are an unnecessary item and unknown beyond a certain area. Expanding the market for contraptions require capital beyond the need for capital improvements. Expanding or creating new markets also introduce an element of risk. The contraption company becomes incorporated by government to enhance their ability to collect and distribute capital through people known as shareholders and investors, while at the same time reducing the level of risk to the investment to expand.

Even without government multiple shareholders and investors diffuse the risk taken, but the government charter of corporations reduces risk further by limiting the liability of capital providers should something go wrong. Incorporation also provides the legal structure for money to be redistributed to people who provide no labor for producing or selling contraptions, making the investments of contraption shareholders a lucrative venture without having to provide the merits of productive labor. Finally, government adjusts fiscal and monetary policy to assist the capital supply and flow to the corporation. Government intervenes with this type of assistance in order to encourage the expansion of markets and, by extension, the growth of wealth. The problem for shareholders and investors comes when government expects to encourage or discourage certain types of market practices in return for encouraging the pursuit of wealth through the corporation.

Laissez faire economists have an answer for this "problem:" government should intervene in the market economy to benefit corporations without no stinkin' strings attached. Government should "let corporations be" with everything except providing the infrastructures needed for charter, commerce, capital markets and contracts. Providing these infrastructures grants a competitive advantage to business corporations over proprietorships. Fair competition practices need to exist between different business corporations, but government should not compensate for disadvantaging proprietorships. Some coercive market practices are allowed under the philosophy of "buyer beware," treating "free" exchange as the only real component of "free" markets. Laws that treat business corporations as individuals provide the legal and rational foundation for government to both intervene and not intervene in the economy for the sake of nurturing the survival and success of business corporations.

Many *laissez faire* economists base their appeal to this greed-based system on what is inherently right and good for the free market and capitalism. These are the free market libertarians, but we will come to know them by another name later on. Either free market libertarians do not understand economics very well, or they are trying to pull a fast one. A free market exists when private goods and/or services are freely exchanged according to the known costs and benefits that resulted solely from production. No inherent aspects of capitalism, corporations or *laissez faire* policy contribute to the necessary conditions for a free market. Capitalism exists once income in excess of production costs can be generated through the private exchange of goods and services. No inherent aspects of corporations or *laissez faire* policy contribute to the necessary conditions for capitalism. Business corporations exist once government provides the structure and protection for shareholders to invest.[3] No inherent aspects of *laissez faire* policy contribute to the necessary conditions for corporations.

Indeed, at the point that corporations enter the picture you no longer have the natural conditions for a free market. The intervention of government on behalf of corporations manipulates the "free" exchange towards certain products. Furthermore, at the point that *laissez faire* policies restrict government's inclination to regulate greed, capitalism no longer exists for enhancing the future production of goods and services. *Laissez faire* corporatism outright coerces markets away from the free exchange that would have occurred based solely on this productive merit. Permitting shareholders to receive income without exchanging the merits of labor or without stipulations for the public good means capital investment exists mainly for the purpose of enhancing the redistribution of capital away from production to further serve capital.

The World Economy model developed by Immanuel Wallerstein provides some insight for *laissez faire* corporatism.[4] In this model the age of colonialism resulted in three types of countries throughout the world. Core countries pursued market expansion through corporations and colonies; periphery countries had their resources exploited and redistributed as capital in core countries; and external countries remained apart from this colonial economic system. Some of the key characteristics of Wallerstein's core countries reveal the necessities for *laissez faire* corporatism. Core countries enhanced shipping and the infrastructure for commerce. Core countries created markets of comparative advantage, where they used raw materials from periphery countries to produced refined goods of higher value, thus funneling capital from the periphery to the core. Core countries exploited labor, at times even turning to slavery, in order to expand markets and capital by minimizing labor production costs. Finally, core countries created trading companies where capital served only capital, thus providing steady fuel for continued colonial/market expansion and concentrations of capital. From the

---

3 This describes business corporations, not necessarily non-profit or government corporations.
4 Wallerstein presented this model in a book series titled *The Modern World System*. For our purposes we have adapted material from *The Modern World System II: Mercantilism and the Consolidation of the European World Economy, 1600-1750* (1980).

very beginning strong government has been a necessary condition of *laissez faire* economics, and exploitation has been an inevitable result.

The Conservation of Consumption

Science has developed two similar laws about nature, the conservation of matter and energy, which state you cannot create something from nothing. Let us extend this principle to the economic world, in what we will call the "law of conservation of consumption." You can't consume something from nothing in a market economy; somewhere something was produced that enables whatever consumption can occur in the markets of goods and services.

A spear that you produce from your own labor can be used in one of three ways. Kinetic consumption involves the use of the spear to kill a wild boar; potential consumption represents the future wild boars that same spear might kill until lost, broken or worn out. You could also use the spear for trade, in which case you have created wealth to go along with the consumption you made possible by your production. Unlike consumption, wealth can be created without production, since only trade creates wealth. An antique spear has a limited amount of potential consumption but can be used, in theory, to generate an unlimited amount of wealth.

What you will not be able to do with the one spear you produced is to consume two spears. You may be able to use the same spear repeatedly, until the potential consumption has been used up when the spear breaks, but if the wild boar you are hunting at the moment necessitates the consumption of a second spear before you are gored, well, tough luck. Enabling your spear to become valued as an antique might mean a lot more wealth in your hands, but not the consumptive capacity of two spears. To consume a second spear another one has to be produced.

Both wages and capital represent, in essence, a line of credit for consumption in a market economy. In the case of wages the credit is backed by the merits of the wage-earner's production. Capital can also be backed by production, such as when a portion of income that might have gone to wages gets redistributed as capital improvements. But capital also can be credit backed by wealth that has been obtained through such trade enhancement tools as control, or by government monetary policy increasing the flow of money. In other words, capital can be credit that is backed by essentially nothing. Lots of capital floating around that is not backed by production causes instability and inflation.

A historical example of how this works occurred with the Spanish Empire.[5] Spanish exploration infused huge amounts of gold into the treasury.

5 An account of this is provided by Kevin Phillips in his book *Wealth and Democracy* (2002), along with other examples of how excess capital inflates the costs of goods. Our own economy in the fall of 2008 provides another example, with the housing market substituted for gold.

While this at first appeared to make Spain extremely rich, the costs of goods that could be consumed skyrocketed. The extra capital in gold did not enable people to consume "something from nothing;" only increased production can increase real consumption. Hence, the surplus capital in gold served only to inflate the value of the goods that could be produced.

Capital therefore can have a liberating or destabilizing effect on free markets. Capital liberates when backed entirely by the merits of production and used to extend the possibilities for future production and consumption. Capital destabilizes when infusing markets with credit that was not earned through production, thus inflating the costs of what can be consumed by the production that exists. Since excess capital can be generated more easily from the unlimited potential of trade than the finite potential of production, large supplies of concentrated capital tend to reflect the greed of questionable trade practices rather than the actual merits of production.

A recent hedge fund transaction made by Goldman Sachs, an investment bank, drives home this point. A hedge fund is basically a secret investment fund, immune to regulation, designed for accredited (wealthy) investors. Hedge fund managers get a healthy cut of the action through a performance fee. To give you an idea of the quantities of capital we are talking about, one justification CEOs offer for their large compensation packages is that their income is meager in comparison with hedge fund managers. A hedge fund thus originates from an obscene concentration of capital, typically billions of dollars, with the goal of concentrating capital further. In August of 2007 Goldman Sachs invested $2 billion of their own money to help buy out one of their own troubled hedge funds, allegedly for the sake of relieving their investors. The hedge fund recovered slightly and Goldman Sachs made $300 million for the month, while the "rescued" investors lost a fifth of their investment.

Making trades such as these is nice "work" if you can get it; if "work" is what you want to call the electronic trading of nothing but capital. Either Goldman Sachs was just plain lucky, or smart but dishonest. In either case neither the loss of capital by investors nor the gain in capital from hedge fund managers in this transaction reflected the merits of producing goods and services. When financial investors can trade lots of capital back and forth, backed by the monetary policy of government to cover the excesses in capital being created, they can generate and concentrate a whole lot of wealth. But, like the antique spear, they have not increased production. Instead, they have inflated the future costs of consuming the production that exists, with the effects hurting mainly those who do not get to pocket the wealth gained from merely trading capital.

Capital Serving Capital

If a proprietorship were to generate a large amount of capital they could invest this to expand the market for their goods, entice shareholders to come on board and become a business corporation. If a proprietorship generated a large amount of capital gains that they did not reinvest, but rather grew "fat" on profits, they would be undersold and out competed by their small business competitors, whose sales covered little more than the costs of labor and raw materials. Thus, a proprietorship that remains small inevitably has a small amount of capital gains in proportion to their production costs.

A large business corporation needs to generate a larger amount of capital gains in proportion to their production costs. Because of production efficiencies and economies of scale, the large business corporation is seldom undersold by a small proprietorship. Even if they could be undersold by proprietorships the marketing and lobbying advantages of large business corporations to influence markets would work to negate this. On the other hand, a large corporation needs to be attractive to current and potential investors. They need to maximize their "bottom line," i.e. capital gains, or they will lose investment capital to other large corporations. This means that a large corporation redistributes capital away from capital improvements upwards to shareholders, and to decision makers that will maximize profits for shareholders, in order to compete in their particular business climate. These shareholders can be motivated only by capital gains, unlike proprietors where the merits of their labor account for at least a portion of their income.

Let us now contrast large business corporations with smaller proprietorships in light of what we know about the supply of capital. Large corporations form a multilevel redistribution pyramid where the top levels of decision making are motivated only by capital gains. Most shareholders receive these capital gains without ever providing productive labor in exchange. In other words, the capital gains they receive are a form of welfare, if we are to respect the definition of that term. For a proprietorship even the top level of decision making is motivated to some extent by the merits of production. Even the profits hoarded by a greedy proprietor could be considered an inflated exchange for past labors, and thus do not constitute welfare as normally defined. As corporations increase in size so does the amount of capital gains concentrated at the top, in relative proportion to capital improvements for production. Increasing the size of business corporations thus increases the extent that capital serves capital rather than production, and the amount of welfare siphoned off for shareholders.

A favorite mantra of *laissez faire* economists is we need to consider the trade-offs for regulating corporate greed. If we were to insist on capital improving the merits of production, rather than providing welfare gains to shareholders and investors, we would do serious harm to the business climate in which corporations compete. This harm would be passed on to middle class consumers and our economy in general. Let us take the reverse approach and instead look at the major trade-off we have conceded by allowing the concentration of capital for serving capital.

Providing welfare capital gains to shareholders and investors is a disincentive for them to contribute the merits of their own labor to our economy. At least, that is what free market libertarians claim about unearned welfare distributed to the poor. The bitter might claim that "fat cats" have no labor of worth to contribute to our economy, but that is nonsense. Even shareholders and investors grown totally dependent on concentrated welfare capital can produce something of value for our economy, if we wean them from their feelings of entitlement.

Laissez faire economists insist that allowing welfare entitlements through capital gains are necessary because people are motivated chiefly by greed. Allegedly no one would invest to help the economy, even with the reduced risk that government intervention insures, if they could gain but a moderate return of welfare through capital gains. This becomes a self-fulfilling prophecy. When government structures the economy for greed, then of course greed becomes the normative function for the economy. We just might find that if government did not help to promote greed then even those born with entitlements to wealth might strive to meet our higher expectations of providing productive labor for the wealth they gain, and desire at most a moderate return of welfare from capital "earning" more capital.

Part of the problem that lies behind our greed-based economic system is addressed by simply recognizing that providing capital gains in return for no productive labor is a form of welfare, by literal definition of the word. However, the root of the problem lies in the assumption that natural competition is purely a matter of survival of the fittest, with the greediest individuals coming out the winners. We need to take a closer look at the ecological evidence for what competition really accomplishes in a system.

Competition for Capital

Natural competition evidently confuses many economists. Since the days of Spencer, *laissez faire* economists have maintained that competition leads to survival of the fittest, thinking they are bringing the revelations of Wallace and Darwin to the discipline of economics. In their view competition naturally favors large corporations in a capitalist system, since large corporations can better compete for the large supplies of capital needed to make the economy run well. Supply-side and *laissez faire* economists maintain that a concentrated supply of capital in the coffers of corporations is a natural result of market competition.

The ecological principle that fits this view of economics is known as competitive exclusion. When one species starts out with a slight advantage over another species in competing for resources they will accumulate more of those resources. These extra resources now give the "fit" species both an inherent and an acquired competitive advantage, and the fit species accumulates an even greater proportion of the resources in the future. Through this pattern a slight natural advantage progresses into a huge overall competitive advantage and the "unfit" species becomes excluded from the competition, i.e., goes extinct.

There is a slight ethical problem with applying the competitive exclusion principle to economics. Large corporations, like "fit" species, eliminate the competition not just on inherent advantage alone, but on their ability to convert resources into an even bigger competitive advantage that is not inherent to their production. One obvious example of this is the ability of large corporations to get no-bid contracts through their name recognition, connections or lobbyists, rather than on continued merit. Thus, competitive exclusion as an economic practice corrupts merit and free markets.

If anything, this might increase the appeal of competitive exclusion to *laissez faire* economists. There is an earthy attraction to unleashing the natural consequences of "survival of the fittest" to an effete cultural world. The problem with this attraction hints at why some economists should be forced to take ecology classes: contrary to the desire of *laissez faire* economists, natural competition may lead to survival of the fittest within a species, but not between species. Survival of the fittest may be an apt metaphor for moving up the multilevel pyramid within an organization, but does not describe what should naturally occur between all the businesses in a free market driven by merit.

The survival of the fittest implies that many do not survive. If this were true for the competition between species only a few super species would survive. A few super trees would be decomposed by a few super fungi, and then consumed by a few super bugs, which would in turn be eaten by a few super insectivores, which would be devoured by a few super carnivores. Thankfully, the natural world does not work that way.

On the second day of ecology class you learn that organisms follow an alternative path when confronted with being excluded from competition: they adapt to different niches. Different species of trees adapt to compete for different types of climate, different types of soil and different types of terrain. Fungi, bugs, insectivores and carnivores likewise adapt to compete for the increasing array of niches being created by organisms lower down on the food chain. The gift that competition between species brings to the natural world is not survival of the fittest super species but incredible diversity through adaptation. The speciation that occurs in a natural system is like the specialization that occurs in an economic system.

Diversity has a romantic appeal in the world of economics that rivals the survival of the fittest. Specialization is the precursor to trade and wealth. We welcome the diversity that ever-branching technology brings us. Most of all, we applaud the resourceful entrepreneur who adapts to carve out a new niche in the business world. Indeed, we view this as the fulfillment of the American Dream, or at least we used to before corporate media created televisions series for CEOs like Donald Trump.

Concentrating capital is not a natural result of free market competition; it simply could not happen without intervention from some form of government or power structure. Nowadays the successful CEO who excludes competition from smaller businesses receives as much or more acclaim than the entrepreneur who adapts and diversifies with his own. Society does not view the loss of jobs at a large corporation as an opportunity for smaller businesses to fill diversified economic niches, but as a doomsday consequence that requires further government intervention to restore the fitness of the large corporation. Our idolatry of an economic system and CEOs that concentrate capital suggests that we do not support the natural or free tendencies in a market economy. Given all the consequences of concentrating the supply of capital, this is a mistake.

Concentrated Capital and Wealth

Competition that favors the diversification of proprietorships minimizes the redistribution and concentration of capital. From ecology we learn that diversity also increases the resiliency and stability of systems. What tradeoffs to these advantages might make us reluctant to allow competition to proceed on a more natural course of diffusing capital resources? The tradeoffs currently of biggest concern in this country relate to wealth and progress. Quite frankly, we can maximize wealth by concentrating capital. Wealth is created by trade and concentrated capital can be used to induce trade that otherwise might not occur, the reason for the business corporation model to exist.

Even in our greed-based economy there are some methods of inducing trade we allegedly prefer not to encourage. One of the ways to increase the trade value of goods is through the control of production. In the extreme such control becomes a monopoly. In theory there are no future tradeoffs to consider here. Our economic system considers this antithetical to a free market and regulations already prevent this means of increasing wealth. In practice the past thirty years have witnessed a deregulatory atmosphere that has favored mergers, if not outright monopolies. We will explore later the political consequences of deregulation in regards to media consolidation. For now, let us assume that we do not intend to encourage merger and monopolization through deregulation. We do not condone concentrating wealth or increasing trade value in this manner.

Expanding markets often occurs through hype or stylish innovations; the effects of which are often indulgence, waste and neglect. Not all that extra stuff we get for providing welfare capital to shareholders and investors is useful extra stuff. In the previous essay we covered the material costs of indulgence; in later parts we will touch upon political and cultural costs as well. Large corporations are adept at increasing wealth through either marketing or lobbying hype. We have few regulations against hype; indeed, our culture seems to thrive on overstated claims, misleading advertisements and hyped (disproportionate) influence on legislators. Even the Supreme Court supported hype when they ruled that money is the equivalent to free speech. This particularly disturbing topic will be explored further in the political and cultural essays. Money as free speech and corporate media consolidation go well together.

Since we apparently covet wealth created through over inflated value, maybe our current system of rewarding hyped value with large supplies of capital should continue. After all, hyping the value of goods increases our standard of living, raises the stock market and inflates all those other wealth indicators. But are they worth the tradeoffs? Do we really want to forego the stability to a system that a diversification of proprietorships would bring? If hyped wealth is so important maybe we can make provisions for small businesses to advertise and lobby on the same scale as the "big boys," thus providing more economic stability while yet preserving all the wonderful hype to which we are accustomed .... Or we could limit the hype from the "big boys" to be no greater than can be achieved by proprietorships.

While we might not be enamored with concentrating the supply of capital for the sake of controlling production, or even hype, these are not the only means of increasing wealth and our standard of living indicators. One other means of generating wealth, substantive innovations, provides useful goods and services as well as merited wealth. Concentrating supplies of capital to shareholders and investors would be desirable if this was necessary for stimulating substantive innovations.

Concentrated Capital and Progress

Progress is driven by substantive innovations, not stylish innovations or hype. Here are examples: redesigning a car to provide a sexy look is stylish; redesigning a car to get better gas mileage is substantive. Most of us want progress, such as getting better gas mileage from cars. We might even accept a tradeoff of redistributing wealth up multilevel marketing and management pyramids for the sake of progress. But is such a tradeoff necessary?

Many of us in the middle class have adopted this abiding faith that the increasing rise of business corporations in our market economy goes together with progress. We need to distinguish between the two. Corporations are the primary tool for expanding markets; specialization is the primary tool for progress. As long as entrepreneurial incentives and a free exchange of ideas can thrive, the empirical evidence reveals no great advantage to large business corporations for substantive innovations. In fact some empirical evidence reveal that start-up proprietorships are the businesses most frequently introducing substantive innovations, while business corporations tend to manipulate patent laws for the sake of controlling and expanding markets for these innovations.

The Model T brought to us initially by the proprietor Henry Ford got better gas mileage than the current average for the entire U. S. fleet of cars, which currently hovers around 21 miles per gallon. Large corporations have made some recent strides with better gas mileage, such as nonhybrid cars that get up to 45 mpg, and hybrid cars that can get in excess of 60 mpg. But even the hybrid cars are bloated gas guzzlers compared to the hundreds of miles per gallon achieved by some expensive three-wheel prototypes. The gap between 60 mpg and hundreds of mpg suggests the potential for future substantive innovations to deliver very high gas mileage at an affordable price.[6]

Three current efforts to produce an affordable car that exceeds 100 mpg feature different technologies and different entrepreneurial approaches. Steve Fambro, of Accelerated Composites, is an inventor and small business entrepreneur using a carbon composite frame to minimize weight and drag. He claims he will be able to get 300 mpg at a production cost of around $20,000. Charles Gray, the director of EPA's Advanced Technology Division, is working with a hydraulic engine that will increase the efficiency of recycling the energy from braking, a similar strategy used by hybrids. He predicts 70% increases in fuel efficiency and 40% decreases in emissions. Mark Holtzapple and Andrew Rabroker, two academics from Texas A&M, have developed technology to emulate jet engines for improving automobile combustion. They predict a two or threefold increase in gas mileage.

None of these substantive innovations being explored come from a large business corporation. Instead, they represent three common origins for much of the technological progress that occurs: government, entrepreneurial inventors and companies that spin-off from academic research. Such grand innovations as atomic energy and genetic engineering initially started through a combination of these approaches. Business corporations later entered the picture after government helped concentrate the supply of investment capital to attract their involvement.

When innovations require a modest investment of capital, proprietorships often get things started. When they require a huge investment at substantial risk, government historically has set the table for business corporations to profit later on, such as with nuclear energy. In either case business corporations are not

---

6 The information for fuel-saving technologies was obtained from "The Race to 100 mpg" (March 15, 2007), written by Billy Baker for *Popular Science*.

responsible for progress so much as making progress profitable. One inevitable cost to making progress profitable through the business corporation is an increase in wealth disparity.

Concentrated Capital and Wealth Disparity

Economists consider goods, labor and capital as separate but concurrent markets affected by supply and demand. Large corporations require a large amount of capital gains in proportion to their production costs, with much of the extra going to shareholders. Yet boons to capital generally come at an expense to labor. Some recent numbers involving the Katrina reconstruction efforts will illustrate this point, with the help of our buddy Hans.[7]

Hans is a local laborer from New Orleans who wants to do his part in rebuilding the region after Hurricane Katrina. He hears about the federal aid that will be provided through Operation Blue Roof, a reconstruction program that temporarily patches roofs by covering them with blue tarps. Hans needs only a modest amount for his efforts, perhaps twenty cents per square yard of tarp laid down will compensate him fairly, but he discovers that the federal government does not reimburse laborers directly with such modest amounts of market exchange.

Hans approaches one of the contractors being paid directly by the Army Corp of Engineers, the Shaw Group, a corporation based in Louisiana that employs over 20,000 people.[8] The Shaw Group receives $1.75 per square yard for attaching blue tarps to roofs, an exorbitant amount to Hans, but they explain to him that there is a lot of overhead to pursuing government contracts. In any case, Hans can't work for them. While they have expertise at various types of construction, and at getting federal contracts for their work, they do not specialize in attaching blue tarps to roofs. The Shaw Group hires a subcontractor for the work of attaching blue tarps, and the determined Hans goes to the next level down on the contracting pyramid.

Hans discovers that the subcontractor does not specialize at attaching blue tarps to roofs so much as coordinating other subcontractors from areas outside Louisiana to do so. They explain to Hans that arranging the logistics for subcontractors coming in from all over the country to repair roofs requires a lot of money. Hans appreciates their efforts at coordinating the reconstruction but, unfortunately, he can't work for them. He leaves to seek a subcontractor one more level down the pyramid to offer his services.

In the end, the local Hans works for a subcontractor from Ohio. Though

---

7 There are a plethora of reports about the contracting shenanigans in regards to Katrina. You should use Google to start your own investigation, but one recommended source is Joby Warrick's "Multiple Layers of Contractors Drive Up Cost of Katrina Clean-up," written for the Washington Post on 3/20/06

8 Information about the Shaw Group was obtained from their web site.

these subcontractors from other areas are siphoning money from the people devastated by Katrina, Hans bears them no ill will. After all, this is the same approach we take to reconstructing Iraq. He appreciates that these outsiders want to help, and after a disaster of such magnitude there is plenty of work for all. But while many can work, only a few control the money. Funds are disbursed in a manner most beneficial to those further up the contracting pyramid; they have more demands for capital gains than the laborers at the bottom. That helps to explain why Hans ends up receiving less than ten cents per square yard of blue tarp he attaches to roofs, half of what he thought would be a moderate amount and seventeen times less the rate granted to the Shaw Group.

Some of the money that disappears into the top rung of the contracting pyramid goes to high-priced professional labor instead of capital—lawyers and lobbyists do not come cheaply. Even so, most journalists, public interest groups and even some of the Katrina contractors concluded that the government doled out more than what the operating costs actually warranted, and that the benefactors of this excess were not the laborers at the lower levels of the contracting pyramid. Multilevel contracting pyramids achieve the same objectives as multilevel marketing pyramids: accumulating wealth through redistributing money upwards.

The Katrina catastrophe illustrates the impact of multiple levels inherent in large corporations. Whether these levels correspond to marketing, contracting or management the effect is the same; the supply of capital gains are redistributed, concentrated and controlled at the upper levels of the pyramid, enriching upper level managers held accountable to investors motivated only by the supply of capital. Amway may have had flaws in their business model, but their multilevel marketing pyramid that redistributed money upwards, away from the actual labor that earned the money, made them no different than any large corporation.

As a supporter of a capitalist system Hans enthusiastically accepts that a portion of the income from production in our society gets diverted from wages to capital gains, and that this is redistributed upwards. Hans also has come to accept, based on faith more than reality, in the supply side economics that increases the supply of capital as a stimulus. In theory, today's concentrated capital will trickle down as tomorrow's wage. Of course, the natural recipients for increased proportions of capital are large business corporations. Hence, supply-siders maintain that capital will trickle down in a business model where the flow of money naturally tends to be redistributed and concentrated upwards for the sake of shareholders. You will find supply-side and *laissez faire* economists employed by the same corporate (mis)information network; even though "supply side" refers to government boosting capital markets and "*laissez faire*" calls for government abstinence. Confused? You have to be an economic scholar to sort through these nuances.

There is one other means of redistribution affecting Hans, which would temper his favorable regard for our economic system if he clearly understood. The lucky Hans, and millions of Americans like him, believe that our taxes redistribute wealth downwards, since higher income brackets pay a higher proportion of their income in taxes. Yet over the past thirty years the percentage of income that the wealthy has paid in taxes has decreased while the proportion of wealth they control has increased. This has been accomplished in large part by reducing the tax on welfare capital gains in relation to earned production income. The wealthiest segments of our society, many of whom obtain more wealth from capital gains rather than production income, now pay a lower proportion of our taxes than the proportion of wealth they control. Over the past thirty years our tax system has been revamped to further redistribute and concentrate money upwards, unbeknownst to the lucky Hans.[9]

To recap this redistribution system: income determined by a market equilibrium of supply and demand is redistributed from the merits of production to capital gains for investors; capital is concentrated and redistributed by government to the upper levels of a corporate hierarchy, from where only some of the capital trickles back down; and government shifts taxes from capital to wages to redistribute the burdens of redistributing capital away from those with the most redistributed capital to begin with. From the perspective of the middle class this redistribution of wealth upwards has become a tad excessive. America stands for capitalism, but America also allegedly stands for a free market; a real free market that is, not what wealthy executives or investors would have us believe passes for one. If large business corporations cannot compete without the welfare entitlements from the triple redistribution of capital, we should have the courage to allow those corporations to fail.

Concentrated Capital and Market Diversity

When only super species exist, ecosystems are super screwed. Nothing is perfect, neither super species nor diverse species. A deadly virus attacking one out of many diverse species hardly affects the overall ecosystem. The niche filled by one diverse species, both the resources consumed and the resources produced by the species, is modest. Other species can adapt to fill this vacant niche, or not, and the ecosystem recovers quickly nevertheless. On the other hand, if a deadly virus or fungus wipes out a super species, then major impacts follow on both resources consumed and produced in the ecosystem. Wiping out the yellow birches in a northern hardwoods forest has minimal impact; the ecosystem still functions as a northern hardwood ecosystem appearing the same to anyone who wants to stroll through a vernal wood. Wiping out the hemlocks in a forest that is 80% hemlock changes the whole ecosystem structure and function. A shaded forest becomes

---

9 The number crunching behind these claims will be presented in Essay 7.

open to sunlight and invites formerly excluded sun-loving species to enter.

Just as with ecosystems, an economy is in danger of major disturbances when dominated by a few "super" corporations. Instead of a virus, corruption can be the cause of deterioration. A huge corporation could hide the bottom line from investors and resort to other accounting tricks that enable them to gobble up capital they do not deserve. When the truth comes out that capital has disappeared into the upper levels of the management pyramid, and much of the profits are imaginary, the large corporation starts to crumble. The ripple effects of this deterioration include cheated investors, unemployed workers, dissolved pensions and even increased taxes in some states. Enron comes to mind.

The "virus" that afflicts a large corporation may not be corruption in the legal sense. A large corporation could use disproportionate influence with Congress or the President to get huge perks and no-bid contracts. The corporation could influence policy making through lobbying or well-connected individuals in high places to benefit themselves, though detrimental to millions of ordinary people all over the globe. Halliburton comes to mind.

Sometimes even a large corporation can lose their competitive edge. Their market share transfers to other large corporations. When this happens to small businesses only tens or hundreds of workers are affected with minimal damage to the rest of the economy. With a large corporation thousands of workers are affected and other businesses suffer as well. This is one aspect of a trickle-down economy that is more than just theory. General Motors comes to mind.

Diversity provides stability for both ecosystems and economic systems. We blame rogue corporations when large-scale corruption or corporate greed impacts our economy, but these problems are endemic to our "survival of the fittest" system that seeks to concentrate the supply of capital whenever possible. If not for one dominant corporation creating instability in a *laissez faire* economy there would be another. The best defense against this type of instability is a capital supply system that declines to help large business corporations get fatter and, instead, allows the mechanisms of natural competition to stimulate the growth and diversification of small proprietorships.

Concentrated Capital and Market Stability[10]

Financial advisors and economists should stop implying my Dad was dumb. This relates to another way capital is supplied in our economic system, through retirement plans. My father did not have one, which means he committed the number one cardinal sin according to financial advisors interviewed by corporate media everywhere. Actually, my father did have an old-style retirement plan: save money in a bank and work at something he enjoyed doing, at least part time,

---

10   May I point out, once again, that this particular section was written in 2006.

until he died. The second part of his retirement plan was leaving a few warm bodied sons, rather than loads of cool cash, to care for his wife after he died. This retirement plan worked just fine for Mom up until her last six declining months with Alzheimer's.

My father's retirement plan was based entirely on savings and Social Security extracted from his wages, which grew at the rate of inflation. There was an accounting for whatever he consumed in his old age through the deferment of his previous production. In no sense did he attempt to create "something from nothing" with his consumption in a market economy. In contrast, our economy now features investments and retirement plans that can be quite lucrative. One reviewer of these essays, my colleague Mark Brown, pointed out that the elderly are being transformed into consumers the likes of which has never occurred before in history. Mark's concern was the environmental stress this may be creating (after all, he works for a conservation organization), but there is also an economic stress. Not all this extra consumption credit has been accounted for by the retirees own production. Either the extra capital in our retirement plans must be accounted for by other people's production—we are retiring on the backs of other people's labors, such as our children or people overseas—or the extra capital being created by government to cover these funds creates a destabilizing, inflationary effect on the economy. To the extent that our retirement plans are in the hands of investment banks like Goldman Sachs, who can generate lots of extra capital simply by making a mistake, you can bet the destabilizing scenario is more likely.

Lucrative retirement plans are but one type of investment that draws money at a faster rate than inflation, without having to produce anything through the merits of labor. That we cannot "consume something for nothing" is hard to accept by anyone involved in the investment community. They might argue that their increased consumptive potential from high yield investments derives from the merited labor of smart thinking. This ignores the fact that "smart thinking" of this type produces no more for our economic system than completing the Sunday crossword puzzles. It also ignores that many "smart" investments are simply lucky investments.

The investment community also might argue that their capital fuels our economy. They admit that they use money to make money, rather than producing something of real substantive value, but without their investment capital the economy would stagnate. They ignore or discredit other means of concentrating capital, such as government providing research money to universities. They ignore or discredit the notion of attaching strings to concentrating capital, so that the capital might be put in the service of merited production. They also ignore the fact that substituting greed for merit has costs. Unfortunately, Milton "no free lunch" Friedman never intended his own slogan to be applied against his own philosophy in this manner.

Both of these disingenuous rationalizations—high yield investments reflect the merited labor of smart thinking, or high yield investments provide a public service to the economy—are attempts to block from our consciousness the unsavory pursuit of "something for nothing." We are loathe to accept that our increased consumption potential has been diverted from other people's labor, or by infusing destabilizing currency into an economy that is not backed by any kind of production.

Regardless of the drawbacks of unearned capital, financial advisors and economists do have a point. In my father's day a house, college tuition and insurance were more affordable to the middle class than those essential ingredients of the American Dream are today. Back then the middle class did not need retirement plans beyond savings and Social Security. But times have changed. Now that we are blessed with a much higher standard of living more of the middle class go into debt while making our house, college tuition and insurance payments. Once we acquire some debt we might as well go a bit further in the hole and invest in a retirement plan, if one is not already supplied as a means of keeping us hooked to the same employer. Plus, adding together the investments in a retirement plan and the interest paid on debts floods the economy with more capital than the savings deposits we no longer can afford to make to a local bank, a welcome condition to both supply-siders and *laissez faire* advocates.

Yes, financial advisors and economists may be right; the contrast with how my father paid for the college education of his five sons lends credence to their advice. We sons earned Bachelors, Masters, and Doctoral degrees; our upward mobility afforded us a much higher standard of living than our father who merely earned a GED; and we accumulated more debt. Our father the salesperson did not borrow capital even for our education, while his sons the professionals must provide a steady supply of capital for corporations in the form of retirement accounts and interest payments on debt.

Today many people draw down from a retirement plan to finance their children's education. With three teenagers soon to enter college I may use the strategy myself.[11] Using a capital investment source to pay for our children's education seems only fitting. Since capital investment and higher education both aim to accomplish similar goals of upward mobility, why not trade one for the other. If my father had borrowed capital to pay for our education he could have used the extra flow of dollars to buy more stuff. More importantly from the point of view of *laissez faire* economists, he would have contributed more capital to a market structured to provide a competitive advantage for business corporations over proprietorships.

My father was not perfect. As a middle-aged salesman he smoked and was overstressed, a bad recipe for his health. On the other hand, putting his sons

---

11 Oops! Written too soon!

through college without a borrowed supply of capital seemed to please my father immensely. His health actually improved during his golden years as he quit smoking, walked regularly and enjoyed his work on a part time basis right up until his death. He left this world contented that he had fulfilled the promise of the American Dream for his family. If given the choice to borrow throughout his life and retire early, he actually might have declined. Some folks are just hard for financial advisors and *laissez faire* economists to figure out.

Irrational Greed

Financial advisors and *laissez faire* economists could learn something from game theorists. The allocation game "Traveler's Dilemma," invented by Kaushik Basu, unveils a paradox in the assumption that a market economy runs best when everyone acts rationally based on greed.[12] In the case of "Traveler's Dilemma" the most rational greedy behavior does not provide the optimal outcome of the game, indeed, the worst individual and overall outcome occurs as the result of greed.

The details of "Travelers Dilemma" are a little involved, so let us turn to another game used by the cultural anthropologist, Edward Fisher, with both his American students and with Mayans from Guatemala. The players are teamed up in pairs. One person in the pair is given a profit, such as $100, and instructed to divide the money up however he/she wants. The split could be 50:50, 99:1 or any other possibility. There was an important caveat: the other person in the pair could choose to accept or reject the offer. If the offer was rejected no one received money.[13]

Professor Fischer's game generated three types of results. The economists in his class tended to choose a lopsided split such as 99:1, intending to keep most of the profits for themselves. The other people in his class tended to choose an even 50:50 split. The Mayans he studied often chose a split that was favorable to their partner, such as 49:51, explaining afterwards that the partner probably needed the money more.

The free money provided by the professor shares two important properties with how our economy uses capital. The capital was gained without any labor by the recipient, such as what occurs with inherited wealth or investors, and initially was concentrated rather than diffused, such as what occurs with business corporations. The economist offer, based on their "rational greed," usually was rejected by the other person in the pair. People preferred not getting any money at all rather than legitimize greedy behavior. The types of offers made by the other students and by the Mayans were accepted. Thus, the economists came up with the worst overall solution based on their "rational" decision of greed.

12 "The Traveler's Dilemma," *Scientific American* (June 2007).
13 From *Peoples and Cultures of the World* (2004), a Course on CD taught by Professor Edward Fischer and provided by The Teaching Company.

Even if the offers of economic students were accepted their solution would not be optimal for a market economy. Let us assume that Professor Fischer's classroom contained a market economy involving Mayan spears with a production value of $45. When capital gains are diffused in a 50:50 split, everyone can buy a Mayan spear for $50, providing a $10 profit for two spears. When the capital gains are concentrated in a 99:1 split only one spear can be consumed. Granted, the extra concentration of capital means the spear merchant can get an inflated profit of $10 or more for just one spear, but the demand and consequent production of the market economy has been cut in half. The Mayan response of charity is just too irrational to take seriously, of course, though it also leads to better results than those produced by rational economists.

Henry Ford is famous not only for assembly line production, but for the generous wages he gave his workers. He gave them $5 an hour back in the early twentieth century, touting the philosophy that he wanted them to be able to buy the Model Ts they were making. Wall Street capitalists were in an uproar over the charitable Mr. Ford, but the result was better workers and greater demand for Model Ts. One of the most successful and famous entrepreneurs in history allocated money more like a Mayan than the *laissez faire* economists whose greed ultimately loses the game.

To date the only empirical evidence that rational decisions of greed coexists with a free market economy is, um, well, there is none. Granted, there are some scholarly deductions made from presumably infallible axioms, whether from the *laissez faire* economist or the neoliberal; the Chicago School or the Austrian School; the minarchist or the anarcho-capitalist. We get lots of talking heads on corporate media platforms telling us how rational greed and free markets work together, but they cannot point to an example that is free of some sort of coercion, ultimately backed by government. Nor can these libertarian folks point to empirical evidence that proves private property to be a natural right as declared by John Locke, rather than a cultural entitlement bestowed by political governments. That little stickler of a detail puts a crimp in many of their scholarly dogmas deduced from "infallible" axioms.

Ecologists stress how all things are connected in a natural system. Good and bad economic trends that coincide for thirty years or more are probably connected, even dependent on each other. Over the past thirty years our supply-side approach to capital, coupled with our multilevel pyramid schemes for corporations, has generated tremendous wealth and great retirement plans. During that same period we have trended towards greater wealth disparity, higher costs for essential goods such as housing, less market stability and more debt. Only a *laissez faire* economist would fail to recognize these steady, noncyclical trends are connected.

We should not assume that any economic system is perfect, including capitalism. Despite our love for capitalism we need to at least acknowledge that people in power have structured the supply of capital to give a competitive advantage to business corporations over proprietorships. While this version of the competitive exclusion principle may be favored by economists from Spencer to Friedman, and no doubt is enthusiastically supported by all *laissez faire* economists, competition does not work that way in the natural world and need not work that way with capitalism. More effective systems for concentrating capital and redistributing wealth upwards are better known as feudalism or colonialism, depending on the scope of the redistribution. The economists in Professor Fischer's class, in fact, had the same economic philosophy for distributing unmerited wealth as feudal lords.

Where are the Henry Fords in today's greed-based market economy? They certainly are not to be found in the CEOs that make hundreds of times the amount of money as the workers on the lowest rungs of the corporation pyramid; nor are they to be found among the hedge fund managers and investors that trade nothing but ethereal capital. Yet the greedy seem to be winning, not at doing what is best for the economy of course, but at what is best for the greedy. Laborers are accepting the 99:1 allocation of unmerited wealth instead of walking out the door. Part of the reason large corporations get away with this is because government has their backs, to the detriment of both productive laborers and the proprietorships where they might turn for an honest deal. The next essay on the self-interests of labor provides more understanding of how greed wins in today's economy.

ESSAY 4 – THE SELF-INTEREST OF LABOR

Overview

- Our commitment to wealth has consequences outside of economics.
- The *laissez faire* view of self-interest necessarily exploits resources and labor.
- *Laissez faire* economists refer to Adam Smith's "invisible hand of self-interest" to justify greed.
- Large corporations are governed by selfish self-interest in relation to laborers.
- Proprietorships are governed by mutual self-interest in relation to laborers.
- Laborers are governed by holistic self-interests of personal growth, family obligations, community service, political involvement and economic productivity.
- *Laissez faire* economists strive to convince the middle class we have more leisure than really exists.
- As apologists for *laissez faire* economics, "free market" libertarians are really puppet libertarians.
- Since the seventies corporations sponsored think tanks, endowed academic positions, funded lobbyists, hired public relation firms and acquired media to self-promote and convey the *laissez faire* message.
- This corporate funded cabal depends on an academic pedigree and faulty applications of empirical data as tools of persuasion.

The Self-Interest of a Family Man

I once lost my job. I worked as a high school teacher at a time when teacher salaries were being raised substantially; the taxpayer response was to cut positions. My position as a science teacher was not cut but, being untenured, I was bumped by a tenured alternative education teacher who was certified in science. As the principal gave me the bad news, he asked me not to look for jobs at other high schools. The teacher that bumped me was looking elsewhere for alternative education positions and the plan was for me to return to my job as a science teacher when he left.

No one likes losing a job, especially after trying your best. Two small children with a third one on the way provided ample motivation to be a good breadwinner. My first year as a teacher I worked in excess of 70 hours a week and almost 60 hours a week the following two years, while Cindy stayed home with the young kids and my elderly Mom. The hard work was rewarded with excellent job evaluations and a principal that did not want to risk me finding a job elsewhere. Unfortunately, my hard work did not achieve my number one objective as a breadwinner: financial security for my family.

I abided by my principal's wishes not to look for a high school job elsewhere, but I sent an application to graduate school—just in case. Everything came to a head in the month of June. On the third Thursday of that month Cornell University offered me a teaching assistantship. The assistantship would provide both money and free tuition, but not enough compensation to motivate a good breadwinner. That changed on Friday, the very next day, when the principal called me into his office to inform me the alternative education teacher had not found another job so I had better start looking elsewhere. A few days later my Mom passed away. Our biggest reason for staying at home passed away with her.

Do you ever feel that a related sequence of events happens for a reason? Though the teaching assistantship was guaranteed money my family's income would be below poverty level for the next few years. On the other hand, I was not optimistic about looking for a teaching job in late June. I accepted the teaching assistantship; the rest, as they say, is history.

From that ordeal I learned some invaluable lessons about one's self-interest and the labor market. In working 60 hours a week I spent less time with my family than I would have liked and, in retrospect, less time than what they really deserved. I sacrificed the labor of being a good father for the labor of being a good breadwinner, without the desired result. Being a good father was the only type of labor completely within my control and, I realized, the more important of the two objectives. Investing only three years of my life to discover that was a blessing. Some people never find out. With our market economy driven by greed rather than merit, the self-interest of our labors has been influenced accordingly, affecting the lives of the middle class in ways that extend beyond economics.

The Self-Interests of K-species versus R-species

Ecologists once again provide some useful insights on economics, this time in regards to the "virtues" of selfishness. An abandoned farm will go through a series of changes that ecologists call succession. Shrubs succeed pasture, sun-loving trees succeed shrubs and shade-tolerant trees succeed sun-loving trees. Shade tolerant trees form what ecologists call a climax community, meaning that no other species succeed them without some external help from the forces of nature or culture. These forces are called disturbances, which can range from windstorm, to fire, to logging. Such disturbances renew the process of succession.

Succession reveals a dirty little secret about the presumed harmonious natural world deep ecologists call Gaia. Some species are greedy bastards; and through their selfishness they create the conditions for their own demise. All trees need the sun, but sun-loving trees are the ones that germinate and grow best with plenty of sunshine. They grow and spread to soak in as much of this resource as quickly as possible, inhibiting other species from getting their share. Eventually they turn a sunny area into a shaded area, thus changing their own environment to the benefit of future shade-tolerant species.

The same dark secret applies to many animal species. Take Bambi and his kin, for example. In a case once described in most introductory ecology texts, deer were allowed to thrive on an island plateau in Arizona that was void of hunters, natural predators or competing livestock. The selfish vermin proceeded to gobble up all the vegetation while reproducing like mad. The population eventually crashed.

Not all species exhibit such selfish indulgence. Shade-tolerant trees display what we might anthropomorphize as patience. Wolves, who for so long have been vilified, are role models of restraint. They cull rather than gobble up resources, hunt down the infirmed and the weak and apply internal controls for limiting their own population. These are the type of species that dominate a climax community of plants or occupy the top of an animal food chain.

Ecologists use the terms r-species and k-species to distinguish between organisms that gobble up resources quickly and ones that "pace" their consumption of resources through their own behavior. Let us borrow and adapt these ecological terms for contrasting self-interests. People who equate self-interest only with greed endorse the indulgent r-species approach to resources; people who equate their self-interest with at least some unselfish motivations endorse the restrained k-species approach.

In an extensively-cited essay titled "The Tragedy of the Commons" (1968, for the journal *Science*), Garrett Hardin portrays a village that provides a commons for villagers to pasture their livestock. He maintained that if this activity was not regulated, each villager would attempt to maximize the benefit gained by their own livestock from grazing in the commons. In so doing the commons would be overgrazed and rendered unfit for future grazing. This scenario assumes self-interest to be greedy, and that humans impact resources the same as r-species. Hardin's conclusion that we need regulation to avoid "the tragedy of the commons" suggests that, unlike k-species, we need external restraints in order to stabilize our demand on resources.

I will discuss later whether Hardin's assumptions apply to all cultures; for now let us explore whether they apply to a corporate culture. Do greedy *Homo sapiens* impact markets the same way they do resources? Or should labor markets in particular be unregulated to actually encourage greed, thus allowing the divine guidance of the invisible hand? Are CEOs, corporate-funded think tanks and *laissez faire* economists correct that government should turn the reigns of the economy over to corporations in the best self-interests of everyone?

The Game of Self-Interest

Adam Smith, the recognized father of economics, described markets as being guided by an invisible hand of self-interest.[1] In the case of the goods market a business seeks to supply a gadget for as much money as possible; the consumer demands a gadget for as little money as possible. The invisible hand of self-interest steers supply to meet demand at an acceptable price for the market. In the labor market a business demands labor to build a gadget for as little money as possible; the laborer seeks to supply that labor for as much money as possible. The invisible hand of self-interest steers the supply of labor to meet the demand at an acceptable wage for the market.

A battle of self-interests can be like a game of chicken. You veer from the challenge first, you lose. If a business veers from their self-interest they become uncompetitive; if laborers veer from their self-interest they become exploited. In a market economy the consequences of such a game of chicken extend further. If one side veers from their self-interest, everyone is harmed. Uncompetitive businesses are bad for a market economy, as are consumers who do not earn a decent wage to spend on goods or save towards capital.

Unfortunately, the laborers always lose at this game of chicken when they come from the middle class and the business is a large corporation. Middle class laborers are more likely to have unselfish motives that they equate with their self-interest; middle class laborers are more likely to be influenced by obligations to family and other factors outside of markets. Consequently, middle class laborers are more likely to have sacrificed something when they pursue a game of self-interested greed in the market.

Even Adam Smith cautioned that large corporations were in a position to exploit this game of self-interest. He advocated safeguards against greedy corporate collusion that would thwart the otherwise infallible guidance provided by the invisible hand of self-interest. *Laissez faire* economists tend to ignore an earlier work by Smith, *The Theory of Moral Sentiments* (1759). Smith insisted that sympathy should be a prime motivator for humans, and that our own self-interest is heavily influenced by societal interest. Society, as a result, was held together by concepts of what was merited. In the later essays on culture, this "sympathy" that Smith promotes corresponds to what will be called our sense of belonging.

Laissez faire economists insist that the middle class should abide by the invisible hand of self-interest in a market economy driven only by greed, not by motivators of sympathy or merit. They show far less concern about the potential abuses of corporations in this game of self-interests than did the father

---

1 The "Bible" of economics is Adam Smith's *The Wealth of Nations* (1776).

of economics. Once again, let us not trust their beliefs, but rather examine more closely the following *laissez faire* rules for the invisible hand of self-interest:

* Self-interest means greed.
* No one should veer from their own self-interest.
* Self-interest is determined only by markets.

Selfish Self-Interest

Consider the plight of our pal Hans, who abides by the *laissez faire* rules for self-interest while working for a large corporation. Large corporations offer jobs aplenty at the lowest entry level, making job hunting easier. They also use their economies of scale to offer better pension and health care benefits than can most proprietorships. One need not even be selfish to find this attractive. Thus there are many laborers just like Hans seeking to maximize their economic self-interest by working for a large corporation.

There are two ways for a family to increase income: by getting a better wage, or by working more hours. Guess which one of those options a corporate economy prefers to offer. The irony is that the greedier the labor force, the more a large corporation can resort to maximizing the income of laborers through more hours rather than through a better wage. This is basic supply and demand at work. If the middle class creates so much supply for jobs because both adults in many families expect to work long hours, and if the demand for jobs can be controlled through a few large corporations, then the labor supplier sacrifices the ability to dictate the wage and hours to satisfy demand. Census data confirms that over the past thirty years family income for the bottom two quintiles have remained relatively constant, but the amount of hours worked has increased.[2]

When neither side veers from their self-interests in a game of chicken, then the winner becomes the side with the most control. Metaphorically speaking, when two vehicles choose to stay in the middle of the road, the cement truck obliterates the subcompact. Large corporations control the labor market when self-interest becomes pure greed. Large corporations can provide the greatest supply of jobs for those in desperate economic situations, with the additional bait of the best pensions and health care, enabling them to dictate the conditions for hours and wages. Since smaller businesses already lose out on other economies of scale, they often need to follow the corporate lead with labor practices. Thus, large agribusinesses employ large numbers of cheap immigrant labor to maximize their profit margin while many family farms need to follow suit just to compete.

In our society the invisible hand of self-interest would become more "even-handed" if we took better steps to temper the influence wielded by large

---

2 Refer to Essay 7 for the empirical data behind these assertions.

corporations. As long as self-interest is defined only by greed, one could argue that this does not matter. Why not work longer hours if there is nothing better by which one's self-interest is determined? So what if Hans is motivated only by selfishness? What are the alternatives? This may seem like an odd alternative for the game of self-interest, particularly for *laissez faire* economists, but what if both sides veered from selfishness?

Mutual Self-Interest

The carpenter I hire for home improvement projects too large for my attention is a personal friend of mine. We met when he participated as a high school student in an alternative education program I organized, which involved backpacking the Long Trail. He went on to backpack the entire Appalachian and Pacific Crest Trails, as I also have done. Given our mutual backgrounds and friendship, I am concerned now about what he charges me for labor. Occasionally, the guy sneaks a "freebie" in on me. With every job he starts I admonish him to charge me more than what he was going to do. In this labor market, the battle of self-interests finds both sides shaking hands and tackling the challenge together.

I undergo a similar "battle" of self-interests with my employer. After my forced hiatus from this geographic area, I returned with multiple advanced degrees and a highly technical trade. I could have demanded a hefty salary in the corporate world. Instead, I chose to work for a local nonprofit organization where I not only get paid less but I actually (gasp) volunteer some of my time for free. For starters my organization does good work for society, but they also provide the means for me to stay in this area and to organize my schedule around my family first. Indeed, my boss accepts that if a conflict for my time arises between family obligations and work obligations, my family always comes first. Here is another labor market where the battle of self-interests has diffused into a cooperative endeavor.

You won't find large corporations adopting an unselfish approach to self-interest and the labor market. There is nothing inherently conspiratorial or malicious about the selfish pursuits of large corporations (though, in practice, some of these selfish pursuits turn out to be criminal). When the top and the bottom of a labor pyramid in a large corporation are so far removed from each other, the self-interests related to the market economy are all that they have in common. Can you imagine a policy by the CEO of a Fortune 500 to chat with all the clerks from the mailroom and allow them to go home whenever called by some type of family obligation?

Such consideration can only be afforded by smaller proprietorships. This is not to say that this is inevitable; a sole proprietor could be a greedy, uncaring jerk. Still, the potential of good faith, interpersonal interactions between the highest and lowest rungs of labor exists only with these smaller businesses. We see this better blending of self-interest in regards to goods and capital as well. Smaller businesses need to gain the trust of middle class consumers in their local area, not dupe them through hype or renewable demands. Proprietorships divert less money to the capital market than a business corporation, which means less incentive to please wealthy capital suppliers with investment welfare and more to please middle class labor suppliers with earned wages. With ample unselfish regard for each other the hand of self-interest remains not only invisible but impotent.

The small business ideal is where the owner knows all the employees. At worst, the sole proprietor may have as one level a management team that, in turn, knows all the employees. The employer-employee relationship thus transcends the self-interest of selfishness. The ideal of a large corporation by definition has at least two additional levels of separation automatically built in: the shareholders who know only the top levels of management, and a "metamanagers" level. In regards to the latter, the national and multinational jurisdiction of a large corporation needs to transcend the management of production to managing the management of production at dispersed locations.

The extra two levels of separation in the corporate business pyramid (and, in reality, there are more than just two extra levels) alienates the top from the bottom. This alienation relates to both intimacy and purpose. For the top of the pyramid, the shareholders, their self-interests relate only to capital. For the bottom of the pyramid, the laborers, their self-interests relate only to wages. Even if the shareholders and laborers of a corporation were well-acquainted they are still far apart in terms of their corporate self-interests. Without shared intimacy or purpose with the bottom of the corporate pyramid, there is little to temper the greed at the top. The laborers who do not like the rules of self-interest established at the top of the corporation have no alternative if they wish to retain their employment. Abiding by these rules imposes extra costs on the laborer that transcends economics.

Holistic Self-Interest

Ecologists would love to pretend that something functions in a closed system. Unfortunately, that simply is not reality. One organism is affected by another organism, one population is affected by another population, and one community is affected by another community in the overall landscape of different ecosystems. Meanwhile, the structure and function of organisms, populations, communities and even landscapes are constantly changing over time. Oh, the enviable fantasy of *laissez faire* economists that assume an invisible hand of selfish self-interest operates in a closed market system whose laborers are motivated only by economic factors.

Our economy is not a closed system regardless of how convenient that assumption may be for *laissez faire* economists, large corporations or corporate funded think tanks. To function as good citizens we need to distribute some of our labors to political and cultural systems in addition to a market economy. Extracting long hours from laborers that want to maximize their self-interest of selfishness is a terrific solution for the large corporations that control the supply of jobs; but the cost to society are citizens who renege on their political and cultural obligations.

Our self-interest goes beyond our role as citizens; our self-interest includes personal growth and maintenance. For those of us that have families the self-interest for growth and maintenance at least doubles. This is not just a matter of getting enough rest and eating right, though those two factors alone should take up at least one-third of a 24-hour day. We grow emotionally, socially and spiritually. In today's complex society few would deny the need for emotional and social growth. Some may balk at the concept of spiritual growth, but what would life be without the beauty of music, nature or compassion. Everyone should get a healthy dose of spiritual growth on a daily basis.

All this self-interest requires labor and time. Let us assume the time for our self-interest should be partitioned equally between economics, politics, community, personal growth and family growth. If we have 15 hours a day to spend on our self-interest—with the other 9 hours devoted to eating, sleeping, and other maintenance activities—that leaves 3 hours for each obligation. Over the course of a week that amounts to 21 hours devoted to the labor market, in the same ballpark as what foragers devote to their "economic" activity. Combining the hours for two adults equals 42 hours a week devoted to the labor market by one family. This may be considered an ideal fantasy in our society now, but this "fantasy" of a 40-hour work week total for a family unit was once the middle class reality on Emerson Street only forty years ago.

The similarity between the amount of labor for two adults in a "primitive" hunting and gathering society and the now quaint ideal for an "advanced" market economy may not be mere coincidence. Foraging cultures lasted for thousands of years in this country, until they were forced to change, and still exist in pockets of the world. Individuals from these societies demonstrate the mental ability to adapt to our world, but not always the emotional ability. In particular, frustrated colonialists reported difficulties with employing former foragers because they are accustomed to a more leisurely work week.[3] This suggests that they maintained their societies for so long through actual intent. There may be something either innately adaptive or satisfying to a work week of 40 hours or less shared by two adults. But even innate drives can be overcome with the right amount of enculturation.

One could construct a believable paradigm about behavior based on holistic self-interest. Maybe the greater proportion of self-interest that the middle class needs to devote to our market economy these days creates an imbalance. Not

3 As chronicled by Marshall Sahlins in *Stone Age Economics* (1972), reporting on the Yamana and other South American cultures.

only do we have insufficient time for politics, community, family and ourselves, but our imbalance causes waste of the time we do have. The holistic self-interest paradigm may only have circumstantial evidence in way of support. Still, that's more support than for the selfish self-interest paradigm championed by *laissez faire* economists.

Leisure Studies of the Federal Reserve Banks

Recently, *laissez faire* economists have been claiming that our economic system actually increases leisure. Perhaps they anticipate the danger from a labor force sensing that greed is not in our overall best self-interest. In their 2002 annual report, "The Fruits of Free Trade," the Federal Reserve Bank of Dallas hints that self-interest in the labor market must go beyond economics. You might be surprised by this confession, given that Texas is home to oil companies and other large corporations that would gain from manipulating laborers who equate self-interest only with greed. But in their report they extol the benefit of free trade to save labor. They contrast this with our overburdened forefathers who labored so hard to be self-sufficient.

In reality, the burden of labor has less to do with the degree of self-sufficiency than with how much material stuff the laborer wants. The 20 hour work week for early foragers was due to their production only for what they used. The large increase in work weeks were the result of cultures producing for exchange in addition to use.[4] Maybe the economists for the Federal Reserve Bank of Dallas are not aware that the trend from the seventies until the present has been an increasing work week for the family unit in our increasingly dependent global economy. They probably were unaware that, while our "American pioneers" may have worked from "sunup to sundown," the Native Americans during the same era had the sparse work week typical of foragers, part-timers at best and far less hours than laborers in our present global economy. Then again, perhaps a financial institution in an oil-driven economy has selfish reasons for falsely claiming that dependency on global markets saves labor.

This desire to convince us how much labor is being saved these days has spread through the Federal Reserve System to the Federal Reserve Bank of Boston. They sponsored a study done by Mark Aguiar and Erik Hurst, titled "Measuring Trends in Leisure: The Allocation of Time over Five Decades" (2006). A news article written by Steven E. Landsburg for the online magazine *Slate*, titled "The Theory of the Leisure Class" (March 9, 2007), sums up nicely what Aquiar and Hurst found out about leisure since the sixties: "First, leisure (like income) has increased dramatically across the board. Second, though everyone's a winner, the biggest winners are at the bottom of the socioeconomic ladder."

---

4 From *Stone Age Economics* (1972), by Marshall Sahlins.

We rely on reporters of research to do our thinking for us just like we use calculators to crunch numbers for us. Yet when we use a calculator we make quick mental checks just to make sure we did not make an error in our method of using the calculator. For example, if we multiply two long odd numbers with a calculator and we get an even number we know a mistake was made with the data entry. Similarly, we should check Landsburg's claim with our own common experiences regarding the matter of work and leisure. Since I live in the house I was raised in, I have an excellent longitudinal perspective to draw upon for a mental check.

According to the trends reported in the study Cindy and I should be working one more market hour a week combined than did my Mom and Pop. This negligible increase in employment is swallowed up, in theory, by less work and far greater leisure in our time spent away from our paying jobs. Cindy and I generally have worked part time since coming back to the area, in order to accommodate our schedules to our kids without using day care. Even at part time employment when our kids were young we worked, on average, about ten hours a week more than my father (the man with a GED), in order to maintain the same socioeconomic status in the same middle class house on the same middle class street in the same rural town. With our kids as teenagers we now work twenty hours more a week than did my father.

Our reality of greater market work hours surpasses the study's theoretical increase of 14 leisure hours combined per male and female. Similarly, more houses on this street have both adults working, and the same adult working multiple jobs, than in the sixties and seventies. Finally, day care was rare in the sixties in the seventies, common now. Do Aguiar, Hurst and Landsburg all suggest that adults put their kids in day care nowadays to better enjoy their theoretical increase in leisure, or that we do so for the sake of one extra hour of employment per family unit? It's time to recheck the data entry.

Laissez faire Reliability and Validity

I mentioned earlier that all scientific research is based on assumptions that make a tradeoff between reliability and validity. The greater the number of assumptions that need to be made to make empirical evidence reliable, the further the researcher is from valid reality. The study done by Aguiar and Hurst involves so many assumptions they could just as well have been researching the *Matrix*, but then, they are economists (as is Landsburg). Their "five decades" analysis (which actually spans forty years) involves synthesizing the results from five different time-use surveys done over that span. Each of these surveys had their own assumptions about how to sample the population, since no researcher has the resources or the cooperation to get everyone in the population to be a part of their research. Each of these surveys had their own assumptions about how to measure the sample. Each of these surveys had their own assumptions about how to generalize the measurements of a sample to the reality of a population. Making comparisons between the time-use surveys required even more assumptions about how to resolve different assumptions of how to sample, measure and generalize.

To ground their assumptions for comparing different surveys of different samples at different times they compared these results to the Panel Study of Income Dynamics (PSID), a longitudinal survey. This survey has the advantage of drawing from a much larger sample of the population and a standardized methodology over time. However, this survey makes additional distinct assumptions about sampling, measurement and generalization. So, the results and conclusions presented by Aguiar and Hurst are based on their assumptions about grounding their assumptions about comparing surveys with different sets of assumptions, using other surveys with different sets of assumptions. They detail all these assumptions quite well. They have a whole lot of reliability going for them but, unfortunately, they fall a bit short on validity.

Though Aguiar and Hurst grounded the time-use results with the PSID, one is left to wonder how well grounded the results are with reality. For example, when a sixties family went out to dinner that was a leisure activity. When one parent and the kids eat out today they often are squeezing in a meal between soccer practice and a play rehearsal. This one simple example has several implications for the changes in the meaning of behaviors over time. The increase in adult supervised activities these days is an inexpensive and necessary alternative to day care for many parents. Eating out between the activities is no longer leisure so much as "nonproductive work" as defined by Aguiar and Hurst, but they categorize this as leisure. Eating out more often also means grocery shopping less often. Being "on the go" more because of children activities also means less time spent on household chores, but not necessarily an increase in leisure time. This is just one single example of why comparing behaviors across decades of time requires more grounding than can be achieved through simplistic classification and statistical maneuvers, based on a plethora of assumptions.

Aguiar and Hurst mention how sampling and measurement bias could have affected the results. They mentioned that excluding retired individuals biased the amount of leisure time downwards. Fair enough, though this bias disproportionately underreports the leisure of upper classes. They mentioned that there may be a good amount of leisure occurring at work, where people are surfing the web and using email. Fair enough, though this bias disproportionately underreports the leisure of the well educated. They mentioned that the time-use surveys do not measure vacation time well. Fair enough, though the researchers also mention that vacation time and wages are correlated, meaning that this bias disproportionately underreports the leisure associated with higher incomes. What seems lost on Aguiar and Hurst (and Landsburg) is that these biases undercut their claims about growing leisure disparity being the inverse of growing income disparity.

Aguiar and Hurst do not acknowledge one source of bias common to surveys, response rates. Survey literature documents that response rate improves with level of education.[5] Accordingly we can expect the time-use surveys to be a more accurate representation of the well-educated, save for the potential underreporting of leisure as admitted (perhaps unknowingly) by Aguiar and Hurst. For those less educated the ones with less leisure are the ones less likely to respond to a time-use survey, particularly one that requires estimating how precious time blocks have been spent. Thus throughout the decades we would expect the surveys to overestimate leisure for the lower socioeconomic classes by not documenting those with the least leisure. Ironically, the less leisure that occurs over the years, such as we would expect for increasing numbers of families headed by a single parent, the more leisure will be overestimated for lower and middle classes by surveys that omit their responses.

Aguiar and Hurst use more assumptions to derive their conclusions than do the ecologists who develop climate models. Here is but one possible suggestion for a much simpler approach that can be easily communicated to the middle class. Track the number of hours spent by children in day care and divide by family size. This has the advantages of uniform measurement over time, without the problem of sampling and response bias. The assumptions needed are minimal. We would assume that each day care hour is an additional "nonproductive work" hour a parent would otherwise have to spend. Most of us would then assume that the reason parents do this is due to an overabundance of productive work hours. However, economists like Aguiar, Hurst and Landsburg might assume that parents ditch their kids in day care to gain more leisure time, in which case we should be prepared to do our own mental checks on their research.

Puppet Libertarians

Why did the Federal Reserve Bank of Boston sponsor a study that needed so many assumptions, when more straightforward approaches are at hand? Recall Landsburg's statement that income has "dramatically increased across the board." In real dollars income has decreased for the lowest quintile, remained about the same for the middle quintiles and increased "dramatically" only for the highest quintile. The numbers are crunched here in Essay 7, but this is so well established at this point that only people with a certain type of philosophy attempt to dispute it with convoluted studies or reasoning. The concluding paragraphs of the article written by Landsburg provide some further insight into his philosophy:

5 While at Cornell I was involved with the Human Dimensions Research Unit, based out of the Department of Natural Resources. Survey response rates and biases were one focus of our research.

"First, man does not live by bread alone. Our happiness depends partly on our incomes, but also on the time we spend with our friends, our hobbies, and our favorite TV shows. So, it's a good exercise in perspective to remember that by and large, the big winners in the income derby have been the small winners in the leisure derby, and vice versa.

Second, a certain class of pundits and politicians are quick to see any increase in income inequality as a problem that needs fixing—usually through some form of redistributive taxation. Applying the same philosophy to leisure, you could conclude that something must be done to reverse the trends of the past 40 years—say, by rounding up all those folks with extra time on their hands and putting them to (unpaid) work in the kitchens of their "less fortunate" neighbors. If you think it's OK to redistribute income but repellent to redistribute leisure, you might want to ask yourself what—if anything—is the fundamental difference."

Ouch! Landsburg seems to have a huge chip on his shoulders. You wonder what some parasitic single parent basking in leisure did to make him so resentful (perhaps refused to do his household chores for minimum wage?). Landsburg is a self-proclaimed free market libertarian; these are really *laissez faire* economists on a public relations mission for corporations. A more accurate term describing their behavior would be puppet libertarians. The strong tones at the end of this article are an apprehensive attempt by a puppet libertarian to ward off public disapproval over a greed-based market economy that favors the self-interests of corporations over labor. We are still a democracy; if the public decided not to abide by the rules of self-interests being promoted by puppet libertarians their corporate sugar daddies would suffer some consequences.

The Powell Cabal

The self-interests of large corporations align with two types of people: those who are at the uppermost levels of the wealth pyramid and those who want to be. This presents a problem for large corporations who want to have their way in our society. The wealthy make up just a small proportion of any population; they have little influence via their numbers alone. Large corporations and the wealthy must therefore swell the ranks of those who mistakenly think what serves the interest of the upper class serves their self-interest as well. This would have been a daunting task in the sixties, when middle class was cool and even the wealthy wanted to belong to the club. Where there's a will there's a way, however, and for over thirty years large corporations have demonstrated a determined will to convince the public that greed is good and, as Landsburg suggests, the "less fortunate" wealthy are deserving of some compassion.

The initial strategy for this public relations campaign was outlined in a correspondence from Lewis Powell to the U. S. Chamber of Commerce, known as the Powell Memorandum, written in August 1971 just before he became a Supreme Court justice. At the time of the memorandum Powell's vocation was corporate law and he served on the board of Phillip Morris. Bad publicity and recent unfavorable regulations caused Powell to fear the mounting backlash against corporations "from the college campus, the pulpit, the media, the intellectual and literary journals, the arts and sciences, and from politicians." In other words, Powell feared the opinions of groups that were the most informed and rational segments of society. Powell recommended that a major goal of corporate America needed to be cultivating opinions favorable to corporations among these segments. This directive was to become as important to corporate executives and shareholders as turning a profit.

Fight fire with fire, as they say. If you want to combat the opinions of the most informed and rational segments of society, you best do so with an academic pedigree. The corporate PR campaign included funding think tanks such as the Heritage Foundation and Cato Institute. The campaign included endowing academic chairs at respected universities, along with funding fellowships for people doing corporate-friendly research. The campaign included funding media venues where corporate-sponsored pundits can share their opinions with a false pretense of objectivity. The campaign included pressure on Federal Reserve Banks to do bogus studies on leisure. The campaign included puppet libertarians reporting on bogus leisure studies by the Federal Reserve Banks.

From the time of the Powell Memorandum to the present large corporations have sunk billions of dollars into buying an academic pedigree with which they claim that their selfish self-interests are best for America. Let us refer to this conglomeration of corporate sponsored think tanks, corporate endowed academic positions, corporate funded lobbyists, corporate hired public relation firms and corporate owned media as the Powell Cabal. The Powell Cabal is, in essence, an elaborate misinformation network to increase the demand for large corporations. Through this demand follows the concentration of capital supplied to large corporations. With the control of capital comes the ability of large corporations to dictate the terms of labor in accordance with their selfish self-interests.

Funding an Academic Pedigree

Large corporations do not throw away profits frivolously. Buying an expensive academic pedigree would be a waste of money to large corporations if, eventually, the informed and rational segments of society would come around to their way of thinking anyways by looking at the empirical evidence and applying inductive reason. Perhaps a short term public relations campaign would be warranted to overcome certain misconceptions about America's self-interest of greed, but not the sustained funding of the Powell Cabal that corporations have provided for over thirty years. Corporations must divert large sums away from profits for funding the Powell Cabal on a permanent basis, with the mission of preventing the informed and rational segments of society from developing alternatives to selfish self-interest.

How does buying an academic pedigree work? We already have witnessed one example with the reports funded by the Federal Reserve Bank, dutifully echoed by a good soldier from the world of academia in an online magazine. A book titled *Trust Us, We're Experts* (2001), by John Stauber and Sheldon Rampton, gives other illustrative examples. The web site for the Center for Media and Democracy promotes the book with several excerpts, including one about the tobacco industry that spawned Powell and his Memorandum.

> "You think that if a scientist says so, it must be true? In the early 1990s, tobacco companies secretly paid thirteen scientists a total of $156,000 to write a few letters to influential medical journals. One biostatistician received $10,000 for writing a single, eight-paragraph letter that was published in the *Journal of the American Medical Association*. A cancer researcher received $20,137 for writing four letters and an opinion piece to the *Lancet*, the *Journal of the National Cancer Institute*, and the *Wall Street Journal*. Nice work if you can get it, especially since the scientists didn't even have to write the letters themselves. Two tobacco-industry law firms were available to do the actual drafting and editing."[6]

Understanding corporate sponsored academic pedigrees gives us an enlightened perspective on puppet libertarians and the Powell Cabal. Corporations can only thrive through the protections of strong government, as Alexander Hamilton was quick to note as the first Federalist (hence, by remote lineage,

---

6 From www.prwatch.org/books/experts.html.

the first Republican). Yet puppet libertarians fault government as the biggest impediment to the free market. If that sounds mad, well, there is a motive to their madness. Corporations replace the natural merits of a free market economy with culturally infused greed. When government acts to temper the effects of greed in markets, this undermines the primary objective of most business corporations. Economists such as Friedman and Landsburg are libertarians in the sense that they want maximum liberty for business corporations that specialize in capital, but they are puppets in their advocacy for a system that undermines free markets.

The irony of this campaign by puppet libertarians and the Powell Cabal is the general support provided by proprietorships. The academic pedigree sought by large corporations has been couched as one beholding to business in general, or to free enterprise, or even to our American heritage. There are no think tanks named the "Large Corporation Foundation" or the "Concentrated Capital Institute." Proprietorships tend to think that large corporations serve as big brothers advocating their interests. Many small businesses fail to understand that this academic pedigree includes economists and think tanks whose interpretation of competition not only butchers the concept from an ecologist's point of view but is detrimental to the self-interests of small businesses, and by extension the middle class.

The irony is driven home on web sites like the one for a proclaimed "Small Business Advocate" that included an advertisement for IBM. As detailed in the biography titled *Think* (1969), written by William Rodgers, the success of IBM was due to an extremely ruthless man who gobbled up and/or destroyed any small business that stood in his way. The Powell Cabal have convinced both graduates from respected business schools and proprietors, either explicitly or at least implicitly, that this model of merge and conquer is the normative expression of the entrepreneurial spirit.

The Academic Black Box

During my forced hiatus from Emerson Street, I did some research about the technology that has now become my trade—using computers to make maps and solve spatial problems. The late seventies and eighties witnessed a flourish of computers being introduced into the service of all levels of government. These computers were introduced as infallible and impartial black boxes that generated impartial truths. In reality, the information that came out of those black boxes was determined by the information put into them. This information was controlled by political and/or technocratic elites that could use their mysterious black boxes to generate any "impartial truth" they wanted.[7]

---

7 The major research in this area was done by James Danziger, Kenneth Kraemer, Rob Kling and William Dutton, *Computers and Politics: High Technology in American Local Governments* (1982).

This brings us back to the study on leisure sponsored by the Federal Reserve Bank of Boston. My first degree was in mathematics with a minor in statistics. Though that was ages ago I have enough residual knowledge to navigate through the maze of assumptions used by Aguiar and Hurst. Most of us middle class citizens would read the simply worded introductory paragraphs and then—after we received the message we were meant to internalize—our eyes would glaze over. Or, more likely, we would not read that study at all and just accept whatever a puppet libertarian disguised as an impartial journalist tells us. With a concept as familiar and important to all of us as leisure that should not happen. We should be willing to question scholarship and dogma when our own experiences tell us something different.

Economists have a mystique about them similar to that of computers and maps: they are objective number crunchers. Society perceives them as "black boxes" where mysterious inputs of data disappear and out come impartial truths. For their part economists love reinforcing this mystery, and not just by a web of assumptions and statistics. Unemployment is bad; but some unemployment is good for making wages competitive. Debt is bad; but some debt is good to stimulate growth. Growth is good; but too much growth is bad for inflation. This bewilders Hans, but he trusts in economists to mysteriously decipher the acceptable levels of unemployment, debt and growth. Just as mysteriously, these acceptable levels change depending on what policies seem to be affecting them, and how they affect the corporate world at the time.

In reality, economists are like political and technocratic elites, some can be quite passionate about what they believe and quite unscrupulous about passing off as truth the information that best serves their corporate benefactors. While ecologists have their public detractors, particularly if one should run afoul of the Powell Cabal regarding global warming, economists have been granted a relatively free pass in public discourse. The evidence reveals no greater commitment to the truth by economists; in fact, reason suggests that economists have greater incentive outside the realm of academics to bias their thinking and their research. The leisure study demonstrated how the validity of their empirical evidence suffers; the happiness study reported in Essay 1 demonstrated how the reliability can be suspect as well.

The *laissez faire* economists that serve the Powell Cabal contribute much to the best academic pedigree corporations can buy, a pedigree that becomes another type of black box. The agenda of economists providing the inputs for this black box needs to be exposed. Do not think for a moment that Milton Friedman, a Nobel Laureate in Economics, understands the effects of natural competition on different species, or on schools, as well as ecologists or even the middle class.

Large corporations maintain that economic happiness is all about wealth. They provide abundant resources to the Powell Cabal of think tanks, endowed chairs of economic departments, public relations firms, lobbyists and media for convincing Hans and the middle class of this. Such a worldview favors business corporations over proprietorships in an economy. Empirical evidence and inductive reason confirm that large corporations are best at maximizing the overall wealth of society, through the mechanisms of mass-produced goods, concentrated capital and selfish labor. What no evidence supports is that maximizing wealth brings happiness to a culture.

In contrast the empirical evidence indicates that maximizing overall wealth increases the disparity of wealth between classes. The evidence indicates that increasing the disparity of wealth increases debt and the cost ratio to family income of important goods such as housing, education and health insurance. The evidence indicates that affluence can be achieved without an unquenchable demand for goods, that progress can be achieved without a concentrated supply of capital and that ones self-interest goes beyond striking a greedy bargain for labor. The evidence indicates that proprietorships are better than business corporations for the pursuit of happiness by middle class America. It is precisely because of what valid and reliable evidence reveals that billions of dollars must be sunk into an academic pedigree that operates through black boxes.

Ah, but what about freedom? What about the reverence our nation holds for breaking the yolk of aristocracy? The free market ideal is revered in our society because of who we are and how we came to be. We have established that our corporate economy has been culturally biased towards greed, rather than a natural free market based on merit, but let us put aside the motivations behind our economic system. If large corporations prove to be more efficient at the mechanisms of a free market, despite their cultural preference for greed, this alone provides a ringing endorsement for them. That would explain why puppet libertarians like Landsburg are so bullish about the income disparity that large corporations create, while apparently unaware about how the self-interests of labor works in a market economy driven by greed.

Before we further discredit the self-interests of *laissez faire* economists or hypocrisy of puppet libertarians we should give the following question some consideration:

Despite their bias towards greed, are large corporations yet the most efficient means to pursue free market capitalism?

ESSAY 5 - FREE AND EFFICIENT MARKETS

Overview

- Economic freedom has become harder for proprietorships and the middle class; and easier for business corporations.
- The Heritage Foundation created an Index of Economic Freedom to provide misinformation about free markets.
- Large corporations obstruct the free flow of information required for a free market.
- Large corporations ignore or hide negative externalities that corrupt a free market.
- Large corporations restrict the free exchange of ideas that fuel a free market.
- Large corporations seek to dominate markets through deregulation.
- Large corporations seek to capture and privatize joint commodities that do not conform to supply and demand equilibriums.
- A valid Index would include indicators for private coercion and be able to distinguish between free and *laissez faire* markets.

Economic Freedom and the Entrepreneur

In the previous essays there was a common theme that proprietorships offer some advantages over business corporations, yet government does more to help out business corporations. Perhaps we should overlook the advantages provided through commerce and contracts as a necessity of big government in a big country. Harder to overlook are the various ways that government concentrates capital to the advantage of business corporations. There also are subtle ways by which government commands the economy to favor investment in certain business sectors that invariably correspond to the largest of corporations. For those of us that have been entrepreneurs at a small scale this is hard to accept.

I once started my own business. Like many budding entrepreneurs my goal was, to quote Robert Frost from "Two Tramps at Mud Time:" "to unite my vocation and my avocation, as two eyes make one in sight." Basically, I wanted to get paid for long distance backpacking. There was another stipulation for my new business; the product had to provide something useful for society. I settled on a Big Brother/Big Sister theme. T.R.A.I.L., Inc. grouped together adults and family-disadvantaged youth for the common goal of completing five-week wilderness journeys, under the umbrella of an educational nonprofit organization.

Admittedly, there proved to be little demand for such a market, but I did not intend to run a business that would go public after I made my first one hundred million. We provided a great product for society, if I do say so myself, but we operated for only two years. Actually, the state still thinks we operate; but every year I simply ignore their request to report T.R.A.I.L.'s income.

In truth, there never was real income associated with T.R.A.I.L., Inc. First of all, how can you charge the youth from family-disadvantaged homes? Family-disadvantaged means single parent homes, most of which hover around the poverty level (though they enjoy lots of leisure, according to puppet libertarians). Second, how can you charge the adults who were willing to give up five weeks of their time to be a mentor for youth? I couldn't do it. That left grants and donations as our only sources of income. T.R.A.I.L., Inc. lost money both years. The late Kenneth Lay and I share the dubious distinction of running our respective businesses into the ground, except that when T.R.A.I.L., Inc. folded my pocketbook was the only one that suffered. I lacked the ability of a corporate tycoon to concentrate capital from other sources into my own pockets.

I might have continued longer if cash flow was the only problem with running the business. Being able to pursue your hobby while helping needy kids certainly merits some out-of-pocket expense. The far greater annoyance was the paperwork. I spent five weeks backpacking and ten months filling out paperwork, not exactly the means of supporting my hobby that I had envisioned.

Still, as they say, better to have loved and lost ... or, with economic markets ... better to have started a business and lost than to never have experienced the thrill of being an entrepreneur. There is something invigorating about starting your own business; something that stirs the heart, mind and soul; something that gets to the essence of what freedom and democracy and liberty is all about. No wonder the entrepreneurial spirit has been so revered in this country.

The costs are rising of "losing" as an entrepreneur, or even as simply being middle class consumers. Small business entrepreneurs face increasingly stiff bankruptcy laws because their first "fling" with markets burned them like a jilted lover. You may be dismayed that recent legislation for stiffer bankruptcy laws targets middle class consumers and was promoted by large corporations. Apparently, corporate lobbyists don't want "Mom and Pop" disrupting their government supported markets. The late Senator Paul Wellstone framed the issue succinctly in a letter to Senator Trent Lott requesting to debate the law:

> "I continue to be puzzled by the false urgency for
> this bill. As bankruptcy rates fell steadily in the
> past two years, the rhetoric about the "crisis" in
> filings became even more shrill. But even more

perversely, projected increases in bankruptcy filings for the coming year – as a result of layoffs and falling income due to a cooling economy – is now being used to justify rolling back the bankruptcy safety net. In other words, now that more working Americans will be forced to file for bankruptcy because of circumstances beyond their control, we should make it harder for them to do so. I for one will have difficulty making that argument to the newly unemployed steelworkers in my state," wrote Wellstone.

How did the "false urgency" Senator Wellstone refers to get generated? The Powell Cabal obliged as usual. Here is an excerpt about how they worked.

"You think that a study out of a prestigious university is completely unbiased? In 1997, Georgetown University's Credit Research Center issued a study which concluded that many debtors are using bankruptcy as an excuse to wriggle out of their obligations to creditors. Former U.S. Treasury Secretary Lloyd Bentsen cited the study in a *Washington Times* column and advocated for changes in federal law to make it harder for consumers to file for bankruptcy relief. What Bentsen failed to mention was that the Credit Research Center is funded in its entirety by credit card companies, banks, retailers, and others in the credit industry; that the study itself was produced with a $100,000 grant from Visa USA and MasterCard International Inc.; and that Bentsen himself had been hired to work as a credit-industry lobbyist."[1]

You might think that incompetent large corporations also disrupt markets, but we have a different solution for them; we use a triple redistributive welfare system that includes taxpayer money to subsidize their endeavors. This adds to the list of why proprietorships do more than large corporations to benefit the middle class. To recap: Proprietorships are more likely to cultivate satisfaction from local or regional customers; large corporations do more to cultivate want

---

1   From www.prwatch.org/books/experts.html.

from generic consumers everywhere. Entrepreneurial proprietors diffuse capital; merging large corporations concentrate capital. Proprietors relate self-interest to the merits of production; large corporations associate some self-interest with the welfare of shareholders. Proprietorships have minimal impacts that markets can easily absorb; large corporations have huge impacts with ripple effects through several markets.

Business corporations must be better at something, since government intervention with commerce, capital and contracts favors them over proprietorships. Large corporations may be worse for the middle class in terms of goods, capital, and labor markets, but perhaps they operate in a market economy more efficiently than proprietorships. Stiff bankruptcy laws for the middle class and bail outs for corporations might be warranted if, after all, large corporations are the more naturally efficient components in a market economy.

The Index of Economic Freedom

The free market involves the supply and demand for goods, capital and labor by the private sector only, without the use of coercion. In contrast to the free market, a command economy is the intentional influence by government on aspects of supply and demand. We have a command economy in the energy sector, where a number of government policies and legislation over the years prop up oil prices and protect investments into oil over other energy alternatives. Markets are not free in a command economy since they do not reflect the free expression of the costs and benefits individuals are willing to accept in a market exchange.

The same problem applies to private coercion, which can be viewed as gaining an advantage through circumventing or breaking free market principles. For example, when large corporations obtain a monopoly they can inflate the price that individuals would otherwise be willing to pay when there are alternatives to the supply. The coercive act of hiding or distorting information about the costs and benefits of goods handicaps a free market more than most types of government interference, save for the type of command that government provides industries such as oil.

Laissez faire economics, as advocated by puppet libertarians from the Powell Cabal, subverts free markets by structuring competition to favor large corporations over proprietorships. Since government is required to provide this structure, *laissez faire* economics is really a more insidious and ubiquitous form of commanding an economy. Because of their strong incentive to maximize wealth, allowing large corporations to operate with little oversight results in various forms of market coercion. No think tanks dedicated to serve corporations—such as The Heritage Foundation—advocate a genuine free market economy based on merit.

The Heritage Foundation think tank, founded in 1973, is practically a charter member of the Powell Cabal. Since 1995 the good people at the Foundation have provided consistent, available data for an Index of Economic Freedom, contrasting the economies of different countries in this regard.[2] The Heritage Foundation defines economic freedom as: "individuals are free to work, produce, consume, and invest in any way they please, and that freedom is both protected by the state and unconstrained by the state."

There are fifty variables corresponding to ten economic categories, each one ranked from one to five in a feigned display of objectivity, with lower scores indicating greater economic freedom. All indicators were peer-reviewed, adding further to the aura of objectivity created by the large quantity of numerically ranked variables. The data from the 2006 Index suggests that the United States is tied for ninth in regards to economic freedom, out of 157 countries measured, and that the United States has generally trended towards greater economic freedom since 1995. Another significant finding, indeed the whole point of these indicators from the Foundation's viewpoint, is that economic freedom correlates strongly with per capita GDP.

The fifty indicators are so flawed that one suspects the Index must have been developed and peer-reviewed only by *laissez faire* economists. Indicators should be derived from the meaning of the construct being measured. The free market has two simple components: no government influence, no private coercion affecting exchanges of goods or services. The Heritage Foundation provides their interpretation of what no government influence really means, namely that: "freedom is both protected by the state and unconstrained by the state." Whether the protections offered by government might favor some businesses over others is not considered or explored. Also, economic freedom can be unconstrained yet nevertheless selectively applied if government policies command an investment advantage towards one industry over another, such as with oil. The Heritage Foundation provides no interpretation of private coercion, and their Index avoids this major assault to freedom and free markets.

Their emphasis on individuals, though outwardly all very libertarian of them, is a little misleading as well. For a new category on labor freedom that they used for their 2007 Index the indicators were minimum wage, rigidity of hours, difficulty of firing and cost of firing. Every indicator, and thus the entire category for labor freedom, was ranked according to potential burdens for the corporate side of the "individual" labor contract. Recall that this is the side with the greater bargaining strength from the start, the side that is a licensed operator of the State in addition to being an "individual." The Heritage Foundation's definition of economic freedom would more accurately be stated as: "*corporations* are free to work ... in any way they please." Granted, our courts treat corporations and individuals as the same, but the middle class entertains unscholarly notions that

---

2 Visit the web site www.heritage.org to explore the Index.

corporations and individuals are somehow different.

The ten categories of the 2006 Index were trade policy; fiscal burden; government intervention; monetary policy; capital flows; banking and finance; wages and prices; property rights; regulation; and informal markets.[3] Nine out of ten of those categories focus entirely on government influence, only the category of informal markets (which includes black markets) relates in some way to the types of coercion that might originate from the private sector. The Heritage Foundation's assessment of economic freedom lumps fifty indicators into one black box of an Index. The inputs and output of this black box become as subject to obfuscation as computer models, statistics or even maps. You could have an Index where forty-nine of the indicators are as irrelevant to economic freedom as the colors in each country's flag, but if just one indicator can discriminate countries based on economic freedom then the unscrupulous might credit the entire Index. Naturally, when faced with a situation like that a well-intentioned researcher's instinct is to test the validity of all the different indicators. The Foundation addressed this concern with a principal components analysis (PCA); they got some interesting results.

A principal components analysis determines the ability of different indicators to discriminate.[4] Of the ten categories used for the Index, you would expect differences in economic freedom to be dependent on some factors more than others. Informal markets, the only category related to private coercion, was the best of the ten categories at discriminating between countries in the Index of Economic Freedom. In contrast, fiscal burden (i.e., taxes imposed by government) provided little discrimination between countries rated high or low by the Index. Limiting taxation is an important issue to the good people at the Foundation, especially on corporations, so they did some extra analyses to explain why taxation on corporations is so detrimental to economic freedom after all. Meanwhile, they dropped informal markets for their 2007 Index. Their handling of their principal components analysis is reminiscent of the scene from the Wizard of Oz when Dorothy and friends are instructed to ignore what is going on behind the screen.

Hans the Proprietor

The only category related in some way to private coercion of markets contributes to one-tenth of the Index. Even if the Index were to weight the informal markets category the same as all the others combined—in order to give private shenanigans and government influence equal importance for compromising economic freedom—there is still the significance of using just one category to represent one of the two

---

3 For the 2007 Index the ten "freedoms" were changed slightly and rankings were based on percentage scores rather than on a 1-5 scale.

4 No principle components analysis was available yet for evaluating the 2007 index, the major reason why 2006 was used for discussion here.

major components of a free market and nine categories to represent the other one. To understand this significance let us turn to our friend Hans, an entrepreneurial proprietor.

Hans claims to be a staunch advocate of the free market and turns to the Index of Economic Freedom for a better understanding of what his free market libertarian ideals are all about. Since Hans is not a scientist he does not question the validity of different indicators, his eyes glaze over when he reads "principle components analysis." He has one hour to spend on his review of the Index and he splits his time evenly among the ten different economic categories.

Hans spends six minutes reviewing that government limits on free trade are bad for economic freedom, as defined by the good people at the Heritage Foundation. He spends another six minutes each on the negative impacts of government's role in consumption and ownership in the markets, regulatory burdens, restrictions on banks, wage and price controls, and interfering with foreign investments. So far Hans has spent thirty-six out of sixty minutes reviewing just how bad government influence can be on free markets, but zero minutes on how coercion by large corporations can be equally bad.

Now things get a little tricky for Hans, our entrepreneurial proprietor. Depending on which part of the Foundation's web site he visits, he discovers that the level of government taxes does not discriminate well between countries measured by the Index, or he may have stumbled on the Foundation's extra analyses that claims they do. Hans spends twelve minutes finding out that a competent government need not be all bad, if the courts can protect the property rights that have been institutionalized and the government sets monetary policy to successfully control inflation.

That leaves six minutes for Hans to review the problems with informal markets, such as bribery and other forms of corruption. But wait a minute! On page 73, Chapter 5 of their Index of Economic Freedom document for 2006 the authors explain that: "an informal market activity is one that the government has taxed heavily, regulated in a burdensome manner, or simply outlawed in the past." They even got a quote from a Harvard professor stating that: "corruption may be preferable to the enforcement of bad rules." You know that anything a Harvard professor says must be true. In this view, the blame for private coercion still rests with government after all. Of course, whoever deserves the blame for informal markets in 2006 no longer matters to the good folks at the Heritage Foundation, since they dropped this indicator for 2007.

Hans has spent 42 – 48 minutes of his hour reviewing how bad government can interfere with markets being "unconstrained," 12 – 18 minutes reviewing how good government can "protect" markets (though with little attention paid to how "protections" might be favorably distributed) and zero minutes reviewing how large corporations coerce and corrupt markets. Hans and other entrepreneurs think they have the complete picture of what interferes with economic freedom; what they have is only the part of the picture that interferes with large corporations ruling the roost. These proprietors take pride that their "libertarian" ideals translates to a fast growing Gross Domestic Product (GDP), not realizing that their ideals are libertarian only for corporations; not knowing that *laissez faire* economics over the past few decades have brought the middle class skyrocketing housing, tuition and insurance cost ratios to family income; and not aware that lobbyists paid by the Powell Cabal are earning their pay making sure bankruptcy laws are tougher for proprietors and the middle class than for large corporations.

The Index of Economic Freedom provides a good case study for false empiricism. The fifty numerical indicators of the Index create the snazzy appearance of real empirical evidence from which objective researchers have induced the importance of *laissez faire* economics for overall freedom. There is little validity to this empirical evidence, since the ability of private coercion to corrupt economic freedom is not even considered, nor the ability of government to command the economy in a certain direction through "protection." The Index is valid for *laissez faire* economics only and not economic freedom. Even more striking, their empirical data lacks reliability. The purpose of a PCA is to weed out the less important indicators from the more important ones. The good scholars at the Heritage Foundation did precisely the opposite. They went to extra lengths to retain and justify a bad indicator, and threw away the best one. No scientist repeating this method in the way the PCA was intended would come up with the same results, the precise benchmark for empirical reliability.

Surely the good people at the Heritage Foundation did not intend for entrepreneurial proprietors like Hans to be so thoroughly misled about economic freedom, so let us help them out. Let us explore the ways in which markets can be privately coerced, anticipating that the Foundation will be eager to incorporate these factors into future Indexes of Economic Freedom. We need only to focus on what causes markets to be inefficient, and how corporations directly impose these inefficiencies to gain a market advantage, or to indirectly impose on government to command that these inefficiencies be allowed to benefit business corporations. Judging by their peculiar use of the PCA the Heritage Foundation may not want indicators that are too relevant, but let us proceed undaunted by this peculiarity.

Free Flow of Information

The primary condition for efficient markets is the free flow of information. Since the alleged purpose of trade is to increase wealth for both sides, people should know all the costs and benefits affecting a market exchange before they agree to such a transaction. Markets never achieve an entirely free flow of information—how often do we know everything about anything? Still, intentionally hiding or distorting information about costs and benefits is coercing the market to manipulate exchange. One of the biggest factors for both creating and bursting the stock market bubble in the new millennium was corporations such as Enron "cooking the books."

Perhaps the most amazing example of private coercion preventing the free flow of information features the chemical company Monsanto and their bovine growth hormone (BGH) for cattle.[5] Studies have documented increased health risks associated with BGH; the hormone is actually banned in every industrialized nation except the United States. If you are a command economist you think that the United States should join other developed countries in curtailing the demand for these goods. If you truly believe in free markets (as opposed to the beliefs of puppet libertarians) you let the free flow of information decide whether this substance should be contained in dairy products. If you are a *laissez faire* economist, like the puppet libertarians from the Powell Cabal, you defend any means a large corporation employs to prevent information from being circulated that incriminates business corporations.

The fate of BGH would have been the same with either the command or free market approach. The market message was clear as far back as the early nineties, neither consumers nor small organic farms in the United States wanted BGH in dairy products. If Monsanto paid homage to the free market that might have been the end of the story. Instead, what has transpired the past 15 years clearly reveals Monsanto, like many large corporations, to be ruthlessly opposed to either free market efficiencies or libertarian ideals.

Monsanto withheld data they had about the impacts of BGH. That's one strike for the free flow of information. Monsanto arranged for farmers to use BGH secretly. That's two strikes for the free flow of information. Monsanto used lawsuits to prevent journalists from reporting on the corporation's BGH misdeeds, though they never denied the activities the reporters were about to reveal. That's three strikes for the free flow of information. At this point Monsanto decided that withholding information was an American ideal that should be universally applied. Through the courts they were able to prevent small organic farmers from labeling that their own products were free of BGH.

To do such yeoman's work at obstructing the free flow of information Monsanto needed a little help. Corporate-employed scientists provided a favorable analysis of BGH that differed from scientists not connected to corporations. Corporate-hired public relation firms provided a favorable view of Monsanto's use of BGH. Corporate-owned media killed the story to be reported by their journalists. Corporate-funded lobbyists influenced laws to ban labeling. The Powell Cabal should have a tag line that reads: "We help corporations coerce the free market for profit!"

---

5 You can review an electronic "paper trail" of the bovine growth hormone saga at www.organic-consumers.org.

If the Heritage Foundation really wants to provide an honest Index of Economic Freedom, they should include a "free flow of information" category. The elements of the Powell Cabal provide a template for individual indicators. Corporate think tanks, lobbyists, public relation firms, and advertisers dish out lots of information, but some of that information is distorted and/or covered up to gain an advantage in markets for large corporations. The Powell Cabal would deny this, of course, claiming they convey nothing but the truth about the fine goods and services large corporations have to offer. One needs to cross-reference any claims of the Powell Cabal with sources not receiving funds from large corporations, though this can be tricky when the Cabal wants to be anonymous about their influence. Distorted information hides the costs and benefits of a market exchange, as does withheld information. Indicators such as the percent of GDP spent on advertising, or the amount corporations provide lobbyists to wine and dine lawmakers reflect constraints on economic freedom as much as government interference with foreign investments.

Negative Externalities

If you have an odd sense of humor you might get a chuckle from the comic image of corporate lawyers scurrying like ants to desperately stem the free flow of information at every turn. Unfortunately, some of the games Monsanto plays are deadly serious in every sense. They are, after all, the large corporation that brought us both PCBs and Agent Orange. This leads us to another source of inefficiency with markets: negative externalities.

As the foundation of wealth, efficient trades benefit all parties involved. Some inefficient trades involve unintended parties with harmful consequences; these are known as negative externalities. The government gave money to Monsanto to benefit from Agent Orange as a defoliant for their herbicidal warfare program in Vietnam, but the chemical is a powerful dioxin that created health problems for soldiers and others that were exposed. Businesses gave money to Monsanto to benefit from PCBs as an additive in pesticides, paints, or various other products, but these durable chemicals created an environmental hazard along with public health problems. Lest you should get the impression that only Monsanto engages in inefficient market activities, General Electric also produced PCBs, while Dow Chemical also produced Agent Orange.

In truth, markets are rife with negative externalities ranging from the noise pollution near an airport to the global warming occurring everywhere. Some negative externalities are harmful enough to be restricted from use, such as PCBs. Taxes may be levied on some markets to cover the external costs, such as cigarettes. Some gimmicks attempt to convert negative externalities into a separate market; such as the trading of emission vouchers between polluters. Despite these and other measures we will never eliminate all negative externalities that occur in nation states.

Corporations cannot be blamed solely for this, as tempting as that may be. Government, proprietors and even individuals produce "negative externalities" (for example, second hand smoke). We should no more condemn corporations for being a source of negative externalities in a market economy than we should condemn ourselves. Having established that, we still need to remediate negative externalities, and we need to clear up some misconceptions the Powell Cabal has perpetuated about the roles and responsibilities of large corporations in regards to this.

One of these misconceptions stems from an assertion that proprietorships are held to a lesser standard than large corporations for remediating the unintended costs they generate. The assertion is often true enough, mainly because proprietorships do not have as much capital as large corporations to spend on anything other than production. However, the assertion creates the impression that more negative externalities created by proprietorships harm society than those created by large corporations. The Powell Cabal makes this contrast not to suggest that small businesses should be held more accountable for negative externalities, but that large corporations should be held less so. Yet the harmful consequences of PCBs and Agent Orange alone probably exceed the combined harmful consequences generated by all proprietorships.

The Index of Economic Freedom constructed by the good people at the Heritage Foundation reflects the *laissez faire* position held by the Powell Cabal. Regulations to ameliorate unintended harmful consequences are considered an intrusion by government in the free market and do not score well in the Index. Though regulations should not score well as they relate in a strict sense to economic freedom, neither should negative externalities. We must return to the foundation of what markets are supposed to be about: trade that benefits all involved, making them wealthier than before. Involving unintended parties with harmful consequences, thereby gaining advantage without accountability or remedy, assaults the free market.

If the Heritage Foundation really wants to provide an honest Index of Economic Freedom, they should include a "harmful consequences" category. Examples of indicators would be the numbers of unintentional lives lost or livelihoods destroyed through market activity. Admittedly, including such a category in the Index creates a no-win scenario. Governments could take a hit if either they combat harmful consequences in a market with regulations or allowed those harmful consequences to occur. This no-win scenario would be more honest than an Index that implicitly rewards the spillover harmful consequences of a market that government has, in effect, commanded. The only other alternative would be to institute a real free market economy, which means no government licensing and protection of corporations.

Positive Externalities

Ironically, the Heritage Foundation considers intervention by government a plus with another type of market inefficiency: positive externalities. This occurs when benefits are reaped by parties not involved in the trades that created them. While this might sound like a good deal, positive externalities can disrupt a free market. If you spend a lot of money making a movie, but could only sell a few tickets and/ or DVDs because the movie was being freely copied and distributed on a large scale, you would go out of business. The "freeloaders" gain something in the short term but everyone loses in the long term if markets cannot be maintained because of positive externalities.

An innovation can become a positive externality. Inventors seek patents for their work to prevent someone from stealing their idea and, consequently, their profits. Patents level the playing field for entrepreneurial proprietorships. Without the exclusive rights insured by a patent, a large corporation with greater capital could start mass production of a new invention much better than the original inventor. With exclusive rights granted by a patent a budding entrepreneur can control the production of their new invention, or make money renting or selling the rights to a large corporation with better means of production.

While positive externalities can be a problem, they are not all bad for small businesses. My profession as a computer cartographer is a perfect case in point. Most of the digital geographic data I work with was free, and I provide digital data I produced freely to others. I have used software extensions provided by other computer cartographers for free, and I make extensions I created available for free. I have used the methods of other computer cartographers to analyze geographic data freely, and they have used some of my methods freely. You do something similar to this when you provide and acquire "freeware" over the Internet.

Are those of us in the field known as GIS (geographic information systems) just being naive? GIS is still a relatively new technology with lots of new discoveries and applications to be made. When GIS specialists insist on being paid for all our data, extensions and ideas we restrict overall access to current innovations and limit the development of new ones. This situation holds for other innovative fields besides GIS. Much of our technological progress over the years has come when ideas were freely shared rather than restricted by patent laws.

The goal of the Human Genome Project was to code all the genes in human DNA.[6] This was tackled by the collaboration of several governments and by the independent work of a private corporation, Celera Genomics. Actually, the term "independent" should be interpreted loosely as applied to the corporation. A repository for genomic research was set up to move the project along for all involved. The governments stuck to the agreement, contributing their research to the repository. The private corporation "took" but never "gave back" in turn, not

---

6 The HGP web site: www.ornl.gov/sci/techresources/Human_Genome/project/privatesector.shtml.

surprising given their goal to acquire patents for the codes of over 6000 genes. So much for corporations holding to free market ideals, but Celera is far from the only corporation to seek profits by sponging off of government. Once again, the oil industry makes a general habit this. *Laissez faire* corporations are blind to such inconsistencies in their myopic view of the "free" market. The government trumped Celera, however, when they declared that the code could not be patented. This was bad news for Celera, but many entrepreneurs benefited from this free exchange of ideas even before the code was broken. From the HGP web site:

> "In the genomics corner alone, dozens of small companies have sprung up to sell information, technologies, and services to facilitate basic research into genes and their functions. These new entrepreneurs also offer an abundance of genomic services and applications, including additional databases with DNA sequences from humans, animals, plants, and microbes."

My wife Cindy provides another case in point that a free exchange of ideas promotes progress. As a licensed WOCN (Wound Ostomy Continence Nurse) for a visiting nurse agency in a rural part of the state, she offers something in little supply. Another visiting nurse agency besides her own once requested her expertise. She followed her instinct and went out to help with a patient, no questions asked or bills submitted. Now that agency will contract with Cindy's agency for her to provide training for all their nurses. Yes, this training will be at a cost, but a one time cost that will then enable the other visiting nurse agency to "compete" effectively in providing this service. Of course, the two agencies "compete" primarily by serving different geographic areas.

Which approach to positive externalities, free or restrictive, best suits proprietorships? That depends on the ambitions of the proprietor. If you want to join the "big boys" someday you want to control the patent of a really useful (or hyped) innovation that can garner a mass market. A visiting nurse agency driven by profit would want to offer a unique service not limited by geography. If you are satisfied with remaining a small business, and you are confident in your abilities, you want as free an exchange of ideas as possible that can enhance your own small but sufficient piece of the pie. In the case of visiting nurse agencies with a limited area, there always will be enough patients to go around for any particular service.

Many large corporations profit through mass production; they depend on the exclusive rights to something useful or hyped to maintain a large flow of capital. They favor strict government enforcement of patents and other intellectual property rights to eliminate positive externalities (if only they were so concerned about negative externalities). Yet government intervention by pure definition interferes with a free market, no matter how beneficial government's protective arm may be for a large corporation. The pace of innovation and the exchange of goods and services in the marketplace would be affected if government did not impose laws for intellectual property rights. In the case of the Human Genome Project progress was accelerated because government withdrew its usually protective arm that enables corporations to tie up patents.

Through their Index the good people from The Heritage Foundation have established the ironic position that government restrictions on the free access to ideas contributes to economic freedom. They might protest, with dubious intentions, that a market is not free if people are inhibited from generating new ideas because someone else will profit. Yet there is an important distinction to be made between protecting a budding entrepreneur from predatory large corporations with superior access to production and capital, and protecting a large corporation from losing their manipulation and control of production and capital.

If The Heritage Foundation really wants to provide an honest Index of Economic Freedom, they should include an "exchange of ideas" category. Not surprisingly, this creates a conundrum much like the potential "harmful consequences" category, being somewhat at odds with the portion of the Index that promotes property rights. This conundrum might be resolved through a better understanding of property rights, a topic explored in the essays on politics and culture.

Market Domination

Taking extreme measures to control positive externalities contributes to a different type of market inefficiency: market domination. Patent rights typically are granted for 20 years, much longer than needed for most inventors to make a decent profit from their thoughts. The Powell Cabal might counter that some inventions are the result of a person's obsessive life's hobby, which amounts to millions of dollars worth many years of protected compensation. If an inventor can "ride their invention" all the way to becoming a business corporation they have been justly compensated. The moment an inventor sells a patent to a large corporation they have, according to market theory, been justly compensated. Inventions by corporate employees are justly compensated, according to the terms of their contracts, when they pick up their paychecks. Just compensation for corporations should amount to no more than the just compensation to the original inventors, plus some overhead costs. If a corporation wants additional income from an invention they should have to earn this through the merits of production, rather than the control of production.

The instances where 20-year patents, granted through government intervention, accurately compensate the amount of time and effort invested by the original inventors are few. The instances where 20-year patents enable business corporations to dominate a market are many. Let us be clear that the latter motivates the howling from the Powell Cabal and fuels The Heritage Foundation's Index.

The domination of some markets cannot be avoided. If you are a famous artist whose products are branded with your name, you necessarily dominate that market. When domination and hype are combined in a market, as is often the case with famous artists, the market price can become absurdly large. A painting was sold recently for 135 million dollars. If billionaires want to spend that much on aesthetic objects that's their problem, but when necessary goods come from markets dominated by a large corporation, the middle class must endure inflated expenses and/or limited choices.

For better or worse, drugs have become necessary goods in our society. Drug patents grant large corporations like Merck or Pfizer the exclusive rights in this country to produce necessary, life-sustaining drugs. Since they dominate the markets for these drugs over a long period of time they can charge inflated prices. Drug companies maintain that the profits from these inflated prices provide needed capital for further research and development (R&D) of essential value to society, but the numbers suggest otherwise. A consumer health organization, Families USA, examined these claims for nine large drug corporations.[7] Revenues that turned into net profits exceeded those committed to research and development for six out of nine of these companies. Bristol-Myers Squibb had the greatest discrepancy with 26% of revenues turned to profit and 11% committed to R&D. Even more to the point, all these large corporations committed significantly more revenues to marketing/advertising/administration than R&D, spending anywhere from 150% to over 300% more on the part of their business plan that includes wining and dining politicians.

Advocating market domination through patents requires government intrusion to an extent that might make some of the Powell Cabal feel hypocritical. Fortunately for them, they can seek market domination through the avenue of deregulation instead. The deregulation of a large industry sounds very libertarian on the surface, but you need to keep in mind the economic system that provides the context for deregulation. If our current economic system favors large corporations—through the means by which the demands for goods are created, through the means by which the supply of capital is concentrated and through the means by which the self-interest of labor is contracted—what is the predictable result of deregulation? (Hint: the answer is not good news for proprietorships).

Deregulation has led to industry mergers and consolidations by allowing large corporations to exploit competitive advantages that were artificially instituted. Enron is an example of deregulatory consequences in the energy industry; WorldCom is an example of deregulatory consequences in the communication

7 For some fun (or revulsion) with numbers, refer to the charts provided by Family USA at www. actupny.org/reports/drugcosts.html.

industry. Not only were these deregulatory consequences antithetical to the free market, they were disastrous for the economy. Perhaps more disturbing than either of these examples is the consolidation of media that has been occurring through deregulation, but this topic is better suited for our future part on political liberty.

Deregulating merger activity does not increase economic freedom. As government influence is removed private coercion steps in. Either scenario makes markets less free. Deregulation of mergers and consolidations only serves *laissez-faire* economics and large corporations.

If the Heritage Foundation really wants to provide an honest Index of Economic Freedom, they should include a "market domination" category. This would be a corollary to their current category for government intervention. If I had to choose between the two, government intervention or market domination, I daresay the latter compromises a free market more, but no doubt the Powell Cabal disagrees with that assessment. Even if neither can be considered worse in terms of free market abuse, private coercion to dominate markets hurts the middle class more.

Joint Commodities

When supplies of goods or services can be offered only to groups of people, they become joint commodities. National defense is one example of this. When we send our troops abroad they defend everyone, not just males or females, conservatives or liberals (whatever those terms mean), folks from Kentucky or folks from Montana. Likewise, the costs of defense are born by the general public through taxes. Joe Doe from Kokomo cannot negotiate for what piece of the defense budget he is willing to cover. He cannot bargain for lower taxes in order to be defended by the Navy only, nor can he kick in a few million to have an Army battalion stationed at his home.

The costs and benefits acceptable to each individual in a group being provided a joint commodity cannot be expressed through free market behavior. Information about the market that might be meaningful to one member of the group could be meaningless or unavailable to other members. You could make assumptions about the costs and benefits an average member of the group might accept, but assumptions must then be made about who is average. The costs extracted from the group might be born equally by each individual, or according to their varying means, but neither approach will reflect the true costs individuals are willing to bear or the benefits they desire.

Even the Powell Cabal accepts some joint commodities as legitimate. No one questions the need for taxes to pay for defense provided by the government, very few people even question or pay close attention to how that money is spent. Reasonable libertarians accept joint commodities simply because there are no reasonable alternatives. One could argue for or against turning some elements of defense into a private market, depending on how comfortable you feel with introducing a profit motive to markets that thrive best during war. In either case, a private corporation like Blackwater cannot charge citizens directly for their mercenary services, but rather must rely on indirect taxation filtered through government.

If goods and services have to be supplied or applied to everyone at the same level, economic freedom is not affected by whether that supply is provided by government or privately. Since there is no freedom of choice to begin with, the only pertinent market consideration is efficiency. Privatizing a necessary joint commodity compromises the efficiency of supply. Education provides a telling example.

Levels of education could be a market negotiated privately by individuals if economic mobility or similar individual goals are the only reasons for education. However, our primary and secondary schools also provide a necessary function of training citizens. Outside of the armed services, the public schools are the only supply of training citizens widely available, and the only training many citizens receive these days in a society that dishes out tax cuts in a time of war. Privatizing all levels of education turns citizenship training into a negotiable service for individuals, rather than something provided jointly to all in order to infuse society with good citizens. Economic freedom is not at issue because training to become good citizens is, in theory, a nonnegotiable expectation of individuals who choose to live in this country. They are required to have the training; the overriding question is whether the supply will be adequate, or whether some children will be inefficiently deprived of this required service because their lack of demand for education fails to stimulate enough supply.

Health care in this country provides a glimpse of what education might become if all schools are privatized. Health insurance by necessity is supplied jointly. People typically become part of a group health plan, often through their place of employment. There is a good reason for this: contrary to the workings of a free market the people with the greatest demand for health insurance are the people that insurance companies least want to supply. If you have health problems you want health insurance, but the insurance company makes less or even loses money by insuring you. The way out of this mess is to place people of varying health into a group where each member pays the same price for the same type of coverage. An insurance company can make a profit because the average cost of insurance exceeds the average compensation given back.

Eliminating insurance companies turns health care into a normal market, with supply and demand determining the costs of everything from a check-up to a heart transplant. This has the advantage of reducing a significant amount of health care costs, namely, the labor and profits owed the insurance companies.

Unfortunately, a person who needs a heart transplant may not be one of the wealthy few who can afford this rare service; for this reason developed countries are more likely to use an opposite approach, universal health care. In essence, this approach treats an entire country as a joint market for health. Everyone is covered in this joint market, at costs that would be more efficient than compensating both the laborers and shareholders of insurance corporations. An additional advantage to this is enabling proprietorships to compete better in the labor market. The Powell Cabal cares little about proprietors when they advocate for privatized health; they want both the financial industry and business corporations to thrive at the expense of proprietorships negotiating satisfactory contracts for labor.

Let us compare our mix-and-match approach of profiting from health insurance supplied to groups with Canada's approach of universal health care provided by government.[8] In Canada you have to wait longer for some treatments when you have an illness that is not life threatening. Occasionally, Canadian citizens will come to this country for faster service. Wealthy Canadians also come to this country for the most advanced treatments that medicine has to offer. These factors weigh in favor of our health care system, though not as heavily as the Powell Cabal would have us believe. If a Canadian needs urgent treatment for a heart attack he does not have to come to the United States to avoid waiting three months. We should also be aware that only wealthy Canadians tend to receive the most advanced medical treatments available in this country, the same exclusionary effect that occurs with Americans.

Canadians have a few benefits from their health care system that offset the inconvenience of longer waits for some treatments. They have lower infant mortality rates, higher longevity rates and fewer uninsured. Actually, to merely say Canada has fewer uninsured sugar coats a particular problem for our health care system. Canada has no uninsured citizens, we have 46 million. You would think that the cost of health care is enormous in Canada, but theirs amount to 10% of their total GDP; ours amounts to 16%. This might suggest that all the good doctors choose to operate in the United States where we spend more of our GDP on health care. The ratio of a doctor's salary to the average Canadian citizen is 5:1; the ratio in this country is 6:1. Many doctors in Canada gladly accept this slight disadvantage in return for a huge reduction in litigation costs.

Wait! There is more evidence confirming the folly of turning health care into a profitable market. For profit hospitals in this country have incurred 19% higher operating costs than nonprofit hospitals. That might be acceptable if for profit hospitals had lower death rates, but the opposite is true. By virtually all important measures (total costs, infant mortality, death rates, universal supply), privatizing health care is inefficient. Being victimized by abominable inefficiencies

8 Most of this information was gleaned from a program on public radio, WAMC, which aired at 1:00 p.m. on 4/6/2006. The program featured a panel of doctors and health care experts. Similar information has been subsequently presented in the documentary "Sicko" by Michael Moore.

in a joint commodity market should not be considered economic freedom.

Small businesses suffer from a privatized system where large corporations can offer a better health care package for workers. In order to get puppet libertarians and the Powell Cabal involved in calling for change the opposite would need to be true: large corporations would need to be suffering at the hands of proprietorships. Lost in the mix either way is the deprivation of 46 million uninsured from the middle and lower classes.

If the Heritage Foundation really wants to provide an honest Index of Economic Freedom, they should include an "inefficient market" category. Some ingredients of inefficient markets include: privatized goods or services that must or should be provided at a minimum level to everyone in society; privatized goods or services that must be provided jointly; or privatized goods or services that do not abide by the normal principles of supply and demand. Privatized markets with these characteristics will detract from economic freedom because of being inefficient and their failure to best supply the intended goods or services. The cost of inefficiency to society could be a warlord aiming for a military coup; wealthy elites monopolizing the best schools; or insurance corporations forming a bloated layer of bureaucracy that absorbs much of the money for health care.

Creating a Better Index

As currently constructed the Index of Economic Freedom validates *laissez faire* economics, the extent that corporations are indulged by government to behave like spoiled children. The correlation with per capita GDP demonstrates that indulging corporations, like indulging spoiled children, will lead to a large accumulation of play things overall, but there is no guarantee that all working people will attain the necessities of life. The good people from The Heritage Foundation ought to change the Index to gauge real economic freedom, and to determine if all the hard working people of a society are receiving what they merit.

Creating a legitimate Index of Economic Freedom requires three radical departures from what The Heritage Foundation has been offering. First, economic systems are not binary. Markets are not determined by a simple choice between increased freedom of exchange and increased command by government. Throughout the world there currently are three distinctive types of market: free, command and *laissez faire*. Nation states in the current world economy do not fall on a continuum between free and command markets but generally have mixtures of all three. A legitimate Index needs to account for how all three components relate to economic freedom.

Second, the importance of economic freedom applies ultimately to individuals, real individuals instead of corporations or even proprietorships. Unconstrained corporations do not promote liberty if government and corporations effectively collaborate to constrain the economic choices of laborers. Per capita GDP does not reflect economic freedom if the wealth is concentrated among the few. A legitimate Index needs to provide some reflection on the liberty or economic freedom of a real individual. Assuming that the middle class would choose compensation to be diffused according to earned merit, rather than concentrated according to greed, wealth distribution reflects on economic freedom more than any current indicator in the Index.

Third, citizens should not have to be economic scholars to fathom the meaning of information being provided for general consumption. There are three simple measurements that together characterize market exchange. The proportion that proprietorships contribute to Gross Domestic Product indicates free market activity; the proportion that governments contribute indicates command markets; and the proportion that business corporations contribute indicates *laissez faire* markets. In addition, a variety of simple measurements can determine the impact of economic freedom on individuals. Contrasting mean and median incomes, or the proportion of wealth controlled by different classes, provide reliable indicators of wealth distribution.

If the number of indicators is kept low there will be no need for the misleading consequences of combining them all into one. There may be one or two more to include, such as those reflecting market efficiencies. Coming up with straightforward indicators for the free flow of information and exchange of ideas should be considered.

I'm afraid our economic system will not rank quite as highly with this new Index. Essay 7 provides data that reveals our economy is trending towards both *laissez faire* markets and wealth disparity, some would conclude dramatically. Nor are we doing well at promoting a free flow of information and exchange of ideas, topics that are discussed more thoroughly in the parts on politics and culture.

The good people from The Heritage Foundation can use these suggested improvements for their Index free of charge, in the spirit of promoting a free exchange of ideas. They can even take the credit if that makes them willing, but their corporate sugar daddies may have too strong a grip on the Foundation to allow indicators that reflect increasing control of the economy by business corporations along with increasing wealth disparity. If that is the case the Foundation should just change their name to the American Heritage Organization for *Laissez-faire* Economics. They will never advocate policies that provide economic freedom to the middle class, via a free market driven by merit, but at least their new acronym will provide us some comic relief.

The Inefficient Corporation

What causes large corporations to be so inefficient in a free market economy in so many ways? The answer: the very ingredients that cause them to be large. Their need to create demand surpasses their need to create new and improved goods and services and they subvert the very reason for why they were granted incorporation. In this subversion they will do anything, such as monopolize a market, to stimulate the extra demand. Their desire to concentrate capital at the top levels of an organizational pyramid surpasses their desire to use capital to enhance production. They will do anything, such as ignore or deny harmful negative externalities, to maximize profits and minimize taxes or penalties. The large separation that exists in a large corporation between the genuine self-interests of labor and the self-interests of those motivated entirely by capital creates a culture of greed not only within the corporation but in the context of society as well. Believing wholeheartedly that greed is good, large corporations will do anything such as obstruct or distort the free flow of information to get the society at large abiding by that principle.

Large corporations are not better than proprietorships at free market efficiencies. In fact, the benefits of proprietorships in the goods, labor and capital markets indicates they are the ones most suited to promote economic freedom and make efficient use of free markets. That brings us back to our original dilemma: finding the rationale for favoring large corporations over proprietorships in the economy of a democratic nation. The real answer is probably political but we can explore one more economic possibility.

We have gone from a society whose citizens used to overestimate who was in the middle class to a society whose citizens overestimate their wealth status. That implies the economic wishful thinking of our citizens has shifted from wanting to be middle class to wanting to be wealthy. The Powell Cabal has succeeded in one of their important missions: greed has become good.

Hope springs eternal, as they say. The reason people play the lottery may be why our country favors large corporations over entrepreneurial proprietorships. After all, many people only play the lottery once the jackpot has reached new heights, even though they have better odds all along at winning a more moderate prize. If your greatest hope is to become enormously wealthy why not favor a system that concentrates wealth for a few, even at the expense of the many. Our complicit support for large corporations and *laissez faire* economics may be as irrational, yet as irrepressibly hopeful, as playing the lottery.

If hope be the cause of pandering to large corporations, then hypocrisy should serve as a type of antidote. Hypocrisy breeds distrust; distrust breeds contempt. Even the most naively optimistic person would stop playing the lottery if they discovered that the chosen numbers were fixed. Here is a hypothesis we can make from this assumption: If eternal hope causes us to indulge corporations, then corporations are not undermining this hope through hypocrisy. Let us explore this hypothesis next.

ESSAY 6 - CORPORATE HYPOCRISY

Overview

- Greed creates double standards that benefit the wealthy and large corporations.
- Inflation is bad; *except* when inflating the money supply of the wealth elites.
- Welfare is bad; *except* when providing welfare capital to the wealth elites.
- Feeling entitled to welfare is bad; *except* for entitlements to capital gains.
- Economic mobility is good; *except* when this interferes with school privatization.
- Morality is good; *except* when this interferes with globalization.
- Free trade is good; *except* when countries would freely decide not to participate.
- Empirical evidence is good; *except* when the evidence must meet standards of validity or reliability.
- *Laissez faire* economics coevolved with corporations to champion greed-based hypocrisies.

Double Standards

My family went on a Church work camp trip to Philadelphia. We had gone on work camps as a family for a few years. The decision to continue with this type of "vacation" was easy, considering that after our first work camp our oldest daughter said she preferred doing that to going to Disneyworld. We have done work for both the rural and the urban poor in this country, and also for the poor in another country. Work camps can be considered an inexpensive vacation alternative that fits most middle class budgets. More middle class families should do this; you won't be disappointed.

People become inspired by work camps; those in poverty are not the uniformly shiftless bunch the anti-welfare zealots from the Powell Cabal would have you believe (anti-welfare for the poor, that is, they support welfare for shareholders). I became inspired by the efforts of a Puerto Rican community with their community gardens near Norris Square. At one time the neighborhood was riddled with drugs, crime and condemned houses. Help was not on the way from the city due in part to communication problems, and due to the fact that ratting on a drug dealer is a risky business in an area where police otherwise do not make an appearance. The police had a habit of stopping at the informant's place first for questioning, thus drawing the attention of drug dealers to the informant.

The community devised a brilliant plan. They congregated and hung around in areas where they knew drug dealing was prevalent. They did nothing, said nothing, but their mere presence was uncomfortable for the drug dealers. The dealers moved their dealing away from the center of the neighborhood. Members of the community would follow up with the same plan, pushing the dealers farther out until the illicit activity was being done in neighborhoods that were of greater interest to the city. The city then took action.

The second part of this plan consisted of beautifying the neighborhood with murals and community gardens. During our first morning in Philadelphia we worked at a community garden that served as the focal point for their efforts. There we were told their inspiring account of a recovering neighborhood. In the afternoon we worked in a different community garden where we heard a more sobering tale.

The second community garden was owned by the city of Philadelphia, a common fate since typically these gardens were once condemned buildings. Our hostess mentioned that this and other gardens were now under threat to be sold and developed. The Puerto Rican community had been successful enough at making their neighborhood desirable as to jeopardize its continued existence.

This unpleasant reality hit home all the more for us because of recent events. The urban garden that was being seized by the city of Los Angeles to use as warehouses had made national news. Having celebrities nearby like Darryl Hannah climbing trees and getting arrested on your behalf certainly helps to publicize your cause; a Puerto Rican community in Philadelphia does not have the same resources.

Not that publicity would matter; our own state became famous recently for a Supreme Court case that ruled in favor of the city of New London taking the property of long-time residents for upscale malls and condominiums. Ostensibly, the reason for such heavy-handed action was to promote the greater good. These days society interprets the greater good solely through the cynical lens of capital investments. Upscale malls and condominiums induce more economic investment than someone's modest home that they treasured for a lifetime. A community garden may be nice but let's face reality folks; growing flowers generates little tax revenue. Never mind that you could spend your whole life working hard to do what society requests of you, to use mainly your own resources to overcome the hardships you face. If such models of responsibility and hard work are judged not to promote the greater good, well, who ever said life was fair.

Affordable housing promotes the greater good, particularly since the ratio of housing costs to family income has been skyrocketing.[1] Regardless of the need, you can bet your very last dollar that upscale property will never be taken for the

---

1 The empirical data for such claims will be presented in Essay 7.

sake of desperately needed affordable housing. Nope. Not going to happen. The Supreme Court would adopt a renewed faith in substantive due process. That is why the hopes of people like the Puerto Rican community at Norris Square are forever burdened by the threat of hypocrisy. In regards to treasured homes or places the wealth elites will never giveth, but they may see fit to taketh away. This is one of the many consequences of markets driven by greed instead of merit. This essay will explore a few more hypocrisies in our greed-based market system.

Inflation Hypocrisy

The inflation of property value causes the problem faced by the Norris Square community. If the community could match any developer's offer for one of their community gardens they undoubtedly would. Inflation troubles communities and corporations alike. The efficiencies of scale that corporations offer for mass produced goods are all for naught if offset by inflation. During inflationary times people concentrate on the necessities. This depresses the demand for many mass produced goods, thus compromising the volume of production that corporations need for their economies of scale. Because of this corporations consider the control of inflation as one of the most important economic functions of government. It even makes the Index of Economic Freedom! If corporations contributed to inflation that hurt the lower and middle classes, at the same time they demanded government intervention to curb inflation, then that would be an example of corporate hypocrisy.

Fiscal policy determines the distribution of money through taxes and spending; monetary policy determines the flow of money through interest rates and the printing of money. The Powell Cabal of corporate sponsored think tanks, corporate endowed chairs of economic departments, corporate hired public relations firms, corporate employed lobbyists and corporate owned media wants government to control inflation through monetary policy only. Many economists use the phrase "too many dollars chasing too few goods" to describe what causes inflation. Interest rates set by the Federal Reserve Board reflect monetary policy intended to limit "too many dollars chasing too few goods." As interest rates increase borrowing decreases, thus limiting the flow of money in the economy that can be used to purchase goods.

Have you ever wondered why government could not just print whatever money they needed to solve their economic problems? One reason is this would create "too many dollars chasing too few goods." The prices of goods would inflate in proportion to the extra dollars available, creating economic instability. Counterfeiting has precisely the same destabilizing effect.

As does wealth disparity.

If everyone made the same amount of money, the cost limit on expensive goods would be determined by this standard income. If some people make more they can pay more for expensive goods; if they make a lot more they can pay a lot more. If they make a thousand times more, similar to the disparity between a bottom level worker at Wal-Mart and the corporate CEO, they can pay a thousand times more. Some disparity is necessary for markets to operate. A free market requires that people earn more according to the merits of their labor and pay more according to the merits of goods and services desired. Unfortunately, enormous wealth and wealth disparity occurs from greed being substituted for merit as the driving factor in markets.

For the very wealthy, a large portion of their wealth comes from capital gains instead of wages. They receive the capital from investments or inheritance rather than earning the income through the merits of their independent labor. Consequently, the wealthy can and will pay more for goods not just because of merit, but because they greedily want to outbid someone else who is wealthy. This has a trickle down effect. A real estate agent finds a wealthy client willing to pay one million dollars for a home that might be worth a half million based on other market factors. The next bidder might have been willing to overpay by "only" $250,000 for the half million home, and instead outbids considerably for a $400,000 home. This pattern continues, thus affecting even homes of modest quality that might otherwise have been purchased for a modest sum by a lower middle class family.

This has been called expenditure or spending cascades, a research specialty of Robert H. Frank. One study on this phenomenon compared the housing costs in two small Midwest towns. Mount Vernon, Illinois possessed a higher median income, lower maximum income and less income variance than Danville, Illinois. The median housing cost was more than double for the town with the lower median income, Danville, due to trickle down inflation.[2]

Mortgage rates exacerbate the problem in the housing market as low mortgage rates have the opposite effect of higher prime interest rates designed to curb inflation. With tax deductions providing an additional incentive more money is borrowed; more money is chasing too few houses; and housing costs become inflated. The corporate-owned media keeps us well-informed about the relationship between interest rates and inflation. In regards to mortgage rates the corporate media "buzz" is more about the risk of the loans than the rate amounts.

When the filthy rich provide too many dollars for chasing too few of the expensive but necessary goods, this trickles down to affect the entire economy and inflates some essential items beyond the normal means of the middle class. Not to worry, though, the middle class can just incur more debt (which, of course, adds even more dollars chasing too few goods). To add insult to injury, the Powell

---

2 Reported in "Expenditure Cascades" (2005), a mimeograph by Robert H. Frank, Bjornulf Ostvik-White and Adam Seth Levine.

Cabal pushes relentlessly for cuts in capital gains taxes to stimulate the economy. Even if some of the extra capital is reinvested, even if some of the extra capital trickles down as claimed, a good portion of that capital welfare remains in the hands of the wealthy that control the supply. The result: more dollars chasing too few goods, inflating the costs of goods such as houses and making the trickle down leftovers for the middle class a zero-sum game at best. This is why the often repeated mantra from the Powell Cabal that wealth disparity does not matter, as long as the least well off still increase their wealth, smells of hypocrisy from the same people who otherwise are so concerned about inflation.

Welfare Hypocrisy

The means by which we supply "too many dollars" to the wealthy adds an intriguing dimension to this hypocrisy. We receive wages for producing goods or services. We receive welfare for producing nothing. However you might feel about people getting something for nothing, welfare to the poor does not disrupt markets much, if at all. Some of the biggest welfare states, such as Denmark, score high even on the *laissez faire* Index of Economic Freedom developed by the Heritage Foundation and have a high per capita GDP. The impact on markets from providing welfare to the poor would be to actually dampen inflation. Giving welfare to the poor does not make them rich, but lessens the ability of the wealthy of having "too many dollars chasing too few goods." Since providing welfare to the poor is fiscal policy you will not hear monetarists like Milton Friedman recommend this as an approach to curb the inflation they dread, but the point remains that no concrete evidence has ever shown that welfare to the poor inflates or destabilizes markets.

Welfare to the rich, on the other hand, contributes to the inflationary problems caused by redistributing and concentrating "too many dollars" in the hands of the wealthy. We provide welfare for large corporations and wealthy individuals in a few ways, like hyping the compensation of CEOs to be a thousand times that of the bottom level workers in the same industry, such as with WalMart. Executives have not earned such compensation through merit only, but have benefited from the hype and levels of managerial hierarchies integral to the corporations they manage. Even if white collar to blue collar ratios became reasonable by J. P. Morgan's standards, merit-based wages do not cover the majority of income for many wealthy people and corporate shareholders.

Much of capital investment amounts to welfare, by our operational definition of receiving money for producing nothing. While the middle class benefits somewhat from investment capital, mainly in the form of retirement accounts, the capital that flows to the middle class is not concentrated as is the capital redistributed for the wealthy and large corporations. Retirement welfare for the middle class has no more impact on market prices and wages than traditional welfare for the poor, since retired people from the middle class would otherwise have income below the poverty level.

Capital gains from corporations provide substantial welfare for the wealthy. Sure, some gets invested in the infrastructure of production, and some may even trickle down to the merited labor of production, but in an economic climate where greed is good much of the capital ends up as mansions that serve as vacation homes and airplanes used only for the personal needs of executives. Corporate capital also provides welfare through stock options. For example, the compensation for William Steere, Chairman of Pfizer was a cool $40 million without unexercised stock options.[3] This is probably more than one thousand times the wages of the janitors in the company, but a trivial amount compared to the compensation such executives get with their stock options included. In Steere's case that amounted to over $130 million. That's a lot of patented Lipitor, baby! Not even this type of welfare, however, is as hypocritical as the most unmerited source of entitlements for the wealthy: inheritance.

The desire of the wealthy to perpetuate large inheritances seems strange to this middle class citizen. My middle class parents did not leave us much money. With assistance from public schools they did something better; they raised us to be able to attain our own goals. I doubt Cindy and I will be leaving our children much money when we pass away, but we have devoted ourselves to providing an education and an independent spirit for the most precious people in our lives. We have confidence they will be able to attain their own goals without us giving them large amounts of welfare.

Many people who by their own merits acquire great wealth appear determined to prevent their progeny from doing the same. One reason wealthy parents may not wish to restrict what their children inherit would be a lack of confidence in their children's ability to succeed on their own. You have to feel sorry for this "silver spoon" progeny. Though our commercial world portrays these rich young adults as people to be envied, they must sense the lack of faith their parents have in them. Another reason for the wealthy depriving their children the opportunity to succeed on their own merit would be if they considered their own means of acquiring wealth as having been unpleasant. If a self-made man equated success with being ruthless and hypocritical, he understandably might want to spare his children this process by enabling them to inherit their wealth instead. The inheritance is still welfare that provides a disincentive for labor, whether done through loving concern or not.

Puppet libertarians protest that people should have the "liberty" to give the money they earn to whoever they please. They have a valid point, for the money that people earn. On the other hand, large returns on investments or on formerly

---

3   Refer to the charts of compensation provided by Family USA at www.actupny.org/reports/drug-costs.html.

inherited money do not satisfy the definition of "earned." A strong case can be made that neither does compensation that exceeds twenty-five times what the least compensated worker in the same industry receives. This is just welfare derived from welfare, or greedy indulgence. This whiffs of hypocrisy from the same folks that protest the loudest that we should not be dishing out welfare.

Entitlement Hypocrisy

Once "new" wealth becomes "old" wealth the explanation for using inheritance to hoard riches without merit becomes easy to understand. Providing welfare to the wealthy through inflated wages, capital or inheritance induces a feeling of entitlement. Feeling thus entitled they will not tolerate any threat to that entitlement, even by the poor whose meager income could not possibly inflate market prices. This attitude of entitlement by the wealthy leads to one more layer to the hypocrisy: the large amounts of time, money, and effort large corporations will spend to maintain and increase this welfare through fiscal policy.

No one documents these hypocrisies better than David Cay Johnston. His book titled *Perfectly Legal* (2003) describes the varied and clever ways that business corporations and the wealthy rig our tax system to suit their purposes. One note of caution: don't read his book if you have a violent nature or are dealing with depression. Let us adapt from his research how our friend Hans, the small business entrepreneur, thinks that both the tax concerns and the tax cons devised by corporations and the wealthy are on his behalf.

Business corporations express concern that their profits are taxed at a high rate. Through the efforts of the Powell Cabal the capital gains tax rate becomes lower than the rate on some wages. Hans believes the argument that freeing up more profits for business means more stimulation for the economy through investment. He neglects to consider that corporations are structured to compete for private investments better than proprietorships. Shifting the tax burden to wages penalizes proprietorships with a higher ratio of wages to capital gains, not to mention the laborers earning the wages.

On behalf of business corporations and the wealthy, the Powell Cabal expresses concern that the income tax should be a flat rate rather than having a progressively higher rate on progressively higher wealth. They succeed in having the highest rate reduced to less than half the level of forty years ago and applied to a broader level of income. Hans believes their argument that the wealthy have been burdened with paying an unfair, disproportionate share of taxes. As a small business owner he earns pretty much what his labor warrants and does not realize that the wealthy benefit from a redistribution of money upwards through inflated wages, hyped goods and concentrated supplies of capital. Any redistribution back downwards through a progressive tax could be viewed as just compensation in a system whose purpose is to redistribute money upwards. Instead, Hans falls for the con, not realizing that while the top 20% of the rich pay 80% of the taxes, they control 90% of the wealth.[4] In other words, they have rigged the system to actually pay less than the share of wealth they received, which is considerably more than the wealth they earned through the merits of their labors.

Large corporations and the Powell Cabal express concern that government, and the Internal Revenue Service in particular, is much too intrusive and their activities need to be curtailed. Because of their influence Congressional hearings are held to publicize and vilify gun-toting IRS agents. Hans becomes agitated over the heavy-handed IRS auditors and is all for slashing budgets that will curb these audits. He does not realize just how well the government responds to the squeaky wheel of the Powell Cabal, contingent on campaign contributions. The IRS budget does get slashed, auditors are laid off, and the ones that remain are discouraged from auditing the wealthy. The working poor are nine times more likely to be audited than multimillionaires, even after controlling for the greater numbers of poor. Hans has been conned once again, in that the lost revenues from concentrating on poor tax cheats instead of rich tax cheats creates an additional burden that shifts to the middle class and his small business.

Large corporations and the Powell Cabal express concern that the government imposes death taxes. The real term is estate tax, a tax on inherited wealth, but death tax has so much more pizzazz. They claim that the death tax— excuse me, estate tax—has led to the foreclosing of small family farms. Fortunately, not even Hans has been conned by this one yet, since the estate tax only affects inherited wealth in the millions. Still, the Powell Cabal does not give up easily. One recent initiative in Congress linked a repeal of all estate taxes in exchange for increasing the minimum wage. For years large corporations, backed by *laissez faire* economists, have been vigorously opposing minimum wage increases, claiming that wage controls corrupt markets. Giving up this battle means that the sense of entitlement to inherited wealth is so great that the rich will abandon their principles, based on economic theory, against wage controls. Condemning entitlements to the poor and feeling entitled to fiscal policy serving the wealthy reeks of hypocrisy.

Economic Mobility Hypocrisy

The Powell Cabal has a backup plan for their "wealth disparity does not matter" approach to justifying *laissez faire* economics. As long as there is economic mobility in a society, as there is in ours, then the lower and middle classes should have no complaints about the economic system. Economic mobility provides an escape hatch. If you do not like being on the bottom rung of a multilevel pyramid,

---

4   The number crunching will be done in depth for Essay 7.

fine, just do what is necessary to move up the levels. If you don't take the necessary steps you are the only one to blame.

This reasoning implies that our economic system is responsible for our economic mobility. That is not true, at least not for upward mobility. A good education fuels the ability to specialize, the "energy" that drives markets. Since we still have the best system of higher education in the world our greed-based market economy cannot eliminate economic mobility even though structured to favor business corporations and the concentration of resources. A bad education policy would be needed to seriously cripple economic mobility. Corporations, *laissez faire* economists and the Powell Cabal claim to value economic mobility highly as a justification for the concentration of wealth, any policy they recommend that decreases the availability of a good education to all would be hypocritical.

Milton Friedman led the way in advocating school vouchers as a means of improving our educational system with an essay titled "The Role of Government in Education" (1955), easily found on the web. His position on school vouchers resonates with his economic ideology, expressed in works such as *Capitalism and Freedom* (1962), that *laissez faire* economics can solve the basic economic, political and social goals of our country through the promotion of economic freedom. Friedman is an icon in economics due to his many significant contributions in the field, his Nobel Prize in economics and his lead advocacy for *laissez faire* economics. As an icon to the pop business culture his opinions get the "black box" treatment, as inscrutable to the layperson as computer models, statistics and maps. Let us first apply some rare scrutiny to demystify the icon and then apply some scrutiny to his beliefs as they impact upward mobility.

No one can be sure of another person's intent but I believe Friedman's brand of *laissez faire* economics stems from an idyllic allegiance to his beliefs, not from a cynical allegiance to business corporations. He is not a prototypical member of the Powell Cabal, though puppet libertarian think tanks such as the Cato Institute clearly worship his dogmatic views. *Laissez faire* dogma unmistakably guides his life's work, in contradiction to his "Essays on Positive Economics" (1953) recommending economic research be conducted empirically. Friedman touted utility and profit as unbiased, empirical measuring sticks. Make no mistake; this was a normative declaration by Friedman, with no natural evidence in support of his "norm." In other words, Friedman's view of "positive economics" was totally subjective. This important distinction appears to be totally lost on all the economic icon's followers; but we must keep in mind these are economists, not scientists.

Scientists championed empirical research long before Friedman; indeed, Friedman no doubt was influenced by the empiricism of the Scientific Revolution. Yet even natural scientists understand that empirical data gets filtered through the subjective lens of human interpretation, through the paradigms of understanding that guides all disciplines. Friedman may not be aware of the extent that his ideology shapes his interpretation of the economic information he amassed in his life. Failure of both one's self and one's admiring public to understand how ideology shapes interpretation is an obstacle to wisdom. You become resistant to changing your beliefs in the face of valid and reliable empirical evidence. You instead change the meaning of what is valid and reliable to fit dogmatic beliefs. Scholars like Friedman easily can mistake to what extent their interpretation of data shapes ideology and to what extent ideology shapes their interpretation of data.

Friedman's positions reveal a similarity to the *laissez faire* economics of the nineteenth century. His view of free market competition stems from a belief that competition leads to survival of the fittest producer, and government should stay out of the fine tinkering that would otherwise naturally occur with free markets. When a *laissez faire* economist like Friedman steps outside the bounds of his own discipline to butcher an ecological concept such as competition, and when that butchering leads to beliefs that undermine economic mobility, such error needs to be corrected.

Survival of the fittest occurs within a species, with the faster gazelles surviving and the slower ones becoming lunch for lions. Between species competition typically has the opposite effect; species adapt to competition by fitting different resource niches, thus increasing diversity. Survival of the fittest may occur within a corporation, as long as a nephew of the CEO does not need a job. Diversity is what natural competition would create between businesses, if governments did not exist to facilitate the concentration of resources. Misinterpreting competition contributes to Friedman's rather misguided view of school vouchers.

To understand why school voucher advocates are misguided about education let us first explore why spending advocates are misguided about improving schools simply with more money. Educational research shows that an extremely important determinant of a child's success in education is the support, involvement and availability of parents.[5] Students who attend private schools tend to do better than public school students in general, but not those whose parents strongly support their education. Wealthy students tend to do better than economically disadvantaged students, but not if the disadvantaged parents strongly support their children's education. The research also shows that parent participation enhances the quality of schools as well as their children's education.[6] Money is a necessity, of course, but more important is a critical mass of parents demonstrating their support of schools and education through their time and/or money.

If money is not the answer, then what is the big deal about school vouchers

---

5 Numerous studies confirm this. See the Educational Testing Service (www.ets.org), Child Trends Data Bank (www.childtrendsdatabank.org), and Educational Resource Information Center (www.eric.ed.gov). The ETS publication "Parsing the Achievement Gap" (2003) provides a good overview.

6 Go to the web site www.education-world.com/a_special/parent_involvement.shtml for a good resource on doing your part as a parent supportive of education.

funneling money away from the worst schools?[7] The main problem lies not with the money but the supportive parents. There always will be an abundance of parents who are not concerned about education. Populate schools with children from just these parents and no amount of money will save the day. Such schools cannot succeed either at providing economic mobility or even with training good citizens.

Concentrating the supportive parents in certain schools emulates a strategy of concentrating the supply of capital in large corporations. While not surprising that Friedman or the Powell Cabal should champion both strategies, their support for school vouchers reveals either their ignorance of competition or their hypocrisy, depending on the intent. If they truly want every school to meet certain standards they need to reveal a better understanding of how competition works. To attract a critical mass of supportive parents to each school through market principles you need to identify the resource for which these parents are competing and devise a means of diffusing that resource throughout all schools.

Here is an example of how a market approach can be used to actually improve school quality. Subsidize the tuition and books at a public university in accordance with the high school standing of students. Students who graduate near the top of the class get a full scholarship, regardless of the quality of high school they attended. Those at the bottom get nothing from government, again, regardless of what high school they attended. Since governments subsidize higher education to some extent already this could become a stipulation for providing those funds. If every school could hold out this carrot, you would have the opposite effect of a school voucher. Supportive parents would tend to diffuse over time to those schools where they see a higher chance for their children graduating high in their class. In other words, you would have a diversity of competitive choices for schools much like what occurs with real competition in the diversification of resource niches, and unlike what occurs in our market system driven by greed, where supplies of capital are concentrated to business corporations through the assistance of government. Draw enough supportive parents to any public school and the combination of resources, involvement and concern that they bring will improve the quality of education.

We must accept the possibility that Friedman and the Powell Cabal are not ignorant about competition at all; they know exactly what they propose. One of my professors at Cornell advocated school vouchers. In a departure from some of the rhetoric being voiced by school voucher advocates at the time, he freely admitted that vouchers would not improve education. For him that was not the point. He believed that vouchers were about maximizing choice, not improving

---

7 There are actually many answers to this question. For an overview see "The real promise of public education and the false promise of vouchers" (2002) by Nat LaCour. I found this article on a business web network (www.bnet.com). The Friedman cult must be severely disappointed with these business folks.

education. If some parents wanted to make bad choices, hey, that's their problem. Such honest opinions can be respected—if the same person or group does not staunchly advocate economic mobility as the defense for wealth disparity. In that case, championing policies that make a good education impossible for the lower rungs of the multilevel corporate pyramids stinks of hypocrisy.

Moral Economic Growth Hypocrisy

These essays have explained how maximum growth requires people to buy many things they do not need to be satisfied. One attribute of our society that helps to accomplish this is the "Keep up with the Joneses" syndrome described in Essay 1. Driven by cynicism, vanity and apprehension this motivation for acquiring more stuff can hardly be considered moral. Indeed, as the negative attributes that fuel our greed spills over to other areas they become distinctly immoral. Case in point: some Americans appear to be so vain and apprehensive about our way of life being threatened, and cynical about basic human rights, that they accept the use of torture as a means for achieving our security ends. Corporations actively play upon these negative character attributes to create hype for their products. If they were to justify these dubious actions on the basis of promoting moral consequences from economic growth that would be more corporate hypocrisy.

Let us turn our attention now from Milton to Benjamin Friedman, author of the book *The Moral Consequences of Economic Growth* (2005). Like his namesake, Benjamin Friedman is a renowned economist in his own right, a former chairman of the Economics Department at Harvard and the recipient of awards for his writings on economics. He is not quite an icon in his field—pop economists are not predisposed to treat Benjamin as reverently as Milton—so let us uncover a few more details about Benjamin to keep him distinct in our minds. Benjamin's book does not reveal him to be a slave to a normative economic ideology, as is Milton. Milton feels that by virtue of his *laissez faire* dogma everyone, including the middle class, will benefit. Benjamin feels that observable results of benefiting the middle class are the primary consideration, and this serves as a litmus test for his ideology. Milton might accuse Benjamin of using normative beliefs to guide his interpretations; Benjamin might counter that at least he does so openly. Indeed, grounding evidence in measurable benefits to the middle class represents more of a legitimate empirical norm than any dogma preached by Milton.

The basic thesis of B. Friedman's book is that economic growth has created moral benefits. The biggest problem for B. Friedman is the title he used. If B. Friedman had titled his book *A History of Economic Growth* he might have played the traditional scholar, using his beliefs that economic growth and morality are linked to deduce and cherry-pick historical events that fit his dogma best. Much to his credit, B. Friedman uses the title instead to shout out his belief. Unfortunately for B. Friedman, his honesty in titling the book transforms his work from a scholarly account to a scientific theory. The title practically begs an empiricist to treat economic growth as an independent variable and moral consequences as a dependent variable and to test the alleged causal link with empirical evidence and inductive reasoning.

An empiricist would first define the independent and dependent variables without introducing a tautology. For example, defining both economic growth and moral consequences in terms of economic progress would verify the hypothesis, but make it absolutely meaningless as well. In essence, the hypothesis would be claiming that economic progress spurs economic progress, not a very helpful observation. Linking the meaning of both variables to economic mobility, or to a work ethic, involves the same circular reasoning.

An empiricist determining causation would also define the independent and dependent variables in ways that are valid and reliable. Political and social progress would not be held up as examples of moral consequences without defining the specific aspects of such that are moral and measurable. For a consequence or benefit to be moral, by definition someone's morals or values must have been positively affected. Political and social progress may be nice benefits, but a person or society enjoying such benefits could still be greedy and immoral. When B. Friedman alludes to general economic, political and/or social progress—as he does occasionally—he blurs rather than strengthens claims of moral causation from an empiricist's point of view.

While B. Friedman occasionally works tautological and/or vague indicators of moral consequences into his discourse, he also cites valid indicators such as openness, tolerance, fairness and democracy. This provides empiricists something they can work with. The next task would then be to test whether the independent variable, economic growth, is necessary and/or sufficient for causing the dependent variable, moral benefits. Economic growth would not be necessary for moral consequences if such consequences could be found in the absence of growth. Economic growth would not be sufficient for moral benefits if cases were found where economic growth contributed to negative moral consequences. If evidence revealed that economic growth was neither necessary nor sufficient to increase openness, tolerance, fairness and democracy, then any relationship between economic growth and moral consequences is weak at best and possibly spurious.

B. Friedman discusses the Native Americans in his book. This is precisely the type of culture that empiricists might study to see if economic growth is necessary for moral consequences. They could be used for baseline data, since many tribes of Native Americans remained foragers for centuries until they were forced to change their lifestyle. However, B. Friedman uses a curious methodology for studying the moral consequences of the Native American cultures. Rather than refer to the extensive works of cultural anthropologists on some of the moral and immoral behaviors of Native Americans, he reviews the opinions of Enlightenment philosophers. Some of these philosophers viewed the Native Americans as moral (Jean-Jacques Rousseau), some as primitive (Adam Smith, Anne Turgot), but all did their "research" from their "armchairs." The Enlightenment philosophers were great thinkers indeed, and B. Friedman impresses his readers with his knowledge and understanding of their opinions, but none of their ruminations about Native Americans would count as real evidence in either a scientific journal or a court of law.

B. Friedman's strange methodology may be why he did not realize that Native Americans were forced out of their "primitive" culture and did not naturally "progress" to commerce in the inevitable manner predicted by Smith and Turgot. Their subsequent assimilation into our culture revealed them to be no less intelligent, indicating that they remained foragers for centuries by intent. Were all the tribes moral? No, but neither were they all immoral. Some of their behaviors reflected the "nobility" and some the "savagery" of Rousseau's armchair characterization. In the absence of economic growth the Native Americans pretty much covered the whole spectrum of what we would consider moral and immoral behavior. Some were tolerant of other tribes, some weren't. Some were egalitarian in their structure, some not. The conclusion an empiricist would draw from this would be that economic growth is not a necessary condition for moral consequences.[8]

Could economic growth be sufficient to cause moral consequences? There is plenty of modern day evidence to tackle this question. Jack Abramoff refutes that economic growth is sufficient for moral consequences at the individual level. Monsanto refutes this hypothesis at the corporate level. China refutes this hypothesis at the national level. Oil based economies refute this hypothesis at the global level. When a hypothesis can be falsified at so many levels most scientists would conclude that the hypothesis is false, though I already have described how *laissez faire* economists follow a different standard for evaluating evidence. The conclusion in this case: economic growth is not sufficient to cause moral consequences.

B. Friedman did stipulate that the distribution of wealth matters. Good for him! Perhaps economic growth is sufficient to cause moral consequences if that growth is widely distributed. I would love to prove B. Friedman right on this score, because he supports the middle class and because such proof would strengthen my own advocacy for markets driven by merit instead of greed. Unfortunately, the historical evidence still does not cooperate for Friedman. There are some problems with how B. Friedman handles the affluent post World War II era. He highlights the moral successes, chiefly the Civil Rights movement and environmental legislation,

---

8 *The World of the American Indian* (1989, revised edition), by the National Geographic Society, provides a good overview of Native American history and culture.

while glossing over something like McCarthyism as a situation that eventually resolved itself. He fails to mention completely that we probably struck our single most dastardly blow against democracy during this era, when our CIA sponsored the Iranian coup in 1953, a deed whose repercussions are still haunting us a half century and a hemisphere away.

Nevertheless, the most disturbing thing about B. Friedman's conclusion regarding this era would be if he is right. Consider that the future likely will not bring a more affluent time than the post World War II era, when our economic growth was nurtured by the additional Keynesian demand for goods stimulated by two more foreign wars and the Interstate Highway System, and government intervention in the form of the GI Bill enabled the lower and middle classes to experience the upward mobility that results from higher education. B. Friedman professes to be an optimist, but there is little cause for optimism if an era featuring McCarthyism, CIA coups, copious KKK violence, J. Edgar Hoover, multiple wars, multiple assassinations of foreign leaders and race riots represents the moral heyday of our country's history.

Whether or not economic growth contributes to moral benefits, such growth is neither necessary nor sufficient, and there appear to be other factors at work that are much more important. The two decades after World War II ushered in a period of apprehension induced by the Cold War, a period of vanity due to our great military and economic successes and a period of cynical realization that being advanced did not mean being civilized. The mood of the country trumped economic growth in determining our moral compass. Moral consequences appear to be more a product of moral intent than material fortune. Imagine that.

The cynicism, vanity and apprehension that influenced our politics after World War II now affect our economics in the new millennium. We are by far the wealthiest nation on earth. How many political leaders or corporations have the courage and humility to turn their back on that to acquire more allies and security in the world? How many political leaders or corporations have the faith to pursue a moral course of action, if a cynical immoral approach brings a better economic return sooner? Economic growth not only fails as a necessary and/ or sufficient condition for moral consequences, the very factors that obsessively drives economic growth can have immoral consequences, particularly when large corporations are involved. A call by large corporations or the Powell Cabal to expand economic growth on moral grounds has the stench of hypocrisy.

Free Trade Hypocrisy

Large corporations play the morality card in regards to free trade. Multinational corporations pressure developing countries to open up their markets on the moral grounds that this will better the lives of impoverished citizens. They preach that through *laissez faire* economics free markets will bring prosperity to these countries. This message can be hypocritical on three fronts, all of them connected to the fact that large corporations are the ones delivering the message. The moral hypocrisy we already have discussed. If large corporations also: 1) limit free choice and 2) increase wealth disparity in order to open up "free" markets for the sake of the poor, we have a trifecta of corporate hypocrisy.

As discussed in the previous essay large corporations often restrict the free flow of information, harm outside parties not involved in the market exchange, stifle the exchange of ideas and dominate markets. To sum up, large corporations spend considerable time, money and effort making markets less free or efficient. You might call it an obsession of theirs. At the international level multinational corporations have added a few more tricks to compromise free markets.

In theory, goods, labor and capital are different but interconnected parts of the same free market. Multinational corporations like to sever the bothersome interconnected part when developing international "free" markets and trade. In particular they like to separate the wages of labor in a developing periphery country from the prices of goods in a developed core country. Without this interconnection of markets multinational corporations can pay labor at one market equilibrium and charge for goods at another. This is a great way of increasing capital welfare gains, much of which can be used to profit investors who have never set foot in the developing country. While the great thinkers of the Powell Cabal appear to love closed systems, this takes the concept a bit too far. Isolating the market equilibriums for labor from goods subverts free market principles for the sake of greed, and the wealth disparity that results has the same inflationary effect on a global economy as with a national economy. Of note: localized businesses are incapable of subverting the free market in this manner.

Large corporations also exploit comparative advantages in trade. The concept of a comparative advantage in economics, first theorized by David Ricardo, seems harmless enough.[9] One explanation for how this works describes how an executive might be both a better manager and a better typist than a secretary. If burdened with both activities the executive would spend less time at the labor of greater value to the company. While there might be an absolute advantage at having the executive both manage and type, there is a comparative advantage of having the executive just manage while the secretary just types. In terms of international trade, maintaining a comparative advantage means a country that excels in the production of many things, such as the United States, produces goods of high value and trades freely with countries who focus on producing goods of low value.

Producing goods of low value necessitates labor of low value. Though

9 Ricardo introduced the concept of comparative advantage in *Principles of Political Economy and Taxation* (1817).

free trade based on comparative advantage may be good for the overall global economy, most of the benefits go to the countries producing the goods of higher value. Consider the case of a secretary asking the boss for training to become an executive. The boss says no, since this would provide no comparative advantage to the organization. The secretary receives a Christmas bonus instead. The executive may be satisfied with this arrangement but not the secretary. Similarly, developing countries on the global economic periphery may be given financial aid, or provided debt relief, as a token of appreciation that they are forced to trade the goods of lower value to core countries. This is a satisfactory, wealth-enhancing arrangement for multinational corporations and the overall global economy, but not for developing countries.

Corporations are assisted in these endeavors by organizations such as the World Bank and International Monetary Fund. They provide much needed capital to fund projects in developing countries, the Christmas bonus so to speak, with a slight catch. The developing countries must open their markets to multinational corporations according to a set of principles called the Washington Consensus, named after the city where these lending institutions are located. Though intended to expand free markets and free trade, the Washington Consensus actually deprives developing countries of economic freedom. Multinationals are the most adept of all corporations at corrupting free markets through obstructing the free flow of information, dominating markets and creating negative externalities; these can be achieved with less hassle in developing countries whose markets have been opened up by the Washington Consensus.

The principles of the Washington Consensus include trade liberalization, welcoming foreign investment, privatization and deregulation. Through the hook of national debt these principles of the Washington Consensus can be imposed, additionally depriving countries of free choice. At least if the governments of developing countries commanded their own economies or developed their own corporate structure the responsibility for success or failure would lie within their own borders. Instead, forcing countries to abdicate their responsibility to multinational corporations for promoting "free" trade practices and economic mobility has the rancid taste of hypocrisy.

You won't hear the Powell Cabal complaining about this assault on freedom by multinational corporations. They may be just a bit concerned, however. The Washington Consensus has proved to be an abysmal failure at helping Latin American countries. On the one hand you have Pinochet's Chile, an economic success to a degree but at the price of a brutal, repressive government. The cause for repression is not embedded in the economic principles of the Washington Consensus, but rather the political policies of the U. S. State Department. Operation Condor, spearheaded by Henry Kissinger, propped up repressive regimes that implemented the economic policies favored by the United States.[10]

There also have been countries like Argentina, who played by all the rules set out by the Washington Consensus, and went bankrupt. Such setbacks have been enough to bring back the old Keynesian economists advocating a role for governments to stimulate economic growth. The Powell Cabal may need to pursue their *laissez faire* policies at a more moderate pace or risk the perception by the global community that wealth disparity caused by greed is not such a good thing after all.

A Corporation's Corporation

One of our family "vacations," sponsored by a Church from a neighboring town, involved a work camp mission trip to the Dominican Republic. In addition to helping rebuild a school devastated by a hurricane, we learned a bit about how global economies affect developing countries. Large corporations such as IBM have a large presence in the Dominican Republic. IBM dutifully serves their wealthy shareholders, isolating the prices of computer goods sold in developed countries from the wages of factory workers in the DR. The difference between the two market equilibriums for goods and labor provides a tidy sum of capital, most of which leaves the country to provide welfare to corporate shareholders.

The perks for large corporations in the global economy do not stop there. One of the more heavily publicized corporate tax cons is the use of offshore headquarters. The "headquarters" can be no more than a post office box number in a Caribbean country, since the purpose of the "headquarters" is only to avoid corporate taxes in the United States. Sometimes a company wants greater service than just a box office number and tax exemption. From the web site of Witherspoon, Seymour & Robinson (http://www.wsr-corporation.com/en/offshore.html), a company formation corporation, here are some of the advertised perks of setting up an offshore company, as copied and pasted from their web site.

Anonymity, limited liability, asset protection, tax exemption!
Offshore companies are the preferred company structure to achieve anonymity and privacy protection, keep all business details confidential and combine all this with limited liability and tax exemption. All companies we offer are fully legal and able to conduct their activities worldwide.

---

10 Documented *in The Condor Years* (2004), by John Dinges.

The main advantages are:
- anonymity
- nominee services through lawyers
- highest level of privacy protection
- limited liability without any paid up capital requirement
- legal tax exemption
- no taxation on any kind of income
- no accounting requirements
- no reporting requirements
- no fees for accountants
- no auditing
- no requirements on profession or financial standing
- business can be conducted internationally
- and much more

As this advertisement makes clear, WSR is a corporation to help corporations avoid all responsibilities. You want to obstruct the free flow of information? Thanks to WSR and developing countries like the DR you have all the privacy you need. You want to escape all accountability for negative externalities? WSR will help you find the right developing country to exploit. You want to cook your books? WSR knows you don't need no stinkin' accountants. You want to accumulate lots and lots of corporate welfare for the wealthy? Look no further, WSR is a corporation's corporation serving your entitlement needs. You just can't beat that now, can you?! Corporations like WSR must make *laissez faire* advocates and puppet libertarians from the Powell Cabal tingle with ecstasy. They are the perfect embodiment of a market economy being driven by greed instead of merit.

Since the demand for corporate goods on a global scale dwarfs the demands for local goods in a small country, the Dominican Republic is totally dependent on the whims of global markets. If a global corporation like IBM goes belly up the economy of the United States would suffer, but the Dominican Republic would be devastated. A recession that increases unemployment by a percentage point or two in the United States leaves a much larger percentage unemployed in the Dominican Republic, such as what occurred while we were there in the summer of 2003.

Walking the streets of Los Alcarhizzos, a suburb of Santo Domingo, my family witnessed how much of the labor force in the Dominican Republic lives. We were prepared ahead of time for some of the negative sights we saw. Rutted dirt roads with sewage flowing down open side canals weaved through shacks of corrugated metal, with various types of livestock in the street. What surprised us were the "positive" sights. The sky was a web of makeshift power lines connecting to the government's electricity grid. This enabled almost every corrugated shack to have a radio and/or television. The rutted dirt roads were moderately trafficked by scooters, motorcycles and even minivans. The essentials for middle class satisfaction—such as good housing and health services—took a back seat to the mass produced goods that can boost a country's wealth indicators. The DR's standard of living has been boosted even as hospitals are flooded because of the unsanitary living conditions. Such are the benefits for many developing countries in a global economy of "free trade" structured to benefit multinational corporations.

Cindy and I brought our kids on these mission work camp trips to have our kids feel the positives of helping the less fortunate. Instead, they were confronted by the anomaly of people living in poverty and squalor yet owning mass produced stuff made by multinational corporations. Faced with this anomaly our kids were forced to weigh the advantages of affluence—having the important stuff you need—and indulgence—coveting the hyped stuff mass produced by business corporations. Our children may not have resolved this moral dilemma the way puppet libertarians from the Powell Cabal or either of the Friedmans would have liked.

All the corporate hypocrisy would seem to dampen the hopes of even the most Hans-like optimist, but that would be true only if Hans was aware of the hypocrisy. Large corporations want small businesses and middle class citizens like Hans to be emotional rather than rational. At the subconscious level, however, Hans must be getting suspicious. When corporations bemoan "too many dollars" inflating the economy, but strive to put "too many dollars" in the pockets of the corporate elite; when the Powell Cabal decries entitlements for the poor and seeks to protect large inheritances; when *laissez faire* economists defend economic mobility while advocating school vouchers; when puppet libertarians preach the gospel of free markets but support the private coercion of markets; at some point the putrid hypocrisy makes you aware of the decomposing body that is being hidden under the floor boards.

Neither economic satisfaction, nor economic freedom, nor irrepressible hope for wealth justifies support for business corporations that generally are more impersonal, coercive and hypocritical than proprietorships. We are back to the same perplexing question: Why should government bias the hyped demand for goods, concentrated supply of capital and greedy self-interest for labor to favor large corporations in our market economy?

Economic Evolution

Laissez faire economists could charge that these essays lack the authority to make economic claims. Through a body of scholarly work the discipline of economics authoritatively establishes that organizations created through government intervention, and dedicated to private coercion, are consistent with free markets.

These essays stray from this scholarship and make wild assertions that business corporations and the free market are mutually exclusive concepts, if you actually bother to take the meaning of words literally. These essays have the audacity to suggest that the meaning of welfare should be class neutral and applicable to both the rich and the poor. Economic scholars might assert that unscholarly, middle class schleps outside the field of economics have no authority to write essays that make such ignorant claims.

The counter charge to this is that economics appears to be a fake science. Scholarship counts for only a little in real science. Yes, you have to apply accepted methods of gathering and interpreting empirical evidence, but the beliefs you have prior to investigation are supposed to be vulnerable. Applying the basic scientific methods of observation and generalization can be done by an economist, an academic or even us middle class schleps lacking in economic scholarship. The empirical evidence is supposed to be capable of changing whatever beliefs you formerly held, whether based on a long tradition of scholarship or not.

When confronted with a conflict between the very definitions of free markets and corporations, *laissez faire* economists keep their fixed belief that they coexist by allowing the meaning of free markets to change. When confronted with the similarity between welfare and capital investments, they keep their fixed belief that welfare goes only to the poor and alter the meaning of capital investments. Their scholarship ignores the standards for validity and reliability of empirical evidence. Their scholastic approach nevertheless gets labeled as positivistic by a pop economist with perhaps the most dogmatic views that ever penetrated the field of economics.

The economics I have described is the economics championed by the Powell Cabal. I am no economist myself, I do not keep up with economic journals and cannot claim that the *laissez faire* paradigm governs the society of real economists. I suspect, or at least hopefully wish, that most are rolling their eyes in disgust at the shilling that *laissez faire* economists and puppet libertarians from the Powell Cabal are doing for business corporations. Perhaps what has occurred is a coevolution of only the *laissez faire* branch of economics with business corporations.

Maybe we are dealing with something similar to the evolution of comparative anatomy in this matter. The fins and arms of different mammals are comparative structures with a common evolutionary background that have developed different forms and functions. Natural evolution does not continually build from scratch but rather works with the materials at hand; maybe the same thing holds true for cultural evolution. Our market economy has evolved from colonialism and feudal systems; perhaps large business corporations remain the focus of our economy as the comparative structure that evolved from feudal lords and colonial powers. Feudal lords were undeniably greedy and undeniably obtained their wealth from the merit of others. Perhaps our current economic lords had no choice from an evolutionary viewpoint but to infuse markets with their greed as well.

Once colonialism evolved from western civilization perhaps the die was cast, and we must now accept *laissez faire* economics as a vestigial growth from this cultural evolution, though as potentially poisonous as our appendix. Such economists are doomed to confuse anything driven by greed to be an indicator of merit. Yet the shilling of puppet libertarians from the Powell Cabal aside, perhaps business corporations are inevitable to the smooth functioning of a market economy. The consequent greed may present some problems, but the quaint idea of free markets absent of private coercion is mere whimsical fantasy.

After throwing the pretense for free markets aside, perhaps we might discover that reducing the role of business corporations compromises the overall stability, resiliency and health of a market economy. Before moving on to political explanations for why Hans has been "trading down" economically let us run a check on how well our market economy has been functioning. A systems analysis needs to be done. Since *laissez faire* economists appear incapable of empiricism; instead let us apply our own empirical investigation based on some ecological criteria to devise an economic report card.

ESSAY 7 – AN ECONOMIC REPORT CARD

Overview

- A systems analysis was used to grade the changes in our economy since the seventies, focusing on components important to all ecological systems.
- The only passing grade was for specialization of the goods market.
- The system diversity/diffusion of capital, adaptability of labor, and stability of wealth distribution all failed.
- Government provides the continuity for our economic system to function in accordance with greed.
- The absence of negative feedback loops for homeostatic monitoring of *laissez faire* propaganda is the underlying cause of our economic problems.

Economic Indicators for the Middle Class

Cindy and I have worked out a strategy for the pursuit of happiness that works well for us. Cindy earned Bachelor and Masters Degrees, plus RN and WOCN certifications for nursing. I hesitate to admit how much education I have had, but my in-laws once joked that my son would be done with school before I would, and that my eventual career would be working for him. Together, our educational backgrounds enable us to live a middle class lifestyle on Emerson Street. Education serves as an economic indicator; upward mobility depends on education more than any other factor. As we will soon see, higher education is one of only a few economic indicators important to the middle class that has tracked well over the past thirty years.

Cindy and I used our education to get precisely the jobs we wanted, working for small nonprofit organizations not too far from Emerson Street. Our employers have allowed us the flexibility of determining how much and when we will work. We did not have one wage earner working forty hours a week, as occurred in this house forty years ago, but during our children's formative years our combined work week hovered only slightly beyond that ideal. You could say our work week, with both adults working part time and adjusting our schedules to raise our children, more closely resembled that of early foragers than a typical middle class family from twenty-first century America. Now that we soon face the costs of college for three teenagers Cindy and I have ratcheted up the combined work hours closer to sixty, in line with many other two-parent families.

Since we were both professionals our earlier work strategy provided us enough income to get by. True, we have more debt than previous generations of home owners on Emerson Street. We secured a home equity loan for improvements on an old house and to negate future student loans, but we are not buried in debt to the current extent of many middle class citizens. We worry about having three kids in college all at the same time in the near future, but we will cross that bridge willingly when the time comes.

Admittedly, not many choose the same economic strategy for a middle class pursuit of happiness that we did. Those who have as much education typically choose to work full time in more lucrative employment, seeking to become upper middle class or wealthier. The typical middle class strategies are to accept risk as a small business entrepreneur, accumulate large debt, or have multiple jobs between both parents.

The dubious strategies for pursuing happiness as a middle class citizen reflect problems with our overall economic system. Scientists, particularly ecologists, spend a great deal of time evaluating systems. Some essential functions of natural systems apply to economic systems as well. Instead of focusing on the stock market and other corporate backed wealth indicators, we will use this systems approach, filtered through middle class lenses, to interpret how well these essential system functions are being met.

The Economic System Report Card[1]

Any measurement or indicator needs context in order to be meaningful. The Gross Domestic Product (GDP), a measure of the total goods and services our society produces, is around thirteen trillion dollars. What does that mean? The GDP as a stand alone indicator tells us nothing. OK, then, in the context of the rest of the world our GDP is by far the highest. That's a feel good statistic that indicates our economic system produced well in the past, building the foundation for the current superiority, but our current economic system could be improving or deteriorating now without the magnitude of our GDP reflecting that. For the proper context we need baseline data, just as a natural scientist who really wanted to learn something about a system would gather. We need to compare how our economic system currently functions with benchmarks from the past, whether we have fluctuated around those benchmarks or trended steadily away.

A trend away from the "baseline data" implies that some intervention occurred to cause that trend. The intervention of spending billions of dollars to manipulate the public perception of corporations and *laissez faire* economics should affect how our economic system functions, or why else would corporations

---

1 The data was first obtained in 2006. Updating the results based on 2008 tables did not change the grades much from the original report card.

spend all that money. Let us use the seventies for our baseline data, soon after the Powell Memorandum of 1971 initiated a Powell Cabal of corporate sponsored think tanks, corporate endowed chairs of economic departments, corporate hired public relations firms, corporate employed lobbyists and corporate owned media.

I prepared a report card that examines the market specialization, diversity, adaptability and stability of our economy now, relative to the seventies. The preferred time period for analysis was thirty years, extending from 1976 to 2005 (mid-decade to mid-decade). When data was lacking for either of these specific dates, or when conveniently provided in one table, a different time period that stretches back to the seventies was used. When particular data is not available for the seventies the time period went back as far as possible.

Middle class economics does not require complex assumptions, statistics and/or indicators in order to prove or shroud a claim. For each of these system functions several indicators were graded using the following criteria: A = improved by more than 15%; B = improved from 5 to 15%; C = within +/- 5%; D = worsened from 5 to 15%; and F = worsened by more than 15%. Note that the 10% increments reflect the typical report card scheme; that is the only rationale for using those delineations. Focusing on the percentages rather than the letter grades will be more revealing. As you will see, the letter grades soften the actual changes occurring.

An overall grade point average for each system function was determined using a traditional formula of: A = 4; B = 3; C = 2; D = 1 and F = 0. A brief discussion follows the grade for each indicator and for each system function. A summary report card is provided, though you are not likely to proudly display these results on your refrigerator.

Market Specialization and the Demand for Goods

Natural systems ultimately depend on the energy of the sun. Organisms can change this energy into different forms but cannot augment the energy along the way. The total amount of energy is conserved, or remains the same, according to the first law of thermodynamics. Eventually, energy dissipates into a state of random disorder, a process known as entropy, or the second law of thermodynamics. Because of the laws of thermodynamics healthy systems need a constant input of energy to retain all their other functions. Turn off the electromagnetic and thermal energy of the sun and living systems will cease, with the needed energy for life dissipating into the void as barely detectable heat. Think about your desk, your room, your house or your yard and you understand the cultural corollary to entropy. Without constant inputs of energy anything becomes disordered.

The energy of the markets, the force that breathes life into a demand for goods, is specialization. If everyone stopped specializing in something, if everyone suddenly became self-sufficient in everything they did and demanded nothing, markets would cease. The ultimate source of specialization is the mind, as supplemented by existing education and technology. The greater the quality and quantity of developed minds in a society, the greater the potential for specialization to infuse energy into markets. Measures of both educational support and success reflect the future potential for the specialization of markets.

For this report card market specialization indicators were:
- high school graduation rates,
- advanced degrees earned,
- public school revenues,
- funding of research and development, and
- relative adult literacy rates.

High School Graduation Rates:

Estimates of graduation rates differ according to the methodology used for measurement. The federal government approach using census data gives higher estimates; the typical state government approach using administrative data gives lower estimates. Since we are comparing graduation rates from the time that the Powell Cabal started a coordinated effort to influence public policy and perception, the objective is to use a consistent method that covers that time span. "State-Level High School Completion Rates: Concepts, Measures, and Trends," a peer-reviewed article written by John Warren in the journal *Education Policy Analysis Archives* (Vol. 51, No. 13), provides graduation rates from 1975 to 2002. The method used for this article indicated a 76% graduation rate in 1975 and a 72% graduation rate in 2002. Our goal for this report card is not to judge whether either 76% or 72% are acceptable graduation rates, only to quantify positive or negative changes that occurred since the Powell Memorandum.

We might hastily conclude that the relative graduation rates have decreased by 4%. That would be wrong. The 4% decrease is relative to the absolute of 100%, not relative to the 76% base rate in 1975. Relative rates are more indicative of the level of change than absolute rates. For example, an increase of 1% to 2% federal funding as a proportion of the GDP seems insignificant, but actually represents a doubling of investment. For this and other items in the report card increases and decreases are determined relative to the base year used. There was a reduction of 5.3% in high school graduation rates from the 1975 to 2002 level ({76-72}/76).
Grade: D

Advanced Degrees Earned:

The federal government makes available many informative tables of data on the

Internet. For example, the U. S. Census Bureau provides hundreds of tables, covering virtually every facet of our society, in a series of documents called Statistical Abstracts (SA). While these may not be the most stimulating reading material for middle class citizens, there is a wealth of unbiased data that reveals much to a discerning eye. Information obtained from federal tables provided on the Internet will be referenced by the type of table and document in parentheses.

The number of people earning a college degree increased from 1,666,000 in 1975 to 2,850,000 in 2005 (Table 292, SA 2008). During that time the resident population increased from 215,973,000 to 296,940,000 (Table 2, SA 2007). As a percentage of the population those earning advanced degrees in a particular year increased from 0.771% to 0.960%, or a 24.5% increase from the 1975 level. Much of this is due to an increase in women earning degrees, a good thing. Some of this is due to an increase in foreign students earning degrees, overall a good thing, but not reflective of American students. Regardless, these statistics confirm we are a great nation for higher education.

Grade: A

Public School Revenues:

Revenues from federal, state and local government for our public schools represent our overall financial commitment to developing young minds that will increase the specialization of markets. Comparing levels of revenues or expenditures requires an accounting for inflationary effects and a standard for comparison. This was addressed by using the GDP for the years being compared as a common denominator. Thus, if revenues for public schools were 1% of our GDP in 1976, greater commitment would be indicated by an increased percentage of the GDP by 2005. The GDP can be obtained most easily from the National Income and Product Accounts (NIPA) tables provided by the U. S. Department of Commerce via their web site.

In raw terms we increased federal, state and local revenues for public schools from $70.803 billion in 1976 (Table 236, SA 1978) to $477.408 billion in 2005 (Table 230, SA 2008). That sounds impressive, except that you have to account for inflation and the increase of wealth. Our GDP increased from $1,825.3 billion to $12,421.9 billion (Table 1.1.5, NIPA) over the same time period. The proportion of GDP used for public school revenues decreased from 3.88% to 3.84%, a relative decrease of 1.0 % from 1976 to 2005.

Grade: C

Funding of Research and Development:

To foster specialization we not only need to invest in the development of minds, but in the application of minds as well. We discussed previously that corporations often spend more on marketing than on the research and development (R&D) that fuels progress, but perhaps our overall commitment to progress has continued. R&D expenditures from all sources amounted to $39.435 billion in 1976 and $323.546 billion in 2005 (Table 775, 2008 SA). This represents 2.16% of the 1825.3 billion GDP in 1976 and 2.60% of the 12421.59 billion GDP in 2005 (Table 1.1.5, NIPA). The funding of R&D as a proportion of GDP has increased by 20.4% from 1976 to 2005.

Grade: A

Relative Adult Literacy Rates:

"The Twin Challenges of Mediocrity and Inequality: Literacy in the U.S. from an International Perspective" (February 2002), a policy information report created by the Educational Testing Service, explored the results of the International Adult Literary Survey done from 1994-1998. The basic findings correspond to the title: the United States lies in the middle of the pack for 20 high income countries in regards to relative adult literacy rates for ages 16-65, though ranking near the top for both extremes of most and least literate categories. This country's literacy disparity mirrors our wealth disparity.

The Powell Cabal might point out that the National Adult Literary Survey documenting rates in our country showed an increase from 1992 to 2003, in seeming contradicting to the flunking grade assigned in this report. The National Institute for Literacy, a federal agency, reports this in positive terms but there are two problems with their official optimism. First, the raw scores for two measures, prose and document literacy, remained flat; only the quantitative measure increased. Second, literacy scores on these surveys tend to get higher over time for all countries, thus the flat scores for prose and document means we are falling still farther down the rankings relative to other wealthy countries, while merely keeping pace with other countries for the quantitative measure.

The report also provides a basis for comparing our relative literacy rates to other high income countries over time. The old-timers in our country scored better relative to their foreign counterparts than did our young people. The age category 56-65 ranged from 2nd to 5th out of 20 countries for three different measures (prose, document, quantitative) while the age category 16-25 ranked 14th for all three measures. The biggest drop in our relative rankings came between the 26-35 and 36-45 population groups, where we fell from 25-30% lower in rank for the three measures. Of note: the 26-35 year olds in the survey were the first to be affected by the Powell Cabal's charter to extol the virtues of business corporations and *laissez faire* economics.

Grade: F

Our country continues to fuel our market economy with the specialization needed for trade and wealth. There are some caveats to mention. The training of citizens in terms of literacy and public education appears either to be waning, or falling in relation to other developed countries. Also, the original analysis for this report card focused on federal funding for R&D, which correlates more with substantive innovations, as opposed to stylish innovations funded by corporations to recycle demand. Federal funding of R&D has decreased by about 75 % in relative terms (Table 775, SA 2008). Our market specialization may be providing us with recycled demand for different lipstick, but our commitment to advances in significant technology may be decreasing.

Market Specialization GPA: 2.2 (C)

Market Diversity and the Supply of Capital

Diversity provides resiliency to a system. In a natural system diversity results from a diffusion of resources (plants, fungi, predators, prey, etc.), leading species to develop different strategies for obtaining those resources. A great diversity of species means the trauma or elimination of one species has less impact on the overall ecosystem. In contrast, concentrating the resources of a natural system in just a few species puts the system under greater stress when catastrophe strikes one of those dominant species.

Towns, states or countries dependent mostly on one type of market leave themselves vulnerable to the problems that could beset that market. For example, if you had the opportunity to rebuild a country's economy for that country's own benefit you would not want to concentrate on one resource such as oil. Resiliency in the marketplace is achieved through a diversity of businesses. Such diversity is achieved when labor competes for income, just as species compete for resources, by specializing in the production of different goods and services. Diverse businesses are built around this specialized labor. In contrast, capital investments do not specialize. One man's dollar "produces" the same investment "service" as another's. The income returned for that capital investment still depends on the competition of specialized labor and not how one dollar bill performs differently from any other. In other words, competition for employee compensation induces diverse production of goods and services; competition for dividends induces the concentration of capital in large corporations. Measures of where and how capital is supplied reflect the diversity of markets.

For this report card market diversity indicators were ratios of:
- proprietor to private enterprise income,
- corporate profits to employee compensation,
- net dividends to corporate taxes,
- "welfare taxes" to GDP, and
- federal subsidies.

Proprietor to Private Enterprise Income:

Proprietors are owners of businesses that divert no capital to shareholders. Private enterprise income includes proprietors and all other business income. Proprietors income was $132.2 billion in 1976 and 959.8 billion in 2005 (Table 1.16, NIPA). Total private enterprise income was $594.1 billion in 1976 and 5,273.6 billion in 2005 (Table 1.16, NIPA). The proportion of proprietors to private enterprise income went from 22.3% in 1976 to 18.2% in 2005. This is a decrease of 18.4% of income to those businesses that do not divert capital to shareholders.
Grade: F

Corporate Profits to Employee Compensation:

Employee compensation is income in exchange for labor; corporate profits are capital income in exchange for investment. Employee compensation was $1059.4 billion in 1976 and $7037.2 billion in 2005 (Table 1.10, NIPA). Corporate profits amounted to $146.8 billion in 1976 and 1208.5 billion in 2005 (Table 1.10, NIPA). The ratio of corporate profits to employee compensation has increased from 13.9 to 17.2%, in relative terms an increase of 23.7% for the priority of redistributing and concentrating capital over the priority of directly rewarding diverse labor.

I hate to let anything go to waste. An original analysis for this report card included 2002, the year before we invaded Iraq. The ratio at that time was actually 12.0%. The current increased diversion of capital away from employee compensation to corporate profits has occurred since our occupation of Iraq. This boost to the concentration of capital was one of the few things our invasion of Iraq seemed to help, and perhaps is closer to the mark of why we are there than any of the official reasons provided. We probably would need access to the information from Cheney's private energy meetings to confirm any conclusions drawn.
Grade: F

Net Dividends to Corporate Taxes:

As recorded in the NIPA tables corporate profits are split between corporate taxes, net dividends, and a third category called "undistributed." Net dividends are the return on the capital investment made by shareholders. Corporate taxes compensate the public good in return for government protection of shareholder assets from liability, and for providing the structure by which shareholders can get income from capital investment rather than from the merits of their labor. Corporate taxes also level the playing field by a diffusion of capital in return for the competitive advantage over proprietorships that government intrusion provides corporations. The remaining category, undistributed corporate profits, has varied purposes that range from trickling down to labor to providing a company executive with a corporate jet.

Net dividends went from $30.1 billion in 1976 to $628.8 billion in 2006 (Table 1.10, NIPA). Taxes on corporate profits were $65.3 billion in 1976 and $468.9 billion in 2006 (Table 1.10, NIPA). The year 2006 was used because an obvious anomaly to net dividends occurred in the year 2005, when they sharply decreased only to sharply increase again. The ratio of net dividends to corporate taxes increased from 46.1% to 134.1%, a change of 191%. Thirty years ago the return from corporate profits to benefit the public good more than doubled the return for concentrating capital to the wealthy, a just compensation for government intruding on markets to empower and protect corporations. The return for the public good is now much less than the service government provides corporations for allowing them to concentrate capital.

Grade: F

"Welfare Taxes" to GDP:

Societies that aspire to be meritocracies place taxes on large inheritances and gifts, transfers of wealth that were not earned through merit. In our country these are officially known as estate and gift taxes, though the Powell Cabal refers to them as "death taxes," understating their great compassion for the wealthy who "can't take it with them." This spin occasionally persuades middle class people like Hans that the government unjustly dictates how hard earned wealth be distributed. Of course, the "hard earned" money might have come mainly from capital investments that diverted income away from actual labor. Even if once "hard earned," providing large amounts of this welfare to the wealthy inheritors discourages latent entrepreneurs to spend much effort in the merits of their labor in the future. Finally, since estate and gift taxes target wealth that was not transferred for the production of goods and services—i.e., they target unearned wealth—they could be called welfare taxes with greater accuracy than death taxes.

Welfare taxes—excuse me, estate and gift taxes—at both federal and state levels amounted to $7.3 billion in 1976 and $30.3 billion in 2005 (Table 5.10, NIPA). This amounts to 0.400% of the $1823.5 billion GDP for 1976 and 0.245% of the $12429.1 billion GDP for 2005 (Table 1.1.5, NIPA). That is a decrease of 38.8% in welfare taxes, or an increase of 38.8% of welfare dollars retained for the wealthy, unattached to any merits for the production of goods or services in the market. Whether or not there is a legitimate cultural argument to be made for large inheritances the economic impact is less capital to provide an incentive for diverse labor.

Grade: F

Federal Subsidies

In some cases government protection from liability is not enough to satisfy corporations, nor is allowing more capital to be concentrated rather than to serve the public good. In some cases corporations survive through subsidies handed back to them by government. Subsidies from federal government have increased from $4.9 billion in 1976 to $58.9 billion in 2005 (Table 3.13, NIPA). As a proportion of GDP (see above), subsidies have increased from 0.269% to 0.474%, a relative increase of 76%.

The original analysis factored in subsidies from state governments. Those increased from $0.2 billion to $0.4 billion. That is not much of an increase compared to federal subsidies but here is the kicker. Concentrating capital for corporations is more effective at the federal level. Proprietorships are more likely to be helped by the state. Large corporations no doubt appreciate federal government making the concentration of capital easier for them than if they had to go through a bunch of smaller governments. The extra costs for lobbyists alone for corporations would be horrendous.

Grade: F

To paraphrase: "There but for the grace of government goes corporations." Government limits the liability of shareholders in a corporation to only their investments; their additional assets cannot be touched. The corporation could be grossly incompetent and/or corrupt, the corporation could cause damage to the government and/or public that amounts to billions of dollars, and the shareholders need only relinquish the money they invested in the corporation. In contrast, proprietorships could lose all of their assets, business related or otherwise, when something goes wrong.

This is why the bitching and moaning from puppet libertarians and the Powell Cabal about the double taxation of corporate profits has to be taken with a grain of salt. First, why should anyone in a meritocracy expect to retain a greater percentage of their capital gains than from the merits of their labor? As long as shareholders receive some return from their investment they have no moral reason to expect a huge income from what are essentially welfare dollars. This same logic applies to inheritances. What incentive does that provide for the wealthy to do something productive with their actual labor?

People would not choose to become shareholders of companies obsessed with maximizing profit, if not for government. Why risk your personal assets for some of the corporate misdeeds that occur? The alternative to becoming a shareholder for a person seeking wealth is becoming an entrepreneur, a real one that is, one willing to invest some labor as well as capital into carving out a new niche for a business. If the Powell Cabal does not like the idea of government exacting a price through a "double" tax in return for the greater liability protection, fine, let's abolish the added protection for corporations and give the real entrepreneurs favorable status.

As long as Hans is willing to believe corporate America about "death" and "double" taxes, we can expect the supply of capital to be further concentrated. This spells trouble for both the middle class and proprietorships that diversify in their attempts to earn income predominantly through the merits of their labors.
Market Diversity GPA: 0 (F)

Market Adaptability and the Self-Interests of Labor

Adaptability also provides resiliency to a system. All natural systems experience at least minor disturbances. Organisms in a well-functioning system adapt to these disturbances, at times even turning them into a positive. For example, trees in an arid climate often have seeds that germinate after exposed to fire. Low availability of prey depresses the birth rates of some predators. Some organisms adapt to the scarcity of resources in winter by hibernating. Adaptability and diversity often are interrelated, as when an organism adapts to a new niche as a competitive response.

Even in healthy, diverse economic systems disturbances will occur. Inflation, recession, natural catastrophes and war can all disturb markets. Just as a chain is as strong as the weakest link, the resiliency to market disturbance depends on how well the most vulnerable type of market can adapt. In our economic system capital can be stored and/or borrowed for times of disturbance fairly easily, provided greed does not skew our ability to use capital. The production of goods and services can be increased or scaled back as needed. Most problematic, however, is the adaptability of our labor market in times of disturbance. Workers who are burdened with lack of time and money have little opportunity to adapt to changes in the labor market. They can not afford retraining or other employment risks when a disturbance such as a recession comes. Measures of the burdens faced by workers reflect the adaptability of the labor market.

For this report card market adaptability indicators were:
*   student debt,
*   ratio of household liability to personal income,
*   proportion of multiple jobs per family,
*   ratio of wage and salary supplements to disbursements, and
*   ratio of nonbusiness bankruptcies filed to number of households.

Student Debt:

Student debt starts a new college graduate out on the wrong foot. Since 1978 the costs for attending college have more than doubled after controlling for inflation, as detailed in a report by the Center for Economic and Policy Research called "Student Debt: Bigger and Bigger" (September 2005). As these costs have dramatically increased, government assistance has dramatically cut back. Pell Grants from the government used to cover about 84% of the costs of college in 1975; they now cover about 39%, as cited by the State PIRG's report called "The Burden of Borrowing: A Report on the Rising Rates of Student Loan Debt" (March 2002).

Perhaps the best web site for exploring the issue of student debt is provided by the Project on Student Debt, whose tag line is "Keeping College within Reach." There you will discover that since 1990 the proportion of students graduating with debt has risen from about one half to two thirds, with the average amount owed increased by 58% after inflation. More strikingly, the web site reports that the number of graduates with serious debt, which they define as $40,000 in current dollars,[2] has increased more than tenfold, from over 7,000 students in 1990 to now over 77,000. This turn of events spans only half the time period for which other trends in this report card have been reported, and many assumptions would be needed to form one indicator from this data to cover thirty years. That will not be necessary. The middle class should award but one grade when an economic system more than doubles the costs of higher education in real dollars, more than halves the amount of assistance for that education and witnesses the number of students in serious debt increase by tenfold.

Grade: F

Household Liability to Personal Income:

Unfortunately, college graduates are not alone in accumulating debt. On Emerson Street in the sixties middle class families had the debt of home mortgage and, um, that's about it. Now we have home mortgage, home equity, credit cards, debit cards, and one or more finance plans. This level of debt increases our stress and decreases our options in the labor market. Our debt pushes us to equate our self-interest in the labor market purely with selfishness, maximizing our labor to earn money, much to the delight of corporations and the Powell Cabal. We incur costs to parenting, community service, political participation and our own growth as multidimensional human beings as a result.

Our total household liabilities in this country were $868.9 billion in 1976 (Table 828, SA 1977) and $11,916 billion in 2005 (Table 1153, SA 2007). Our total personal incomes were $1,474.8 billion in 1976 and $10,239.2 billion in 2005 (Table 2.1, NIPA). You will first note that we went from a nation with more total personal income than household liability to one with less. The proportion of household liability to personal income has increased by 97.6%, a doubling of overall household debt.

Grade: F

---

2 One reviewer of these essays mentioned the importance of relating student debt to what they can expect to make as a starter salary. The comparison of debt in current dollars effectively controls for this.

Proportion of Multiple Jobs:

More debt means the need for more work. In terms of multiple jobs per person, 4.5% of the civilian labor force in 1976—mainly men—had multiple jobs (Table 648, SA 1977); 5.3 % overall had multiple jobs in 2005 (Table 595, SA 2007. This is an increase of 17.8% for individuals holding multiple jobs. For the sake of simplicity we will use this figure for our report card, but there are a few caveats worth noting. In 1976 the labor force, including the armed forces, was 61.2% of the total population (Table 626, SA 1977); by 2005 the civilian labor force had increased to 66.0% of the civilian population (Table 573, SA 2007). Much of this increase comes from multiple jobs held by one family. In 1975 36.7% of mothers with children younger than 6 years old worked, already a high number if you consider adult contact important for raising children; in 2005 this proportion increased to 59.8% (Table 584, SA 2007).

Finally, there is evidence that we have reached our limit in expanding the work force. The percentage of mothers from two-parents home with children under six years old increased from 3.9% in 1970 to a high of 7.8% in 1995 (Table 580, SA 2008). In recent times that percentage has declined and appears to be hovering around a maximum limit of around 7.3%. This segment of the labor force, mothers with both husbands and toddlers, should be viewed as a last resort for expanding productivity. Thus 17.8% is likely an underestimate of the increase in work for a family unit, and in any case we are ill-equipped to expand that work load further. This runs contrary to what Federal Reserve Banks and a few puppet libertarians would have us believe.

Grade: F

Ratio of Wage and Salary Supplements to Disbursement:

Employer-controlled pensions and insurance have a variety of negative impacts. They give a competitive edge to large corporations over small businesses in the hiring of employees, but the problems extend insidiously beyond that. Pensions and insurance are speculative compensation being substituted for a current exchange of wages in the labor market. This speculative quality induces employees to stay with an employer beyond the point where their happiness and productivity starts to decrease. People burn out with many types of jobs, such as teaching, but when your pension is tied into how long you stay everyone suffers. The current system works for only one reason: we have been convinced that "greed is good" and "self-interest is selfishness" so burned out laborers hang on for the sake of employer-controlled speculative compensation. Increasing the costs of pensions and insurance increases the dependence of the labor market on the corporations that best supplement those costs. The increased costs coerce continued employment with an employer when otherwise the best free market exchange of wage for labor might be found elsewhere.

Wage and salary disbursements were $899.6 billion in 1976 and $5671.7 billion in 2005 (Table 2.1, NIPA). Employer contributions for employee pension and insurance funds were $105.2 billion in 1976 and $926 billion in 2005 (Table 2.1, NIPA). The ratios of these speculative supplements to actual wages were 11.7% in 1976 and 16.3% in 2005. This is an increase of 39.3%.

Grade: F

Bankruptcies Filed to Number of Households:

For each bankruptcy that is filed there is at least one household whose pursuit of happiness has been thwarted by credit problems and lack of income or prospects for the immediate future. In 1976 there were 518,000 bankruptcies filed and pending (Table 867, SA 1977), which was 0.71% of the 72,867 thousand households. In 2005 there were 3,387,816 bankruptcies filed (Table 754, SA 2007), which was 2.99% of the 113,146 thousand households. The ratio of bankruptcies filed per number of households increased by 321%. More of the civilian population is working than ever before, with households featuring both parents working, sometimes with multiple jobs. Yet since the Powell Cabal began their campaign for *laissez faire* economics in the seventies, based on their misunderstood concept of how competition works in the natural world, we have more than four times the bankruptcies per household.

Grade: F

These are not the type of indicators provided to us by either the Powell Cabal or even the government. They usually provide labor statistics void of proper context. We often are informed how many new jobs are created in a month, without being told how much the population has grown and how many jobs were lost in the same month. We often are informed of unemployment rates, without being aware of how this statistic is determined and what they mean by employment. *Laissez faire* economists are quick to point out the higher unemployment rates in Europe; they fail to mention that 40 hours worth of work in a week between two parents is better able to support a household.

We are mainly a nation employed, but employed at a cost. We leave college in debt and that debt continues while raising our families. We have too much debt to save, which makes us increasingly dependent on employers that can provide "perks" such as pensions and insurance. This dependency allows large corporations to better dictate the conditions of employment. One of these conditions is for the middle class to work more. The other condition, explored in the next system function, is to receive less. Working more for less perpetuates the debt and dependency that works well for large corporations, but prevents labor from adapting to personal or national disturbances that occur in markets.

The untold story of how the economy impacts the middle class does serve a purpose, whether intended or not. We judge an economy in large part on productivity. If families produce more by having more adults working more jobs, they have increased the productivity of our economy. Increased productivity by middle class families means increased capital for corporations, without a troublesome investment in education, research and development or increased wages for an individual in real dollars. For government and the Powell Cabal this productivity increase is what the economy is about, regardless of the impacts on labor to fulfill obligations for citizenship, community, family or personal well-being at the same time we are working more for less.

Even at the macro level there are drawbacks to increasing productivity by increasing how much the family has to work for less income in real dollars. Consider World War II. In a time of emergency many Americans were called to sacrifice, working additional hours in industries that supported our war effort. Americans have less leeway to sacrifice or change their quality or quantity of economic production for the sake of their country. Of course, these days we only call upon soldiers to sacrifice, while dishing out tax cuts that disproportionately benefit wealthy citizens and corporations.

Market Adaptability GPA: 0.0 (F)

Market Stability and Wealth Distribution

Even when adaptability and diversity make a natural system resilient, conditions or disturbances cannot be too extreme for the species that live in that system. A fire in the southwest perpetuates the same mix of vegetation; a fire in the northeast sends a forest community back to the earliest stages of succession. Only the most limited of natural systems survives on the slopes of a volcano with periodic lava flows. The environment must provide some stability for a diverse natural system to thrive.

The Powell Cabal would have us believe that the distribution of wealth should not matter to the middle class. As long as the least well off are gaining in wealth, no worries mate! In our current economy there are two problems with that assumption. First, only the wealthiest have been gaining appreciable wealth in real dollars. Second, a wide disparity of wealth inflates important markets beyond the normal means of the middle class. Great disparity in the distribution of wealth is an inflationary force which destabilizes economic systems. Measures of "too many dollars" distributed to the wealthiest, and of inflated costs of essential items in relation to the middle class share of this distribution, reflect instability in the markets for the middle class.

Shares of income and wealth held by the wealthiest should not steadily

increase over time, neither should the gap widen between the amount of income and overall wealth controlled by the rich. If net dividends rises much faster than economic productivity this has the effect of "too many dollars" pumped into the economy, inflating costs of expensive but essential items that cannot be reduced by economies of scale. Even beyond the economics, increasing shares of costs with decreasing shares of income psychologically compromises the pursuit of happiness over time for the middle class. For this report card market stability indicators were:
- share of income held by the top 5%,
- share of wealth held by the top 1%,
- increase in net dividends to GDP,
- increase in medical care costs to personal income, and
- increase in home sales prices to median family income.

Share of Income Held by the Top 5%:

A variety of reports cite the increasing disparity between CEO compensation and blue collar wages. In *The State of Working America, 2006-2007* the Economic Policy Institute reports that the CEO to average worker pay ratio was 24:1 in 1965 and 262:1 in 2005. An earlier report in *Business Week* (April 1999) cited this ratio as 42:1 in 1980 and 419:1 in 1999. While these ratios provide an insightful glimpse into corporate greed, they are not useful for this report card. One could suggest, albeit unconvincingly, that this concentration of "too many dollars" in the hands of CEOs alone does not imply "too many dollars" being concentrated in the hands of the wealthy in general.

Fortunately, there are more accessible statistics in the Statistical Abstracts relating to the concentration of income. In 1976 the 5% wealthiest families received 15.6% of aggregate income (Table 734, SA 1978). In 2005 the 5% wealthiest families received 22.2% of aggregate income (Table 675, SA 2008). Data compiled by Thomas Piketty and Emmanuel Saez, available at http://elsa.berkeley.edu/~saez/TabFig2004prel.xls, paints a bleaker picture. Without considering income from capital gains, the wealthiest 5% of the population had a 21.03% share of income in 1975 and 31.00% share in 2004 (Table A1), the last year available for this dataset. The data easily obtained from the government indicates an increase in the share of income of 44.9%, the data from academic researchers indicates an increase of 47.4%. In either case the grade is the same.
Grade: F

Share of Wealth Held by the Top 1%:

Wealth consists of more than income, particularly for the wealthy. Assets related to both goods (e.g., real estate) and capital (e.g., stock) contributes to potential wealth that goes beyond yearly income. The share of all wealth held by the richest 1% of the population was 24.1% in 1972 (Table 753, SA 1977). Unfortunately, this important government statistic for illustrating how much wealth was being concentrated at the top was discontinued after 1972. In his book, *Top Heavy* (2002), Edward Wolff calculated the top 1% share of household wealth to be 19.9% in 1976, the low point for being rich according to this study, and 40.1% in 1997, the last year reported.

These figures exceed those obtained by Piketty and Saez. The amount of wealth controlled by the richest 1%, both from income and capital gains, was 8.87% in 1975 and 19.47% in 2004, an increase of 122%. The numbers for the richest 0.5% were 6.07% in 1975 and 15.42% in 2004, an increase of 154%. The corresponding numbers for the richest 0.1% were 2.56% and 9.18%, an increase of 259%. The numbers for the richest 0.01% were 0.85% and 4.25%, an increase of 400%.

Which of the absolute numbers provided by the Statistical Abstracts, Wolff, or Piketty and Saez are more correct does not matter. Nor does it matter if the absolute numbers for concentrated wealth are even less than the low end of Piketty and Saez's report. We are more concerned about trend rather than magnitude, irregardless of how obscene the magnitude may be. Trends based on consistent, standardized methodologies reveal that for the past thirty years the control of all wealth has been increasingly concentrated at the top by astonishing rates.
Grade: F

Increase in Net Dividends to GDP:

The concentration of wealth at the top is but a trickle of wealth being shifted to net dividends in relation to the productivity of this country. Net dividends amounted to $39 billion in 1976 and $577.4 billion in 2005 (Table 1.16, NIPA). This amounts to 2.13% of the $1823.5 billion GDP for 1976 and 4.65% of the $12429.1 billion GDP for 2005 (Table 1.1.5, NIPA). This is an increase of 218% for the amount of capital diverted from productive labor and concentrated for investors.
Grade: F

Increase in Medical Care Costs to Personal Income:

The Powell Cabal asserts that the inflation of the GDP in relation to MFI should not matter to us. In their view the middle class should be content if our incomes have been increasing relative to time and ignore the relationships to other factors. But some factors are hard to ignore, like the increase in medical costs. Medical care costs totaled $109.1 billion in 1976 and $1491.3 billion in 2005 (Table 2.4.5, NIPA). Personal income increased from $1474.8 billion in 1976 to $10301.1 in 2005 (Table 1.7.5, NIPA). Medical care costs as a proportion of personal income went from 7.40% in 1976 to 14.48% in 2005, a relative increase of 95.7%.

Perhaps the Powell Cabal's response to this is that the middle class should just stay healthy.

Grade: F

Increase in Home Sale Prices to Median Family Income:

Let us be fair to the Powell Cabal, though at this point it may not be clear why we should. As essential as medical care may be to the happiness of the middle class, some of the inflationary impacts are due to cutting edge technologies that impact only a few people. In contrast, owning your home might be considered the cornerstone of happiness for every middle class family. The inflationary impacts of wealth disparity on housing costs goes to the very heart of the matter.

We have been faithful to the use of the Statistical Abstracts and the National Income and Products Account for our analysis whenever possible. For the most part these are unbiased datasets not serving a political agenda, but that is not entirely true. What they choose to represent housing costs changed in 1983, with the effect of the new definition lowering average costs. Also, it is not easy to tease out per family costs from NIPA, while the SA does not go back far enough for this data. In contrast, a study by the Pew Research Center contrasted home sales price to median household income based on the same definitions between 1970 and 2005 (pewsocialtrends.org/pubs/?chartid=546). Based on 2008 dollars, median income rose from $41,748 to $50,811. Home sales rose from $109,940 to $233,915. According to this study housing costs rose 419% faster than median household income.

Grade: F

The percentage of people in poverty could have been used as a single indicator in place of the five indicators used for this report card, since poverty is a result of both wealth disparity and the inability to acquire necessary goods. After the Great Depression the amount of people in poverty steadily decreased until the low point in 1973, the same year The Heritage Foundation set up shop. The Statistical Abstracts provides percentages of people in poverty based on a weighted average poverty level that ultimately depends on the costs of a "basket of goods" that the average consumer purchases. In 1973, 11.1% of the population was below the government defined poverty level (Table 745, SA 1977), and 15.8% were below the 125% poverty level (Table 746, SA 1997). In 2004, these indicators were 12.6% and 16.8%, respectively (Table 689, SA 2008).

Why should we wade through five indicators when one easy to understand indicator gives a similar result? All the other indicators provided in this report card, while corresponding to only two points in time, reveal a steady trend when the data for all intervening years are considered. Some of this trend data is available on my web site, The Middle Class Forum (www.middleclassforum.org). For example, the share of wealth held by the richest 1% decreases steadily to around the year 1976 in the data gathered by Wolff. After 1976 the share of wealth increases steadily to the present. This can be correlated with other large scale events that have occurred steadily during that time, say, the constant input of dollars from corporations to manipulate public perception of the economy. The poverty level goes through greater fluctuations than the other indicators used for this report card, meaning that short term events could be the primary cause for any of these fluctuations instead of the misinformation network that was set up in the seventies.

There is another reason not to use an indicator based on the government defined poverty level. While easy to understand as an indicator, poverty level is not easy to derive and contributes to "black box" economics. Also, the poverty level indicator was changed one year after the low point was reached. The current indicator being used underestimates poverty in comparison with the old indicator. There have been other changes in other years as well, including 2005. The indicators used for this report card, including all the ones for market stability, involve easily obtainable data, consistent methodologies over time and simple calculations. If any of these indicators do not look right to you, please, look up the data and do your own simple analysis. The middle class needs to get out of the habit of accepting the claims and rationalizations of economic experts without any cross-examination or investigation. The concluding essay on economics will discuss "black box" economics and poverty levels further.

Market Stability GPA: 0.0 (F)

Indicator	% Change	Grade	GP	GPA
High school graduation rates	-5.3	D	1.0	
Advanced degrees earned	+24.5	A	4.0	
Public school revenues	-1.0	C	2.0	
Funding of research & development	+20.4	A	4.0	
Relative adult literacy rates	> -15.0	F	0.0	
Market Specialization				2.2
Proprietor vs. private enterprise income	-18.3	F	0.0	
Corporate profits vs. employee compensation	-23.4	F	0.0	
Corporate taxes vs. net dividends	-190.9	F	0.0	
"Welfare taxes" to GDP	-38.8	F	0.0	
Federal subsidies	-76.0	F	0.0	
Market Diversity				0.0
Student debt	>> -15	F	0.0	
Proportion of multiple jobs	> -17.8	F	0.0	
Household liability to personal income	-97.6	F	0.0	
Ratio of wage and salary supplements to disbursements	-39.3	F	0.0	
Bankruptcies filed to number of households	-321	F	0.0	
Market Adaptability				0.0
Share of income held by the top 5%	-44.9	F	0.0	
Share of income held by the top 1%	-122	F	0.0	
Increase in net dividends to GDP	-218	F	0.0	
Increase in medical care costs to personal income	-95.7	F	0.0	
Increase in home sale prices to med. family income	-419	F	0.0	
Market Stability				0.0
Overall Economic System Grade				0.55

ECONOMIC SYSTEM REPORT CARD

GP = Grade Point (4.0 is highest possible score), GPA = Grade Point Average

% Change = relative change since the seventies

+ = positive change for middle class, - = negative change

>15%=A; 5 to 15%=B; -5 to 5% = C; -5 to -15% = D, <-15% = F

Continuity and Government

Carbon based life forms do not switch to become silicon based life forms. The genetic code does not switch from nucleic acids to right-handed amino acids. The energy molecule of cells does not switch from ATP to ethanol. Every natural system includes some means of continuity for the same basic "rules of the game" over time. Natural systems achieve continuity through the reproduction of a genetic code, a function that also assists with enhancing diversity and adaptability.

Governments are necessary for all economic systems, as they function to continue the existing economic system over time. In our economic system government is crucial for enhancing long distance commerce, capital markets that serve capital over production, and the legitimacy and enforcement of contracts benefiting those with greater bargaining strength. All of these market interventions by government grant advantages to business corporations over proprietorships, over laborers and over the middle class.

There is a breed of economists known as anarcho-capitalists that recommend the abolishment of government from economic systems, allowing business corporations and the free market to maximize wealth and liberty for all. This philosophy is beyond absurd. Business corporations and free markets cannot coexist in a literal sense, as has been covered in some depth. On the other hand, capitalism cannot exist without governments. At least, there is no record in the entire history of civilization of capital markets being able to exist without nation states. They, in fact, evolved together. Restricting governments from economic systems means restricting capitalism, hardly what the puppet libertarians from the Powell Cabal really envision. Finally, business corporations already have influenced governments to structure economic systems to their advantage; abolishing government as the "middle man" in the process of coddling business corporations will not mitigate the long term trends harming proprietors, laborers and the middle class.

One of the figureheads for anarcho-capitalism is David Friedman, son of Milton. Milton was not quite that radical, perhaps this is a case of the son trying to outdo the father. Both father and son demonstrate an ability to let their ideologies distort their perceptions of reality.[3] Yet there also is an insidious purpose to the mere discussion of an economic philosophy by respected economic scholars that otherwise should be treated with scorn and laughter by any thinking person. By giving anarcho-capitalism even an ounce of scholarly credibility the *laissez faire* alternative appears all the more moderate and legitimate as a pursuit of free markets.

In this country we have a big government by the necessities of geography and federalism, quite independent of whatever economic system might continue functioning. Our government is big and will decide what economic system continues over time; those are nonnegotiable realities. The decision left to a democracy is who our big government serves in their decisions of intervention or nonintervention. Government could serve the interests of the military, aristocrats, large corporations or the middle class.

We have the strongest military in the world, yet the potential for them to take over the country is close to nil. They are a blessing not because of their strength but because of their restraint. Our intelligence agencies are more likely to pose a threat to who our government serves than our well-trained armed forces.

---

3 With some regret I continue to make reference to Milton Friedman. After the bulk of these economic essays had been written, Milton Friedman died at the age of 94. He was a great intellect and I do not doubt that his heart, in contrast to his subjective *laissez faire* ideology, was in the right place.

We also have avoided a true aristocracy commanding our government. Some government officials are corrupt, and some aristocrats can cheat the IRS all they want without ever having to fear an audit, but their shenanigans are done in the shadows precisely because we view them as cancers to the ideal of meritocracy.

That leaves corporations and the middle class as the two main interests competing for the type of economic system our unavoidably big government will continue. Our report card indicates a failing grade for the economy, but that is only from the point of view of the middle class, proprietorships and a free market. From the point of view of business corporations, puppet libertarians, *laissez faire* economists and the Powell Cabal our economy has functioned increasingly well since the seventies.

Homeostasis and the Free Flow of Information

Whether a current economic system is desirable or not depends on the perspective. This report card does not evaluate the current state of our economy from a neutral perspective; that would not be possible. Perspective always matters and perspective always exists, regardless of hypocritical claims to the contrary by Nobel Laureate economists. The appropriate system functions vary according to these different perspectives. While a diversity of businesses benefits the middle class citizen seeking the satisfaction of essential but expensive needs, a diversity of investment strategies benefits the shareholders of corporations seeking to accumulate wealth. While the middle class seeks adaptable strategies for the self-interest of labor, corporations seek adaptable strategies for concentrating the supply of capital.

We have impressive numbers in terms of GDP and other wealth indicators, and those numbers reflect an economy where lots of people have lots of stuff. *Laissez faire* economists would give our economy high grades[4] from their perspective that maximizing wealth is all good, and the negative consequences that result from concentrating wealth in order to maximize wealth stem more from the frailties of individuals and government than the bottom line of corporations. Large corporations, small businesses who want to become like large corporations, people of great wealth, people who covet substantial wealth and anyone who has fallen under the spell "greed is good" share this perspective.

The dismal grades in this report card stem from evaluating the change in the economy from a middle class perspective for the pursuit of happiness, which relies more on merit than greed. The report card reveals that though we have a wealthy economy where lots of people have lots of stuff this has been accomplished through lots of debt, lots of labor, lots of instability and lots of dependency on corporations. We also have a wealthy economy with lots of poverty and an increasing proportion

---

4 Or at least *laissez faire* economists would have award high grades for the years corresponding to this report card. Not even these economists are giving our economy high marks for 2008.

of people who have neither lots of stuff nor even essential stuff.

How the perception versus the reality for middle class economics developed over the past thirty years relates to the system function known as homeostasis. Homeostasis is the mechanism natural systems use to stay in balance. An example of how homeostasis works is the thermostat in your home. You set your thermostat to 68 degrees Fahrenheit and your house will fluctuate slightly around that temperature. When the house is too cold the thermostat turns the furnace on and the house is heated. When the temperature gets too high this provides negative feedback to the thermostat to turn the furnace off and the house is cooled.

A natural example of this with great relevance these days is the equilibrium of gases in the atmosphere. Plants take in carbon dioxide and produce oxygen. An increase in carbon dioxide in the atmosphere induces the system to spur more plant growth, unless humans are cutting down large tracts of forest at the same time the carbon dioxide is increasing. The conversion to oxygen by plants mitigates the concentrations of carbon dioxide. This mechanism helps to keep the concentration of gases mildly fluctuating around a steady state. In essence, natural systems monitor information (too much prey, too many predators, etc.) just like the thermostat in your home.

Wages and prices in a free market driven by merit will stay in a mildly fluctuating equilibrium if a free and unbiased flow of information about true costs and benefits can serve a homeostatic function. Large corporations naturally will attempt to bias the flow of information to increase their profits at the expense of laborers and consumers. Negative feedback loops, in the form of laws and public opinion, serve to counteract this bias. The Powell Memorandum of 1971 set in motion a campaign to obliterate these negative feedback loops. The Powell Cabal turned the thermostat on high for greed and then jammed the sensors for merit and wealth distribution.

Granted, we are still a democracy and the sensors still work up to a certain degree. We have been analyzing changes over thirty years of time. If any of those changes had happened over one year, the homeostatic mechanism of public opinion would kick in and corrective policies and laws would follow. Spreading the changes out gradually numbs the senses to those changes, like the ability of the sense of smell to habituate to an obnoxious odor. Unless you live on the same street in the same type of neighborhood for over fifty years the context for comparison dissipates and you are vulnerable to accept whatever the corporate owned media tells you about our economy.

Hans the small business owner, the middle class citizen, is kept too confused to know the thermostat needs to be fixed. There have been times when corporate media reported that the increase in GDP was slowing down and another on the same day that the stock market was continuing in a cycle of rapid growth. Just the juxtaposition of that news would confuse Hans but the conundrum goes further. Part of the slowdown for the GDP was due to a falling housing market, a pity for developers and people who treat homes as investments, not such bad news for Hans and his family chasing the American Dream of owning a home for the first time. The stock market was bolstered by indicators that interest rates would be curbed, but lower prime interest rates could lead to the borrowing of "too many dollars" that inflate housing costs. Which trend really affects Hans more and how?

Hans continues to hear about the stock market and the GDP day after day after day, relying on only the word of corporate owned media of what the indicators mean for his life. What he seldom hears about are indicators such as the ones in this report card. Hans is no longer capable of serving a homeostatic function for the economy; neither, for that matter, is a government enslaved to the public opinions manipulated by corporate media. The Powell Cabal has created this predicament through the use of information that is neither valid nor reliable. We need a guide for identifying the tricks that the Powell Cabal plays in order to demolish our homeostatic function. The concluding essay on economics turns to this need next.

ESSAY 8 – THE POWELL CABAL PRIMER

Overview

- The Powell Cabal manipulates concern over small businesses to gain competitive advantages for large corporations.
- The unacknowledged fourth important question of economics is "Why?"
- The Powell Cabal network has grown rapidly since the Powell Memorandum.
- The Powell Cabal uses "black box" economics to obscure invalid evidence.
- The Powell Cabal uses "black is white" economics to distort unreliable evidence.
- The Powell Cabal discredits economics based on merit.
- The Powell Cabal neither can be blamed nor relied on for fixing our economic system.
- Corporations "bargaining from a position of strength" must be mitigated for the labor market.
- Corporations concentrating "too many dollars chasing too few goods" must be mitigated for the capital market.
- "There is no free lunch" must be understood for the tradeoffs between free markets and corporate capitalism.

A Concern for Small Businesses

Corporate hypocrisy and wealth disparity have not interfered with the Powell Cabal's ability to manipulate public perception. Over the course of thirty years they have honed their message. Prior to the 2006 elections I received a flyer in the mail supporting an incumbent congresswoman. On behalf of small businesses, the organization sending the flyer wanted readers to know where the congresswoman stood regarding tort reform issues. The flyer began like this:

> "One Piece of Paper... 'You are Hereby Summoned'...can RUIN a Lifetime of Work. Due to out-of-control lawsuits, small business owners in Connecticut go to work each morning wondering if this is the day a greedy trial lawyer makes them a target."

This pithy opening contains all the elements corporations use to create demand. "RUIN" is in bold, red, capital letters to let the middle class know we need to be apprehensive about the lurking dangers. "A Lifetime of Work" appeals to our vanities; no one should be interfering with our livelihoods. "Out of control lawsuits" and "greedy trial lawyer" let us know how cynical we need to be about the rule of law. We are primed to take matters into our own hands on behalf of all those beleaguered small business owners trembling over the threat of lawsuits "each morning." The horror! How do we as good citizens act to eliminate this abomination that plagues the small business owner every morning of every day? The flyer informs us that the only action needed from us to remedy such a dire situation is to simply vote for the congresswoman.

The flyer provides further reasons for us hapless victims to have no faith in the rule of law: "By filing frivolous lawsuits, predatory lawyers are cashing in on enormous settlements." Note that predatory lawyers, not middle class plaintiffs, cash in on these "enormous settlements." The flyer informs us of the necessary solution: the federal government passing "real" legal reform. We need government intrusion to save free markets from the courts attempting to remedy problems that interfere with free markets! The distributors of this flyer should not be mistaken for advocates of liberty, though they no doubt are puppet libertarians.

We are informed of the specific issues the congresswoman champions on our behalf. One is to ban "ridiculous lawsuits such as blaming restaurants for obesity." Yes, sir, I bet the first priority for plaintiffs from my town would be to blame the local pizza place for their obesity, while giving Pizza Hut a free pass. Maybe we are to assume that even if plaintiffs wanted to sue a large corporation the greedy lawyers would steer them towards a frivolous lawsuit against the local restaurant instead.

Another solution would be forcing the plaintiffs of frivolous lawsuits to pay their "fair share" of legal fees. Funny, when frivolous lawsuits lead to "enormous settlements" the lawyer wins; when these lawsuits get thrown out of court the plaintiff needs to bear the brunt of losing. Let us overlook the peculiar logic; a bigger problem lies with determining a "fair share." The expense of counsel for small businesses is miniscule compared to large corporations. What middle class consumer wants to risk paying the "fair share" of corporate counsel? In essence, this is a deterrent to lawsuits that grows with the corporate size of the defendant.

The objective behind a third issue listed on the flyer does indeed benefit small businesses: capping punitive damages to small businesses. The organization's web site reveals their support for the Small Business Liability Reform Act, targeted for businesses with fewer than 25 employees. The problem lies not with the objective supported by this organization, but the strategy to be used.

The Small Business Liability Reform Act was a federal law to overrule state laws regarding punitive damages. The federal government was not to intervene in all states, mind you, only the forty-three states that allowed punitive damages exceeding the level recommended in the Act. The seven states with greater restrictions on punitive damage could continue to function without the feds intervening. This is a surprising strategy to employ on the behalf of small businesses.

Limitations in size and influence necessitate that small businesses pool their resources in organizations such as the National Federation of Independent Businesses to lobby at the federal level, and even then they will not receive any pork at the expense of corporations such as Halliburton. Seeking intervention from the federal government to aid the producers in an economy, as a general strategy, gives a competitive advantage to large corporations over small businesses. Small businesses are better situated to directly lobby lawmakers in state legislatures on their own behalf. The fact that seven states have greater restrictions on punitive damages suggests that small businesses can and do indeed effect change in state legislatures, but the problem has not been as urgent an issue to them nationwide as the flyer suggests. Phew! We can be comforted that most small business owners do not really "go to work each morning wondering if this is the day a greedy trial lawyer makes them a target."

The other peculiarity behind this organization's strategy for capping punitive damages, though we should not be surprised by now, is the abhorrence this demonstrates for the free market. Economics 101 tells us that caps are one of the most disruptive forms of interfering with market equilibriums, whether the caps apply to price controls, wage controls or negative costs. Allowing fifty states to independently work out what this cap should be, if there should be any, restores some free market credibility to limiting unintended costs. The organization that distributed the flyer supports federal intervention with the large majority of states that would allow greater punitive damages to be assessed and a more *laissez faire* approach in those very few cases where the states would restrict damages further. This is the kind of hypocrisy that makes the Powell Cabal of corporate sponsored think tanks, corporate endowed chairs of economic departments, corporate hired public relations firms, corporate employed lobbyists and corporate owned media proud.

In fact, the distributor of the flyer should make the Powell Cabal very proud. They are the U. S. Chamber of Commerce, original recipient of the Powell Memorandum in 1971.

The "Why?" of Economics

Traditionally, the three fundamental questions of economics, as dictated to us by economic scholars, have been: "How?", "How much?", and "For whom?" At a macro scale the United States has answered the question "How?" by allowing capital to serve capital instead of production. We have answered the question "How much?" by maximizing wealth. We have answered the question "For whom" by increasing the disparity of wealth. There is a fourth fundamental question of economics that determines the answer to the other three: "Why?" Large corporations have persuaded us that the motives for producing goods and services are that "greed is good" and "self-interest is selfishness." As a result we as humans have behaved more like the ecological r-species that gobble up resources heedless of the consequences, rather than the k-species that pace themselves with motives other than to purely maximize consumption. When "greed is good" is our mantra we exhibit the voraciousness of vermin more than the wisdom of wolves. Maybe the reason *laissez faire* economists and textbooks leave out "Why?" as one of the fundamental questions of economics is they don't want the middle class thinking too much about such questions and forming their own judgments.

Rather than equating their "self-interest with selfishness" (a subjective judgment if ever there was one) the middle class would benefit more from a different motive for economics: the exchange and reward of merit in resource distribution. Quite simply, not everyone can have a maximized amount of goods and services. If happiness were to depend on that, then Hans is out of luck. On the other hand, if happiness depended on acquiring essential goods and services relatively debt free, then wealth needs to be distributed more in accordance with the merits of labor than investments that reward only greed. At the least this prevents inflating markets from huge amounts of welfare dollars concentrated in the hands of the wealthy. In a capitalist system wealth will follow the capital. Diffuse the supply of capital to proprietorships and wealth will be more attuned to merit.

Enabling proprietorships to drive the economy and reduce the amount of debt conflicts with the interests of large corporations, the one sector of the economy that greed and *laissez faire* economics serves well. That the U. S. Chamber of Commerce should cultivate apprehension, vanity and cynicism in middle class citizens should come as no surprise, considering what is at stake for the Powell Cabal. More disturbing is their shameless cultivation of proprietorships as advocates for competitive advantages to be granted to business corporations.

Corporations have an upside but let us make no mistake: the components and function of our current economic system enable business corporations to exploit the middle class and proprietorships. For the middle class and proprietorships to truly take charge of the situation we need to focus on the "Why?" of economics, rather than react to urgent messages intended to get our votes. This calls for a guide for knowing the enemy better, who they are and the basic strategies they employ to convince us that greed should drive economics instead of merit.

The Powell Cabal Network

Much of the information used here about the Powell Cabal comes from www. endgame.org, compiled by George Draffan, unless otherwise stated. Let us start with the U. S. Chamber of Commerce (USCC). This business association was created in 1912, but did not become very active until the seventies (hmm, what occurred in 1971 that might have spurred such activity?). Throughout that decade of the seventies the USCC membership and budget grew exponentially; by 1980 they had 45 full time lobbyists. From the years 1998-2004 the USCC spent more on lobbying than any other organization, over 204 million dollars, more than double the next highest amount.[1] The USCC has a Council for Small Businesses, and boasts that small businesses form the great majority of their membership. Those facts did not comfort the American Small Business League when the USCC lobbied to have Fortune 1000 corporations considered as small businesses in the granting of federal contracts.[2]

The original mission of the USCC was to advocate uniform business and trade policies, an issue of some concern for all businesses, but of greatest concern for corporations. Since the seventies they have advocated reducing taxes in a manner that shifts the burden from capital gains to wages, giving corporations a competitive advantage over proprietorships. The USCC promotes welfare reform, though they have nothing to say about the welfare the corporate world enjoys through large inheritances and concentrated capital gains, money that could be diffused to ultimately benefit proprietorships. We already know their position on tort reform, and the craven tactics they will use to push their agenda. The USCC engages many small business owners like Hans in their appeals on one hand, but advocates economic policies tipping the scales for large corporations on the other.

We already have met the Heritage Foundation and their Index of Economic Freedom, which fails to account for how large corporations make markets less free. Here are some other fun facts you should know. The Heritage Foundation was founded in 1973 by Richard Scaife, who enjoys a vast welfare entitlement—oops, I mean inheritance—from Mellon oil and banking fortunes. In 1999 alone pundits from the Heritage Foundation had 125 television appearances, 180 newspaper articles and over 200 radio spots. They created the Center for Media and Public Policy to further facilitate the interface between corporate funded think tanks and corporate owned media. One Heritage trustee was a former chairman of the USCC.

The Cato Institute was founded in 1977 by billionaires from corporate oil and corporate finance. The Institute is perhaps the most "principled" of the Powell Cabal in their commitment to libertarian ideals. Much is made of the Cato Institute's criticisms of subsidies to large corporations, particularly agribusinesses such as Archer Daniels Midland, as evidence of their pure libertarian intent.

1 This data is available from opensecrets.org, the web site for The Center for Responsive Politics.
2 As reported here: americansmallbusinessleague.blogspot.com/search?q=US+Chamber+of+Commerce.

Strange, then, that a think tank so "committed" to libertarian ideals has little to say about corporate free market abuse such as obstructing the free flow of information, negative externalities and market domination. Oh, one other thing, they occasionally defend the government commanded advantages provided to oil companies.

The Hudson Institute was founded in 1961 but picked up steam in the seventies. The Hudson Institute is very, very concerned about the harm that small organic farming can do to consumers. The Institute is funded by chemical and biotechnical corporations such as Ciba-Greigy, ConAgra, DowElanco, DuPont, Sandoz and, of course, Monsanto. How wonderful that these corporate citizens have got our backs covered against sinister organic farmers seeking to put labels on their products.

The Hoover Institution on War, Revolution and Peace deserves some recognition, despite their deceptive title and the fact that they were founded way back in 1919. They provide a comprehensive package for manipulating public perception with an academic pedigree. Stanford University provides significant funding along with some benefits of their tax-exempt status and campus facilities. A Media Fellows Program provides residency for people dedicated to influencing newspapers, magazines, and television. They provide their own media, called "Uncommon Knowledge," through a local PBS station. The Hoover Institution also sponsored the Boskin Commission, which will be discussed soon. Their board includes billionaires from oil, agribusiness and industrial military corporations.

We have covered merely a sample of some prominent think tanks, which have gone up in numbers from under one hundred before 1970 to over fifteen hundred by 2006.[3] Powell's charge that an academic pedigree was necessary to persuade the most reasoned segments of society spurred a significant part of this growth. These think tanks rely on direct corporate funding only in small part. More funds are provided by wealthy individuals and corporate sponsored foundations, a more tax friendly/evasive way of funding the message.

Some wealthy families do yeoman's work in funding the mission of the Powell Cabal. The Koch family owns an oil corporation, sponsors several foundations and founded think tanks (including the Cato Institute). The Scaife family formed the same type of oil-based triumvirate with The Heritage Foundation. Integrating oil industry interests, funding and advocacy works well when they lobby Congress to command a variety of economic advantages for the oil industry at the same time their profits are escalating.

Another important corporate vessel was the John M. Olin Foundation. The Foundation terminated in 2005 based on the wishes of the founder, whose family was involved in chemicals and munitions. This provides additional insight into the character of the Powell Cabal. John M. Olin was too vain to think any other beliefs

---

3   From a presentation by James McGann on "The Development of Think Tanks and Their Role as Catalysts for Ideas and Actions in the U. S. Political System."

but his were worthy and too apprehensive to trust anyone else to promote them. He stipulated that when his handpicked trustees died out, so would the fund. You can have the best academic pedigree money can buy, but without allowance for evolving wisdom that pedigree will go the way of the Dodo bird. Presumably the same myopic vision afflicts the Professorship in Humanities that Olin endowed, who also became president of the Hudson Institute.

The Powell Cabal has made significant inroads with providing fellowships and other funding, but they also boast corporate owned media with specifically intended corporate biases, such as Rupert Murdoch's 24 hour *Fox News* channel. Public relation firms have been a key ingredient as well, particularly for corporations that need such assistance in the following areas: corporate and issues advertising; corporate communications; corporate social responsibility/communications; crisis communications; government relations; issues management; media relations; or social education/government education. These are a few of the areas of practice expertise listed in the Council of Public Relation Firms' database.[4]

One function of public relation firms has been to provide a means of getting around some lobbying restrictions. But we need not feel bad about the lobbying industry over these "restrictions." In the space of ten years, from 1998 to 2007, the amount of lobbying investment essentially doubled from 1.44 billion dollars to 2.82 billion.[5] The NIPA tables reveal that the Gross Domestic Product only increased by two-thirds over this same time span. In case you are interested—and why shouldn't you be—the industry sectors that feel the greatest need to influence our legislators are financial institutions and pharmaceuticals/health products. The one organization that spends the most on lobbying is—you guessed it—the U. S. Chamber of Commerce, with more than twice that of the financial institutions Freddie Mac and Fannie Mae combined.

At the international level the Powell Cabal has the World Bank, International Monetary Fund (IMF) and World Trade Organization (WTO) going for them. In theory, the World Bank stimulates investment in developing countries; the IMF lends money to developing countries to foster trade; and the WTO establishes international free trade rules. All of that sounds admirable in terms of actual goals; in terms of strategies there are conditions attached to investment, lending and free trade that betray what the ultimate goal is: facilitate the endeavors of multinational corporations in developing countries. The boards for these organizations read like a Who's Who from the corporate world; they represent multinational corporations more than developing countries.

Black Box Economics

This conglomerate of associations, think tanks, foundations, public relation firms, endowed academic positions and media use a few tried and true methods

4 This database can be searched at www.prfirms.org/index.cfm?fuseaction=PageviewPage&pageId=477.
5 Data on lobbyists is available at http://www.opensecrets.org/lobby/index.php.

of persuasion. Cynicism, vanity and apprehension works well for establishing the desired emotional state among the middle class, but occasionally the Powell Cabal must make at least a nominal attempt to support their claims with empirical evidence. "Black box" economics is one valuable means for convincing Hans that what's good for corporations is good for him. The black box symbolizes an obtuse method of generating results. You put a bunch of empirical data into a "black box" where mysterious things occur and out come the statistics and indicators you want to be generated.

The black box is a useful tool for obscuring invalid evidence. Hans accepts conclusions drawn from "objective" statistics and indicators because he does not have the foggiest idea how they were derived. Thus fifty economic indicators can be manipulated as an Index of Economic Freedom without addressing private coercion. A plethora of assumptions, surveys and statistics can be manipulated to convince us how much leisure we have as we send our kids off to day care.

For the government's weighted average poverty threshold the empirical data are the "basket of goods" chosen by the Bureau of Labor Statistics that represents the minimum a household needs to get by. The black box changes this basket of goods into the Consumer Price Index (CPI), which in turn transforms into a weighted average poverty level for different size households. The biggest mystery is the logic behind the basket of goods.

In 1976 the government's defined poverty threshold was $5,815 for a family of four (Table 732, SA 1977).[6] In 2005 the threshold was $19,971 (Table 688, SA 2008), increasing by a factor of 3.43 over those thirty years. From the NIPA table 1.7.5 we learn during that same time span the GDP went from $1825.3 billion to $12433.9 billion, inflating by a factor of 6.81. Personal income went from $1474.8 billion to $10301.1 billion, inflating by a factor of 6.98. These figures must be adjusted by impact of population increases alone. We had 218,035,000 people in 1976 and 296,940,000 in 2005 (Table 2, SA 2008), inflating by a factor of only 1.36. So the poverty level and underlying CPI are not keeping track with either our productivity or the resulting income. Ah, but maybe while we all are getting richer our "basket of goods" is getting relatively cheaper.

From the NIPA table 2.4.5 we see that personal consumption expenditures have gone from $1151.9 billion in 1976 to $8707.8 billion in 2005, inflating by a factor of 7.55. Housing costs have gone from $162.2 billion to $1298.7 billion, inflating by a factor of 8.01. Higher education costs have gone from $11.6 billion to $126.4 billion, inflating by a factor of 10.90. Health costs have gone from $124.7 billion to $1782.1 billion, inflating by a factor of 14.29. The costs of each of these essential items have gone up at least twice as fast as the poverty threshold, indeed, even faster than the GDP or our income. Either the "basket of goods" used for the CPI must not include a good home, good health and/or a good education,

---

6 As detailed in the previous essay, SA refers to the Statistical Abstracts easily accessible over the Internet. Numbers crunched here, as in Essay 7, are from these tables.

or the Bureau of Labor Statistics employ extraordinary bargain shoppers on their staff for these costly but essential items.

Changes in the methodology determining the CPI and poverty thresholds contribute to this problem. In 1973 the government went to a new method of calculating poverty that would have underestimated the values from previous years. In 1983 the government decided to substitute rental costs for housing ownership costs in the "basket of goods." Houses are treated as investments rather than castles these days; the adjustment was made to control for the investment aspect of home ownership. But rental costs are not as prone to be inflated by "too many dollars" concentrated in the hands of the wealthy, nor do they represent the importance of owning a home to the American Dream. The "basket of goods" does not include property taxes or house insurance either. The effect of this substitution would be—you guessed it—to underestimate the true poverty threshold.

Being the fair-minded folk that they are, various elements of the Powell Cabal have expressed dissatisfaction with the Consumer Price Index (CPI) and the weighted average poverty threshold, though not exactly for the same reasons expressed here. The Heritage Foundation complains that the poverty level does not consider government assistance programs, and thus we are overestimating the real poverty threshold. Ah, there you have it. The reason that the poverty threshold has lagged behind GDP and essential consumer costs must be that government welfare has increased over those thirty years to make up the difference! Except...

The amount of government assistance has grown even slower than the poverty threshold. The Middle Class Forum (www.middleclassforum.org) provides data for this. Meanwhile, government subsidies to corporations have grown faster. Not factoring in the taxpayer's contribution to subsidized goods underestimates real consumer costs, a detail that escapes The Heritage Foundation. The Heritage Foundation experts—whether explaining the Index of Economic Freedom, poverty thresholds or other "black box" economics—always seem to miss something important from the perspective of the middle class.

The most notable critic of the CPI from the Powell Cabal is the Hoover Institution or, more specifically, the Boskin Commission put together by the Institution. Headed by Michael Boskin, the charge of the commission was to explore why the CPI overestimates inflation. Yes, you read that right. Rather than illuminate why the CPI fails to keep pace with housing, medical or tuition costs they were charged in 1995 to explain why the CPI might be overestimating inflation. There are several reasons for giving such a charge to a commission. Social security payments are indexed to the CPI; an inflated CPI means doling out too much money to the middle class. An inflated CPI also means overstating the numbers of former middle class citizens falling below the poverty threshold. The Powell Cabal naturally wants to prevent us middle class citizens from pulling a fast one with our social security checks and claims of increasing debt or poverty.

Let us examine one of the criticisms the scholarly institute connected with Stanford University levied against the CPI, something referred to in obedient economic texts as substitution bias. The CPI fails to account for consumers choosing less of an item that increases in cost. If the mortgage or rent goes up everywhere Hans should choose less or different housing; if medical care costs go up everywhere he should choose less or different health care; if tuition goes up everywhere he should choose less education. As the cartoon characters in the Guinness commercials would say: "Brilliant!" As a long-distance backpacker I am better equipped than most to choose less housing by setting up my tent somewhere, but most middle class folk would object to that option. Incidentally, housing costs are by far the greatest portion of a middle class consumer's budget, though apparently too negligible an amount to counter those other nasty CPI biases.

The Powell Cabal gets away with this utter nonsense of invalid information because of black box economics. The esteemed scholars on the Boskin Commission do not expect the middle class to understand how the CPI is derived, or to understand what biases exist besides the ones they spoon feed the public. Even if we did understand, how many of us have the perspective to know how things have changed. If you are too young you cannot draw from experience. The typical older middle class family has moved several times; they can lose perspective and believe that inflated costs result only from their upward mobility in moving to a new area. Here on Emerson Street, a middle class neighborhood in a town that has remained rural, the evidence that the costs of essential items have inflated tremendously over the past thirty years, independent of upward mobility, becomes inescapable. This inflation has occurred because "too many dollars" are being concentrated in the hands of the wealthy. No black box can change that reality.

Black is White Economics

"Black box" economics works best with statistics, indicators and numerical data that appear to be objective, making the derivation of that "objective" data hard for the average person to comprehend. When working with less objective concepts the Powell Cabal may resort to "black is white" economics as well. We have covered a few of the hypocrisies of the Powell Cabal, each of them an example of "black is white" economics. For example, inflating dollars is not inflating dollars when the abundance is being concentrated in the hands of the wealthy. Welfare entitlements are not welfare entitlements when the wealthy receive capital without having to provide labor. The Washington Consensus of lending money to desperate developing countries with strong corporate strings attached promotes "free" trade. You get the idea.

Black is white economics is based on unreliable evidence that would not be interpreted the same way by empirical standards. Statistics and indicators generally do not fall victim to this tactic because people, particularly scientists, are hard to convince that two plus two can equal either four or five. There are exceptions, though. These exceptions become both entertaining and alarming when they occur in the number crunching discipline of economics.

As we previously discussed in Essay 6, the title of Benjamin Friedman's *The Moral Consequences of Economic Growth* (2005) shouts out Friedman's thesis, that economic growth creates moral benefits. The essay established that economic growth was neither necessary nor sufficient to create moral benefits, and that any relationship between the two was either weak or spurious. That reality did not deter B. Friedman from promoting his thesis, the crux of which occurs in a graph on page 316 relating economic growth to rights and liberties.

Leading up to that graph, B. Friedman provides another one on page 313 to show the relationship of per capita income with rights and liberties. On the graph are close to two hundred points, each one representing where a country stands in terms of the per capita income along the x axis and the rights and liberties along the y axis. The indicator for political rights and civil liberties created by the Freedom House organization is a type of "black box" which may lack validity but that is not the most intriguing part of the graph. Let us assume that widely scattered points give a "black" appearance to the graph and indicates that no real relationship exists between per capita income and rights and liberties. When the distribution of points on the graph neatly fall along a sloped line that gives a "white" appearance instead, meaning that a relationship exists where changes to one variable correlates with changes in the other. By these definitions the graph on page 313 has a gray appearance. Points are scattered all over the place, but there is one cluster that indicates a relationship between high income and rights and liberties.

B. Friedman acknowledges the "grayness" of the first graph, but the relationship between economic wealth and rights and liberties is not his main point. A country needs sustained growth, not absolute wealth, to reap moral benefits. He presents the graph on page 316 to show the relationship of average annual growths in per capita income with rights and liberties, from 1978-2003. He claims that this new graph helps to establish that wealth is the causal variable in the previous relationship, and that a distinct relationship exists between growths in per capita income and rights and liberties. Metaphorically speaking, B. Friedman is claiming that the graph appears "white," meaning that a neat linear relationship appears. Hans might be convinced easily of this, but statisticians would claim the graph appears not even gray, but "black." Points are once again scattered all over the place. There is a cluster of points for the countries with strong political rights and civil liberties, but this occurs just beyond the 0% growth mark.

To double check my own "senses" for what I saw on these graphs I went out and bought my own copy of the 1978-2005 World Development Report put out by the World Bank. I transferred tables of data to Microsoft Excel where I ran my own correlation analyses. The relationship of per capita income with rights and liberties produced an r factor near 0.5 (on a scale of -1 to 1), meaning pretty much what both B. Friedman and I saw in the graph of scattered points on page 313, a "grayness" suggesting a relationship that kicks in mainly at the higher levels of wealth. The r factor for the relationship of annual GDP growth from 1990-2003 with rights and liberties was close to 0.05.[7] In terms of grayscales this means the relationship was 95% gray, or effectively black, but B. Friedman nevertheless wrote an entire book claiming the relationship was white.

There are fewer examples of economists abusing empirical reliability than validity. The researchers for the Pew Happiness Survey qualify as abusers by their creative lumping of income categories (Essay 1), but B. Friedman's sloped line on page 316 provides a more illustrative case. How on earth did B. Friedman statistically generate that line? We do not know because he never includes this detail. Perhaps he used some complicated statistical model that would make the Federal Reserve Banks envious, rather than a simplistic correlation analysis. Complexity appears impressive, and certainly helps to hide the validity of a method, but simpler methods of empiricism should trump complex approaches.

On the other hand, perhaps B. Friedman inserted the sloped line based solely on the scholarship that formed his beliefs. Perhaps this scholarship caused him to see "white" where any empirical interpretation would see "black," and judged that he needed no stinkin' reliability standards for creating a line that conforms to his belief. Since the majority of his readers would be from the Powell Cabal something as trifling as reliability was not important for presenting evidence.

I ran one other analysis, the correlation of the Gini coefficient with the rights and liberties indicator. The Gini coefficient is not as mysterious as some other economic indicators. The coefficient is a ratio of how much wealth the rich controls to how much wealth the poor controls. Higher coefficients mean greater wealth disparity. This analysis tested an important caveat behind B. Friedman's thesis, that the growth benefits must be well distributed to stimulate moral benefits. We should not lose sight of the fact that B. Friedman at least pretends to be a champion of the middle class.

The r factor correlating the Gini coefficient with rights and liberties was 0.1, twice that of the r factor calculated for economic growth but hardly a convincing relationship. Considering that these essays promote affluence for the middle class, why should I share this bit of damning evidence that significant growth has little relationship with the quest for rights and liberties? For that matter, why should we in the middle class bother debunking a book that claims black is white when the author attempts to represent us?

B. Friedman's thesis attempts to refute a foundational economic principle made famous by none other than Milton Friedman: "there is no free lunch." In this

---

7 The data available in the World Development Report did not allow for going back to 1978.

one regard Milton had the better perspective. Economists in general caution that there are tradeoffs to consider with any economic policy, but the Powell Cabal and *laissez faire* economists apply this principle selectively to discourage interference with the private coercion of markets. When economic growth is the policy allegedly there are no tradeoffs to consider—not for political rights, not for civil liberties and not for moral benefits. By this reasoning we should, of course, maximize economic growth. But to maximize economic growth, to be driven by the desire for the trade that creates wealth, we have to subscribe to greed and selfishness as moral virtues. This paradox is the ultimate in "black is white" economics practiced by the Powell Cabal, combining Orwellian doublespeak for "there is no free lunch—but there is" and "greed and selfishness are immoral—but moral." To move forward Hans needs to snap out of the stupor being imposed by these messages. There are tradeoffs to consider with the economics of maximizing growth, with greed and selfishness as purely immoral attributes chief among them.

The "grayness" in the r factors and graphs indicate a spurious relationship; other variables play a greater causal role in affecting both economic and political ends. B. Friedman alludes to this, but he never lets the reality interfere with his main thesis. Let us look at the problem from the perspective of the U. S. Chamber of Commerce's flyer in support of a congresswoman. The driving force behind our social systems lies not in whether tort reform provides more restrictive punitive damages or less. The driving force lies not in whether federal intervention overrules the states or not. The driving force lies with the extent that cultural attributes such as cynicism, vanity and apprehension are employed by groups like the U. S. Chamber of Commerce to achieve both economic and political ends.

False Tradeoffs

Maybe these essays will make an impact with Hans and the middle class. If so, we can expect the Powell Cabal with their puppet libertarians to respond in kind, using some of the strategies we just covered to discredit our message. They will warn us that there is "no free lunch" and to consider the dire "tradeoffs" if we were to convert to an economic system of merit. We need to be honest and concede that such a system would mean owning less mass produced goods for the sake of indulgence, waste or neglect. Other than that, let us be prepared to refute some of the false tradeoffs the Powell Cabal might claim.

The Powell Cabal could cynically counter that happiness and greed are intricately linked. In truth, they have been making this argument for years. To back up this counterintuitive position (though seemingly persuasive) they need to explain why rigorous surveys reveal that increased wealth driven by corporate driven greed has not increased happiness over the past thirty years. They also need a clever explanation for how large numbers of hard-working poor people filled with greed can be happy with their situation. If this proves too daunting a task the Powell Cabal could argue instead that happiness is independent of economics, but that assumption likewise contradicts their goal of pursuing maximum wealth.

The Powell Cabal could appeal further to our vanities by alleging that these essays call for a halt to wealth. Maximizing wealth requires greed, but merely increasing wealth is accomplished through further specialization and the increased merits of labor. Maximizing wealth by necessity leads to maximizing the concentration of capital, the regrettable consequences of which have been well documented, regardless of the Powell Cabal's attempts to excuse, ignore or hide them. Maximizing wealth also requires favoring business corporations as the centerpiece of your economy. If we abandon maximizing wealth as our goal then maybe the concentration of capital can be tempered; conscientiously distributed away from corporate welfare to favor the specialization and diversification of proprietorships, improve production, stimulate substantive innovations and perhaps even trickle down to the merits of labor.

The Powell Cabal might claim that these essays are a socialist attempt to subvert capitalism, thus playing on our apprehensions. Capitalism could be the "wetlands of the free market." Wetlands serve the invaluable function of absorbing surges of precipitation during storms and releasing the water in moderation during times of drought. Capital could be the monetary corollary to wetlands, serving as a moderating tool for the surges in costs that affect production. Prices in goods and wages for labor could be buffered by capital to prevent fluctuations. Capitalism could indeed be a great tool for stabilizing market economies. However, our *laissez faire* economy shuns capital as a moderating tool for the free market in favor of a speculative wealth enhancement tool biased towards greed. For example, when oil prices have spiked over the past few years, so have oil profits. The strategy is simple enough: produce oil under a low cost climate, keep them as reserves, and sell them under a high cost climate. The inflated value has nothing to do with "private production creating profits," the literal meaning of capitalism, and more to do with creating profits out of speculative air. It is as if the oil industry replaced the potential "wetlands" benefits of capitalism with a "cement channel," funneling the storm surges of business costs straight to the pocket book of the middle class consumer.

The Powell Cabal also might play on our apprehensions by claiming that these essays call for large businesses to be abolished, along with the goods and services that only a large scale operation can produce. While abolishing business corporations sounds tempting, we do not need to halt all large businesses. Diversity is the key. A diverse economic system still can include a few large businesses. We do need to be mindful that incorporation includes perks that subvert the free market; the larger the incorporated business the greater the subversion. At the scale of business where nonworking shareholders are being lucratively rewarded, we can be sure that greed has replaced merit. Consequently, neither fiscal policy (tax breaks, earmarks, etc.) nor deregulation should provide added advantages to business corporations over proprietorships. If corrupt and/or incompetent business corporations cannot succeed on superior merit alone, if huge no-bid contracts are their mother's milk, if they need the federal government to usurp state legislatures, then simply let the greedy bastards fold.

The Powell Cabal might push the apprehension card further towards outright fear, warning that allowing corporations to fold when they cannot compete on merit alone will throw workers out on the street. This would be a serious charge, and one to take seriously if made by actual workers instead of corporate financed pundits being interviewed by corporate owned media. Workers—and junior executives for that matter—should keep in mind that the Powell Cabal has manipulated attitudes for more than thirty years. At one time the American ideal for an entrepreneur was the self-made man willing to brave the markets on his own terms. In contrast, the Powell Cabal wants workers and junior executives alike to be apprehensive about the jobless fate of corporations folding and fearful about starting up or working for proprietorships on their own terms of self-interest. They want workers and junior executives alike to be vain about their employment with a business corporation and prefer that to working for a lower profile proprietorship. They want workers and junior executives alike to be cynical about the old-style entrepreneur and the ideal of the self-made man, to have them remain in the clutches of business corporations like addicts in the clutches of their next fix.

A combination of cynicism, vanity and apprehension has led aspiring entrepreneurs to change their image of what smart, successful and respected means. At one time Ben Franklin fit the ideal of an entrepreneur; in our current time Jack Welch has been idolized as smart, successful and respected. That simple observation reveals much about what we have become and where we are heading. Workers and junior executives would require no small amount of faith, humility and courage to buck the current system, but the rewards would be all the greater for both them and our overall society.

The Powell Cabal may play their "progress" card in response to a movement championing proprietorships over business corporations. Are we willing to sacrifice the type of progress that requires huge concentrations of capital for satisfying a romantic fancy about the self-made man? The short answer to this is yes, if the huge concentration of capital must be achieved through the fiscal policy of government. More to the point, if government needs to concentrate capital on behalf of a business corporation like Halliburton to float their endeavor, then instead let government run the show. In either case government is, in effect, commanding the economy to the advantage of preferred businesses. The Powell Cabal cautions us against the unaccountability of corrupt government but government holds the potential of serving the middle class, while corporate executives are obligated to satisfy only their shareholders looking for welfare. Fixing an irresponsive government that at least is supposed to serve the middle class is better than shifting the responsibility to large business corporations that would just as soon shift operations to Dubai to enhance their bottom line of greed.

But this answer overlooks the important role that proprietorships have had, and should continue to have, with progress. Progress tends to feed upon itself. Like the science adage that every answer leads to a hundred new questions, every progressive innovation opens the door for a hundred more, just as we are witnessing with the Human Genome Project. Thus the pace of patents granted has accelerated throughout our country's history, independently of whether the GDP was dominated by production from proprietorships or business corporations. Actually, that last statement is not entirely true. During the new millennium, a time that has witnessed large corporations ruling the roost, the pace of patents granted actually has fluctuated. There certainly is much left to learn and invent. There are 80,000 proteins in our bodies with vital functions, the structure and synthesis of each representing a few patents waiting to happen with profound implications for human health. Unlike the development of an F-14 fighter jet, this research could be facilitated better through a diffusion of capital to various universities and smaller businesses willing to freely exchange ideas. A diffusion of capital for worthy efforts such as these might stimulate a steady increase in the pace of patents once again, though such a movement may make the Powell Cabal howl.

The Powell Cabal could attack the methods behind the message. Methods of research always can be made better; this definitely holds true for the economic report card used for these essays. Two discrete points in time were picked to examine changes, one to correspond with the seventies and one with the new millennium. Anything might have happened in between. Maybe all the negative changes occurred in the seventies, and Reaganomics righted the ship at a level plateau ever since. The continuous data in the NIPA tables and Statistical Abstracts suggest an ongoing continuous degradation of these economic factors, but a correlation analysis—though not quite as simple—would establish this better than comparing two discrete points in time. If the Powell Cabal should challenge our report card on these grounds let us make a counterchallenge. Let us urge the good scholars at the Hoover Institute to set up a new commission to do a regression analyses on housing, medical care and tuition costs since the seventies, in relation to such variables as GDP and median family income. They can use the results of these analyses for their reexamination of the real flaws in constructs such as core inflation, poverty and the Consumer Price Index. While we await further action from these good scholars, The Middle Class Forum (www.middleclassforum.org) provides data for some of these trends.

The Powell Cabal could attack the audacity of invading their scholarly realm with empirical methods and ecological principles. They have no one to blame but themselves in this matter, for *laissez faire* economists themselves sought to apply principles of natural selection and competition to their discipline, though butchering the concepts in the process. Puppet libertarians trumpet their indicators and statistics as empirical evidence, though they sacrifice validity and reliability to their god of greed. If they want to borrow from other disciplines without proper understanding they should expect no less than to have their academic pedigree challenged by those disciplines.

The Powell Cabal could justify their large expenditures to guide public perception as a corrective measure for the alleged anti-corporate venom being spewed in the "mainstream" media. The "mainstream" media is actually corporate media, which should automatically discredit such a charge, unless we think business corporations are so altruistic as to attack themselves through their own investments. Yet the public does appear to be that gullible, as evidenced in the popularity of twenty-four hour news networks. Let us test the hypothesis of an anti-corporate media with a quick survey. Do you know more about stock market indicators than the poverty threshold? Do you know more about how high interest rates control inflation than how low mortgage rates contribute to greater housing costs? Do you know more about the GDP than median family income levels? Do you know more about how government interferes with free markets than how business corporations interfere with them? Do you think the estate tax affects small businesses and family farms? If you answer "yes" to a majority of those questions, the Powell Cabal has nothing to complain about with "mainstream" media. "Mainstream" media serves corporate owners, which the gullible Hans desperately needs to comprehend.

Sympathy for the Devil

Though the Powell Cabal exists to promote corporate interests at times harmful to the middle class, we should not be blaming them for the trends that have occurred since the seventies. In one sense, they deserve more sympathy than blame. Peel away the academic pedigree and the façade of confidence in their mission and you discover the afflictions that plague people addicted to wealth, power and dogma. They operate in isolated spheres of greed and ruthlessness. Communal contentment eludes them.

Even the members of the Powell Cabal who originated from middle class neighborhoods, but who long since aspired to be connected with wealth, no longer understand the middle class mindset. They dwell in a world where self-esteem stems from wealth. With cynicism they equate morality with economic growth, as they lack the faith that the human spirit, and human worth, transcends material boundaries. With vanity they impose a corporate brand of globalism on the world, as they lack the humility to think that other cultures can develop markets of merit without the greed of multinational corporations. With apprehension they vigorously pursue entitlements such as huge capital gains and repeals in the estate tax, as they lack the courage to face an economy where they must survive entirely on their own merit. Filled with cynicism, vanity and apprehension the Powell Cabal knows no better than to persuade the middle class and proprietorships that we should similarly lack character as well.

There are now two books about the middle class being at war. The conservative Lou Dobbs wrote *The War on the Middle Class* (2006), while the liberal Thom Hartmann penned *Screwed: the Undeclared War against the Middle Class* (2006). Both Dobbs and Hartmann understand what is happening to us in our corporate society better than economists like Benjamin Friedman, but their titles are similarly misleading. Yes, wealthy shareholders and corporate executives devise schemes to shift income from labor production to capital welfare that becomes concentrated in their pockets. Does anyone really believe those same shareholders and executives are also discussing how they can specifically screw the middle class?

Investors and executives are merely sticking out for their own self-interests, as slaves to greed, not intending a war on the largest segment of society. Most of them probably think that what is in their best interests is in everyone's best interests. Even many of those with enough intuition or awareness to realize that greed naturally contributes to disparity, and capital enables that disparity to occur independently of production or merit, still think they are actually promoting free market ideals. Puppet libertarians probably think they really are libertarians.

The middle class cannot expect wealthy shareholders, corporate executives or the Powell Cabal to change their self-interests just because they do not align with what is best for proprietorships and the middle class. The middle class needs to stick up for what is in our best self-interests in return. We need to reject corporate greed. We need to value on a level with our jobs our other labor obligations for citizenship, community, family and ourselves. While fully supporting the use of capital to serve labor and goods, we must be leery of the use of capital to serve capital, which means we should demand indicators such as the ratio of housing costs to median family income rather than the standard of living. Most importantly, we need to realize that merit and greed are mutually exclusive ends; maximizing the pursuit of one compromises the pursuit of the other.

The report card featured in Essay 7 revealed that for more than thirty years the median family income has not kept pace with productivity, housing costs, health care or tuition, yet the amount that middle class families work has increased, as has consumer debt. While the report card compared two discrete points in time, a close examination of the unbiased and transparent data reveals consistent trends throughout the intervening years.[8] Do not trust what "black box" indicators

---

8 As documented on The Middle Class Forum (www.middleclassforum.org)

devised by economists have to say when that conflicts with your own experiences. You can turn to tables of unbiased data and determine for yourself with simple calculations that housing costs, the single most important and expensive portion of a middle class budget, requires an ever-increasing percentage of your income. Do not be persuaded by complicated studies about leisure if you are placing your kids in day care for much of the week. Place this in the context of valid and reliable data revealing that the disparity of wealth has grown over those thirty years while happiness has not.

We might be waiting for hell to freeze over before *laissez faire* economists, the dominant economic cult of the Powell Cabal, acknowledges these striking trends. Unlike the empiricism that accompanied the Scientific Revolution, economics appears to be caught in a dead zone where for the past few hundred years scholars in that field have been incapable of improving on the stagnant and flawed business corporation model of maximizing the returns of stock. This flawed stagnancy is underscored by the very pearls of wisdom the Powell Cabal uses to convey important economic principles. Let us close this part on economics by reexamining a few of these economic chestnuts.

Bargain from a Position of Strength

Government has declared business corporations to be individuals, up to a certain extent. They receive the same protections due to an individual in our system of law, but not quite the same liabilities. You can use the courts to take away everything a person owns. For the persons investing in an "individual" business corporation you can only take away the assets invested in the corporation. Other individual, umm, personal assets cannot be touched. This is part of the package of being licensed by the State, something not available to individuals, umm, persons.

This dual status for business corporations comes in quite handy in regards to contracts. Perhaps to fully understand this we need to be fully aware that contracts are not necessary for all market exchanges to take place, including those involving labor. Granted, the law requires contracts for labor, but people are being paid under the table everywhere, all the time, with the parties involved in the exchange freely and reliably depending on each other. Contracts are for creating conditions backed by government where "individuals" are forced to honor an economic agreement. For the "individual" known as a business corporation economic agreements are the sum total of their existence. For the "individual" known as a person there are other aspects to existence for which the contract may come to be a conflicting burden.

Government is not obliged to consider the "individual" as more than an economic creature in regards to contracts, but the business corporation is well aware of the extra obligations of persons outside of normal economics. The previous functions of communities have been woven into contracts. Care for sickness and old age has been transformed into economic "goods" for which the corporation can substitute speculative compensation in the future in return for binding labor in the present. Health insurance must be provided as a joint commodity, which makes privatized approaches economically inefficient. This inefficiency of escalating costs merely contributes to the bargaining strength of the entity offering the privatized and speculative compensation of health insurance.

In this and many other ways business corporations structure labor contracts from a position of incredible strength. In essence they use contracts to extort from those at the bottom of the labor pyramid and concentrate the benefits to the upper levels of a management hierarchy whose main obligation is to satisfy shareholders. Thus compensation ratios can reach one thousand to one in relation to the bottom levels of the pyramid, even for the upper management of corporations not performing well in the market. This bargaining strength has been granted effectively by government, though the Powell Cabal ironically views this as a "free market" attribute.

Should the government waiver in regards to the backing they provide business corporations there has been a safeguard put into place. In short, money has become free speech, bestowing the blessings of extra liberty on those "individuals" who can afford to "speak" the most, regardless of the accuracy of the content. This is a problem with broader implications than economics, as will be covered in future parts.

Too Many Dollars Chasing Too Few Goods

We all readily understand that counterfeiting money is bad. We condemn this practice because counterfeiters do not earn the money they make. However, if not outlawed counterfeiting also would wreck havoc in an economy. Dollars would be created without the economic productivity to back those dollars. The economy would be inflated and destabilized.

We have come to the point where too many dollars chase too few goods in our economy, causing the costs of expensive and essential items to inflate faster than our incomes. Puppet libertarians and the Powell Cabal focus our attention only on how this important principle applies to monetary policy. Critiquing how government sets interest rates and prints money does not threaten their corporate sugar daddies. Yet there are broader applications of "counterfeiting" going on that is causing our economy to destabilize and inflate. Just like with the printing of illegal money, these other applications of "counterfeiting" also involve receiving welfare in return for no economic productivity. Let us review some of these applications.

Unlike all other goods and services that naturally depreciate in worth after the initial purchase, the housing market features a good that appreciates in value.

As long as there is reasonable upkeep in a house the value increases over time, sometimes dramatically. Houses have become investments, but when no real economic productivity increases the value of the investment the extra dollars being "counterfeited" are inflating and/or destabilizing the economy. The evidence of increased housing costs as a proportion of our incomes is emphatic.

Part of what enables housing costs to inflate is the inflation of credit, another form of "counterfeiting." The credit is backed by future economic productivity on the part of the debtor, a good portion of which becomes interest rate payments. Yet no real economic productivity on the part of financial institutions really earns all these interest rate payments generated from expanded credit. Some labor is involved, just as there is labor involved in printing out counterfeit money. Yet nothing has been produced for consumption as a result of the inflated value of interest rates added to the costs of goods. Furthermore, too much credit means too much future productivity than can realistically be delivered by the debtor.

The wealthy do not have to rely on expanded credit, but they have been involved in counterfeiting at the grandest scale of all. Nothing generates capital without productivity as much as investments in capital markets. Obscene sums are involved in trading that involves no productivity at all, such as futures trading. Even when economic productivity may be occurring somewhere to back the capital, inflation still occurs through this wealthy form of welfare. The unearned capital may be gained from the economic productivity of developing countries. Aside from the ethics of diverting capital away from the country that is producing it, the result is similar to the Spanish Empire infusing their economy with unearned Aztec gold. Instead of everyone getting richer, the overall costs of goods at home inflate in adjustment to this unearned capital from abroad being concentrated among wealthy investors.

Even if the welfare gained by investors comes from labor at home, inflation still occurs. As long as the balance of unearned income flows in the direction of the wealthiest the effect on the money supply is the same as with expanded credit. Money supply as a limit is being removed and the costs of goods not made by children in Southeast Asia inflates.

"Too many dollars chasing too few goods" is one of the most profound principles for market economies. Too bad *laissez faire* economists only know how the concept works with monetary policy.

There Is No Free Lunch

The members of the Powell Cabal are not the real villains in a society that justifies greed, increases wealth disparity and diverts our labors away from our other obligations as citizens. We, the middle class, are both the victims and the villains. We have been convinced that greed is in our best interests. Consequently, we have consented to an economic system bad for satisfying needs without debt, bad for small businesses, bad for free markets, bad for wealth distribution, bad for hope and bad for the middle class. At the heart of this is how we have come to apply the wisdom of "There is no free lunch" selectively.

The free market ideal is a barter system where two parties make a voluntary exchange of products that are both free from exploited labor, in full awareness of who and what they are dealing with. The "unfree" opposite of that would be a system where the labor of production was coerced, the agents of exchange anonymous, information about the exchange hidden and/or distorted, the infrastructure necessary for the exchange dependent on government, and the economy commanded to benefit this exchange by government. In other words, the extreme "unfree" opposite to free market is corporate capitalism, not a socialism that really goes only halfway at best at making markets less free.

Given that government provides the blessings for any economic system, whether through intervention or nonintervention in various aspects, "There is no free lunch" is meaningful only in the context of whether the blessings of government favors the free market or corporate capitalism end of the dichotomy. Socialism does not move us in the direction of free markets, but even further removed is a system where government "lets be" all the actions needed to counter the command favoritism government bestows to business corporations protected as both "individuals" and licensed wards of the State.

If government decides to "let be," as advocated by the misinformation network of *laissez faire* economists, puppet libertarians and the Powell Cabal, the tradeoffs include the furthest point away from free markets that we can get, along with the tradeoffs of greater wealth disparity, greater labor exploitation, greater inflation of essential items and greater difficulty for entrepreneurial proprietors to survive. The gains are greater amounts of mass-produced stuff, greater maximized wealth, greater power and greater ability to impose dogmatic beliefs. Only the first gain truly benefits the middle class.

In reality, most people want a compromise between both the limitations and liberty of a barter system and the expanded consumption and constraints to liberty brought to us by corporate capitalism. Politics determines where that compromise lies. Middle class economics will be achieved through middle class politics. Let us turn next to the function of our political system.

PART TWO

POLITICAL LIBERTY

ESSAY 9 - AUTHORITARIANISM OR WISDOM

Overview

- Humans naturally trust authority, enabling authoritarianism.
- People with authority do not need empirical evidence to promote their beliefs.
- People naturally conform, particularly at war time.
- Natural trust and conformity gives rise to groupthink and party loyalty.
- The authoritarian quest for power is linked to wealth.
- Wisdom involves the accumulation and prioritization of experiences.
- The necessary conditions for collective wisdom are diverse, independent, decentralized and aggregated experiences.
- The ideals for collective wisdom correspond to ideals for liberty and democracy.
- Wise democracy is sometimes evident in small town government.
- A political system of wisdom derives from empiricism and the middle class.

The Milgram Experiments

As a freshman at the University of Connecticut I enrolled in a Psychology 101 course, as did a few hundred other students. Professors of introductory psychology courses often enlist large numbers of undergraduate students as guinea pigs for the experiments of their graduate students. To fulfill a course requirement I chose to participate in an experiment that was reported to be about learning. I later discovered I participated in a replica of the Milgram shock experiments, but I did not know that when I showed up to fulfill my obligation.

The researcher explained to me that another volunteer in a separate room was about to be given a learning task. If he failed at a task I was to give him a mild shock. If he kept failing I was to increase the voltage. The learning tasks were easy and I administered the first shock without much reservation, thinking the subject would quickly learn. I wondered what was wrong with the guy when I increased the voltage once, and then a couple more times. After that I stopped, though the researcher put pressure on me to continue. The researcher later informed me that the real focus of the experiment was the shocker, not the "shockee." The purpose was to determine how far people would go with obeying authority.

How could I go along with shocking people for a stupid experiment on learning? Save your condemnation, dear readers, as it turns out I was a relative model of restraint. In comparison to the original shock experiments done in the sixties by Stanley Milgram from Yale, I desisted far sooner than most.[1] For that study the "shocks" began at 45 volts and were increased in 15 volt increments. Though the "learner" in the next room followed a scripted sequence of yells, banging and complaints about his heart, no one quit before the 300 volt level. Eventually, the sounds from the next room stopped all together before the final 450 volt shock was administered. How many went all the way, you ask? How many subjects agreed to shock another human being after yells, banging and pleas, followed by "dead" silence? The answer might upset you, but stay tuned.

Authoritarianism

The natural sciences, as usual, provide a good explanation for such shocking behavior. Creatures adapt to maximize their energy budget. Predators target the weakest prey; leafy plants close their photosynthesis factories at night; bears hibernate; and people watch television. When we trust authority, when we believe and obey the people we consider to be in charge of certain areas of our lives, we save ourselves a whole lot of energy that we can budget for other activities. Trusting authority saves the energy of having to research whether they are right. Obeying authority saves the energy of flailing away at your own uncertain plans to meet your own uncertain goals. If we trust authority, and authority delivers on that trust, we can budget energy for more desirable activities. Or we can keep that energy "in reserve" while we watch more television.

Trusting authority is adaptive in other ways. Zorg and his Neanderthal mates are out on a hunt. Zorg instructs his fellow hunters to circle around the mastodon. The hunters all start asking questions instead. Why must they circle the mastodon? If they must, then why does Zorg get to stay where he is? During this rebuke to authority the mastodon charges and flattens the hunting party. Eventually the Neanderthals go extinct.

The corollary to Zorg in a nation state would be the authoritarianism of a benevolent dictator. Such a dictator is like a caring parent. If a monarch always pursues what is best for his/her subjects, there is no need for those subjects to waste their time and energy on citizenship. Like the children of responsible parents, the citizens of a benevolent dictatorship can budget their energy to satisfy their own personal interests while trusting in their good and steadfast ruler. As counterintuitive as this may sound to those who live in a democracy, a truly benevolent dictatorship forms a utopia.

But there are at least three problems with authoritarianism. First, people sometimes change, including benevolent dictators. As the saying goes, absolute power has the potential to corrupt absolutely. Second, there are limits to the

---

1 For a full description of Milgram's work refer to *Obedience to Authority: An Experimental View* (1974).

wisdom of any one person, even Solomon made mistakes. When everything is put into the trust of one authority, there are no checks and balances for these mistakes. Third, the next dictator to come along may not be so benevolent. Unleashing a new, ruthless ruler on citizens who habitually obey their leaders without question could have shocking consequences.

A country can pass laws to counteract these problems, but trusting completely in laws has similar shortcomings. Laws can change. For good or bad, the USA PATRIOT Act represents a restrictive change in our liberties. Laws can be misguided. At one time only white males could vote. Laws can be circumvented. During war time presidents will use their executive authority to ignore laws they believe hamper their war plans.

Authoritarianism, though adaptive in some ways, leads to complete vulnerability. That may be a worthwhile tradeoff for intimate partnerships or tribal hunting parties but not for the citizens of a nation state. To shake their vulnerability citizens need not be openly rebellious or even automatically skeptical, thereby reenacting the plight of Zorg and his recalcitrant tribe. At the least, however, true political liberty requires citizens to be well-informed about both their leaders and their liberties.

Scholasticism

Authoritarians promote their beliefs without the need for valid or reliable evidence. They instead change the meaning of experience to align with their fixed beliefs. Authoritarians use rhetorical arguments to persuade others. The quality of their rhetoric is determined largely by their authority, independently of empirical evidence. In our economic essays a good example of authoritarianism was the influence of Milton Friedman, a man convinced in the belief that positive economics confirmed his faulty, normative view of economic freedom that included the role of corporations in free markets. His pop authority blinded puppet libertarians to the empirical contradictions inherent in their beliefs. Acclaimed scholarship often commands authority, whether or not merited by empirical evidence.

Marilyn vos Savant is, by the measure of one particular IQ test, the most intelligent person in the world. She has a column in *Parade* magazine, "Ask Marilyn," where she answers the questions posed by readers. Most of the questions pose a word, number or logic puzzle for vos Savant's sharp mind to solve. However, a few questions call for the application of wisdom rather than intelligence. One reader asked vos Savant if she supported the death penalty. In her column of February 16, 1997 her basic reply was "Yes."

Since the basic thrust of this essay is to not blindly trust authorities, we should seek a second opinion of a different sort. Let us go with world opinion; or, at least, the world opinion of secular democracies; or, to take our opinion out of the equation, secular democracies besides us. Not one of them implements the death penalty. The collective governments that rule by collective consent seem to refute vos Savant's authoritative "wisdom." Are they all being foolish?

The death penalty provides two confirmed benefits: retributive justice for the State and individual satisfaction for some victims. Perhaps those benefits directly relate to past experiences of vos Savant. However, there are costs associated with those benefits.

- As vos Savant acknowledges, whatever retribution the State seeks against the individual also provides legitimacy for similar retribution, in the minds of many individuals, against the State or other individuals. In other words, the death penalty perpetrates violent retribution as a goal throughout the fabric of society.

- While some victims express satisfaction with the death penalty, others express satisfaction with forgiveness. Forgiveness tends to provide greater and more permanent satisfaction than retribution, by the testimony of those who make that choice.

- Even supporters of the death penalty, including vos Savant, fault the method as being an uncivilized means. The company the United States keeps, in terms of nations who resort to the uncivilized death penalty, is dubious.

- Mistakes are made in implementing the death penalty; mistakes with the ultimate severity in consequences that cannot be rectified.

Vos Savant makes several of these points in attempting to persuade the reader she is making a rational, intelligent assessment of both sides of the argument. She then presents her one rationale (yes, she has only one) for supporting the death penalty, couched in a preemptive, authoritative strike against those tempted to disagree:

"At best, it is surely a deterrent of the strongest possible magnitude. I suggest that most who believe otherwise are probably rationalizing an obviously justifiable abhorrence for the death penalty. When emotions are involved, it is more difficult to be free of bias, and this is a good example. My definition of bias is the inability to give credit to "the other side" when it is due, usually combined with the inability to accept debit to one's "own" side when it is due. These are the hallmarks of a biased argument. And this is why the issue of capital punishment -- a highly emotional issue -- bursts with bias, and why so many bad arguments are made about it."

This statement resembles the *modus operandi* of the Powell Cabal: feigned objectivity disguising a biased agenda. In truth, the overall body of research suggests that the death penalty does not deter violent crime at all. There is, as with all things being researched in this dogmatic age of cherry-picking evidence, conflicting studies. Some very smart folks orchestrate studies that conclude the death penalty has been a deterrent. Not surprisingly, some of these studies have been done by economists using "empirical" black box techniques.[2] There have been two serious flaws to these studies. They do not adequately control for other variables that could be affecting the outcome,[3] and they do not triangulate well with other types of evidence. For example, states without the death penalty have less violence than those with, even when the states are neighbors, and democratic countries without the death penalty are, at worst, no more violent than us.[4]

Conjecture that the death penalty deters violent crime is therefore based more on biased opinion than adequate research and vos Savant spends most of the paragraph "rationalizing" her own "bias," which must have been the product of her "emotions," in the absence of her actually researching the facts. There was, in fact, no reference made by vos Savant to actual research. As a consequence, she displays an "inability to accept debit" to her central thesis and presents quite a "bad argument." Yet, by virtue of her authoritative intelligence, many readers probably misconstrued her position as wisdom.

Trusting in the scholarship of authorities is known as scholasticism. The basic epistemological tools of scholasticism are deductive reasoning and rhetoric. From the traditional wisdom of authorities one deduces the meaning of experience to fit these beliefs. In the preceding example, vos Savant offers no empirical evidence that the death penalty is a deterrent, she has deduced that based on her emotional beliefs. She uses rhetoric, or persuasive language, such as "surely" and "strongest possible magnitude" to strengthen a case that is based solely on belief rather than any empirical evidence.

Conformity

Natural trust in authority works in tandem with conformity. The Asch conformity experiments explored the impact of groups on the judgment of individuals. Conducted by Solomon Asch in the late 1950s, his series of experiments embedded one subject in a group of confederates whose responses were scripted by the

---

2   Such as Isaac Ehrlich's "The Deterrent Effect of Capital Punishment: A Question of Life and Death," in American Economic Review (1975).
3   Deterrence and the Death Penalty, A Critical Review of New Evidence (2005), by Jeffrey Fagan and The Death Penalty (2006), No Evidence for Deterrence, by John J. Donohue and Justin Wolfers, are two recent articles exposing the habitual methodological flaws in studies attempting to prove the deterrence belief.
4   See the Death Penalty Information Center web site (http://www.deathpenaltyinfo.org/deterrence) for data.

researcher.[5] For several trials the group was provided a visual of different lines drawn on paper and asked questions about comparative lengths. The confederates would give the wrong answer, such as claiming that two lines were the same length though they might differ by a few inches. All subjects showed discomfort with the prospect of providing the correct answer; the subject went along with the misleading confederates in a third of all trials; and two-thirds of the subjects went along with the misleading confederates in at least one trial.

Keep in mind that the correct answers were neither a matter of opinion nor of knowledge. In this experiment the correct answers were a matter of observing empirical evidence; indeed, everyone judged the comparative lengths correctly when not influenced by the beliefs of the confederates. One might doubt their own sound opinions or knowledge for any number of reasons but denying what your senses tell you is not an easy thing to do. What is going on? And what does this imply about our liberty?

Once again, a prevalent psychological behavior can be linked to a natural adaptation. There is safety and strength in numbers. Zorg and his tribal mates go off to hunt a saber-tooth tiger. All his buddies stick together and go up the nearest mountain. Zorg believes they are on the wrong track and leaves the others to search by the river, where he has often seen the tiger hunting. By golly, Zorg was right, but without reinforcements Zorg becomes the tiger's next meal.

One would think that conformity in a large nation state would be difficult to achieve. To whom does one conform? As Robert Pullman documents in *Bowling Alone* (2000), the amount of civic involvement in our society has decreased steadily. We spend more time with electronic entertainment (television, video games, etc.) than with community activities. Meanwhile, more people seem to agree with the sentiments expressed in a Frost poem: "Good fences make good neighbors."

But we still conform, indeed. If not to groups we know personally through community involvement, then to groups we know symbolically through mass media. Scholars have branded different forms of this modern day conformity with labels such as groupthink, mass culture and herd mentality. We can add party loyalty to that list as well. Conformity to the masses no longer holds the same adaptive advantage that would have prevented Zorg from being eaten. There is less immediacy to the beliefs of a group spread out across the land. Indeed, some conforming beliefs may have no adaptive advantage whatsoever for the individuals that hold them. Consider, for example, the dreaded "death" tax—excuse me, I mean inheritance tax—we discussed in Part One. Abolishing the tax benefits only multimillionaires, yet many a blue collar worker has been convinced that this "welfare" tax—oops, inheritance tax—on large amounts of unearned income hurts them as well.[6]

---

5 For a full description of the Asch conformity experiments refer to the *Scientific American* article, "Opinions and social pressure" (1955).
6 As reported in *Perfectly Legal* (2003) by David Cay Johnston.

If groupthink, mass culture, the herd mentality, party loyalty, et al, no longer provides a natural survival advantage, what does such conformity provide? Once again, organisms (especially humans) want to conserve energy. The subjects in the Asch experiments may not have conserved energy by conforming against what their senses told them, but that is precisely what makes the results of those experiments compelling. In contrast, consider the time and energy an individual saves by conformity of opinions and knowledge. Constructive opinions require thought and useful knowledge requires research. If we are willing to abandon our senses for the sake of conformity, we certainly would be willing to save time and energy through the allegiance of our opinions and knowledge to an interest group or party we trust.

Conformity and War

The assault on liberty via conformity resembles the assault on liberty via a complete trust in authority. Through conformity, as with a complete trust in authority, we the middle class can be manipulated. Let us illustrate this with our good friend Hans and one of the best tools for conformity and trust in authorities, a rallying cry for war.

Hans gets back to town after a few months of deep-sea fishing, and the first thing he does is patronize a local bar. The television above the barkeeper's head reports that the country is now planning to go to war. Hans acknowledges the atrocities of war but is willing to support a just war. He asks the customer on the bar stool to his right what the war is about, and the man replies: "Atlantis is a threat to our security, we must protect ourselves." Hans asks the customer on the bar stool to his left what the war is about, and the woman replies: "They have such a repressive government; we need to help those poor people out." Hans asks the barkeeper what the proposed war is about, and the barkeeper replies: "We have vital interests in that country, we need to protect those interests." A biker sitting at the end of the bar shares his opinion: "We need to kick some ass, show the world who is boss!"

Hans recoils at the notion of going to war to "kick some ass;" he has a teenage son that could end up in any war, and he disdains armchair warriors. Yet he observes that the opinion, if not the motive, conforms to the majority. Meanwhile, Hans considers security, noble missions and protecting one's interest to all be just causes. Hans has little knowledge of the facts at this point but his mind is made up; he conforms to the majority opinion expressed in the bar.

Despite the death and destruction there is something for almost everyone in war. Some people are motivated by doing good deeds; if packaged right war appeals to the noble. Some people are motivated by the glory of war; if packaged right war appeals to the vain. Some people are motivated by security; if packaged right war appeals to the apprehensive. Some people are motivated by the spoils of war obtained through might; if packaged right war appeals to the cynical. Some people are motivated by death and destruction; war needs no packaging for these folks.

If packaged right war can appeal to a variety of folks for a variety of reasons all at the same time. When that happens an added appeal kicks in for a sizable majority of the population; war appeals to those who conform. Add to this the fact that foreign wars are extremely good for an economy, especially an ailing economy. War may be one of the worst atrocities afflicting mankind but, considering the various appeals of war, one can understand why war is a constant in global politics.

Conformity and Party Loyalty

Party loyalty encourages the herd mentality at a shocking level. Consider the 2004 election. Eighty-nine percent of Democrats voted for John Kerry and ninety-three percent of Republicans voted for President Bush II.[7] In addition, we can assume that virtually everyone who identifies themselves as conservative Republicans voted for President Bush II, and virtually everyone who identifies themselves as liberal Democrats voted for John Kerry. Maybe liberal Democrats and conservative Republicans contrast sharply and distinctively with their opposing agendas; or maybe they both are conformists with much more in common than they would like to admit.

Supporting an unproven candidate from your party can be explained as a matter of faith. The higher percentage of Republicans showing solidarity in the 2004 election is the more revealing statistic because their candidate was a known incumbent. Conventional wisdom says that an election with an incumbent becomes a referendum on that incumbent's record. Once that candidate acquires a well-known record of accomplishments and misdeeds party members can determine whether their previous faith was warranted.

The solidarity of conservative Republicans in the 2004 election defies this conventional wisdom. Conservatives advocate fiscal responsibility; a budget surplus became a record deficit during the Bush II administration. Conservatives want controlled spending; the Bush II administration had not vetoed a single pork-filled bill by the 2004 election. Conservatives favored states rights in the Reagan-Clinton era; the Bush II administration constantly fought states rights on issues ranging from the environment to security.

Conservatives historically have favored restraint bordering on isolationism, as evidenced in their opposition to intervention in Kosovo. Once no WMDs were found in Iraq President Bush II professed that the main reason for intervention was

---

7 As reported on 12/3/04 by Bob Burnett in the *Berkeley Daily Planet.*

to spread democracy, a contradiction to conservative restraint (though consistent with neoconservative ambition). Conservatives led the charge to curb the power of the executive branch during FDR's reign; the Bush II administration's push to concentrate power in their hands harkens back to the Alien and Sedition Acts of 1798. If President Bush II was a Democrat you could bet that many conservatives would have called for impeachment, hoping to stop the relentless assault on the principles they hold dear, but more than ninety percent of conservative Republicans gave this incumbent's record a thumbs up.

Maybe the conformity exhibited in the 2004 election was a referendum on the President's pedigree and competence and not his ideology. George W. Bush was a second generation president. He also is fourth generation oil, fourth generation military industrial complex, fourth generation finance, and third generation intelligence.[8] Such a pedigree should not have been important to middle class Republicans, unless they are employees of Halliburton or similar large corporations connected to President Bush II's heritage. That leaves the question of his competence. You have to admire party members who put aside their ideology to vote for competence, but this was an unlikely factor in the ninety percent support of Republicans for President Bush II in either the 2000 or 2004 elections.

President Bush II was a mediocre student at best. That should not be automatically a strike against him, though he seems to lack curiosity in a striking way. A competent president of a complex country needs to be a little bit inquisitive. President Bush II failed at the majority of his business ventures. His greatest success was as co-owner of the Texas Rangers, an endeavor where the partner fronted much of the money and the city of Arlington kicked in additional amounts. His most notorious failure was Harkin Energy Corporation, an oil company that crumbled while President Bush II was connected to insider-trading shenanigans. Similar incompetence had conservative Republicans up in arms in regards to the Clinton involvement with Whitewater.

Competency while in office matters most, of course; perhaps ninety percent of conservative Republicans were expressing approval of President Bush II's job performance in the Oval Office. President Bush II handled the immediate response to 9/11 masterfully. This showed in his approval rating among both parties. His approval rating remained high through the initial phase of the Iraq War, back when the President boasted "Mission Accomplished." By the time of the 2004 election, however, opinions of the Iraq War had soured with realizations of faulty information and faulty occupation strategies. Three months before the elections two disturbing bits of economic news came out on the same day: both poverty and the amount of uninsured were rising. Even though the news came out on a Friday and got very little air time, many people considered President Bush to be incompetent in the handling of the economy leading up to the 2004 election,

---

8   This information is in *American Dynasty* (2004), by Kevin Phillips.

including some former members of his own administration.

If ideology and competence means little for party loyalty, to what forces of nature do we attribute such resolute conformity? The political herds of both Democrats and Republicans stampede to the same instigating factors that hold so much economic sway. First, these manipulated herds apprehend what would happen if a different herd gets the choicest political feed. They fear that the country would suffer greatly should some other herd control the politics of the nation. Second, political herds are vain. The status of political control satisfies this vanity, regardless of what ill-advised gains might result from this control. Third, and most tragically, political herds are cynical. Even if one of their own should prove incompetent this matters not because everyone knows that all politicians are the same. A political herd might as well stick with the "devil they know" than the devil from a different herd. Power trumps both ideas and competence in commanding loyalty to incumbents from either the Republican or Democratic Party. Ninety percent support for President Bush II from conservative Republicans was first and foremost a referendum on maintaining power, driven by apprehension, vanity and/ or cynicism.

Power and Wealth

Power shares many of the same attributes as wealth. As with wealth, concentrating power maximizes the effects of power. As with wealth, the concentration of power creates an unearned, disproportionate disparity of power. Certainly we identify these conditions to be true with monarchies, where a king can decree unearned benefits and positions of power for his friends and family. But even in our country we have seen that being born or related to families of power bestows no small measure of that power on offspring quite apart from their merits or actions. As the only superpower the United States wields influence disproportionate to our stake in the world, as evidenced by our preeminent role in the Middle East, a hemisphere away. Inside our borders the concentration of power in the executive branch of government has reached levels that Republicans from the 1940s through the 1960s would judge to be disastrous.

Power and wealth are, in fact, intricately linked. Corporations seek to maintain their wealth through the power of politicians to legislate. Politicians seek to maintain their power through the wealth of corporations and interest groups funding their campaigns and other activities. In broad terms a primary goal of wealth is to secure power and a primary goal of power is to secure wealth. Disparity of wealth accompanies disparity of power. Comparative studies of developed countries reveal that a lack of veto power, multiple party systems and proportional representation correlate with greater economic equality than occurs with our political system.[9]

We should not be surprised, then, that of all the indignities and complaints that the Powell Cabal of corporate sponsored think tanks, corporate endowed chairs of economic departments, corporate hired public relations firms, corporate employed lobbyists and corporate owned media may lay at the feet of government intervention, we seldom hear from them a call for term limits or campaign finance reform. No, the good people at The Heritage Foundation are not likely to incorporate in their Index of Economic Freedom an indicator for how much average wealth is required to win a federal election, or to wine and dine a legislator.

Ah, but I have picked on corporations and *laissez faire* economists enough in our previous part on the economic pursuit of happiness. For this new part on political liberty I will shift attention away from the corporations wielding wealth to the politicians wielding power. As with corporations and the wealthy, we know that politicians are an entitled bunch, going to such lengths as gerrymandering to maintain their power regardless of merit. We know that politicians wield the emotional tools of apprehension, vanity and cynicism to solicit the continued support of constituents.

This leaves us with a conundrum similar to the one faced with the pursuit of happiness. Considering that we all are "slaves to our emotions," politicians spend a large amount of time enslaving us to apprehension, vanity and cynicism in order to maintain power. Being motivated by apprehension, vanity and cynicism to exercise our political liberty diminishes the pleasure of having that liberty. Consider, also, that this emotional enslavement goes for naught when the "wrong politician" acquires power. Seeking political power as an expression of our independent liberty makes no more sense for the middle class than basing the pursuit of happiness on greed.

Wisdom

What should political liberty entail for the middle class? Certainly, we want to avoid the pitfalls associated with political power. We want to avoid a political system that creates large disparity between those with the most power and those with the least, as the middle class will be periodically—if not perpetually—aligned closer to those that have the least. We want to avoid a political system where politicians covet power to the extent that they will play upon our apprehension, vanity and cynicism to maintain that power. Above all, we want to avoid a political system that thrives on groupthink, with political liberty being wasted on conformity and trust in authority.

In many ways the opposite of authoritarianism is wisdom. Granted,

9 Reported in "Why do so many jobs pay so badly?" by Christopher Jencks, a chapter in *Inequality Matters: The Growing Economic Divide in America and Its Poisonous Consequences* (2005), editors James Lardner and David A. Smith.

conventional wisdom as currently derived through the efforts of mass media causes conformity, but real wisdom arises from the coalescence of independent thought. Once independent thought is removed as a foundation for belief and behavior what remains is just convention without wisdom. A more accurate term for the coalescence of independent thought would be collective wisdom. While conventional wisdom may become outdated, collective wisdom implies a continuous process of gathering ideas generated by independent thinking. While power can be wielded wisely, a relentless commitment to the power of authoritarianism necessitates conformity and interferes with a pursuit of collective wisdom.

Two studies provide a foundation for what wisdom means and the value of collective wisdom as a libertarian goal. The first study was a Masters thesis titled *Effectively Evaluating the Meaning Behind a Wilderness Learning Experience* (1989), done by yours truly. Similar to my motivation for once starting a nonprofit business, my Masters thesis was a shameless ploy to earn a degree while backpacking long distances. The learning experiences of twelve members of the 1985 Connecticut Continental Divide Expedition—a seven-month, 3,000 mile backpacking expedition—were evaluated using a variety of methods, including concept maps.

Concept maps involve enclosing the key concepts to an idea in boxes, and drawing arrows between boxes to indicate how the concepts are linked together. My overall hypothesis was that pursuing a strenuous goal in the wilderness for seven months would induce various types of learning. The amount of concepts on concept maps, and the links between them, would increase over the course of the wilderness journey.

On the contrary, for a majority of the concept maps the number of concepts decreased, while the number of links between concepts increased for only half the maps. One of the concepts that had to be mapped was interdependence, a combination of emotional and social learning. Objective surveys, essays and interviews all confirmed that interdependence increased significantly for the group during seven months of supporting each other, as we traversed through mountains and desert with heavy packs. On the concept maps created for interdependence before and after the hike the number of concepts decreased by almost half.

No matter, being proven wrong by the empirical evidence provides a more stimulating challenge than having your beliefs supported. We typically associate learning with gaining an increased complexity of conceptual knowledge, but the concept maps assessing emotional, social and spiritual learning refuted this. I concluded that the emotional, social and spiritual learning that occurred through intense experiential education was a function of gaining wisdom through the simplification of conceptual relationships. Wisdom involves the weeding out of experiences to focus on those most valid and reliable for giving us meaning.

Many answers to life can be gained through complex knowledge, by accumulating loads of information and working out all the details embedded in the data. But you also can get answers to life through wisdom, by seeing past the complexities into the essence of things. Thus, wisdom is not confined to the "best and the brightest." Anyone can acquire wisdom through their experiences. The Continental Divide Expedition members did not work out elaborate philosophical discourses on the meanings of interdependence; they came to know the essence of interdependence through the experiences of wilderness backpacking together as a group.

There are tremendous advantages to the simplicity of wisdom. Wisdom, in a sense, is another approach to conserving our energy budget. Wisdom saves time and effort, similar to memorizing your multiplication tables rather than having to work out the answer with your fingers each time. Wisdom also can be more reliable than intelligence.

The hardest course I ever took was "Taxonomy of Vascular Plants." I figured that as a backpacker I knew about trees, thus, I knew about vascular plants. After day one in the course I learned that the trees of the United States make up but a small fraction of the hundreds of families of vascular plants, many of which can be distinguished from each other only by small complex details. I prepared elaborate study guides to help me key out the vascular plants that were presented on herbarium sheets. I struggled nonetheless.

Another student in the class almost always identified the families of vascular plants correctly. As a graduate student who had gone on field trips to South America with the professor, she was the one student who had experienced almost every family in the field. I asked her once what characteristics she used to correctly identify one particularly difficult plant that had confounded the rest of the class. She shrugged her shoulders and replied: "I just knew."

The tables were turned only once in that class. Out of the hundreds of families of vascular plants there was one that I identified correctly on a herbarium sheet and the star pupil did not. The family was the Urticaceae or, as commonly known by backpackers, the family of stinging nettles. These are found, sometimes in painful overabundance, along the Appalachian Trail. I needed none of my study sheets of complex details to identify this one; based on the past experience of itchy legs that nearly drove me crazy, I just knew.

Empirical Wisdom

You will note the two key ingredients to wisdom: accumulating experiences and prioritizing those most valid and reliable to give us meaning. Everyone accumulates experiences over time, but some people accumulate them faster. These people may be bold, willing to try new things. They may be creative, with a propensity to "think outside the box." They may be intelligent, able to grasp the meaning of different experiences quickly. By virtue of these various attributes we may come to think of these people as authorities whose wisdom we can trust. However, a greater ability to accumulate experiences provides no guarantee for wisdom.

Intelligence, boldness and creativity are not necessary for wisdom, since everyone accumulates experiences over time. Furthermore, as vos Savant demonstrated in regards to the death penalty, intelligence is not sufficient for wisdom, or even for sound reasoning. Great intelligence can be employed in scholastic fashion to make any experience seem to be valid and reliable. In regards to the death penalty and other questions seeking wisdom, do the beliefs of intelligent individuals or numerous democracies worldwide have greater validity and reliability? Should we go with scholastic authoritarians or the empirical collective experiences of people in forming wise policy?

James Surowiecki, a *New Yorker* columnist, wrote a book called *The Wisdom of Crowds* (2004). His main thesis is that crowds of people, under the right conditions, can derive more accurate answers to problems than authoritative experts. The conditions that Surowiecki cites for extracting wisdom from crowds are the precise opposite of groupthink. They are as follows:

- Opinions must be diverse.
- People must form opinions independently from each other.
- Opinions must be based on decentralized knowledge bases.
- Opinions must be aggregated in a way that reveals the mean or the mode.

Let us go through these criteria for collective wisdom again, this time inserting the word freedom. The freedom to have diverse opinions, the freedom to be independent and the freedom to have decentralized knowledge sound much like a working definition for individual liberties. The freedom to aggregate such opinions into the mean or mode sounds much like a working definition for democracy. Individual liberty provides the accumulation of experiences and democracy the process of prioritizing these experiences to gain collective wisdom.

There is another familiar analog to Surowiecki's concept of collective wisdom. One of the main themes of the Enlightenment was replacing the epistemology of scholasticism with empiricism. Forming theories from observable experience was now judged to be superior to dialectic rationalizations from "infallible" axioms (dogma) that inevitably proved to be fallible. Patterns or consistencies are detected from a collection of experiences. Meaning is induced, or generalized, from these collective experiences, just as a democratic process generalizes the collective wisdom of citizens. Conventions of logic are used for generalizations; with both the empirical experiences and conventions of logic being more open to shared cross-examination than the beliefs and rhetoric wielded by authoritarian scholars (or leaders). Concepts of empiricism and democracy coevolved during the Enlightenment. What people consider to be good knowledge determines what they consider to be good decisions.

The only criticisms I have read of Surowiecki's thorough research to support his theory run along the lines of: "fascinating, but unlikely for common practice because of the mass media and groupthink."[10] Yes, that is precisely the rub. To produce collective wisdom a group can be neither conforming nor blindly trusting of authority. You will not extract collective wisdom from the devoted readerships and viewerships of mass media with their special interest group pundits and celebrity news talk show hosts. The last place to find collective wisdom would be among the devout rank and file members of a political party determined to maintain the power of their incumbent politicians.

This places the pursuit of collective wisdom, and the pursuit of democracy, in a Catch-22 situation. Blind trust in authority contributes to the herd mentality. Since this conformity of the masses produces less than optimal results, we trust further in the wisdom of authorities. These political essays will explore further why this represents a real danger; why negative feedback loops that should provide homeostasis to maintain liberty and democracy are being transformed to positive feedback loops that could overload and break the political system, turning authoritarianism into totalitarianism.

A Case Study in Wisdom

For forty-two years my small town had their version of Zorg, the tribal leader. For forty-two years John J. Curtiss held the office of first selectman, running unopposed on both the Republican and Democratic tickets for much of that time. This may seem like a power grab but quite the opposite was true. During his tenure the first selectman received part time compensation, and managing a small town provides none of the power or wealth perks enjoyed by politicians at the federal or state level. A first selectman for a small town mainly serves. Mr. Curtiss did a fine job serving his town and no one else wanted the burden; he was the one and only choice for the townsfolk for as long as he wanted to be our public servant.

The reign of John J. Curtiss may sound like a benevolent dictatorship as described earlier. The difference between the two lies not with the leaders but the followers. Mr. Curtiss managed, but much of the policies, or politics, were generated by town commissions and town meetings. At the small town level of government liberty involves making up your own mind about the issues independently of your party affiliation; democracy involves having each unique opinion expressed and counted; politics involves the negotiated and wise resolution of diverse and independent positions. This pattern of government has continued for this small town even now that we have candidates from both parties running for

---

10 From one of the reviews of the book on amazon.com.

first selectman.

Our town recently faced a large scale development proposal for a "world class" golf course and upscale residential development. The development team featured a cadre of elite experts including one of the most expensive engineering firms in the state and one of the most expensive golf course architects in the country. The developer was once the co-owner of the Texas Rangers with President Bush II. Since owning a baseball team proved to be George W. Bush's only competent business endeavor you figure the savvy of the co-owner must have had much to do with that. Now his savvy and cadre of experts would be used to influence decisions by small town government.

The development proposal probably had more proponents than detractors initially, and at first was treated favorably by the press. However, two points of concern plagued the proposal from the start. The water-thirsty world class golf course would be located in water-sparse headwaters, affected by a climate inhospitable to golf. Secondly, though the public relation phase of the proposal prominently featured the upscale residences also to be developed, the development team only applied for a golf course in round one of the application phase.

These two points of concern collided when the team of experts claimed that there was little room for alternative layouts of the golf course. They were willing to make small adjustments in response to ecological concerns about amphibian habitat but were adamant against the larger adjustments needed to address public health concerns over water flow. The elite experts stated that the steep slope gradients of the headwater region prevented them from shifting the layout away from pristine headwaters. Though they had 780 acres of property to work with, the steep slope gradients allegedly were too pervasive for relocating a few acres of golf course. The elite experts never explained why the prohibitively steep slopes were better suited for the upscale residential development waiting in the wings, alleging that there may never be any houses built and they could not be legally considered as part of the current application.

Only after the Inland Wetlands Commission of our small town rendered their decision did rather less expensive experts in the specific field of elevation modeling prove that the elite experts had made false claims about slope gradients. The slope gradients where they were proposing to locate the golf course were similar to other areas of the 780 acre property, thus negating that as a real factor in preventing them from shifting away from pristine headwaters. This information was provided to the federal and state agencies required to review projects affecting watercourses and wetlands; combined, these agencies required the elite experts to relocate two holes and provide better quality and quantity of data on the hydrological impacts of their proposal. Apparently, these state and federal agencies no longer had faith in the opinions of these elite experts.

Without the benefit of the elevation modeling information being provided, the Inland/Wetland Commission of our town nevertheless took a cautious approach. The initial two points of concern served as a counterpoint to the alleged economic benefits and excitement of having a world class golf course come to a small town. The citizens of the town were energized and exercised their liberty to express diverse opinions both in support and against the development proposal. The collective wisdom of this input spurred the Inland/Wetland Commission to approve the proposed development—with over 100 conditions attached. In other words, the wisdom from the "crowd" of informed townsfolk came to a similar conclusion as supervisory agencies and people with very specific expertise evaluating the proposal—they allowed the golf course in concept but were suspicious of what the elite experts really had in mind.

Milgram Revisited

The results from the Milgram shock experiments are deeply disturbing. In the original experiments no subject quit before administering a shock at the 300 volt level. At this point the scripted sequence of screams, banging against walls and eventual silence led some to drop out, but only some. The proportion of subjects that continued with the full sequence of shocks in the initial experiment, ending at 450 volts, was sixty-five percent. A substantial majority of people obeyed authority and were willing to shock people even after the screams stopped. Subsequent repetitions of the original experiment done by other researchers, such as the one I was involved in, support this initial finding. Out of every three strangers that you encounter, two of them would be willing to do you serious harm, in response to authoritarianism. The chances are good that you are one such person.

Let us assume some experimental bias. The subjects were largely self-selected and perhaps not truly representative of a free-thinking population exercising their liberty. Maybe at best (or worst) "only" 50% of Americans would obey authority to shock another human being beyond the point of silence. That is enough people abandoning critical thinking and trusting authorities to thwart the efforts of more involved citizens. That is enough people willing to conform to prevent open debate. That is enough people to empower leaders that thirst for power. That is enough people to enable the corporate agenda promoted by the Powell Cabal to do economic harm to the middle class. That is enough people to support slavery, Japanese internment camps or torture. That is enough people to implement the death penalty in a democracy.

The necessary antidote for the dangers of blind trust and conformity includes fostering diversity, independence and decentralized knowledge among citizens. The antidote necessitates aggregating the will of a democracy in a representative manner untainted by wealth or dogma. The antidote requires public servants rather than politicians. The antidote demands that we value wisdom over authoritarianism.

Few would claim that small town government can be emulated at state and federal levels; few would claim that small town government always works well, as in the case presented here. But this case in small town government confirms that wise decisions can and do result when political liberty and democracy is being exercised by a "crowd," and that wise decisions can temper or contradict what the experts and/or leaders are advocating. This is not the current *modus operandi* for national politics. Authorities tell their parties or interest groups what policies to support and the herds fall into lock step to provide bases of power.

Historically, we know that wisdom was intended to be a product of our political liberty. We know this from the advocacy for education by religious groups coming to this land, wanting Christians to autonomously interpret the Bible for themselves. We know this from the First Amendment provisions in the Bill of Rights for free speech. We know this from the checks and balances set up in our three branches of government. Our occasional shortcomings in regards to wisdom will be explored in the remaining essays for Part Two. The common themes throughout describe how our political system:

- Favors authoritarianism over wisdom;
- Favors politicians over public servants;
- Undermines the conditions needed for exercising liberty;
- Undermines the conditions for wise democracy; and
- Employs falsehoods and secrecy to fool middle class people like Hans.

This essay contrasted authoritarianism with wisdom as the functions of a political system. The next essays in this part on politics will cover the major components of our political system: leaders, political parties, media, citizens and the rule of law. They will uncover serious flaws in these components. Based on the empiricism of natural experience an alternative foundation of our natural conditions and rights will be suggested for our political system. Our concluding essay in this part on politics provides a guide for detecting how authoritarians exploit our natural trust to trample our natural condition and rights.

ESSAY 10 – CONFORMING TO PATERNAL DEMOCRACY

Overview

- The invasion of Iraq was a consequence of paternal democracy.
- Apprehension, vanity and cynicism are tools of a paternal democracy to persuade us that our authorities know best.
- Paternal democracy adorns the cloak of presumed infallibility.
- Presumed infallibility caused us to miss the truth about conditions in Iraq.
- Presumed infallibility caused us to impose the dogma of security over liberty.
- Presumed infallibility caused us to use ineffective rationales for preemption.
- Paternal democracies fool citizens with unreliable information.
- Paternal democracies exclude the valid experiences of citizens.
- Our political system attracts politicians to rule in a paternal democracy.
- To strive for wise democracy we must be realistic about the shortcomings of our current paternal democracy.

A Lost Bet

A representative democracy presents a paradox. Democracy implies collecting wisdom from citizens, yet this wisdom must be represented in a few people with authority. In our political system the authorities we empower often act first in their own best interests, or the best interests of their party. This alone is not reprehensible or corrupt. People have a natural tendency to think that what is good for them is good for you. In their minds they think they do what is best for you as they serve their own interests. This is paternal democracy. While not always corrupt this form of democracy resembles authoritarian dictatorship in some ways, with the exception that we get to choose periodically who we want for our dictators, er, representatives.

These essays make a distinction between politicians and public servants. Politicians seek to maximize their authority in a paternal democracy, whether for reasons of knowing what is best for us or purely to advantage themselves. Public servants seek to fulfill the collective wisdom of a representative democracy. To make representative democracy work citizens must avoid the natural adaptation to save energy and blindly trust authorities. Yet even when citizens are willing to spend energy to exercise their political liberty the outcome of a representative democracy depends largely on whether the authorities behave as politicians attempting to preserve and enhance their power or as public servants willing to serve our collective wisdom. The unfortunate consequences of paternal democracy led by politicians are no more evident than in our invasion of Iraq.

The last bet I lost was in 2003, thanks to our leaders behaving as authoritarian politicians rather than as public servants. As a cautious person in regards to bets I only bet pizzas that my opponent and I can share together, that way there are no real losers. As a further precaution I generally make bets where I am privy to some type of "insider's knowledge" that gives me an edge. In the build up to the invasion of Iraq—excuse me, Operation Iraqi Freedom—I had access to such knowledge.

I knew that a former chief weapons inspector in Iraq declared quite emphatically that there were no weapons of mass destruction over there. I knew the CIA ombudsman reported that more field operatives complained about their work being distorted to show a link between Hussein and Al-Qaeda than for any other assignment. I knew that most of the information incriminating Hussein came from an untrustworthy man at the head of a puppet organization set up by neoconservatives seeking to impose their agenda. I knew that the fanatical Islam group in northeast Iraq that authorities claimed to be aligned with Hussein actually wanted to assassinate the dictator. I knew that key members of the administration had made emphatic statements that they were against nation building. I knew that Republicans in general had a history of isolationist tendencies, as evidenced in their recent opposition to military intervention in Kosovo.

This information was available to the administration; available to the "opposition" party in our two-party democracy; and available to the public in 2002, the year before the invasion of Iraq. Granted, such news was seldom available from mainstream corporate media, but in the blossoming age of information technologies anyone could have possessed this information. I considered this insider's knowledge only because most citizens do not spend the energy to research the stated reasons given by authorities for going to war, outside of listening to 24-hour news networks.

Self-defense is the one cause that justifies any action, particularly when the conditions are urgent, but our security was not threatened by Iraq, certainly not in an urgent manner. Surely, I thought, the administration must have a hidden but rational motive, other than invasion, for collecting and disseminating false information. The current weapons inspectors in Iraq constrained Hussein's power considerably. I thought, naively, that the administration intentionally distorted information in order to talk tough and keep weapons inspectors in Iraq while working out a more comprehensive strategy to meet their hidden objectives for the region.

I bet a friend, via email, that President Bush II would not go to war in Iraq unless he was in alliance with the Arab League. Once again, being cautious (and cheap), I included the alliance as an added safeguard against paying for pizzas, fancying how clever I was by adding that stipulation. If the administration really did want war they would need regional alliances, and getting these would be problematic unless the case for invasion truly was a "slam dunk." The Shiite neighbors of Syria and Iran no doubt would be willing partners for removing a Sunni regime, but we already labeled Iran as part of the axis of evil. No disrespect intended, but the willingness of countries such as Kuwait and Qatar to host some aspects of our operations is not a sufficient substitute to the full alliance of the more influential Middle East nations. The Arab League remained the best bet, with precedence for their alliance established in the first Gulf war. While such an alliance was possible, we needed to provide the Arab League with more credible evidence than what corporate media was feeding the American public.

Certainly, even the neoconservatives in the administration were not so vain as to think a Christian dominated country from another hemisphere could impose our will on an Arab nation without a strong Arab alliance; or apprehensive enough to attach a great deal of urgency to such an objective; or cynical enough to authorize dubious preemptive attacks on behalf of hidden objectives. Even if neoconservatives were that foolish there was yet one more safeguard protecting my bet. While citizens have a natural inclination towards authoritarianism, an opposition party has a natural inclination to oppose the party in power whenever they see a possibility to do so. That very mechanism of providing opposition is the means by which a two-party system can draw out debate and collective wisdom in a democracy. The opposition party in Congress could have had a field day destroying the silly assertions that the secular Hussein was in cahoots with the religious fanatic bin Laden. They would be like sharks in a feeding frenzy, with even better evidence available to them than an ordinary citizen such as me possessed by sampling various media sources outside of the corporate mainstream. Pleased with my cleverness and insider's knowledge, I counted on winning another pizza.

Well, so much for the advantage of insider's knowledge. My problem was thinking that valid empirical evidence was important. Anything goes when the evidence presented does not have to pass a smell test.

The obstacles to genuine public debate will be discussed in other essays. For now the invasion and occupation of Iraq serves as a focal point for exploring what can go wrong in a paternal democracy. Whether or not invading and occupying Iraq proves to be advantageous in the long term, the dogma used to unite public opinion compromised our political liberty. Using the invasion of Iraq as a point of reference, let us examine in depth the methods and consequences of authoritarian induced conformity.

Apprehension and Iraq

The support for invading Iraq reached as high as 80% in the months prior to our invasion, despite abundant evidence that might temper people's support for a preemptive strike. In a society as diverse as ours such a high level of support for something as questionable as a preemptive strike of a remote country with a strikingly different culture is a remarkable display of groupthink. One strategy used to achieve this was providing faulty information to induce apprehension. For the selling of the war on Iraq the purported threats were twofold: the threat of weapons of mass destruction and the threat of links between Saddam Hussein and Osama bin Laden.

We know now that there were no WMDs in Iraq and, in fact, substantial evidence refuting this existed even before we attacked. Even had there been legitimate supporting evidence for WMDs, wise counsel would suggest no threat was posed to us. Here are two undisputable facts about Hussein and Iraq: 1) Hussein loved power; 2) even if Iraq had WMDs, that country could not withstand an attack from the United States. Combine these facts with a little sound reasoning and you conclude that Hussein would never take on the United States directly whether he had WMDs or not. If he employed WMDs against the United States, Iraq gets annihilated. That is not a good way to retain power. If authorities wanted to use fear as a selling point they needed to come up with an indirect way by which Iraq could use WMDs to make such a threat plausible.

Ah, yes, the War on Terror, there's the ticket. Support terrorists and you become an immediate threat to the United States. Hussein's Iraq no doubt harbored terrorists, just like virtually every nation in the Middle East. The critically thinking citizen might point out that what makes Iraq special out of all these countries are the comparatively large reserves of oil, but that revelation does not reinforce the selling point of fear as well as an alleged link with al-Qaeda. Once again, simple reasoning should cause doubt that such a link existed. Hussein instituted secular reforms in Iraq, in part to diffuse the hold of Islam on his subjects and increase his own power. These reforms angered bin Laden, a religious fanatic who once referred to Hussein's Baathist Party as infidels.

Some extraordinary supporting evidence would be needed to back up such unlikely claims that Hussein and bin Laden were linked. That is where the Iraqi National Congress comes in. The Iraqi National Congress came into existence in the nineties, with help from an American public relations firm called the Rendon Group.[1] The head of the Iraqi National Congress was Ahmad Chalabi, a person convicted of embezzlement in Jordan and with known ambitions for wielding power in a new Iraq. The INC provided much of the "evidence" that Hussein was linked to al-Qaeda. One might think that information from the Iraqi National Congress would be considered suspect. Our own CIA considered the "evidence"

---

1 As reported by the Center for Media and Democracy on their web site, SourceWatch.

provided by the INC to be false, but such a conclusion interferes with our paternal democracy's strategy of employing fear to sell the war for our own good. Provide lots of faulty information that a link exists between Hussein and al-Qaeda and the problem of them being former adversaries goes away.

Vanity and Iraq

Regardless of how well any particular strategy works, one should always have a backup plan. For those people who refuse to be motivated by fear, perhaps a different button can be pushed, such as vanity. You might wonder how vanity could have been used as a selling point for the Iraq war. Great vanity seeks vast military and economic advantages, the likely motives for an administration infiltrated with neoconservatives and oil industry executives, but these motives never were used as a selling point. How, then, was vanity used to gain conformity? Let us turn to our neighbor Hans to personalize the psychology at work.

Hans is a well-meaning resident of a neighborhood filled with middle class Christians. He helped save the marriage of his next door neighbors, Bob and Mary, providing liberal doses of Scripture when appropriate. He became a pillar of strength when his neighbor Ted lost his job and stopped going to church. Hans was the anchor in the neighborhood for resolving problems.

Unfortunately, this magnanimous role filled Hans with a false pride. A friend of Hans, named Mostafa, confides that his own neighborhood has gone to hell. Hans thinks: "If I can rescue my own neighborhood I can help my friend's as well." While staying at Mostafa's house Hans attempts to work his magic. Unfortunately, Hans could not relate to the troubles of Mostafa's estranged neighbors, Ahmal and Farishta, who did not respond well to quotes from the Bible. Hans knew how to counsel Ted, but did not have a clue what to do about the concern that Sardar no longer prays to Allah. In short, Hans's vanity got him into a situation where he did not belong and could not be effective.

This brings us to the backup plan for selling the war in Iraq; we conformed to the opinion that we could accomplish a good deed. When the war was "over," and our apprehensions were exposed as groundless, vanity for doing good deeds became the focus of our continued involvement. To think that the United States is the best country to be in charge of good deeds for a "neighborhood" like the Middle East takes a great deal of misguided vanity. Sure, we can throw a lot of money around and flex our muscles, but many problems simply cannot be resolved by money and muscle. Good deeds like "stabilizing a region" or "spreading democracy" have more to do with being able to resolve regional disputes using regional wisdom. Good deeds targeted to change behavior require large measures of understanding, common experience and trust building, all in short supply in regards to our relationships with Arab nations. Quite frankly, by this set of criteria the United States is probably the single most country likely to fail at doing a good deed in the Middle East.

The RAND Corporation seems to agree. The Pentagon hired this nonprofit organization to assess the effect of the "surge" of 30,000 American troops in 2007. Increasing troops in Baghdad neighborhoods had the predictable short term effect of reducing insurgency attacks. The administration and various neoconservatives in corporate media and think tanks reported this temporary tactic to be a huge strategic success for our overall goals, but the Pentagon did not want to take their word for it.

The Pentagon has intelligence analysts. If they needed to come up with information that would confirm predetermined policy decisions they were capable of doing so. For that matter, the Pentagon could have hired a number of think tanks with real expertise at manufacturing data to fit an agenda. The good scholars at the Hoover Institute could have organized something like the Boskin Commission that evaluated the Consumer Price Index by discounting the costs of the most expensive and essential goods for the middle class. The good scholars at The Heritage Foundation could have invented an Index with many wonderful indicators that correspond only to what the Pentagon wanted to see. For that matter, the Pentagon could have turned to the Iraqi National Congress, the puppet organization set up by neoconservatives to provide the information they wanted to hear for invading Iraq in the first place.

The Pentagon had a need instead for empirical research. They wanted the meaning of what actually happens on the ground to shape their beliefs, rather than the scholarly research so many think thanks and special interest groups can provide. Thus they hired the RAND Corporation, a think tank that actually specializes in doing nonpartisan, empirical research on global issues for the military. The RAND Corporation reviewed 89 insurgency conflicts since World War II, placing them into categories of government wins, mixed outcomes and government loses. In their list of major conclusions internal factors were more important than external intervention in dictating the outcome. Their report branded our occupation in Iraq as "at best inadequate, at worst counter-productive, and, on the whole, infeasible."[2] The report concluded that "foreign forces cannot substitute for effective local governments, and they can even weaken their legitimacy." Wow! The empiricists at the RAND Corporation will not be on any scholarly neoconservative's Christmas card list this year.

In case you might be convinced of the irrationality of a Christian nation imposing democracy in fundamentalist Muslim lands, there is a back-up vanity plan. The phrase "cut and run" conjures an image of a cowardly marine knocking over women and children as he heads for his quickest helicopter exit. Perhaps the

---

2 From *War by Other Means – Building Complete and Balanced Capabilities for Counterinsurgency* (2008), by David C. Gompert, John Gordon, IV, Adam Grissom et al, available for review at www. rand.org/pubs/monographs/2008/RAND_MG595.2.pdf

same person who came up with that phrase does PR work for the U. S. Chamber of Commerce. How embarrassing to fail in our mission to do a good deed! How embarrassing to waste the past deaths of soldiers in a noble cause, even though we might avoid the deaths of future soldiers! The fact that chicken hawks are the ones admonishing us not to be chickens apparently escapes notice.

The term "honor" gets bantered about as a similar vanity ploy. Perhaps, if the truth came out, we might agree that our soldiers must be in Iraq out of necessity for some currently unmentionable goals, but claiming their occupation amounts to honor is a bit of a stretch. The mightiest nation on earth "shocks and awes" an impoverished country in the Middle East to protect ourselves, and that is honor? We impose democracy through occupation rather than diplomacy, and that is honor? We grant no-bid contracts to American companies to rebuild a country that we destroyed, and that is honor? We protect the oil ministry immediately while allowing weapon dumps to be pillaged, and that is honor? Our response to a politician using the "honor in Iraq" card for getting elected should be like Andre the Giant's delightful quote in the movie *Princess Bride*: "I don't think that word means what you think."

Cynicism and Iraq

There are several reasons why the public accepted the shaky evidence and faulty reasoning behind fear and a good deed as motives for war. Some people need no persuasion for war, any more than they need persuasion to do crimes. Many of those who need to be persuaded conform to authoritarianism, because that conserves energy and makes life more convenient. Corporate media will not vigorously expose bad information for going to war, as that jeopardizes their future access to authorities that generate the bad information. Corporate mass media, in fact, likely plays the most crucial role in groupthink. Presidents have achieved 80% support only a handful of times during times of crisis, all of them coming in the age of mass media, with the earliest being FDR.[3]

Most citizens now believe a primary reason for our presence in Iraq is to secure and control more oil. What makes this extraordinary is that no leader, no neoconservative, no expert, no authority on Middle East affairs aligned with the administration has told the American public that oil is indeed a reason why we occupy that country. None of the corporate mainstream media reporters have pressured the administration consistently to provide explanations for how oil might be linked. The authorities were quick to offer us any other reason we might believe for invading Iraq, not suggesting oil and energy policy as another reason reeks of cynicism for democracy.

---

3 As reported by Ron Feaucheaux for Campaigns & Elections in the article "Ups, Downs, of Presidential Popularity," February 1, 2002.

Whether or not you agree with the policy, invading Iraq for oil has both the strength of valid and reliable empirical evidence and solid inductive reasoning, unlike the arguments for WMDs or links to al-Qaeda. Iraq has the second largest deposits of oil in the Middle East. In addition to the obvious economic benefits of securing that oil there are military benefits. The main reason that the Middle East became such a focus for western powers throughout the twentieth century was the military advantage gained by controlling their oil. Indeed, if securing oil never occurred to the administration as an important reason for invading Iraq, we could brand them in all fairness as idiots.

The administration viewed oil as having strategic importance. Many of the key decision-makers in regards to the war in Iraq belong to an organization called the Project for the New American Century (PNAC). If you visit their web site you will find a Statement of Principles; the signatories for that principle include Dick Cheney, Donald Rumsfeld, I. Lewis (Scooter) Libby and Paul Wolfowitz.[4] The web site presents the views of neoconservatives, calling for whatever actions are necessary to entrench America as the premier global leader. You will note from this web site that the importance of oil for world dominance does not escape their attention.

Many of our executive authorities also had close relationships to the oil industry. They stood to gain financially, at least indirectly, from an economy whose government went to bat for big oil by securing oil reserves abroad. In our paternal democracy no doubt our authorities, well-connected to oil, thought our economy would work best for everyone if our government acted to benefit this industry. The extent to which our economy has been commanded to support the oil industry could be accused as socialist with some justification. Yet our paternal leaders had not the faith in the basic principles of democracy to admit that controlling oil was at least one of the reasons for invasion.

The cynicism authorities held for democracy is now returned in kind. Another shift in the polls has been a decrease in our trust for the president. A majority now believe that he is not honest and trustworthy, nor do they trust his decisions about the war.[5] Our belief in oil as a reason for invading Iraq and our decrease in trust go hand-in-hand. You would have to be cynical about what authorities have been telling us in order to trust your own instincts that oil is an important reason why we invaded Iraq.

Unfortunately, we needed some help to move away from our trust in authority and conformity to trust in the wisdom of our own divergent opinions. The war became drawn out and the media (with the exception of *Fox News*) reported more diligently on the faulty evidence and reasons provided by authorities before the war. In the face of these falsehoods we were forced away from our natural instincts towards authoritarianism and relied on our own collective wisdom, and

4 Visit www.newamericancentury.org.
5 USA Today polls from December 2006 reported these trends.

that wisdom shouts out "OIL!", though the authorities in charge of the war to this day never mention this as an objective.

Our accumulated experiences with American politics contribute to both our cynicism and our wisdom in this matter. We have experienced authorities from both political parties who were apprehensive about telling the truth. Whether their objectives were to maintain power or paternally guide us in ways they felt only they knew best, authorities have and will be dishonest in order to reach those objectives. We have experienced authorities too vain to admit they were wrong. Confessions of error contribute to wisdom but undermine the power of authority. We have experienced authorities too cynical to have faith in the democratic process. They go beyond falsehoods to orchestrate cover-ups and suppress information in clouds of secrecy. As a consequence of these past experiences in American politics the public is not so naïve that we would refuse to believe oil is a reason for invading Iraq simply because authorities never told us to think that.

We have paid a high price for our paternal democracy. What would have happened if we demanded some resolution between what authorities and what our own wisdom told us were the objectives for invading Iraq? If oil was admitted as a primary objective from the start would our strategies for invasion and occupation have been any different? Could the current occupation strategies actually be viewed as successful in regards to a primary objective of keeping the oil secure? Would we democratically approve of this objective even if the strategies were working? At this point these are unanswerable questions because our collective wisdom came too late.

Infallibility and Paternal Democracy

Iraq illustrates how citizens could benefit from wise governance that tolerates divergent opinions, but what about the authorities? A true democracy must tolerate diverse opinions, but such opinions are a thorn to a paternal democracy. Either a true democracy must be created by refusing to empower authorities or the empowered authorities must be convinced by reason or laws that tolerating diverse opinions enhances their own best interests.

John Stuart Mill, in his book *On Liberty* (1859), presented several excellent reasons for protecting independent thought as a basic liberty. Mill expressed his concerns in regards to overwhelming majorities convinced that they are right about a particular issue, but his reasons can be applied to a paternal democracy fostering this groupthink just as well. As a precondition for other reasons justifying independent thought, Mill first established the dangers of presumed infallibility. For example, no one has an infallible memory. Any person will remember some things better than others, but no one can be certain that they have remembered all the details of even the most important events. As a precaution against our flawed memories we take notes.

A delusion of infallible wisdom poses dangers, even if assumed sparingly for certain situations. Infallible wisdom must be grounded in infinite experience, something beyond the grasp of mortals. While taking notes supplements one's own flawed memories, the corollary to this for supplementing one's own flawed wisdom is drawing upon the collective experience of others. When authorities fail to nurture and consider diverse opinions from the collective experience of others they presume themselves infallible, whether intentionally or not.

There may have been two "infallible" sources behind the "wisdom" to invade and occupy Iraq. One of these sources was God. Representative authorities of a democracy have no business assuming they embark on infallible missions endorsed by God. The chief executive of a true democracy is charged to execute the collective wisdom of citizens, not the infallible wisdom of a deity that, in reality, cannot be fathomed by any lone individual. At times President Bush II indicated he was serving God through his Iraq mission. This claim may have been just for show, a few actions by President Bush II suggest he has no intention of serving God; but if he does sincerely believe his claim he becomes unfit to execute the collective wisdom of a democracy that can only succeed by acknowledging the inherent flaws of leaders and allowing for diverse opinions, both good and bad.

Neoconservatives were the other "infallible" source behind the invasion and occupation of Iraq. They probably would not claim themselves to be infallible but their writings reveal arrogance in their convictions and intolerance of opposing views. This neoconservative intolerance has crept into executive decision-making, with seeds planted during the Clinton administration and blossoming during the Bush II administration. The unwarranted certainty of neoconservatives such as Dick Cheney, Donald Rumsfeld, Paul Wolfowitz and Douglas Feith (not to mention neoconservatives in the media such as Rupert Murdoch, William Kristol and Christopher Hitchens) has resulted in as much dogmatic folly as if they thought they were on a mission from God.

Cloaked in presumed infallibility as neoconservatives tend to be, they were prone to suffering the consequences.

Infallibility and Ignorance

An example of unwarranted certainty turned to folly was the neoconservative assumption that we could get the grateful Iraqis to help us topple Hussein. As reported in *Cobra II* (2006), a book about the invasion and occupation of Iraq written by Michael R. Gordon and General Bernard E. Trainor, neoconservatives instituted a program that spent millions of dollars to train an Iraqi opposition force that ended up with only 73 members completing the training.[6] This illustrates the

6 Numerous book reviews cite the account of Gordon and Trainor as one of the most unbiased and authoritative. There is even a supportive quote from Dick Cheney on the cover jacket.

most obvious reason Mill provides for acknowledging that our convictions are prone to error: sometimes those convictions are missing important elements of truth.

Cobra II provides ample material of this in describing Defense Secretary Rumsfeld's micromanagement of the war. Rumsfeld's primary objective was not to fulfill neoconservative ambitions (though he is a signatory to PNAC) but to transform the military into a lean, mean fighting machine. Instead of superiority through numbers Rumsfeld envisioned superiority through mobility and stealth. He, along with many other Republicans, faulted prolonged nation building efforts in the Balkans during the Clinton administration. The duty of the military according to Rumsfeld was quick intervention to meet American objectives, followed by a quick exit to prevent being bogged down with matters not pertinent to American interests.

Rumsfeld relied on his past experiences as a CEO for a pharmaceutical company to manage the military with a heavy hand. Rumsfeld was lauded for his corporate management, receiving awards from both the Wall Street Transcript (1980) and the Financial Times (1981). Rumsfeld can boast such accomplishments as getting aspartame, better known as NutraSweet, approved by the Food and Drug Administration despite health concerns. He also received generous compensation for his company's sale to Monsanto, a chemical giant that never was too concerned about health issues.

The removal of the Taliban from governing Afghanistan was accomplished using Rumsfeld's vision for a transformed military. The initial success of that effort caused Rumsfeld to gloat that his methods provided far better results for our interests than the ongoing process of nation building that occurred in the Balkans.[7] With giddy confidence he suggested that using a streamlined military force would probably work even better for a country like Iraq.

Let us assume that being designed for stealth and mobility is the best direction for our military. Nevertheless, life deals us many exceptions to the rules, and Iraq proved to be such an exception. As *Cobra II* reveals, Rumsfeld believed in the infallibility of his transformative vision and his CEO experience to an extent that prevented him from accepting diverse opinions from either military commanders or the State Department. In the end, Rumsfeld's presumed infallibility was to his great detriment, even before his resignation. His vision for transforming the military received a serious setback that could have been averted had he acknowledged the diverse opinions expressing the pitfalls to be faced in Iraq. To add insult to Rumsfeld's injury, diverting resources to Iraq now has hampered our once "model" engagement in Afghanistan as well. Based on Rumsfeld's own criteria for limited engagement, our past intervention in the Balkans now looks like the model for military and nation building efficiency compared to what has been

---

7 From his speech titled "Beyond Nation Building," given upon his reception of the Intrepid Freedom Award on February 14, 2003.

happening in Iraq, and even Afghanistan.

The former Secretary of Defense would have been better off, in terms of meeting his own stated objectives, if he accepted diverse opinions. We are involved in prolonged nation building in both Afghanistan and Iraq, with the prospects for success much dimmer than our Balkans engagement during the nineties. Rumsfeld once bemoaned the 500 million dollar price tag involved in stabilizing and rebuilding the Balkans, a now paltry sum compared to our current commitments. Transforming the military very well may be a desirable goal but the folly of Rumsfeld's once presumed infallibility, not allowing diverse opinions to be factored into consideration, has compromised his own vision.

Infallibility and Dogma

Mill cites the avoidance of dogma as another advantage to encouraging diverse opinions. If diverse opinions are not allowed as a challenge to our convictions we increase the likelihood of not understanding what they really mean. With the lack of understanding that accompanies dogmatic belief we risk betraying our own convictions.

We cherish America as the Land of the Free and the Land of Liberty. Our most cherished monument is the Statute of Liberty. We fancy ourselves as pioneers of democracy (literally not true, but the important thing here is the perception) and the primary guardian of the free world. Our belief that America stands foremost for liberty is so strong, and so unquestioned, as to reach the level of dogma.

In recent times our representative authorities have instilled a competing dogma among the citizens of America, that a commitment to security trumps everything, including liberty. If diverse opinions were encouraged and aggregated from citizens we would find some Americans value liberty over security, and some treasure security more. As a third possibility our collective wisdom could arrive at Mill's utilitarian understanding of liberty, which holds that only through a devout commitment to liberty can real security be achieved. Instead, authorities have reversed Mill's premise, persuading America that only through a devout commitment to security can liberty really be achieved.

The leading authority in the current administration for instilling the dogma of security first is Vice President Dick Cheney. Just as an aside to expose my own biases, I cannot think of a better poster boy than Cheney to exemplify the cynicism, vanity and cowardice alluded to in these essays as the foundation of our current woes. He manages to comprehensively incorporate all three vices together with his frequent assertions that disputing the administration's objectives or strategies in Iraq aids the terrorists. Fearing diverse opinions on Iraq shows cowardice, chastising people for exercising their liberty demonstrates cynicism for a democratic ideal and assuming the moral authority to make such chastisements reveals vanity. Cheney has been effective, though; even pundits from the "opposition" party automatically accept the dogma that security trumps liberty.

Establishing two competing dogmas—liberty first in Iraq and security first at home—has backfired for our authorities. On the one hand we have a security-conscious citizenry unwilling to make the sacrifices of the World War II generation to fight for liberty. This will limit the administration's ability to commit troops and money, and to prolong the engagement in Iraq. On the other hand we have instilled doubt throughout the world regarding both our sincerity and effectiveness for promoting liberty abroad. We are not becoming the respected global leader that neoconservatives like Cheney envisioned. By shunning diverse opinions that would have prevented the formation of dogmas, indeed, by branding diverse opinions as unpatriotic or even traitorous, our authorities have compromised the ability to maintain either liberty or security, while damaging their credentials and credibility as representative authorities.

Infallibility and Incompetence

Invading Iraq appears to be a mistake at this point, but even if in the cosmic order of things the invasion proves to be the right thing to do history will judge the Bush II administration harshly. The cause relates to one final advantage cited by Mill for allowing diverse opinions: by allowing opinions to be challenged authorities are forced to make effective cases in their defense. The best case, by default, involves letting valid and reliable experiences guide the formation of opinions. Authoritarians want the easy task of preaching to the choir, with anything they say determining the meaning of experience instead. They discourage diverse opinions and use rhetoric to captivate the citizenry, rather than delving into the type of empirical evidence and reason that will withstand the test of time. Consequently when things go wrong, as they most certainly have in Iraq, the old rhetoric becomes ineffective.

Without effective justification for action having been offered historians discount the rhetoric of previous authoritarians entirely. Neither future historians nor leaders will conclude from our Iraq experience that hyped suspicions are a legitimate cause for a preemptive attack. Thus, should any legitimate cause ever exist for preemptive attack against a remote, less advance nation, our current authoritarians have rendered as ineffective for the future their own opinions for taking this course of action.

Lately, authorities have been telling us that the Iraq War has enabled us to fight the terrorists over there so they will not fight us here at home. Such an assertion derives from presuming our original motives for security as infallible. Terrorists must have both the motivation and the means to do harm. Let us assume that our presence in Iraq has limited the means of terrorists in Iraq to do harm. By so doing we have not limited the means of terrorists in other countries, while increasing the motivation of terrorists everywhere. Since Iraq was never the country where most of the terrorists congregated, eliminating the means for a small subset of terrorists while universally increasing motivation is a fool's bargain. Effective strategies would target both the motivation and the means of terrorists everywhere.

In addition to being ineffective, our strategy of "fighting the terrorists over there" has been costly. We went eight years between foreign terrorist attacks here at home, which occurred between the first years of the Clinton and Bush II administrations. By the time the Bush II presidency ends we will have lost more people than during the 9/11 attack, with additional high costs in failed infrastructure investments and collateral damage. Of course, authorities have been cultivating an attitude that the loss of soldiers abroad does not matter as much as security at home, since only soldiers should be willing to risk their lives while all other citizens should fear for ours. There is much to doubt about our authorities these days, and their claims that Iraq is still being fought as a security measure ranks high on the list. This leads us to a disturbing possibility that our representative authorities simply are ignorant about how to collect wisdom from anybody.

Unreliable Paternal Democracy

I assumed for the sake of discussion that some of our policies for Iraq represented the best course of action, whether the goal be transforming the military, promoting liberty or enhancing our security. I examined how refusing to consider diverse opinions prevented authorities from meeting their own stated goals. In so doing I provided evidence that nurturing independent thought as a basic liberty is in the best interest of authorities whose own opinions and policies become amended and strengthened. The value of independent thought would be all the greater for authorities if their initial policies were flat out wrong, and considering diverse opinions served as a corrective measure that saved them from future embarrassment. In theory, then, representative authorities and a true democracy devoted to wise governance can coexist and thrive.

But in a paternal democracy authorities mainly want the power to implement their objectives without alteration, and are not compelled towards wisdom by either good sense or law. In a paternal democracy authorities hide policies and objectives if they suspect that a true democratic process would compromise those objectives. In a paternal democracy authorities value deceit more than diversity, if they believe deceit helps them do what is best for their constituents. An example of this would be hiding and distorting information related to our invasion of Iraq, if authorities in our paternal democracy suspected that the citizenry would not go along with this objective based on the truth. Under such conditions a paternal democracy views independent thought as a threat, and the information authorities provided would be unreliable indicators of what they really believed.

In the politics of deceit we gain a better understanding of real independent thought. The advantages of such thinking come from only the freedom of honest thought. We should expect that diverse opinions include many bad ones, but as long as they are honest and representative of the vastly different experiences of citizens aggregating those opinions through sound democratic processes we should yet arrive at collective wisdom. However, if our independent thought should be corrupted by dishonest and manipulative authorities then we have sabotaged the liberty necessary for our collective wisdom to bloom. Let us illustrate this with Neanderthal politics, which you may or may not find similar to our own system.

Nine Neanderthals need to form a hunting party. Six Neanderthals think that killing a mastodon would bring the best return on meat for the tribe. Three Neanderthals think that killing a saber-tooth tiger would be best, because of a belief that eating tiger meat bestows a special quality of fierceness. Two of the six Neanderthals who think that the mastodon would be best for the tribe nevertheless want for themselves the excitement of hunting a saber-tooth. Assuming that majority rules, the beast the hunters decide to kill depends on the advantages or disadvantages of being honest.

If Neanderthal politics required the hunters to eat last, jeopardizing whether they might receive a portion of meat, then hunters would make reliable decisions about what is best for the tribe. Though some of the hunters have misguided opinions, the collective wisdom evident in the majority leads them to bag the mastodon. If Neanderthal politics protects the hunters from suffering the same consequences as the rest of the tribe by getting first dibs on the meat, then two of the hunters have more to gain by being dishonest and their decisions are unreliable. Adding the two unreliable opinions to the three misguided opinions leads the hunting party to bag the saber-tooth tiger. Because of the dishonesty of self-serving hunters both wisdom and the food supply suffered.

We seldom know for certain the reliability of policy decisions. Vice President Cheney may be passionate about security or he may be passionate about Halliburton. If he valued stabilizing the Middle East for our security as much as he claimed, considering diverse opinions and challenges to his authority would have served his objectives better, and we can expect that he is duly chagrined about how his dogmatic leadership style compromised his plans for Iraq. If Vice President Cheney cared more about getting his former company "first dibs" in a war-induced gravy train, then he gained from being secret and dishonest. He would have compromised his hidden objectives if he explained that they were more about oil and the military industrial complex than about security through stability. We likely would not be comforted that his hidden objectives are being met in Iraq as we build permanent military bases and control the oil ministry.

Invalid Paternal Democracy

When a paternal democracy keeps citizens uninformed about hidden objectives the reason relates in some way to security. The stated reasons for secrecy, when they must be given, call for national security: securing us from foreign or domestic enemies, or foreign competitors, who would prevail if they knew how we planned to deal with them. The actual reasons often are to "secure" objectives or actions against the criticisms of citizens, political opponents or other branches of government. Citizens need to distinguish which type of security authorities really seek, and when this poses a threat to our liberty and collective wisdom. The 1997 Congressional Report of the Commission on Protecting and Reducing Government Secrecy declared:

> "secrecy has significant consequences for the national interest when, as a result, policymakers are not fully informed, government is not held accountable for its actions, and the public cannot engage in informed debate."

In other words, secrecy reduces the validity of what is being decided. Wisdom comes from experience. Our experiences determine the meaning of any information that government might provide for us. The "Wisdom of Crowds," as advocated by James Surowiecki in his book of that title, develops from the wide array of diverse experiences providing meaning to information. While few citizens qualify as experts in regards to government policy, nevertheless by aggregating the wealth of meanings from public experience we produce collective wisdom. Citizens do not need to be informed about all the workings of government, just those details for which their own experiences add validity to what is being decided.

Most details affecting national security have no impact on our liberty, simply because most of us do not have the experience for these details to be meaningful. Knowing the identity of a covert CIA operative means nothing to most citizens; we do not have the experience to suggest who could do a better job. When President Bush II declassified information relating to the identity of Valerie Plame he did not enhance our liberty or independent thought, though he did seriously infringe on the liberty of Plame's future career aspirations.

The type of information that most impacts our independent thought relates to what we want from government and how we want government to operate. Vice President Cheney's confidential energy task force meetings, which mainly involved donors to his campaign from the oil sector, likely included important details about government's objectives and strategies for securing energy. Let us assume, just hypothetically of course, that securing oil in Iraq was one of the topics addressed at those confidential meetings. We should not consider this too bold an assumption. If oil executives did not have securing global oil as one of their chief concerns, we must conclude that the oil industry sector is run by mentally challenged executives.

The strategy of using force to secure foreign oil holds meaning for citizens. Our sons and daughters would be involved in the use of force, and we all have our own ideas regarding our dependence on oil. Removing this basic issue from our consideration thus restricts our liberty and the nation's ability to draw from our collective wisdom. Exposing these issues, stripped of certain details, would not have enhanced the ability of foreign enemies to prevail. If we want to use force against a grossly overmatched country we will not be stopped. The only real security purpose for such secrecy was securing objectives and strategies from the validity of public criticism and debate.

If Iraqi oil was brought up at the confidential meeting, and relevant objectives and strategies then brought to the public's attention, one of two things might have happened differently in regards to the eventual invasion and occupation. If in subsequent public discourse our democracy provided our support to securing oil by means of force, then we would not have to be so concerned now about stabilizing Iraq. We build our permanent military bases, we control the oil ministry, we protect our own soldiers and allies and we let other events play out however they might. This may sound callous, but the report provided by the RAND Corporations confirms that we are not the best option for stabilizing Iraq. On the other hand, if the collective wisdom of our experiences judged that securing foreign oil by force was not a valid course of action for security or democracy, then we do not invade in the first place.

We could assume instead that the authorities and energy experts at Vice President Cheney's confidential energy meetings were not competent enough to realize that Iraqi oil could relate to our own energy objectives. We do not know if such details escaped the oil industry executives at these meetings, since the Supreme Court ruled that Cheney's meetings could remain secret. The pretext given by the administration was that you cannot expect executives to provide honest input unless they can trust that their input is confidential. While we should not be surprised that corporate executives have a hard time with honest input, a redacted version that protects the identity of the guilty still could have provided the necessary details with which citizens could exercise their political liberty. Then again, we should not be surprised by the Supreme Court's decision. Throughout its history, the Supreme Court repeatedly demonstrates a lack of comprehension regarding Surwiecki's wisdom of crowds or Mill's independent thought; but that is a topic for another essay.

The "Best and Brightest" Politicians

When politicians decline to serve the wisdom of collective democratic experience, what masters do they obey in their quest for power? The answer lies in what we use to attract politicians to office. We provide financial perks to our elected officials unavailable to most citizens. We are told this must be done in order to have "the best and the brightest" running our country. The irony of this seems to be lost on most citizens these days. We have assumed that there is a higher correlation between merit and being motivated by wealth, than between merit and being motivated by integrity. For the highest authorities that "serve" our country, we have instituted a system to attract politicians rather than public servants. Let us explore some of the ways that we allow wealth to be the master of our highest elected officials.

You can come from a humble background and run for President, as Ronald Reagan and Bill Clinton proved. However, you cannot aspire to remain middle class in our political system. The level of finance required to run a campaign necessitates being well connected with wealth. The sources of wealth become masters that steer politicians away from serving wisdom. The 2000 election featured large contributions from energy corporations, most of which went to President Bush II, a man who failed as an oil executive. Bush received over $110,000 from the coal industry, $290,000 from nuclear power, $447,000 from electric utilities, and over 1.8 million dollars in campaign contributions from oil and gas (maybe Bush II's fellow oilmen judged that his failures in the oil industry necessitated some extra cash for him to succeed at anything).[8]

President Bush II did not have the entire energy industry wrapped up. Al Gore received the most campaign contributions from alternative energy industries, which collectively infused his campaign coffer with $8,300 of cool cash. If Al Gore had become president and held his own confidential energy meeting, you need not fear that only wind geeks would be at the table discussing their secret plans, leaving the poor oil industry out. Gore received over $140,000 from oil and gas, more than ten times the amount he received from alternative energy contributions, but less than ten times the amount President Bush II received from the same energy sector.

Once a politician gets elected they become well-compensated, at least from a middle class perspective. The president receives an annual salary of $400,000, eight times the median family income, with an expense allowance of $50,000. Once President Bush II leaves office he will receive a pension of about $150,000 a year, with up to another $150,000 provided to maintain an office and staff. The president's salary started at $25,000 for George Washington, an amount that quadrupled to $100,000 by 1949, one-hundred and sixty years later. The salary quadrupled again by 2001, fifty-two years later.

---

8 Statistics were obtained from the Center for Responsive Politics, at their www.opensecrets.org web site.

Receiving eight times the income of a middle class family may be more than enough compensation for public servants, but we need to consider that many elected officials come from the corporate world, where many CEOs make more than 200 times the amount of their blue collar employees. Given such disparity, the compensation we provide elected officials may not be enough to attract many potential politicians from the corporate world. That is why the pot needs to be sweetened with a revolving door between the corporate and government sectors, facilitated by lobbying and public relations firms.

By the way, George Washington refused the salary he was offered for being president, but that was before our country knew that the "best and brightest" authorities were supposed to serve wealth instead of democracy.[9]

Faith in Wisdom

We no doubt have precisely the type of government our culture deserves when we create the expectations that our "best and brightest" should be attracted to wealth and power instead of wisdom. Yet in all my experiences with work, community and various organizations the people who served others best were the ones most motivated to serve, regardless of compensation. Granted, they were not all Ivy Leaguers like our president, but most appear to me just as bright or brighter. Dear reader, please consider all the true public servants you have known—the people who do yeoman's work at the PTO, the church fair or the community association—and see if your recollections of the type of people motivated to serve well have greater allegiances to people or wealth.

Throughout these essays we describe the problems of being cynical, yet these essays also suggest that we should not blindly trust authorities. Resolving this apparent conflict warrants some further explanation.

When you approach a used car salesman you should not pay the initial asking price. Instead, you negotiate for the best deal, with an understanding of how buying used cars works. Thinking a good friend would cheat you out of money is cynical; thinking a used car salesman wants to maximize profits is realistic. These essays claim that the ideals of democracy and liberty would produce wisdom. Doubting that wisdom could be produced from these ideals would be cynical. Knowing there are kinks in the system to be negotiated is realistic.

We have created a political system that values authoritarianism over wisdom. We are not being cynical to observe when authorities behave in ways dictated by that prioritization, we are being realistic. If our political system breeds politicians rather than public servants, then citizens need to "negotiate" with them accordingly. Either we change the political system to one that entices public

---

9 Statistics on presidential compensation comes from the Congressional Quarterly's *Guide to the Presidency*.

servants and serves wisdom or we "trust" politicians to behave in a certain way, as we would a used car salesman, and play an aggressive role in exercising our political liberty.

Protecting our independent thought from politicians is a necessary part of this negotiation, but not sufficient for either liberty as described by Mill, or collective wisdom as outlined by Surowiecki. In addition to diverse freedom of thought Mill cited the necessity of self-actualization as an important ingredient in our liberty. We must be allowed not only to think, but to be who we truly are. The meaning we take from our experiences must be uniquely our own. This relates to Surowiecki's criteria of independence and decentralization as conditions for collective wisdom.

Anything that tends to homogenize us, to dictate how we provide meaning to our experiences, constrains the wisdom that can come out of our aggregated experiences. The greatest "homogenizers" in our culture are special interest groups. There are no other special interest groups as powerful and influential as our political parties. Let us turn to them next.

ESSAY 11 – DEPENDENCE ON PARTY DEMOCRACY

Overview

- Political parties seek to enhance and maintain their authority.
- Our early leaders, government and culture disdained political parties.
- Negative campaigning was the initial impetus for party democracy.
- Our founding fathers predicted that parties would promote self-interests over the public interest and become corrupted.
- Party democracy shuns wisdom by concentrating wealth, power, and dogma.
- Political balance through the negative feedback of an opposition party has failed.
- Political balance through the negative feedback of party fragmentation has failed.
- Political balance through the negative feedback of corruption is failing.
- Our political system links wealth, power and dogma in a way that overcomes negative feedback.
- Without negative feedback party democracy becomes totalitarian.

Party Confusion

I once ran to be elected as a local representative on a regional Board of Education. My qualifications for the position were solid. I was a teacher in both high school and college. My Masters degree was in education. I did some graduate research on educational administration and finance. I volunteered to serve on a committee that reexamined our school district's current approach to regionalism. Most importantly, I have terrific name recognition in this small rural town of 1700 people. I have many relatives in town, with some of us residing here longer than most of the voters.

People congratulated me after the election for my impressive showing. That was small consolation, considering that I lost with only about 25% of the vote. My biggest handicap was that I did not then, never had before and up to this day do not belong to a political party. For awhile I thought I might someday join a party; there is pressure in our society to do so. But I was having trouble understanding what each major party believed. Initially, I gave each the benefit of the doubt that they stood for a few principles, but whenever I thought I had identified one such principle a party would violate that very principle at a national level.

In general terms I understand that Democrats are supposed to be liberals and Republicans are supposed to be conservatives. Leaving aside the inherent inconsistencies of those ideological labels, neither party can claim to be consistent adherents. We have explored already just how "unconservative" the Bush II administration has been at times. Let us examine briefly now the record of the Clinton administration. Much of the media consolidation took place under the watch of President Bill Clinton, as did consolidation of the oil industry. In addition, his administration cracked down on welfare recipients, shifted the tax burden away from capital gains to wages and social security, strengthened the health insurance industry, consolidated financial institutions, delivered balanced budgets and was the first administration since before FDR to make some gains at shrinking government. Some of these achievements were good for the middle class, some bad, but none of them could be called liberal, at least not in accordance with what the "liberal" or conservative brands mean at this current hour.

Throughout most of the twentieth century Republicans were the ones against overreaching power. Teddy Roosevelt was known as the trust buster in his campaign against large monopolies. The Republicans in Congress during the multiple terms of Franklin Roosevelt introduced legislation to curb the increasing power of the executive branch. Dwight Eisenhower warned us of the looming dangers being presented by the military industrial complex. Nowadays if you want to join a party that wants to curb the overreaches of power you best look towards the Democrats. On the other hand, you could paraphrase the advice provided by Mark Twain about New England weather: if you don't like the direction in which the political winds are blowing for your party, just wait a few election cycles.

Teasing out what has remained consistent about either party we find that each holds to exactly one inviolate principle, which happens to be one and the same for both parties: the enhancement and retention of authority. This goal necessitates demands for party loyalty. Party members that waiver in commitments to their party undermine the influence and authority of their party. By creating loyalty to a party platform, as changing as it might be, parties rob the independence of their members. Both political parties are, in essence, the most powerful of all our special interest groups. Identifying this has made my political future clear: I never will join either major party. I do not care if my future for local public office remains bleak; I'll serve my town in other ways.

Granted, there are some slight distinctions that can be made between Democrats and Republicans. Republicans attempt to exploit the link between power and wealth by pandering more to corporations. Democrats attempt to exploit the link between power and dogma by pandering more to interest groups. Should anyone choose to challenge me on this, to lay claim that both parties pander equally to both corporations and interest groups, I shall concede the point without argument. For those convinced that our two major political parties have been a boon for our democracy that, in theory, is supposed to aggregate wisdom for wise governance, I hope to persuade you otherwise.

Party Disdain

Nothing in our Constitution calls for the creation of political parties. This omission reflects the sentiments of our founding fathers. The person who best encapsulated—or perhaps successfully influenced—middle class attitudes in colonial times was our favorite pamphleteer, Thomas Paine. He wrote:

> "It is the nature and intention of a constitution to prevent governing by party, by establishing a common principle that shall limit and control the power and impulse of party, and that says to all parties, thus far shalt thou go and no further. But in the absence of a constitution, men look entirely to party; and instead of principle governing party, party governs principle."[1]

Even the aristocracy most responsible for forming and leading our early government disdained the notion of parties. Alexander Hamilton, who favored a strong national government, stated: "Nothing could be more ill-judged than that intolerant spirit which has at all times characterized political parties."[2] Others like Hamilton that favored a strong national government thought that parties, through power struggles of self-interest, would only fracture a consensual approach to establishing the national interest. Alexander Hamilton eventually would form and lead the political party known as the Federalists.

Thomas Jefferson, who championed states rights, agrarian virtue and individuals as independent moral agents, had this to say about parties: "If I could not go to heaven but with a party, I would not go there at all."[3] Others like Jefferson feared the power that would be wielded by a strong national government, and thought that wise governance arose directly from the liberty of citizens, not parties, to have a direct impact on more localized government. Thomas Jefferson became the figurehead for the party created by James Madison, first known as the Democrat-Republicans.

How did opponents of parties, in a political system designed not to have parties, in a culture that generally disdained parties, come to be the leaders of parties? Let us check in with a young colonialist named Hans.

---

1   From First Principles of Government (1795)
2   Federalist #1 paper (October 27, 1787).
3   In a letter written to Francis Hopkinson Paris (March 13, 1789).

Party Evolution

The Federal Convention of 1787 that led to the framing of the Constitution reflected the spirit of the times. The Articles of Confederation were not working well and needed to be changed. No parties existed to promote a particular agenda; people gathered with a common sense of purpose to make their exciting new government better. The convention was nevertheless contentious. Factions developed over the central issue facing the colonialists: the balance of power between national and state governments.

An excited Hans kept track of the debate over the balance of power with keen interest. He favored states rights over a strong national government, as did the majority of agrarian colonialists at the time, with the conviction that they had rid themselves of the centralized English rule and did not need a surrogate. History would judge that Hans was on the losing side of this issue, but he was not as disappointed as one might think. The Constitution that was crafted did not impose the will of one faction at the total expense of the other. Alexander Hamilton did not do a bawdry victory dance in the metaphorical end zone of the convention hall. Instead, a humble compromise had been designed to make both factions feel that their input and concerns were being addressed.

The Constitution granted more power to the national government than did the Articles of Confederation, but to make sure the states rights faction approved nine out of thirteen states had to ratify the Constitution to make the document the law of the land. The promise had to be made to include a Bill of Rights that would protect the independence of citizens from centralized power. The factions that resolved this issue could now dissolve with good will, though involved colonialists like Hans would be ready to support different factions with different alliances of people over the next important issue to arise.

The factions formed for the sake of this one issue never fully dissolved. The resulting government was dominated by the people from the faction that had supported a strong national government. In retrospect this was a natural development; a government designed to be stronger attracted in disproportionate numbers public servants who wanted stronger government. Colonialists like Hans started to feel disenfranchised. He was OK with the compromise reached through the crafting and ratification of the Constitution, but what started as an issue to be resolved now appeared to be an ideology that was entrenched, as were the people running his government. Hans joined an organized special interest group called the Democrat-Republicans as a means of providing a stronger voice to his concerns.

Over time the voice of the group grew stronger. The people that favored a strong national government organized their own special interest group in response. To counterbalance the influence of each other both groups grew in strength and outreach. From factions formed to work out the solution to a single issue they became parties devoted to promoting a comprehensive ideology over time. Each party formed as a negative reaction to neutralize the power of the other, more than to positively promote their own agenda. Negative campaigning was once the impetus, and now the lifeblood, of political parties.

Party Ideology

We should appreciate what our founding fathers did, but not blindly trust all their actions. That would be like having blind trust in authorities. Corporate media and politicians cite the acrimony among the different factions of our founding fathers as justification for the current venom used in our public discourse. If they grew belligerent towards each other, as started to occur between colonialists engaged in the states rights squabble, then belligerence must be natural and good for our government. Yet the hyperbole used by our forefathers undermined their ideals for government, resulting in the political parties they knew would compromise their very own political ideals.

There are significant differences between the sides of an issue that leads to factions and the ideologies that become the foundations of parties. Factions dissolve once an issue has been addressed. Different groups of people form new factions to influence the next important issue. The faction that supports a new educational funding plan has both some of the proponents and opponents of a former state income tax resolution.

In contrast, adherents to party ideologies do not independently coalesce with new groups of people as specific issues and their conscience dictates. The multiple fracturing of a party over different interests would prevent the party from presenting a united front over their core interests, or to even agree on what those core interests should be. Instead, dependency is created to a package of beliefs over the long term, with the faith that supporting the total package provides the best chance of success for their important issues embedded within that package. This may lead them to support some issues that they might view differently from an independent angle, but that is the price to be paid for dependency on the party's dogma.

The founding fathers were concerned about special interests replacing the public interest of republican government. They feared that the politics of government would involve partisan battles rather than a nonpartisan commitment to what worked best for all. Such battles would sacrifice virtue as a goal of governance (or campaigning). In the absence of a monarchy for establishing order, the colonialists anticipated that party politics in a republic would lead to corruption.[4]

If our founding fathers are watching us from the grave, they no doubt

---

4 This assessment of early attitudes towards political parties is from *The History of the United States, 2nd Edition* .(2003), a course on CD by Allen C. Guelzo, available from The Teaching Company.

are shocked at being used by corporate media apologists to justify our current incivilities. While taking some amount of justified pride in their communal approach to establishing our constitutional government, they are chastising themselves for allowing special interest politics to corrupt what they created. Now that the fears of our founding fathers have come to pass we need to address an important question. Do people need to be dependent on political parties in a democracy, or does party democracy need to instill dependency in people? Should we be more vigilant at enforcing laws to remove the corrupt politicians that flock to our existing system of government, or create new laws or a new system that minimizes the number of potential public servants being corrupted by party democracy?

The Party System

With interests and members united a political party gains greater power to influence policy. The power to influence becomes an increasingly important end apart from the ideology. In fact, ideologies may be adjusted in order to maintain or enhance the power to influence policy. Party members adapt to these adjustments of beliefs, just as they adapted to the original package that might have compromised some of their beliefs over specific issues. Parties that adapt to maintain authority prove themselves worthy of investment for wealthy interests that want a piece of that influence. A political party thus embodies a synergy of dogma, power and wealth that occurs over time.

Some interesting evolutions of parties resulted from this natural adaptation to coalesce interests, power and wealth. The lineage of present day Republicans can be traced to the original Federalist Party. The party of Alexander Hamilton was all about promoting commerce and corporations through the means of a strong national government at the expense of state autonomy. Yet corporations settle for the intervention of any level of government to concentrate capital. While a strong national government is still essential for corporations to be successful, business corporations are chartered by state government. Hamilton's party and conservatives backed states rights through much of the twentieth century, though in the new millennium they did not practice what they recently preached.

Political parties, in effect, shun wisdom; their dependency on wealth and dogma to maintain power results in conformity to a party platform. The aggregation of citizens achieved by a political party does not collect the localized experiences of members in a grassroots movement, but imposes doctrines based on what seems to work best for synthesizing interests, power and wealth at the national level. This fostered dependency on doctrine that divorces political parties from wisdom also guarantees the eventual corruption of parties.

Albert Einstein made famous the premise that we needed to trust the empirical data over our strongly held theories, in essence a renewed support for empiricism. Former doctrines needed to be abandoned in order to accept that light could bend or that time could slow down. We need to apply empiricism to our political system of parties. Trusting the data leads us to conclude that party politics will never be suited for the pursuit of wisdom. A two-party system is no better than a one-party system in that regard. Our party democracy has not been the vanguard for the wisdom that a democracy truly seeks, but a hindrance. If we can just let go of that sacred cow we just might be able to make the appropriate adjustments to both enhance wisdom and minimize corruption.

Having stated that, there already are some natural safeguards in place for our two-party system. As with many systems there are homeostatic mechanisms to prevent the extremes from knocking the system out of balance. These mechanisms include:

- Opposition parties fostering debate,
- Majority parties becoming fractured and
- Public abhorrence to corruption.

Our current tribulations stem not so much with the inherent flaws of political parties, but the weakening of homeostatic mechanisms in our political system that keep parties from becoming too powerful and foolish. We will see how the cause of these weakening mechanisms relates to the growing phenomenon of echo chambers and media consolidation.

Homeostasis and Party Opposition

I have given the administration of President Bush II considerable flak for the Iraq War. Viewed from a system perspective the Democrats deserve greater blame. Foolish mistakes are to be expected in a party democracy, but homeostatic mechanisms prevent these mistakes from getting out of hand. Let us look at this problem another way. Bad information and decisions about Iraq are like viruses, the Bush II administration is like a circulatory system and the opposition party is like an immune system. The circulatory system may be at fault for spreading the virus, but the task of the immune system is to contain the spread.

In a two-party system where one party clearly rules, as occurred in the early millennium, the other party must clearly oppose. The value of opposition is no more evident than in the compromises worked out for our Constitution. George Washington had this to say about the process:

> "Upon the whole I doubt whether the opposition to
> the Constitution will not ultimately be productive
> of more good than evil; it has called forth, in its

defense, abilities which would not perhaps have been otherwise exerted that have thrown new light upon the science of Government, they have given the rights of man a full and fair discussion, and explained them in so clear and forcible manner, as cannot fail to make a lasting impression."[5]

Washington's words foreshadow Mill's defenses for preserving the liberty of thought in *On Liberty* (1859). The opposition insured that important elements were added to the Constitution; the opposition forced the proponents to ground their advocacy in rationality; and their advocacy for national government only grew stronger through the challenge. Thus, the opposition party not only provides a check on power, but an important medium for wisdom. We could praise opposition parties for this crucial role but that would be too generous on our part. The opposition party opposes for reasons of self-interest, just as they did when they first formed. Yet this mechanism for preserving balance utterly failed us in the months before the Iraq war. The facts were there to at least generate heated opposition and debate but the will to expose these facts was lacking.

To illustrate the problem more specifically let us focus on one particular Democratic senator, Hillary Clinton. By all accounts former Senator Clinton has a sharp mind that she can wield for the sake of exposing facts and generating debate. In addition to providing opposition for the sake of her party, one could reasonably expect Senator Clinton to have provided opposition for her own sake. After all, she has witnessed one dynasty take hold of the presidency, the possibility of her continuing a Clinton dynasty as well as becoming the first women president had to at least cross her mind even before the Iraq invasion. When the discussion begins about increasing executive power for the war on terror and, by extension, a possible preemptive invasion of Iraq, one might think that Senator Clinton would relish the chance to sully the ruling party a bit. Throw in one other factor, that there is a moral obligation to review all the facts before unleashing the atrocities of war, and you would figure that a heated debate over the topic was inevitable.

Senator Clinton certainly had the material for initiating such a heated debate. Independent of any information our intelligence agencies might gather, or what *Fox News* might report, the world at large knew that Hussein and bin Laden were enemies. As a secular Sunni with a thirst for power Hussein feared the fanatic Sunnis that included bin Laden. Hussein had, in fact, issued a decree against the Wahhabi religion, bin Laden's puritan brand of Islam, and violators warranted the death sentence. Bin Laden, for his part, had issued a fatwa against Hussein and the secular infidels governing Iraq. The two alleged collaborators had issued death sentences against each other prior to our government's call for a

---

5   In a letter written to John Armstrong (April 25, 1788).

preemptive strike.

You could imagine how someone with a sharp mind like Senator Clinton might react: "Hmmm. The alleged ties between Hussein and al-Qaeda do not seem to reflect reality. I should investigate these claims further." With such an inclination she might fact-check some of the administration's intelligence regarding the ties between the two enemies. She would then discover, for example, that the medical assistance Iraq provided an al-Qaeda operative, as criticized and deemed extraordinarily significant by the administration, was done unwittingly. They thought they were treating a Jordanian citizen. When informed that the patient was al-Qaeda they immediately turned the patient over.

Once again, you could imagine how someone with a sharp mind like Senator Clinton might react to this: "Hmmm. The administration appears to be stretching the truth a bit. I should see what other intelligence agencies have to say about this." With a little bit of investigation Senator Clinton would have discovered that the CIA could not uncover any real evidence for ties between Iraq and al-Qaeda and, in fact, consistently found problems with the administration's intelligence linking the two.[6]

Given their status as the opposition party the spineless behavior of Congressional Democrats now seems totally bizarre. They had the ammunition; they had the moral obligation; they had the self-interested motive, twice over in the case of Senator Clinton. What on earth were they thinking?!

The answer to that, of course, is what the public was thinking. War is, and always has been, an easy sell. Add to that the events of 9/11 and the successful invasion of Afghanistan and you have a public primed for continued war. The administration cultivated this climate further by nurturing fear in everyone not meant to play the role of soldier. In such a climate of apprehension, being the opposition party changes from a golden opportunity for being the good guys to risking being the bad guys. The Democrats might have laid the foundation for being considered wise detractors if the war goes bad, but they reinforce an image of being soft on defense if the war goes well.

Still, the abundant materials for discrediting the administration's intelligence and the moral obligation to resist unnecessary war might have persuaded Democrats to serve their homeostatic function, even in the absence of self-interested opposition as a motive. In the past this might have been true, but there are some unique conditions affecting politics in the new millennium. War always has been an easy sell, but only now do we have in this country such massive consolidation of corporate media. We have been threatened in the past, but only now do we have echo chambers to reverberate these threats. Administrations have played on the public's fears in the past, but only now do corporate media supply such large amounts of news time for exploitation by fear mongers. If the age of the echo chamber works against you, exposing facts and generating heated debate

6 There are multiple meanings for the word "intelligence" used in this sentence.

goes for naught.

That leaves a moral obligation as the only remaining motivator for Democrats to perform their homeostatic function of opposition. While a moral obligation may be sufficient motivation for many segments of society, such a motivation will never suffice for a political party adapted to synthesize interests, power and wealth. A moral obligation did not compel Hillary Clinton and other Democratic senators to do even some rudimentary fact checking.

Homeostasis and Party Fragmentation

Should the opposition party fail to oppose dubious claims and actions by the ruling party, there are other mechanisms that kick in to preserve wisdom in the political process. When ruling parties face little opposition they tend to grow larger and stronger. People love to back a winner. However, as the party expands dissenting views that formerly came from without now come from within. As more people contribute to the party more diverse interests are represented. As long as these diverse interests maintain their independence to be heard the expansion of a party serves as a homeostatic mechanism for maintaining wisdom within.

Party leaders want to discourage independent dissent. The administration of President Bush II is not unique in this manner, but a few examples revealing how they terminated independent dissent among their very own Republican ranks help illustrate the point. Let us review the nature of the dissent, and the subsequent retaliation, for a few of those who dissented.

Scott Ritter

Scott Ritter was a Marine assigned to do intelligence work and weapons inspections for both Russia and the Middle East. This self-described conservative Republican worked under President Bush I, whom he admires, and President Clinton, whom he loathes.

Ritter's dissent consisted of active and vocal lobbying during both the Clinton and Bush II administrations for continued weapons inspections of Iraq. He criticized on a consistent basis the use of weapons inspections as merely a political ploy by both administrations to prop up movements for regime change, rather than for their intended purpose of disarmament. He alleged that claims about Iraq as a security risk were being used by the Bush II administration as an acceptable excuse to the public for furthering neoconservative objectives.

The Clinton Administration had the FBI investigate Ritter for possible spy connections with Israel (an ironic move, though Ritter worked with Israeli intelligence in the weapons inspections of Iraq, he was openly critical of Prime Minister Ariel Sharon's policies). During the Bush II administration charges were brought against Ritter in relation to an Internet sex sting, but those charges were dropped. The dismissed charges suddenly reappeared as a media target, despite sealed court documents, in the months preceding the invasion of Iraq, limiting Ritter's effectiveness as a speaker promoting forbearance.

Richard Clarke

Richard Clarke was a counterterrorism expert whose public service began with the Reagan administration. He received praise for his work throughout his service, in particular for how seriously he took the threat of terrorism and his dedication to thwarting our terrorist foes.

Clarke's dissent consisted of advising the Bush II administration, while he still worked for them prior to 9/11, that they were not taking the terrorist threat seriously enough. This dissent later became public when Clarke wrote *Against All Enemies: Inside America's War on Terror* (2004), in which he revealed that the administration was focused on Iraq immediately after 9/11, and that this focus has been counterproductive to fighting terrorism.

The Bush II administration reacted to Clarke's work-related dissent by replacing him with "experts" who shared their views of how to handle (or ignore) the intelligence they received. They responded to Clarke's book by claiming the man was attempting to make money and influence the 2004 elections. The establishment forces could not quite get their spin straight. Dick Cheney went on Rush Limbaugh's show to claim that Clarke was out of the loop at the same time Condoleeza Rice was telling reporters that Clarke was the central figure in counterterrorism. Senate leader Bill Frist denounced Clarke's testimony under oath to the 9/11 commission as being contradictory, then later admitted he could not point to any specific contradiction. Rather than fact checking any criticisms of Clarke, corporate media and pundits from the Powell Cabal joined the bandwagon, adding their own wild speculation that Clarke was perhaps jockeying for a position in a Democratic administration. While most authors do attempt to make money, the release of the book was many months before the elections, an incompetent decision if the purpose was to influence election results.

Paul O'Neill

Paul O'Neill was the Treasury Secretary for the Bush II administration. He came to the job with experience as a CEO for Alcoa and chairman for the RAND Corporation. He was known as a fiscal conservative with allegiance to *laissez faire* economics.

O'Neill's dissent consisted of criticizing the Bush II administration for fiscal policy that turned a budget surplus into a large budget deficit. He also provided documents that indicated the administration was more concerned about

Iraq, both before and after 9/11, than al-Qaeda.

The Bush II administration replaced O'Neill with John Snow, someone less finicky about running up deficits. In response to O'Neill's providing documentation about the administration's peculiar decision-making they had the Treasury Department investigate him for possible treason.

The Bush II administration is not the first to squelch party dissenters. Their actions were notable because at times they squelched traditional Republican principles along with their critics, and they received little backlash. Indeed, the Bush II administration managed to increase their support among Republicans for the 2004 election. A certain amount of wiggle room accompanies party principles, but are we to believe that Republicans no longer care about fiscal responsibility or fighting terrorism?

For there to be a backlash against party leadership the rank and file would need to be aware of a problem. While virtually everything gets reported somewhere, somehow, the numbers of investigative reporters are declining constantly through media consolidation. The emerging pro-authoritarianism media giants such as Sinclair Broadcasting Corporation or News Corporation were not going to put the Bush II administration on the hot seat, even for the sake of conservative values. As will be examined in the next essay, news talk show hosts are more concerned about "liberal" media ignoring "positive" economic indicators than the precipitous fall from budget surplus to large budget deficit. The echo chambers will not reverberate about the increased rates of terror attacks or deaths since the Bush II administration took office. Twenty-four hour news stations do not need to appease fiscal conservatives like Paul O'Neill for a steady stream of opinionated material.

An anecdote told by Scott Ritter sums up the supreme challenge we face in this brave new world of corporate media. Before being interviewed on CNN Ritter had to meet with executives for hours to make sure a conservative marine who was a former weapons inspector in Iraq had credibility about WMDs. "Good for CNN!" you say, "We need the media to be vigilant about their sources." Well, except that the Bush II administration never was subjected to an *a priori* credibility check for any type of information they provided. In fact, corporate media seldom does any follow-up fact checking on what the administration reports. "But they are our leaders!" you protest. Yes, that is precisely the point. We now support a media that will support authoritarianism without cross-examination; while threats to authoritarian positions are given the third degree, regardless of their expertise. That is the complete opposite of how wise democracy works.

Homeostasis and Party Corruption
Corruption functions as the last resort to steer a political party back towards wise

democracy. History repeatedly has verified the founding fathers' suspicions about parties; but every time corruption soils a party's reputation citizens take corrective action. We have witnessed a sweeping homeostatic response twice in recent decades. In 1994 Congress went from being controlled by Democrats to Republicans, due to the public reaction against corruption. In 2006 the reverse occurred. Some might argue that the occupation of Iraq had much to do with the citizen revolt of 2006, but from Mark Foley to Tom Delay a series of scandals seriously weakened Republicans as the elections approached.

We all prefer democracy without the corruption, but let us appreciate the valuable role corruption plays in the democratic process. Because of our natural trust in authority—which had an adaptive function in simpler, prehistoric eras—we depend on policy making to be in our best interest. This dependence allows party leadership to adapt their ideologies over time to best combine dogma, power and wealth. This path towards power leads a party farther away from wisdom. Once a party, or party leadership, has been identified as corrupt the trust that began this path is broken. We emerge as if out of a fog to think and act independently of our former trust. Though we might be willing to shock/torture another human being because of our trust in authority, corruption awakes us from our stupor.

Though we have had our "success" stories in recent times, when sweeping change for restoring balance followed corruption, there are also signs for concern. In the two decades before 1980, which marks the dawn of twenty-four hour news, we had a president with personal peccadilloes (Kennedy) and one who overreached for power (Nixon). The president who would have been impeached was the one who overreached, though he resigned and was pardoned. Since echo chambers and news talk show hosts ruled the airwaves we likewise have had one president with personal peccadilloes (Clinton) and one who overreached for power (Bush II). This time the House impeached the president with the personal peccadilloes. The actions of Congress probably reflected the opinions of citizens in these matters, since politicians seldom take drastic action that might incur public wrath. In the absence of echo chambers, Nixon's thirst for power was reverberated directly among citizens; in the era of echo chambers, Clinton's peccadilloes were reverberated indirectly for citizens by corporate media. Breaking our once adaptive, now vestigial blind trust in authority depends on what gets "reverberated." Corporate media decides, and we respond.

Beyond the kinds of corruption that breaks our trust, there are types of pervasive corruption that lie under the radar. They are, in fact, forms of institutionalized corruption, inherent in how our political system operates. Citizens cannot remove the corruption through voting or impeachment, because the corruptive aspects of the system are still in place. These forms of corruption correspond to how we have integrated wealth and dogma into the politics of acquiring and wielding power.

The Political Gravy Train

During the 2004 election cycle the Democratic Party spent $710,416,993 and the Republican Party spent $875,704,006.[7] In the 2004 election the average campaign expenditure was $1,034,873 for a House seat and $7,173,260 for a Senate seat. This is about twenty times and one-hundred and forty times the median family income, respectively, but amounts to chump change in comparison to the presidential campaign. From 1976 to 2004 the amount spent on presidential elections increased by just under a factor of eleven, from over $66 million to over $717 million; the median family income during that time span increased only by about a factor of four.[8]

The Financial/Insurance/Real Estate sector contributed the most with over $338 million. Either these contributions provided the financial sector with disproportional access to power or corporations that specialize in money wasted theirs. Some special interest can align with public interest, but big dollars would not be as necessary to empower those special interests that the public would overwhelmingly support. Therefore, when the sharp-minded Hillary Clinton suddenly became incurious about the Bush II administration's evidence for sending middle class sons and daughters to war, we can assume she was not disappointing the special interests that filled her campaign coffers more than other members of Congress. Out of the fifty largest contributors to campaign finance from industry sectors, eleven of them judged the incurious senator from New York to be the best at representing their special interests.

Out of 80 industries tracked by opensecrets.org, lobbyists came in 32nd for campaign contributions in 1990. By 2004 lobbyists ranked 12th, but the real influence of lobbyists comes after politicians get elected. As with campaign contributions, industries would be spending irresponsibly to wine and dine politicians in direct proportion to how much their special interest aligns with the public interest. The greater need comes when lobbyists must convince politicians to legislate counter to the public interest. In 2004, the special interest with the greatest need was that old friend of the Powell Cabal, the U. S. Chamber of Commerce. They spent over $353 million, almost three times the amount of the interest group that came in second, the American Medical Association.

Two other health care industries joined the AMA in the top ten as well, the American Hospital Association and the Pharmaceuticals Research and Manufacturers of America. The housing industry also made the top ten with Freddie Mac and the National Association of Realtors. If you recall our economic report card, housing and health care costs have increased far faster than median family income; faster, even, than Gross Domestic Product. No doubt these industries

---

7 All numbers for political finances are from the organization/web site opensecrets.org, a source that is low on opinion pieces and high on straight tables of facts.
8 Median family income is derived from the Statistical Abstracts, as reported in the economic essays.

would claim they lobby for many things in the public interest. But of particular interest to the middle class is that housing and health care costs remain affordable. When these costs outpace both the median family income and even the GDP, while their respective industries are leaders for lining lobbyist pockets, one can conclude that the public interest is being subverted.

The merger of beliefs, wealth and power goes beyond campaign contributions and lobbying. Politicians leaving public office can join the same lobbying firms that used to provide them favors. If not lobbying firms, then think tanks, public relation firms or any other members of the Powell Cabal will suit politicians just as well as they seek to enhance their wealth through special interest. This happens at the state as well as the federal level. One study revealed that in 2005 alone 1300 former state legislators registered to become state lobbyists.[9] The revolving door also involves government employees in addition to elected officials, particularly if they "serve" in certain agencies. Close to one hundred senior executive branch officials, whose "patriotism" led them to serve on the new Department for Homeland Security that was created after 9/11, left that agency within five years for more lucrative ventures with corporations that fed off of the bureaucracy. Here is how they did that:[10]

> "Federal law prohibits senior executive branch officials from lobbying former government colleagues or subordinates for at least a year after leaving public service. But by exploiting loopholes in the law — including one provision drawn up by department executives to facilitate their entry into the business world — it is often easy for former officials to do just that."

The revolving door for politicians betrays the vision of Benjamin Franklin and Thomas Paine regarding what public servants would do once they left office. They thought that, wearied from public service, public servants would forever leave politics behind them. Instead, too many either make a career out of their "public service," or go through a revolving door of influence between the public and private sectors. Our political system is rigged to corrupt politicians in ways that stay beneath the radar of what would break our trust in authorities. No doubt even career politicians like Hillary Clinton once had good intentions of serving the public interest over any and all special interests; perhaps some even fool themselves into thinking that they are immune to the systematic corruption.

---

9 From "Statehouse Revolvers" (October 12, 1006), by Kevin Bogardus, for the *Center on Public Integrity* (www.publicintegrity.org/hiredguns/report.aspx?aid=747).
10 From "Former Antiterror Officials Find Industry Pays Better" (June 18,2006), by Eric Lipton, for the *New York Times*.

Party Authoritarianism

The ability to think independently contributes to wisdom; dependence on a party democracy to do our thinking for us reinforces authoritarianism. Parties organize to consolidate dogma, wealth and power. To maximize wisdom a democracy cannot be controlled by parties, hence, party democracy is an oxymoron. Not everyone becomes corrupted by our party system in the legal sense, but at the least career politicians maximize their own self-interest over serving the public interest, or else they would not make a career out of their "service." Very few people could make a career out of selflessly devoting themselves to the public interest over what is ultimately best for them. Our founding fathers knew this to be true, as do you. The greed that corrupts free markets also corrupts democracy.

Our two-party system of democracy has devised mechanisms where power is kept in check through the negative feedback loops of homeostasis. These mechanisms include incentives for the opposition party to expose facts and generate debate; party fragmentation with increased party size; and the breaking of trust through corruption. Yet homeostatic mechanisms are not invulnerable. One natural example of homeostasis being broken is when fever has driven our body temperature up so high that we stop sweating. In a similar vein, there is a point where corruption no longer restrains power by breaking our trust.

Corruption checks power by providing a negative feedback loop. In democracies power stems from the trust of the people. When authorities or parties undermine that trust through corruption they also diminish their power. However, in political systems where citizens have no real means to infuse the political process with collective wisdom corruption now becomes a valuable tool for authoritarians. Corruption becomes a positive feedback loop where corruption is used to reinforce power, which in turn reinforces corruption. The litmus test of a democracy is whether corruption diminishes or enhances the power of authorities. At the point that corruption changes from a negative feedback loop to positive feedback, democracy has changed to totalitarianism. The conditions that may provide such a turning point for our democracy are growing.

As intended by Paine, Jefferson, Hamilton and the rest of the colonialists democracy was both the right thing to do and the wise thing to do. Our founding fathers must have had some slight pangs of guilt when their political squabbling, petty and strident at times, led to political parties. In fairness to them, they could not know some of the problems of our political system that would develop to make their concerns about political parties come true. They did not know the extent that corporations and special interest groups could influence power through campaign contributions, lobbying and revolving doors. They could not have foreseen one most ominous Supreme Court case that would take place on the 200th anniversary of our independence, *Buckley v. Valeo* (1976). This case will be discussed when these essays turn to jurisprudence.

Beyond the actual legislative process, our founding fathers certainly could not anticipate how the system outside of the legislative branch would be complicit in the corruptive power of parties. They might have anticipated the yellow journalism that developed over the next hundred years, with newspapers using the founding fathers own tactics of hyperbole to critique the establishment. They could not have guessed to what extent newspapers would become consolidated along with radio, television and the Internet; nor imagine how hyperbole would come to be used by the fourth estate to actually limit critique of authoritarianism. Indeed, if our founding fathers had the foresight to know to what extent a conglomeration of power, wealth and interests would become centralized in this country thus thwarting democratic intent, even Hamilton and the Federalists might have recommended more curbs for our national government.

ESSAY 12 – CENTRALIZED CORPORATE MEDIA

Overview

- News media in the sixties focused on events independently of party politics.
- Localized news media provides one of the ingredients for political wisdom.
- News media norms should be localization, a focus on events over opinions, and a slight anti-authoritarianism bias.
- Media consolidation has led to centralized news with a pro-authoritarian bias.
- Centralized twenty-four hour news proliferate opinions over actual events.
- Centralized echo chambers obscure opinions and events harmful to corporations.
- Centralized news talk hosts foster negativity for entertainment value.
- Centralized news entertainment degrades our civility as a nation.
- The FCC acts in the interest of *laissez faire* economics rather than the public.
- The purpose of localized media is not to eliminate bias, but to enable diverse opinions to flourish for the sake of democracy.

News Media Independence

The news hour started at 6:00 p.m. every weekday evening. Local news would be first, with a menu of local news, sports, weather and some brief clips on national events. That would be followed at 6:30 p.m. by Walter Cronkite on the CBS Evening News, which consisted mainly of video clips of places far away from my rural town. The time slots for news were limited—early morning, evening, and late night—and evening news worked best for my parents. I watched the news with them because we only had one television to feed my young addiction to video images. Even had there been another television in the house, we received only four stations and three of them were networks. After we had supper, I had no choice as a teenager but to learn about current events.

I did not mind being a captive audience because there were two spectacles to watch: the one on the television and the one in our living room. On the television were spectacles of riots and wars; in our living room was the spectacle of my father's animated opinions about what was on the television. The half irate, half pleading exclamation, "Mother of God!" still rings in my head.

Though I could tell you plenty about what my father thought of world and national events, I had no idea what the newscasters thought. My father, who voted for every Republican president except one, loved Walter Cronkite. Only in recent times, when much of the news has become about the newscasters, did I learn that Cronkite was one of those Democrats my father otherwise disliked. In the sixties newscasters were only known by their personalities. They gave little clue to their politics during newscasts, and no special interest groups were discrediting the messengers of news to deflect attention from the content of news.

There were a few other aspects about newscasts during my teenage years that, only now in retrospect, were striking. Pundits espousing their opinions had yet to become a big part of the news. The only polls with saturated media coverage were exit polls on the first Tuesday of every fourth November. The only guides for interpreting what the news meant were the opinions of my parents.

Our political liberty depends on our freedom of thought and the ability to form our own independent opinions. We rely on the information provided to us by news media to achieve that goal. The biases of anonymous pundits spouting their opinions are hidden to us, unlike the biases of our parents or other close acquaintances. We do not need to know what the polls say everyone thinks; we need to know what we think when presented with the original details. Over the twentieth century we have conformed more to paternal democracy and depended more on party doctrines in large part because of trends affecting news media. These trends result from media consolidation, thus centralizing the news being provided to inform our democracy.

News Media Norms

Imagine if we obtained our news straight from the "horse's mouth." Imagine that we could listen directly to the president, governor, senator or any other authority making the important decisions in our governance simply by tuning into any channel on our radio or television. Imagine if we eliminated biased news critiques of government completely.

Fiction writers have portrayed such scenarios, the most renowned work of this genre being *1984*, by George Orwell. This may have been fiction but there are some real life corollaries. Most notably, fascism evolved as a totalitarian urge to centralize the control of information. Stalin's Soviet Union has been linked to Orwell's book, but Hitler's Germany is perhaps the better fit.

Our cultural evolution has predisposed us to trust ordered government as an alternative to chaos. But ordered government can be structured to promote either authoritarianism or wisdom. Since imposing ideas on a democracy and deriving ideas from democracy contradict each other you cannot maximize both. Having our freedom of thought shaped only by what authorities tell us maximizes authoritarianism, even if our authorities were to be as wise as Solomon.

We refer to the media as the fourth estate. The media counterbalances the authorities in legislative, executive and judicial branches of government to preserve our political liberty. News media serves two crucial functions for preserving democracy: reporting on the original events that shape opinions and giving voice to the diversity of opinions that are shaped from those actual events. When the news mainly provides a centralized report of the opinions of authorities the media has failed at both functions and our democracy has suffered.

Let us review once more the ingredients for obtaining collective wisdom, detailed in Surowiecki's *The Wisdom of Crowds* (2004). Wisdom requires the systematic, unbiased aggregation of diverse opinions, derived from the independent and decentralized experiences of citizens. Thus, even though ye olde town pamphleteers were strident and opinionated, whether they proved to be zealots in favor or against government, they contributed to the wisdom of a democracy through their decentralized perspectives. Creating uniformity in voice through centralized news media disintegrates the foundation for collective wisdom and the main function of a democracy.

Let us view this now from John Stuart Mill's seminal work, *On Liberty* (1859). In addition to the freedom of thought, Mill proposed self-actualization as a key ingredient of liberty. This is the right of individuals to become the persons they want to be. Mill cites a variety of cultural phenomena that interferes with this goal: such as social customs, Calvinism, socialism and mediocrity. He criticizes communication that indoctrinates the norms of the majority, recognizing ahead of his time the problems of mass media that arose a century later.

Finally, let us take one step further back in time to one of history's most famous pamphleteers, Thomas Paine. Paine contributed significantly to our country's views on rights and liberty. He distinguished political wisdom from authoritarianism in this way: "… Governments arise either out of the people or over the people." His views were not unique, the essential points in the *Rights of Man* (1791) were expressed in the Declaration of Independence, nor did they provide as lucid a description of liberty as Mill would provide later. Still, Paine was a better writer than Mill, at least in the opinion of this reader; he persuaded people to agree with him at a time in history when the virtues of democracy over aristocracy was not evident to all. The *Rights of Man*, in fact, was a counterargument to a book touting the virtues of aristocracy in England. That Paine succeeded as a local pamphleteer was as much a contribution to true democracy as his views. You do not need to be a leader, aristocrat or famous philosopher to contribute to wisdom; you just need to resonate with the independent, decentralized experiences of other citizens.

Linking the ideas of Surowiecki, Mill and Paine we conclude that news media must transcend the role of providing information; news media plays the pivotal role of brokering wisdom in a democracy. News media must be the vessel of collective wisdom for citizens who want to exercise their political liberty and for authorities who want to be public servants. With such an exalted role in our democracy we can and should apply normative guidelines as to what constitutes good news media.

First and foremost, news media should be independent and decentralized or, in the jargon of media experts, most news media should be localized. Second, news media should report mainly events, not the opinions of authorities about events. To the extent that opinions are inevitable, and that some amount of bias is inevitable, the nature of those opinions and bias should, on balance, be slightly anti-authoritarianism. Anti-authoritarianism should be taken in a broad sense, guarding against authoritarianism regardless of whether authorities actually have earned the public trust. News media needs to investigate the authoritative opinions of experts, as follows from Surowiecki; to question the conventional mores of the majority, as urged by Mill; and to resist the tyrannical impulses of government, as advocated by Paine.

Since the days of Walter Cronkite news media have been moving away from all these norms. Through corporate acquisition media has become more centralized. The same corporation now can own the newspaper, radio and television outlets of the same town, and dominate any of these markets throughout the country. A high proportion of the news reports on opinions rather than events. One news blurb I heard on radio, regarding an upcoming speech at a Republican National Convention, reported a pundit's opinion about what one party's future opinion would be about what the other party's future opinion would be about the president's future opinion. Corporate media has an authoritarianism bias. This is not entirely corporate media's fault. They are chastised for being unpatriotic with news coverage that is anti-authoritarianism, and their access to news from authorities becomes restricted unless they abide by certain rules.

One of the most prominent corporate media conglomerations is News Corporation, of which *Fox News* is a part. *Fox News* viewers were more likely than viewers of any other news programs to think that Iraq was connected to the events of 9/11, or that the majority of the world favored the United States invading Iraq. The misconceptions of *Fox News* viewers holds true across education levels; you could be a genius and still be clueless thanks to *Fox News*.[1] Another study involving *Fox News* provides somewhat humorous, somewhat troubling evidence about the impact of these conglomerations on our collective wisdom. People who got their news from *The Daily Show* were better informed about the 2004 election issues than people who got their news from *Fox News*.[2] What makes this humorous is that *The Daily Show*, in the words of the host, is "fake news," with the main goal

---

1 Results from the Program on International Policy Attitudes/Knowledge Networks Poll "Misperceptions, the Media, and the Iraq War." Program on International Policy Attitudes October 2003.
2 Results from the National Annenberg Election Survey, September 21, 2004.

of getting a laugh. What makes this alarming is *Fox News* intends to be taken seriously.

Though specializing in "fake news" *The Daily Show* provides one service not provided by real news media. They will often take the sound bites of politicians, both Democrats and Republicans, and juxtapose them with earlier sound bites from the same politician contradicting what they now say. What better way to convey the message that citizens need to take their political liberty seriously and not take everything authorities say at face value?

However, there was one excellent target of ridicule and humor that *The Daily Show* never touched: the follies of then chief FCC commissioner Michael Powell in trying to shove media consolidation down the public's throats. This is not surprising, since *The Daily Show* is owned by the corporate media giant Viacom. Exposing the hypocrisy of politicians may be an admirable goal of *The Daily Show*, but their public service falls short of exposing the hypocrisy of their own industry.

Media Consolidation

You might be surprised to learn that giant media corporations, like most large corporations, thrive on government intervention. These folks spend millions in public relations campaigns to condemn regulations, but they will also spend millions to support regulations if they provide a competitive advantage over small businesses. In the case of allotting radio airwaves corporations favor regulating wide bandwidths to prevent station signals from interfering with each other, even though in the digital age this has become a limited problem. A side effect for restricting airwaves, or perhaps the main intent of corporations, is the restriction of local competition.

The federal government accepts the responsibility of regulating airwaves as a public service. The Radio Act of 1912, prompted in part by airwave complications with distress signals from the *Titanic*, required that airwave operators be licensed and conforming to standards that were intended for the public good. The subsequent Radio Act of 1927 and Communications Act of 1934 provided more details for what Congress considered to be the public good and created the Federal Communications Commission (FCC) as an independent regulatory agency to enforce this goal for all forms of media. Among the primary objectives associated with the public good were diversity, localism and competition.[3]

Since the fifties communication rules and legislation have served to undermine the public good of diversity, localism and competition. In 1953 the caps for the number of radio stations the same corporation could own were set at

---

3 Unless otherwise indicated, the factual details (dates, percentages) about media regulation and consolidation come from Eric Klinenberg's book, *Fighting for Air: The Battle to Control America's Media* (2007).

seven AM and seven FM. In 1984 these caps were raised to twelve and twelve; in 1992 they were raised to eighteen and eighteen; in 1994, twenty and twenty; and in 1996 national caps were eliminated, though a corporation could not own more than eight stations in the same local market. Other media forms have mirrored this pattern of consolidation as well. In 1945 about 80% of newspapers were privately owned, now 80% are corporate owned. Cross-media consolidation has occurred as well. The Chicago Tribune conglomerate of newspapers, radio, television and Internet sites reaches 90% of the Chicago market.

Corporate media's love affair with protective government regulation in regards to bandwidth does not include encouraging diversity, localism and competition with media ownership. This has led to dual lobbying efforts. Lobbyists for the National Association of Broadcasters (NAB) and National Public Radio (NPR) persuaded Congress to flex some regulatory muscle by passing the Radio Broadcasting Preservation Act of 2000 that severely constrained the number of low power FM broadcasts allowed. The title of the act reeks with Orwellian doublespeak, as what was being preserved was corporate media's mission to minimize local competition. On the heels of this regulatory success the lobbyists went to work on further deregulation of media consolidation caps, assisted by Michael Powell, the person in charge of providing media oversight. Based on their successes in the 1990s, and with an ally chairing the FCC, corporate media figured they would be able to eliminate ownership caps entirely.

As with the Bush II administration's approach to invading Iraq, there are reasons corporate media publicly states for eliminating caps and reasons they do not share. The early 1990s proved to be a downturn in the business cycle for corporate media. Business cycles are to be expected, as are efforts to push through favorable legislation during downturns. Mind you, small businesses have limited ability to influence government during their downturns but that is their problem, not the problem of large corporations. Corporate media claimed that the proliferation of media venues such as the Internet and cell phones guaranteed a competitive climate that puts them at a disadvantage. This begs the question of why government should help large corporations overcome this type of competitive disadvantage at any point in a business cycle.

The answer, according to corporate media, is to benefit the consumer. As if all corporate media would wither and die if government did not come to their rescue during a downturn, the media giants maintained that consumers would miss out on the innovations that only large corporations could usher in. There are three flaws to this argument. First, corporate media was NOT going to wither and die simply because of a downturn. Once the downturn was over, and bolstered by the elimination of national caps in 1996, corporate media consolidated with alarming speed and vigor. Clear Channel Communication, for example, now controls over a thousand radio stations.

Second, no evidence supports a claim that big businesses are more innovative than small businesses. Throughout our history the diversity and free exchange of ideas typical to a small business climate has competed well for stimulating innovative production. In terms of the actual quality of news product, corporate media actually stiffed consumers. Corporations need to maximize profits for the sake of their shareholders. One means to this end is to increase efficiency through operation cuts. Many of the operation cuts made through media consolidation were the elimination of local news staff and content, replaceable by packaged programming at centralized corporate locations.

Finally, media consolidation has increased prices for the consumer. Since the Telecom Act of 1996 lifted national caps, cable rates have increased by three times the inflation rate. More stations have been added to cable and satellite packages, but not in response to the choices of consumers. A consumer cannot select ten of their preferred stations and pay only for them. Cable and satellite packages, and the associated costs, are compiled according to what fits best for corporate media.

Though media consolidation provides fewer benefits for consumers than claimed by corporate media, the real causes for concern are the costs of centralized news packaging to citizens. Local investigative reporters, the modern day corollaries to Thomas Paine the pamphleteer, are disappearing. For example, the events leading to the Enron implosion were not exposed by the local Houston Chronicle, whose gutted editorial staff made excuses for the first signs of trouble at Enron.

The centralized programming eliminates the independent and decentralized function the fourth estate could provide for stimulating collective wisdom. The Sinclair Broadcasting Corporation, who owns the most television stations in the country, created NewsCentral as a means of putting their spin on the news. The politics of that spin was documented by Eric Klinenberg, in *Fighting for Air* (2007, pgs. 88-89):

> "With NewsCentral, Sinclair aimed to establish a national network of outlets that would transform local news broadcasts into platforms for the management's favorite conservative causes. For example, after 9/11, Sinclair forced all of its stations to have on-air personalities pledge support for President George W. Bush and the War on Terror during their broadcasts. It forbid its Fox affiliate in Madison, Wisconsin, from airing ads produced by the Democratic National Committee during the summer of 2004. During

the 2004 presidential campaign, Jon Leiberman, then the Washington bureau chief, complained that Sinclair was using its local stations to air 'propaganda meant to sway the election,' and that the news manager, citing pressure from the top, consistently denied requests to report on the torture scandal at Abu Gharaib. An ex-producer at Sinclair said he was ordered not to report 'any bad news out of Iraq—no dead servicemen, no reports on how much we're spending, nothing.' And the producer that Sinclair sent to Iraq to report on the war called the resulting coverage 'pro-Bush.' 'You weren't reporting news,' she explained. 'You were reporting a political agenda that came down to you from the top of the food chain.'"

Rather than present a slightly anti-establishment bias that would encourage viewers to think independently of authorities, Sinclair Broadcasting and News Corporation attempt to do the direct opposite: to have their viewers conform to biases these corporate media giants support, providing a centralized package to achieve this. Some editorial bias can be expected from any news station, but these corporate giants influence a high percentage of the population with the same centralized biases because of media consolidation. In addition to extra coverage, corporate media has developed a way to increase the frequency of communicating their centralized biases as well: through twenty-four hour news programming.

Centralized Twenty-four Hour News

The advent of twenty-four hour news stations, beginning with CNN in 1980, presented an opportunity for politicians and corporate media to assist each other with mutual goals. Corporate media giants could, in theory, fill up a day with a mixture of local, county, state, regional, national and international news. This would be a public service indeed, contributing much to the independent, decentralized localism needed to generate collective wisdom. Our freedom of thought and political liberty would be all the better from such programming. However, this would necessitate expanding rather than shrinking local news staffs. Profits would suffer.

Without much in the way of local, county, state or regional supply of news to supplement programming, corporate media must be accommodating to centralized suppliers of news. For the most part these suppliers are authorities connected with government or corporations.[4] Some authorities understand that they are not supposed to use news media as a propaganda tool, and that the media is supposed to play an investigative and even critical role. However, even fair-minded authorities will seethe at what they perceive to be unfair criticism, and will view most criticism against them as unfair. Since corporate media needs more news than they can obtain just through investigative reporting, since they need to draw from the extra supply that authorities can provide, they avoid anti-authoritarianism bias that might promote liberty, as viewed by Mill or Paine, but would antagonize their news suppliers.

Another way to increase the supply of news is to go beyond the reporting of events to include the reporting of opinions … and the reporting of opinions of opinions … and the reporting of opinions of opinions of opinions. There exists a prodigious and obliging supply of opinion providers throughout our society. A Google Search (in June 2007) provided 751,000 hits for "conservative blog" and 659,000 hits for liberal blog;" 274,000 hits for "conservative think tank" and 70,100 hits for "liberal think tank;" 130,000 hits for "conservative pundit" and 23,100 hits for "liberal pundit;" and, of course, 192,000 hits for "conservative talk show" and 45,000 hits for "liberal talk show."

In case you were wondering, there were 605 hits for "middle class blog," 65 hits for middle class think tank," 9 hits for "middle class pundit," and 6 hits for "middle class talk show." If you read the blurbs provided the sources are often bloggers that have peculiar ideas about the middle class. Apparently what qualify as middle class talk shows are the afternoon spectacles where bodyguards are on hand to prevent the guests from ripping each other's eyes out. Bring on the gladiators!

The blogs, think tanks, pundits and talk shows all cross-reference each other (though the middle class networking is obviously a bit limited), so that essentially the same opinion can be aired incessantly, even when filling twenty-four hours of news. With twenty-four hours news we are not to make up our own minds as a result of the reporting of events by local news staff. Instead, our minds are being made up for us by centralized corporate media profiting shareholders and placating authorities.

Centralized Echo Chambers

Media groups refer to the regurgitation of opinions during news programming as the echo chamber. The echo chamber provided by twenty-four hour news started a decade after the Powell Memorandum challenged corporations and their special interest groups to control public opinion. From that time on the echo chamber

---

4 In his well-regarded book *Rich Media, Poor Democracy* (1999), Robert W. McChesny elaborates on the connections between corporate media and government and corporate news suppliers.

and the Powell Cabal coevolved, relying heavily on each other. To borrow a catch phrase from our economic essays, the echo chamber is the means by which "the Powell Cabal of corporate sponsored think tanks, corporate endowed chairs of economic departments, corporate hired public relations firms, corporate employed lobbyists and corporate owned media" harnesses the fourth estate to serve their purpose.

Only select news items are featured in the echo chamber. A nice illustration of what "makes the cut" happened during the 2004 election. In August of that election year two separate but related news releases occurred on the same day: one stating that the percentage in poverty had increased and the other that the percentage of uninsured had increased. Though the statistics were released on a Friday to minimize coverage, news media with a slight anti-authoritarianism bias could have provided sustained coverage juxtaposing these statistics, if they were judged to be "newsworthy." They could have even tinged their coverage with emotional bias, something they can do quite well when they have a mind to. Can you imagine the video clips and other methods corporate media could have used to hype uninsured people falling out of the middle class? Alas, nary a word could be heard in the echo chamber about poverty or being uninsured.

Instead, the echo chamber focused mainly on two topics during that month: the character of John Kerry, as portrayed by the Swift Boat Veterans for Truth; and the character of George W. Bush, as inferred by the quantity and quality of his service during the Vietnam War. Corporate media took some heat for their lack of investigative reporting to determine if the more outrageous claims were true. Conservatives used the Bush II focus as evidence of liberal bias while liberals used the Kerry focus as evidence of conservative bias. If anything, these cross-accusations of media bias had to please corporate media, since no one noticed if there might be corporate bias at work. The echo chamber focused the public's attention on character issues of political candidates rather than economic issues that could be damaging to corporate media and other corporations.

Documentaries can supply chunks of news time. Since this requires more resources than airing people's opinions, documentaries must be judiciously selected. John Stossel has a particularly impressive track record for ABC's *20/20* which make that corporate media giant's investment worthwhile. His programs include "Freeloaders," which critiques how the poor can get something for nothing; "Greed," which champions the ways that the greedy can get something for nothing; "Are We Scaring Ourselves to Death," which defends pesticides and chemicals; and "The Food You Eat—Organic Foods May Not Be as Healthy as You Think," for which Stossel was caught fabricating facts.[5]

Stossel escaped any serious repercussions for fabricating data about organic foods, or for pressuring children in yet another program to respond that

5 Sheldon Rampton and John Stauber provide greater detail for the news reporting of John Stossel in their book, *Banana Republicans* (2004).

they had been terrorized by environmentalists. He had established appreciative friends among the Powell Cabal of think tanks and foundations who came to his rescue when he needed them most. In fact, his corporate employer showed Stossel some love by promoting him to co-anchor of *20/20*.

Access to authorities, echo chambers and documentaries reveal how corporate media can provide a twenty-four hour "news" supply. However, people are naturally interested in their own local news. Substituting an echo chamber of national pundits for localized news means adding some pizzazz to the programming that will help stimulate demand. The news talk show has proved a valuable asset in this regard.

Centralized News Talk Show Hosts

Scientists sample events. Trained to accept that we can never acquire data that represents the total population of events, we instead go for a representative sample that reliably reflects the population. From this type of sampling I concluded that Rush Limbaugh loves to complain.

I knew that Limbaugh was popular before I heard him for the first time. While channel surfing the radio in my car his name came up and I decided to see what his popularity was all about. After listening to him complain about something for a few minutes straight I switched the station to something that would keep me in a better frame of mind for my commute. This was only my first sample of Limbaugh, which was not enough to be confident about what he was really like.

Over a period of years I continued to sample Limbaugh. The experiment that evolved was to see how many seconds would transpire before this news talk show host would start complaining about something. At that point I would switch the station, unless I felt compelled to listen just enough longer to better gauge what he was complaining about. The longest interval before the complaints began was twenty-six seconds. I eventually reached a confidence level that Limbaugh was indeed a whiner and stopped my sampling.

I was confident, but there still remained some room for doubt. I had acquired numerous samples but not the total population of "Limbaugh" events. Anything could have biased my samples. Perhaps I always sampled on days when the news as a whole was bad from his perspective, or perhaps I always caught him on days when he was experiencing personal problems, such as the drug addiction he had. I decided to obtain one last sample. My previous sampling informed me as to Limbaugh's politics, not through what he championed, of course, but through what he complained about. A week after the 2004 election, a time that should have witnessed Limbaugh glowing, I sampled his program one last time.

Limbaugh complained about Democrats complaining about the election. He could have taken the opportunity to emulate Ronald Reagan, infusing his audience with positive feelings about the "morning in America" that lay ahead with executive, legislative and judicial branches of government controlled by Republicans. Instead, he used his radio pulpit to enrage listeners during a time of triumph. I was certain. Limbaugh neither uplifts nor even informs; he seeks to cultivate meanness in his listeners through incessant complaints. The most depressing aspect of Limbaugh's show is that his meanness apparently entertains so many Americans.

A couple years ago I was commuting at an unusual time when I tuned to the radio station with the most powerful signal in our region, WTIC, a little before noon. I immediately heard whining, leading me to conclude I must be listening to another "news" talk show, but I also heard a falsehood of considerable interest to me. I continued listening.

The host stated that 96% of the indicators about the economy are positive, citing one of the Powell Cabal's think tanks as his source of information. This claim is at odds with the inflation of housing, health care and education costs in relation to median family income, as well as several other economic issues we explored in our economic essays. Still, this was corporate media and, unlike the middle class, none of these inflation pressures damage the rarified economic stratosphere of corporate executives. As viewed by the host—or at least by the Powell Cabal providing the statistics and the media giant paying the host—maybe 96% of the economic indicators are positive.

"Unlikely!" would exclaim the scientist. You seldom get such a high percentage of agreement for variable phenomena, natural or cultural. The only way you could expect such uniformity with the indicators would be through "stacking the deck." For example, out of 100 indicators you could have four that include housing, health care and education costs, in addition to rising debt. The other ninety-six indicators might correspond to strategically selected stocks of various technologies. Presto! You have your 96% positive economic indicators. But you don't have a valid sample of the economy, not even from the point of view of corporate executives. These are the kind of economic indicators you might expect from The Heritage Foundation.

Citing positive economic indicators may not sound like whining, but the host tossed out another percentage as well. We never hear about how well our economy is doing, the host lamented, because 85% of the journalists are liberal. Once again, such an unnaturally high percentage sets off an alarm regarding biased samples. Let us forego the statistics for now and evaluate the claim that 85% of journalists are liberal based only on logic.

As earlier data from the Google searches suggest, most talk shows, think tanks and pundits are conservative. The authorities are conservative. Corporations, including corporate media, tend to be conservative. The host of the show no doubt would claim that a majority of Americans are conservative, and that he is also conservative. Yet in response to both the greater supply and demand for conservatism, we are to believe that the conservative corporate media hires liberal journalists in overwhelming proportion. This suggests bungling incompetence in the hiring practices of large corporations who naturally would want journalists that agreed with their point of view.

The "incompetence" extends even further than this logic so far suggests. There is a network for grooming conservative journalists that liberals lack. Sheldon Rampton and John Stauber documents in Banana Republicans (2004, pgs. 74-75):

> "Liberals do not have an organized system for recruiting, nurturing and promoting the careers of left-leaning journalists, but conservatives do. It begins on college campuses, where the Collegiate Network, which began as a project of the Institute for Educational Affairs, serves as a networking resource and spends more than $300,000 per year funding 80 conservative student newspapers. From 1995 to 2002, the Collegiate Network received more than $4 million from conservative funders."

Regardless of the inaccuracy of either claim, why should a news talk show host whine about 85% of the journalists being liberal, rather than be enthused about 96% of economic indicators being positive? Why should Rush Limbaugh whine about Democrats whining, rather than be excited about Republicans controlling all branches of government? What is to be gained by such whining negativism in the echo chambers of corporate media? To answer this, let us check in with Hans.

Centralized News Entertainment

After supper Hans settles into his favorite recliner for an evening of prime time news. Unlike many families Hans has only one television, but he does have TIVO. This allows Hans to record his children's favorite programming that occurs during prime time. Meanwhile, the kids are upstairs on their computers, connected to entertainment on the Internet. No compromise is needed in this family. Hans can watch what he wants without protest and the kids do not have to burden themselves with watching news programming with their parent.

Hans turns on the TV and a chart of stock market indicators appears. A news anchor briefly describes the bullish economy (this essay was written in 2007), which makes Hans feel proud to be a wealthy American, but he has little knowledge about stocks. Hans knows by now that reporting on the stock market will take only a minute. To best emphasize this pro-corporate economic news corporate media provides the stock market information incessantly but briefly throughout the day. Hans has developed less patience than the minimal amount required for the stock market indicators and he begins to channel surf with his remote.

An image comes up of a well-known news talk show host and Hans settles in for what really amounts to entertainment. Often this host is merely whining about something but tonight he goes a step further with a display of anger. The host has a guest he obviously dislikes, or at least pretends to dislike, and he rips into his guest without mercy. Had Hans been watching this "news" program with his kids he would have been a bit uncomfortable at this point. After all, Hans treats his neighbors with civility, an example he wants his kids to emulate. But his kids are not in the room; Hans can entertain himself with some outright rudeness and anger, staged or not.

Corporate media knows that kids are not a factor in whatever Hans watches, and that Hans wants to be entertained as much or more than he wants to be informed. All they need to do is make sure that Hans does not get angry about certain topics. Economic news relevant to the middle class, like health care costs, will be treated more briefly than the stock market, and without the incessant reinforcement. Only rogue corporations will be featured in the echo chamber, as an exception to the rule of our necessary corporate economy. Even then, you would not expect something like WorldCom or Tyco to get as much airtime as Anna Nicole Smith or Britney Spears. Corporate media has found a formula to get the maximum entertainment value out of "news:" get rid of localism, get rid of civility and maximize opinions over actual events. When they go to the FCC to lobby for deregulation, this is the news programming they claim represents "progress" over what localized media can provide.

The FCC and the Public Interest

We could have focused on the domination of corporate media as an economic issue. We could have explored the methods by which they create demand for the centralized packaging of their news programming. We could have explored how they use their large market share to concentrate the supply of capital provided by advertisers, hogging what might otherwise be provided to local media. We could have explored how they control the labor market for news reporters; subsequently reducing their overall numbers, changing their job to require more entertainment than investigation and requiring longer hours for the average reporter. We could have illuminated further why cable rates have increased three times the rate of inflation since the Telecom Act of 1996.

Yes, we could have adapted this essay for the part on economics quite nicely, using corporate media to elaborate how large corporations and the Powell Cabal seek to strengthen and entrench a competitive advantage over proprietorships. If we had done that we would not have featured the biggest problem with media consolidation and the centralized packaging of news. We should be upset by the degradation of free market diversity as government acts on the behalf of corporate media, but we need to be even more vigilant about the impacts on our political liberty and the ability to achieve wise rule from our democratic system.

Persuading government to enhance the competitive advantage of corporations at the expense of proprietorships turns economics into politics. Lobbying for increased regulation of airwaves and decreased regulation of media consolidation may seem like a double standard if you take the espoused doctrine of corporations and *laissez faire* economists seriously. What corporations really want is to maximize profits for shareholders, in which case the increased regulation of airwaves and decreased regulation of media consolidation are inconsistent means to a consistent end. The objectives for which Congress empowered the FCC— enhancing localism, competition, and diversity—requires the precise opposite means of decreased regulation of airwaves and increased regulation of media consolidation. The track record of government confirms that with the air waves, as with so much of society, they will side with *laissez faire* economics over the public interest.

This brings us back to Michael Powell, the former head of the FCC. Powell first came to the FCC from the U. S. Department of Justice Antitrust Division in 1997. This sounds like an ominous background for corporate media, until you realize that the way our political system tends to work these days is to let the foxes run the chicken coops. Powell was quoted in *Wired* magazine as saying: "Monopoly is not illegal by itself in the United States. People tend to forget this. There is something healthy about letting innovators try to capture markets."[6]

Powell headed the FCC during the first term of President Bush II, corresponding to the time that Michael's father, Colin, served as Secretary of State. This was soon after corporate media succeeded in getting stricter regulations on the allotment of airwaves through the Radio Broadcast Preservation Act of 2000. Giddy from this success, and with an ally now in charge of the FCC, corporate media was confident they could eliminate media ownership caps entirely.

Powell led a campaign to achieve this goal for those plucky corporate media "innovators." He set a target date of June, 2003 for eliminating national ownership caps. Powell had once admitted that the FCC was supposed to serve the public interest, but claimed to not know what that meant. His campaign to eliminate ownership caps not only illustrated his ignorance, but revealed that he actually had no interest in the public interest. Citizens and interest groups of varying backgrounds and beliefs united against deregulation, including noted libertarians

---

6 In "Big Media or Bust" by Frank Rose (March 2002).

such as William Safire (though the "libertarian" think tanks of the Powell Cabal, such as the Cato Institute and Heritage Foundation, offered no protests against media monopolization).

In the eight months prior to the target date Powell met privately with corporate media interests over seventy times, and only five times with public interest groups.[7] Of course, corporate media provides better incentives for meeting privately with them. Up until the target date for eliminating ownership caps corporate media had sponsored the travel and entertainment for 44 trips taken by Powell at a cost of $84,921, with the most frequent destination being Las Vegas.[8] These are the kind of frequent "work" trips that contribute to the reports of the Federal Reserve Banks claiming that the working class has more leisure than the fat cats. Under pressure Powell held public hearings, but after the public informed him they did not like his plan he stopped attending them. Instead, he announced that the FCC would be better served to get the process over with as quickly as possible. Powell cited the information gathering process as outdated in the electronic age; though he also had to acknowledge the 750,000 emails the FCC received that condemned further consolidation.

Instead of public input Powell relied on research done by economists to justify his crusade for deregulation of ownership caps. Oh, oh. We know now what kind of research is done by *laissez faire* economists and Powell Cabal think tanks. We witnessed how they can use multiple indicators and multiple assumptions to obscure the validity of their data. This same approach was used for supporting the economics of deregulation. You might be interested to know that, at least by the clever analyses backed by the FCC, the Dutchess Community College television station has a greater impact on the public than the *New York Times*. Attorney Harold Feld, vice president of the nonpartisan telecommunications law firm known as Media Access Project, gave the following assessment of these indicators:

> "They used proprietary data that the commission would not release to other researchers. No one could replicate their studies or validate their findings. ... The truth is that the FCC doesn't do real social science. They spend too much time listening to Heritage (Foundation) and Cato (Institute), and all the free-market ideologues who do 'research' to prove what they already believe. ... And I've seen them distort the research to

---

7   From "Behind Closed Doors: Top Broadcasters Met 71 Times with FCC Officials" (May 29, 2003), an article by Bob Williams posted on the Center for Public Integrity's web site.

8   From "On the Road Again—and Again" (May 22, 2003), an article by Bob Williams and Morgan Jindrich posted on the Center for Public Integrity's web site. As a quick aside, I wonder if this type of "work" was factored into the study sponsored by the Federal Reserve Bank of Boston bemoaning the comparative lack of leisure for the upper class.

support the results they wanted."[9]

On June 2, 2003 the FCC voted to support Powell's deregulation plans, with the 3-2 vote following party lines. By this time, however, public outrage had been duly noted by a Republican Congress, if not by the Republican members of the FCC. Here is a timeline of subsequent events.

- In July, 2003, the House displayed unusual bipartisan support for maintaining the current ownership limits in a 400-21 vote. A battle ensued with the FCC, corporate media and the Bush II administration maneuvering to get the new FCC rules in place and the rarely "bipartisan" House and Senate pushing back.

- In September, 2003 the Courts got involved, with the Third Circuit Court placing a stay on the FCC rules.

- In June, 2004 the Court upheld compromise legislation passed by Congress and refuted Powell's contention that ownership caps were unconstitutional.

- In 2005 Powell resigned as FCC commission and went through the revolving door to work for a firm handling investments from corporate media. In his new job Powell no longer has to suffer the nuisance of the public interest.

This series of comic missteps would have provided great fodder for something like *The Daily Show*, except that the fake news show is owned by Viacom, one of the corporate media giants that contributed to Powell's Vegas trips. You cannot get too upset with *The Daily Show* for not satirizing the shady and comical politics behind media consolidation; they are, after all, fake news. You can get upset that such a topic will never reach the centralized corporate media echo chambers that focus our attention on the travails of Paris Hilton and the character issues of political candidates.

Understanding Bias

I get my news these days from a wide variety of media: localized and centralized, conservative and liberal, print and broadcast. Aware of my knowledge regarding different news sources, my oldest daughter came to me for advice on a school project she did in 2006. Her Civics teacher assigned the class to do a report grading

9 As told to Eric Klinenberg in an interview for *Fighting for Air* (2007).

President Bush II. Bless her heart; my daughter wanted a variety of sources with different types of ideologies from which she could base her grade. I suggested the web site TruthOut.org for the input of anti-authoritarian media, and the *Fox News* broadcast for the input of authoritarian media. I resisted the temptation to provide my own input.

Both my daughters are "A" students (please forgive a father's pride for the moment). My oldest daughter had not received a grade lower than A- in her Civics course up until her project. She received a C for her President Bush II report card, which was still a better grade than what she gave the Bush II administration after her attempts at researching contrasting perspectives.

My daughter's project grade was to be expected; her Civics teacher supported the authoritarians currently in government. She could not expect to give the Bush II administration a very low grade and still receive a very high one for herself. You have to make choices in this complicated world. The only thing that really bothered me about my daughter's project was the teacher's comments regarding her news sources. One hopes that teachers can identify biases, even as they may agree or disagree with these biases. The teacher faulted TruthOut. org for being a source with an anti-authoritarian bias, certainly guilty as charged, but made no comment about *Fox News*. Maybe he believes that a news station directed by Roger Ailes—a former media consultant for Republican presidential candidates—can be as "fair and balanced" as they claim. This particular teacher did not last long; he now works in the business world.

Everyone has biases, of course. The point of having independent and decentralized news reporting is not to eliminate bias, but to enable diverse opinions to flourish. Yet even with diverse opinions based on independent and decentralized information, wisdom still might elude a democracy. The trick lies in how well we can aggregate our opinions into a form of collective wisdom. Like it or not, this involves some responsibility on the part of us, the citizens.

ESSAY 13 – CONVENTIONAL CITIZENSHIP

Overview

- Authorities encourage citizens to be less willing to die or serve than soldiers.
- Authorities burden citizens with a similar emotional hell experienced by soldiers.
- Apprehension for our security has become conventional.
- Cynicism regarding democratic double standards has become conventional.
- Vanity for material and libertarian indulgences has become conventional.
- The voting booth often aggregates a conventional input of citizens.
- Experiential learning can increase our independent thought.
- Service can enable citizens to acquire independent and diverse experiences.
- A Universal Service System would commit citizens to service in ways that could foster wisdom and democracy.
- Authorities could lead by their example of public service, but instead we have career politicians.
- Career politicians steer government in the direction of greed and authoritarianism.

Mr. Harrington's Horror

My father joined the Navy at the tender age of 35 to fight in World War II. His service as a boatswain on a battleship led to the loss of hearing in one ear but he came back with more stories about exotic islands than fierce battles. He repeatedly told anyone who would listen: "I was as safe standing on the deck of a battleship as I am standing right here." Many people who have been in battle tend to minimize their own experience in honor of those who had it worse; I never was sure if my father expressed his true apprehensions he felt during battle. I also had one brother in the Army Reserve during the Korean War, and one brother in the Air Force during the Vietnam War. Fortunately, neither one saw combat. Whatever wisdom I gained about the horrors of battle came not from listening to my family but from watching television and from Bob Harrington.

The Vietnam War occurred in an era before twenty-hour news networks and news talk programs. No pundits were called in frequently to give their opinions. Politicians and the military did not control the access by journalists to the extent found in this "sellers market" for news. With only a couple hours per day to devote to news the networks had to fill much of their programs with actual news reporting and film footage of events. During the Vietnam War both the reporting and the film footage conveyed atrocities. Perhaps the graphic images of the Vietnam War, as much as the atrocities experienced during World War II, contributed to my father's reticence in portraying his own experience in battle.

Those images and stories were sufficient to convince me that war was indeed hell on earth, but the exclamation mark was provided by Mr. Harrington. He had returned from a tour of duty in Vietnam and became involved in a different type of service—helping coach the Babe Ruth team I was on. During one practice he was working with the shortstop with his back to the outfield. The head coach was hitting balls to the outfielders. The left fielder caught a fly ball and threw the baseball back to the infield, heading for the general vicinity of Mr. Harrington.

From my vantage point near second base I shouted: "Look out!"

Many of you may be able to guess what happened but to a somewhat blissfully ignorant teenager the next moment was astonishing. Mr. Harrington threw himself down on the ground in sheer panic—seemingly to avoid a tiny baseball. The practice came to a halt as we all watched dumbfounded while he picked himself up again. He yelled for us (me) not to do that again and then relaxed. He explained what caused his behavior. In his mind, of course, were all too real images of bombs exploding around him; he responded how he was trained to respond when in the thick of battle.

Mr. Harrington had gone through hell on earth for his country. That should be the one characteristic that makes a soldier distinct from a citizen. Instead, soldiers have become more distinct for their willingness to die and to serve, something that the rest of us citizens should feel some remorse about. In contrast, the rhetoric of authorities often seeks to place all other citizens in an emotional hell, while making them less willing to serve or die for others. Making citizens less willing to serve, less willing to die and more exposed to an emotional hell ripens us for groupthink. Authorities can indoctrinate the conventional "wisdom" that supports their continued political agenda, rather than having to aggregate the collective wisdom of a democracy. This essay explores both problems and solutions for citizens indoctrinated with conventional "wisdom."

Soldiers and Citizens

Soldiers are required to do things on behalf of all other citizens. The differences between soldiers and citizens have expanded in recent times, but for the wrong reasons. Authorities apparently think the courage and altruism of lesser mammals fails ordinary citizens.

Politicians often chide citizens to support the troops that are willing to die for their country, but willingness to die for a cause is neither heroic nor unique to soldiers. As any naturalist can tell you there are many species that instinctively die for their young, including humans. Many of us will instinctively die for our land as well. If we were invaded by a foreign country many people would exercise their Second Amendment rights rather than "come out with their hands up." Maybe fewer would risk their lives now than in an earlier era, for reasons we will get to shortly, but the fact remains that dying for a cause is part of the inherent nature of many mammals and should be considered neither heroic nor unique in humans.

In addition to our willingness to die for a cause humans are among the creatures of this earth distinguished by their altruism. In early cultures altruism was not just a distinctive characteristic; it was how we survived as a species. Authorities do little to nurture this altruism. Instead, they partition us into the soldiers that are supposed to serve and be altruistic while for the rest of us this remains optional at best. Oh, we are a great nation for volunteering and our authorities will encourage this. But this is a matter of doing something good for those disadvantaged by our systems, and not a matter of taking individual responsibility for making our systems run better. For us citizens such responsibility need extend no further than the voting booth.

Let us take a moment now to understand what is supposed to be unique about the soldier. War is the closest thing to hell on earth. For those who die in battle the hell ends with their life. Understanding this, we can appreciate fully the soldier who laments that: "the lucky ones died in battle." Due to the human capacities to remember and feel emotion the hell never ends for those once embroiled in battle and returned home. Mr. Harrington showed me all I needed to know about that.

We train and require soldiers to experience hell on earth so that citizens can remain in a civilized bubble. When in battle at no point can soldiers relax and be unconcerned about what might happen the next moment. This apprehension must be maintained on a 24/7 basis so that citizens can feel secure in their homeland. For soldiers to fulfill their duty in battle sometimes their vanity must grow to a point where they view the enemy as subhuman. This vanity contributes to successful combat, while citizens can lead normal humble lives. Surrounded by carnage and "subhumans" no one should be surprised that some soldiers become cynical and break their rules of engagement. Yet due to the efforts of our soldiers abroad—including the unavoidable atrocities that people succumb to in hell—citizens back home can maintain their faith in a democracy and the rule of law.

A mind once conditioned to constantly apprehend danger, demonize enemies and justify atrocities cannot easily recover. Many soldiers continue to deal with such personal torments even after they return home and adapt to life as "normal" citizens, seeking to join the rest of us in our civilized bubble. We need to understand this because these former soldiers are the ones we tend to neglect most. Out of one side of their mouths politicians and certain special interest groups praise soldiers lavishly for being willing to serve and die for the causes the politicians themselves choose, portraying this willingness to serve and die for a cause as something extraordinary and unusual among the human species. Out of the other side of their mouths politicians will at times vote to cut benefits to the soldiers who have returned home, giving no thought to the real nature of their sacrifice, the sacrifice of having to go through hell.

As politicians succeed in making citizens afraid to risk our own lives the willingness to die by soldiers becomes more heroic than what should be natural. As politicians encourage us to think of liberties as an entitlement rather than a responsibility the service of soldiers becomes more heroic than what should be natural. But if citizens get to the point where we have constant apprehension, regard enemies as subhuman, and can justify atrocities what has the heroics of soldiers gained for us? Let us pay a visit to Hans to explore further how the gap has narrowed between soldier and citizen experiencing hell on earth.

Conventional Apprehension

Hans lives in the state of New Hampshire, where his license plate declares: "Live free or die." With this constant reminder Hans is willing to die not only for his family and his home but for the cause of freedom as well. Hans has understood that freedom is a package of both rights and responsibilities ever since President Kennedy challenged him in the 1961 Inaugural Address to: "…ask not what America will do for you, but what together we can do for the freedom of man." Hans willingly accepted that this freedom package justified risks to life not only for soldiers but for citizens as well.

After a terrorist attack killed over 3,000 people, Hans was ready to do his part for freedom. All he needed was leadership. Though terrorists killed less than two-thousandth of a percent of the population, authorities convinced Hans of an urgent and immediate reality that this could very well happen to him. Mushroom clouds from nuclear weapons could appear on the horizon in the very near future.

Apprehension of terror was made conventional by authorities. Hans subconsciously picked up the subtle inference that "live free or die" was just a figure of speech, at least the "die" part. He was told that security topped all priorities, and that was what all Americans like him should want and demand from government. Unless Hans intended to become a soldier he needed to become not just apprehensive but outright terrified of risking his life, even for the cause of freedom.

There is more to this conventional apprehension than just the fear of terrorism. Security has been trumped up by authorities and philosophers alike as the primary goal of a nation state. We are not to face life on its own terms, as we naturally evolved to do as early foragers. Life is to be made secure on our behalf, independently of our own actions. Authorities are the ones to make the world secure while citizens do the only thing required of us, vote for the right authorities.

Some of our dependency for security lies with corporations. Laborers and potential entrepreneurs are not to be relied on as an alternative to the corporate economy when things go south. If corporations go through a downturn, such as with corporate media in the early nineties or the current housing market, they are to be protected for the sake of our security. Corporations in general are to be saved because our perceived economic security lies in their empowerment and not to be entrusted to citizens coming up with alternative entrepreneurial plans on their own behalf. Meanwhile, a downturn for middle income families and proprietorships calls for making bankruptcy laws more severe, because this is a threat to corporations and the "security" they provide us.

A newspaper recently featured the opinions of a few citizens on what to do about the ailing economy. One citizen rhetorically asked: "Why would we tax the wealthy, they provide us jobs?" Note that we are not to look to ourselves or even the help of friends or community for economic production. Filled with conventional apprehension regarding our own abilities to survive, we are to rely on those folks who are wealthy to secure our employment, which is to say we are to rely on corporations or the authorities that legislate on their behalf.

Conventional Cynicism

After 9/11 authorities encouraged Hans to cynically believe that democratic standards should be applied selectively. This conventional cynicism held that our quest for freedom should impose freedom abroad, forcing the conversion of countries according to what works best for our timetable, not theirs. This conventional cynicism held that the self-interest of one country should trump the Geneva Convention or the United Nations, both products of a democratic process. This conventional cynicism induced Hans to support the USA PATRIOT Act, which restricts our liberty for the sake of liberty.

The USA PATRIOT Act applies a double standard: citizens should have less privacy while government has more. If we do not have the urgency to abide by this double standard we allegedly will fail to obtain the information to warn us about future terrorist attacks. Unknown to Hans, we had the information to warn us about 9/11 but that information did not get processed with due diligence. The USA PATRIOT Act addresses the information part of the issue, the part that was not the problem, and provides greater means to hide the problematic part of due diligence. As citizens we are to cynically support the abandonment of checks and balances and government oversight for the sake of democracy. That is to say, we are to embrace paternal democracy at the expense of true democracy.

Along this same problematic vein energy policy vital to the nation was decided in secret meetings because we allegedly needed to protect energy executives for advising what they thought was in the country's best interest. This raises two interesting questions. Why would there be repercussions to energy executives for advising our country's energy policy, unless their advice was driven by self-interest rather than the public interest? Even if there might be repercussions, should not energy executives be willing to suffer consequences for doing what they think is best for our country? Yet the executive branch decides that government privacy, unlike individual privacy, is to be upheld at all costs while the judicial branch provides legal cover. Vice President Cheney gets his privacy while the rest of us wonder why the executives and justices of our political system must protect the confidences of people supposedly doing their civic duty.

Authorities are granted executive privilege and executive authority not just to run the country but to keep their decisions and actions hidden from citizens. We trust that they have the public interest in mind, but what evidence do we have that is the case? Mainly the evidence of whatever they tell us. The only decisions we are asked to make is which authorities to trust for making all our important decisions. A conventional cynicism has invaded the land regarding the very foundations of democracy. A true democracy cannot function but through the involvement of citizens being provided pertinent information for their own decision making.

Corporate media nurtures conventional cynicism with news talk hosts and pundits from special interest groups that glorify our democracy as we attempt to impose democracy abroad. Corporate media and their think tank pundits encourage us to support free trade even as we coerce developing countries into these "free trade" agreements through loan entrapments. Corporate media encourages us to be cynical about corporate media itself, proclaiming loudly that conservative corporate media owners are powerless to stop the tide of liberal journalists, thus drowning out the more real issue of whether corporate media has, in fact, a corporate bias.

Conventional Vanity

The apprehensive and cynical Hans yet wants to know if there might be something he could do to serve his country for freedom's sake. Authorities let Hans know that asking what he could do for his country was a quaint sentiment but totally unnecessary; all he had to do to be a good citizen was vote the right way to make the country secure. Hans can proceed with only a vain concern for what his country could do for him and, if he happened to be wealthy enough, enjoy a tax cut in a time of "war." In return for only his vote politicians promised to indulge Hans with material comforts and liberties.

Being materially indulged creates vain desire for more material indulgence. This is the essence of greed. We are willing to work for this material indulgence, to contribute to our country's economic productivity in return, but that presents a problem. As a higher proportion of family labor goes to economic productivity a lower proportion goes to the equally important tasks of self-improvement, family obligations, community service and political involvement. This is precisely how authoritarian leaders would want our labors to be divided up. If we are wrapped up in economic productivity we relinquish the political responsibility to hold representative authorities accountable. We are willing to settle for the quick fix of whatever corporate media and think tank pundits can sell us with sound bites.

A liberty provided by the State corresponds to either a natural right or a cultural entitlement. We are born with natural rights that include unexploited labor, freedom of thought and the free will to belong (see Essay 15). These are physically evolved traits which Nature bestowed and cannot take away. Unfortunately, the State has greater influence over our lives than Nature. Governments around the world, including our own, can and have deprived us of these natural rights. On the other hand, the State can call these natural rights liberties and grant them to us. The State also can grant libertarian indulgences not bestowed by Nature, such as the rights to property, security and privacy.

Sometimes libertarian indulgence conflicts with our natural rights. For property, which only can be guaranteed through provisions and protections of the State, we are willing to exploit and be exploited towards that end. For security, provided and protected by the State, we are willing to abandon our freedom of thought to blindly follow the authoritarians that promise us this security. For privacy, provided and protected by the State, we are willing to abandon the free will of belonging to others. Instead of belonging to others, we seek belonging to the interest groups that best indulge our beliefs while enabling us to maintain privacy apart from our community.

Libertarian indulgences become conventionally vain entitlements. Just as wealthy investors come to feel vainly entitled to capital without having to produce anything in return, citizens come to feel vainly entitled to various liberties without bearing the responsibility of citizenship. A conventional vanity has been induced through hypnotic hyperbole and dogma about how government is to "let be," with little thought as to how we are to responsibly self-govern.

In the absence of politicians detailing our responsibility as citizens, corporations have provided their view. We need only the "responsibility" to be selfishly self-interested to work out all the kinks in our economic, political and cultural systems. We accept by vain convention that the economics of property should be fueled by greed. We accept that the politics of security should be driven by authoritarianism. We accept that the culture of privacy should worship the dogma of special interests.

Leadership since 9/11 has molded Hans to "live free," though afraid to die and unwilling to assume democratic responsibilities. He need not have the courage of his convictions; he need not be humble enough to think he needs to serve, rather than be served, by his country; and he certainly need not have enough faith in freedom or the law to hold his country accountable to either in times of perceived peril. Hans now feels he need not be willing to "die" for anything, indeed, he believes that reducing risk of death should be cherished above all else—unless you are a soldier you need not display the courage or altruism of a lesser mammal. The reformation of Hans's emotional state would seem to devalue the sacrifice by soldiers going through hell on the battlefield. On the contrary, soldiers have become more heroic now than ever before, since their devotion to real service sets them apart from ordinary citizens whose service goes no further than the voting booth.

The Voting Booth

What happens at the voting booth provides the litmus test for democracy. Ideally, voting expresses the collective wisdom of citizens. But for this wisdom to occur citizens must not be driven by conventional apprehension, cynicism or vanity nurtured by authoritarians. Each vote must reflect the independent and decentralized perspectives of a diverse citizenry. When the reelection of incumbent authoritarians surpasses ninety percent—as occurs in both totalitarian regimes and in our own country—the voting booth reflects citizens ruled by totalitarian convention.

Since citizens have a natural instinct to conform and trust authority, encouraging nothing else but voting as a rite of citizenship works to the natural advantage of incumbent politicians. Emphasizing the other necessary ingredients for expanding individual liberty and collective wisdom—encouraging citizens to draw upon their own experiences and think critically about the claims of authorities—would detract from an incumbent's ability to maintain power. As John Stuart Mill described in *On Liberty* (1859), aggregating opinions that merely conform to the established power structure leads to a conventional tyranny of the majority. Essay 10 on paternal democracy described further how conformity has infected this country.

Political parties are dependent on both wealth and dogma in order to succeed. By belonging to a political party we in turn become dependent on their ability to merge the right blend of wealth and dogma in order to maintain power. We transfer this dependence to the voting booth where we can pull the party level or otherwise support the conventional party ticket, without ever having to suffer through our own independent thought. Essay 11 on party democracy described further how dependence has infected this country.

Too often our opinions have not been formed by the events we experience or observe, but rather by the opinions we receive from consolidated media providing centralized news. This news media has been consolidated by corporations, as allowed by government to subvert the natural tendency of competition to create diversity. We substitute the perspectives from our own individual experiences with the conventional experience of the legally designated and protected "individuals" known as business corporations. Essay 12 on corporate media described further how centralization has infected this country.

Too often the voting booth aggregates the input of citizens conforming to authorities, dependent on political parties and informed by centralized opinions. Many of us have traded the freedom of thought for promises of security and entitlements. We have become herds of sheep ruled by convention. Ironically, the silver lining at the voting booth has been voter apathy.

Though voting is the only encouraged rite of citizenship these days, we have been apathetic even with this minimal requirement. This is actually a better fate than an electorate voting in large numbers in totalitarian convention. Apathy at least signals that there is a problem with our democracy's ability to collect wisdom. The response to apathy should not be merely getting out the vote, but engaging citizens in a larger process of exercising our independent thought for the sake of a functioning democracy. At the heart of our own independent thought are our own experiences.

Experience and Independent Thought

Expressed in the terms of logic, voting is a necessary but not sufficient condition to extract wisdom from the political liberty of citizens. Referring again to the conditions for wisdom derived by James Surowiecki in *The Wisdom of Crowds* (2004), voting provides a means of aggregating opinions but no guarantee that those opinions will be diverse, independent or decentralized. Diverse, independent and decentralized opinions derive from the most important liberty for democracy, the independent thought.

Independent thought must draw from diverse experiences. Our country values the liberty to have diverse experiences and opinions enough to provide guarantees for this in our Bill of Rights. Authoritarians in a paternal democracy do not like diversity. From their point of view diversity slows down the ability of authoritarians to get precisely what they want; at worst, diversity may derail their ambitions. Yet opinions born out of diverse experiences bring to light all the possibilities for consideration that even the most accomplished expert or leader would otherwise miss.

Independent thought necessitates that citizens maintain their independence from authoritative agents and agencies. We need not rebel or break laws to do so; but we do need to weight the validity and reliability of messages and not the authority of the messenger, particularly when the messengers are party loyalists. Forego our independence and we subjugate our potential wealth of diverse experience to the opinions of experts we assume must know better than us. An expert may know more than any individual citizen regarding an issue but does not have the wisdom of an entire citizenry exercising their independent thought to express informed opinions. Not only do they lack such democratic wisdom, experts and authorities may subjugate the public interest to their own self-interest, an affliction that our forefathers warned us about.

The freedom to think independently from authorities provides no great advantage for collective wisdom without the benefit of decentralized experiences. We might be the best situated nation on earth to draw from a plethora of decentralized experiences, as our Statute of Liberty welcomes the masses from varied cultures all over the world. Unfortunately, this advantage has been lost since we are also the world leader in mass media and conformity to a corporate culture.

Fostering the independence and decentralized experiences needed for independent thought could be achieved by local public education. Attending school already is a mandatory rite of citizenship in this country. However, our primary and secondary schools must serve multiple functions; energizing young people with the responsibility of political liberty falls behind other priorities. The classroom curriculum at the secondary level primarily prepares our children to choose a career path and be productive citizens economically. The common mode of instruction in the classroom is authoritarian; an expert shares his/her knowledge with little contribution of knowledge from students. There are many excellent teachers and lesson plans providing a stimulating learning experience for our youth, but in most classrooms neither the curriculum nor the instruction is geared towards engaging students with aggregating the wisdom of their diverse, independent and decentralized experiences.

Extracurricular school activities come nearer the mark of providing the type of experiential catalyst we need. A wider range of experience and more autonomy is provided in these club settings. However, by their very definition extracurricular activities are not mandatory. Even if they were mandatory the main intent is to broaden cultural interests, not training students to make the most out of independent thought and collective democracy.

If we want to catalyze the independent thought gained from experiences, then experiential education would be a logical catalyst. Most experiential education takes place outside the classroom and, in fact, outside our schools. Two of the more famous venues for experiential education are Outward Bound and the National Outdoor Leadership School (NOLS). Both of these programs place students in an intense, strenuous wilderness setting that requires a mixture of teamwork and self-reliance. No specific economic, political or cultural interests are promoted as part of the experience. Participants develop their own unique wisdom from individual experiences of self-discovery.

One drawback of many experiential education programs such as Outward Bound and NOLS is their brevity. A program whose term is measured in weeks does not ensure a life-changing experience, regardless of the intensity. Even with the numerous long-distance backpacking expeditions I have participated in, whose terms are measured in months, the effects of the experience wear off over time for some of the participants. The benefits of intense experiential education activities become internalized only if changes in normal, everyday behavior occur as a result.

Experiential education that focuses only on self-discovery also fails to broaden the horizons of participants who have previously experienced only one economic class, one political ideology and/or one cultural setting. Collecting wisdom from the diverse experiences of citizens is facilitated if each citizen in turn has diversified personal experiences contributing to individual wisdom. This personal collection of diverse experiences could become a first step in an approach to federated wisdom and federated democracy.

Service and Wisdom

One of the best venues for learning from the experience of others is through service. In addition to the military there are a variety of opportunities to serve in this country. The Peace Corps provides service to underdeveloped countries. AmeriCorps provides service for education and other community needs. The Student Conservation Association provides service for our public lands. Habitat for Humanity provides service for people struggling to afford a home. You can browse the website at www.networkforgood.org to appreciate the wide range of service opportunities available and, perhaps, to find one that will capture your own heart and mind.

There remain at least three problems that limit the potential of volunteer service for enhancing liberty and democracy. First, voluntary service by definition cannot become a mandatory rite of citizenship. Second, people tend to volunteer for service that is in line with current interests, not use the opportunity to expand their wealth of experiences. Third, voluntary service holds no expectation for volunteers to apply what they have experienced beyond the particular service opportunity. Each of these problems needs to be remedied in order for service to become the rite of citizenship that catalyzes individual and collective wisdom in a democracy.

There was a time when one type of service was mandatory for citizens. Congress passed the Selective Service Act of 1940 which created the Selective Service System, more commonly known as the draft. The draft expired in 1947 but was reinstated in 1951 by the Universal Military Training and Service Act. We associate the draft with times that the country has been at war, but the draft also occurred during times of peace, such as the late fifties and early sixties. To catalyze full participation in liberty and democracy, we need something along the lines of "Universal" Service, rather than "Selective" Service. We also would need to expand the opportunities beyond that of the soldier.

There are good reasons to not make soldiers out of all citizens, as in the case of ancient Sparta. Serving our country should not require heroism, as many politicians and special interest groups like the American Legion would have us believe. As asserted earlier, soldiers should not be viewed as heroic for their service but for their willingness to go through a hell of apprehension, vanity and cynicism that are the emotional consequences of war. For all other citizens service should help alleviate these afflictions. Service should reduce vain attachments to one's own economic, political or cultural interests, while at the same time reducing apprehension of different interests. Service also should reinforce faith in a country of laws and principles aimed at promoting the common good.

There is another aspect of military service that would not be appropriate for a universal rite of citizenship. Soldiers are the one category of citizens for whom conformity and blind trust in authority are not just natural attributes but necessities. Indeed, you have to wonder who our leaders are really talking about when they discourage dissent because of the demoralizing affects they claim this will have on our troops. Surely they don't mean to degrade our well-disciplined soldiers. We should trust our military leaders to train our soldiers well enough to ignore dissent outside of their ranks. The only type of dissent that should affect a well-trained soldier would be widespread dissatisfaction expressed through a democracy, aggregating the collective wisdom of citizens exercising their independent thoughts. Considering what an easy sell war generally is for nation states, widespread dissatisfaction from a citizenry necessarily would be based on substantive concerns developed through this independence.

In addition to providing for traditional military service, a Universal Service System could tap into the existing infrastructure of organizations providing other types of service opportunities. Enlistment into this system would be mandatory as a rite of citizenship. As part of their mandatory obligation citizens could be placed in service situations that broaden their horizons. Some of the wealthy could serve in urban schools; some of the urban poor could serve in our National Parks; and all walks of life could serve at those necessary but unpleasant jobs that corporations and "libertarian" think tanks patronizingly tell us that no Americans want.[1] As an additional bonus, the current problem of soldiers being represented overwhelmingly by the lower and middle classes could be remedied through a Universal Service System structured to balance this representation.

In response to the longevity of the current war embroiling our country we have been relaxing our recruitment standards for soldiers. Rather than recruiting more soldiers from the wealthy we have set the bar lower for standards of behavior and intelligence. At the time this essay was first drafted most ardent proponents

---

1 As an aside, my favorite work on the farm where I spent summers earning money for college was haying, a very physically demanding and uncomfortable job. Then again, I'm only middle class, and don't fit well in Karl Rove's America that sees such work as demeaning for Americans.

for the successful democratization of Iraq were calling for even more troops to be deployed. A return to the draft would seem to be the logical resolution of this evolving dilemma but an odd dynamic occurred. For the most part the politicians in favor of our continued occupation in Iraq are against a draft; the current proponents of a draft come from politicians who have tepid support at best for continued occupation.

You do not have to dig too deeply to understand what is behind this apparent enigma. Churchill once said: "Play for more than you can afford to lose, and you will learn the game." Without a draft wealth and power elites are not playing for more than they can afford to lose, since their sons and daughters are underrepresented in the military. Some politicians dissatisfied with our involvement in Iraq figure that decision makers would "learn the game" better, be more astute with the facts in the future handling of the war, if there was a draft. The draft also would personalize the war for all Americans. Politicians could not continue the strategy of cultivating wimpy citizens who concern themselves with tax cuts during a time of war. Churchill's quote could be paraphrased: "Make service a rite of citizenship for all and collectively you will make wiser decisions."

Public Servants

One potential source of inspiration for how citizens could serve would be from our elected leaders. But there are several reasons to think that the term "public servant" is a misnomer, as applied to elected officials. Many politicians will promise a tax cut to appeal to our vanities concerning our hard earned money. The tax cut may be just a cynical ploy, if current economic conditions make the tax cut irresponsible, but that does not factor highly for the politician that mainly wants to be reelected for the twelfth time. Many politicians exhibit a stubborn reluctance to curb earmarks to their states in order to pay for a tax cut; that strategy risks upsetting both their constituents and bloated corporations providing funds for politicians.

The safer (more cowardly) means for politicians to implement a tax cut is to slash programs that benefit the working poor, who are never a key constituency for keeping a politician in power. Meanwhile, tax cuts over the past thirty years have been applied frequently to capital gains, once again benefiting most those who can help the politician maintain power most. To justify this many politicians will claim that providing corporations more capital gains will translate into jobs for America. Never mind that capital gains, which provides welfare for investors, will just as likely benefit corporate executive sugar daddies as bolster the blue-collar job market. They count on us citizens being too apprehensive about losing corporate jobs and lacking the courage to start up or work for proprietorships. How politicians have utilized the promise of tax cuts over the past thirty years has not been about serving the country, but themselves.

The cynicism our elected leaders breed for service to country extends much further than campaign promises. We are told that running this country requires "the best and the brightest." Behind that claim is the cynical inference that "the best and the brightest" generally are a greedy lot, and thus we need wages and benefits for our elected leaders that are at least three times the median family income. We do not need to reward them as much as corporations would, since they are public servants after all, but we certainly must provide much, much more in wage and benefits than an average citizen would get. Otherwise, the "best and brightest" would never condescend to be a "public servant" that works in government.

Engaging in service is radically different than engaging in a career. Because serving is all giving and little getting at the material level you cannot fulfill the ideal of service for long stretches of time. You do not serve for long terms as you would work for a career, unless your ego/self-esteem has grown dependent on being recognized for your service, or you have the spiritual makeup of Mother Theresa. A public servant, by definition, should be giving to the country much more in time and effort than he/she would be receiving from any kind of compensation. Hence, one sure indicator that our elected officials do not fit the role of public servants is their eagerness to keep on "serving." The longer an incumbent stays in office, the greater the certainty that the position is being used as a lucrative career opportunity, signaling wealthy interests to come calling.

If expecting leaders of a democracy to be altruistic is naive, you can count the founding fathers as simple-minded idealists. Benjamin Franklin warned that salaries for the executive would attract "ambition and avarice, the love of power and the love of tyranny."[2] He suggested that the compensation for legislators be moderate. Our first president, George Washington, declined the salary offered to him. Thomas Paine, explaining our constitutional form of government in the *Rights of Man: Part the Second* (1792), reflected that "Government is not a trade which any man, or any body of men, has a right to set up and exercise for his own emolument ..."

This begs the question of whom, but the aristocracy, could afford to serve over a long period of time. Paine assumed that those who served government would be willing to make such a sacrifice for only a limited time. The framers of the Constitution instituted short terms in the House. They varied in their opinions on term limits for the President, but the sentiments put forth by Franklin prevailed: "In free governments the rulers are the servants and the people their superiors and sovereigns. For the former therefore to return among the latter is not to degrade but to promote them." Moderate compensation over a short term made public service more feasible to people outside the aristocracy.

For the most part we citizens have only ourselves to blame for how far our

---

2 As recorded by James Madison, and recounted by Catherine Drinker Bowen in *Miracle at Philadelphia* (1966)

current system departs from this ideal. We are ten times as likely to elect incumbents over challengers. One argument put forth in support of long term incumbents is the stability they provide to the political system. Their experience enables them to get things done in an efficient manner. People who fit the traditional definition of conservative feel that a high turnover rate for elected officials changes government too much and, by extension, our economics and culture. Many people feel more secure when the status quo is maintained.

In nature, stability is provided through a process of homeostasis. Change occurs, but negative feedback loops cause the changes to oscillate around an equilibrium. If there was a high turnover rate for our elected officials the same type of oscillation would occur with our political system. Liberal actions cause conservative reactions; conservative actions cause liberal reactions. As citizens oscillate between these actions and reactions, and our short term public servants responded accordingly, our politics would never stray too far in either direction.

Long term politicians will institute directional change, rather than oscillate with the citizenry. This may sound counterintuitive. You may have an image of an old fossil voting the same way for the same things year after year. This would be true only if a long term politician found the political system to be ideal for his objectives when he first became elected. Otherwise, you would expect an incumbent politician to consistently tinker with "improving" the system. In the case of incumbents, these improvements would include legislation that facilitates making a career out of being a politician. Incumbents reward the support of constituents by tinkering earmarks and other bits of pork for the industries of our states. They reward the support of corporations by tinkering with legislation that favors greed. All this tinkering amounts to constant directional change; the longer the incumbency the more steadfast the direction of change caused by career politicians.

Indexing the compensation of elected legislators to indicators such as median family income or the poverty level would seem to be a wise thing to do for public servants. A politician interested in real service to the country should want his/her pay and benefits to be related to how the country is doing economically, and not to be much greater than citizens who elected them to "serve" their country. Indexing the compensation of policy-makers to the poverty level likely would have the added benefit of producing a more accurate poverty level indicator, though the good scholars from the Boskin Commission and the Hoover Institute might not agree. In theory, a public servant would cringe at the idea of being provided excellent health insurance as an elected official, when 24% of Americans are without such insurance. In practice, our "best and brightest" politicians have no such altruistic pangs of conscious.

Simplifying tax codes and legislation would assist those who are less than the "best and the brightest" but earnestly wish to serve. In fact, this simplification might enable some of our "less bright" legislators currently in office to read bills like the USA PATRIOT Act before they are passed. Such actions also would make government more accessible to citizens who wish to make earnest use of their political liberty. Transparency works against the goals of authoritarians, however. They have no greater desire for laws or government to be transparent than they wish for citizens to vote against convention.

Rites of Citizenship

With Vietnam looming urgently and immediately on the horizon I considered my options for what to do if I was drafted. When you are young you feel invincible to begin with; I was young at a time when politicians did not work hard to convince citizens they should be unwilling to die for a cause. With images from television and Bob Harrington diving to the ground I was more concerned about what Vietnam would do to my mind than my body. Specifically, I wondered what effect killing someone might have on my conscience. In response to this concern I planned to become a medic if drafted, figuring that helping to save lives would alleviate some of the other horrors I might experience.

During the draft there were many ways for young people to avoid service in Vietnam. As always, children from wealthy families were more likely to employ these means than those from lower and middle class families. Still, the willingness to die for a cause back then even by the wealthy was not corrupted as much as now by politicians looking to stay in power. As we proceed now with not only the war in Iraq but the "war on terror" citizens will need to be vigilant about our independent thought or politicians will effectively make cowards of anyone not in uniform.

Fortunately, I never needed to implement my plan to become a medic; the draft was discontinued the same year I had to register. I make no apologies for not enlisting to serve in Vietnam after the draft ended; but I have mild regrets I did not do something like join the Peace Corp. Instead of a rite of citizenship based on service I pursued a rite of passage similar to what is done in "primitive" cultures. Spending a few years and many thousands of miles in wilderness travel did much to promote my independent thought, as "primitive" as some may consider that endeavor to be.

One way to serve the country is supposed to be by holding public office, to become public servants. However, our current political system institutes barriers to public service, citizenship, independent thought, wisdom and, ultimately, democracy. Every branch of government has placed these obstacles in our way, and they all reinforce authoritarianism at the expense of wisdom.

There is one conspirator limiting diversity, independence, decentralization and the democratic aggregation of wisdom that has yet to be examined with much detail. At the time that the Constitution was ratified by the states, the role of the judicial branch of government was still uncertain. Throughout the terms of George Washington and John Adams the Supreme Court was almost an afterthought in our system of government. For much of that time the Supreme Court simply had nothing much to do. That would change with the nineteenth century.

"Good," you say. After all, a strong judicial branch could only enhance a wise system of checks and balances. This assumes that the branches of government are coequal. In regards to the Constitution, the Supreme Court established superiority to all other branches. With this power, some Supreme Court decisions helped to usher in the darkest moments of our history, and they may yet usher in that final turning point that eliminates any vestige of wisdom from our "democratic" process. Let us turn to those well-respected Supreme Court justices next.

ESSAY 14 – LEGAL DOGMA

Overview

- We expect Supreme Court justices to be the most paternally wise of our leaders.
- Party politics led to the Supreme Court being the final arbiter of the Constitution.
- Supreme Court justices are authoritarians appointed by authoritarians.
- Judicial doctrines are legal dogma used to justify the beliefs of justices.
- Doctrines and philosophies are selected to support the decisions of justices.
- Greed trumps merit with the Supreme Court.
- Property jurisprudence contributed to the Civil War.
- Contract jurisprudence contributed to the Great Depression.
- The federal judicial system profiles cases on behalf of wealth and power elites.
- The hyped issue of voter fraud is an authoritarian smokescreen imposed on our political system, assisted by a "diligent" national press.
- Averting further judicial disasters requires commitments to true liberty and an empirical foundation for law.

Judicial Bias

We all have our addictions. I once received a letter long ago from the University of Connecticut asking me to justify why I was still going to school with so many credits (the trick is to keep switching majors, even into your 4th year). That my compulsion to learn has been an end in itself, rather than a means of moving out of the middle class, has left a few in-laws scratching their heads. Currently my addiction leads to researching matters affecting the middle class. Since nearly everything affects the normative middle of society, my research should prove to be permanently ongoing.

I thought I conquered my addiction the last time I graduated. Before making my final parting from the Cornell campus I went to look at and listen to the historic clock tower. Filled with emotion I paraphrased Chief Joseph and declared out loud: "I will go to school no more, forever." I returned to schooling three weeks later when I ordered my first of "The Great Courses" on CD, available from The Teaching Company. If there is a twelve step program for people like me, please let me know.

Two of the earliest courses I purchased were *Civil Liberties and the Bill of Rights*, taught by Professor John E. Finn of Wesleyan University, and *The History of the Supreme Court*, taught by Professor Peter Irons of the University of California at San Diego. I listen to these courses now, after many years spent as a student and teacher, with a totally different perspective than I would have had as a young adult. Some professors are truly gifted as teachers and the wealth of knowledge they bring to their subject truly inspires. Yet all professors, even the gifted ones, have biases. Getting the most out of a course as a student—not to mention maximizing your grade—depends on understanding that the professor has a bias and placing course material in that context.

Identifying the bias of Professor Irons was easy because at the beginning of his lectures he proclaimed his affinity for civil liberties. His frequent references to Thurgood Marshall in the context of his lectures then came as no surprise. Professor Finn took more of a *Fox News* approach, never pronouncing his bias and, in fact, peppering his lectures with the phrase "you decide." Ah, but this middle-aged student is not fooled easily. If I had to take an exam crafted by Professor Finn I would be well versed in the property cases of the Supreme Court, as well as the writings of Antonin Scalia.

As different as the biases of Professors Irons and Finn may be they share at least one common bias: their admiration for early Chief Justice John Marshall. Perhaps all constitutional scholars and lawyers share this bias since Marshall is credited for empowering the Supreme Court with judicial review of the Constitution. In an early case known as *Marbury v. Madison* (1803) Marshall established the Supreme Court as first among the "equal" branches of government in regards to interpreting the Constitution. Anyone who champions the current structure and function of the Supreme Court would admire John Marshall by association.

The public ranks Supreme Court justices high on the list of people they trust. With Supreme Court justices our instinct to trust authorities is reinforced by expectations that learned scholars trained to sit in judgment of the law will utter pearls of wisdom. Furthermore, Supreme Courts justices are not elected but appointed for life. Supreme Court justices thus become the most paternal figures in a paternal democracy.

The perceived paternal wisdom of justices further gains by association. The Constitution was wisely written, achieved through much collaboration and compromise, following the basic principles for a wise democracy as discussed in these essays. The Constitution was backed by wise intent, excluding provisions for political parties and including provisions for checks and balances, both intended to minimize the concentration of power. We naturally assume that now the Constitution is wisely interpreted, due to the experiences of nine justices removed from electoral politics. But Supreme Court justices have their own biases, just like the professors that teach Constitutional law, and the students who seek to learn about Constitutional law. Since these justices represent another type of authority, and indeed the most paternalistic of all government authorities, whether or not actual wisdom survives their biases should not be conventionally accepted by citizens.

Scrutinizing our Supreme Court justices and their decisions becomes all the more crucial given the political conditions we have explored so far. When paternalistic leaders seek conformity to dogmatic policies; when political parties and other special interests command dependence on their dogmatic platforms; when corporate media centralizes our sources of news infused with dogmatic opinions; when patriotic vanities and security apprehensions become conventional dogma for citizens; our one remaining recourse for infusing the political process with empirical wisdom appears to be what we can codify in law, and in particular the Constitution. If even our Supreme Court justices and their decisions accommodate the marriage of power, wealth and dogmatic beliefs at the expense of empirical wisdom a chill wind blows through our total democracy.

The task, then, is to scrutinize the biases of those whose job is to interpret the Constitution for the sake of our democracy. Similar to Professor Irons, the middle class should not be reluctant to acknowledge our own biases. We are biased by expecting the normative middle segments of society to receive the normative benefits of democracy; we are biased by expecting wisdom to be the normative goal of good government; and, by extension, we are biased by expecting our paternal justices to seek wisdom at the expense of their own dogma. With this in mind let us focus on four issues related to Constitutional interpretation.

- Why does the Supreme Court have the final say for interpreting the Constitution?
- Who are the Supreme Court justices that do the interpreting?
- What doctrines have the Supreme Court used to guide their interpretations?
- How do justices interpret who wins a Supreme Court case?

Dogmatic Court

The Supreme Court has the final say on the Constitution mainly because of party politics. Though our government did not begin with political parties they soon formed for the very reason they first were being avoided: they concentrated the self-interest and power of different factions. Our inaugural government was dominated by Federalists, who wanted a strong national government and strong commerce. That the party most interested in concentrated power and wealth had the initial advantage with party politics should come as no surprise. Initially, our homeostatic mechanisms for keeping a party's power in check were excellent. The opposition party provided copious debate and criticism; dissension grew within the ranks of Federalists; and citizens put party leadership on a short leash when they overreached for power.

The "smoking guns" for the Federalists were the Alien and Sedition Acts of 1798. Though ostensibly these laws were for preventing French sedition, they evolved into an attempt by the Federalists to make criticism of Federalism illegal. This turned out to be a particularly foolish and damning piece of legislation for the Federalists, but we do not expect empirical wisdom to be produced by dogmatic party politics. In the next presidential election the Republicans were ushered in with Thomas Jefferson at their head. The Federalists, as an official party, would never again gain the presidency. In an ironic, confusing twist of party evolution, by the next time this party would gain and hold power for an extended amount of time they would be called Republicans, while the former Republicans evolved to what we now call Democrats.

The Federalists had a final trick to play before handing over the keys to government. They increased the size of the judicial branch that they then stacked with Federalists. One of these new appointments, intended for William Marbury, was not completed by the time Jefferson entered office and Marbury was denied his appointment. Marbury sued the federal government and the Supreme Court, headed by Federalist Chief Justice John Marshall, ruled in favor of the Jefferson administration. This would seem like a defeat for Marshall's own party, except Marshall ruled that Marbury had no case before the Supreme Court according to the Constitution, thus establishing the precedent that the ultimate judges of what the Constitution meant were those justices that sat on the Supreme Court. The profound result of *Marbury v. Madison* was establishing the Supreme Court as the authoritative, final interpreter of the Constitution, a position that is not written into the text of the Constitution.

We can assume that Marshall as a lawyer would be biased in favor of the judicial branch having the final say with interpreting the Constitution. But Marshall also was motivated by maintaining a strong national government. The Jefferson administration came in with promises of a return to small scale economics, states rights and agrarian virtue. Marshall wanted to mitigate these anti-Federalist goals by making the Supreme Court, stacked with Federalists, dictate what the Constitution means for government.

Chief Justice Marshall was involved in two other cases to solidify the power of national government and the authority of the Supreme Court to uphold that power. *Martin v. Hunter's Lessee* (1816) was a case that involved the state court of Virginia declaring an Act passed by Congress to be unconstitutional. The Supreme Court decided against the state court, in the process declaring that federal courts had authority over state courts in regards to the Constitution. There are times when state courts might want to refer a case to the Supreme Court for further interpretation, but now that is irrelevant. The Supreme Court decides, with full dogmatic autonomy, which cases from the states to hear, and the Supreme Court alone decides when the timing to hear each case is ripe.

McCulloch v. Maryland (1819) settled a long standing controversy over whether the federal government can institute a national bank, though no provision for that was included in the Constitution. The Supreme Court ruled that objectives for the federal government stated in the Constitution, such as the regulation of commerce, automatically implied the power to accomplish those objectives by whatever justifiable means. The final interpreter of these justifiable means would be, of course, the authoritarians on the Supreme Court.

Taken together these cases solidified the Federalist objective to maintain as much power as possible in the federal government, a condition necessary for corporations to thrive, with a federal Supreme Court having the final say in disputes that might arise. We will examine further whether the path charted by the Marshall Court would infuse the interpretation of Constitutional law with wisdom, but from the start dogmatic politics determined this path. The judicial branch, like the other two branches of government, seeks to wield and enhance power even at the expense of empirical wisdom.

Dogmatic Justices

The Supreme Court justices are, for the most part, experienced lawyers. Since wisdom depends on experience this seems to provide a good foundation for interpreting the Constitution. However, the wisdom that benefits democracy is collective, and that should be the standard we apply to the entire "crowd" of Supreme Court justices as well. For us to suspect that something is amiss with the collective wisdom from the club of lawyers who become Supreme Court justices, we need only point to one relatively recent example of Supreme Court interpretation that overtly sacrifices wisdom to accommodate power and wealth.

In the case of *Buckley v. Valeo* (1976) the Supreme Court decided that money was a form of free speech. Given that the Constitution as a whole was a document intended to facilitate wise democracy we might assume justifiably that the free speech provisions of the Bill of Rights has the same intent. As originally intended free speech is the expression of free thought. The writings of John Stuart Mill made clear that both free speech and free thought are essential to our liberty. Democracy, collective wisdom and our basic instincts regarding fairness require that everyone's liberty be worth the same. By extension so, too, would everyone's free thought and free speech.

Equating money with free speech subjects liberty to an alleged merit system that proves to be disastrously false. You have an Orwellian situation where everyone is equal, but some are distinctly more equal than others based on the "merits" needed for aggregating money. Since the income of some CEOs are one thousand times that of their lowest level employees that would make their liberty, as expressed by money-funded free speech, one thousand times greater. CEOs need not limit their "expression" by using just their own money; they can influence the of use corporate money to further their "expression," even if that runs counter to the "expressions" of many employees in the corporation. Furthermore, as we have explored in our economic essays, much of the concentrated wealth amounts to entitlements for a few, amassed through such means as inheritance, subsidies and tax laws. Thus free speech as expressed through money also becomes an entitlement for a few; totally abrogating any role free speech might have in terms of genuine merit, democracy, collective wisdom, basic fairness or "liberty for all."

Concluding that money is an expression of free speech reflects a mindset with greater allegiance to power and wealth than to wisdom. How could this have happened with wise, paternal Supreme Court justices? For starters, Supreme Court justices are appointed by the President; the same party politics that influences presidential policies affect presidential appointments. Only lawyers are appointed, even though this is not a necessary requirement in the Constitution. At times the Supreme Court has been dominated by corporate lawyers, as was the *Laissez Faire* Court that established the liberty of contracts at the turn of the twentieth century. Collective wisdom works by canceling out the errors of bias from different perspectives, but the selection of Supreme Court justices institutes systemic bias from limited perspectives generally divorced from the middle class.

The life terms of justices, while immunizing them from electoral politics, makes them even greater pawns for dogmatic party politics. Thus the retirement of a Supreme Court justice usually accommodates a desire to maintain similar political ideologies in the court, rather than to infuse the Court with a constant, randomized influx of current perspectives. In essence, the Supreme Court is an "old boy's network," albeit with an occasional female thrown in. They strive to reinforce the key dogma for which they were selected rather than draw from the empirical wisdom of a democracy.

In our economic essays we observed just how connected to wealth and power a Supreme Court justice can be. The Powell Memorandum that initiated the Powell Cabal came from a corporate lawyer and future Supreme Court justice. Justice Lewis Powell rather predictably supported the ruling that money should be considered an expression of free speech. We do not know his precise opinion on this affront to wisdom, since the Court's written opinion in *Buckley v. Valeo* was per curiam. This means that no single judge wanted to provide an individual rationale for interpreting that money is an expression of free speech. Given the tortuous logic needed to make such a claim, who could blame such timidity?[1]

Dogmatic Doctrines

No justice, regardless of background, wants to be accused of arbitrarily making up decisions without legal basis; justices employ doctrines to defend their decisions. Justices frequently cite the doctrine of stare decisis, or the precedence of previous decisions made by the Supreme Court. Relying on precedence prevents the rule of law from chaotically changing over time. Through the use of precedence justices also observe the Golden Rule. Since they do not want their own decisions being reversed easily, they are reluctant to overturn previous decisions of the Court.

The dogmatic nature of precedence as a doctrine occasionally conflicts with wisdom. Adhering only to precedence means either ignoring that experiences enhance wisdom over time, or concluding that wisdom is not as important as authoritarian dogma. Once the Supreme Court decided to equate money with free speech in 1976, that unwise decision became fossilized as subsequent campaign finance cases referred to that precedent. We can expect money-as-free-speech to remain the law of the land unless Supreme Court justices prioritize wisdom over authoritarianism as the foundation for law.

Other doctrines used by Supreme Court justices conflict with wisdom as well. Textualism holds that a Supreme Court decision should draw only from what is in the text of the Constitution. The Constitution is a sparse document that leaves much of the details for governance to be filled in through the laws passed by Congress and the states. If the Supreme Court rejects these laws as unconstitutional, based strictly on the text of the document, Congress and the states still can prevail by going through a process of amendment.

Amending the Constitution, like the original process of ratification, could be viewed as a wise process, involving super majorities from federal and state governments. Textualism could be viewed as a wise doctrine for setting this process in motion. However, politics have changed since the time of the Federal Convention in 1787. Different factions once debated the crafting of the Constitution for the sake of wise governance, now different parties invested with wealth and power seek political gain. Localized media fostered independence throughout the colonies; now corporate media uses echo chambers to "centralize" our opinions, and gladly accept the money to accommodate "free speech" from their corporate brethren.

As a result, howling about textualism does little more than enable the Supreme Court to avoid a confrontation with empirical wisdom. Textualism is

---

1 I admit to some cheekiness here. Per curiam decisions often reflect an attitude of justices that there are no unique or insightful rationales to put forth in defense of the decision. While the rationale for equating money with free speech may be self-evident to corporate lawyers, middle class citizens would have benefited from some more extensive enlightenment on this matter.

actually a hypocritical means for a justice to support his/her own dogma. Nothing in the text of the Constitution calls for the judicial branch to be the sole interpreter of the Constitution, as the Supreme Court decided in *Marbury v. Madison*. Nothing in the text of the Constitution calls for the federal courts to have power over the state courts, as the Supreme Court decided in *Martin v. Hunter's lessee*. Nothing in the text of the Constitution states that there are federal powers to be implied from Constitutional objectives, as the Supreme Court decided in *McCulloch v. Maryland*. Any justice that truly believes in textualism should be willing to revisit and overturn these early decisions as a top priority; opting instead to allow a wise process of amendment to expressly state these powers for them. Alas, a justice allegedly committed to textualism that has the integrity to recommend this path never existed and never will with our current political system.

Even if there were enough justices with the integrity to advocate true textualism we would then be depending on the legislative branch to take constitutional responsibility. The Military Commissions Act of 2006, passed amidst controversy, reveals this to be a dubious wish. Even Congressmen who voted in favor of the bill suspected that clauses in the Constitution for challenging detentions and for prohibiting ex post facto laws were being violated. Arlen Specter, Chairman of the Senate Judiciary Committee, gave this rather extraordinary defense: "Congress could have done it right and didn't, but the next line of defense is the court, and I think the court will clean it up."[2] In other words, we should not go too far in blaming justices for not committing to true textualism when they know the responsibility for interpretation will get tossed back to them; but we should not tolerate when justices hypocritically wield this doctrine as a smokescreen for imposing their own dogma.

The way out of feigned textualism, at least in the minds of some justices, is to use a combination of doctrines. Originalism seeks to interpret the original meaning embedded in the text of Constitutional provisions, as John Marshall did in *Marbury v. Madison*. Framer's intent seeks to interpret what the people who crafted the Constitution meant, as was the rationale for interpreting *McCulloch v. Maryland*. Through a combination of these historical doctrines Supreme Court justices can decide most court cases to suit personal biases. After all, the original construction of the Constitution involved framers with varying intents. Therefore, whose "intent" and "original meaning" applies is often a matter of—as you would guess—dogmatic judicial interpretation.

This leads us to the doctrine considered to be the opposite of textualism, namely, structuralism. Structuralism interprets the meaning of the Constitution as a whole for deciding cases. One branch of structuralism views the Constitution as a living document, with meaning that changes over time. Our privacy liberties resulted from Supreme Court justices interpreting the Constitution as a whole.

---

2 As quoted in "Pass the Buck" (October 7, 2006), by Dahlia Lithwick, for the online magazine *Slate*.

Neither the text of the Constitution nor what we know about framer's intent provides a basis for these liberties. The doctrine of structuralism appears to be tailor-made for extracting the wisdom of experience over time, but appearances can be deceiving.

In the absence of strict textualism as defined here, all judicial interpretation includes a pliable mixture of precedence and other doctrines that amounts to structuralism under many guises. Whether the myriad forms of structuralism produces empirical wisdom reverts to the questions of who are doing the interpretation and why they do so. The Supreme Court justices may all be experts at law, but relying only on the experts from one field fails to collect wisdom from the wider experiences of those not indoctrinated by that narrow field. Most of the justices only have remote connections to the normative middle class; many of those who started from humble beginnings turned from those roots in their quest to reach the halls of power and/or wealth. Doctrines aimed at justifying the narrow perspectives of an old boy's network, influenced by wealth and power, will favor dogmatic authoritarianism over empirical wisdom.

Dogmatic Decisions

There are two opposing philosophies behind the decision-making responsibility of justices, judicial restraint and judicial activism. Judicial restraint means letting legislatures pass laws without interference from Supreme Court decisions, giving them the benefit of the doubt in all but obvious violations of the Constitution. Judicial activism means overturning any law justices think conflicts with the meaning of the Constitution. These philosophies coalesced around legal interpretations of due process ever since the Fourteenth Amendment stated: "nor shall any State deprive any person of life, liberty, or property, without due process of law." Advocates of judicial restraint tend to support a doctrine of procedural due process, concentrating on whether legislatures observed a legitimate "due process" for enacting laws. Advocates of judicial activism tend to support a doctrine of substantive due process, insisting that due process is embedded in the substance of the Constitution which, of course, is the duty of Supreme Court justices to interpret.

Judicial activism versus restraint is a misleading dichotomy about making decisions, as is the dichotomy between procedural and substantive due process. For allegory about these false dichotomies, I refer to my vocation of natural resource management. As any forest ranger could tell you, harvesting timber and preserving wilderness are both management decisions. Though wilderness requires the restraint of human activity, the decision to preserve wilderness is still actively made by humans. Every intended decision of a resource management agency is active management, no matter if the intention involves restraint.

Just so, the intended decision to employ either judicial restraint or activism, either procedural or substantive due process, is still up to Supreme Court justices. Even if a justice remains consistent with either philosophy the choice to do so was the justice's, unguided by any other source. Every decision of a Supreme Court justice is essentially active and substantive, ultimately in service to the dogmas they hold dear.

Just as there is no external condition requiring justices to choose between doctrines of philosophies for making decisions, there is no external condition requiring justices to remain true to any from one case to the next. With such a loose system for making decisions justices have free reign to decide in favor of their biases. The governing factor in our evolving legal system is not a matter of what doctrines or philosophies are used, but who is using them to serve which dogmas in their decisions.

Supreme Court cases are like contests, often featuring the interests of a state or federal government (both will be referred to as the State) contested against the rights of an individual. The interests of the State, as stated in the Preamble for the Constitution, are to: "…establish Justice, insure domestic Tranquility, provide for the common defense, promote the general Welfare, and secure the Blessings of Liberty to ourselves and our Posterity." The State's interest falls into one of two categories:

- Compelling: such as protecting citizens from imminent danger or harm.
- Rational: such as labor laws to promote health.

The rights of an individual are codified in the Bill of Rights. The greater the alleged social interest, the more likely the State will be the winner. The more basic the alleged individual right, the more likely the individual will be the winner. An individual's right falls into one of two categories:

- Fundamental: such as the right to free speech.
- Conditional: such as the right to vote, given certain conditions.

Over time patterns evolve as to which interests and rights triumph over others. This evolving pattern of court decisions is known as jurisprudence. Historically, jurisprudence tends to form cultural entitlements for wealth, power and special interest elites that are best represented in our paternal and party democracies. Let us review the jurisprudence behind two of the most entrenched cultural entitlements.

Property Jurisprudence
During the Enlightenment John Locke proclaimed property to be a natural right;

the courts have supported this as legal dogma ever since. James Madison, father of the Constitution, claimed that "property is a fence to liberty." This meant that while protecting the "Blessings of Liberty" was an intangible goal of our Constitution, property was the tangible expression of liberty that a system of laws could directly protect. Madison also thought that a Bill of Rights was unnecessary, as words on paper could not do justice to the range of our inherent liberties. We owe Madison thanks for our Constitution, but perhaps being a propertied landowner caused him to be wrong on both these counts.

Historically, there have been at least three problems that stem from equating property with liberty.

- One person's property can thwart the Blessings of another person's Liberty.
- Unequal amounts of property bestow unequal "Blessings of Liberty."
- Property can be obtained legally without any merit of productive labor.

Taken together, these three problems mean that property can be a fence for unequal "Blessings of Liberty" apportioned in a way that undermines merit, labor and economic productivity. Underlying these three problems is a fourth: the wealthy benefit at the expense of the middle class when unmerited property results in unequal liberty. A fifth problem, the focus of our discussion, is that a Supreme Court created and staffed through power politics, containing justices-for-life that disproportionately come from a narrow cross-section of society connected to wealth and power, using doctrines that do not draw upon empirical wisdom, establish property jurisprudence that amounts to cultural entitlements.

That one person's property can deprive another person of liberty was evident in Madison's own time, through the existence of slavery. A case called *The Antelope* (1825) came before the Marshall Court to determine the fate of slaves first stolen from Portuguese and Spanish ships and subsequently seized by an American naval patrol. Marshall ruled that the slaves needed to be returned to their owners. Though Marshall personally detested slavery as an affront to natural law, he judged this inferior to international property law that legitimized slavery. Property as a fence to liberty trumped virtually everything we might hold truly dear about real liberty.

Roger Taney, a wealthy landowner that supported slavery, replaced John Marshall as Chief Justice in 1836. Taney ruled in the *Dred Scott v. Sandford* (1857) case that no blacks could be considered as citizens with rights to be protected. This decision went beyond entrenching slavery in the South, the good old boys on the Taney Court declared that no black anywhere in the United States could seek protection or redress through the federal courts. Marshall's establishment of Supreme Court power through judicial review of the Constitution worked well for the Taney Court. They struck down laws to mitigate slavery, such as the *Missouri*

Compromise (1820), and upheld pro-slavery legislation such as the *Kansas-Nebraska Act* (1854). This provides an excellent example of how the pliable use of judicial restraint and judicial activism renders these "opposing" philosophies of interpretation meaningless.

Most whites in slave states shared the view that blacks were property, but only wealthy whites benefited significantly from such an interpretation. Had the slaveholders of the Taney Court refrained from overturning legislative attempts to curb the spread of slavery, our country might have navigated a path to the reduction and abolition of slavery without the horrors of the Civil War. One easily can imagine a different course for history if blacks had federal protection and redress in the northern states and new territories. Over time, a market system would favor the states that provided protection to blacks and the South would eventually need to fall in line to survive economically. Instead, judicial interpretation that disproportionately benefited the wealthy led to over 600,000 deaths from all classes, in a war that failed to reduce the oppression of blacks.

An assumption could be made that early jurisprudence on slavery had more to do with racism than cultural entitlements to property. A series of modern Supreme Court cases rules out racism as the cause for bestowing unequal "Blessings of Liberty" through property entitlements. In *Kelo v. New London* (2005) homes were taken from middle class residents by the city of New London, Connecticut for the subsequent use of a private developer, in accordance with a public economic development plan. This decision seems to reject property as a fence to liberty, but justices defended the decision based on the Fifth Amendment clause: "nor shall private property be taken for public use, without just compensation."

Taking property without the homeowner's "Blessings" is an affront to liberty even if they are compensated justly. Furthermore, taking property for a private developer is a questionable interpretation of "public use." To understand what is really being protected in *Kelo v. New London* let us place this decision in the context of two other modern court cases.

In *Nollan v. California Coastal Commission* (1987) the Supreme Court ruled that the State (Coastal Commission) could not enforce an easement on a property that would allow public access to a public beach. By enforcing the easement the property owner would not be able to invest in the further expansion of his home and this was viewed as a taking without just compensation. In *Lucas v. South Carolina Coastal Council* (1992) the Supreme Court decided that the State could not prevent a lot owner from developing property near the shore. There was no proposed "taking" in any literal sense by the State; the compelling interest was to prevent environmental degradation of sand dunes. The owner would still have the property, but not the investment potential.

These three cases appear to be inconsistent on the surface. The State can take properties for the "public use," as administered by private developers, but must protect the development potential of property regardless of the public interest for either recreation or the environment. A closer look, however, reveals a consistent winner. The investment potential of property wins out against either the public interest of the State or the liberty to obtain and hold property through free market exchange. In other words, greed trumps the merits of either the State or the individual in deciding these cases.

This brings us back to the misguided assumption of property as a natural right. The next essay provides an empirical foundation for natural rights; private property does not qualify. Essay 22 on The UnEnlightenment explores how mistakes such as proclaiming property to be a natural right occurred. Essay 24 provides an example from early cultures of how property belonged to merited "users," rather than something that was privatized by the State and could be used independently of merit. These add some further understanding to property jurisprudence in this country.

Without the State or any kind of power structure the Kelo home could not be taken away without their "Blessings." They bought the home with hard-earned money, they were making good use of their treasured home; they did not want to freely trade the merited use of their home away. Without the State or any kind of power structure the Lucas property could not be hoarded for potential future development. As a natural right Lucas could claim only the property that his current use merited.

What these modern court cases confirm is that private property is a cultural entitlement, not a natural right. The greatest purpose of this cultural entitlement provided by Big Brother is to guarantee the potential of future uses to generate capital over currently merited uses directly or indirectly resulting from labor. The intent of property jurisprudence is to guarantee the primacy of greed over merit. What else would we expect from Supreme Court justices?

Contract Jurisprudence

After the Civil War the Supreme Court became dominated by corporate lawyers. They decided in civil rights cases brought by five states in 1883 that private discrimination was allowed, and established the infamous "separate but equal" doctrine in *Plessey v. Ferguson* (1896). Rather than overcoming the problems of property being individuals, these corporate lawyers instead considered corporations to be individuals as well. In *Santa Clara County v. Southern Pacific Railroad Co.* (1886) the Supreme Court decided that corporations were entitled to the substantive due process rights granted to persons under the Fourteenth Amendment. This decision set the table for the contract jurisprudence to follow.

In *Lochner v. New York* (1905) the majority of the Supreme Court interpreted that the "right to free contract" was part of the substantive due process entitled to individuals, including corporate individuals. Justice Holmes wrote in dissent that Supreme Court justices were infusing their economic dogma into law, rather than interpreting what was in the Constitution. The Supreme Court continued to advocate the liberty of contract up until the Great Depression, apparently without any sense of the irony.

We should not be surprised that lawyers would champion contracts, and contract law does have a legitimate role in protecting the rights of individuals. But contracts were seldom used in agrarian culture. Two farmers agreed to an exchange or a loan based on a handshake, with local gossip and community standing providing incentives to keep agreements. As the country urbanized, and we relied on commerce between distant parties, the contract formalized economic obligations between strangers. Contracts prevent anonymous individuals from being cheated.

When one of the anonymous individuals involved in a contract is a corporation, the ironic reference to liberty becomes apparent. If we are to believe what corporations and economists themselves tell us, that bargaining should be done from a position of strength, then we must believe that individuals with more power and wealth have the greater "Blessings of Liberty" to maneuver contracts to their benefit. Historically, the side with greater liberty tends to be corporations, and the side with less liberty tends to be laborers. In other words, a tool for binding "individuals" to economic agreements bestows disproportionate liberty on the wealthy and powerful corporate individuals, not that this would bother the corporate lawyers on the Supreme Court.

Many contract cases take the form of a corporate individual's "Blessings of Liberty" to dictate and enforce the terms of a contract versus the State's interest in protecting the "general Welfare" of citizens with less bargaining power. Lochner v. New York effectively required states to demonstrate a compelling interest in order to prevail against the fundamental right of corporate individuals. The corporate lawyers on the Supreme Court became fans of substantive due process, since this allowed them to uphold their interpretation of corporate contract rights over the due process of State legislatures attempting to protect ordinary individuals.

Protecting corporations as individuals implemented a double standard in contract cases up until the Great Depression. For the State to promote the "general Welfare" of people in a contract case they must have a compelling interest. In contrast, protecting the "general Welfare" of corporate individuals required only a rational interest. The handicapping of true individuals goes yet a step further in that corporations are licensed wards of the states, people are not. People cannot enjoy the limited liability for wrongdoing that the corporate wards are granted.

As with the Dred Scott decision, one can easily imagine an alternative history for this country had not the corporate good ol' boys on the Supreme Court established legal dogma to protect corporations as individuals and contracts as another fence to liberty. The superior bargaining strength of corporations as both individuals and licensed wards of the State allowed the coercion of contracts to overwhelmingly favor the corporation, with states helpless to assist the "general Welfare" of laborers. Laborers worked more for relatively less as wealth disparity climbed. The Great Depression descended on a work force that was not compensated in just measure for their economic productivity, with government protected contracts in true *laissez faire* fashion concentrating too much unmerited capital in the hands of a few, and the economy collapsed. Hmm. That sounds like a script that could be written for 2008.

Over time the Supreme Court is forced to correct the problems generated by their own legal dogma. Empirical events such as the Civil War and Great Depression demand such remedies. This begs the question of why Supreme Court justices could not be governed by empiricism in the first place. Sure, they are selected by party politics from wealth elites, but why not follow a code of empiricism once placed in the highest court in the land for life? Unfortunately, the dogmatic approach to law infiltrates our entire political system.

Authoritarian Profiling

Judicial interpretation throughout the federal court system mirrors the affinity for wealth and power demonstrated by the Supreme Court. The Seventh Amendment of the Constitution guarantees a trial by jury for lawsuits involving more than twenty dollars. But just as Supreme Court justices have full autonomy in deciding which cases to hear, federal judges have the discretion to determine whether a lawsuit can be tried. They can bypass the guaranteed jury if they feel the plaintiff's case is weak or frivolous. This begs the question of what type of cases federal judges might choose to preempt.

When Monsanto prevented a Fox affiliate from airing an expose of Bovine Growth Hormone, as pointed out in Essay 5, they did so via the threat of litigation. The corporate lawyers for Monsanto had little going for them in terms of winning the case. What they had on their side were the financial resources for a prolonged legal battle, the financial incentive to engage in such a battle and the assurance that no judge was likely to throw out their case, no matter how weak or frivolous. Monsanto was like a poker player who got his opponent to fold by raising the stakes too high.

Federal judges are less accommodating when citizens are the plaintiffs. In an online article from *Slate*, titled "The Jury Snub" (12/18/06), Seth Rosenthal reported a growing tendency for federal judges to throw out cases brought by consumers before they could be heard by a jury. He cites the claims of earlier appointees to the bench faulting their newer colleagues, recent Bush II appointments, for throwing out cases that were potentially winnable for the consumers.

Weeding out consumer initiated cases is a matter of judicial interpretation, and we should tease out the real logic behind these interpretations. In our recent political climate conservatives tend to advocate judicial restraint; led in this call by conservative Supreme Court justices, such as Antonin Scalia and Clarence Thomas. But usurping the role of juries shows little restraint on the part of federal judges, hence, we can rule out conservative judicial restraint as the logic behind the interpretation. This is not surprising, since out of all the reasons offered by judges to defend their interpretations, their calls for judicial activism or restraint should be taken the least seriously.

On another front the Powell Cabal makes the charge that there is simply too much law these days and cases need to be weeded out. If judges were responding to this logic, then cases with corporate plaintiffs should be weeded out at least as much as those with consumer plaintiffs. Since this is not the case, we must look for yet another possible cause. Through the process of elimination, we must conclude that selectively depriving consumers of their Seventh Amendment right to trial by jury satisfies only a goal of protecting the "Blessings of Liberty" for helpless corporate individuals against an avaricious middle class.

Power elites can expect similar protection from our judicial branch of government. U. S. attorneys, who also are chosen through party politics, employ a selective process for prosecution even before cases reach the federal courts. During the Bush II administration was not a good time to be a Democrat in public office. Research by professors Donald C. Shields and John F. Cragan revealed that from 2001 to 2006 more than four times as many Democrats as Republicans were investigated by the Bush II Justice Department.[3] As reported by the authors:

> "We believe that this tremendous disparity is politically motivated and it occurs because the local (non-state-wide and non-Congressional) investigations occur under the radar of a diligent national press. Each instance is treated by a local beat reporter as an isolated case that is only of local interest."

We could quibble over how "diligent" corporate media bosses allow the national press to be, but political profiling in federal prosecutions or jury case selections are forms of power politics designed to lie under the radar screen. Yet even when the "diligence" of the corporate media is engaged the result still reeks of authoritarian profiling, as with the hyped attention of voter fraud.

---

3 Their study can be found at www.epluribusmedia.org/columns/2007/20070212_political_profiling.html.

Authoritarian Fraud

As we explored the structure of our political system we went from the paternal democracy, to party democracy, to centralized media, to conventional citizens and on to the legal dogma framing our political system. Let us now examine an issue that draws all these components together. The "diligent" national press has focused our attention on the issue of voter fraud, which refers to the practice of placing illegal votes. If you have voted more than once, if you are a convicted felon or if you are dead then your vote should not count. We have become familiar with voter fraud because the failure to investigate this issue contributed to authoritarian leadership in the Bush II administration firing eight U. S. attorneys in a manner that everyone, including Republicans in Congress, concluded was party politics.

Why not investigate voter fraud? First, the attorneys did investigate the occurrence of fraud, upon the direction of President Bush II and Senators such as Pete Domenici (R-NM), but found little evidence for prosecution. One reason why there would be little evidence is that voter fraud is no longer an efficient means of influencing an election. Rather than having a few confederates stuff ballot boxes, to be effective voter fraud must now be accomplished by numerous confederates voting multiple times with electronic machines. The much more efficient, modern day corollary to voter fraud would be computer hacking into those electronic voter machines. A party that chose old-fashioned voter fraud as a means of influencing an election could be charged, justifiably, as bumbling incompetents (come to think of it, this charge has been aimed at Democrats).

Meanwhile, there are other means of influencing elections that can happen at a scale that actually could impact elections, do not receive much attention from our "diligent" national press and escape investigation from the U. S. attorneys serving the "president's pleasure." In the *Rolling Stone* article "Was the 2004 Election Stolen?" (6/01/06) Robert F. Kennedy Jr. details some of these practices. For example, one out of every four citizens who registered to vote in the swing state of Ohio discovered they were not listed on the rolls when they showed up at the polls. Many had trouble even getting to the polls because in certain districts too few voting machines were provided for too many people, creating huge lines to vote. Those are stories deserving more attention from U. S. attorneys and the "diligent" national press, rather than investigations into the sparse occurrence of votes coming from the grave.

Vote caging is another method of depriving people the liberty to vote. This is only now gaining much attention; though, in reality, vote caging delivered the 2000 election to President Bush II. Vote caging works by sending out registered mail to potential voters not likely to be home. When the mail gets returned, the people who sent the mail lobby for those voters to be stricken from the rolls. For example, if you sent registered mail to blacks that you expected to be away at college, or serving in the military, then you would get much of the mail returned and you could cite their lack of a current address as a reason for not allowing them to vote in your state. This happened in Florida for the 2000 election and received coverage from international media not long after.[4] Vote caging only received attention from our "diligent" national press once an incidental reference to the practice was made by Monica Goodling in her testimony for the firing of U. S. attorneys based on profiling. This "diligence" occurred in 2007.

What becomes the focus for our "diligent" press becomes the focus for the nation. Voter fraud was a successful practice when Mayor Daley could have ballot boxes stuffed in Chicago, but now with electronic venues the practice is ineffective and antiquated. Nevertheless, a Google search of "voter fraud" on June 15 of 2007 (around 8:30 a.m.) produced 941,000 hits. Vote caging is effective and, in fact, determined the outcome of the 2000 presidential election. A Google search of "vote caging" on the same day produced 45,200 hits, or less than 5% of the attention given to voter fraud, and this was after the Monica Goodling testimony.

The disproportionate attention given voter fraud may have been greater even than what the Google search suggests. Google's algorithms may be affected by the disappearance of the American Center for Voting Rights (ACVR). This was an interest group devoted to pushing the issue of voter fraud, and lobbying to get practices with the same objectives as vote caging instituted as law throughout the country. They folded their operations around the time of Goodling's reference to vote caging in her testimony to Congress, and their former counsel has struck all references to having worked for that interest group.[5]

While they existed the ACVR was very productive. They influenced the passage of the Help America Vote Act (HAVA), which charged the Election Assistance Commission to develop national statistics on voter fraud, and provide recommendations for eliminating this national "problem." Job Serebrov (Republican) and Tova Wang (Democrat) did the research and drafted a report concluding that voter fraud was not a problem. The only person they interviewed that claimed voter fraud to be a problem was from ACVR, the special interest group that lobbied for HAVA.[6] That one dissent provided enough "evidence" for the Election Assistance Commission, another lobbying target of the ACVR, to change the original report to state that there is much debate on the topic of voter fraud.[7] The ACVR has folded but not before contributing to the "diligence" of the national press on voter fraud, getting an Act passed by Congress designed to promote voter identification laws and doctoring a report by an official commission to promote

4 Much of this reporting has been done by Greg Palast, an American who writes for *The Guardian*. The 2000 election foibles also are covered in his book, *The Best Democracy Money Can Buy* (2002).

5 The disappearance of the ACVR was researched and documented by Richard L. Hazen in "The Fraudulent Fraud Squad" (May 18, 2007), for Slate on-line magazine.

6 Go to graphics8.nytimes.com/packages/pdf/national/20070411voters_draft_report.pdf for the draft report.

7 Go to www.eac.gov/docs/Voter%20Fraud%20&%20Intimidation%20Report%20-POSTED.pdf for the final report.

these ends. You might think they would be proud of such accomplishments, rather than to get out of Dodge when a whiff of vote caging finally reaches the "diligent" national press.

A case could be made that being deprived of voting threatens democracy more than voting multiple times, if both occurred at similar scales. Voting multiple times means, in a sense, exercising additional liberty, something the Supreme Court already has blessed by equating the money used to finance campaigns as an expression of free speech. Yet the Supreme Court considers the extra liberty from voter fraud differently than the extra liberty from money as free speech.

An Arizonan case, *Purcell v. Gonzales* (2006), pitted the problems of voter fraud against the problems of voter identification laws. There is legitimacy for hearing this case apart from the voting issue. The Supreme Court overruled a federal circuit court of appeals which, in turn, had overruled a federal district court in upholding a state law to curb voter fraud, passed just before the 2006 elections. By siding with the federal district court, the Supreme Court allegedly adhered to a doctrine of procedural due process, legitimizing a law passed by a state legislature. However, since we know that such doctrines are pliable as wielded by Supreme Court justices, we should look further as to why the Supreme Court decided to intervene.

The Supreme Court justices acknowledged that protecting the fundamental right to vote was important for judges to consider, but deemed that voter fraud was the greater concern, providing the following gem of a rationale:

> "Voter fraud drives honest citizens out of the democratic process and breeds distrust of our government. Voters who fear their legitimate votes will be outweighed by fraudulent ones will feel disenfranchised."

This rationale has a familiar ring. Recall the rationale provided by the U. S. Chamber of Commerce for tort reform (Essay 8), citing the insomnia of small business owners who wake up each morning terrified they will get sued. Apparently the Supreme Court feels that you and I, as honest citizens, have been refusing to participate in elections because we are worried sick about this voter fraud issue. Never mind that no evidence yet suggests that voter fraud is a problem. Never mind that citizens upset by voter fraud would likely get MORE involved in the democratic process. The good ol' boys on the Supreme Court have interpreted the situation differently. This rather remarkable opinion provided by the Supreme Court justices was per curiam, just as in the case of *Buckley v. Valeo*, reflecting a similar unwillingness to claim individual responsibility for some of their legal dogma.

UnJust(ice) Compensation

You may think this portrayal of Supreme Court justices as unfair, but we evaluated them only from the perspectives of what is good for the middle class and empirical wisdom. Constitutional lawyers and scholars certainly hold Supreme Court justices in higher esteem, as no doubt do people connected to power and wealth. We must also acknowledge the inaccuracies and injustice of branding individuals with the stereotypical characteristics of a group. Certainly, there have been Supreme Court justices, like Louis Brandeis, who never divorced themselves from middle class roots. Yet small town lawyers generally have a different interpretation of public service than most Supreme Court justices. For comparison's sake let us contrast Hans, a small town lawyer, with current Chief Justice John Roberts.

Both Hans and Chief Justice Roberts provide expertise to benefit government. Hans retains his practice in civil and criminal law, while providing a public service in his free time for a local town commission. Chief Justice Roberts left his corporate law practice for a variety of political appointments, culminating with becoming the "Honorable" Chief Justice. Through his law practice Hans has worked for a wide spectrum of humanity. Chief Justice Roberts has worked only for the power and wealth elites in corporations and government. Hans volunteers to interpret legal documents for his commission. Chief Justice Roberts gets paid $212,000 to interpret the Constitution. Hans never asks for any type of compensation. Chief Justice Roberts accepts speaking engagements that enables him to campaign for higher pay, an unusual practice even for Supreme Court justices who covet wealth. Hans believes that citizens have an obligation to serve government. Chief Justice Roberts believes that government has an obligation to handsomely compensate the "best and the brightest" who "serve" on the Supreme Court.

Hans legally could serve on the Supreme Court; there are no requirements to be a corporate lawyer or even a Constitutional scholar. Yet Hans would never get asked because he never avails himself to the power elite. This suits Hans just fine. If endearing himself to power elites was important Hans would never waste his time providing true public service for local government. Hans graduated at the top of his class, but that is irrelevant. Had he been merely a competent lawyer he would be able to serve his town commission just as well. The will to serve finds a way.

The will to authoritarianism finds a way as well. You no more have to graduate at the top of your class to wield power as to provide service. Certainly, President Bush II provides evidence for that. But Chief Justice Roberts comes from a background where $212,000 amounts to the biweekly paycheck for some of the lawyers in his profession. Naturally, Chief Justice Roberts thinks of himself as one of the "best and the brightest." He figures that he deserves more than four times the compensation of the average family, and that all the "best and the brightest" lawyers must naturally have that expectation. The possibility that all lawyers, and all people who might be qualified to interpret the Constitution, do not covet wealth as much as corporate lawyers must seem like pure fantasy to Chief Justice Roberts. Or maybe he does understand that there would be highly qualified people ready to serve if the politics of choosing Supreme Court justices were different, but he wants a majority of comrades well-connected to wealth and power to aid him with an authoritarian interpretation of the Constitution.

Averting Judicial Disaster

The middle class needs to burst the protective bubble of public opinion that surrounds Supreme Court justices, much like we need to burst the protective bubble that surrounds "objective" number-crunching economists. The Civil War and the Great Depression were at least augmented, if not outright initiated, by prior judicial interpretations of the Supreme Court. These two worst domestic tragedies in our history were fueled by an old boy's network catering to wealth rather than wisdom, as expressed through legal dogma regarding property and contracts.

If you think this overstates the case of Supreme Court impact, let us briefly examine two Supreme Court decisions that did not relate to property. In the case known as *Minersville v. Gobitis* (1940) the Supreme Court upheld the expulsion from school of a Jehovah's Witness for refusing to salute the flag. The Jehovah's Witnesses were wary of the saluting that was being forced on people by Hitler's Germany, and viewed forced flag saluting as a similar infringement on their religious beliefs. Since a religious group does not carry the same status as corporations, the Court viewed the State's interest in this matter as more compelling. The decision opened up a flood gate of harm against those unpatriotic and dangerous Jehovah's Witnesses, so virulent that the Supreme Court admitted to their mistake and reversed their ruling only three years later in *West Virginia v. Barnette* (1943). The Supreme Court remedied their mistake by striking down the expulsion of a Jehovah's Witness for refusing to salute the flag. Let us not underestimate the influence of the Supreme Court and the consequences that result from their legal dogma and allegiance to authoritarianism.

Quite possibly, we are due for a third catastrophic domestic tragedy in our near future, thanks again to our judicial branch of government. We have at least two ingredients for a substantial assault on democracy. On the one hand, significant numbers of middle class and lower middle class citizens are being deprived of their liberty to vote because of reactions, fueled by a "diligent" national press, against voter fraud. On the other hand, corporations and wealthy citizens are being granted additional liberty through their ability to influence elections and policies with money, much of which was not even obtained through the merits of their labors. Who knows how these assaults on democracy will initiate or augment a tragedy? Perhaps the looming tragedy already has been set in motion.

The Supreme Court, for their part, shows no signs of abating their dogmatic affront to wisdom. In 2006 they struck down a Vermont law that limited campaign contributions and expenditures. Justice Stephen Breyer, writing the majority opinion for *Randall v. Sorrell* (2006), provided yet another corker of a rationale. Justice Breyer warned that Vermont's law would be ``preventing challengers from mounting effective campaigns against incumbent officeholders, thereby reducing democratic accountability.'' At least a Supreme Court justice took responsibility for an irrational opinion this time.

Let us unpack Justice Breyer's claim a bit. According to such logic we need money to hold democracy accountable. We should not curb the control that wealth and power have on elected officials, since this would presumably reduce democratic accountability. Rather, according to the old boy network at the Supreme Court, we are to increase the obligation of any would be "public servant" to these "accountability" tools before they can effectively challenge an incumbent. If the wisdom of that escapes you, you must be merely middle class.

But wait, here's the real wonder in Breyer's logic, at least in the implications for the middle class. If Breyer's assumption that challengers need big money to succeed is false, then we have a bogus rationale for obligating our politicians to power and wealth elites. If Breyer's assumption is true, then middle class interests are put at a serious disadvantage in the political arena. No person who wants to forsake the power and wealth elites to remain true to the middle class stands the remotest chance of being elected, or even being heard. Corporate media certainly will not go out of their way to provide such a voice.

Some unusual allies support the use of wealth and power as accountability tools for democracy, though they have to make strange alterations to their usual goals. The ACLU sees no need for the diversity of candidates that would result if all did not have to establish connections with wealth, power and/or special interest groups. The puppet libertarians at think tanks like the Cato Institute support the political dependency on corporate media that equating money with free speech induces. Advocates of judicial restraint as a guide for maintaining voter identification laws—such as Justices Antonin Scalia and Clarence Thomas—think judicial activism is cool when overturning state or federal campaign finance laws.

There were good reasons for the founding fathers to equate property with liberty. Madison himself took an expansive view of property, including the property of one's thoughts and one's health under this same umbrella. In Madison's day property in the form of land could be had merely through the willingness to labor for a harvest. Property and the merits of use were more closely linked in yesterday's agrarian society than in today's world of hedge funds. But the wisdom of experience gained through time is like the wisdom of experience collected through democracy. We now have more than sufficient evidence to refute the claim that property is a fence to liberty. Indeed, we know now that abundant property can be gained through such means as inheritance, capital gains or hype. Among the wealthiest segments of society property actually undermines merit while bestowing extra "Blessings of Liberty."

Since the time of Madison, we also have gained sufficient understanding to consider liberty as something that contrasts with property. Thanks to the works of people like John Stuart Mill and James Surowiecki we can identify and protect the real ingredients for liberty. These ingredients are diversity of opinions, independence of thought and decentralization of information. Through protecting the essence of liberty we promote a democratic process dedicated to wisdom instead of power.

Yet there is more to be done than to promote the real ingredients to liberty. We must shun the legal dogma framing our current political system for a more empirical foundation to doctrines and jurisprudence. In particular, we have faltered in our judicial interpretation of liberty due to cultural interpretations for the "unalienable" or "fundamental" rights of nature. From a focused understanding of natural rights we can determine the true benefits and costs associated with the tension between individual rights and State interests. Understanding these true benefits and costs then enables us to construct a system of political liberty dedicated to the democratic pursuit of wisdom. Let us turn to this endeavor next.

ESSAY 15 – NATURAL CONDITIONS AND RIGHTS

Overview

- Our political system of liberty is not based on a foundation of natural rights.
- Liberties that are not natural rights are entitlements provided by the State.
- Property, security and privacy are cultural entitlements.
- Natural rights are evolved adaptations in humans for survival and well-being.
- Our natural right to independent labors enables diversity.
- Our natural right to independent thoughts enables adaptability.
- Our natural right to independent belongings enables stability.
- The State can deprive us of natural rights.
- The State has a compelling interest in the diversity, adaptability and stability gained by protecting our natural rights.
- Self-defense should be the only compelling interest that constrains natural rights.
- State police powers can be prompted by retaliation or preemption.
- Preemptive jurisprudence reflects cowardice that has led to tragic consequences.
- Free speech jurisprudence uses State police powers to protect false speech.
- Property jurisprudence sacrifices natural rights for cultural entitlements.
- Sense of belonging jurisprudence has a limited track record that we should steer further in the direction of equal protection and nondiscrimination.
- The Constitution allows us to develop a political system based on natural rights.

Natural Rights

Up until now I attempted to "stand on the shoulders of giants" to link political liberty with wisdom. However, in at least one particular aspect these giants, including Mill and other great thinkers of the Enlightenment, are found lacking. They did not have much experience with Nature and, consequently, have invalid and unreliable views of natural rights or our natural condition. This confuses their applications of what is "unalienable" or "fundamental" and, in turn, has misled our interpretations for which interests of the State are compelling. An unambiguous political system of liberty, one not as prone to self-interested and corrupt political manipulation or interpretation, one not as prone to decry cultural entitlements to the poor while providing greater entitlements to the rich, needs to be grounded in regards to those rights that are truly natural.

In regards to wisdom derived from wilderness experience I have a leg up on the great thinkers of the Enlightenment, and even on most of our founding fathers. For a crucial period during my young adult life I spent what amounted to three years in the wilderness, with my bed on the ground and belongings on my back. These wilderness journeys were done with groups, providing a closer approximation to the social life of early foraging bands than even an American pioneer would experience. I have extensive experience with distinguishing between what amounts to rights that evolved naturally for all humans and entitlements that only can be provided by culture..

Let us begin with counterexamples for natural rights. In Essay 14 the "natural" right to property was exposed as an entitlement that only the State is capable of providing and protecting. We have not naturally evolved with a right to security. During the times I found myself face-to-face with a bear, hanging off a cliff by my fingertips or succumbing to the first stages of hypothermia I knew that Nature had no intention of making my life secure. I was blessed to make it through those natural mishaps, just as most of us are blessed by living in a culture that, for the most part, is dedicated to providing us security. We may desperately want the security of our lives to be considered an "unalienable" right, but neither cultural nor natural evolution works to guarantee that we live forever. In these essays you will note that I do not treat the "right to life" as Jefferson intended, simply because the literal interpretation of this being unalienable does not make sense.

We have not naturally evolved with a right to privacy among others. To be left alone in the natural world you must be alone. You can hike, backpack, fish, hunt or meditate by yourself in the wilderness, and in so doing have privacy. However, you cannot live in the wilderness in close proximity with other human beings and be guaranteed the same privacy. Quite the opposite tends to be true. In the wilderness you know everyone's business of the company you keep, and they know yours. Secrets do not exist. Only the State offers the potential for forming secrets, or to be left alone while amongst many, and even then there are no naturally evolved constraints that prevent the State from intruding.

Protecting rights to security and privacy, like the right to property, are cultural entitlements that the State attempts to provide. The State seeks to attract and bind individuals through these cultural entitlements for which Nature provides no guarantees. No absolute constraint evolved from Nature forces the State to provide these cultural entitlements, nor prevents the State from taking those cultural entitlements away. As entitlements the State may deem to provide them selectively without merit, as inevitably occurs with property.

A meaningful basis for "unalienable" or "fundamental" rights would depend on what is naturally provided, rather than what must be entitled by the State. Being deprived of a cultural entitlement makes an individual no worse off than if the State did not exist to provide the entitlement in the first place. However, depriving humans of a natural right interferes with how we naturally evolved. While there has been plenty of evidence that great scholars think that cultural evolutions improves on natural evolution, there is also plenty of evidence that these great scholars delude themselves. Some of the cultural essays in this collection provide greater details for this assertion.

A right naturally provided amounts to our universal adaptations for survival and well-being. They are "fundamental" to who we are as individuals, apart from any action of the State. They are "unalienable" in the sense that, if State action does take them away, we sacrifice our natural tools for individual survival and well-being.

Individuals may willingly relinquish cultural entitlements provided by the State. Relinquishing cultural entitlements may be done with noble intent and noble effect, such as soldiers who forsake security. In contrast, relinquishing or being deprived of those rights that are "fundamental" and "unalienable" due to natural evolution means a genuine deprivation has been caused by the State that could not have occurred otherwise. This calls into question the validity of the corresponding State interest, no matter how noble the intent or effect. We will explore three such natural rights that should provide the foundation for our political system of liberty. These natural rights are:

- Independent labor;
- Independent thought; and
- Independent belonging.

Independent Labor

Fads come and go, even with long-distance backpacking. When I first hiked the Appalachian Trail in 1975 heavy packs enhanced your status. Now light packs are in and the dogmatists of the day declare that anyone wearing a heavy pack is a fool. For my own part I loved my craft, so to speak, and experimented with all types of backpacks and all types of backpacking. I spent eleven days traversing the Bitterroots with nothing but a daypack, relying in part on outdoor survival skills. I tolerated a night spent at over 10,000 feet by stripping a fallen pine of branches for my bedding. On the other hand, I spent eighteen days in the Sierra Nevada with a pack that started at 102 pounds, as weighed at an airport hangar. The abundance of food I carried enabled me to refute the claim of other backpackers that I would not make it through a remote, high-altitude stretch without hiking out for more supplies.

In truth, there are advantages to both types of backpacking. Carrying a light pack provides greater mobility, which helps in some types of survival situations. Carrying a heavier pack allows for more gear and food, which helps in other types of survival situations. Carrying a light pack means more energy conserved. Carrying a heavy pack means more luxuries. Carrying a light pack minimizes the negative impact of weight on aggravating injuries. Carrying a heavy pack maximizes the positive impact of weight training that all serious athletes use to enhance performance and durability. I owe my longevity and intensity in the "sport" to mainly carrying heavy packs when I started backpacking and lighter packs as I grew older.

We naturally evolved to have an independent choice in the costs and benefits our labors merit. Those who choose to carry heavy packs incur one set of costs and benefits; those who choose to carry light packs incur a different set. One can not expect increased mobility from carrying a heavier pack, increased strength is the laborer's due instead. People who are out of shape when they start backpacking experience both greater costs and benefits than those already in shape. Our independent choices of labor are a natural right that determines how we survive. By natural right we choose to catch a fish and we can eat a fish. By natural right we choose to build shelter and we can stay warm. By natural right we choose to migrate to environments where we think we will thrive better. The independence of our labors enabled a species originating in Africa to adapt and survive all over the world, forming a wide variety of diverse cultures.

Not all organisms naturally evolved with independent choice for their labors. Many organisms survive through a strict regiment of stimulus-response behaviors. They are limited in the range of their responses and the environments in which they can thrive. Sometimes they can be supremely good at their labors, such as the bacteria that can survive with hydrogen sulfide as an energy source, but they have no independent choice in the matter. Humans evolved to survive and prosper by independently choosing different labors to survive in different environments. Nature does not present us with uniform stimuli that encourage us to thrive with uniform responses, supremely fine-tuned. Constraining our natural right to independent labors can be done only by the State.

Independent Thought

I embarked on my first thru-hike of the AT with the eager anticipation that everyone I met would share my views. On the surface, there were some consistent similarities among us. Very few thru-hikers were minorities (unfortunately), while the great majority of them were male (thirty plus years ago). Yet behind these demographic similarities were a wide range of economic, political and cultural beliefs. There were Democrats, Republicans, third party advocates and unaffiliates. There were conservatives, liberals, moderates and radicals. There were anarchists who thought people should overthrow government and anarcho-capitalists who thought corporations should. There were members of every special interest group from the NRA to the NEA.

Most thru-hikers were likely to have the same opinion on some issues. Only two out of the hundreds of thru-hikers I have met, to my knowledge, advocated privatization of the National Parks and Scenic Trails (those crazy anarcho-capitalists, invite one to your next party!). The great majority of thru-hikers, with a few alarming exceptions, believe in low-impact camping. Still, even those slight deviations from the norm reflect greater diversity than the proportion of NRA members who favor strict gun controls, or the proportion of NEA members who think teachers get paid too much.

Nature does not have the power to constrain our thoughts. Nature cannot imprison, torture, or lobotomize us for thinking one way instead of another. Months spent in the wilderness enable one to think about anything they please, unfettered by the herd mentality. For most of the time we dwell on the mundane and the mainstream. Heck, most of the time we only think about food. Yet even while visions of pepperoni pizzas dance in our heads an independent thought or two creeps in, giving us our own unique perspectives for how life ought to be.

As with other thinking organisms, we naturally evolved to think empirically. Our thoughts are a response to our experiences. We could not have adapted to such diverse environments, even with our ability to labor independently, unless our minds could evaluate the changing conditions of real experience and respond appropriately. Plato may have been a great scholar, but his purely scholastic approach to knowledge would have left him and his followers for dead in a prehistoric world driven by changing experiences. Fixed dogma and dialectic reasoning have little adaptive value for much of what a migrating social band needs to survive.

Our independence of thought allows us to think both empirically and scholastically, but there are two caveats that apply to even the most dogmatic of scholars. We cannot lie to ourselves. We may fool ourselves into believing what we want but we cannot intentionally deceive our own thoughts. In other words, we can not pretend to believe in something we don't without being aware of the pretense. Similarly, we can not hide our thoughts from ourselves. An idea or information may be forgotten, but we can not consciously block what we consciously know. Our independence of thought is an honest and open communiqué we have with ourselves to determine the meaning of experience, even for dogmatic scholars.

Independent Belonging

Our expedition of thirteen backpackers explored potential routes for the unfinished

Continental Divide Trail by splitting up into as many as four smaller groups. We often did not follow a trail at all, as none yet existed, but instead navigated cross-country routes with map and compass. Through the Wind Rivers of Wyoming I separated from the others to hike cross-country along the crest of the mountains. The rest of the expedition hiked the Highline Trail, but split up further into groups hiking the same route at alternative times.

Two cliques formed. Going by the titles they bestowed on each other, the expedition divided into the "Three Hour Coffee Break" and the "Go, Go, Go" groups. One group preferred their leisure at the beginning or middle of the day; and at the beginning of the section. The other group preferred to have more leisure at the end of the day, and at the end of the section. This pattern of forming smaller groups according to individual preferences reoccurred throughout the journey, with different sets of backpackers forming new cliques. A few backpackers ended up together often, but no one felt compelled to stay with a certain group of people.

Four different methods of evaluation revealed that the Connecticut Continental Divide Expedition grew close to each other. Even as backpackers independently rearranged themselves into smaller groups, there remained for individuals a powerful sense of belonging to both their group and for all expedition members. On a survey evaluating physical, emotional, spiritual, social and family self-esteem, the two constructs for which expedition members recorded the most growth was social and family. Yes, that's right. From an experience that gets people into the best shape of their lives and provides daily, awe-inspiring beauty, the most profound effect of traveling in small social bands appears to be on our belonging.

This sense of belonging transcends social bonds. Through long periods of time spent in the wilderness people develop a sense of belonging to Nature herself. If we may stretch the meaning a bit further, long-distance backpacking nurtures an independent belonging to yourself, enhancing feelings of "to thine own self be true."

This independent belonging is another natural right that evolved for our survival and well-being. We work and survive better in groups than in isolation. Beauty and awe inspires belonging in us in ways that enhance order. Whether we want one or not we have a conscious that helps us to function better in small social groups (if not in anonymous suburbs or large nation states). When we deny these belongings we feel individual alienation and social groups suffer. In a word, our belonging creates stability.

State Deprivation of Natural Rights

All of our natural rights, even our independent belonging, are vulnerable to the compelling interests of the State. What Nature provides, the State can deprive.

The State can deprive us of independent labors, either by constraining the labor of which we are capable or by redistributing the costs and benefits. Such deprivation is not necessarily diabolical and may, in fact, provide the arrangements necessary to bind people to the State. Imprisonment for crimes provides an example of constraining labor that individuals consent to as they collect to form the State. Fueling capital markets by redistributing earned income to unproductive shareholders is another example. Redistributive taxation for the general good, in partial compensation for the costs of redistributive capitalism, is yet a third example.

Each of these examples, which we accept as legitimate, can be abused by the State. The State sometimes imprisons individuals that have committed no crime. The State can structure and protect an economic system that redistributes too much income away from compensating our independent labors to concentrate as capital gains for the wealthy. The fiscal policies of the State can serve large corporations and special interests rather than the general good. Thus empowered by the State, large corporations have the bargaining strength to coerce contracts in a way that constrains the independence of our labors. When large corporations dominate an economic system, diversity suffers.

The State can deprive us the independence of our thoughts. The State, or wards of the State such as licensed corporations and special interest groups, can bombard us with false ideas and misinformation. The State also can hide or outlaw ideas and information deemed to be harmful. In a word, the State can brainwash. This may be harshly put, but no more accurate term describes the practice of changing what people might otherwise think by hiding or distorting information and ideas. Unlike choosing our labors, for which we might have a just cause to forfeit, we never have a just cause for allowing ourselves to be brainwashed in a democracy. To succeed at brainwashing the State needs to diminish our independence, centralize the information we receive and limit the diversity of our opinions. When the State seeks to manipulate thoughts, no matter how just the cause or benign the intent, our collective wisdom and adaptability suffers.

The State can deprive us the independence of our belongings. Jim Crow laws, besides depriving blacks the full merits of their labors, also served to constrain the sense of belonging to each other that might have developed between different races with similar class backgrounds. The "separate but equal" doctrine imagined by the old boy network of the Supreme Court legitimized a prejudice that poor blacks should not expect to feel accepted by poor whites or vice-versa. The State also can force a sense of belonging that otherwise might not be felt. One would expect a certain amount of patriotism from the individuals of a State, but constraining the meaning of patriotism to performing certain rituals and sharing a narrow set of beliefs in a democracy inhibits individuals from becoming patriots based on the love of their land or their people. The State can force us to abandon our independent conscious, using propaganda to justify abhorrent means to achieve the ends deemed necessary by authoritarians. When belonging is forced in contradiction to our nature both the stability of the individual and the society is threatened.

State-Enhanced Natural Rights

Why would individuals want to be governed by the State, given the various State actions that can deprive us of our natural rights? Part of the reason lies with those cultural entitlements protected by State laws or good will that have not naturally evolved. Wilderness is portrayed often in literature as something to fear, where our life is at greater risk than in the comforting arms of civilization. Laws protect us from each other while technological innovations in medicine and manufacturing protect us from ourselves. Many also appreciate the anonymity that can be protected better by the State than by Nature. And, if one wants property that they are not using, one must come to rely on some type of power structure.

These entitlements alone do not buy our allegiance to the State. Property can be awarded to the few at the expense of the many without merit. The State protects privacy in some ways, but invades privacy in others. Sacrificing natural rights for greater security may seem like a bargain for some, but to others an atrocity. Certainly, Patrick Henry falls into the latter category, having proclaimed: "Give me liberty, or give me death!" New Hampshire license plates echo these same sentiments. State induced stress, crime, and/or pollution actually increase mortality rates. Neither a law nor good will by the State amounts to guarantees for any cultural entitlement.

The major reason to be governed by the State is that, rather than sacrificing natural rights, individuals anticipate those rights being enhanced. Both the individual and the State benefit from independent labor. Individuals can focus on certain types of labor, and explore new types, with the assurance that they do not need to labor at everything they need in order to survive. The State that features diverse opportunities for labor increases the willingness of individuals to be governed by that State.

Both the individual and the State benefit from independent thoughts. The reasons for the majority in a democracy to tolerate independent thoughts resemble the reasons not to empower a benevolent dictator. As with the benevolent dictator, a majority government may fail at times to serve the best interests of that same majority. As with the benevolent dictator, the majority government may have insufficient wisdom to attain their ends. As with new dictators, the future majority government may be serving the interests of a different majority. Attracting and tolerating independent thoughts provides adaptable wisdom for the governance of the State to benefit the individual.

Both the individual and the State benefit from independent belongings. Different belongings lead to different cultures with different perspectives. These varying, decentralized perspectives contribute to the ingredients of collective wisdom. They are also critical for our human identity. If we all felt the same thing, developed the same attachments, acted on the same loves, we would become a special class of robots. Finally, the ability to blend different cultural beliefs and behaviors stabilizes and advances civilizations, which will be explored in the cultural essays.

Compelling Interests of the State

The State is, essentially, a large collection of individuals. Given the potential enhancement of natural rights provided by the State, a greater enigma is why a collection of individuals would do anything to constrain the diversity, adaptability and stability that ultimately attracts them. Why would the State want to provide a disincentive for choosing diverse labors by allowing wealth to accumulate independently of merit? Why would the State employ falsehood and secrecy as means to their ends when these circumvent the adaptable wisdom of a democracy? Why would the State support media consolidation that homogenizes culture and discourages independent belongings, when this makes us no more advanced than an early social band of foragers, and less stable?

Unfortunately, out of a large collection of individuals there will be some obsessed with accumulating wealth, wielding power and/or promoting dogma. Because of these very attributes, such individuals will seek to rise to the top of the State's hierarchy. These same individuals then find that allowing diversity, adaptability or stability through natural rights undermines their goals. In States without the rule of law, or with laws arbitrarily designed to benefit the individual(s) at the top, natural rights can be abolished totally. Our Constitution and laws serve as safeguards against the lust for wealth, power and dogma that degrade a democracy.

Natural rights translate roughly, but not perfectly, into liberties protected by Constitutional government. Our mentor on liberty, John Stuart Mill, sums them up in this way, from *On Liberty*:

> "This, then, is the appropriate region of human liberty. It comprises, first, the inward domain of consciousness; demanding liberty of conscience, in the most comprehensive sense; liberty of thought and feeling; absolute freedom of opinion and sentiment on all subjects...
>
> Secondly, the principle requires liberty

of tastes and pursuits; of framing the plan of our
life to suit our own character; of doing as we like,
subject to such consequences as may follow:
without impediment from our fellow creatures, so
long as what we do does not harm them,

Thirdly, from this liberty of each individual
follows the liberty, within the same limits, of
combination among individuals; freedom to unite,
for any purpose not involving harm to others: …"

Mill's liberty of conscious corresponds to independent thought. His liberty of tastes and pursuits, subject to such consequences as may follow, corresponds to independent labor. Mill's freedom to unite corresponds to independent belonging. But natural rights sometimes suffer in our interpretation of liberties, even when we use Mill for guidance. For example, elevating the status of property obtained through the pursuit of investment welfare comes at the expense, not the reinforcement, of our natural right to productive independent labor.

As covered in Essay 14, the rule of law occasionally deprives us of our natural rights and/or liberties. For example, the Supreme Court overturned the rational interest of the State for protecting fundamental rights of individual people in favor of a rational interest for protecting individual corporations, in *Lochner v. New York* (1905). Yet the State should be viewed as having a compelling interest in protecting the natural rights of people, since protecting the diversity, adaptability and stability that springs from these rights enhances the survival and well-being of the State as well.

Overturning the compelling interest of the State to protect independent labors, thoughts and belonging should go beyond merely a rational interest, though corporate lawyers such as Chief Justice John Roberts probably would object. We should require an interest more compelling than preserving diversity, adaptability and stability through independence. We can turn once more to Mill for further guidance. Instead of his list of liberties, Mill regarded his most important principle to be the conditions under which these liberties may be restricted.

"That principle is, that the sole end for which
mankind are warranted, individually or
collectively, in interfering with the liberty or
action of any of their number, is self-protection.
That the only purpose for which power can
be rightfully exercised over any member of a
civilized community, against his will, is to prevent
harm to others. His own good, either physical or

moral, is not a sufficient warrant. He cannot be
rightfully compelled to do or forbear because it
will be better for him to do so."

If we use Mill for guidance, the most compelling interest of the State is essentially self-defense. The diversity, adaptability and stability gained through independence may be thwarted when preventing harm to others. This begs the question of how the State should prevent harm in self-defense.

State Police Powers

The Constitution provides for police powers to compel the State's interests. The term "police powers" is intended figuratively, as in the sum total of efforts by the State to protect compelling interests, including the laws that are passed. The means of policing comes in two basic forms, preemption and retaliation. These forms contrast greatly in how they constrain natural rights and protect the compelling interests of the State.

Preemption debilitates. Consequently, we seldom pass laws to preemptively protect ourselves from harm. Instead, the laws we make tend to be in retaliation to problems that have occurred. We notice a pattern of car accidents from people using handheld devices and we "retaliate" with a law. When current laws do not sufficiently curb drunk driving, we "retaliate" with tougher laws. Even seat belt laws are, in a sense, "retaliation" to the existing problem of people having been hurtled through windshields.

If we took the preemptive approach to protecting ourselves from car accidents we would run into two problems. First, we would need to flood our legal system with laws and regulations anticipating every probable cause of car accidents, including some that seldom happen. Second, our limited foresight means that even after we take all these preemptive measures car accidents will still happen. We might selectively preempt to be more efficient, but this makes preemption less effective and presents another set of problems, as our foreign policies help to illustrate.

The Bush II doctrine of permitting preemptive strikes must be selective by necessity. In order to preempt every possible threat of foreign origin the United States would need to subjugate the entire world. While this indeed may be what some neoconservatives have in mind, such a mission does not square with practical reality. We would debilitate ourselves from too much activity, much like flooding our legal system with preemptive laws to prevent car accidents, stretching our military resources to the point of breaking. Meanwhile, the act of world subjugation would motivate a whole lot of enemies. Even if we regard preemption as desirable foreign policy, we nevertheless must preempt selectively by targeting what we perceive are our greatest threats. We invaded Iraq preemptively as allegedly our greatest threat.

There are three different types of drawbacks to selective preemption, depending on the target. Selecting a target that is bigger than what a nation can handle—such as if Iraq had targeted the United States to preempt our preemption— invites destruction. Selecting a target that is a nation's equal—such as when we propped up Iraq to take on Iran—invites escalation. Selecting a target that a nation can overwhelm—such as our invasion of Iraq—invites global animosity that resembles the fear and disdain held for the neighborhood bully.

Because of the problems inherent in selective preemption, selecting targets need to be a sure thing. You select to preempt the greater foe when your position already has been rendered next to hopeless. In retrospect, preemptively attacking the United States would have been a rational strategy for Saddam Hussein. Since Hussein was about to be destroyed anyways, his only hope for inflicting damage was through preemption. This lesson no doubt has been internalized by Islamic fundamentalists and, ironically, our destruction of a toothless foe makes their fanatical acts appear more rational to the world.

You select to preempt the equal foe when there are some principles for which citizens as well as soldiers are willing to die, a likely consequence when the aggression is returned and the conflict escalates. Our experiences with Iraq could prove to be ironic in this regards. Though no foe exists that is our equal at the moment, authorities have orchestrated the war on terror on the hidden message that citizens should think differently than soldiers. Soldiers should risk their lives for liberty, citizens should not. Security trumps everything, if you believe chicken hawks such as Vice President Dick Cheney. Though the attraction of the State includes the potential for greater security than Nature provides, we should be wary of any Faustian bargain by which we forfeit our natural rights for that security. Also, as Mill suggests, only through liberty does real security prevail. Thanks to the "leadership" of chicken hawks such as Cheney and other neoconservatives encouraging us to think cowardly about our security, citizens will have a harder time in the future finding the resolve to prevail against attacks from a truly formidable foe.

You select to preempt the lesser foe when you have concrete proof that the foe would have harmed you without the preemptive strike, and you willingly risk global animosity as a necessary consequence. In the case of Iraq our authorities alleged that they had such concrete proof, a "slam dunk" in some respects. When that "proof" turned out to be false we further induced hostility towards us reserved for the "neighborhood bully." This made the war in Iraq totally different from the war in Afghanistan in terms of world perception.

Our retaliatory strike of the Taliban in Afghanistan had near unanimous support of the global community, and we had the military resources to retaliate effectively. When we preemptively invaded Iraq we lost the support of the global community, stretched our military forces thin and increased the numbers and intensity of those who hate the bullying acts of the United States. Admittedly, the costs of waiting for retaliation can be severe, such as the people we lost in the 9/11 attacks. Yet the immediate retaliation based on the certainty of having been attacked was effective, as we ousted the Taliban with global support and made the world safer for a few months. Since our preemptive strike of Iraq we have lost more soldiers than the citizens we lost on 9/11, not to mention the additional thousands of innocent Iraqi citizens killed in the process. We also rendered our actions in Afghanistan less effective. The result: 86 % of national security experts polled by Foreign Policy magazine think that the world has become more dangerous for us; 87% think that invading Iraq specifically has hurt our national security.[1]

Very few nations in the history of the world have sought to protect themselves from harm through a foreign policy of preemption. The great majority of aggressive military acts have been for one or more of those three bugaboos: consolidating wealth, power and/or dogma. Certainly, these have been the reasons for the most aggressive country in overthrowing governments in the past century, the United States. Thorough documentation of our actions and motives has been provided by Stephen Kinzer in his disturbing but entertaining book *Overthrow: America's Century of Regime Change from Hawaii to Iraq* (2006).

A rational mind with an understanding of how natural selection works would wonder about this. If preemption works, then the nations that have selected the practice over the course of history should have been geopolitically favored over other nations. The fact that this has not happened should provide a clue obvious enough even for neoconservatives. Preemption in the overall scheme of things invites retaliatory harm, rather than prevents harm, even for the biggest bully in the neighborhood.

A foreign policy of preemption is such a dumb idea that this should increase our suspicions further about our invasion of Iraq. Ironically, the global community might have accepted with less apprehension the United States revealing that we mainly wanted to control Iraq's oil. Such a motive for aggression may have been unpopular, but expected and tolerated more by the global community than the spectacle of the mightiest nation on earth spinelessly preempting a Third World foe.

Perhaps our authorities weighed the risks between exposing to us the objective of securing oil, or hiding that rational objective and allowing the global community to perceive us as bullies. Perhaps they decided that risking the world's wrath under a false pretense was better than having their real objectives vetoed by citizens at home. This is actually hopeful speculation, inferring that citizens in this democracy really do have the ability to influence how authoritarians act, if

---

1 From a June 2006 poll. Poll results are here: www.americanprogress.org/kf/terrorsurveypoll.pdf.

allowed our diversity of opinions, independence of thought, and decentralization of information provided.

Preemptive Jurisprudence

We have reviewed why laws and foreign policy work better at retaliating against known harms that have occurred rather than preempting possible harms yet to exist. We should apply this same principle to determining the compelling interests of the State to protect citizens. Doing so occasionally requires more courage than citizens, lawmakers and Supreme Court justices have demonstrated.[2]

A set of Supreme Court cases decided in 1919, on the heels of World War I, provides telling testimony to this matter. In the first case, *Schenck v. United States*, a "clear and present danger" doctrine was established for determining the compelling interests of the State. Charles Schenck was a Socialist against the military draft. He circulated leaflets to drafted men encouraging them to peacefully petition for the repeal of the Conscription Act. Schenck was arrested under the Espionage Act of 1917 for allegedly attempting to cause insubordination in the military; his imprisonment due to that arrest was upheld by the Supreme Court. In an opinion written by Justice Oliver Wendell Holmes, Schenck's leaflets calling for a petition represented a "clear and present danger" to the security of the United States.

As applied to Schenck and subsequent cases, a test of "clear and present danger" has been preemptive and, as so often happens with preemptive actions, the applications have been cowardly and false. In truth, Schenck was not attempting to overthrow the military or the government. In truth, even if Schenck had such intent, his leaflets represented absolutely no clear and present danger of doing so. The State has access to every media outlet in the country, patriotic civic groups and the natural trust of most citizens. Charles Schenck had access to a cheap printing press. If Schenck's leaflets could overcome the massive resources of the State, then he would have to be peddling a very, very powerful idea, an idea whose time had come in a true democracy regardless of State actions.

Charles Schenck was relatively lucky, compared to the defendants of another case heard that same year by the Supreme Court. The defendants in *Abrams v. United States* also were tried under the Espionage Act for circulating two "harmful" leaflets, which they distributed by anonymously throwing them off the top of a roof. The defendants were Russian immigrants and the leaflets called for the United States to not intervene in Russia's civil war against the Bolshevik

---

2   As in the previous essay, much of the factual information regarding Supreme Court essays were first gleaned from two courses on CD offered by The Teaching Company: *The History of the Supreme Court*, taught by Professor Peter Irons, and *Civil Liberties and the Bill of Rights* taught by Professor John E. Finn. I also use *The Oxford Guide to the Supreme Court* (2005), ed. Kermit L. Hall, as a reference.

regime. The leaflets were slightly more "violent" than Schenck's call for petitioning government, as these encouraged munitions workers to go on strike. Still, their intent was not to stop the war with Germany; one leaflet stated that the distributors hated the Germans even more than the U. S. government. Rather, their intent was to limit bloodshed against workers with whom they felt both a nationalistic and class kinship.

The effects of the Abrams leaflets were the same as the Schenck leaflets. That is to say, they had no effect. Imagine that. Leaflets expressing the thoughts of a few radicals have little power to persuade the same public exposed to the government's collective resources for persuasion. The defendants received 20 year prison terms. They were subsequently deported and, considering that their criticism of the Bolshevik government was more substantial and real than their "threat" to ours, persecuted upon return to their homelands. Some died at the hands of that persecution.

The same justice that established the "clear and present danger" doctrine in the Schenck case dissented eight months later in the Abrams case. In the interim, Justice Holmes conversed with legal scholars who convinced him that allowing dissension in the form of free speech was a necessary aspect of good government. In the Abrams case Holmes did not renege on his "clear and present danger" doctrine but stipulated that, in the absence of such dangers, the expression of free speech must be protected as contributing to the "marketplace of ideas." The majority of the justices nevertheless wielded the "clear and present danger" doctrine in traditional preemptive fashion, with the same type of cowardly and false assumptions driving the same type of outcomes which prove "dangerous" only to those who attempt to exercise freedom of speech.

The "clear and present danger" doctrine was altered eventually, but not in the way you might think. Remember, we are dealing with the old boy network of the Supreme Court. The power and wealth elites that make up this old boy network have greater fears for losing what they have than the average middle class citizen, and are prone to act on these fears. The case of *Whitney v. California* (1927), upheld the conviction of Anita Whitney for helping to establish the Communist Labor Party in the state. The opinion of the Supreme Court diluted a "clear and present danger" doctrine for limiting free speech, to a doctrine that condemns speech that merely encourages a "bad tendency." The "bad tendency" in this case was advocating reform through democratic ballot measures at her party's convention.

Justice Louis Brandeis wrote a concurring opinion that nevertheless refuted the "bad tendency" claims of the majority opinion. Brandeis claimed that citizens have an obligation to participate in the governing process, and that this can occur only if unpopular views are allowed to be expressed. Eventually, the attitudes of Holmes and Brandeis regarding the necessity to protect free speech would prevail in *Brandenburg v. Ohio* (1967). What sort of extraordinary circumstances would lead a majority of the old boys on the Supreme Court to not preempt inflammatory free speech? Clarence Brandenburg was a Ku Klux Klan leader who advocated acts of real violence (not strikes or petitions) against Jews and blacks, and who denounced our government (not Russia's) for suppressing the Caucasian race. While the Supreme Court did protect the free speech of the KKK, the irony here is that convicting KKK leaders of inciting violence against minorities would have been retaliatory, rather than an act of cowardly and false preemption against a "clear and present danger" or "bad tendency."

Preemption on behalf of the State's compelling interest has led to many more tragedies than so far cited here. The false tendencies of preemption led to the torture of pacifist Mennonites, who had the misfortune of a German heritage during World War I. The cowardice of preemption created the Japanese internment camps during World War II, an act of Congress subsequently upheld by the Supreme Court. The costs of preemptive paranoia are extraordinary, and should not be the basis for establishing the State's compelling interest in usurping natural rights. The same cowardly impulse that drives individuals or the State towards preemption also causes them to almost always apply the doctrine falsely.

False Speech Jurisprudence

Using preemption as the basis for a compelling interest to protect citizens from harm erodes both the liberty of free speech and the natural right to independent thought. Other erosions of this same natural right have occurred because of a flawed understanding of how free speech represents independent thought. Evidence of this is in the same Schenck case that established the doctrine of "clear and present danger."

Holmes wrote in his opinion that: "The most stringent protection of free speech would not protect a man in falsely shouting fire in a theatre and causing a panic." This statement makes the assumption that falsely shouting fire is an expression of free speech. Perhaps that fits the traditional view of free speech as an expression of liberty, but does not fit with how free speech represents a natural right. By natural rights you cannot be false to yourself; hence, being false to others cannot be considered a real expression of independent thoughts.

Falsely shouting fire in a crowded theatre fails to qualify as free speech, if the purpose of free speech is to protect the liberty of a natural right. If natural rights were our guide an appropriate statement from Holmes would be: "The most stringent protection of free speech would not protect a man from falsely shouting anything, regardless of the consequences, since false speech is not free speech." Truthfully shouting fire in a crowded theatre and being correct would only bring thanks. Truthfully shouting fire in a crowded theatre (from one's deluded perspective) and being wrong might bring condemnation and/or a trip to the sanitarium, but would not bring conviction even under a preemptive "clear and present danger" litmus test.

If Charles Schenck truthfully thought that conscription is a violation of liberty, then the leaflet he distributed exercised the freedom of speech that represented his natural right to independent thought. Denying the speech inhibits the natural right of independent thought, which places the State in a quandary. One of the premiums the State can offer the individual is enhancing natural rights through diversity. Inhibiting the natural right to independent thought harms one of the advantages for individuals to be governed by a State. In addition, limiting diversity of opinions harms the State's ability to collect wisdom. When limiting free speech, ostensibly to protect citizens from harm, an allegedly democratic State inflicts harm to the very foundation of its existence.

The intent of Schenck's speech was similar to the intent of Vietnam War protesters, whose expressions of speech helped to end our involvement in Vietnam. There are those who still insist terminating our involvement in Vietnam was wrong, but they need to consider one of our most important objectives for that mission. Vietnam now has the economic system we fought over there to protect. We could have had the same end result with much less carnage, or we could have continued with the carnage for the sake of claiming we also spread "democracy" via a few million extra deaths and napalmed acres of landscape. The wise choice should be clear, and that was the choice made when the collective wisdom of citizens could be expressed through free speech.

Speaking of wisdom, or lack thereof, we now can understand another aspect of the foolish decision in *Buckley v. Valeo* (1976) to equate money with free speech. How many well-funded campaign ads do you think contain neither falsehoods nor secret omissions? Virtually every expensive ad fails to reveal the thought that created the message, which would require the following disclaimer:

> "Irrelevant to whether we think our candidate is
> best for the job, or will keep his/her campaign
> promises, we mainly want you to vote for him/
> her to enhance the authoritarian presence of our
> party in government."

Keep in mind that hyped speech is, in essence, false speech. If you state the worth of something to be greater than what independent thinking truly believes, or that the opposing candidate is worse than what you truly believe, that is being false. False speech is not the expression of our natural right to independent thought. Interpreting the Constitution to offer protections for false speech may be justified by a distorted view of what liberty really means—if liberty is the real intent of such a decision—but in no way preserves a natural right. This is true whether or not money is involved, but money adds greater incentive to use falsehoods and secrecy to achieve one's ends. More money also means the potential for greater false hype and distortions, and thus greater undermining of our natural right to independent thoughts and our ability to collect wisdom in a democracy.

The police powers of the State can be used to either punish or protect. Using the police powers of the State to punish false speech may prove unfeasible, but certainly those police powers should not be employed to actively/substantively/ structurally protect false speech. We know with certainty that money is used as an expression of false speech; in a system devoted to our natural rights the Supreme Court would not be protecting this from campaign finance laws. Quite frankly, the precedence established in *Buckley v. Valeo* is something that we, the middle class, need to be extremely concerned about. The decision has the same "quality" as the Dred Scott interpretation that no blacks had any rights anywhere. Grounding our interpretation of rights with what is truly natural may help restore some rationality to campaign finance jurisprudence, and perhaps avoid yet another looming tragedy spurred in large part by the good ol' boys on the Supreme Court.

Property Jurisprudence

Grounding our interpretation of the Constitution and the law with an understanding of our natural rights would affect property jurisprudence. Property is not a natural right, like enjoying the merits of our independent labors, despite what authoritarians and corporations wish us to believe. The free market provides for an exchange of goods produced through diverse labors that were chosen independently. Property can be a placeholder for the merits of these independent labors; but property also can undermine this natural right. Instinctively, we know this to be true. The property of feudal lords undermines the natural right to independent labor. The property of slave owners undermines the natural right to independent labor. What we have more trouble accepting—thanks to corporate media and the Powell Cabal—is that property in the form of capital welfare undermines this natural right as well. The economic implications of capital welfare were covered in Essay 3, but we now will explore further the political implications.

Capital welfare includes inherited property. Nature tends to reclaim the fruits of our independent labors that we do not consume in a timely manner. Accumulated property, in addition to representing the merits of an individual's labor, requires the consent of a State that provides a system for hording. Large inheritances are a form of capital welfare that the State allows to be diverted from both the labor and the system creating the hoarded capital to a third party recipient. The natural right of the recipient to their choice of independent labor would not be violated should the property be returned to the State that enabled the hording. In fact, large inheritances are a disincentive for the recipient to exercise their natural right for any independent labor. The State may grant a cultural right to inherit hoarded property up to certain amounts, but otherwise recipients have no natural claim based on the natural right of independent labors.

Capital welfare can be provided in the form of investment property. A real estate investor might buy 100 acres for $500,000 (this does not reflect market reality; we are just keeping the numbers simple). She carves a lot out for herself, which is merited to the extent that the money used for the investment was obtained through the merit of her previous independent labors. She then carves out forty two-acre lots which she intends to sell for $20,000 each. The $800,000 of investment potential does not result from the merits of labor.

Let us assume that the State prevents ten acres of wetlands on this property from being developed. If the investor sued for entitlement to the extra $200,000, the State likely would prevail against the investment potential of the property. The State's interest in wetlands is generally regarded as compelling for protecting public health and safety, and would warrant a decision from local boards and state courts in favor of limiting the investment potential without compensation. If we were concerned with protecting property only as a placeholder for the merits of independent labor, then the decision becomes even easier. If the choice of our labors, not property, was the direct target for liberty, no liberty of the individual was violated by diminishing the investment potential of property for a compelling interest of the State.

While local boards and state courts generally find the protection of wetlands as a compelling interest of the State, the good ol' boys on the Supreme Court tend to think differently than us plain folk. In the case of *Lucas v. South Carolina Coastal Council* (1992), mentioned in the previous essay, the Supreme Court decided that a developer was due just compensation for the full development potential of land near the shore, despite the State's interest to prevent the degradation of sand dunes. Mind you, the developer was not due just compensation of the purchase price of the property for the State to gain ownership. That could be interpreted as compensation for the merits of independent labor that enabled the developer to purchase the property. The developer was due the "just compensation" of 100% the full development potential of the land...and he could retain title to the land. If any kind of property can be considered a "fence to liberty," then the Supreme Court can fancy that they took the side of individual liberty. If only the value of property gained through merited labor represents liberty, then the decision in Lucas merely took the side of greed.

This principle of protecting property gained only through merit can be extended to contracts as well. If contracts are viewed as an exchange of the self-interests of independent labor, we must acknowledge that the exchange can and has been skewed without merit to the side with the greater strength to bargain.

Thus contracts, like property, can undermine merit and, in so doing, undermine the natural right of independent labor. Because of the virtues of protecting natural rights, the State has at least a rational interest to neutralize unmerited advantages in the bargaining of contracts, and often may have a compelling interest.

The wealthy and powerful, and those who hunger to become so, are not likely to be enamored with this distinction of property as a placeholder for merited labor versus capital welfare. Making such a distinction calls too much attention to the undermining of liberty through greed. Unfortunately, this means we can expect the current power and wealth elites, ranging from the Powell Cabal to the good ol' boys on the Supreme Court, to vigorously refute such a concept of natural rights. We must, in turn, consider whether we should blindly trust these authoritarians when they present their arguments.

Belonging Jurisprudence

The Constitution represents the natural right to independent belonging through the First Amendment right to freedoms of assembly and religion. These have not been discussed in depth yet; jurisprudence involving freedoms of assembly and religion has evolved more recently and has less of a track record. Still, there are a few lessons to be learned from history so far, and a few principles that could be applied to future belonging jurisprudence.

The freedoms of assembly and religion alone have not sufficiently established the compelling interests of the State to protect independent belonging. The State, in fact, has taken cowardly preemptive action against this independence. McCarthyism falls under this category. No dire event deserving of retaliation caused Senator McCarthy to begin his investigations of communists, just political opportunism. What turned into the Red Scare had no basis in anything but cowardice. In many countries the leaders look over their shoulders in paranoid apprehension of a military coup. In our country the military ultimately rescued us from the paranoia of dogmatic elites when they took the initiative to refute McCarthy.

Historically, the paternal authoritarianism of power and wealth elites in our democracy constrained other freedoms besides those of assembly and religion. McCarthyism confirmed that dogmatic elites are instead the particular threats to our natural right of independent belonging. This seems to present a paradox, since many people identify religious beliefs as fundamental dogma. Indeed, dogma established by great religious scholars drove the scholasticism and universities that formed prior to the Enlightenment. This paradox suggests that constraining religious dogma constrains religious freedom, though the authoritarianism of dogmatic elites also forms the biggest threat to religious freedom.

The way out of this paradox lies in the distinction made throughout *Systems out of Balance* between empirical experience and scholastic beliefs. The natural right to independent belonging is something we experience. Whether we describe this experience as belonging to Mother Nature, God or some other transcendent being depends on the social beliefs we construct from our individual experiences. The State should have a compelling interest to protect individual experiences of transcendent belonging, yet no interest in protecting any set of social beliefs constructed from those experiences. By extension, the morality that nurtures the experiences of belonging should be a compelling interest of the State, but not the morality framed by social beliefs. What constitutes the morality of belonging will be discussed further in the cultural essays.

By preserving independent belonging as a natural right, diverse affiliations form. Some of these affiliations could be construed as harmful to the State. A doctrine of preemption aimed at limiting these affiliations has and will lead to false and cowardly movements such as McCarthyism, and degrade the stability that the natural right for independent belonging provides to the State. Retaliating against an affiliation that already has done tangible harm against the State is warranted, but until tangible harm can be conclusively documented we would, on the balance, do the greater harm through preemptive action.

There is one other footnote to add. Independent belonging thrives by virtue of acceptance and the absence of prejudice. The State must therefore consider the elimination of institutionalized prejudice as a compelling interest. Individual bigotry cannot be forcefully eliminated by the State, and attempts to do so would only jeopardize the very liberty the State meant to protect. But combating discriminatory practices and extending equal protection under the law qualify as compelling interests of a State that wishes to protect the natural right to independent belonging.

Exercising Our Political Liberty

We have uncovered a few basic principles for a political system of liberty, through which we might simplify and strengthen our democracy by the rule of law and the flourishing of collective wisdom. These principles are based on rights that evolved naturally for our survival and well-being. The State can provide enhancements to these rights for individuals, and protecting these rights for individuals enhances survival and well-being for the State. Protecting natural rights form a compelling interest for the State that should be trumped only by retaliatory self-defense.

A few extra caveats were attached to our natural rights. The natural right to independent labor contributes to diversity, a diversity that is fostered through merit and robbed by greed. The natural right to independent thought contributes to adaptability, but requires open and honest information that cannot abide false speech. The natural right to independent belonging contributes to stability, but only if we seek to harmonize the beliefs formed from our belonging with the belonging experienced by others.

This political system of liberty was established without input from the good old boys of the Supreme Court. What nerve! This system lacks the following:

- The respect of a John Marshall, a fierce party loyalist, as he interpreted law guided by party politics.
- The backing of a Roger Taney, a wealthy slave owner, as he interpreted law to selectively apply liberty.
- The scholarship of Oliver Wendell Holmes, an aristocrat, as he interpreted law to preemptively compel the interests of the State.
- The connections of a Lewis Powell, a corporate lawyer, as he interpreted law for the benefit of corporations.
- The idolatrous following of Antonin Scalia, professed advocate of judicial restraint and textualism, as he conveniently abandons these doctrines whenever they don't serve his idolized agenda.
- The pedigree of a John Roberts, another corporate lawyer, as he wails about the low pay collected by the "public servants" on the Supreme Court.

The alternative to entrusting our political system to the authorities is for middle class citizens to draw from our own collective experiences. There will be many that judge an attempt to simplify our political system of liberty to be presumptuous; many who might claim these doctrines for jurisprudence simple-minded. We can rely on the Constitution for some support, as there is nothing in the Constitution, which has not been subsequently amended, to refute the principles we offer here. Nothing in the Constitution states that greed should be rewarded in property disputes, or that falsehoods should be protected. No Article or Amendment calls for preemptive laws based on cowardice. Yet, in the end, we are only middle class. What do we have going for us?

What, indeed, except for the exercise of our political liberty and the collective wisdom a true democracy can offer. The obstacles we face in overcoming authoritarianism lie embedded in the natural trust we have for authorities. In an earlier time of our natural evolution this trust was adaptive; now this trust interferes with our homeostatic function of keeping authoritarianism in check. Similar to the tricks played by the Powell Cabal, our political system is feeding us invalid and unreliable information that we are trusting. We will conclude our political essays with a guide for identifying these authoritarian methods of exploiting our trust.

ESSAY 16 - THE WAGGLE DANCES OF POLITICIANS

Overview

- Corporate news media reporting is often invalid and unreliable.
- Corporate news media provides political theater at the expense of real news.
- Politicians waggle angles of public interest to achieve goals of self-interest.
- The "black box" waggle dance obscures the validity of empirical evidence through complexity or secrecy.
- The "black is white" waggle dance uses bravado, morality, or bait and switch tactics to champion unreliable policies for the public interest.
- Detecting waggle dances depends on recognizing authoritarian dogma.
- Authoritarians and corporate media waggle about issues that undermine wise democracy.
- Intense waggle dancing infects citizens with vanity, cynicism and apprehension.
- The success of authoritarian waggle dances derives from cultural conditions.

Invalid and Unreliable Information

Most journal articles begin with abstracts. These provide just a very few sentences of the background, methods, results and conclusions of scientific research. For the sake of brevity, abstracts contain little opinion except for suggesting the importance of the research. The researcher reads the abstract first, and then decides whether the rest of the article is worth reading based on: 1) the material in the abstract reflecting his/her interests and 2) the apparent validity and reliability of the research. What our democracy could use is something like abstracts being issued by the various politicians and authorities about their policy decisions. What we get are echo chambers and news talk hosts. This last essay on politics provides a guide for detecting when authoritarians and corporate media are providing invalid and unreliable information for the functioning of a wise democracy (this essay was crafted in 2007 and refers to the Bush II administration).

In the absence of abstracts there are other tricks to preview the content of a written document. Sometimes bullet points provided at the beginning of a news article help out the interested reader, similar to the overviews provided for these essays. My own favorite trick is to read a news or magazine article backwards until I decide whether or not the article should be read forwards. The concluding paragraphs of an article are usually to the point, while at the same time revealing the type and intensity of bias affecting the writer. For example, here is a concluding paragraph we first quoted in Essay 4 that reveals much.

> "Second, a certain class of pundits and politicians are quick to see any increase in income inequality as a problem that needs fixing—usually through some form of redistributive taxation. Applying the same philosophy to leisure, you could conclude that something must be done to reverse the trends of the past 40 years—say, by rounding up all those folks with extra time on their hands and putting them to (unpaid) work in the kitchens of their "less fortunate" neighbors. If you think it's OK to redistribute income but repellent to redistribute leisure, you might want to ask yourself what—if anything—is the fundamental difference."

There are numerous invalid and unreliable claims in just this last paragraph. Over the past thirty years there has not been just "any increase in income inequality," there has been a steady and dramatic increase, as the numbers crunched in Essay 7 reveals. The article refers to "redistributive taxation," but fails to recognize that this is a corrective measure for "redistributive capitalism," which concentrates as capital gains a portion of the income that the free market otherwise would have awarded the merits of production. This explains the "fundamental difference" between redistributing income and leisure, which seems to escape the writer.

Corporate capitalism does not redistribute labor, just income. The poor, beleaguered office manager has not stayed at work late to push brooms for the lazy janitor. Government policy should only correct what has been redistributed previously. Finally, the alleged 40 year trend for increased leisure counters the intuition for anyone over 40 years old who knows about the tremendous rise in day care services. Overall, the paragraph reveals typical ignorance from the Powell Cabal and *laissez faire* economists about the economics of the middle class.

The concluding paragraph above was remarkable for poor quality, misleading information, false conclusions and snide tone. It was perfect to feature in Essay 4, which dealt in part with how the Powell Cabal misleads the public. In a similar vein we now will explore how corporate media misleads the public when providing the invalid and unreliable information that authoritarians want us to have.

Political Theater

For much of this essay we will focus on a newspaper article that I will keep anonymous for now. Part of our challenge will be not only to evaluate the merit of information and opinions provided, but also the type of newspaper that might print such an article. The article refers to other articles reporting on the testimony to Congress by James Comey, former Deputy Attorney General under John Ashcroft, about the National Security Administration (NSA) wiretapping controversy. We know already that rather than a news piece, or even an opinion piece, this is more like an "opinion of opinions" piece. Opinion meisters like echo chambers, news talk shows and *Fox News* immediately come to mind as potential sources for such a piece. Please remember as we go along that this is a newspaper article, not something transcribed from the entertainment industry, though we might end up judging the content to be geared more for entertainment than news. Here are the last two paragraphs.

> "What's really going on here is a different form of political theater: Democrats are trying to whip up an aura of 'illegality' to create the political leverage to strip a Republican President of his surveillance authority in wartime. They've tried to do this since the program was revealed, and back in 2006 Russ Feingold compared it to Watergate. But unfortunately for the Democrats, wiretapping aimed at America's terrorist enemies is politically popular.
>
> So, rather than arguing the legal merits, Democrats are spinning a yarn about shady deeds perpetrated in a hospital room at night. They are using half-truths to achieve a partisan goal that is dangerous policy, and they shouldn't get away with it."

The very last clause of this "opinion about opinions" article urges us to hold Democrats accountable for their dangerous half-truths. Depending on your party affiliation that last paragraph either makes you dubious, since both parties continually indulge in half-truths at the expense of the public interest, or angry, since there comes a point at which we should halt such partisan politics, and your implicit trust in the scholarly source of the article convinces you that only Democrats have crossed the line.

If we back up one paragraph, two unreliable innuendos will steer us more towards one of these possibilities. The first innuendo implies that Democrats do not want wiretaps on terrorists. There may be a few flaming news talk show hosts that would claim that, but no newspaper staff with any common sense truly believes that the bulk of Democrats, despite their many follies, do not want terrorists to be wiretapped. This leads us to the other innuendo in the same sentence: that the controversy is over fighting terrorism. The real issue is about accountability: whether there should be checks and balances for the executive branch as they do their wiretapping. Both innuendos fail a test of reliability; an impartial observer would not come to the same conclusions, and the last paragraph amounts to something even less than a "half-truth" from the author.

The article attempts to frame the issue with these innuendos in the same unreliable manner as the echo chambers of pro-authoritarianism corporate media. We can guess that the newspaper is either aligned with the wealth and/or power elites, or that it is a second rate rag without the journalistic integrity or competence to be independent from mainstream corporate newspapers. Let us back up further to get a better sense of this.

More false innuendos infiltrate the first paragraph quoted above; let us tackle them in reverse order. The "wartime" being alluded to is not the occupation in Iraq, which still presents the conditions of war, but the fight against terror, which has little to do with actual "wartime" activities. We may refer to the "war on crime" or even a "war on drunk driving," two violent and criminal activities that claims far more American lives than terrorists, but we realize those are just emotional figures of speech. The efforts to prevent those types of violence, though they might include killing bad guys in responding to crime, do not qualify as real "wartime" behavior. We do not battle for territory or resources with drunk drivers; nor do we get criminals to surrender en masse. You would think that no freethinking journalist or editor seriously thinks we will get terrorists to capitulate to our will and sign a treaty, which means "wartime" is an invalid reference. We might conclude, once again, that this is a second rate rag that truly believes fighting terror qualifies as "wartime," or that this mainstream corporate newspaper dutifully channels the rhetoric of the administration, designed to generate fear in citizens.

The same sensational sentence refers to the "surveillance authority" of the President. Anyone who has paid attention to this controversy knows that the ability of the President to authorize surveillance has not been called into question, only whether he must notify the judicial branch in some manner. Thus, the President is not in danger of being stripped of anything. Democrats may desire to strip the President of something, but Democrats are much too wimpy to initiate such a thing unless they think corporate media has got their backs. Democrats just might follow our lead if citizens, to whom they pander for power, provide the backbone for them. Otherwise, Democrats will not risk the alienation of the pro-authoritarianism corporate media.

Actually, Democrats alone did not orchestrate this "political theater." For a key section of testimony the questioner was Republican Senator Arlen Specter and the entire testimony was being provided by James Comey, a conservative Republican. Since the article's intent was to provide the omissions of other news stories, perhaps the Democrats being targeted most are in the media. Corporate media, for whatever purposes, loves to brand "mainstream media" as liberal; liberals are Democrats; ergo, Democrats are attempting to manipulate public opinion through their stranglehold on mainstream media. Presumably, even though supply and demand both favors conservatism (see Essay 12), conservative corporate media bosses do not have the business acumen to make this ideological market work for them, and are helpless to stop the onslaught of liberal/Democrat journalists.

The reference to "political theater" implies that these Democrats/thespians orchestrated the hearing with the sole objective to "strip" "surveillance authority" in "wartime." Once again, many Democrats probably would have loved to actually impeach the President Bush II, but they did not have the guts to attempt that unless the smoking gun was the size of a mushroom cloud. No doubt the Democratic senators wanted to provide some opposition and embarrassment to the President through these hearings. That is, after all, the homeostatic role of an opposition party in the interest of preserving democracy. If one party with some power is not going to provide opposition to another party with greater power, the party system has no contribution to make to a wise democracy. Such nuances are lost on a newspaper that either must be a loyal soldier of the pro-authoritarianism corporate media, or an inept rag lacking both the resources and the integrity to be independent of corporate media.

Corporate news media provides the real political theater. I neither have the will, nor you the attention span, to enumerate all the false innuendos throughout the article, though we will come back to them periodically. We will refrain, charitably, from accusing the newspaper of providing false news, since the article was chiefly an "opinion of opinions" piece, reacting to previous news stories. We have yet to determine what kind of newspaper produced the article. We can conclude, however, that the newspaper was providing cover for a political waggle dance.

Political Waggle Dances

The waggle dance was discovered and interpreted by ethologists studying bees. Honey bees use a waggle dance to communicate to the hive where pollen can be found. Upon returning to the hive a honey bee will walk a vertical path that resembles a figure eight. During the portion of the dance that gets repeated the bee waggles at an angle to the sun that reveals the direction of the pollen. The number of waggle dances reveals the distance. Since the waggle is done at a vertical angle from the sun, the bees do not communicate the actual direction of the pollen, but all the bees in the hive know how to break the code.

Politicians communicate with a waggle dance of their own. The content of their messages correspond to the orientation of a waggle dance, while the intensity of their messages correspond to the numbers of waggles that bees make. Just as the angle honey bees waggle represents a code, politicians waggle a public interest angle really intended to achieve a goal of self-interest. The important difference with the waggle dance of politicians is they do not intend for citizens to break the code that translates the public interest angle they profess to the self-interest they want to achieve.

The Constitution provided for limited term lengths, precisely because the founding fathers did not want politicians to make careers out of governance. When Congress passed the Twenty Second Amendment to the Constitution in 1947 they reinforced this wisdom by limiting the number of terms for the President. They did not, however, see fit to apply such wisdom to themselves. The reason why is simple. Rather than viewing public office as a temporary public service, many politicians seek public office as their permanent career. When public office becomes their career, their livelihood that they are motivated to maintain, politicians have little choice but to put their self-interest above the public interest.

Our career politicians use some types of waggle dances frequently, such as the war waggle. The current war in Iraq, as with most foreign wars, had been good for our economy in important ways. Indicators that truly reflect middle class interests, such as the ratio of housing costs to median family income, have been going south for some time, but prior to the Iraq invasion even some of the wealth indicators that corporate media broadcasts were hurting as well. Invading Iraq postponed our economic stress, just as the Korean and Vietnam Wars helped boost our economies throughout the fifties and sixties, and just as World War II helped to deliver us out of the Great Depression. Unemployment indicators typically improve with foreign war, since demand for labor at home increases with many young adults abroad. When war takes place in foreign lands you do not have to suffer the economic destruction of war, but you receive the economic stimulation.

This would seem to suggest war as being in the public interest, with the boost to the economy serving politicians and citizens alike. There remains the problem of deaths in battle, and lives destroyed for those who cannot recuperate from going through hell. These problems disproportionately affect the middle and lower classes whose sons and daughters fight in war, rather than the power and wealth elites who most influence policy. This is not to suggest that politicians start a war for the sake of the economy, just that if foreign wars hurt our pocket books, in addition to all the other costs that start to accrue, politicians would have greater incentive for ending wars sooner when they bog down. Should a middle class citizen be directly asked whether he/she prefers a stronger economy or fewer lives destroyed by war, the choice would be to terminate the war. However, the waggle dance of war makes sure that the choice is never framed in that manner, relying instead on more obscure codes, such as security or spread of democracy.

Another waggle dance politicians use frequently advocates diverting the use of capital for capital gains, rather than for capital improvements. Capital improvements benefit the entire workforce, enhancing the production of goods and services in proportion to the merits of production. Redistributed capital gains disproportionately benefit the wealthy, including our legislators in the House and Senate. For example, members of Congress invested between $386 and $1,165 million in just the "Financial, Insurance, & Real Estate" sector in 2007.[1] You cannot be more invested in capital serving capital instead of economic productivity than with that particular sector, which dwarfs all other sectors of the economy in terms of investments from elected officials. It's easy to pick on politicians investing in the financial sector now, given the recent collapse of the economy. In reality, the continuous trickle down waggle done by politicians over the past thirty years has enabled a long term shift in fiscal polity to protect their capital gains at the expense of capital improvements or wage income.

Let us explore some of the nuances of these political waggle dances in greater depth, in order to break the code. Similar to our interpretations of Powell Cabal economics there are two categories of waggle dances. The black box waggle obscures invalid information and the black is white waggle distorts unreliable information.

Black Box Waggles

The black box waggle seeks the same objective of hiding the source of invalid information as the black box economics we discussed in Essay 8. Economists like to work with assumptions and indicators. Some, such as the economists who serve the Powell Cabal, stuff a whole bunch of assumptions and indicators into a black box, metaphorically speaking. There the ingredients are stirred and shaken in ways only transparent to the manipulator of the data. One of the reasons for this behavior is need-based, since the inflationary wealth that these economists ultimately seek to justify requires complicated assumptions. The other reason is that out of the "black box" come results that are hard for the middle class to question, since we do not fully understand the process of how those results are derived.

The closest waggle dance correlation to black box economics can be found in Congress, where legislative bills have reached staggering lengths and levels of complexity. Sometimes the lengths of bills are designed to embed nuggets of self-interest, known as pork or earmarks, in legislation for the public interest. Sometimes the length and complexity of bills stems from a desire to obfuscate the entire legislation. A prime example of this is the *Uniting and Strengthening*

---

1 From the Politicians & Elections/Personal Finance Disclosure/Sectors section of opensecrets.org.

America by Providing Appropriate Tools Required to Intercept and Obstruct Terrorism Act of 2001 (Public Law 107-56), otherwise known by the acronym USA PATRIOT Act. The Act was over 300 pages and rushed through Congress before the full text could be read. Most middle class folk do not sign things before reading them, but our elected officials waggled to us that signing this complex bill, virtually sight unseen even by them, was urgent for our security at the time.

The black box waggle can use secrecy as well as complexity, a popular tool when security is being used as the public interest angle. Deciphering how much the self-interest of the waggle dancers departs from this proposed public interest angle depends on the type of information being hidden.

Information falls into the general categories of Who, When, Where, How, How Much, What, Which and Why. The collective wisdom of a democracy does not depend on knowing all the details of all these categories of information. We derive wisdom from our experiences, and many of the details of governance have no relationship to our experiences. For example, CIA documents from the seventies recently were declassified revealing, among other things, plans to assassinate Fidel Castro. With the safety of hindsight going for us we can evaluate that information for what we did not need to know at the time, and what we should have been told as a functioning democracy.

Citizens never needed to know details like Who might kill Castro, When or Where the assassination would take place or even How the assassination would occur. Very few of us, even considering the wide range of our decentralized experiences, have the knowledge to evaluate which assassin in our government's employment might do the best job of knocking off a dictator. We are not likely to consider May 13 as a better alternative to February 5. Most of us would not care if it was done in the Conservatory with a Candlestick, or in the Kitchen with a Knife … if we supported the objective of assassinating dictators we do not agree with. What does matter to citizens, with our great range of decentralized experiences to draw from, are the details relating to What, Which and Why. Citizens are capable of deciding whether our general foreign policy should include assassinating leaders we do not agree with.

Some citizens might support assassinating leaders we do not like. Most citizens probably do not, which is precisely why the CIA has refrained from overtly doing so despite their inclination for the sport. The news that the CIA planned to assassinate Castro was leaked decades ago, and received widespread incredulity back then. Our collective wisdom draws from multiple experiences the meaning of "an eye for an eye," and collectively we do not wish to initiate that type of eye-gouging. Hiding the details of What, Which and Why for the assassination of Castro meant the self-interested angle of the waggle dancers departed greatly from the public interest.

We are not going to get rid of classified information entirely in our government, nor should we. Classified information, and unclassified information that has been redacted, may cover up details that have no relationship to the collective wisdom of our experiences but provides for the success of a political endeavor. For example, citizens have no need to know the identity of covert CIA agents, such as Valerie Plame. For some strange reason this was the one bit of previously classified information that Vice President Dick Cheney's office wanted the public to know. This information does not help us exercise our political liberty one iota. On the other hand, the leak of this information restricted Plame's liberty severely, while compromising future missions for which she might have been the CIA's best choice.

The Plame leak stands out dramatically because, apart from this striking exception, Cheney proved to be the champion black box waggle dancer for the Bush II administration; the head drone, if you will. The secret energy meetings held by Cheney provide another good example of how the categories of information being hidden reflect the self-interest of the waggle dancers rather than the public interest. Let us assume, just hypothetically of course, that one of the topics at those secret meetings was securing Iraqi oil by invading the country. This topic involves many details that might be pertinent to exercising our political wisdom and seeking the collective wisdom of a democracy. Still, we can concede that some details are more important than others.

Protecting Who said what at those meetings, a concern the Supreme Court found persuasive in upholding their secrecy, hardly impacts our liberty. Whether someone from Enron or Halliburton advocated building numerous permanent military bases in Iraq does not matter so much as being aware of the possible mission. Names could have been stricken from the record to protect high-powered executives that are too timid or modest to be credited for what they think is best for the country. We did not need to know details of When and Where acts of aggression might occur so much as the possibility for our sons and daughters to be used for those acts. If only details such as Who, When and Where were hidden, their waggle dance represented just a slight departure between the self-interests of energy executives at the meetings and the public interest. Hiding from us the additional details of What and Why discussed at those secret meetings meant the difference between the public interest angle and their actual self-interests were significant.

The public should have been provided a thorough listing of all the general topics covered and why they were being discussed at those energy meetings. Knowing the omitted topics for discussion was of equally great concern to the collective wisdom of our democracy. We all have a stake in whether renewable energy sources get much attention from the Cheney waggle dancers, one topic that may have escaped the attention of the particular energy executives invited to these particular meetings. For that matter, we would want to know if securing Iraqi oil was not discussed at those meetings. After all, if this was never a consideration for our invasion, if our top energy executives and elected officials embedded in the energy industry never considered the importance of Iraqi oil in their energy discussions, that would be a danger sign that we have a bunch of incompetent boobs steering the ship. Dilbert's pointy-haired manager comes to mind for the managers of a country invading an oil-rich nation without oil being considered.

Advanced Black Box Waggles

Invoking executive privilege is an advanced level of the black box waggle dance. Executive privilege allegedly protects the liberty of the president to conduct business in secret, which in turn promotes the liberty of people advising the president through hiding their identity and advice. Bruce Fein, a lawyer with 38 years of experience working with administrations, mostly Republican, had this to say about the validity of this reason for executive privilege.

> "I have never heard any high or low executive-branch official so much as insinuate that presidential advice had been or might be skewed or withheld if confidentiality were not guaranteed. The gravity of advising the president universally overcomes anxieties over possible embarrassment through subsequent publicity."[2]

The wise justices on the Supreme Court apparently were not aware of this as they upheld Vice President Dick Cheney's right to meet with Halliburton and oil executives in secret. Cheney and his staff waggle at the most advanced levels. They not only seek to classify documents, they classify what they classify.

> "Across the board, the vice president's office goes to unusual lengths to avoid transparency. Cheney declines to disclose the names or even the size of his staff, generally releases no public calendar and ordered the Secret Service to destroy his visitor logs. His general counsel has asserted that 'the vice presidency is a unique office that is neither a part of the executive branch nor a part of the legislative branch,' and is therefore exempt from rules governing either. Cheney is refusing to observe an executive order on the handling

---

2 From "Executive Nonsense," an online article in Slate (7/11/07).

of national security secrets, and he proposed to abolish a federal office that insisted on auditing his compliance."[3]

The federal office the Cheney dancers wished to abolish was the National Archives, tasked with arguably the most important function for future governments to gain wisdom from our current experiences. Though President Bush II could not provide this level of assistance to the waggle dancers, he did invoke the executive privilege not to enforce executive orders. Invoking executive privilege often assists the advanced level of waggle dancers who seek to remove oversight and accountability. The alleged war on terror has provided some fine opportunities for this invocation. The Bush II administration, the original authors of the USA PATRIOT Act, did not appreciate the alterations made for reauthorization, some of which provided for greater oversight when the government restricts civil liberties. President Bush II signed the Act, which allowed him to continue restricting liberties in the way his administration proscribed, but included a signing statement also declaring that he was not obligated to inform Congress about how expanded police powers of the State were being used.

Black Is White Waggles

This leads us back to the newspaper article we have been examining. The controversy over wiretapping without FISA approval stemmed from the President's signing statement. Another paragraph in the article does the Cheney waggle dancers proud:

> "So where's the smoking gun here? When the program was reauthorized by the President alone, Mr. Comey and others planned to resign in protest. So, Mr. Specter asked, does that mean the program went forward illegally? Again, negative: "The Justice Department's certification . . . was not [required] as far as I know." That's because, as even Mr. Comey conceded, many judges and scholars believe a President has the Constitutional authority to approve such wiretaps, especially in wartime."

This paragraph employs the artistic use of epsilons to omit some of Comey's

3   From "A Different Understanding of the President" (June 24, 2007), written by Barton Gellman and Jo Becker for The Washington Post.

testimony, and parentheses to insert an important waggle word of the article's choosing. These both are fine black box waggle techniques, but this paragraph is most striking because of a different type of waggle. The paragraph communicates that Comey did not personally question the legality of the President's action, when in fact he did, as a less edited version of his testimony reveals.

> "In the early part of 2004, the Department of Justice was engaged -- the Office of Legal Counsel, under my supervision -- in a reevaluation both factually and legally of a particular classified program. And it was a program that was renewed on a regular basis, and required signature by the attorney general certifying to its legality. And the -- and I remember the precise date. The program had to be renewed by March the 11th, which was a Thursday, of 2004. And we were engaged in a very intensive reevaluation of the matter. And a week before that March 11th deadline, I had a private meeting with the attorney general for an hour, just the two of us, and I laid out for him what we had learned and what our analysis was in this particular matter. And at the end of that hour-long private session, he and I agreed on a course of action. And within hours he was stricken and taken very, very ill... (Question from Senator Chuck Schumer)
> We had concerns as to our ability to certify its legality, which was our obligation for the program to be renewed."4

But there is a "half-truth" to the newspaper article's claim that Mr. Comey thought that the "Justice Department's certification ... was not (required)." Here is perhaps the most pertinent part of Comey's testimony, sans epsilons or parentheses.

> "Well, I suppose there's an argument -- as I said, I'm not a presidential scholar -- that because the head of the executive branch determined that it was appropriate to do, that that meant for

---

4 Quotes by James Comey were taken from the transcript of the May 15, 2007 U. S. Senate Judiciary Committee Hearing on the U. S. Attorneys Firings.

purposes of those in the executive branch it was legal. *I disagreed with that conclusion* (italics mine). Our legal analysis was that we couldn't find an adequate legal basis for aspects of this matter. And for that reason, I couldn't certify it to its legality."

Perhaps the author of the newspaper article had trouble deciphering Comey's words on this matter. Let us supply that service. Comey, a conservative Republican, did not believe that authorization of the wiretapping program without the Department of Justice's consent was legal. However, he was uncertain as to whether the President can decide legally to be above the law. Certainly, there is just cause to think that the current administration may indeed feel this way and, as long as no one attempts to reprimand them, that makes them correct in their interpretation. That does not mean that either Mr. Comey or the middle class has to agree with such an interpretation. Certainly no Republicans agreed with such an interpretation seventy years ago.

The article chastises Democrats for challenging the legality of wiretapping, contrary to the public interest. The actual angle of self-interest the article wishes to promote—if not intentionally, then as an unwitting stooge for authoritarian politicians or corporate media—is to preserve the administration's wish to wiretap without accountability. The article waggles the public interest angle that Democrats undermine democracy. The actual self-interest angle is to prevent Democrats from serving their democratic function as an opposition party. The entire article, therefore, uses the dance steps of a black is white waggle. Let us now explore this dance step in further depth.

Bravado Waggles

In middle class neighborhoods we regard the people with a lot of bravado with skepticism. The collective wisdom of many people's experiences verifies the old cliché that action speaks louder than words. We at times suspend this wisdom when our authorities display bravado. Bravado is a black is white waggle to convince us of actions benefiting the public interest, when in reality actions of self-interest are having the opposite effect. The more pronounced the bravado waggle, the more strenuously politicians are compensating for actions harming the public interest. The choreographer for the Bush II administration's bravado waggle is alleged to be Karl Rove.

Karl Rove, the political advisor for President Bush II, has been characterized by some to be a genius and by others as the devil incarnate. Events like the false allegations about John McCain's adopted child in the 2000 South Carolina primary and the Swift Boat Veterans for "Truth" attack on John Kerry in the 2004 election provide fuel for both positions. Admirers and detractors both credit Rove for orchestrating these political maneuvers while at the same time keeping his role in these slime crimes hidden. His comments before the 2004 election that the war in Iraq would work to the President's advantage added to this mystique of an aloof "Shogun" with omniscient control and limited scruples.

This mystique of Karl Rove may be exaggerated. First, since his maneuverings are kept hidden, who is to know what they really are? Perhaps Rove himself is just the fall guy, a rather witless middle man being manipulated by Cheney or others to absorb the allegations of political mischief. Second, Rove's alleged "genius" has resulted in one of the most unpopular presidents in history and the ousting of his party's control of Congress. That does not look good on a resumè, though in our current political climate Rove probably can find steady employment.

Rove allegedly is adept at turning the opposition's strengths into weaknesses. Assuming Rove deserves such praise this brand of deception may be a deception in turn, a metadeception. Rather than turning the opposition's strengths into weaknesses, Rove's particular brand of genius may be choreographing bravado to turn this administration's weaknesses into strengths. Take, for example, fighting terrorism.

First, let us consider the aspect of efficiency. President Bush II claimed, when all other reasons for invading Iraq started to sour, that we "fight the terrorists over there so we don't have to fight them here."[5] Granted, that is a neat little sound bite, but let us unpack what that really means. Fighting terrorists elsewhere would be an efficient choice if we lose fewer citizens in the process. Unfortunately, we have lost more soldiers than the casualties from the 9/11 attacks, with huge collateral damage thrown in as well. We know that in this administration's universe a soldier's life is more expendable than citizens urged to be cowards; but that should not be the attitude of middle and lower class families whose sons and daughters have been made disproportionately expendable. In addition to the costs of lives "over there" we have restricted civil liberties at home, not an efficient tool for discouraging people who allegedly want to see our liberties restricted. Regardless of how effective the public perceives the fight to be, we have chosen extremely inefficient means to be effective.

We might be forgiven somewhat for overlooking the inefficiency of our fight against terror. In a fit of panic we went for expediency rather than efficiency. More puzzling is the basis of anyone's perception that the fight has been effective, in the absence of any empirical evidence. One common metric presented to justify this administration's success with fighting terror—excuse me, I mean their "wartime" activities against terror—is the lack of a terror attack on our soil since

---

5 William Kristol actually coined this slogan first in the Weekly Standard (10/20/2004), a neoconservative magazine funded by Rupert Murdoch, for which Kristol is editor.

9/11. You would think this to be a strange metric to use, since they cannot possibly do better than their predecessor in this regard. Islamic fanatics attacked us the first year of the Clinton administration but then no more occurred for the rest of his presidency. There were attempts to be sure, such as the Y2K attempt intended for Los Angeles. Yet without the benefit of color-coded terror alerts, USA PATRIOT Acts or 9/11 fact finding commissions these attempts were thwarted. The Bush II administration simply cannot top that, unless they change the Constitution and allow him to run for a third term. The only factor that might weigh in the Bush II administration's favor in this matter would be that terrorists have greater motivation to attack us now than during the Clinton administration, thus our efforts at preventing these attacks must have increased.

During this administration's tenure the numbers of terror attacks, the frequency of terror attacks, the number of deaths from terror attacks, the recruitment of terrorists and the hatred of the United States all have escalated.[6] Yet the bravado increased as well, with good results. The bravado waggle dancers of the administration convinced us in 2004 to vote as if only Republicans were interested in fighting terror. They waggled their way into office with tough talk about the public interest for security at the same time their actions on behalf of their own self-interests made the country less secure. They even threw in a few orange terror alerts for good measure. The fact that this has been mere bravado has become evident to all but the most devout party loyalists.

Morality Waggles

An insidious form of the black is white waggle relates to morality. Considering that wise democracy is a moral end, yet we engage in the amoral power struggles of party politics, you could consider our whole political arena as a grand waggle dance of this form. We concern ourselves here with not just form, but also with intensity. When politicians overtly bring morality into amoral party politics we can decipher that, as with increased bravado, they are overcompensating for something.

The morality waggle could be as discernible as the bravado waggle, but we must first be able to let go of preconceived notions. Maybe you think this an easy task, and you already have concluded that politicians are not just amoral, but immoral. Please allow a test of your certainty. Do you think Supreme Court justices are moral agents? Or, if you are willing to doubt that a few of them are moral, do you at least believe that the ones who tout traditional values as a doctrine must be among the more moral agents in our governance?

Consider then, the following opinion by Antonin Scalia, current Supreme Court justice and advocate of originalism and traditional values.

---

6 As reported in all the Country Reports on Terrorism, which began in 2004, compiled by the U. S. State Department as mandated by Congress. Also refer to The Terrorist Threat to the U. S. Home-land, a National Intelligence Estimate prepared by the National Intelligence Council.

"Justice Scalia responded with a defense of Agent Bauer, arguing that law enforcement officials deserve latitude in times of great crisis. 'Jack Bauer saved Los Angeles . . . . He saved hundreds of thousands of lives,' Judge Scalia reportedly said. 'Are you going to convict Jack Bauer?' He then posed a series of questions to his fellow judges: 'Say that criminal law is against him? 'You have the right to a jury trial?' Is any jury going to convict Jack Bauer?'

'I don't think so,' Scalia reportedly answered himself. 'So the question is really whether we believe in these absolutes. And ought we believe in these absolutes?'"[7]

The short answer to the last question from a true originalist would be "Yes, we do believe in absolutes, since that is a condition of morality. That is also why we are not in favor of structuralism." Then again, perhaps Justice Scalia thinks torture is a traditional moral value. Thankfully, Scalia was not asking this of his fellow Supreme Court justices, who might have been all too ready to agree, but judges at an international conference in Ottawa, who tended not to agree. For those who are not acquainted with Jack Bauer, he is a fictitious character on a TV show that catches bad guys and extracts confessions in the nick of time to prevent disasters. Basing opinions on fictitious events may be as sound as how Scalia applies other doctrines for legal interpretation, but real life facts about the application of torture do not match the fiction portrayed in film.

Torture does not work at preventing a terrorist plot that will destroy Los Angeles in the next twenty-four hours.[8] People being tortured are either too eager to falsely say anything their captors want to hear, or they cannot be broken down in such a short time. Effective torture takes time, but then, so do other methods of extracting the truth. Brainwashing is at least as effective as torture. If time is required to extract necessary information regardless, then the choice of torture is neither moral nor necessary. Still, advocating torture may be backed by better logic, if not greater morality, than advocating money as an expression of free speech. Unfortunately, Scalia and other Supreme Court justices consider that precedent as one of our traditional moral values as well.

When religion becomes infused with politics, identifying the morality

---

7 This excerpt is now plastered over the web. I could not find an official transcript, but copied and pasted from here: http://blogs.wsj.com/law/2007/06/20/justice-scalia-hearts-jack-bauer/
8 A Question of Torture: CIA Interrogation, from the Cold War to the War on Terror (2006), by Alfred McCoy, reports on the ineffectiveness of torture. The One Percent Doctrine (2006), by Ron Suskind, provides evidence specifically related to our 9/11 response.

waggle as a charade becomes particularly difficult for many. A few years ago the Christian Coalition hired a new Director, Joel Hunter, who was a minister for a large evangelical Church in Florida. His term lasted only a few months before he resigned. He held the traditional convictions of southern evangelicals, but he also reflected their growing concern about environmental issues and poverty. The Christian Coalition deemed that these added concerns would brand their organization as too liberal and Hunter decided to step down.[9] Make no mistake, the Christian Coalition is embedded in politics, and morality is not the litmus test you might believe for a special interest group touting the label "Christian."

Accepting that religious politics in our system is as amoral or immoral as other special interests may be painful for many. With this anguish in mind we will cover the topic further in our part on culture. For the purpose at hand let us use this as a lesson that we must suspend all our preconceived notions for moral intent whenever we witness a career politician do a morality waggle.

Bait and Switch Waggles

Other forms of the black is white waggle by politicians are not discerned easily while the dance is in process, some additional context is needed. For example, the bait and switch waggle occurs when the authorities we instinctively trust are not the real authorities. Politicians sometimes substitute information based on their political self-interest for expert judgment made in the public interest. When politicians cause the Environmental Protection Agency (EPA)[10] or Food and Drug Administration (FDA)[11] to alter reports provided by technical experts, they are substituting political self-interest for scientific judgment made in the public interest.

Deciphering the bait and switch waggle these days requires vigilance on the part of citizens. The claim by trusted authorities of a relationship between Hussein and al-Qaeda provides a good example of this. As a citizen, you would need to uncover that much of this information came from neoconservatives such as Paul Wolfowicz and Douglas Feith, and you would need to know something about the neoconservative agenda. You would need to uncover that neoconservatives obtained much of their information from Ahmed Chalabi, an embezzler with designs for wealth and power in his homeland of Iraq. You would need to uncover that the CIA operatives in the field disagreed with this assessment. You would need to know that the CIA Director is a politically appointed position, with different objectives than CIA field operatives.

---

9 Reported on NPR's All Things Considered on November 28, 2006.
10 "White House Alters EPA Scientific Document on Climate Change" (3/23/07), by the Union of Concerned Scientists.
11 "FDA Scientists Pressured to Exclude, Alter Findings; Scientists Fear Retaliation for Voicing Safety Concerns" (7/20/06), by the Union of Concerned Scientists.

Some resources for identifying the bait and switch waggle are out there. We are, after all, in the information age. For example, a report was prepared that empirically documented the number of misleading statements made by the Bush II Administration.[12] An example of a misleading statement is Vice President Cheney's declaration, made on January 22, 2004, that: "there's overwhelming evidence that there was a connection between al-Qaeda and the Iraqi government." The report tallied 237 misleading statements over less than a two year period: 11 statements claiming that Iraq posed an urgent threat; 81 statements exaggerating Iraq's nuclear activities; 84 statements overstating Iraq's chemical and biological weapons capabilities; and 61 statements that misrepresented Iraq's ties to al-Qaeda.

Unfortunately, the middle class needs to dig up reports like these on their own. Corporate media is more interested in bottom-line entertainment than public service news reporting. Nor can we rely on opposition parties to fulfill their role for issues judged to be popular. Certain issues become popular through the use of echo chambers by corporate media, which tends to oblige authoritarian elites providing enormous amounts of money to corporate media as an expression of their "free speech." Being a good citizen should entail more dedication than we typically have been willing to provide, but recognizing the bait and switch waggle dances of politicians requires greater due diligence from citizens than we would expect.

Detecting Waggle Dances

Let us summarize what we have learned about political waggle dancing. The purpose of the dance is to communicate a public interest angle coded to disguise political self-interest. With black box waggles the keys to breaking this code are identifying what type of information is being cloaked in secrecy and the skill level of the waggle. Here is a typology of skill levels for black box waggles:

- Beginner: Releasing half-truths, redacting information.
- Intermediate: Classified information, secret meetings.
- Advanced: Invoking executive privilege, no oversight or accountability.
- Extreme: Totalitarianism.

In a totalitarian regime the "total" centralized control of information shuts off all diversity of opinion. Not even the Cheney waggle dancers achieved the highest level waggle of totalitarianism. Thankfully, the other levels leading up to this are easy enough to discern. Waggle dances for such things as war and

---

12 "Iraq on the Record: The Bush Administration's Public Statements on Iraq" (March 16, 2004), by the Committee on Government Reform, Minority Office.

protecting capital welfare at the expense of earned income are commonplace; the middle class just needs to decipher when these dances are done in the self-interests of power and wealth elites.

To ward off totalitarianism we need to decipher the black is white waggle dances as well. Not allowing normal biases to blind us should be sufficient for detecting the bravado and morality waggles. More problematic for the middle class are the bait and switch waggles. The average citizen does not know when valid and reliable expertise being employed for the public interest is being switched with allegedly empirical evidence supporting political agendas of self-interest.

The most crucial need in determining the validity and reliability of empirical evidence is establishing the relationship of that evidence to beliefs. With authoritarianism the beliefs of authoritarians are the starting point; research is chosen and results interpreted to confirm the meaning of those beliefs. With wisdom the decentralized experiences of the many are the starting point. The beliefs of a democracy are dictated by the aggregation of those experiences. News media could be the essential component in communicating decentralized experiences. Unfortunately, the fourth estate is being consolidated and subjected to the will of corporations, while opposition parties in turn bend to the will of the powerfully influential corporate media.

Speaking of which, let us return once more to the article we have been critiquing. We have yet to identify whether a second rate rag or corporate media newspaper could have been responsible for such lack in journalistic integrity or content. The second paragraph provides enough of a clue to answer this basic question.

> "Senate hearings can be boring, so we'll assume the press corps dozed through select parts. That would explain why no one reported on the discussion as Senator Arlen Specter questioned Mr. Comey on how the great covert operation actually went down. News stories have suggested a pattern of White House misdeeds to accomplish an ultimately illegal end. The transcript tells a different story."

The article calls to task the press corps as a whole dozing through an important part of the story and, as a result, getting the story wrong. Such an arrogant rebuke of peers no doubt comes from a corporate media newspaper. What makes this reprimand of other journalists delightful is the declaration that: "The transcript tells a different story." The article then used epsilons and parentheses to distort the opinion of James Comey. Then again, perhaps the author of this piece merely "dozed through the selected parts" he himself omitted.

Clearly, we cannot count on corporate mainstream media to be our window into anti-authoritarian, decentralized news reporting. We cannot count on them for valid and reliable news reporting. We must develop our own primer for detecting and deciphering the waggle dances of politicians.

Waggle Dance Primer

Corporate media, like the Powell Cabal, would feel angered or threatened if the self-help guide for the middle class presented here gains a significant audience. They run the risk of looking foolish if they get too worked up about the concerns of the middle class, since we have no designs on great power or wealth. Yet we can expect corporate media to ultimately respond to threats to their authoritarianism. We could expect the entertainment news media to counter with their favorite tool of persuasion, the echo chamber, where one anonymous pundit throws out invalid and unreliable innuendo and the rest of the corporate media establishment echoes this as fact. They may, somehow, craft a message aimed at our natural trust in authorities to persuade us that what is good for the power and wealth elites, such as media consolidation, is good for all. We should be ready if this happens. As a training exercise let us review some of the waggles that authorities and corporate media have done to thwart collective wisdom. I will state the issue, the appeal for the public interest that has been made, the political self-interest behind the waggle dance, and the type of waggle we would expect the politician to employ.

Issue: Attracting the "Best and the Brightest"
Public interest appeal: Public Service
Political self-interest: Authoritarianism
Waggle type: Black Is White, Bravado

Politicians display a bit of bravado in regards to the important work they do for the country. The decisions they make are important, of course, but they are still just decisions. When politicians make an argument about how much more elite professional athletes make, they hope we overlook the fact that Alex Rodriquez is not making $25 million a year for a uniquely superior ability to make decisions. When they make an argument about how much more CEOs make, they hope we overlook the fact that CEOs get paid money for decisions to make money. When they make an argument about pressure and deadlines, they hope we overlook the fact that bills like the USA PATRIOT Act simply get passed without having been read by a majority of the people making the decision. When they make an argument about lucrative compensation to attract the "best and the brightest" to a demanding job, they hope we never consider that an alternative approach is not to hold onto a demanding job for very long, precisely what the founding fathers intended. When they make an argument about the type of expertise needed to make good decisions, they hope we overlook the fact that public servants are automatically supplied with that expertise, in the form of true democracy.

Issue: Preemption of Liberty
Public interest appeal: National Security
Political self-interest: Political Security
Waggle type: Black Is White, Morality

When politicians (including Supreme Court justices) legitimize the use of preemption to curtail liberties, they often make claims based on morality. They claim a moral obligation to protect such important matters as lives or democracy before they are threatened, even though the vain, cynical or cowardly emotional states that induce preemption are immoral. Authorities must be cynical to subvert the normal rules of law to protect the rule of law. Authorities must be vain to think they have the moral authority to subvert these rules. Authorities must be cowardly to take us down such an urgent path. We have a famous cliché in my field of expertise: "Garbage in, garbage out." When immorality is employed for morality's sake, out comes the garbage of trampled liberties for the sake of providing political job security for our authoritarians.

Issue: Echo Chambers
Public interest appeal: Expanding News Coverage
Political self-interest: Control of Opinions
Waggle type: Black Is White, Bait and Switch

When we read an entertaining nonfiction book, we remember the main message and gloss over the footnotes. News reporting has become like the footnotes of a book, while the main messages promoted by news media are driven by echo chambers. You would think that with the advent of twenty-four hour news we would have received more news. After all, they call those talking heads on our television sets "newscasters" and "news anchors." What we have instead are infinitely more opinions that echo each other across media types and media markets. The amount of actual news being reported could still fit in the limited time slots that were offered in the sixties and seventies, but such news would have less repetition, less entertainment value and much less opinions. Even newspapers have gotten into this act. Corresponding to the advent of twenty-four hour news stations was *USA Today* and the proliferation of opinion polls. We have been baited with the advertising of expanded news that is "fair and balanced" and where "you decide," and switched to the echoing of opinions endorsed by corporate media.

Issue: Media Consolidation
Public interest appeal: Economic Freedom

Political self-interest: Corporate Coercion of Media Markets
Waggle type: Black Box, Beginner's Level
There are a variety of half-truths corporate media employs in defense of consolidation. They emphasize how many channels we get now for a modest monthly fee, while omitting that we have limited choice for what goes in that packet, and if we could pay only for the channels we really want, most of us would pay less. They emphasize the proliferation of the Internet and other expanding new sources, while omitting that cross-media consolidation is happening in those arenas as well. They emphasize that their news products have been enhanced with terrific graphics, while omitting that the base of investigative reporters providing real news for those fancy graphics is shrinking. They emphasize that allowing corporations to have their way is merely allowing markets to work, while omitting that they are not talking about free markets.

Issue: Major Parties
Public interest appeal: Democracy
Political self-interest: Power
Waggle type: Black Box, Intermediate Level
Our major parties are hiding something. We cannot precisely say what they are hiding, but we know the purpose. Most middle class people join a party because of principles. Kept hidden from us are the details of how wealth and special interests partner with parties for the sake of consolidating power at the expense of principles. Having only two major parties provides an effective way for corporations and powerful interests to concentrate their influence. The only thing better would be one major party, but that would smack of totalitarianism and, besides, two parties enables opposing interests to both consolidate power and wealth. The two major parties make an elaborate show of how they represent core principles, including well-publicized forums and campaign speeches. What they keep hidden are the closed, back room meetings with leading industry sectors and special interests. Meanwhile, we are left scratching our heads as to why so much consolidation with media and financial institutions happened under the Clinton administration, and why such large deficits and consolidation of executive power occurred under the Bush II administration.

Issue: Money as Free Speech
Public interest appeal: Liberty
Political self-interest: Profits, Influence
Waggle type: Black Box, Advanced Level
Money as free speech strips democratic accountability from information. To merely provide your opinion on something costs nothing and the receiver of the opinion easily can evaluate both the content and context of the opinion. Providing

that same opinion via media requires a moderate amount of money. This inhibits access by individuals but provides an advantage for interest groups and businesses that do not want their information too closely evaluated. Hyping opinions with expensive film footage and other tricks requires a great deal of money. This inhibits access by smaller interest groups and businesses but provides the means for the most influential interest groups and corporations to completely obscure the validity and reliability of the information. The truth can be avoided just as effectively as by invoking executive privilege. Since the Supreme Court provides cover for this scam, authoritarian elites have been encouraged to push the envelope of falsehoods and secrecy through the cover of corporate media. We are told this is a protected liberty, but our natural right to free thought depends on the removal of falsehoods and secrecy.

Waggle Intensity

The number of times that bees do a waggle dance indicates the distance from pollen. In similar fashion the number of political waggles indicates distance between self-interest and public interest. Here is an example of three different waggles in a concise package.

> "Failure in Iraq at this juncture would be a calamity that would haunt our nation, impair our credibility, and endanger Americans for decades to come."

This was testimony provided by Robert Gates at his Congressional hearing to replace Donald Rumsfeld as the new Secretary of Defense. Let us unpack the three different waggles in that one sentence. Failure or success in Iraq is placed squarely on the United States. Such an assumption needs to be placed in some context. Would you ever want failure or success in the United States to be the responsibility of a country from Asia? Would you ever want failure or success with your favorite baseball team to be the responsibility of your favorite football team? Would you ever want failure or success with your own life to be the responsibility of a person from another town? Depriving others of self-determination is a cynical betrayal of the lip service we pay to merit or democracy, and a double standard we would fight with great ferocity should any nation attempt to do this to us.

People and countries alike often request help and support in their endeavors, but the value of such assistance generally increases with the intimacy of the source. Our support may be desperately needed in Iraq, since we broke the country, but no principles of psychology, sociology or even rational statesmanship would point to us as the ones that should possess the lead role in dealing with that particular culture. Of course, if we are mainly there for our own interests, then that elevates the status of the second waggle in the statement by Gates.

Failing in Iraq indeed would impair our credibility, but this begs the question of credibility for what. We shocked and awed enough of the world to retain our credibility for being the most powerful nation on earth. Our credibility for being able to forcefully secure another country's oil remains in tact. Our credibility for acting unilaterally is unquestioned. Our credibility for succeeding unilaterally, however, already has been damaged and will be damaged further if we fail. Only vanity prompts one to think the credibility to succeed while taking the lead in Iraq is crucial.

A plethora of evidence, logic and even authoritative opinion maintains that our continued presence in Iraq has increased terrorist activities and recruitment. Yet we are to believe that removing this stimulus for terrorism will endanger us for decades. We are to believe that the mightiest nation on earth cannot withstand the will of a nationless entity unless we provide some other country as fodder for their terrorist activities.

There no doubt are people that still blindly trust such rationales and the politicians that waggle them. Such people have become the cowards that the administration wants us to be. This reveals that the ultimate price of political waggle dances is not political but cultural. We become a culture where apprehension, vanity and cynicism infiltrate the lives of citizens for the sake of political self-interest.

Uncivil Waggles

The corporate media article we critiqued contained hyperboles, such as the rare occurrences of Democrats behaving like an opposition party as "dangerous policy." Corporate media points to the hostile rhetoric of colonial times to justify their current incivility. We in the middle class are then to believe that our civilization must represent the natural and best order of things. But the intensely venomous exchange between some of our founding fathers resulted in political parties, a consequence that even the party founders would condemn as contrary to the public interest. Perhaps they could not help themselves, and perhaps we should not be too surprised about the intense incivilities of our current corporate media and politicians. This incivility suggests we need to look outside politics for ultimate causes and solutions for our political dilemma.

We started these essays by uncovering how the economic pursuit of happiness has been lacking for the middle class. We have biased markets driven by greed rather than free markets driven by merit. To the extent that this represents a choice of ours, we needed to peel back a layer and uncover the politics behind our liberty. We have discovered a politics driven by authoritarianism, rather than the pursuit of wisdom that should be the goal of a democracy. The founding fathers who least wanted a politics of power waged by parties nevertheless behaved in a manner that led to their creation. We now need to peel back one more layer to uncover important details about the culture that guides what we believe and how we behave, a culture that commits us to a two party system of authoritarianism in spite of original founders' intent.

The article we have examined throughout this essay was titled "Wiretap Tales: What you didn't read about Jim Comey's senate testimony" (May 17, 2007). As we have discovered, there was a good reason why the waggles of this article were not widely echoed even by other corporate media; other newspapers had more journalistic integrity. We may learn something of importance when we turn to cultural explanations and solutions, but any such lesson will likely be lost on this corporate newspaper devoted to authoritarianism.

The article came from *The Wall Street Journal*, before Rupert Murdoch acquired ownership. Perhaps the neoconservative news entertainment mogul that brought us the News Corporation and *Fox News* can now improve this newspaper's journalistic standards.

PART THREE

CULTURAL QUALITY OF LIFE

ESSAY 17 – IDOLATRY OR HARMONY

Bloom County (1987), Berke Breathed (c) Berkeley Breathed, dist. by The Washington Post.
Reprinted with Permission.

Overview

- Being civilized requires social cohesion and responsibility.
- The quality of life depends on our natural rights.
- The quality of life does not depend on technology.
- The quality of life has not been enhanced by Enlightenment beliefs.
- The quality of life is harmed by idolatry of beliefs.
- A sense of belonging surpasses shared beliefs for harmony between neighbors.
- Interest groups idolize shared beliefs across different neighborhoods.
- Communities use shared neighborhood experiences to harmonize diverse beliefs.
- Pluralism and federation give us the potential to become an advanced civilization, but they also make harmony difficult to achieve.
- Merit, wisdom and harmony complement each other in an advanced civilization.
- War is rooted in some form of dogmatic idolatry; peace is rooted in harmony.

Being Civilized

As a college freshman I lived in a complex of dormitory housing called the Jungle. The Jungle was named for the wild behavior that occurs in many young adults experiencing freedom for the first time. I landed in a dormitory chosen that same year to be one of the first on the entire campus to become coed. Rather than begin such an experiment with one of their new or expensive dorms, the university chose instead to experiment with modifying behavior. The strategy worked like a charm. I had some of my most civilized experiences in the Jungle.

Throughout my stay at Litchfield Hall there was a 60% return rate each year. By the time I was a junior I was living in a dormitory well represented by every class and major field of study. That year four of us put two sets of bunk beds into Room 317, freeing up Room 315 for our social gatherings. Room 315 was referred to as the "Hot Dog" room, named for the mural painted on the wall by Blake, my roommate from the previous year. Blake had moved out, leaving to Buck, Rob, Keith and I the opportunity to set up our new living arrangements.

The "Hot Dog" room became a commons for the third floor of guys and, to some extent, the fourth floor of gals. We left the door unlocked. Indeed, we would absent-mindedly leave the door wide open, even on a weekend when the four of us were not around. People gathered, listened to music, played games and partied throughout the year. People made arrangements to use the phone in the room (back when there were no cell phones), and honored their agreements for reimbursement without us having to nag anyone. No vandalism or accidental damage occurred and out of our entire possessions only one record album was missing at the end of the year. The one drawback was that our bedroom, with four young males living in close quarters, tended to smell like a locker room.

Our floor took advantage of the group rates offered for plays, concerts, sporting events and other activities throughout campus. We would leave as a group for the evening's activity and come back as a group afterwards to party. We played pranks on the first floor guys and they played pranks on us. We broke things, but this only served to prove our responsibility. If we broke a window playing soccer in the hallway we repaired it on our own, before we could be "written up" by the RA. In this and other ways we formed a social group distinguished by cohesion and responsibility.

Litchfield Hall was really "life as usual" for me, having come from the village center of a rural town. Only after I became a Hall Director at another college could I appreciate just how unique was my dormitory living situation in Litchfield Hall. Only then did I experience students who would accidentally damage or intentionally vandalize the property of others and subsequently do or say anything to avoid responsibility. I learned that there were people who would urinate in stairwells and defecate in showers. One telling consequence of this jungle behavior was the lack of cohesiveness among residents and the eagerness everyone had to move out into apartments. Many people like to recount their tales about how they "partied hardy" in places like "The Jungle," but no one wants to remain in those places for long. This was the opposite of being civilized.

We think of jungles as places governed only by the law of survival, places wild and brutish where anything goes as long as one can keep going. Civilizations represent advancement over this brutish state. We tend to think that the farther removed civilizations are over time from a natural wilderness state the more advanced and the higher the quality of life must be. The continual advancement of science and technology reinforces this view. But history reveals so many exceptions to the natural advancement of civilizations over time as to negate the rule. Some modern civilizations struggle more with social cohesion and responsibility than did early cultures.

Both the advancement of civilization and the quality of life depends more on social cohesion and responsibility than on science and technology. This essay explores these alternative criteria for being civilized further. In so doing the foundation will be provided for the remaining essays on culture and, in a sense, for the previous essays on economics and politics as well.

The Quality of Life

A classmate of mine once declared, during a discussion in a graduate level course, that we lived in the best of times. When pressed for why she felt that to be true, she referred only to our high standard of living as the cause. Let us refer to this as the "Best of Times" paradigm.

The "Best of Times" paradigm implies that each successive day must be better than the last, since the foundation for the "Best of Times," the standard of living, tends to steadily increase over time. A literal interpretation of this paradigm would suggest that successive generations of upwardly mobile people must have increasingly higher qualities of life. The "Best of Times" paradigm fails to account for why happiness has not increased for the general population over the past thirty years, though the standard of living has more than doubled (Essay 1). We must conclude that all the people from earlier cultures, no matter how content some of them may have been, were miserable compared to us.

Material wealth is a relative concept. Obviously no wealthy senator from ancient Rome thought that an automobile was important for his quality of life, but most middle class Americans would insist that an automobile was crucial. The arbitrary nature of material "necessities" reveals these to be spurious rather than causal variables for quality of life. There must be causal factors for the quality of life that transcend the material differences of cultures, factors shaped by inherent aspects of human nature.

Essay 15 detailed our natural rights: the independence of labor, independence of thought and independence of belonging. We evolved over hundreds of thousands of years to possess these natural rights. A few thousand years of culture may be able to tinker with our basic nature, but not enough to supplant our natural rights for what is essential to being human. We could have the wealth of pharaohs, but if civilization suppresses how we choose to labor, what we choose to think and to whom we choose to belong we have lost our humanity in the process.

In the essays on politics the independence of thought was touted as the most important for maintaining liberty in a culture. The independence of belonging is most important for the very shaping of cultures. To belong to others we must share our life experiences with them in social groups. In this social process we form cultural systems of beliefs and behaviors.

Whereas belonging to others forms cultures, cultures in turn shape other senses of belonging. Many individuals, particularly those from early cultures, sense a belonging to something that transcends humans. In social groups we construct the meaning behind these individual experiences of belonging and develop religions. Individuals also form a sense of belonging to their own self, in the manner of being true to their conscience. Yet what the individual conscience demands depends largely on the social context shaped by culture.

Culture encompasses the entire system of beliefs and behaviors adopted by a social group. Our economic and political systems are shaped by the company we keep: the groups we form, the religion we practice (including materialism) and the conscience we follow. Through these economic and political systems will the independence of labor and thought either be enhanced or diminished. Thus at the root of how well all our natural rights flourish in culture is how our sense of belonging shapes social groups.

Let us now propose that the cultural quality of life depends on the flourishing of all our natural rights, as enabled by the social groups formed by our sense of belonging. Cultural beliefs and behaviors that allow people to freely enjoy their independent labors, thoughts and belongings provide a higher quality of life than a culture that deprives any or all of those natural rights. This empirical foundation for the quality of life enables us to explain material differences between cultures in how people perceive their quality of life. For example, whether an automobile or a chariot provides necessary transportation, the quality of life really stems from the independence of labor (or leisure) either the chariot or the automobile provides.

Proposing that belonging determines our quality of life refutes the "Best of Times" paradigm. There is no empirical evidence or inductive reasoning from real experience to suggest that our sense of belonging changes for the better as a function of the standard of living advancing over time. However, before I go further with this proposed criterion for our quality of life let us consider a different source of empirical evidence that, like the standard of living, relate to the advancement of time.

Technology and the Quality of Life

You may think there is a glaring omission in the claim that "beliefs and behaviors" determine culture and the quality of life. What about technology? First, technology results from the beliefs and behaviors of a culture, due to what counts as knowledge and how that knowledge develops technology. Second, technology does not inherently enhance or detract from the quality of life. A hammer might be used to build something or to hurt someone. Beliefs and behaviors determine not only what technology is developed but how that technology is used.

We might think the exception to this rule would be in the realm of medicine. We might naturally conclude that advances in medicine inherently advance our quality of life independently of our beliefs and behaviors. Yet advances in medicine and applying them to maintain a high quality life still depends on the beliefs and behaviors of culture.

The old saying: "an ounce of prevention is worth a pound of cure" has relevance here. For example, medicine that reduces cholesterol can be used as the ounce of prevention to prevent many afflictions. In this manner pills can prolong a high quality of life. In other situations, pills have become the pound of cure necessitated by the neglect of a healthy lifestyle. Since a healthy lifestyle has many benefits, some relating to a poor sense of belonging, relying on pills and medical technology as the cure for failing to live healthy prolongs a low quality of life.

I once was confronted by students in high school with the statement: "we rather live short but happy lives." At face value such a claim is hard to refute. Why live a long, miserable life? For people that believe in an afterlife this is a penetrating question. If there is "a better home awaitin'" and you can strengthen your belonging to God, why desire to prolong the time spent in a depressing world? Even for people who only believe in the here and now many, if not all, would claim that the quality of their life was decided by other factors than simply how long they are able to live.

Medicine and some other types of technology also can be developed to benefit the few at the expense of the many. As medicine advances, we naturally expect hospitals to be equipped with these advances. Only a few people benefit from the most recent advances in laboratory testing for obscure diseases, but the extra hospital costs are sufficient to reduce the availability of hospital care for many when insurance rates become unaffordable. Widening the disparity in something as essential as health care creates wedges in our sense of belonging to others and to a natural order that we believe should work against gross disparity.

Technology does not enable the enjoyment of a high quality of life; a high quality of life allows the enjoyment of technology, or any other cultural attributes or endeavors. Consequently, we can refute that our quality of life is a function of technology advancing over time. Perhaps, though, that both technology and a high quality of life derive from beliefs that advance over time, such as beliefs about democracy.

Democracy and the Quality of Life

Much of the social and intellectual fruits of the Enlightenment were developed from the seventeenth to the nineteenth centuries. The nineteenth century witnessed a relatively long lasting peace for the six large powers of Europe who made the greatest contributions to the Enlightenment (Britain, France, Russia, Italy, Germany and Austria-Hungary). By the twentieth century these western powers prematurely concluded we had reached the pinnacle of civilization. To use a phrase that neoconservatives tossed around more recently: we had reached the end of history. Some of this euphoria was due to a relative peace, by Europe's low standards, during the nineteenth century. Much also was due to the presumption by the western powers that we had become advanced democracies. We blazed the path of democratization for all other countries to follow.

War obviously diminishes the quality of life. The same western powers that were the standard bearers of the Enlightenment initiated World War I, which came as a big shock to western civilization. The shock was not due only to the barbarism of the war, or to the sheer numbers of deaths alone. Europe experienced many wars, while the Black Death killed a greater percentage of the population. The shock came from the blow dealt to a civilization who fancied they had attained enlightenment. People who assumed they were providing the gifts of democratic rule, free market capitalism and empirical utilitarianism also proved they could induce the lowest quality of life on the planet.

Theories have been proposed to explain how the most "enlightened" democracies of a particular era were involved in the most horrific war of the same era. Edward D. Mansfield and Jack Snyder, in their book *Electing to Fight: Why Emerging Democracies Go to War* (2005), used statistical evidence to distinguish between mature and incomplete democracies. Mature democracies never fight each other, but often engage in war with incomplete democracies. Spencer Weart, in his book *Never at War: Why Democracies Will Not Fight Each Other* (1998), uses case studies to distinguish between democracies and oligarchies. Democracies never fight each other, and oligarchies seldom fight each other (with only one historical example provided by Weart), but democracies and oligarchies fight each other quite often. In both these explanatory systems, Germany was the black sheep of the enlightened democracies by virtue of being incomplete and/or oligarchic.

In the view of Mansfield and Snyder, the proper ingredients and sequencing of the democratic process for all nations leads to peace between nations. The proper sequencing involves first establishing an "orderly administrative powerbase," and "development of the rule of law and institutions of public debate." Only those conditions could prevent authoritarian leaders with nationalist impulses from manipulating the liberty granted to the masses. In Weart's view, peace exists between democracies with similar beliefs of what constitutes the "ingroup." The ingroup is the ruling elite for oligarchies and the total population for Weart's true democracies. Consequently, the wars between oligarchies and democracies are wars targeting "outgroups." *Electing to Fight* was critical of how the United States went about democratization in Iraq, and *Never at War* prescribes diplomacy over military intervention. Yet both books could be used as an apologetic by neoconservatives for spreading democracy. We just need to get the hang of it.

Both theses appear to be taking an empirical approach to establishing their beliefs. After our fling with *laissez faire* economics we should be wary by now about statistics automatically serving the cause of empiricism. The Hellenistic city states and the Roman Republic pose problems for both theories. The city states would be considered mature democracies; some historians claim that Athenian democracy surpasses ours. Yet these democracies fought each other. Mansfield and Snyder do not have to deal with this contradictory reality because their statistical analysis dates back only to the French Revolution. Their main causal factor for war, nationalism, literally could not be applied to city states. When you are posing nationalism as a causal factor, to eliminate from your data everything but nations introduces a serious problem with reliability. Others are not so likely to constrain democracy as applying only to nations. *Electing to Fight* reflects a scholastic approach of allowing beliefs to dictate what counts as data.

Weart addresses the problem of the city states by making distinctions between which ancient democracies were really democracies and which were really oligarchies involving subsets of elites. He needs to make other fine distinctions with democracies involved in war throughout the ages, including cases that involved the United States. We may or may not agree with every one of Weart's distinctions for a true democracy, but the fact he needed to make them is telling. When one has to increasingly "fine tune" their operational definitions a question of validity enters the picture. Not just any democracies will avoid fighting each other, but ones that satisfy a list of conditions. By inference, these satisfactory democracies must also accurately perceive each other as having essentially the same conditions. If we follow Weart's fine tuning to their logical conclusions, then the one valid requirement for preventing war is for all countries in the world to have the same beliefs and behaviors. Hmm. I wonder whose beliefs and behaviors the whole world should adopt.

The views of Mansfield and Snyder or Weart, even if we accept their empirical shortcomings, do not adequately explain the political causes for the horrors of World War I. David Stevenson, a professor of international history at the London School of Economics, offers a more thorough perspective. In the first page of the introduction to his book about the Great War between the leading democracies of the age, titled *Cataclysm: The First World War as Political Tragedy* (2003), Stevenson wrote:

"Its victims died neither from an unseen virus nor

from mechanical failure and individual fallibility. They owed their fate to deliberate state policy, decided on by governments that repeatedly rejected alternatives to violence and commanded not merely acquiescence but also active support from millions of their peoples. Contemporaries on both sides at once hated the slaughter and yet felt unable to disengage from it, embroiled in a tragedy in the classical sense of a conflict between right and right.

When the war descended on a peaceful continent it seemed a reversion to the primitive, an atavistic upsurge of interethnic violence. Yet it engulfed the richest and most technologically advanced societies of the day, transformed by industrialization, democratization, and globalization since the most recent comparative upheaval, the campaigns against Napoleon a century previously."

Notice Stevenson's reference to governments (democracies) on both sides. From the viewpoint of hindsight, used scholastically to fit data to theories, Germany may have been incomplete or oligarchic as a democracy. Germany was nonetheless more "mature" at democracy than 90% of the world, and Germany was not alone in responsibility for the true horror that World War I became. Arguably the most horrible quality of life in history, at least until the most enlightened democracies went at it again in World War II, took the combined work of all the democracies considered to be the proud fruits of the Enlightenment.

Taking any or all of these views together about the democracies involved in World War I refutes the idea that a high quality of life occurs with the advancement of democratic beliefs over time. First, democratic beliefs have not automatically advanced with time. Second, even if they had, the wrong sequencing of democratization could lead to war. Third, the similarity of political beliefs between nations appears to prevent war better than the degree of democratization. Fourth, one slip, one black sheep in the enlightened order of democracies, can unleash inhumane beliefs and behaviors by all of the democracies. We come to these conclusions even by agreeing with Mansfield and Snyder or Weart, whose theses reflect scholasticism more than they do empiricism.

The apparent solution to this, certainly the solution that neoconservatives endorse, is to convert all nations to the type of democracy that is cut from the same American cloth. Never mind that there are people from nations unlike ours that might be enjoying a high quality of life. Never mind that people from mature democracies, at the whim of world events, can be plunged into a cultural abyss. In Stevenson's view, World War I was not a matter of misfiring on the proper ingredients and sequence for democracy, but countries "embroiled in a tragedy in the classical sense of a conflict between right and right." The real danger to peace and the quality of life, as Weart even implies, is not from differences in democratic beliefs between nations, but in the reaction to these differences, and in the idolatry of one's own "enlightened" beliefs.

Idolatry of Enlightened Beliefs

World War I failed to dissuade everyone that civilizations advance naturally with time. Though Europe provided the Enlightenment for the politics, economics and culture of western civilization, America was where those enlightened ideas blossomed. Americans could consider World War I to be more the result of European transgressions or "immaturities" than inherent flaws in the enlightened beliefs of the west. But throughout the twentieth century events closer to home would contribute further empirical evidence that the fruits of the Enlightenment were not an automatic tonic for civilizations everywhere. The Great Depression, dropping the atomic bomb on a civilian population, unethical experiments on minorities, Japanese-American internment camps and CIA sponsored coups of democratically elected governments are but a few black spots on twentieth century America that are hard for historians not wrapped in dogmatic scholasticism to ignore.

Essay 11 uncovered an example of enlightened beliefs actually diminishing the quality of life, when idolizing those beliefs takes priority over everything else. Let us quickly review that here. One faction of our founding fathers believed in democratic rule by a strong central government; another faction believed in maintaining states' rights. These enlightened beliefs were blended nicely in the construction of our Constitution and the formation of a federalist system. Both factions also believed that ideological parties would place self-interest over public interest, which would lead to corruption. The Constitution provided a witness to this concern through the deliberate omission of articles for political parties.

After the Constitutional Convention the different factions of colonialists banded together to form interest groups that idolized their enlightened beliefs. These interest groups became political parties, against the better judgment of the two party figureheads—Alexander Hamilton for the Federalists and Thomas Jefferson for the Republicans. The political parties formed entrenched battle lines to promote their respective beliefs at the expense of civility. The self-interest and corruption of political parties have been a bane to society ever since, just as the founding fathers feared.

The contemporary writings of Voltaire may have contributed to the prophetic beliefs of the founding fathers. In his *Letters on the English*, Voltaire contrasted the multiple religions present in England to the dominant Roman Catholicism in his native France. He warned that one state religion becomes despotic. A one party system, we know, has the same effect. Two state religions, according to Voltaire, would aim to "tear each other apart." Voltaire claimed that England avoided both problems because they had too many different religions to allow the idolatry of religious beliefs to sidetrack economic or political negotiations. With self-interests thus diffused, people were more inclined to collaborate in the public interest.[1]

The Constitutional Convention did not dwell on religion for much the same reason that Voltaire proposed. There were too many different religious beliefs present for anyone to feel emboldened to make theirs absolute. God was important and entered into the conversation, but neither Quaker nor Calvinist could promote the status of their beliefs over others.

The two political beliefs at the Convention that could have "torn each other apart" were central government versus states' rights. Both were enlightened beliefs, but neither had a well-coordinated interest group promoting the absolute status of their enlightenment. Instead, our founding fathers gathered to address a common problem, the ineffectiveness of the Articles of Confederation. They felt compelled first and foremost to resolve this problem, and were able to achieve harmony in the blending of their different beliefs of how the problem should be solved. Fortunately, the most important political act in our country's history took place before the idolatry that accompanies political parties began.

Harmony between Neighbors

Idolatry of specific beliefs is the mission of a special interest group, like a think tank or policy center. A political interest group idolizes beliefs for how to govern; a cultural interest group idolizes beliefs about behavior; an economic interest group idolizes beliefs about fiscal or monetary policy. An antithesis to idolatry is harmony. For a piece of music, harmony involves the artistic blending of differences. In these essays cultural harmony will be treated as a sense of belonging among people that enables them to blend diverse beliefs and behaviors.

In Essay 15 we explained how the State might actually provide an enhancement of natural rights by providing the benefits of diversity. Through diversity we have greater choice for independent labor, thought and belonging. Cultural harmony encourages this greater choice to be available to greater numbers. Achieving the harmony of many beliefs, not the idolatry of any single belief, enhances the quality of life that the State can provide through diversity.

In contrast to interest groups idolizing beliefs, the unit of culture where we

---

1 Voltaire's *Letters* is viewable at http://www.fordham.edu/halsall/mod/1778voltaire-lettres.html.

might expect harmony and the quality of life to best thrive is the neighborhood. Let us visit our neighbor Hans for illustration.

Two new sets of neighbors move in next to Hans at the same time. One set is a gay couple that has moved in to the west of Hans; the other is a bigamist and his two wives that have moved in to the east. Right after moving in the gay couple approaches Hans to sign a series of petitions in support of various gay rights that presumably would enhance their quality of life. Hans fancies that he is an enlightened man and signs every one of them. However, homosexual males make Hans uncomfortable and his support of their beliefs becomes the sum total of his interaction with them in the neighborhood.

The bigamist and his wives similarly approach Hans with a petition to legalize polygamy. They point out to Hans that some other cultures allow multiple wives or husbands. Hans is not persuaded by this and refuses to sign any of their petitions. But Hans enjoys their company and proceeds to treat them like neighbors. He invites them over for dinner, drives any of them to the airport when needed and helps them clear their driveway after snowstorms. Day after day Hans demonstrates in ways both subtle and obvious that he may not agree with the beliefs of his neighbors to the east, but he can live in harmony with them.

A sense of belonging, not shared beliefs, determines who your real neighbors are. A neighborhood where a sense of belonging can be established among neighbors of diverse beliefs has found harmony. This harmony allows diversities of labor, thought and belonging to exist and blend, thus enhancing the quality of life for that segment of the neighborhood.

Community and Harmony

The language of a culture affects the desire for the idolatry or harmony of beliefs. Merely the tone of language reveals a cultural disposition. Aggressive news talk hosts on radio or television, or aggressive blogs, do not concern themselves with harmony. Whining, belligerent or sarcastic personalities—both conservative and liberal—are intent on the idolatry of their beliefs rather than seeking to maintain a sense of belonging among Americans of different beliefs. Whether or not they truly believe in their whining, belligerence or sarcasm as a positive contribution to our culture perhaps depends on how much money they get paid for these "talents."

Language can be distorted to convolute the meanings of words. Steven Poole, a writer for the *Guardian* on politics and culture, uncovers examples of this in his book *Unspeak: How Words Become Weapons, How Weapons Become a Message, and How that Message Becomes Reality* (2006). One example Poole provides relates to the quality of life. He provides the etymology of the word community, derived from Latin roots to mean shared feelings, brotherhood and fraternity. These are all derivatives of a sense of belonging. Unfortunately, the original meaning of community has been kidnapped, as Poole relates:

> "'Community' is among the most perfect political words in English. It can mean several things at once, or nothing at all. It can conjure up things that don't exist, and deny the existence of those that do. It can be used in celebration, or in passive-aggressive attack."

Poole provides examples of how the meaning of community has been convoluted to no longer align with a sense of belonging. Community can refer to a place, such as a local village center, with no stipulation attached as to whether the people in that place have shared feelings or fraternity. Community can refer to a guild or similar group of shared interests, shifting the cause for the formation of community from belonging to beliefs or behaviors. When used in this manner community becomes a synonym for interest group. While interest groups can have a sense of belonging, this belonging actually depends on shared beliefs rather than a bond that transcends beliefs.

Poole cites many ways in which people use community for stereotyping. Demographic categories such as black, gay or Muslim can be called the black community, the gay community or the Muslim community with an implied context of shared beliefs everyone in these "communities" must have. These communities are thus set up as straw men to be torn down; since we can assume that the beliefs of these special interest communities must at times conflict with our own. In other words, community has evolved as a language tool to erect barriers, rather than describe the removal of barriers in fraternal cause.

In these cultural essays we will return to the original, genuine meaning of community. A community is a neighborhood of people with shared experiences and feelings. A sense of belonging has transcended diverse cultural beliefs, creating harmony in the neighborhood. Community is thus the antithesis to the interest group, which seeks out shared beliefs across all neighborhoods. No wonder, then, that some interest groups, most noticeably political parties and "libertarian" think tanks, seek to erode the meaning of community through unspeak.

What defines the neighborhood at which community is achieved? At the typical level of community a neighborhood consists of a street, a few blocks, a village center or perhaps a small town. An ambitious pursuit of community would not stop at those levels, but rather expand the geographic extent of a neighborhood.

Advanced Harmony

Historians use the term civilization to define the interaction of multiple cultures, multiple systems of beliefs and behaviors, through trade and other activities. Let us add a normative stipulation to this: civilizations are civilized. If the interaction of multiple cultures has little to do with trade and more to do with aggression or oppression, then the stipulation of being civilized is not being met. This essay began by asserting that being civilized requires social cohesion and responsibility. Let us now add that being civilized is achieving harmony among multiple cultures, and the high quality of life that results.

Equating being civilized with a high quality of life and harmony shapes the criteria we can use to distinguish between primitive and advanced civilizations. There are two characteristics of the United States that give us the potential to be the most advanced civilization in the history of the world, as determined by the high quality of life achieved through harmony. As a pluralistic melting pot our country attracts people from different cultures with different beliefs. Bound together within the same country the potential sense of belonging to each other would provide the very essence of harmony. Just as four-part harmony in music may be considered more advanced than two-part harmony, so does the pluralism of beliefs that could be harmonized within a culture represents a further advancement of civilization.

The other characteristic that could make us a truly advanced civilization is our pioneering commitment to federation. We think of this mainly in terms of the federation of states within our national government, or federalism. We pursue parallels to federalism at multiple levels of government. Our states consist of a federation of counties, our counties a federation of towns and our towns a federation of neighborhoods. Each level of federation represents an expanded geographic extent where community might be achieved. Each expanded level of community means an advancement of civilization by achieving harmony among diverse cultural beliefs and behaviors.

While pluralism and federations provide the ingredients for us to be advanced, they alone do not make us civilized. The same ingredients that provide the potential for being advanced make harmony and civility more difficult to achieve.

Immigrants tend to form homogeneous enclaves in urban or village centers. These enclaves form precisely to bolster the sense of belonging of new arrivals to a strange land, but neighborhood enclaves do not exist in isolation. A neighborhood enclave implies by definition surrounding neighborhoods that are different. Problems can arise with the harmony between different neighborhoods. Examples of such problems range from the African and Irish Americans in Boston to the Sunnis and Shiites in Baghdad.

Integrated neighborhoods living in harmony achieve our standard for a high quality of life, but the suburbs of twentieth century America complicate this pursuit. The suburb is a different cultural phenomenon than the urban or village center. Many people move to the suburbs in part to become less committed to others in a neighborhood social group. They pursue an individualism that they think is part of the American identity. We will discuss other problems with perceived individualism later, but one consequence is that people become more focused on self-interest than the public interest. Those motivated primarily by self-interest idolize their beliefs with others of like mind outside the realm of neighborhood, rather than seek harmony with those of different beliefs within their neighborhood. They share a neighborhood but not neighborhood experiences.

With people idolizing beliefs at the expense of neighborhood involvement, relative harmony at all levels of our federated system has been difficult to achieve. Different ethnic neighborhoods are estranged within many towns. Rural towns and urban centers are estranged within many counties. Rich and poor counties are estranged within states. Red and blue states are estranged within our country. As this estrangement increases our civility decreases. We are not at a point where we can consider ourselves the most advanced of civilizations, because of our struggles with the incivility born out of the idolatry of beliefs.

An Advanced Trinity

The political essays explored how economic greed and political authoritarianism are linked. Cultural idolatry is in turn linked to both. How does one most efficiently promote their "enlightened" dogmatic beliefs over others? The answer is to wield more power and wealth than competing dogma. Through great power and wealth we currently seek to promote our beliefs in Iraq. Regardless of how enlightened our beliefs may or may not be, a high quality of life will never be achieved if our continued presence interferes with the pursuit of harmony in that region of the world. Greed, authoritarianism and idolatry combine to form an unholy trinity dictating events in Iraq.

The United States has advanced cultural qualities, with pluralistic diversity and multiple levels of federation. These same qualities applied to a lesser degree with the European powers involved in World War I. Yet we know that from 1914-1918 these powers were advanced mainly at being uncivilized. Are we to assume they were civilized in 1913? Or in the intervening years between World War I and II? I am begging the question of whether being civilized is only kinetic, an assessment of how a civilization performs at any moment in time, or reflects the overall potential of a civilization to behave abhorrently in the present or the future.

Most Americans would admit to a potential for our advanced country to behave abhorrently in the future; many would claim we behave abhorrently in the present. This should make us wonder what we might lack to become better civilized. There really are only three natural ends that matter to humans, even in the context of civilization: to freely enjoy or share the merits of our labors; the wisdom of our thoughts; and the harmony of our belongings. Everything else in life becomes only the tools along a journey. Capitalism or communism, monarchies or federations, neighborhoods or federations, are good or bad only in the context of how they help or hinder civilizations with merit, wisdom and harmony.

Merit, wisdom and harmony are interwoven tightly. We do not have the luxury to choose an economy of merit without a politics of wisdom. We cannot choose a culture of harmony without an economics of merit. We will succeed with a politics of wisdom only in a culture of harmony. Cultural harmony exists only in a climate of economic merit and political wisdom. Together, these normative functions of economic, political and cultural systems guide people who are civilized.

This means that greed, authoritarianism and idolatry together rule those who are uncivilized. Many of us in the middle class might vehemently recoil at this suggestion, instinctively recognizing that we belong to a country that pretty much fits these attributes, yet feeling quite civilized in our own individual right. Ideals of greed or merit, authoritarianism or wisdom, and idolatry or harmony may be too abstract for many of us. Let us then conclude with the most practical matter of war or peace.

War or Peace

The great powers involved in World War I and II fancied themselves as the nation states of an advanced civilization, but they were mistaken. They idolized wonderfully enlightened beliefs about market economies, democratic rule and empirical utilitarianism. Together they acted as a global interest group maintaining they were the world's most advanced democracies. Yet by our criteria for harmony and a high quality of life these same advanced powers fell short of being civilized.

The League of Nations and the Treaty of Versailles could have provided venues to achieve harmony between cultures that still fancied they were advanced. Yet distrust even among "allies" went into the war and came out of the war. A spirit of "we are in this separately" prevailed over "we are in this together," with the interests of the "enlightened" countries being negotiated in competing idolatry rather than collaborative harmony.

Many Americans are aware that the seeds for World War II were sown in the aftermath of World War I, in regards to the continued distrust between European powers. Fewer of us are aware that similar seeds of distrust were planted between the American and Japanese "allies" in World War I that would affect events in World War II. Japan proposed a general declaration of racial equality in the League of Nations Covenant, but our mature democracy abstained from approving the clause. In the absence of unanimity our president, Woodrow Wilson, declared the amendment invalid. The desire of Pacific coast states to be able to discriminate against Japanese Americans with economic employment caused our mature democracy to equivocate on advancing our civilization.

Since the European powers also happened to be colonial powers, the repercussions of the World Wars spread not only across time but across the world. Of current interest is how the colonial apportionment of the Middle East after World War I still affects beliefs and behaviors in those countries—and in the countries with a presence in those countries—even today. The fact that the European powers were also colonial powers reveals that they were not as enlightened as they thought. We will explore other shortcomings of the Enlightenment later, but the main point now is the fallibility of presumed infallibility or, in Stevenson's words once again, "tragedy in the classical sense of a conflict between right and right."

This returns us to the reasons John Stuart Mill gave for the majority to allow a diversity of opinions (Essay 10). We should never assume that our "enlightened beliefs" have reached the status of infallibility. Through accommodating a diversity of opinions we plug in the gaps to our knowledge, avoid the dogmatism that inhibits understanding our own principles and strengthen our reasoning for what we believe. Idolization of enlightened beliefs deprives them of further enlightenment and may, in fact, cause them to regress.

Among the reasons that have been offered for why democracies go to war have been improper sequencing of democratic elements; incomplete sequencing (immaturity) of democratic elements; and a mismatch of democratic types and/ or perceptions. Identifying these causes for war provides good news only for establishing authoritarian elites as necessary for manipulating intricate foreign policies. None of these reasons explain why the United States has overthrown the most governments and has been involved in the most number of wars over the past century. As a counterpoint, our inclination towards clever foreign policy led to the CIA sponsored coup of a democratic Iran in 1953.

The research of Mansfield and Snyder or Weart, even if we accept the empirical flaws, does not address the root cause of our aggression; neither do the more common excuses offered by neoconservative or patriotic groups. By virtue of geography we are one of the most secure nations in the world, with ocean forming two of our four borders. If the cause of our continual overthrow of governments during the twentieth century was preemptive security our collective psyche could be characterized as paranoid delusional. If making the world a better place has been the motivation for being the most aggressive nation in the world over the past century, by the valid and reliable empirical standard of overthrowing much less powerful countries, perhaps we need to rethink our strategy.

The United States has fallen victim to the same disease that infiltrated the European powers; we have become idolatrous. Wars are caused by idolatry; if not idolatry of dogma, then idolatry of wealth and power, though the worship of wealth and power may be considered dogmatic as well. The idolatry that causes war need only be present in one nation, if that nation is powerful enough to be aggressive, or relatively secure enough not to be vulnerable to retaliation.

The universal cause of idolatry and dogma for aggression implies that striving for harmony between diverse beliefs creates the necessary condition for peace. Along with this harmony comes the wisdom that diffuses power and the merit that diffuses wealth. This simple proposition would never satisfy the wonks at policy centers and think tanks. Special interest groups such as these prefer complexity, since this helps to justify their existence. What think tank would perform a clever statistical analysis on the problems of idolatry or promoting dogma, the very reason for think tanks to exist?

This is not to say that nothing good comes from special interest groups. But there are two things that every special interest group peddles: dogma and idolatry. No matter how good the beliefs—and in these cultural essays I will make cases for morality and even intolerance—there comes the baggage of idolatry. Mansfield and Snyder produced clever research with quantitative empirical data and even some sound inductive reasoning. Their thesis suffers from trying too hard to justify their idolatrous dogma that mature democracies do not fight, while at the same time reconciling an authoritarian approach towards instituting democracy.

Mature democracies may be more inclined towards peace, but only by being more inclined towards economic merit, political wisdom and, above all, cultural harmony. No special interest groups such as policy centers and think tanks will ever attract enough concentrated wealth and power to explore the egalitarian implications of this proposition. Merit, wisdom, harmony and peace must be pursued in the context of community at increasing levels of federation. By such means civilizations become advanced.

Harmonic Obstacles

Perhaps you personally feel quite civilized right now. No doubt a British aristocrat in 1913 felt the same way. But do you feel that a World War III is possible and that the most influential country in the world could be in the thick of that war? Do you feel that our invasion of Iraq has increased the quality of life either at home or abroad? Do you wonder why we are the only secular democracy to institutionalize the death penalty? Do you puzzle over why the wealthiest nation on earth falls embarrassingly short of having the best child survival rates or the best literacy rates?

If you at this point remain an apostle of the "Best of Times" paradigm, or believe in our mature democracy as the key to our quality of life, you might as well close the cover of this book right now. The remaining essays on culture simply will not make sense, given the lens with which you view the world. Certainly the concluding premise of this essay grates on you: that an advanced civilization does not result from enlightened beliefs, sophisticated technology or even the standard of living. Rather, an advanced civilization results from the quality of life that stems from harmony among diversity, and the United States comes up lacking in many ways. We all are witnesses daily to the lack of harmony displayed by political parties, news talk shows, suburban migration, special interest groups and cultural idolatry. If you think of yourself to be civilized it is in spite, not because, of our prevailing culture. In the remaining cultural essays the following themes will reoccur:

- Vanity, cynicism and apprehension diminish our quality of life.
- Interest groups promote idolatry over harmony.
- Idolatry creates urgency.
- Secrecy and dishonesty are tools of idolatry.
- Our cultural idolatry promotes greed and authoritarianism.

A system of beliefs and behaviors should function to achieve harmony; that is the normative proposition behind this last part on culture. For the sake of policy wonks everywhere these cultural essays will add some complexity to the matter. As occurred in the previous parts on economics and politics, the next five essays in this part will elaborate on the structure of our cultural system. Our systems analysis will then be to harmonize some of the current beliefs of our civilization with our natural condition. The part on culture concludes in similar fashion to the other parts, with a guide for detecting the ways that Hans and the middle class has been fooled into supporting a system of beliefs and behaviors that undermines our cultural quality of life.

ESSAY 18 – THE SENSE OF BELONGING

"The wolf shall dwell with the lamb,
and the leopard shall lie down with the kid,
and the calf and the lion and the fatling together,
and a little child shall lead them.
The cow and the bear shall feed;
their young shall lie down together;
and the lion shall eat straw like the ox.
The sucking child shall play over the hole of the asp,
and the weaned child shall put his hand on the adder's den.
They shall not hurt or destroy in all my holy mountain;
for the earth shall be full of the knowledge of the Lord
as the waters cover the sea."
Isaiah 11: 6-9

Overview

- Our sense of belonging is a natural phenomenon that transcends species.
- Belonging is naturally strengthened by humility, faith and courage.
- Belonging can be culturally thwarted by vain desires, cynical anger and apprehensive confusion.
- Advanced religions readily accommodate multicultural diversity.
- Separating Church from State provides a homeostatic mechanism to balance materialism with humility, faith and courage.
- Uncivil public discourse promotes vanity, cynicism and apprehension at the expense of evidence and reasoning.
- An urgent mindset leads to uncivil and unnecessary behaviors.
- The desire to fulfill destinies stimulates urgency.
- Free will guarantees nothing, but destiny guarantees civilizations will remain primitive.
- Economic and political gullibility contributes to decay, tragedy and incivility.
- Our free will to choose the humility, faith and courage of belonging distinguishes us from machines.

Natural Belonging

In the Moremi Game Preserve of Botswana, leopards and baboons are natural enemies. Since leopards are solitary and baboons travel in troops, usually the leopard comes out on the short end when the two species meet. Occasionally, when a leopard meets a lone baboon, the tables are turned. An article titled "Leopard Lessons" in National Geographic (April 2007), written by Dereck Joubert and photography by Beverly Joubert, describes such an encounter with an unusual twist. The "Lesson" this twist holds for us regards the sense of belonging.

A leopard that the authors called Legadema killed a baboon that was apart from her group, but not quite alone. Only after the kill did Legadema notice the baboon's baby. The orphan reached out to the leopard, yearning for a new protector. An older baboon would recoil from the leopard with fear, but the baboon was too young to know better. We cannot so easily dismiss what Legadema did next. She picked up the baby gingerly in her mouth and transported him to a higher place in the tree. There Legadema kept the baboon company, even snuggling with him to keep him warm through the night. By morning, the baby still died from the cold, but only after the baby's death did the leopard return to the lower branch of the tree to eat the mother.

Some may derive sadness from this account, mourning for the orphaned baby. Some may cringe at the wildness of the leopard eating the mother. But we should also view this unusual bond between two different species as inspiring. The bond may have been unusual, but the yearnings that lead to such bonds are not.

The culture of man creates enemies within our species. From Democrats and Republicans, to the tragic Palestinian/Israeli conflict, humans form groups that reject each other categorically. Yet there can be no greater enemies between cultures than the mortal enemies of the wild, where natural, routine survival depends on killing or avoiding an enemy species. Some might excuse what the leopard did as motherly instinct, and attribute the unusual bond to instinctive behaviors that transcended the usual instinct to be enemies. But if the acceptance by Legadema for the baby baboon was nothing but instinct, perhaps humans could benefit from a little more natural instinct and a little less culture. At the least this should temper possible beliefs that "advancing" civilizations represent a constant and continual improvement on the incivility of primitive nature.

The previous essay established that the senses of belonging we naturally develop forms our cultures. Three basic types of belonging are found in all cultures: belonging to ourselves, to others and to a natural order that transcends humans. The following observations were made: our quality of life derives from our sense of belonging; harmony is a sense of belonging that transcends diverse beliefs; an advanced civilization achieves harmony with increasing diversity. This essay picks up on these themes to explore what ultimately contributes to our sense of belonging and, by extension, what ultimately stands in our way of being civilized. Let us focus on the following points:

- The importance of our sense of belonging transcends cultures.

- Religious belief affects the advancement of civilization for good or bad.
- Urgency and belief in destiny are impediments to becoming advanced.

Separation and Preparation

Our sense of belonging has been described by different cultures in different ways. The theologian Paul Tillich defined sin as separation, categorized further as separation from God, separation from others and separation from our selves.[1] These are the same categories for which we sense that we belong. If we view separation as the opposite of belonging, then the essence of sin is when we deprive ourselves of our belonging.

Our sense of belonging relates to the view of oneness held by Eastern cultures. Buddhists view the means by which we either strengthen or weaken our oneness as karma. Karma is not a system of cosmic rewards and punishments, as western cultures tend to conclude. Rather, the Buddhist views karma as a cosmic training regiment by which we can learn from our experiences on our path towards oneness. As viewed through a Buddhist lens the basic types of human folly that karma addresses are desire, anger and confusion. These could be viewed as the Eastern corollary to Western sin. We are visited by karma not to exploit these follies, but to prepare us to overcome them.

We all have desires. Our very sense of belonging or quest for oneness stems from a type of desire. Unfortunately, the vanity we hold for our own importance sometimes causes us to desire things at the expense of others. Such vain desire is manifested in arrogance, selfishness or greed. In contrast, through our humility we lose the focus on ourselves and strengthen our belonging to others. One purpose of karma then, from the Buddhist point of view, is to provide humility. Christians have the ultimate expression of humility through the Crucifixion of Christ, which involved the humility to give up everything for the sake of others. Of note: unless Christ had the free will to choose this course, His sacrifice was neither humble nor meaningful.

We all have anger. We get angry at many things for many reasons. The Buddhist may view all anger as defeating a quest for oneness; but Christians have the model of Christ, normally a presence of overwhelming calm, expressing deliberate and momentary anger at the merchants in the temple. Both East and West agree, however, that our well-being suffers from festering anger. We come to such anger when we lose faith in natural or cultural orders. Through faith we can handle the setbacks of life with a sense of purpose in the world, or a sense of belonging to God. Cynical anger is thus one root of sin and a major barrier to oneness or belonging. Another purpose of karma is to strengthen the faith in a natural order that overcomes cynical anger. Christians have an extreme test of

---

1 From "You Are Accepted," in *The Shaking of the Foundations* (1948).

faith through the Resurrection, which the faithful interprets as even the darkness of death being transcended. Of note: without the free will to choose to believe in God, faith does not exist.

We all get confused. The reason for our confusion determines whether this weakens our oneness or belonging. I once attempted to learn German, prior to a visit to that country, and found myself in a constant state of confusion. This does not necessarily interfere with our sense of belonging. My German hosts were amused, and no less accepting of me, when I confused the verb and noun forms of the same word and declared that: "I would like to eat myself." On the other hand, sometimes confusion results from lacking the courage of following our conscience. Like when Peter denied knowing Christ three times before the cock crowed, we become strangers to ourselves and who we think we really are, or at least who we wish to be. Acquiring the courage of our convictions eliminates our apprehensive confusion and restores our sense of belonging to our selves. Therefore one more purpose of karma is to nurture the courage that overcomes the confusion we get from apprehension. Christians have a source for courage through the Holy Spirit. After the Pentecost Peter became a changed man and by his courage followed his convictions until he became martyred. Of note: without the free will to choose his path, Peter is more a puppet than a courageous man.

East and West is compared to emphasize the similarities in an inherent natural right that transcends different cultures. Viewing this right as belonging or oneness does not matter. Ethnographers might refer to kinship instead of either term. Whether we focus on sin as separation or karma as preparation we are drawn to the importance of humility, faith and courage for maintaining this natural right.

These moral attributes, like our sense of belonging, flourish in nature. If you need to survive in a small social group, as was the case for early human foragers, humility is adaptive and vanity is maladaptive. A cheerful faith would be welcomed into the group more than a cynical anger. The courage to face the uncertainties of wilderness would be selected over cowardly apprehension. Only culture turns this completely around, so that moral attributes become maladaptive in many modern groups. And, in fact, only cultural agents attempt to persuade us that the immoral alternatives are actually moral.

Advanced Religions

Christianity and Buddhism are two of the three advanced religions in the world today. The term advanced has no bearing on the sophistication or importance of the religious belief. I apply the term advanced to religion as I do for civilization: the ability to harmonize multiple cultural systems of beliefs and behaviors. The foundational beliefs of Christianity do not inherently promote advancement; a debate arose within the early Christian Church as to whether or not only Jews could be Christians. Once Paul's belief prevailed that "There is neither Jew nor Greek" (Galatians 3: 28), Christianity became an advanced religion that could be adopted by multiple cultures, and by civilizations that are multicultural.

Christianity is the offspring of Judaism. Judaism may be considered a great religion in terms of sophistication and importance, but not advanced in regards to harmonizing different cultures. The Hebrew Testament makes clear that the Hebrews alone were God's chosen people and chosen culture, independent of fidelity. Destiny mattered at least as much as the intensity of faith in the scheme of retaining their chosen status. This inhibited Judaism from being embraced by other cultures throughout the world (not to mention upsetting God on occasion, according to the Hebrew Testament).

A similar relationship exists between Buddhism and Hinduism. Certainly, vast numbers of people in the world are Hindus, and their belief system is quite elaborate. Yet the intricacy and uniqueness of the Hindu system of castes and gods does not translate well to other cultures. Hinduism began with Indian civilization and has yet to expand significantly beyond some small parts of Southeast Asia. Buddhism originated in the Indian subcontinent as well, in response to Hinduism. The diminished importance of castes and gods made Buddhism more amenable to other cultures. Buddhism expanded to Chinese civilization early on and, in more recent times, gained a foothold in western civilization.

The two great religions that originated in Chinese civilization, Confucianism and Taoism, perhaps had the ingredients to become advanced. However, Chinese civilization historically was less inclined towards continual expansion than their western counterparts. They had a tendency to absorb, rather than promote, advanced religions.

The third advanced religion in the world today is Islam. Islam arose in the Middle East and, much like Christianity, spread to virtually all other civilizations. In the heyday of Islam, corresponding to what western civilization would call the Middle Ages, the ruling caliphates were tolerant of diverse cultures and faiths. Cultural tolerance no longer appears to be important to some Muslims, nor to some Christians. We should keep in mind that both religions are advanced in their emphasis on personal faith over fixed cultural beliefs and behaviors, but that "fundamentalist" factions within both idolize a more narrow system of beliefs and behaviors.

Separation of Church and State

Advanced religions evolved to advocate some form of separation between Church and State. Buddhism would not have advanced easily into Chinese civilization had the Chinese dynasties perceived the new religion would threaten their rule. Jesus advised Christians to "render therefore to Caesar the things that are Caesar's

(Matthew 22: 21)." The Quran likewise cautioned that preoccupation with matters of the State detracted from religious observance.

The ambivalence of advanced religions for the State has been exploited by authoritarian rulers feigning religious beliefs to gain support, while at the same time behaving in ways that contradict these professed beliefs. This led Karl Marx to charge religion of being an opiate for the masses, implying that religion provides the distraction for authoritarian elites to get away with various atrocities. Religious dogma, whether from an advanced religion or not, frequently have led to war. Atheists and agnostics point to the atrocities that result from this as evidence that civilizations would be better off without religion.

Contrary to this view, the combined presence and separation of the Church from the State provides an important homeostatic mechanism for culture. I have discussed homeostasis repeatedly throughout these essays, hopefully planting firmly in your minds the crucial role of homeostasis for any type of system. Homeostasis works through negative feedback loops. When a room gets too hot, the heat itself sends a signal for the room to cool down. When the room gets too cool, the cold sends a signal for the room to heat up. The ideal Church has a similar relationship as a thermostat to the State, with the purpose of nurturing the sense of belonging in a culture. The attributes of humility, faith and courage that could hinder material State functions are the primary concerns of the ideal Church. When the Church exists and remains separated from the State, these moral attributes provide a negative feedback loop for regulating material excesses of the State.

For example, commerce does not engage the interest of the spiritual Church, thus the spiritual Church normally wishes not to interfere with the State's structuring of an economic system based only on materialism. However, should the State's economic practices strike at core moral values; this activates the spiritual thermostat of the Church. Slavery has been part of the economic system in many civilizations. The economic might of the Roman Empire was built in large part on slavery. But the vanity of treating segments of society as inferior, the cynicism of striving for success through exploitation and the apprehension of life without material abundance draws the condemnation of the spiritual Church. When the assault to core moral attributes gets too high, the Church thermostat turns on to regulate the State. Christianity contributed to a reduction of slavery in the Roman Empire; and drove the abolition movement in American culture. When the State reacts to accommodate the spiritual values of the Church, such as by forbidding the use of slavery, the Church thermostat turns off to once again become ambivalent towards State materialism.

To accommodate the views of atheists and agnostics in this discussion let us expand our definition of the Church as any organized body within a State that serves as a spiritual guide for the humility, faith and courage that strengthens our belongings. Organized religions serve as the Church in most nations, but perhaps the same moral promotion of humility, faith and courage could be achieved through New Age spirituality or the beliefs held by SETI worshippers.[2] When the material greed and power of the State runs rampant and unchecked, this implies one of two problems in regards to our broadly defined Church.

One problem would be the absence of a Church thermostat. One hopes that humility, faith and courage could not disappear totally from a civilization; but without a champion the scope and influence of these moral attributes diminish. The material problems inherent in the communist State result from rulers such as Stalin and Mao obliterating the spiritual thermostat that might otherwise regulate their materialism.

The other problem occurs when the State embraces the Church and/or vice-versa. The spiritual thermostat to regulate greed and power exists in theory, but not in function. When State unites with Church then idolatry joins greed and authoritarianism as triple threats to harmony. The thermostat is broken and provides positive reinforcement rather than negative feedback. The State distorts the beliefs and behaviors of the Church, which in turn serves to support the abuses of the State. Hitler tinkered with the spiritual thermostat of the Church in this manner.

The harmful consequences of switching the spiritual thermostat from providing negative feedback to positive reinforcement for the material State are obvious. A more subtle problem occurs when the type of bond that forms between Church and State maintains the spiritual thermostat, but adjusts the tolerance level for materialism to high. With this scenario Church extends a disinterest for wealth to a disinterest in the concentration of wealth. In return for this disinterest the State reinforces spiritual matters in symbolic ways. Something that only has meaning in terms of a spiritual relationship with God, such as prayer, becomes a cynical talking point for authoritarian leaders who use the Church to concentrate power.

At times the uniting of Church and State serves to idolize the beliefs of the former. The Israeli/Palestinian conflict provides a tragic example of the impact on humility, faith and courage when this happens. Islamic suicide bombers and Jewish soldiers consider themselves to be humble servants to their purpose; but in Essay 19 we will explore the foundations of a truer humility. They both act in faith; but in Essay 20 we will explore the foundations of a truer faith. They both fancy themselves as being courageous; but in Essay 21 we will explore the foundations of truer courage. Current idolized dogma on both sides will need to change for any real solution to work.

We should not be quick to point a finger at other countries idolizing beliefs or engaged in uncivilized conflict. We go through two year cycles where our own idolatry combines with authoritarianism and greed in uncivil displays. We call them political campaigns.

---

2 SETI is the program to Search for Extra-Terrestrial Intelligence, a faith endeavor if ever there was one.

Uncivil Campaigns

When Edmund Muskie cried at the podium during a presidential campaign I was both disturbed and impressed. I hardly knew who Muskie was at the time (U. S. senator from Maine) but I was disturbed that Muskie's wife had been dragged into the campaign with little cause or relevance. That certainly was not how the middle class behaved around here on Emerson Street. On the other hand I was impressed with Muskie's deep concern for his wife that would move him to tears. How could that not play well with the middle class folks in Peoria? Contrary to my naïve opinion, from that point on Muskie's campaign went on a downward spiral based in part on his moment of "vulnerability."

We can consider the incivility of campaigns, assisted by corporate media, to be a cultural constant. Corporate media had little problem with Saxby Chambliss attacking Max Cleland for being weak on defense, during a senate race in Georgia. Never mind that Cleland was a Vietnam vet who lost his limbs in the war. Since corporate media were uncritical of the message the Chambliss accusations only needed to be made a few times before retraction, without ever needing the courage to face the accused. The pundits and news talk show hosts of the echo chambers circulated the message for free, once again without ever having to face the accused or with any type of balanced analysis. This same approach worked well when the Swift Boat Veterans for "Truth" sold their souls for the sake of maintaining their party's power.

In addition to the incivilities that politicians heap on each other, there are uncivil consequences that spill out to the public. While sensationalizing the stances of opponents on taxes and the economy, politicians vaunt our vain desires to maintain great wealth. While distorting the position of opponents on foreign policy, politicians exploit our apprehensive confusion over how we can best maintain security. Meanwhile, the cumulative effect of negative campaigning is to cultivate the cynical anger of a public that believes all politicians are alike; that all seek self-interest at the expense of public interest; that intent to sacrifice and selflessly serve need not be a factor we seriously consider. Political campaigns become a battle of idolized beliefs at best or, worse, an uncivil scrum that undermines cultural harmony. Hardened politicians in a campaign are like the college students that urinate down a stairwell.

Corporate media loves our uncivil campaign culture. Indeed, the one segment of society that stands to lose the most from civil campaigning is corporate media. Consider the old adage: "facts speak for themselves." You do not need graphic or rhetorical enhancement for powerful evidence and logic if clearly presented; you just need the message to be heard and repeated, like the Dow Jones indicators. Nothing beats corporate media for getting a message heard and repeated, especially if that message makes the echo chambers of opinionated pundits and news talk hosts, but there are much cheaper ways of clearly conveying evidence and logic. The greed of corporate media naturally will incline them to favor campaigns that need to use expensive graphical and rhetorical flourishes to legitimize a message void of sound evidence and logic.

The use of corporate media increases the appeal of campaigns for interest groups. Idolized beliefs, like authoritarian politicians or corporate greed, creates a similar demand for graphical and rhetorical distortions over evidence and logic. A report on NPR (8/22/07) described how politicians now spend more time justifying themselves to advocacy groups than to their constituents. As long as we equate money as free speech, we can expect that harmonizing the beliefs of diverse constituents will continue to decline in importance in relation to getting elected by special interests promoting dogma.

Those who would idolize beliefs also would idolize people. Thus the other clear winners in a campaign circus, fueled by corporate media and the use of money as free speech, are people who can best become idols. Dynasties help in this regard. Bush I provided an edge for Bush II. Bill provided an edge for Hillary at first, until a greater idol arrived in Barack Obama. The events of 9/11 provided a heroic sheen for Rudy Giuliani, even though his contributions beyond a few good speeches have been questioned by New York policemen and firefighters.

While some candidates may be better suited to become idols than others, certain issues bring out a uniformity of rhetorical response. During the 2008 campaign Democrats rallied behind the assertions of Biden and Clinton that the blame supporting the Iraq War lies with the administration pulling a fast one on those poor unsuspecting Democrats in Congress. Lacking from their rhetoric still is an assessment of how oil figures into our past and future actions in Iraq. The Republicans rallied behind the rhetoric of John McCain and Mike Huckabee preaching honor for our troops and nation. But without mentioning to the American people how oil fits into the equation they either prove themselves to be totally naïve or less than honorable. This lack of honor in neglecting the truth especially applied to McCain, whose mother inherited substantial welfare from oil. Maybe we are supposed to assume that neither Democrats nor Republicans are competent enough to figure out that Iraq is a strategic country for oil.

Urgent Piffle

Powerful urges for wealth, power and/or dogma drive campaigns and, in turn, campaigns insist that the public becomes urgent. The urgency that infects political campaigns spreads to our entire political discourse. With the benefit of hindsight let us consider one very instructive example of how such urgent discourse played out. Names will be withheld for two reasons. The person that was vilified with this discourse has been beaten down enough and has withdrawn from further public scrutiny. The people who did the vilifying seek attention as a *modus operandi* and we will not reward such a motive here. You may immediately figure out who was being vilified, since the echo chambers of corporate media played a significant role in this. If you are determined to identify the people doing the vilifying there is always Google.

A woman lost her son in the Iraq War and decided to demand straight answers from Bush II. The woman became a symbol for the believers of her cause and came under the scrutiny of corporate media. Corporate media provided abundant coverage of her actions, though little coverage to the actual cause of demanding straight answers. With her actions being the focus she became little more than a media circus, as disturbing as the truth of that accusation might be to her followers. People who did not share her view of getting straight answers really had little to worry about. Actions such as hers play out as a media sensation for only so long before being replaced by some Hollywood scandal. Yet she had detractors who evidently thought this woman was a genuine danger. Here are some of their quotes:

> "She is a disgrace to her brave son … She will
> do and say anything to discredit the US and its
> commander and chief."

> "(She) evidently thinks little of her deceased son,
> his sacrifice or of those left to do his noble work
> in his absence."

> "She is spouting sinister piffle."

Whew! Unfortunately that is just a limited sample of the bullying quotes. Here is a mother whom we have no reason to doubt loved her son and, also with no reason to doubt, was motivated by that love to do something about his death. Muskie and Cleland should consider themselves lucky. Perhaps verbal bullies feel all the more emboldened when their target is a female. Bullying quotes make us enraged with either the person being vilified or the bullies. In either case we are brought down to the level of those doing the bullying. The inevitable effects have not changed since our founding fathers first perpetrated such uncivil discourse, destroying their own vision for a democracy free of party politics.

The men behind these quotes, lets call them the "piffle" people, must have been urgent. Urgency can be either a responsive or an ongoing condition. As a responsive call to immediate action urgency is an adaptive behavior, but this was not the type of urgency that afflicted the "piffle" people. Had they a smattering of patience, or civility, they simply would have waited for the media sensation to burn out. There was no danger that the Bush II administration was going to respect a call for straight answers; nor was there a danger that corporate media would suddenly become tenacious in looking for straight answers. Echo chambers and news talk hosts would have to have the brazen audacity of consistently asking and cross-examining our objectives for oil in relation to Iraq.

The type of urgency possessed by the "piffle" people, along with too many other Americans, is an ongoing condition. The type of urgency that led to their uncivil words was not responding to an immediate call to action, as no action on their part really was necessary to achieve their goal. Whatever made the "piffle" people urgent was not a response to external conditions but rather their own internal state of mind. Their self-generated urgency as a state of mind was brought about by some combination of vain desires, cynical anger and/or apprehensive confusion.

These conditions for internal urgency help to explain why this type of urgent behavior tends to be uncivilized. As vain, they tend to be insensitive to others; as cynical, they tend to be insensitive to a higher order of life; as apprehensive, they tend to be insensitive to their own conscience. The "piffle" people likely are insensitive to all three, which helps to illustrate why uncivilized behaviors prompted by urgency often turn out unnecessary. All these urgent men are plugged in to corporate media, yet they apparently are clueless regarding how corporate media works. Their sense of belonging to the corporate media world should have provided the foresight and patience to allow the aggrieved media sensation to run her course. Vanity, cynicism and/or apprehension instead urged them to spout their own "sinister piffle."

Urgent special interest groups, like urgent "piffle" people, can be infected collectively by poisonous states of mind. This is certainly true for special interest groups that support preemptive strikes against a third world country from another hemisphere. By definition, preemption is not a responsive action. One could argue that a response is in the mind of the responder, and that any urgent act can be defended as an imagined response to a threat, whether real, remote or ridiculous. But if either empirical foresight or hindsight proves an "immediate call to action" was unwarranted, this confirms that the urgency is an ongoing condition and the resulting behaviors uncivil and unnecessary.

Urgent behaviors can prove to be not only unnecessary but self-defeating. No doubt neoconservatives fancy their beliefs about democracy to be the most enlightened in history, much like the attitude of European leaders before World War I. Yet urgent impulses lead them to think that democracies can be imposed everywhere with one exalted superpower in charge of the whole "democratization." Such a fantasy is absurd beyond description, almost as absurd as thinking torture works to thwart terrorists, almost as absurd as accusing an aggrieved mother of spouting "sinister piffle." Even if we believe that democracy is best for all countries everywhere, imposing "democracies" defeats the overall purpose of world support for our system of beliefs and behaviors.

The idolized beliefs of neoconservatives might not have gained any more credibility than used car salesmen, had they not positioned themselves well in the power structure of political parties and corporate media. Can there be anything more urgent, at least in the eyes of politicians, than party politics? Politicians are more than eager to latch on to the urgency of idolized beliefs if they perceive a synergy with their urgency to wield power. Since power trumps principle, party members fall in line even when they might be inherently opposed to the idolized belief. Thus the same party that was opposed to manifest destiny throughout our history now leads the charge for the imposed democratization of a foreign culture in a remote hemisphere, with the rank and file of the party genuflecting with loyalty.

Destiny and Free Will

Destiny often serves as the impetus for urgency. This may not make sense at first, since logically no one need force something already destined to happen. The early Hebrews showed little urgency in their faith while taking for granted their destiny as the chosen people. Putting this exception aside, impatience is the norm for the good things one expects to happen. Your kids urgently waiting for the coming of Christmas provides a clear example of this. The holiday is destined to arrive but once, and the closer the destiny the more urgent your kids become.

Notions of destiny have permeated western civilization throughout history. During the post-classical period of western civilization the Judaic belief of a chosen people evolved into a Christian form. Formulated and championed by St. Augustine, the religious doctrine of predestination held that the kingdom of heaven was for chosen believers. Paul's declaration that there was neither Jew nor Greek allowed this faith in predestination to go global, with no cultural strings attached.

Also during the post-classical period a belief in scholasticism held that the wisdom of the ancients was inviolate and could be used to deduce explanations for all phenomena. The cornerstone of the Enlightenment, more so than the economic and political changes that occurred, was a growing faith in empiricism. Knowledge was induced from observations with the senses, not deduced from the dogma of ancient Greeks and prophets. One might think that with this empiricism the Enlightenment opened the door for both free thinking and free will.

The age of empiricism encouraged independence from many traditional beliefs but not from a belief in destiny. God set the universe in motion with fixed laws of nature, and the destiny of man was no less than to fathom the intricate mind of God. The empiricists of the Enlightenment formed an informal religion of sorts known as deism. Deists were mainly an optimistic bunch. Johann Keppler thought he was on the verge of understanding the universe when he discovered the laws for planetary motion; and virtually all contemporaries of Isaac Newton thought he was on the cusp of this same lofty goal when he discovered the universal force of gravity. Achievements such as these fueled beliefs that a good God set into motion the orderly laws of the universe, and everything happened as destined for the best.

A more direct Enlightenment lineage to the predestination of St. Augustine and the post-classical period was provided by the branch of the Protestant reformation known as Calvinism. Calvinists were strikingly more pessimistic than Deists, but they embraced destiny as well to support their faith in an angry God that had the universe figured out ahead of time, much to the detriment of most sinners everywhere. Calvinists reinforced the Protestant belief to know Christ based on one's own understanding of the Bible, rather than faith in the Pope, but they still denied that free will charted one's destiny.

Skepticism was the one other belief system relating to faith that gained momentum during the Enlightenment. Skepticism should not be confused with agnosticism. Skeptics such as Blaise Pascal and Pierre Bayle had a passionate faith in Christ, while Denis Diderot had a passionate faith that God did not exist. They were all skeptical about faith in the destiny of reason and using reason to support the destiny of faith. They despaired at the notion that the "best of all possible worlds" included devastating earthquakes and human cruelty; they were infuriated by the intolerance of organized religions inflicting judgment and retribution on behalf of an angry God. Reason and faith each had their separate purposes for the Skeptic. Reason could lead to wonderful discoveries, but provided no guarantee that these discoveries would work to the overall good of humanity. The love of others that provided a foundation for the Christian faith could benefit humanity, but not when tainted with arrogant rationality that one's particular dogma was the best. In other words, the Skeptics cautioned against idolizing one's beliefs, whether saint or scientist. The importance of separating the spiritual Church and material State can be derived from this philosophy.

Of these three faith movements prompted by the Enlightenment only Skepticism recognizes free will. The other movements used either reason or faith to make invalid and unreliable claims about an omniscient God and destiny. Free will was subjugated to the inevitable destinies dictated by progressive enlightenment or an angry God. Out of the three movements, Skepticism comes out of the Enlightenment limping in today's world with the least support. Though Pierre Bayle's *Historical and Critical Dictionary* (1695-1697) was one of the charter works placed by Thomas Jefferson in the Library of Congress, how many Americans have heard of him now?

Textbooks are the "echo chambers" of academics. A determined researcher can uncover most historic events, and most contemporary opinions of those events. What most of the public believes, however, is the history that is cross-referenced and echoed in school textbooks. The wealthy and powerful determine in large part the echo to be "heard" from history textbooks, just as they influence the content of corporate media echo chambers. Bayle's humble view of reason and faith did not fit well with *laissez faire* economists and authoritarian democracies at the turn of the twentieth century. The wealthy and powerful fancy the destiny of advancing civilizations as being on their side and do not appreciate a Skeptic like Bayle cautioning against this.

The exercise of free will provides no guarantee for civilization. Free will, by definition, guarantees nothing. Free will does not guarantee an economic system of merit; but destiny favors the greedy who become the wealth elites. Free will does not guarantee a political system of wisdom; but destiny favors the authoritarians who become the power elites. Free will does not guarantee a cultural system of harmony; but destiny favors the idolatrous who become the special interest elites. The wealthy, the powerful and the idolatrous employ urgent means in turn to quickly achieve their "destiny."

Free will does not guarantee we choose the humility of belonging to others; but destiny leads us towards the arrogance modeled by wealth and power elites. Free will does not guarantee we have faith in a higher purpose; but destiny leads us to justify any cynical means to accomplish our ends. Free will does not guarantee we choose the courage to remain true to our conscience; but destiny leads us to cowardly place security above all other considerations of conscience and moral behavior. Free will does not guarantee our civilization becomes advanced; but destiny leads us to become slaves to our vain desires, cynical anger and apprehensive confusion. Free will may not be our salvation, but without free will the destiny of civilizations to remain primitive is certain.

The fact that atrocities were occurring in Europe even as enlightened Deists held to their optimistic beliefs spurred Voltaire to convert from a Deist to the Skeptic that wrote the satire *Candide* (1759). The main character, Professor Pangloss, responded to catastrophes by saying this was, nevertheless, "the best of all possible worlds." The Brothers Grimm, who wrote during later stages of the Enlightenment, provided their own Panglossian caricature with the lucky Hans. Hans was featured throughout these essays, because in many ways we are him. Now the time has come to face the unpleasant truth about Hans.

Economic and Political Gullibility

Our friend Hans from the Brothers Grimm's tale in the Prologue may or may not belong to one of the advanced religions, but he must have a well-developed sense of belonging. Economically, he has been swindled; politically, he has been fooled; culturally, Hans feels lucky. Perhaps Hans feels lucky because of strong roots in a community that nurtured his sense of belonging to others. Perhaps Hans is such a blooming optimist because of a strong relationship with God or some other form of a higher purpose. Perhaps Hans just has good self-esteem. All Hans really needs to be "in luck" is for the sun to shine and the grass to grow. As long as Hans does not know that he has been bamboozled, what real harm has he experienced?

A similar question is raised by the movie *The Matrix*. Machines rule the world, incubating captive humans in pods to tap their energy, while keeping them in an interactive state of virtual reality that resembles normal human culture. The movie provides a provocative and ironic reflection on Rene Descartes' epistemology: "I think therefore I am." Descartes' response to skepticism helped to usher in the Enlightenment's emphasis on empiricism. Do we fault material enslavement, either literally by machines or figuratively by our own desires, if our experiences prevent us from knowing we are being enslaved?

In *The Matrix*, a civilization still exists that avoided captivity. The main character of the movie was once a captive human, Neo, who the free humans have rescued for their own salvation. The most despicable character in the movie betrays Neo to the machines in return for the promise of being provided a lavish virtual reality as a captive. Though we do not blame the ignorant captives who never know they are helpless slaves to machines, we despise the free human for his Faustian bargain to become captive.

Just as we can empathize with the ignorant captives in *The Matrix*, we might excuse and even envy the "lucky" Hans. Likewise, why should we fault those believing in the "Best of Times" paradigm claiming, for any given moment in time, that the advancement of technology and enlightened beliefs up until then has produced the most advanced civilization? If our quality of life truly depends on something as intangible as harmony, then having everyone thinking they are "in luck" regardless of their economic or political situation seems to be a terrific cultural solution for advancing civilizations. There are at least three reasons why economic and political gullibility does not make us culturally "in luck."

- Gullibility contributes to cultural decadence.
- Gullibility contributes to human tragedy.
- Gullibility is fueled by incivility.

The world historian Arnold Toynbee, in his twelve volumes *A Study of History* (1934-1961), has suggested a commonality in the rise and fall of civilizations. Predicating the falls were maladaptive government bureaucracies and a decadent citizenry that lost interest in civic duty. We can point to one recent development in the new millennium that fits nicely with the Toynbee model. For the first time during a war our civilization provided tax cuts that favored the elite. We can forego the discussion of whether we need to be at war or not, civilizations have embarked on lots of wars without coming to an end. However, past civilizations crumbled when their elites were as empty of civic virtue as some of our current elites are, even in a time of war. Watching our civilization crumble as we relinquish our civic duty is not a "lucky" cultural solution.

Another reason to dampen naïve feelings of good fortune is for the sake of avoiding tragedies. There are some things just impossible to feel "in luck" about. In your lucky bliss you could support a war, but become miserable once a loved one is lost. You could feel lucky about our system of privatized health care simply by listening to the Powell Cabal and corporate media, yet be unable to get the care you need at a crucial time. You could happily acquire lots of mass produced stuff from large corporations, yet be on the verge of financial ruin when the costs of inflated, essential items take up too great a proportion of your income.

The most pertinent reason for Hans not to feel culturally "in luck" is when he really is culturally "out of luck" with his belonging. The fairy tale Hans may have a strong sense of belonging, filled with humility, faith and courage. The fairy tale Hans may have no shred of desire, anger or confusion, and have the patience of Job. An abundance of empirical evidence and logic suggests that the same does not hold true for the middle class Hans living in the United States. We have referenced throughout these essays how vanity, cynicism and apprehension have affected us economically and politically. In the next three essays we will turn to how these traits affect us culturally.

Machines or Miracles

If we wish to consider ourselves more than the machines in *The Matrix*, we must place our faith in our free will to belong. I have had experiences that cement this faith; no doubt you have as well. Please allow me to close with one such experience, not unlike the lesson of the leopard and baboon that began this essay.

I have gone on long-distance backpacking expeditions where a support vehicle meets us with supplies every week or so at remote road crossings. This does not keep the pack weight down so much as making access to a town easier for a group of backpackers. I was camped at one such supply point in the Bitterroots of Montana when an extraordinary thing happened. A hummingbird flew in through an open window of the support vehicle, bumped into the windshield and became lodged between the windshield and dashboard.

I rescued the hummingbird from its predicament and the creature remained limp in the palm of my hand. The body was warm, the eyes were open and the breast moved in a way to confirm that the hummingbird was alive; but, in truth, the bird appeared to be all but dead. The poor thing appeared to be gravely injured.

As I contemplated whether or not the humane thing to do would be to put a quick end to the hummingbird's life, a loud buzzing swept by my ears. I recoiled as if I had just been dive bombed, and indeed I had. Another hummingbird had swooped in and now hovered above my head. Within a blink of an eye the docile, helpless creature in my palm disappeared, and both could next be seen weaving in and out with each other in what any witness must conclude were flights of joy. These creatures belonged to each other, and that belonging was the absolute difference between joy and despair.

How many of us get to hold a docile, uninjured bird in our hands? Yet this was not the extraordinary part. Just days before my encounter with the hummingbird I read in an essay of a similar encounter. The essay was by Loren Eiseley, a natural historian who writes with insight and passion. While doing field research on behalf of a museum, Eiseley had additional instructions to capture some live specimens for a zoo. He first attempted to catch a female sparrow hawk. The hawk's mate would not allow this and attacked Eiseley, sacrificing his freedom to allow the female to go free.

The next day Eiseley had a change of heart and decided to let the male sparrow hawk go free as well. He took the hawk out of the small box that served as prison and laid the bird on the grass. Eiseley beautifully describes what happened next.

"He lay there a long minute without hope, unmoving, his eyes fixed on that blue vault above him. It must have been that he was already so far away in heart that he never felt the release from my hand. He never even stood. He just lay with his breast against the grass.

In the next second after that long minute he was gone. Like a flicker of light, he had vanished with my eyes full on him, but without actually seeing even a premonitory wing beat. He was gone straight into that towering emptiness of light and crystal that my eyes could scarcely bear to penetrate. For another long moment there was silence. I could not see him. The light was too intense. Then from far up somewhere a cry came ringing down.

I was young then and had seen little of the world, but when I heard that cry my heart turned over. It was not the cry of the hawk I had captured; for, by shifting my position against the sun, I was now seeing further up. Straight out of the sun's eye, where she must have been soaring restlessly above us for untold hours, hurtled his mate. And from far up, ringing from peak to peak of the summits over us, came a cry of such unutterable and ecstatic joy that it sounds down across the years and tingles among the cups on my quiet breakfast table."[3]

What stirred Eiseley's memory at the breakfast table was an article he had just read in the *New York Times*. The article reported with optimism the wonderful progress of machines that may even be able to make themselves some day. Eiseley's memory was a counterpoint to the article's optimism about machines. In Eiseley's view:

"...the brain they say now is just another type of more complicated feedback system. The engineers have its basic principles worked out; it's mechanical, you know; nothing to get superstitious about; and man can always improve on nature once he gets the idea... I don't deny it, but I'll stick with the birds. It's life I believe in, not machines."

Having read Eiseley's moving account of the sparrow hawk, just days before my own similar experience with a hummingbird, guided my revelation. Eiseley framed his essay to answer the question: "Are we miracles or machines?" Let us close this essay with a similar question: "Do we have the free will to belong?" Machines may provide wonderful labor, and machines may even develop artificial forms of thought, but without the free will to belong a machine remains nothing more than a machine. Without the free will to belong to others, belong to a higher order or belong to our selves we, too, are nothing more than machines.

The same natural stage that contributed to my experiences with belonging also enlightened me to our moral attributes of humility, faith and courage. Unfortunately, for both theists and atheists alike these natural moral attributes have become eroded by culture, particularly by American culture. Without these moral attributes in abundance our cultural harmony and quality of life suffers, regardless of what pride we might take in our wealth and/or power status. Let us now explore some of the specifics of why Hans, despite his optimistic and patriotic beliefs, has run out of luck.

---

3 Eiseley's account is from the essay "The Bird and the Machine," in *The Immense Journey* (1959).

ESSAY 19 – VANITY AND FALSE PATRIOTISM

Hyla Brook
By June our brook's run out of song and speed.
Sought for much after that, it will be found
Either to have gone groping underground
(And taken with it all the Hyla breed
That shouted in the mist a month ago,
Like ghost of sleigh bells in a ghost of snow) –
Or flourished and come up in jewelweed,
Weak foliage that is blown upon and bent,
Even against the way its waters went.
Its bed is left a faded paper sheet
Of dead leaves stuck together by the heat –
A brook to none but who remembers long.
This as it will be seen is other far
Than with brooks taken otherwhere in song,
We love the things we love for what they are. (italics mine)
Robert Frost

Overview

- Patriotism and fanaticism have similarities.
- The support provided by patriots and fans can be either talk or action.
- True love of country targets the people and places of your belonging.
- False patriots vainly target successes and ideals that fuel their self-esteem.
- False patriotism leads to vigilante attacks on constructive criticisms.
- Vain patriotic greed prevents us from proportional giving to the world.
- Vain patriotic arrogance fuels our current global economic philosophy.
- Vain patriotic ignorance supports "great" things that really are not so great.
- The American Legion promotes the idolatrous false patriotism that focuses on lip service to ideals rather than the real service that comes from true love.
- Patriotic service as an expression of true love includes family devotion, community service, political involvement and economic productivity.

Sports Fans and Patriots

I am a passionate fan of the UConn men's and women's basketball teams. I go to a few basketball games each year, watch all other games on television and even record a few for posterity. As I type these words I am wearing my UConn sweatshirt, with a UConn clock above my desk and a UConn wastebasket underneath. I know all the words to the UConn fight song, which I exuberantly sing when the opportunity arises. If UConn were a country people would call my behavior patriotic. There are many similarities between the belonging of fans and patriots. Understanding sports fans in general provides an unbiased glimpse into our patriotism.

My sense of belonging to UConn resembles that of the patriot who loves the people and places of his country. UConn is the primary state university. I first became aware of UConn basketball in the Wes Bialosuknia/Toby Kimball era, when one of my brothers attended the university. UConn later became the first college I attended. Several of my nephews graduated from UConn, and my two oldest children now attend, both initially enrolled in the honors program. My oldest daughter was accepted early, which was fortunate considering this straight-A student and Merit Scholar ignored the advice of even her biased Dad and applied only to UConn.

Life is generally good if you are a UConn basketball fan. Duke may be the most heralded men's basketball team, and Tennessee the most heralded women's, but UConn currently has the upper hand with both of them come championship time. Because of UConn's success there are a number of bandwagon fans, people whose self-esteem and allegiance is wrapped up in backing a winner. I am the other type of fan. As an alumnus of the university I have followed UConn basketball closely even when we struggled just to win one game in the Big East tournament. Like Frost's Hyla Brook, I love the UConn teams I love for what they are: my own.

Passionate fans are junkies for information about their favorite sports teams. We crave to know more about the schedule, the players, scouting reports of players on other teams, evaluations of players being recruited for the future and in depth analyses about everything from the upcoming season to what went wrong with a single possession in a game. We could scour a bunch of newspapers and sports magazines for this information, but the passionate UConn fan inevitably finds his/her way to the Boneyard.

The Boneyard is a message board on the Internet where fans post their own thoughts and provide links to all information related to UConn basketball. I first posted on the Boneyard in the mid nineties, when the fledgling message board was run by the Hartford Courant and neither team had yet won their first championship. The Boneyard was transferred to private volunteers who kept the message board going through their labors of love. During this phase the Boneyard grew in popularity, inviting flamers to post and servers to crash. Time and resources necessitated that the Boneyard eventually go commercial, first as part of a sports network known as Rivals, then later as Scout.

People who post on message boards use pseudonyms known as handles. This maintains the anonymity typical of the Internet. Most visitors to message boards take the anonymity a step further and only read the boards without posting, a practice known as lurking. Since the time I began writing these essays I now only lurk on the Boneyard, reading what others have to say but refraining from providing a response.

I once encountered a post on the Boneyard that bridged the sports fan with the patriot. Let us refer to the poster as Teacher, inventing our own pseudonym to provide an extra degree of anonymity. The post described a classroom incident where students were reciting the Pledge of Allegiance. One student left out the bulk of the pledge in the middle to recite only the words: "I pledge ... liberty and justice for all." Here was the reaction of Teacher to the student's condensed version of the pledge.

> "If he starts it, he will finish it and properly. What he did was disrespectful to those of us who honor and value America ... and for those of us who had family in the military who fought and potentially died to give them the rights to be so inappropriate and rude."

You might first conclude from this that Teacher is a fervent patriot. Many people equate patriotism with defending the honor of their country. But this can be done with just talk, such as what we hear from politicians, pundits and news talk hosts. For that matter the Pledge can amount to nothing but talk, if there are no concrete actions to support the conviction being expressed. Precisely because "talk is cheap," many see the essence of patriotism as services rendered, with little relationship to cheap talk. In this essay we will contrast the patriotism of those who lip serve with those who really serve.

Ethnographic Study of Internet Fans

The allegiance of patriots stems from the sense of belonging that shapes our culture. Precisely because of the close connection between our belonging and patriotic allegiance, this runs the risk of being a sensitive, inflammatory topic. A brief, ethnographic study of fans on the Boneyard provides a less threatening entry point for characterizing the belongings of patriots.

Teacher not only had a low tolerance for students who omitted words from the Pledge, she bristled at any hint of criticism for the UConn women's basketball team, no matter the source. If other UConn fans appeared not to be sufficiently loyal about the team, Teacher sometimes chastised them with messages that had the same tone as the one about the Pledge. Teacher fits the profile of sports fans that I will call vigilantes. There are various types of fans that might draw the wrath of vigilantes.

Some fans are born pessimists; they see the glass half empty even when free refills are available. Some fans are analytical; in their quest to be insightful they include the negative. Some fans strive for balance; they think the gods will strike the message board down if other fans become too arrogant in their support of the team. Some fans are just plain mischievous. They know whose chain to yank to get a little excitement going on the message board; there is no chain quite as fun to yank as the vigilante. Most of the internal hostility that occurs on the Boneyard, or any other message board, stems from exchanges between vigilantes such as Teacher and one or more of these other types of fans.

There are two additional types of fans worth mentioning. Some fans think that free refills for their drink are coming even after the establishment has closed and locked their doors for the night. These optimists might draw some criticism from those fed up with their rosy scenarios, but they are too positive-minded to return the hostility. One Boneyard regular predicted that the UConn women's team would go 195-0 over five years. A few fans challenged him on this rather forcefully (and the prediction did not come true), but his nastiest response was: "you are entitled to your opinion."

The most important fans on message boards are the moderators. The official moderators establish the rules to be followed. Critiquing the performance of players is fine; critiquing their character will get your post deleted. Bringing negative material over from an opponent's message board is discouraged. Topics that fans start obsessing over will get their message threads locked. There are unofficial moderators as well; fans who attempt to moderate discussion not so much to appease the mojo gods but to promote civility.

Moderators receive less criticism than the other types of fans, even less than the eternal optimists. Most fans appreciate the time and efforts spent by moderators and are grateful for the moderation. Moderators occasionally receive criticism for censorship, and this criticism might come from any of the other types of fans except for the eternal optimists. No one has to pay to use most message boards, and since volunteers are responsible in large part for the Boneyard's success, the criticisms directed at moderators do not gain much support from others.

While fans are to some extent the same all over, the basketball programs they follow differ. What is going on with their favorite basketball team dictates the overall tone of the board, whether of optimism or pessimism, moderation or extremism. The two UConn basketball programs went through synchronous periods of ascendancy, domination and slight decline that were reflected in changes of tone on the Boneyard.

The period of ascendancy for both basketball programs was the decade of the 90s. The women's team won its first championship in 1995, but the basketball program was still considered second best to Tennessee. During this time the Boneyard was created and dominated by long time fans buoyed by the positive direction of both teams. The early years of the Boneyard featured the best written posts in terms of wit, creativity and overall positive outlook. RabidHusky, BadDog and Fishy were the most distinguished posters in this regard. Many fans from other programs, such as the Kansas fan beakumhawks, visited on a regular basis to join in the playful banter. Almost all the hostilities that occurred were between UConn fans and the fans from other programs that posted on the message board to "trash talk."

The period of dominance for UConn basketball ran from 1999-2004. The men's team won championships both in 1999 and 2004. The women's team recruited their best ever freshman class for the 1998-1999 season, and they capped the 2004 season with their third straight championship. During that time many new fans arrived at the Boneyard, drawn by the successes of the teams. Many of these newcomers were bandwagon fans; fans that are attracted to a team mainly because of success rather than regional loyalty. The Boneyard grew less creative and witty. Perhaps some of the original contributors grew tired of being creative, while others did not like the change in tone on the message board. The Boneyard was nevertheless an entertaining forum, as the period of basketball dominance ushered in an era of insightful analysis. Analytical posters like zymurg and nyhuskyfan gained in popularity. A fair analysis usually involves some criticism, but if your team is always on top the amount of criticism for the occasional bad play or bad game still amounts to tolerable reading even for vigilantes. Internal hostilities started to grow, however, as some posters either unintentionally or deliberately elevated their "analytical" criticism to a level that bordered on inflammatory.

After 2004 a slight but immediate decline affected both programs. The term decline must be viewed relatively, because bandwagon fans from the state would still find UConn a more rewarding team to back than Quinnipiac or Fairfield. Internal hostilities increased to the point where battles were engaged not only over analytical criticisms of the team, but over provocative criticisms of coaches, media, players, fans and other Boneyarders. Much of the provocation came from fans that arrived at the Boneyard during the dominant era of UConn basketball, and not the old guard who posted during the nineties.

Throughout these periods of ascendancy, dominance and decline the missions of the vigilantes and moderators remained constant. They serve as the yin and the yang to fan activity; one always battling the external, analytical and/ or provocative critics; the other always keeping the battle under control. One continually defends their team's honor through their words; the other serves their favorite team by maintaining a useful forum for all fans. On some message boards moderators may actually be vigilantes in disguise, but not on the Boneyard. My personal thanks goes to Fishy, temery, HuskyNan, JS111 and biffster for their labors over the years.

In doing this ethnographic study I had to identify and distill my own biases in support of UConn basketball. This is not an easy thing to do. Something of striking consistency on all message boards are the complaints about the fans on other message boards. In the eyes of many fans, certainly in the eyes of vigilantes, the charge of fanaticism applies only to the supporters of other teams. Let us keep this in mind as we transfer our knowledge about the belonging of sports fans to patriots.

False Patriotism

The definition of patriotism arose with the creation of nation states and nationalism. People started to identify themselves more with their country than with their local village. Yet patriotism still is rooted in a sense of belonging. In a village your sense of belonging is directly to the people and place of that village. Belonging to a country occurs at a more abstract level of shared experience. The particular object of this belonging determines the type of patriotism found in a nation.

The message from Robert Frost's Hyla Brook identifies one object of our belonging: "We love the things we love for what they are." As an intermittent stream Hyla Brook was no great natural feature, yet Frost loved this stream simply because of geographic proximity. This is the same sense of belonging that we develop for kinship or communal proximity as well. When "we love the things we love for what they are," we develop a belonging for those people, places and things we share our life with directly on a daily basis, regardless of their particular attributes. Harmony ultimately depends on loving things for "what they are."

Americans share common economic, political and cultural systems. Most of us share a common history of migration to this country. Our belonging could be to either these abstract systems or the diverse people and places, known and unknown, with which we share these experiences. If our allegiance is to people and places, our patriotism expresses the sense of belonging found in the local village applied to a national scale. This is patriotism that loves things for "what they are," increasing harmony and our quality of life.

In contrast to loving things for "what they are," a different kind of patriotism cherishes the successes and ideals of a country that enhances personal self-esteem. This type of patriotism is driven by vanity that forsakes the belonging to people and places. By misdirecting belonging to the symbolic idolatry of beliefs, rather than to real people and places, this type of patriotism is less likely to condone differences in beliefs and behaviors. Loving things for ones personal self-esteem threatens multicultural harmony and the overall quality of life.

Politicians and certain special interest groups promote this symbolic idolatry by praising soldiers for defending our greatness as a nation. If we are to believe seriously that this motivates our soldiers we hover on a precipice. What if soldiers vainly idolize our compassion? Do vain soldiers falter in battle after finding out that we have one of the highest infant mortalities rates of developed countries, while many go uninsured in order for a few to benefit? What if soldiers vainly idolize our participatory democracy? Do vain soldiers lay down their arms when they learn that our leaders withheld and altered important information from citizens about going to war? What if soldiers vainly idolize our market economy? Do vain soldiers go AWOL if they discover that our laborers work longer hours and go into greater debt than European counterparts?

We better pray that our soldiers are motivated by loving things for "what they are" rather than the "ideals they represent." We should hope that our soldiers fight for tangible targets of belonging, the land and the people they love, rather than for intangible and idolatrous beliefs in greatness. We should wish that our soldiers wish to serve others because of their humility, rather than for pride in their own self-esteem or in backing a winner. Recall world historian Toynbee's model (Essay 18) that civilizations go through periods of ascendancy and decline similar to sports programs. There may be "sinister piffle" folks out there urgently wishing to bring about the "End of History," but the overwhelming historical evidence weighs in against them. If idolatry, greatness and self-esteem be all we fight for, at some point in history we will be forced to surrender our homeland.

Vigilante politicians and special interest groups rhetorically appeal to the vanity of citizens. They inform us that we need to defend our honor, implying that honor makes a difference for what used to be a natural willingness to sacrifice for others. They demand lip service and idolatry as an expression of patriotism, with the intent that we blindly give allegiance to certain beliefs, rather than open our eyes to how we may best serve each other in a land of diverse cultures. Through this rhetoric vigilante politicians and pundits cultivate citizens that idolize beliefs more than they love their fellow countrymen. False patriotism is this subordination of genuine patriotic love of people and places, the love of things for "what they are," to the vain admiration for ideals and greatness.

False patriotism is like the misguided son of a functioning alcoholic. The son grows up idolizing his father as a good breadwinner, successful businessman and loving father. Only when the son comes of age does he realize his father is an alcoholic. What does he do? If he gets help for his father he is a loving son doing the right thing. If he ignores or covers up his father's problem, he displays the same vanity as false patriotism.

Vigilante Patriotism
False patriots also are analogous to the bandwagon fans of sports programs. When

the team is on top the bandwagon fan provides demonstrative support; in a sense, they are cheering on their own self-esteem. However, for this same reason problems with the team are assaults on their egos. One strategy to preserve their egos and self-esteem is to deny that problems exist and become a vigilante. Vigilante false patriots provide the same "service" as the vigilante fan; they ward off all criticism, even the constructive criticisms born out of true love rather than vain idolatry.

A common mantra from vigilante patriots past and present is: "We are the greatest nation on earth." This begs the question of what makes a country great. Some false patriots in this country take vain pride in being the wealthiest and/ or most powerful nation on earth. Others are vain about our status as the most prominent Christian nation. Merged together, these vanities create a dilemma for the vigilante patriot who wishes to champion our foreign policies.

One of the creeds of Christianity is that: "The first shall be last." Christ served all; hence, our lives should have the same altruistic focus. Providing service to others does not reconcile with aspirations to be the wealthiest or most powerful. This is at the heart of why we never hear the word "oil" when the administration presents information on Iraq. If we wish parents to send their children off to serve in battle, we do not want them to dwell on the empirical evidence and inductive logic that invading Iraq obliges a desire to remain the wealthiest and most powerful nation. Basking in greatness and humbly serving are mutually exclusive goals, unless a country aspires to be the greatest servant.

One possible angle for our country becoming the greatest servant would have been to take the lead role in promoting harmony between diverse cultures across the globe. After all, what nation has more experience at blending diverse cultures than the "melting pot" of the world? Yet actually getting along in harmony with diverse cultures has proven difficult for us to do. We could not get along with the Native American, though we solved that "problem" by putting them on reservations. We could not get along with freed slaves, though we temporarily solved that "problem" with Jim Crow laws and other forms of institutionalized discrimination. Currently, getting along with immigrants has proven difficult, though we propose solving that "problem" by building a great wall. If even our domestic policies fail at achieving harmony, we cannot succeed with this as our mission for becoming the greatest servant abroad.

But being the greatest servant is not really what the vigilante patriot has in mind when they refute any suggestion that we may not be the greatest nation on earth, or even any criticism about being preoccupied with greatness. The type of greatness the vigilante patriot seeks is the greatness that will stroke their vanity, enhance their self-esteem. Achieving cultural harmony holds no importance for them.

When harmony fails idolatry is to blame. The vanities of false patriots seek an idolatrous approach for merging ambitions of greatness with obligations of service. The solution is to "serve" our "great" beliefs and behaviors to the rest of the world in a globalization process. As is always the case with idolatry and dogma, our vain endeavors have had harmful consequences to the quality of life among different cultures and have hindered the advancement of civilization. This has been particularly true in regards to our economic beliefs and behaviors.

Vain Greed

Through the collective generosity of government, corporations and private individuals our country has provided enormous amounts of economic aid to the world. False patriots take vain comfort in the amounts of aid we provide, as this directly supports their conviction that due to our greatness we provide the best global service. They also gain vain pleasure from our role in economic globalization. We are the leader in capitalism, allegedly providing the best guidance for market economies of all nations because of our position on top. When former Secretary of State Colin Powell stated that "We are the most generous nation on the face of the Earth" on ABC's Nightline (12/30/04), he merely echoed the vain pride false patriots have held for decades. We should take notice, however, that Powell made this statement in response to criticisms of our foreign aid policies, prompted by the tsunami that hit Asia on December 26, 2004. Powell's next statement reveals the context for these criticisms: "Now, if you measure it as a percentage of GDP, you can make the case that we're not as high as others."

The "case that we're not as high as others" can be made quite convincingly in a comparison with other developed countries that form the Development Assistance Committee of the Organization for Economic Cooperation and Development. Out of twenty-two nations the United States ranked third to last in 2005, just ahead of Portugal and Greece, providing 0.22% of our Gross National Income for official development assistance.[1] This is actually an improvement over the previous year, when we provided 0.16% of GNI and ranked second to last ahead of Italy. Other countries may come and go, but we are a proud fixture near the bottom of proportional giving. The "jump" from 2004 to 2005 occurred in large measure due to our response to the 2004 tsunami, after the administration had been placed on the hot seat of world and national opinions.

The criticisms served their purpose of stimulating increased giving, but corporate media did not respond kindly to such unpatriotic complaints. Pundits were invited on to the corporate media echo chambers to explain how a country that has increased in wealth as much as ours should not be held to a standard of proportional giving.[2] In other words, the very greatness of our economic system exempts us from proportional giving; we should focus on the greatness of the total

---

1 OECD provides these statistics for 2005 at http://www.oecd.org/dataoecd/52/18/37790990.pdf.
2 "The World's Most Generous Misers," (2005), by Ben Somberg, discusses the media coverage of our generosity.

amount of giving instead. This may be well and good for our fragile self-esteem, but many false patriots cognizant of the Christian creed that "the first shall be last" seem to be unaware of the Christian corollary that much is expected from those to whom much has been given.

Corporate media, politicians and special interest groups have succeeded in fueling the vanities of false patriots, as evidenced in our false perceptions. A survey done by the Washington Post, Harvard University and the Kaiser Foundation in March 1997 asked respondents what was the largest federal expenditure. Sixty-four percent cited foreign aid in response. A survey done by the Program on International Policy Attitudes in March 2005 revealed that respondents thought 20% of the federal budget goes to federal aid. When informed that the actual figure was 1.6%, respondents subsequently refused to believe that was the full amount.

Vain Arrogance

The vain conceit that false patriots have in our generosity aligns with a faith, perhaps unwitting, in trickle down economics. The pride in giving large total amounts rather than large proportional amounts must be premised on your nation having so much more wealth to begin with. Having much greater amounts of wealth must be accomplished through a global economic system that allows for great wealth disparity. If other nations made as much as we did, and gave a higher proportion of their wealth, we could hardly consider ourselves generous. Without first concentrating large amounts of wealth in our control, the trickle-down amounts we provide in "generous" aid would give no cause for vain patriotic pride.

The vain false patriot feels that developing countries should duly note and appreciate our generosity. This reveals another false perception that our trickle down approach to aid represents the best solution to inherent problems with economic globalization. Hearken back to Essay 6, where we explored the fallacy behind the economic principle of comparative advantage. I used the manager's secretary as a metaphor then and will continue with that now. The corporation is best served by the manager sticking to managerial tasks and the secretary doing secretarial tasks, the metaphoric essence of what comparative advantage in global economics is all about. Yet that is not the best scenario for the secretary. Even if the corporation included a lucrative Christmas bonus for the secretary, a better option would be a training program through which the secretary can become a future manager. We are contrasting the proverbial gift of a fish versus the gift of teaching to fish.

We can leave the economic development of third world countries to multinational corporations because they will do the various tasks more efficiently. In that case lots of capital becomes concentrated for the sake of shareholders who live outside the developing countries. Whatever problems this concentration of wealth creates can be resolved through a trickle down "Christmas bonus" of foreign aid. What a cozy arrangement! On the other hand we could assist with the development of local corporations whose obligations and profits are concentrated within the country being helped. That is a less efficient solution no doubt, and provides less profits or vain comfort for this country, but we just might find that our generosity becomes as well regarded abroad as by our own false patriots.

What gets in the way of such a sensible solution is our vain arrogance. We know best. We can do it best. If American stakeholders can get rich in the process, while never setting foot in an impoverished country or contributing to the labor, all the better! Let multinational corporations, modeled after the American business corporation, save the day and exact their price. This is just more western colonialism under a different guise, continuing the same exploitation and filtering of resources away from developing countries that has occurred for centuries. But, hey, let's vainly feel good about the foreign aid (Christmas bonus) we send to these poor folks, fancying ourselves to be extremely generous, even as we refuse to give proportionally from the wealth we have managed to gain from those we exploit.

Vain Ignorance

The greatest travesty lies not in our miserly approach to giving, or even in our trickle down approach to global economics, but in the ignorance of our vanity. People make mistakes; governments make mistakes; corporations make mistakes. Our approach to assisting Latin American governments in the seventies was no doubt well-intentioned and well thought out, but things did not work out as planned. Some countries became bankrupt, some countries became brutal, some became both. The mistakes have been acknowledged, but our approach essentially has not changed. Vanity will do that. We still look to multinational corporations as the shining knights to globalization because for the most part they are American shining knights. The blinders of vanity prohibit a homeostatic evaluation, adjustment and enhancement of the economic services we provide others.

The blinders of vanity lead to forms of hero worship. The creation of the Bill and Melinda Gates Foundation was a feel good story. A multinational business tycoon provides the granddaddy of all Christmas bonuses, both for home and abroad. But let us remove our blinders for what this charitable foundation reveals about greed-driven capitalism. The seed money for the foundation came through the redistribution of a whole lot of capital gained through the near monopolization of an industry, with practices that only can occur through the support or tolerance of government, to the detriment of pure entrepreneurial merit.

This near monopolization did not benefit the consumer. The Linux operating system performs as well without the added costs of Microsoft systems. The near monopolization certainly did not benefit other countries. The biggest key to success was not technological innovation but extorting the political/economic system, and the main beneficiaries were Microsoft shareholders. Thus, the initial generosity was made possible only through exploitation enabled by an economic system backed by government. No doubt we are better off with tycoons like Bill Gates rather than Jack Welch, but let us not mistake tycoon Bill for entrepreneurs like Ben Franklin, or even Henry Ford.

The Gates Foundation distributes 5% of their worth to good causes; the other 95% is invested to keep the endowments growing.[3] The foundation has come under fire for the quality of these investments. While the much smaller pot of money has been used for programs to immunize against polio and measles, the much larger pot has been used for investments that include oil corporations like Eni. Eni is an Italian-based oil corporation with operations in Nigeria. Their pollution of the Nigerian environment includes 250 toxic chemicals with links to respiratory disease and cancer, health problems that ironically negate the good work of immunization. As reported in the LA Times: "The Times found that the Gates Foundation has holdings in many companies that have failed tests of social responsibility because of environmental lapses, employment discrimination, disregard for worker rights, or unethical practices."

Bill Gates created his foundation with good intentions, but the vanity he holds for his objectives prevent him from amassing wealth through open competition or from investing only in ethical corporations. As intelligent a person as he no doubt is, he appears to remain vainly and blissfully ignorant regarding the overall impact of his "charity." Corporate media and vain patriots fall into the same ignorance, idolizing "great deeds" that is fueled by investment into great harm. The ends justify the means when you are vain, whether a vain tycoon, politician, special interest group, vigilante sports fan or false patriot.

Idolatry and Lip Service

Patriotism implies a willingness to serve the country you love. Talk is cheap, and to serve your country by idolizing "honor" or "greatness" requires no greater effort than posting on a message board. Let us return to that post by Teacher about the student that pledged allegiance only to "liberty and justice for all." We obviously know little about this student. Perhaps he is a nutcase whose view of liberating is similar to the students who assaulted Columbine High School. On the other hand he may have a low tolerance for symbolic idolatry and prefers to pledge only to the tangible ways of serving his country. We know nothing beyond his words, and though his words refuse to pay lip service, his redacted version of the Pledge still hold out the potential for real service.

---

3 The details of the Gates Foundation's charitable giving and investments were obtained from "Dark cloud over good works of Gates Foundation" (January 7, 2007) an LA Times investigative report written by Charles Piller, Edmund Sanders and Robyn Dixon.

Ironically, Teacher's post provides greater detail about her own shortcomings with real service. We know from her stance on the Pledge that Teacher, like a good vigilante, pays full lip service to the country she loves. Unfortunately, she may not be willing to truly serve the cause of liberty, since her one recorded action consists of constraining the liberty of someone who was not doing harm to society.

We should not ostracize Teacher for being a vigilante, any more than vigilantes should ostracize people who do not pay lip service. When we reflect on someone's patriotism we should be willing to consider the whole body of allegiance. The American Legion, the largest service organization for veterans, offers their vision for what this whole body of allegiance entails. Their "four pillars of service" are: A Strong National Security; Taking Care of Veterans; Mentoring Youth; and Promoting Patriotism and Honor.[4]

The four pillars could have been borrowed from the city state of Sparta. Real service is for veterans (Spartans), while everyone else only needs to engage in certain types of lip service and symbolic idolatry. Their description of these four pillars makes plain that the American Legion intends to be more than a support group targeting only veterans. By advocating beliefs and behaviors for the entire country, such as with their Flag Amendment initiative, the American Legion is the stereotypical special interest group. Supporting veterans takes up a mere one quarter of their attention, if that much.

Veterans are special. Perhaps they are even more special than they should be, given the encouragement by politicians and special interest groups like the American Legion that anyone not a soldier should be cowardly preoccupied with security, but that is not their fault. They deserve a support group that focuses only on their needs, such as medical care and education, but that is not what they get with the American Legion. The Legion diverts attention and resources away from the core issues that can improve the lives of veterans to a broader cultural agenda. There is a difference between veterans, citizens who truly served, and the American Legion, a big time special interest group that wants lip service from all citizens.

The American Legion occasionally chooses to battle other special interest groups. One of their chosen foes was the ACLU. In the publication "In the Footsteps of the Founders: A Guide to Defending American Values," the ACLU was singled out as the prominent antagonist to the American Legion's mission. The irony of this is that in regards to another special interest issue, protecting money as an expression of free speech, the American Legion would hop into bed with the ACLU quicker than you could salute the flag. Large special interest groups like the American Legion and ACLU love the disproportionate influence and wealth that the "money as free speech" interpretation by the Supreme Court nurtures.

No doubt that Teacher would be considered a patriot in good standing

---

4 From the American Legion website: www.legion.org.

by the American Legion, but there are two troublesome aspects of their vision. First, unless we become a total military state like Sparta, not all citizens in this country can provide the type of active service the Legion idolizes most. This makes the American Legion a special interest group that politicians can embrace with gusto. Once again, politicians looking to manipulate support from citizens love to promote the valor of soldiers while encouraging the rest of us to quiver like cowards for our national security. For cynical politicians a big time special interest group like the American Legion is a critical partner.

The second flaw with the Legion's vision is that even for the Spartans/ veterans the service of a patriot is geared more to loving the country for the "ideals they represent" rather than loving the people and places of this country for "what they are." Missing from their four pillars of service is a humility that acknowledges the pluralism and diversity that distinguishes the United States as an advanced civilization. Such humility provides the impetus for meaningful service that will improve harmony and the quality of our lives. Such humility allows a loving son to acknowledge and help an alcoholic father, or a loving citizen to acknowledge and address the flaws of a wayward nation. Let us turn to the veteran Hans for an example of why real service surpasses the lip service wielded by politicians and special interest groups.

Harmony and Active Service

Let us establish our own "four pillars of service" that is a little more demanding— and less demeaning—than what the American Legion recommends for the average citizen. A true patriot not enslaved by vanity should provide service to the land and people he loves through: Political Involvement, Community Service, Economic Productivity, and Family Devotion. Granted, this is greater service than the American Legion advocates even for veterans, but the flip side of demanding this active service would be relaxing the requirements for lip service and symbolic idolatry. Hans the veteran demonstrates how each of these four pillars work.

In the military Hans encountered people of diverse backgrounds, bound together in their active service. Hans recognized the virtues in the various special interests of Democrats or Republicans, conservatives or liberals, as expressed by the diverse soldiers who served in his unit. Once Hans left the military he decided on two things. He did not join a political party, refusing to engage in the power politics that idolizes their own platforms at the expense of denigrating all other interests. Hans remained politically involved by contributing to local government and independently seeking out different political viewpoints from the diverse people that he loves.

Hans cherished the bonds that developed among soldiers in the military. Many soldiers follow this up by joining the American Legion, but Hans declined to join for the same reason he would not join the Democratic or Republican parties: he would not idolize special interests at the expense of harmony. In addition he was a little miffed that the Legion did not devote their vast resources solely to being a much needed support group for veterans. At one time the American Legion was part of the solution to veteran's benefits like the GI Bill. Since then the American Legion's diverted attention to special interests became part of the problem for why those benefits eroded over time. Hans noted that the three hot special interests for the American Legion were stopping illegal immigration, proper flag protocol and public expression of religion. Taken in isolation, Hans felt that each of these issues had merit, but none of them espoused the virtues of community service, or provided much tangible support to veterans.

The American Legion did advocate outreach "service" to the community, particularly in regard to their platform for the public expression of religion; and the mentoring to youth. The intent of this outreach was not to achieve any harmonic resolution of diverse interests that might differ for each unique community. The American Legion advocated the same tools and objectives that corporate media uses to generate a herd mentality in idolatry of specific dogma. Hans still carried a passion to serve the land and the people he loved and he concluded that the community, not a special interest group like the ACLU or American Legion, was the best outlet for this passion.

Hans works in manufacturing, thus contributing to our country's economic strength and productivity. This alone makes Hans more of an ideal patriot than those involved in investment markets where capital serves capital, contributing only to individual greed and not the country's productive merit. Hans relies on savings in the bank and government bonds, rather than a lucrative retirement account, to prepare him for the future. He does this not because the Dutch and the British empires started to decline when too much of their economy was wrapped up in financial markets. He does this not because pensions and health care plans trap laborers into working longer hours and longer years for the same corporation. He does this not because high yield investments must sometimes be backed by the feds increasing money flow and concentrating capital for the benefit of financial institutions. While all these factors might be reasons for a true patriot to rely on savings rather than retirement accounts Hans has another reason, related specifically to his sense of belonging. He has an uncomfortable feeling that any investments providing high rates of returns, including some retirement plans, ultimately might be living off the backs of this country's children. The true patriot has a sense of belonging to future generations as well as his own.

Hans works twenty-five hours a week, his wife fifteen hours, during the precious formative years of his family. Neither has a pension due to their part time status, but the tradeoff for quantity time with their children made this an easy decision. Hans conceded there were certain advantages to only quality time spent with children, such as earning more money, but there was one major drawback. The only way to convey the message of family devotion is through quantity time. If Hans was unwilling to send this message to his kids, how would they in turn raise his future grandchildren? Hans no more wished to short future generations on family devotion than with money.

Hans resembles the moderators of the Boneyard message board, offering to community and family his labor of love. He quietly serves without much cheap talk. He does not gain the attention of a vigilante politician or special interest group, and he does not require wealth or power be funneled to him as a condition for his service. Nevertheless, he has the respect of his community and family at a level that no vigilante politician or special interest group can match.

Unfortunately, our country makes things difficult for the true patriot like Hans to exist. Unless we spend time in the military we are encouraged to merely pay lip service through the Pledge and symbolic flag-waving, instead of provide any type of true service as a condition of citizenship. We expect our country to indulge us in tax breaks even in a time of war. Political parties encourage us to vote, preferably by pulling the party lever, but they discourage us to independently become informed through exploring different points of view. Corporate media bombards us with their spin on the issues, which can be diverse only as long as corporate interests are not threatened. Our government enables interest groups to offer us perks, such as tax deductions, which cannot be matched by involvement in our communities. The effective result is that government commands an advantage to special interest groups over local communities, a cultural socialism if you will.

While Hans has no misgivings about the lost pension, missing out on a health care plan is a bigger deal. Hans occasionally enlists in a private plan, but plans change as health care continues to escalate and this true patriot, willing to devote his labor for community service and quantity family time, must go through periods without health care. Hans also has to rent an apartment rather than buy a house; a penalty for believing that economic productivity should not be the only service of a patriot. Finally, when his kids are ready for college Hans will find he is in a predicament. Unlike the sixties, when the economic system enabled the middle class to provide for both college and retirement through their own savings, supplemented in part by government programs, Hans must make a choice with his savings. Hans must either sink his retirement savings into his children's education, or allow his children to finish college mired in debt from the start.

These are the types of choices brought to bear on the true patriots who love this land and people so much they feel compelled to go beyond economic productivity, lip service and symbolism in support of their country. Too bad the American Legion's vision does not focus on this type of true patriotism, but you can expect no more from a special interest group.

The Local Hyla Brook

We have our own Hyla Brook, as described in the Frost poem, here on Emerson Street. At the corner of Emerson Street a small stream funnels into a culvert and disappears under a five-way intersection of roads. For most of the year the stream becomes an intermittent trickle. When my kids were small I would take them for a grand adventure down the culvert to the other side of the intersection; they could walk for most of the distance while I crouched and slithered. When they got a little older we went on trips upstream the short distance to where the stream went under Maple Avenue, picking up trash we found along the way. On a summer afternoon with open windows or while working in the yard I could here my kids over by the stream coming up with their own adventures, just as I did when I was young here on Emerson Street.

One other home lies between ours and the small stream at the corner. One former neighbor that lived there would never have been a candidate for the best home or garden award. He habitually started projects without finishing them. The next homeowner that moved in needed a truck to haul away the Budweiser cans that filled half the basement. In many respects not worth mentioning we were different from each other in our beliefs and behaviors. Yet every year this neighbor would go down to where the trickle of a stream entered the culvert and planted flowers with loving care.

As a long-distance backpacker I have seen spectacular bodies of water across this scenic land. While backpacking the Pacific Crest Trail the Columbia River inspired with majesty; Burney Falls inspired with wonder; Crater Lake inspired with beauty. Yet none of those scenic attractions, in all their greatness, inspires in me the love I have for that little stream down by the corner; the type of love that caused my neighbor to plant flowers each year; the type of love that fosters a communal sense of belonging among those who would care for a neighborhood stream.

Perhaps you think that a communal sense of belonging, nurtured by daily attachments to people and place, cannot be achieved at a national scale. If attachments across diverse cultures and advanced levels of federation cannot be achieved, then harmony is a pipe dream. A false patriotism based on vanity and idolatry of uniform beliefs and behaviors is the best that we can do.

Certainly, a false patriotism will be the best that we can do if that is all we think is possible. We need faith to aspire to true service and a greater sense of belonging than what vigilante politicians and special interest groups would have ordinary citizens achieve through our symbolic idolatry. The next essay turns to the matter of faith or, more precisely, the lack of faith and the problem of cynicism, particularly among those who would claim to be faithful evangelists.

ESSAY 20 – CYNICAL FALSE EVANGELISTS

"Let go of anger.
Let go of pride.
When you are bound by nothing
You go beyond sorrow.
Anger is like a chariot careering wildly.
He who curbs his anger is the true charioteer.
Others merely hold the reins.
With gentleness overcome anger.
With generosity overcome meanness.
With truth overcome deceit.
Speak the truth.
Give whenever you can,
Never be angry.
These three steps will lead you
Into the presence of the gods.
The wise harm no one.
They are masters of their bodies
And they go to the boundless country.
They go beyond sorrow."
- From the Buddhist *Dhammapada*

Overview

- Impending apocalypses misrepresent the essence of faith.
- Faith in a higher order fits into one of four main categories from a Christian viewpoint: atheist, agnostic, empirical, and fundamental.
- False evangelism spreads the good news of faith with bad intent and bad effect.
- Empirical faith experiences the peace, love and joy of a higher order.
- Fundamental faith promotes infallible beliefs over spiritual experiences.
- Triangulation of different faith experiences overcomes the relativism of "infallible beliefs" constructed from only one source.
- The three moral norms for social character are humility, faith and courage.
- The three moral norms for social systems are merit, wisdom and harmony.
- The threefold agenda of false evangelists features materialism, integration

of Church and State, and global exploitation.
- Beliefs in predestination and angry behavior distinguish cynical evangelism.
- Idolatry of infallible beliefs, not intolerance of immoral behavior, corrupts our belonging.
- Scholasticism threatens our empirical belonging and cultural quality of life.
- Our own free will, not predestination from God, gets in the way of our belonging.

Apocalyptic Evangelism

Unlike many people, I actually look forward to a Jehovah's Witness bringing their Watchtower publication to my door. The Jehovah's Witnesses are fairly humble people; they are not televangelists wishing to accumulate wealth, and I admit to having a little fun at their expense. The Watchtower prepares people for the second coming of Christ. I have read through the whole Bible twice, not to mention some additional study guides. I am bad at memorizing verses of greater length than "Jesus wept," (John 11:36) but I do well at grasping concepts. There is something cynical about Christians who evangelize about the Apocalypse and the second coming of Christ, almost as cynical as Christians promoting materialism. Uncovering this cynicism is the purpose of this essay.

Standing on my doorstep, speaking to someone with humility, I refrain from charges of cynicism. Before a Witness gets too far along I ask: "What difference does the second coming make? Is it not the first coming that matters to being a Christian?" This question alone generally causes a Jehovah's Witness to reflect, though I may need to throw in the simple observation that there have been at least a hundred generations of Christians up until now. Are we the only generation that, through preparation for the second coming, can get our faith right?

Since the Jehovah's Witnesses are humble people not out to take your money, the conversation generally needs to go not much further than that. They come to your door for your sake (in their eyes), and they are willing to at least respect your contrary view if you have a good grasp of the matter. I sincerely doubt that one could have the same type of conversation with televangelists, not that I would want to come near one. These people make lots of money with what they are selling; they will not abandon their cash cow just to get the meaning of their faith right. Hence, their apocalyptic-tinged messages not only suffer from a false premise, but through false intentions as well. Considering the growing influence of this type of evangelist, their cynicism represents a real danger to both Christianity and our civilization.

A Christian Typology

Religion consists of cultural beliefs and behaviors focused on a higher order. This system of beliefs and behaviors can be divided into matters of salvation, civility and conscience. Matters of salvation strengthen our sense of belonging to a higher order. Matters of civility strengthen our sense of belonging to each other. Matters of conscience strengthen our sense of belonging to ourselves. Christianity qualifies as an advanced religion because the requirements for salvation, civility and conscience could be integrated with different cultural systems of beliefs and behaviors. Thus a Jewish prophet founded a system of beliefs and behaviors for belonging to a higher order that was championed by Gentiles, and now has at least an identifiable presence in every civilization.

In this country our faith in relation to a higher order, after filtering through a Christian lens, takes one of four forms. Atheists have faith that no higher order exists and that Christianity does more harm than good. Agnostics doubt that a higher order exists but they have been indoctrinated into a cultural system of right and wrong based on the life and teachings of Jesus. Empirical Christians have faith in a higher order through personally experiencing a sense of belonging and through the experiences of Christ as recorded in the Gospels. Fundamental Christians have faith in a higher order due to an infallible belief system constructed from the Bible.

For the empirical Christian the second coming of Christ is irrelevant to their beliefs and behaviors. The belonging to a higher order that they empirically sense in the here and now sustains their faith and their religion. Each moment in time is an end within itself, with the end always being the felt-presence of Christ in their lives. The attributes of humility, faith and courage that enhance the sense of belonging are important ingredients for each moment. This means that empirical Christians, despite the immediacy of each moment of cherished belonging, must have the patience not to abandon these natural attributes: "they are those who, hearing the word, hold it fast in an honest and good heart, and bring forth fruit with patience." (Luke 8:15).

In contrast, the fundamentalist Christians that believe in the Apocalypse have some urgency. If not urgent in what they really feel or think, they are at least urgent in the system of beliefs and behaviors they wish to impose in time for the second coming. An urgent heart, as discussed in Essay 18, tends to produce both uncivil and unnecessary outcomes. Let me editorialize that I do not believe this to be true for most fundamentalist Christians, but for an important subset that will be the focus of discussion.

Urgency creates doubt as to whether one's own humility, faith and courage can suffice for the matter of salvation at hand. Urgent people get angry at the world when the beliefs and behaviors of others seem to jeopardize the destiny they seek. Urgent people wish to impose their will, rather than leave to chance the outcomes of free will. The combination of vanity, cynicism or apprehension used to manipulate others undermines the very sense of belonging Christians should wish to nurture.

Both empirical and fundamentalist Christians are called to be witnesses to their faith, i.e., to evangelize. An evangelist brings good news for good effect. For Christians the Gospels that document the experiences of Christ are the good news, and the good effect is establishing a fellowship in Christ. A false evangelist brings allegedly good news in a manner that produces bad effects. Some fundamentalist Christians evangelize to bad effect when they encourage converts to idolize beliefs about the Apocalypse and the second coming, at the expense of experiencing a belonging to Christ in the present.

Cynicism compromises faith intentionally. The cynical false evangelist intends for a belief system, not the experience of Christ, to be the focus of converts. In fact, having a personal sense of belonging to Christ interferes with the belief system, if increased patience detracts from the urgency that the cynical wishes to foster. The bad effects of the cynical false evangelist are to erode the humility, faith and courage which could enhance the sense of belonging of their converts to Christ, and instead fill them with urgency for the idolatry of particular beliefs and behaviors. Perhaps only a few fundamentalist Christians, such as televangelists, should be stereotyped in this manner. But only fundamentalist Christians are capable of becoming cynical false evangelists. For an understanding of this, let us contrast the journeys of two Christian converts.

Christian Journeys

Hans began his Christian journey by experiencing an epiphany. While watching a beautiful sunset from the top of a cliff in the wilderness he became filled with the sense and wonder of belonging to a higher order. His new faith in this higher order filled him with appreciation for being a humble part of this order and with new courage and conviction for how to proceed with his life. Peace, love and joy were the dominant emotions Hans sensed during this epiphany.

Culture provides the context and meaning for our experiences. Having lived in a Christian culture this was the context for how Hans built meaning around what he sensed. He had heard about the Prince of Peace, who came from the God of Love, filling believers with a Spirit of Joy. This all fit perfectly with the belonging and emotions Hans experienced. He decided to join a Church whose members emulated the sense of belonging for each other and for the higher order that Hans felt. Hans started to read the Bible to gather deeper meaning for his faith.

Had Hans turned to the Hebrew Testament first after his epiphany, without already knowing about Christ or Christian culture, he might have abandoned the text before reaching the Gospels. The Bible, taken literally as a whole, can be a wilderness of confusion, even after treating some of the passages as allegorical. There are snippets of the peace, love and joy Hans associated with his new found sense of belonging; but there are also liberal doses of violence and vengeance at the hands of an angry God. Fortunately, Hans knew about Christ before reading the Bible, and he focused his attention on the Gospels to illuminate and reinforce the emotional sense of belonging he felt.

One day Hans had dinner with an old friend, James, whose journey to become a Christian followed a different path. They shared their Christian journeys with each other. Rather than a sense of belonging to a higher order, James began his journey with an epiphany about a belief. He heard a question posed by a preacher on television one day.

> "Suppose you were to die today and stand before
> God, and He were to ask you, 'What right do you
> have to enter into My heaven?'—What would
> you say?"[1]

James did not have a ready answer for this and developed an urgent need to find one. He turned to the Bible as the most logical place for answers. Televangelists and other prominent Christian leaders provided allegorical explanations for the confusing parts that James encountered. In regards to entering heaven these leaders placed a heavy emphasis on salvation through believing precisely the same things they did, rather than an emphasis on experiencing Christ in the present. Because of the impending Apocalypse and second coming of Christ these leaders held their beliefs to be urgent, and needed to be urgently witnessed to others. The initial sense of belonging James felt was not to a higher order, but to a Church fellowship that shared these urgent beliefs.

Since this journey did not begin with actually sensing a higher order, James never placed that at the empirical center of his focus. His first and supreme allegiance was to beliefs that he felt could get him into heaven in the future, not the peace, love and joy of belonging in the present moment. James need not ever sense a belonging to a higher order in order to continue with his urgent Christian journey. He needs to believe that we belong to Christ, of course, but he need not ever experience that belonging. He has been told that as long as he champions the right beliefs his entrance to heaven has been secured, predestined even.

The two old friends departed unfulfilled. James left angry that he could not get his old friend to focus on the right beliefs that would enable the two to be

---

1 Any resemblance between this fictional James and the late D. James Kennedy is intentional. See http://www.coralridge.org/about_djk.htm, and also the chapter "Conversion," in *American Fascists* (2006) by Chris Hedges. If there also happens to be a resemblance to James Dobson, I would not be surprised.

reunited in heaven. Hans left concerned that his old friend was filled with anger at the world for putting up impediments to his beliefs.

Empirical Faith

Ironically, the conversion of Hans relied on the type of empiricism advocated by Enlightenment scientists and philosophers. He began with what he sensed, and through induction provided meaning to his empirical experience. When Hans turned to the Bible he demonstrated a scientist's urge to gather more data. When confronted with a confusing and seemingly conflicting dataset Hans did what any scientist would do: he applied controls to determine if there were correlations between subsets of data. He reclassified the Biblical data into three categories: the life and teachings of Jesus; prophecies and interpretations about Christ; and all the other stuff. Most of the confusion was embedded in all the other stuff, the stuff that even St. Augustine thought superfluous to the Christian faith. Hans found a very high correlation between the life and teachings of Christ and the peace, love and joy discovered in his sense of belonging to a higher order.

Having established his controls, Hans finds the evidence and logic for correlating the Bible to his sense of belonging easy and straightforward. At the heart of his explanatory system are the Crucifixion, the Resurrection and the Pentecost. These are all fantastic events to be sure; to believe in their meanings requires great faith that goes beyond empirical experience. Yet the events all fit with the emotional belonging that Hans has sensed, and no empirical evidence has disproved that these fantastic events occurred.

James did not follow an empirical path, since the "sense data" was not a necessary part of his journey. Should James one day emotionally sense a belonging to Christ he will use deductive reasoning to interpret this experience in the context of his beliefs for entering heaven. He is not likely to dwell on the emotions of peace, love and joy so much as to deduce the sense of belonging as verification that his beliefs are infallible. In this manner James resembles the philosophers and even scientists who practice scholasticism, deferring to the authority of experts rather than building knowledge around the empirical experience of the senses.

The Crucifixion, Resurrection and Pentecost are all well and good for James, but those events alone do not support the urgent belief system being espoused by apocalyptic Church leaders. He places greater "faith" in the meaning he derives from the Books of Genesis and Revelations, the descriptions of the beginning and end times. Together these books provide the carrot and the stick for adopting apocalyptic beliefs. Omnipotent God can welcome you into His glorious kingdom; or He can bring the hammer down with a vengeance. Urgently adopting the right fundamental beliefs avoids the hammer being brought down.

There are problems with attaching urgent beliefs to the beginning and end times described in the Books of Genesis and Revelations. Genesis describes a prehistoric era for which there are no historical records. Revelations describes a dream. Both are imagined accounts that require belief in a long chain of infallibility, rather than the experiences of an empirical faith. For Genesis and Revelations to be true the authors must infallibly have described events they never experienced directly, or even indirectly through documents; historic Church leaders must infallibly have chosen these infallible writings out of possible alternatives for inclusion in the official Bible; current Church leaders must infallibly have interpreted the meaning to these infallible writings chosen infallibly by historic Church leaders; and fundamental Christians must trust in their own infallibility in choosing apocalyptic Church leaders over alternative denominations.

Stringing together such a chain of infallibility actually requires cynicism for the value of empirical experience. The Crucifixion, Resurrection and Pentecost as historic but empirical events must be diminished in favor of an "infallible" belief system that turns a forgiving God into a vengeful God, a loving Father into a domineering Lord. Along the same vein, the empirical emotions involved in a sense of belonging either must be missing or ignored. The "infallible" spin and emphasis on the Apocalypse and the second coming of Christ corrupts the peace, love and joy to be experienced in the present moment. Even if empirical faith once had existed, fundamental belief must subjugate that faith in urgent importance.

Humble Triangulation

Scientists and religious converts alike run the risk of letting their own personal biases distort the meaning of their discoveries. Triangulation is the term used by scientists to describe multiple methods of data gathering and interpretation. This requires the humility of placing one's own experiences or research in the context of others. Personal bias cannot be completely eliminated when building meaning from experience, but cross-referencing one's own experiences with those of others helps to expose biases that result from "wishful thinking." When Hans referred to Christian culture and the Bible to provide greater meaning to his sense of belonging he engaged in a form of triangulation.

Precisely because the starting point for Hans was empirical faith Hans engages in triangulation with a humble spirit. He welcomes any interpretations that will deepen the meaning of the wonderful emotions he experiences through his belonging. Some beliefs, such as satanic worship, clearly conflict with an empirical faith and belonging to Christ. Other beliefs, such as belief in an apocalypse, have no bearing on belonging to Christ; they only serve as an idolatrous diversion. On the other hand there are a range of different Christian beliefs, such as the significance of Communion and Baptism, which Hans can triangulate for attaching greater meaning to his belonging to Christ. His quest need not stop there. Since belonging, not belief, is at the root of empirical faith, Hans does not rule out that other cultures might be able to attach further meaning to the same belonging he feels, using an entirely different belief system that does not center on Christ. For example, Hans draws meaning from the Buddhist belief system of overcoming desire, anger and confusion.

Hans is poised to find harmony among different cultures, different religions, through empirical faith and triangulation. He can tolerate idolatry of certain irrelevant beliefs such as the Apocalypse, as long as no one expects him to diminish his empirical faith through such idolatry. Hans wants to spread the "good news" of his empirical faith to others, but the good effects of this news is belonging to Christ, not an infallible belief system. As long as other belief systems account for this emotional belonging to a higher order, Hans does not feel compelled to spread the "good news" in a way that might diminish this sense of belonging as experienced by other cultures.

James will not triangulate different interpretations of belonging to Christ. James incorporates everything in the Bible into a literal mess of conflicting events and accounts that forms his total belief package. He deems this belief package infallible, conveniently relieving him of making logical sense of anything, including a sense of belonging. The infallible beliefs mainly have to serve the purpose of distinguishing between "us" and "them," between those who will enter heaven at some future date and those who will be left behind. Making this distinction takes priority over the peace, love and joy felt in the sense of belonging to a higher order. While dogmatic in regards to specific beliefs, in other ways this infallible belief system is amazingly tolerant. This infallible belief system can tolerate cynicism in empirical faith. This belief system can tolerate the vanity of infallibility and the apprehension of flexibility. Most notably, this infallible belief system can tolerate materialism.

James needs to have a good memory for retaining all the conflicting beliefs of the Bible, but he need not give much thought to consistency or how closely his fundamental beliefs relate to empirical faith. To spread the "good news" James must then attempt to impose these fundamental beliefs on others, even if he does so while lacking empirical faith. Because he assumes his belief system to be infallible, there is nothing for James to learn from a humble examination of other beliefs. Alternative beliefs only assault and threaten his own. The "good news" therefore involves idolatry of his beliefs, rather than some type of harmony and meaning-enhancement drawn from different cultural beliefs. James naturally thinks that since his beliefs are infallible he has the key to absolute moral truths. But nothing absolute comes from the relativism of a faith that derives meaning relative to only one cultural context, without triangulation.

Moral Norms

Triangulation enables scientists to get closer to normative experience. With the help of triangulation and his empirical faith Hans comes to know moral norms based on the sense of belonging. I have alluded to these moral norms throughout these essays, but let us briefly recap them here. One needs the moral attributes of faith to overcome separation from a higher order; humility to overcome separation from others; courage to overcome separation from one's self. From this foundation we have asserted a few moral norms for social systems. The moral norm for economics should be merit, not greed; the moral norm for politics should be wisdom, not authoritarianism; the moral norm for culture should be harmony, not idolatry. We have provided cultural explanations for these moral norms, but as we will discover in Essay 22 there are natural explanations as well.

For fundamentalists of all religions their moral truths are not absolute as they claim, but relative to their belief system. Fundamental Christians will profess faith, but they behave cynically when they promote their fundamental belief system at the expense of actually experiencing a sense of belonging to Christ. Merely adopting certain beliefs will suffice for evidence that you have been saved, not the peace, love and joy of experiencing a higher order. If their cynicism was followed to a logical conclusion, then small infants or the learning disabled cannot have salvation even if they come from a fundamentalist family, since they are incapable of adopting the proper beliefs. Fundamentalists will make exceptions for contingencies such these, as well as the unborn, though not for people from different cultures who interpret empirical faith in a higher order with a different belief system. Fundamentalists thus mistake diversity for relativism, and mistake their own relativism for a "morality" that need not be grounded on the experience of belonging.

Some fundamental Christians may profess courage, but apprehension causes them to impose a relativistic belief system that they claim to be moral, rather than search for absolute moral truths. Some fundamentalist Christians may profess humility, but vanity causes them to place this relativistic belief system on a higher plane than the universal experience of a higher order. Vain people also are driven by desire. These desires can expand from belonging to Christ to desires for wealth, power and dogma.

The beliefs of others cannot impugn one's own steadfast faith, humility and/or courage. However, the beliefs of others do affect the ability to meet personal desires for wealth, power and/or dogma. This explains the motivations for the fundamentalist Christians that become televangelists or form political special interest groups. They epitomize the cynical false evangelist. They use a large stage to spread their cynicism, vanity and apprehension to bad effect. They work to infect our entire culture with greed, authoritarianism and idolatry. One only needs to listen for a moderate amount of time to televangelists like Pat Robertson, also the founder of the Christian Coalition, to understand the threefold agenda of the cynical false evangelist.

The Threefold Agenda

The agenda of the cynical false evangelist focuses first and foremost on spreading materialism. This would be a mission impossible for an empirical Christian faith journey. The sense of belonging to Christ has no material component of wealth, power or dogma. The life and teachings of Christ as recorded in the Gospels further denounces materialism. One might interpret from the Gospels that we gratefully accept whatever material blessings given to us by the grace of God, but desiring wealth and power are outright sins. The only way to justify materialism for Christians is through the cynical inclusion of beliefs having no relevance in the belonging to Christ.

The Christian materialist is like a member of the Powell Cabal, with a mission to spread the Gospel of Greed. There are only subtle distinctions. Large television ministries, megachurches or special interest groups become the repositories of concentrated wealth, instead of large corporations. Some of the concentrated capital trickles down to mission work; but some of the capital supports the upper class lifestyles of cynical false evangelists. Scrutinize the lifestyles of the televangelist Paul Crouch, the former televangelist Tammy Baker, or Focus on the Family head James Dobson sometime. False evangelists resemble the Powell Cabal when they form special interest groups to spread their mission. The Heritage Foundation and the Christian Coalition might as well set up joint offices.

The Christian Coalition recently hired a Director that went off message. As explained in Essay 16, the Coalition then parted company with Joel Hunter for allegedly not being conservative enough. To get at the real truth of the matter, Hunter was not qualified to spread materialism. The Coalition perhaps assumed that a pastor at a large, evangelical Church in Florida would be all about materialism, but Hunter had to go spouting off about environmental issues and poverty. These simply are not part of the materialistic belief system that defines cynical false evangelists. The Coalition prefers their Directors to have political ambitions and to live large at the expense of others. Pat Robertson and Ralph Reid were perfect matches for the Christian Coalition; Joel Hunter needed to go where his empirical faith could be expressed in doing good works.

The second agenda item for Christian materialists is to control government. This goes beyond lobbying, though their special interest groups join the Powell Cabal in adopting that strategy. They seek to remove the separations between Church and State. They are joined in this endeavor by vain false patriots, such as the American Legion. As will be discussed next, cowardly false neoconservatives get in on this action as well.

Fundamental Christians want to remove the separations between Church and State for allegedly moral reasons. Empirical Christians would view this as a big mistake. The State has to deal with the material concerns of commerce and defense. The Church deals with the spiritual guidance that empirical faith has revealed. To blend the two is to corrupt both. As discussed in Essay 18 the most effective roll for the spiritual Church is to retain a homeostatic separation from the State, providing negative feedback when material ambitions subvert spiritual truths and norms. Once the Church and State become integrated, the natural inclination of the Church is to provide positive feedback, even when the materialism of the State infringes on moral norms. Western civilization has gone the route of integrating Church and State before, resulting in such atrocities as Inquisitions and the Crusades. Hitler merged Church and State to get widespread "moral" support for his material ambitions of power.

But morality is not the real reason that Christian materialists want Church and State integrated. After all, let us not mistake people like Ralph Reid or Tom DeLay for being moral. Televangelists like Paul Crouch and special interest groups like the Christian Coalition want wealth and power. They want materialism. What better partner to feed such desires than the materialist State? If you can get the fiscal policy of government to favor your special interests you can go much farther than you would through television ministry or cleverly targeted mass mailings.

Why stop with the resources of a nation? If you are a Christian materialist, why not reap the resources of an entire globe? This leads to their third agenda item: guiding our foreign policy according to the impending Apocalypse. Two ingredients of the Apocalypse, as interpreted by some fundamental Christians and eagerly adopted by Christian materialists, are the control of Palestine by those of Hebrew lineage, and the Antichrist setting up shop in Babylon. This is where the grand battle at the end of times will be fought, and we are encouraged to get a head start on the grand event through our foreign policy. We need to help Israel secure their control of the region and we need to battle Islam.

Incidentally, Islam happens to be on top of a cauldron of black gold. Controlling the contents of this cauldron has been the key to military and economic successes throughout the twentieth century. To the victor goes the spoils, concentrated in the hands of the wealthiest. To the empirical Christian, whether the Apocalypse happens or not has absolutely no bearing on one's personal relationship to God, experienced empirically through the sense of belonging. To the cynical false evangelist, keeping our government involved in the Middle East is another means of fueling materialism.

Cynical Benchmarks

Fundamental beliefs and materialist goals, absent an allegiance to empirical faith, are necessary conditions for a cynical false evangelist. But these conditions alone are not sufficient. An evangelist has to spread "good news." A false evangelist has to create bad effects by the news they spread. A cynical false evangelist has to create bad effects with intent to abort the empirical faith of others. Most fundamentalist Christians practice their faith without spreading their beliefs on a wide stage, to bad effect. Most fundamentalist Christians have noble intent. Consider also that in our society even empirical Christians have a touch of materialism. We should focus on specific indicators that fundamental beliefs and materialist goals have created a cynical false evangelist.

There has been a tendency throughout history for established religions to believe in predestination. Judaism and the Hebrew Scriptures set the precedent with God's chosen people; St. Augustine drew from these scriptures in applying the doctrine of predestination to Catholicism; Calvin reestablished the doctrine for Protestantism (though Martin Luther also believed in predestination). Predestination fits with the notion of an active God; one who lovingly reaches out to us regardless of our undeserving natures. Predestination fits with the notion of an omniscient God; we cannot accept that God knows absolutely everything without including absolute foresight as well. Predestination also happens to fit nicely with a system of infallible beliefs. Infallible beliefs are not discovered empirically through a sense of belonging; they are handed down in keeping with the scholastic tradition. Learning of predestination through an infallible belief system provides extra incentive for converts to subjugate themselves to religious scholars as proof of their destiny.

Predestination contradicts free will. Free will implies that the initiative to belong resides in us, not God. God can reach out, as with Christ, but the responsibility to follow through still lies with us. But the safety valve of having the right infallible beliefs will not remove the sin of separation if we seek to be vain, cynical or apprehensive. Fortunately, the emotions involved with a sense of belonging to a higher order are motivators for the will to freely pursue humility, faith and courage. One has to wonder if a staunch advocate for predestination ever has sensed a genuine belonging to Christ. If they have, and they still champion predestination as a belief to impose on others, that is a sure trademark of false intent.

If you want to enforce an infallible belief system, then the type of God that nurtures a sense of belonging just won't do. In the Calvinist view an active God can be an angry God. An angry God can condemn you to hell for not having the right infallible beliefs; an angry God can withdraw blessings from whole countries; and an angry God can unleash the Apocalypse. A cynical false evangelist benefits when this wonderful source of our belonging yet turns angry when potential converts do not fall in line with the right beliefs. When we combine predestination with anger we truly arrive at a "mystery of faith." The mystery is: How can a

God who determines your destiny be angry with you for what amounts to His own intent? Talk about blaming the victim! Anger results from cynicism, from a loss of faith in life functioning properly. An angry, omnipotent God means a God who has lost faith in his own omnipotence. There can be no greater benchmark of cynicism than a belief system that incorporates an omnipotent God becoming angry over the destiny He determines.

The anger and cynicism of an angry God becomes channeled into the anger and cynicism of the false evangelist. The cynical anger of Pat Robertson, calling for the assassination of another country's leader; the cynical anger of Jerry Falwell, blaming gays for 9/11; the cynical anger of James Dobson, backing the execution of abortion providers; the cynical anger of Paul Crouch, threatening his critics with violence; the cynical anger of Timothy LaHaye, expressed in vivid and gruesome (and poorly written) portrayals of the end times; these are all marks of cynical false evangelists. Cynical anger added to materialistic goals and predestination completes the transformation of a fundamentalist Christian into a person capable of undermining a whole culture's sense of belonging. Perhaps this happens to but a few fundamentalist Christians, while most are hardly distinguishable from empirical Christians. But just a few cynical false evangelists, once allied with wealth and power, become a few too many.

Tolerance or Harmony

Cynical false evangelists have less of a following than vain false patriots. The cynicism of anger and falseness of materialism becomes so transparent to most that they actually become critical of religion. On the other hand, the cynical essence of these evangelists makes them capable of endorsing the most grotesque behavior that might otherwise be considered off limits. The vanity of a false patriot may cause them to glorify combat, but Inquisitions and apocalyptic visions require an even darker side of the human soul, infested with cynicism. Merging the breadth of false patriotism with the darkness of false evangelism creates the destructive combination of a virulent disease. Like a virulent disease, the combined vanity and cynicism can infect even those who try hard to resist.

Consider the main thesis of *American Fascists* (2006), a book written by Chris Hedges. Hedges rails against the intolerance of what he calls the Christian right or, as his title implies, American fascists. He finds himself gripped in a paradox. He condemns the intolerance of Christian fascism, yet sees no alternative but to be intolerant of such intolerance. This is a paradox shared by a growing number of people. They believe that their faith calls for them to be tolerant, yet responding to some of the cynical anger and materialism of false evangelists calls for intolerance.

The paradox is not real, and reveals the extent to which cynical false evangelists have infected culture. Tolerance versus intolerance does not distinguish empirical and fundamentalist Christians. Both groups are tolerant of some beliefs and behaviors, intolerant of others. For fundamentalist Christians, as well as the fundamentalists of other faiths, tolerated behaviors are relative to their belief system. For empirical Christians tolerated behaviors are absolute norms determined by the universal sense of belonging that characterizes the human species.

The real dichotomy that distinguishes fundamentalist from empirical faiths is idolatry versus harmony. Fundamental Christians idolize an infallible belief system. They can tolerate a wide range of behaviors, from asceticism to materialism, within this belief system. Empirical Christians harmonize different beliefs to enhance the meaning of the sense of belonging they experience. This makes empirical Christians more intolerant in some respects than fundamental Christians. Since vanity, cynicism and apprehension interfere with harmony, empirical Christians tend to disapprove of the beliefs and behaviors that stem from these traits.

The mischievous might suggest that being intolerant amounts to being unharmonious. The difference between the two lies in the arena where harmony occurs. Special interest groups like the Christian Coalition, by their very nature, are not harmonic endeavors. They are founded to do battle, to have their interests win out over those of others even if they must resort to incivility to do so. The relative merits of opposing interests are beside the point; special interest groups do not exist to find any merit in opposing interests, only to promote idolatry of their own. Intolerance is unharmonious for a special interest group promoting specific cultural beliefs and behaviors, but there is no other way for such an interest group to function.

Within a community, the intolerance is precisely for the unharmonious. Idolatry at the community level gets in the way of functioning together. Idolatry may occur if everyone in a community believes the same thing, but this makes the community nothing more than a special interest group with a specific location. People who want to get along need to minimize vanity, cynicism and apprehension in their communal relationships, and will grow intolerant of these unharmonious characteristics.

Fundamentalist Scholasticism

It's not easy being rooted in empirical faith these days, and the threat comes from both fundamentalist Christians and fundamentalist scholars. In the eighties a leading "fundamentalist" scholar was William Provine, a professor at Cornell, who declared that it was intellectually dishonest to believe in both a theory of evolution and God. Let us cross-examine this belief from both the empirical Christian and the empirical scientist points of view.

There once was a religious community in this small town known as the Bruderhof, who departed in many ways from fundamentalist Christians. They had no problem with believing in both a theory of evolution and in God. The important message in Genesis for the Bruderhof is that God breathed spiritual life into humans. The evolutionary journey of humans up to that point does not matter to their faith.

The Bruderhof obviously feel a strong sense of belonging to others; after all, their whole existence revolves around living in community. No doubt they also have felt an empirical sense of belonging to a higher order. Having that empirical faith at their center leads them to interpret Genesis figuratively rather than literally.

For an empiricist to conclude that a theory of evolution refutes the existence of a higher order, conceptually known by most as God, there must be a generalization that can be made from empirical data that is valid and reliable. We can skip the tests of validity and reliability in this case, because empirical data for how evolution occurred cannot be generalized to why evolution occurred, or to reflect on the existence of a higher order independently of evolution. Evolution can be used to empirically refute some literal claims made by fundamentalist Christians, but cannot be used as the starting point for building or refuting an inductive case for a higher order.

Allow me to role play and wear a fundamentalist hat for a moment. My fundamentalist Christian brethren have got it all wrong! My alternative fundamentalist belief is I do not believe God to be a tawdry magician waving a wand that goes "poof" for whatever He desires. For someone as wonderfully omniscient as God evolution is no more than a sequence of complicated moves made by the Supreme Grandmaster of Life. Now, as a fundamentalist would you rather have a trickster God that wields creationism like a magic wand (and, one presumes, occasionally in a foul mood)? Or an infinitely wise Lord that knows all, sees all, and causes all through the patient mechanisms of the natural laws He set into motion? This latter view happens to be the foundation of Deism, shared by such noted scientists as Johann Keppler and Isaac Newton. Just think, by Provine's criteria these revered scientists were intellectually dishonest folk.

The empirical scientist really is neutral in this conflict. From the empirical data of fossils and genetic mutations we logically can generalize as far as a theory of evolution, but no farther. Links to God, refuted or established, result from deductive explanation based on a belief, and are defended by rhetoric; the old scholasticism at work. Whether a fundamentalist Christian wants to deduce there is a link between evolution and a belief in a Grandmaster of Life, or a fundamentalist scientist wants to deduce a link between evolution and a belief in randomness (or determinism, depending on the fundamentalist scholar), makes no difference to the empiricist.

Scientists use both deduction and induction; the departure from scholasticism lies in the starting point. An empirical scientist will not hesitate to use the theory of evolution to deductively predict undiscovered organisms in the fossil record, but the starting point remains the generalization of a theory of evolution from other observable fossils and genetics. These essays resort to rhetoric at times; perhaps you have judged the overall tone to be rhetorical. Persuasion relies on rhetoric and, admittedly, I wish to be persuasive. Yet the starting point for each part of these essays is an empirical break down and analysis of function and structure.

The starting point for claims about a higher order needs to be our sense of belonging. If we only sensed we belonged to others, if no one ever sensed we belonged to a higher order, no "theory" of God ever would have gained traction. If only a few isolated people throughout history claimed to have experienced this sense, then we might generalize that hallucinations were the cause. Given the vast numbers across time and cultures that have experienced a sense of belonging to a higher order, such theories do not fit the empirical evidence. Some Enlightenment scholars and their modern disciples might be quick to claim vast numbers of Native Americans as being too fond of peyote; but even they would have trouble informing C. S. Lewis he was hallucinating. I have read C. S. Lewis; Dr. Provine is no C. S. Lewis (and neither is Sam Harris).

The empirical Christian generalizes directly from the sense of belonging that there is a higher order. Empirical scientists may instead attempt to reduce the sense of belonging to the most basic observable components, leading us to generalize theories about the role of hormones and neurons in the brain. Yet the theory about how we developed these capabilities already has been induced: evolution. Theories about why evolution occurred, or about the observable phenomena of hormones and neurons being triggered by the unobservable phenomena of a higher order, cannot be tested.

A theory of evolution refutes literal interpretations of some of the books in the Bible. The people overly concerned about what Genesis literally means are either the fundamentalist Christians or fundamentalist scientists. Though they are seemingly at odds, these fundamentalists could form a special interest group together; their common mission would be to undermine the empirical sense of belonging that determines our quality of life. Both dogmatic extremes provide a useful service for the cynical false evangelist.

The Narrow Gates

By now you no doubt have guessed that the empirical faith journey of Hans in this essay derives in part from the author's own journey. I consider myself to be both a Christian, one who has experienced the sense of belonging to a higher order, and an empiricist. My study of the Bible and other Christian documents has been that of both empirical believer and empirical critic.

Even the Gospels present some perplexing passages for those who have experienced a sense of belonging to a higher order. I once struggled over the notion of sin. As far as my young mind could tell sin was the opposite of perfection, an ideal possessed only by God. Thus to be human was to sin and to sin was to be human. I had no idea about tautologies and circular reasoning back then, but something told me this view of sin was not particularly useful for anything. As covered in Essay 18, Paul Tillich provided some necessary meaning by linking sin to separation. The consequences of separation were not punishments from an angry God, which would be alien to the joy we sense from a higher order, but something we have the free will to accept or reject.

Another passage I have struggled over for a longer time is the declaration by Christ that the gates to heaven are narrow. Once again, this did not fit with my sense of a loving God that would welcome all. I could have rejected the passage as not fitting in with my empirical experience. Since I already prioritized books from the Bible by designating the Gospels to be more important than Genesis or Revelations, why not consider certain passages within the Gospels as more important than others?

Empiricism requires being faithful to the rules one sets for their logic, until further experience undermines the legitimacy of those rules. Either I was going to use triangulation, thus weighting the evidence from other "Christ" experiences as equal to my own, or just invent my own religion. Not being a big fan of authoritarians or scholasticism (I hope you noticed), I committed myself to triangulation. There must have been some truth embedded in Christ's warning about the narrow gates.

The notion of free will helps with resolving the message of the narrow gates. An angry God is not putting the squeeze on a majority of people, since the advent of civilization and scholasticism we have chosen beliefs that lead us away from empirical faith. Why do we make this choice; which is to say why do so many succumb to vain desires, cynical anger and apprehensive confusion?

Essay 22 provides the natural foundation for answering this question. Before we get to this natural explanation for our cultural woes, let us first uncover one last structural flaw in our cultural system of beliefs and behaviors. Let us turn next to the most apprehensively confused people on the planet: neoconservatives.

ESSAY 21 – COWARDICE AND FALSE NEOCONSERVATISM

Courage considered in itself or without reference to its causes, is no virtue, and deserves no esteem.
- W. E. Channing

Conscience in the soul is the root of all true courage. If a man would be brave, let him learn to obey his conscience.
- J. F. Clarke

Courage is always greatest when blended with meekness.
- E. H. Chapin

Courage without conscience is a wild beast.
- R. G. Ingersoll

The most sublime courage I have ever witnessed has been among the class too poor to know they possessed it, and too humble for the world to discover it.
- H. W. Shaw

I love the man that can smile in trouble, that can gather strength from distress, and grow brave by reflection. 'Tis the business of little minds to shrink; but he whose heart is firm, and whose conscience approves his conduct, will pursue his principles unto death.
- Thomas Paine

Overview

- There are natural, normative standards for moral behavior.
- The neoconservative manifesto is that America needs to spread democracy to spread security and morality.
- True neoconservatism would need to prioritize morality over security to pursue both; false neoconservatism prioritizes security over morality.
- Real courage faces daily apprehensions for uncertainty, truth and

responsibility.

- Neoconservatives cannot overcome apprehensions for uncertainty and truth that undermine their objectives.
- Neoconservatives reject normative standards for moral responsibility.
- Neoconservatives are confused about the requirements for true democracy.
- Neoconservatives are confused with their logic that aggression promotes security.
- Neoconservatives are confused about their relativistic views on morality.
- The confusion of neoconservatives has culminated in the use of torture.
- False neoconservatives network with false patriots and false evangelists to promote zealotry and dogma at the expense of harmony.

Tortured Morals

In the context of these essays, scorn has been applied to the hypocritical; those who use "black box" or "black is white" methods to manipulate the middle class. Neoconservatives have been treated scornfully throughout these essays. Had they been true to their stated vision, we would not be in a variety of predicaments induced by neoconservative influences. This essay explores the consequences of neoconservative hypocrisy.

As a graduate student at Cornell I took a course called Religion, Ethics and the Environment (RE&E). All three topics interested me separately; combined together they formed a most enlightening course. Considering the wandering path I took through different colleges I was generally older than other graduate students. Since RE&E was more of an advanced undergraduate course I was more than ten years older than most of my classmates. I soon discovered this made a big difference in terms of the type of high school curricula we had experienced.

Early on in the course Professor Richard Baer asked the class: "Raise your hand if you think it is wrong for a different culture than ours to have a custom of torturing people for fun."

What an absurd question! I raised my hand just as I expected every other student to do. When some of the students failed to raise their hands I attributed that to a lack of morning coffee. Then the professor asked for those who thought different cultures had the right to determine different standards of morality, torture included. About one third of the class raised their hands.

I learned from this that value-neutral curricula swept through high schools soon after "my day." In an effort to promote pluralism and tolerance schools encouraged students not to judge other cultures by our standards. Though no doubt a well-meaning movement, this relativistic approach to values implies there are no universal standards for being human. There are no natural rights, no natural characteristics that might suggest some types of cultural behaviors to be detrimental to our natural development. That a significant number of people anywhere could believe such a thing gave me a case of culture shock in my own culture.

The previous essay established a basis for morality, one derived from natural attributes of humility, faith and courage that bond us together; and social norms of merit, wisdom and harmony that reinforce our natural attributes. The expressions of immorality are the desires of the vain; the anger of the cynical; and the confusion of the apprehensive. This foundation for morals is not derived from an infallible belief system, which invariably is relative to the culture where the beliefs were created, but from an empirical sense of belonging experienced universally by humans.

Neoconservatives claim allegiance to the pursuit of moral clarity, but their concept of morality includes accusing aggrieved mothers who have lost a son as "sinister piffle," and tolerance for torture under perceived, necessary conditions. Is torture sometimes moral? Or are the morals of neoconservatives dangerously tortured?

The Neoconservative Manifesto

I will present neoconservatism viewed mainly from three sources. The *Weekly Standard,* owned by the neoconservative sympathizer Rupert Murdoch, is essentially the trade publication for neoconservatism. The Project for a New American Century (PNAC) is the major special interest group representing neoconservatism. The book *Neoconservatism: Why We Need It* (2006), by Scottish journalist Douglas Murray, is a recent apologetic, regarded well in terms of message by neoconservatives themselves. *Fox News*, also owned by Rupert Murdoch, may have contributed in subliminal ways to my understanding of the neoconservative manifesto that will be documented.

Let us first establish who qualify as neoconservatives. Douglas Murray doubles as a director of a think tank dedicated to neoconservative domestic policy in England, while his book on neoconservatism concentrates on American foreign policy. Murray traces a philosophical lineage for neoconservatism that originates with Levi Strauss. In Murray's view some of the people involved in the war plans of the Bush II administration are not true neoconservatives because they are not products of this lineage. Yet Dick Cheney, Donald Rumsfeld, Paul Wolfowitz and Douglas Feith are all members of PNAC, and their actions fulfilled neoconservative objectives. While Murray's book was chosen precisely for some philosophical background on neoconservatism, in this essay we will counter that you are what you do. In this regard the whole Bush II administration involved in the war plans for Iraq can be considered neoconservative. In fact, neoconservatism dates back before Levi Strauss at least as far as the administration of Teddy Roosevelt.

In fairness to neoconservatives, they probably would not choose Murray to be their ideological standard bearer. He was only 27 when his book on neoconservatism was published and, despite being a journalist, his writing at the time reflected his youth. Murray relies on a machine-gun fire approach of echo-chamber styled rhetoric, with no empirical foundation provided for anything he writes. His problem is not manipulating invalid and unreliable data; he essentially does not bother with it. Still, though even neoconservatives may fault Murray's writing skills, they acknowledge that he captures the essence of their ideas.[1]

Neoconservatives consider themselves to be an eclectic bunch, with both liberal and conservative ideologue derivatives. The common vision that unites them is embedded in the Statement of Principles on the PNAC web site.[2]

> "Our aim is to remind Americans of these lessons and to draw their consequences for today. Here are four consequences:
> - we need to increase defense spending significantly if we are to carry out our global responsibilities today and modernize our armed forces for the future;
> - we need to strengthen our ties to democratic allies and to challenge regimes hostile to our interests and values;
> - we need to promote the cause of political and economic freedom abroad;
> - we need to accept responsibility for America's unique role in preserving and extending an international order friendly to our security, our prosperity, and our principles.
>
> Such a Reaganite policy of military strength and moral clarity may not be fashionable today. But it is necessary if the United States is to build on the successes of this past century and to ensure our security and our greatness in the next."

---

1 See the web site http://www.claremont.org/publications/pubid.472/pub_detail.asp for one such critique.

2 http://www.newamericancentury.org/statementofprinciples.htm

To break these consequences down into one concise statement of neoconservatism: Neoconservatives view the spread of democracy as a means to achieve ends of greater morality and greater security, at home and abroad. This is the standard by which neoconservatives should wish themselves to be judged, and this essay shall oblige them. Let us start by gathering fuller meaning to their view of democracy, morality and security.

Perhaps because of their professed eclecticism, pinning down precise definitions from neoconservatives is hard to do. Democracy, to the neoconservative, springs from freedom and liberty. Few would disagree with that, but neoconservatives treat freedom and liberty as self-evident constructs needing no further definition. How democracy consequently results from freedom and liberty also is left as self-evident, as is the form that an ideal democracy should take. This would seem to leave much room for interpretation about what they mean about democracy except for one underlying implication, which I will come to shortly.

Neoconservatives fault modern society for a lack of moral clarity. According to Murray's thesis we have a perverse compulsion to criticize our own American values, while at the same time excusing the tribulations of other cultures. The same value-neutral training that was evident in my RE&E class causes Americans to be too devoted to secularism and relativism. In perceived contrast, neoconservatives make a claim to moral clarity. The foundation of their morals appears to be concepts of natural rights and natural law, as expressed by historic scholars such as St. Thomas Aquinas or John Locke; but translation of these rights into morality was never made clear in Murray's particular work. Ultimately, moral clarity for the neoconservative is grounded on something else; again, I come to this shortly.

The meaning of security is plain enough in the neoconservative vision. America needs to maintain our position of strength. We need to maintain our position of prosperity. We need to strengthen ties with people we consider democratic, and consider the rest to be enemies that need to be challenged. There is no mention in the Statement of Principles, or in any other neoconservative documents here reviewed, that an increase in security be gauged by any empirical barometer, such as a decrease in killing or violence.

The ambiguities of the neoconservative manifesto are addressed by making democracy, morality and security relative to America. The meaning of democracy is relative to the United States being the leading democracy; the meaning of moral clarity is relative to American fundamental beliefs as perceived by neoconservatives; the meaning of security is relative to what keeps the United States on top of the world. The only thing that comes close to an empirical grounding of their manifesto is their reference to natural rights. As we touched upon in Essay 15, and will explore further in the next essay, the natural rights that sprung forth from the Enlightenment have their own problems with empirical grounding. The neoconservative manifesto is, in essence, an apologetic for self-absorbed, self-indulgent scholasticism and relativism.

Prioritizing Security

The two different ends of morality and security must at times be in conflict, at least superficially. For guidance in resolving this conflict we can draw parallels to the dual pursuit of liberty and security. In the mind of John Stuart Mill, whose famous works relating to the matter are *On Liberty* (1859) and *Utilitarianism* (1871), liberty must trump security in this dual pursuit. Mill puts forth a rationale that only by moving away from the tyranny of the majority and authoritarianism that real security can be achieved. The wonderful mind of Vice President Dick Cheney, a signatory to the PNAC Statement of Principles, works a little differently than Mill; in his view only by gaining security through authoritarianism and mass conformity can liberty be achieved.

We are not likely to convert many of the self-absorbed relativists that side with Cheney's position, but let us introduce some empirical evidence to the contrary. We had major terrorist attacks on our soil in 1993 and 2001. Neoconservatives no doubt would agree that our response to the 2001 attacks placed security in a more sacrosanct role then our response to the 1993 attacks. Using an empirical measure for security such as American citizens killed, we can compare the two responses for greater success. Between 1993 and 2001 a few hundred additional Americans were killed by foreign operatives, with the most lethal occurrence being the coordinated bombings of the U. S. Embassies in Tanzania and Kenya. Since 2001 a few thousand additional Americans have been killed in Iraq alone, exceeding the number of American citizens killed in the 2001 attack that prompted our new "security" approach. Neoconservatives have vivid imaginations. Even if we accommodated neoconservatives by imaginatively blaming all the 2001 deaths on the Clinton administration's former approach to security, their "less secure" approach still resulted in fewer American citizen deaths than the Bush II administration's approach since then. But such empirical grounding does not oblige the relativism of neoconservative scholarship.

A qualifier could be made that soldiers are, at the same time, both more and less than real American citizens. They are more than real citizens in that they are the only Americans expected by neoconservatives to have the courage to risk their lives for a cause; they are less than real citizens because neoconservatives would not want the lives of soldiers counted in an empirical assessment of security. Neoconservatives (and perhaps the American Legion) may be comfortable with that dual quality of soldiers as American citizens, but middle class fathers and mothers should not be. Yes, soldiers are expected to fight so that the few die for the many. But when the many start dieing for the many or, if we consider innocent people from other nations, the vast die for the few, we have confused our perspective on what security really means. No doubt neoconservatives would prefer a less empirical approach to back their claims on security, but at the least the exponential increase in casualties suffered since 2001 should provide some support to Mill's claim that prioritizing security over liberty jeopardizes both.

Unfortunately, we have no empirical evidence for making the same type of comparison with the dual purposes of morality and security. Our foreign policy in the Middle East has never provided a moral foundation as a basis for comparison, at least not since the CIA backed coup of a democratic Iran in 1953. We could make the inference that since our foreign policy never has been moral, and the Middle East during that time never secure, that morality must be a condition for security rather than vice-versa. We also could make the inference that prioritizing security over morality puts that dual purpose in even greater jeopardy than prioritizing security over liberty. For you cannot expect to torture captives without being tortured when captured. You cannot expect to act preemptively from a position of strength without opponents seeking terrorist retaliation. You cannot expect to use immoral means for preventing harm against you without increasing the motivation of others to do precisely that.

This brings us to our basis for contrasting true and false neoconservatives. The neoconservative manifesto seeks the spread of democracy for the sake of greater morality and security. The true neoconservative would make security subordinate to morality, since that is the only way to pursue those dual purposes. The false neoconservative makes morality subordinate to security, thus ultimately compromising both. In essence, all neoconservatives are really false neoconservatives. At the root of their hypocrisy are apprehensions that have grown into cowardice.

Overcoming Daily Apprehensions

We must understand the real targets of apprehension to understand the real consequences. Politicians and neoconservatives want the middle class to be cowards about dying (if we are not soldiers), and certainly that has had consequences, but overcoming the fear of dying is not where the tests for courage takes place in the daily lives of most people. The three fears we must overcome constantly are the fear of uncertainty, the fear of truth and the fear of responsibility. The mark of courageous citizens does not lie in their sparse moments of facing death, but rather in their steadfast abilities to handle the constant realities of uncertainty, truth and responsibility. Let us turn to Hans the schoolteacher for a lesson on overcoming apprehension in our daily lives.

As a schoolteacher Hans has had some advanced training for overcoming apprehensions. He has been trained to love knowledge. This means he has to be willing to accept uncertainty about his current knowledge base. He has to be able to discern and accept valid and reliable knowledge and disregard false discoveries and innuendo (not to mention echo-chamber styled rhetoric) even if they support current dogma. He has to accept the responsibility of acquiring this new knowledge as a necessary standard dictated by his trade as a schoolteacher.

The training involved in his craft has prepared Hans for the apprehensions affecting his life. The school hires a new principal who shakes things up in the school. The curriculum is modernized; Hans must create and teach the new Environmental Science course. Hans would have liked to continue teaching the traditional Biology courses, for which he honed his lesson plans over the years. But middle class people face worse uncertainty to their employment conditions, including sudden unemployment with families to feed. Hans overcomes his apprehensions for uncertainty and develops new curricula with dedication.

The principal institutes a new program that involves extensive peer evaluation. Other teachers come into the classroom and evaluate how Hans teaches. They later provide feedback, which presents Hans with some hard truths. He tends to ignore the kids that are quiet. No teacher wants to think they purposely leave any kids behind, but teachers also love to be stimulated in the learning process as much as they wish to stimulate others. The quiet kids do not provide immediate positive feedback in this regards. Hans could ignore the truth and continue with the greater stimulation of focusing on the responsive kids. Instead, Hans overcomes his apprehensions for accepting the truth and involves the quiet kids more in his lessons. He allows the empirical evidence to change his behavior.

Hans does not teach merely as a means of earning a paycheck; he wants to make a difference in the lives of students. He teaches at a time that he remembers quite differently from when he went to school. Back in "the day" parents were involved with the schooling of their kids. Whether this perception is really true is not the point; Hans perceives that the responsibility for the learning of students has been shifted entirely to the teacher. He finds the lack of support from parents frustrating. Achieving high standards of learning for his students is much more difficult without that support. Hans could have refused the added responsibility of surrogate parenting. Fortunately for his students Hans overcomes his apprehensions for this responsibility and does whatever he feels is needed to maintain high standards of learning for his students.

Neoconservative Apprehension of Experience and the Unknown

False neoconservatives do not overcome their apprehensions well. The apprehensions to change that neoconservatives have are embedded in *The End of History* (1992), by Francis Fukuyama, a signatory to the PNAC Statement of Principles. Fukuyama interpreted the fall of the Soviet Union as a signal that the American system of democracy was the final answer to government. Fukuyama has been attacked for misreading both what the fall of the Soviet Union meant and for his assessment regarding our brand of democracy, but such criticisms miss the essence of what is really wrong with his thesis.

Fukuyama and other neoconservatives should watch some episodes of *Star Trek*. The Star Trek Federation is a fictional system of government that surpasses our own as an effective democracy. The point of this comparison is not that we should aspire to fictional forms of government, but rather that we always should aspire to be more than what we are. To think any system of government represents an absolute end, without any universal standard of empiricism for making that conclusion, is irrational and foolish. But people with tight links to authoritarianism, such as most neoconservatives, want their comfortable world order to continue in the same manner. Wanting our system of government to be the end without further exploration, given that we are comfortable with the current results, refutes empiricism and cowers in the face of uncertain change.

The neoconservative comeback to this charge is that only the major issues of government have been resolved. Change still is to be expected and welcomed, but only as fine tuning to avoid entrenchment of the status quo. This view of limited change and uncertainty ignores at least one huge question of government that has not been resolved by American democracy, since the question is not even supposed to be asked. This is the normative "Why?" question of economics, allegedly nonexistent according to cult economists and economic textbooks, but in reality answered either correctly or incorrectly by all governments. Imagining that American emphasis on economic greed represents an absolute endpoint for democratic government is greater fancy than produced by the writers of *Star Trek*.

The reality of experience has been painful for neoconservatives. Many people, both at home and abroad, do not want to go along with their plans for world order. Those of us who are balanced overcome our apprehensions to the empiricism presented by our daily experiences and adapt our beliefs accordingly. Apprehension for empiricism turns to cowardice when we use secrecy and distortion to prevent others from knowing the empirical evidence we refuse to accept.

Cowardice in the face of empiricism causes neoconservatives to be false to their own professed ideals for democracy. You cannot spread real democracy without simultaneously spreading openness and honesty. We all know now that secrecy and distortions were implemented by the neoconservative administration to cover up truths about the lack of WMDs and terrorist links in Iraq. We know this was done to better sell the invasion to the public, in a manner that subverts true democracy. Whether or not we agree with invading Iraq, we need to recognize the true cowardice and hypocrisy that neoconservatives used to accomplish this goal. You will not find condemnation of the secrecy and distortion used by the Bush II administration in the *Weekly Standard*, the PNAC web site or in Murray's thesis. But, then, willingness to police one's own actions takes a certain amount of moral responsibility.

Neoconservative Apprehension of Responsibility

Accepting responsibility requires a commitment to standards. We must be willing to "make the grade." We can make the grade in one of two ways: with the courage to meet normative standards or the cowardice to reduce the standards to a level requiring virtually no responsibility.

We get an idea of the type of standards neoconservatives set for themselves in the title of Ron Suskind's book, *The One Percent Doctrine* (2006). This refers to the standard of proof Cheney set for going after rogue states that might do us harm. The crucial moment of the book, indeed, what some might conclude as a crucial moment in the new millennium, reports on Cheney's response to learning that Pakistani nuclear scientists had been meeting with terrorists.

> "If there's a one percent chance that Pakistani scientists are helping al Qaeda build or develop a nuclear weapon, we have to treat it as a certainty in terms of our response.... It's not about our analysis, or finding a preponderance of evidence."

Evidence, logic and truth be damned! This minimal one-percent standard of evidence and analysis abrogates all responsibility to either. On the face of it, this is about as gutless as it gets. We should keep in mind, however, that Cheney saw fit to apply his gutless standard to only one nation. Not even Pakistan, home of the nuclear scientists, or Saudi Arabia, home of the great majority of 9/11 terrorists, have been targeted for regime change by the one-percent doctrine. Cheney saw fit to apply this gutless standard only to Iraq, for whatever mysterious reasons that turn an oil man's attention away from nations posing greater security threats from terrorists.

Even if Iraq is the only nation to which we apply the gutless one-percent doctrine, we have shrunk from our responsibilities in a variety of other ways that marks us as cowards. We fear the responsibilities of treaties, whether they apply to the environment (Kyoto), defense (SALT) or even free trade (Canadian logging). We fear the responsibility of applying the rule of law, particularly in regards to prisoners, though we alleviate some of these fears by simply changing the law. We fear the responsibility of pursuing national security without compromising global security. We set a shoddy standard of fighting terrorists "over there," contributing to unbearable conditions for millions in foreign countries, because we have not the courage to focus on the best defense possible for our national security at home.

We need to distinguish the source of our cowardice as the neoconservatives that have influenced foreign policy, not ordinary Americans. Neoconservatives may have suckered many of us into fearing for our lives, but most Americans are like Hans the schoolteacher, overcoming the apprehensions of uncertainty, truth and responsibility on a daily basis. We could be inspired to overcome such apprehensions at the national and global level, certainly we could be inspired to go beyond a one-percent doctrine, but this is not in the best interest of neoconservative authoritarianism.

Confused Democracy

Either oil was or was not a motive for invading Iraq. If securing the single most important resource for economic and military strength in the world was not a factor in choosing Iraq over nations that posed greater terrorist threats, if this motive did not cross the minds of our neoconservative leaders with extensive backgrounds in oil, then grossly incompetent idiots ran the country during the Bush II administration. If oil was one of the motives, then the anticipated reaction of a democracy to this truth was feared by the neoconservatives in charge of the war plan, and the truth purposely withheld. This reveals confusion about the purpose and mechanisms of a democracy.

Neoconservatives have an excuse for this confusion. As Murray writes about invading Iraq:

"…it was spurred by reasons either too numerous or too opaque for large proportions of the population to go along with.

…in matters of grave importance, occasions arise in which a leader will know best, and in which the less well-informed masses, if given the opportunity to decide on a specific matter, might decide wrongly. There are very few who would disagree with this, and the profession of outrage at the very notion of the "noble lie" is, to put it kindly, an example of faked outrage." (pg. 130)

Maybe we should be thankful that Murray addresses us "kindly," given the overall tone and implications of his rhetorical writing, but the middle class should display some "faked outrage" nevertheless. The claim that an authoritarian "leader will know best," in grave matters affecting a democracy, is far from irrefutable. There is too much historical evidence to the contrary. Having faith in democracy—and having courage in that conviction—means the masses must be trusted for precisely those decisions that affect democracy. As covered in Essay 9, empiricism and democracy are the cultural and political components of the same orientation towards wisdom. We commit to democracy for the same reason we commit to empiricism: we feel the "batting average" for the wisdom gained from collective empirical experience will surpass that of restrictive authoritarian knowledge over the long haul. This does imply, however, that the masses are kept well-informed and can independently make the best sense of their decentralized experiences.

Masses are more or "less well-informed" due to the decisions of government. Government can limit diverse opinions and centralize news outlets to foster a herd mentality; or, alternatively, enable the ingredients for collective wisdom as detailed by James Surowiecki in the *Wisdom of Crowds* (2004), implied by John Stuart Mill in *On Liberty* (1859) and reported in Part Two of this book. Disagreeing with Surowiecki or Mill or the collective wisdom gained through the genuine independence of free thought is one thing; to profess an allegiance to democracy at the same time exhibits confusion.

Murray proposes to thwart the herd mentality of the masses by an alternative means of keeping us in the dark "in matters of grave importance." That amounts to an authoritarian solution of an authoritarian generated problem. Neoconservatives should either openly commit to authoritarianism, and admit their disdain for real democracy, or come up with a democratic solution to the authoritarian problem of "less well-informed masses" in regards to "grave matters." Neoconservatives are much too confused to make sense of that proposition, a confusion that results from recognition of democracy as an American ideal, but with extreme apprehensions about the uncertainty, the experiences and/or the responsibilities that a true democracy might bring.

Confused Security

Murray reported that the neoconservative Jeanne Kirkpatrick once claimed that democratic nations do not start wars. This goes far beyond the confusion of Mansfield and Snyder, reported in Essay 17, overlooking the fact that mature democracies in the Hellenistic era fought each other.[3] To rationalize the view of Mansfield and Snyder you merely need to constrain the meaning of democracy to eliminate most Hellenistic city states and the early Roman Republic, as was done by Weart. At least such rationalizations could be made with a pinch of empirical evidence and logic.[4] The only way to reconcile Kirkpatrick's claim that democracies do not start wars at all, whether or not with other democracies, you have no other choice but to conclude that the United States was never a democracy. Whether we have been involved in eliminating Native Americans (some of these tribes had quite mature democracies), establishing banana republics, instigating coups or "democratizing" Vietnam or Iraq we have been, on the balance, a fairly aggressive nation over the course of our existence. One would think neoconservatives would wish to ban the delusional Kirkpatrick from further neocon status, given the fodder she provides for reasoned antagonists. Instead, Murray fairly glows about her, revealing that many neoconservatives share Kirkpatrick's democratic dementia.

In fairness to neoconservatives, the point they would really wish to make, and most do this with obviously better statesmanship and coherency than Kirkpatrick, is that democracies only start wars when necessary to spread democracy and enhance security. Yet acts of aggression to enhance security involve merely a different type of twisted logic. Fancying that you can crush a foreign enemy's spirit under an authoritarian thumb satisfies those with a certain psychological makeup but ignores the experience of historical reality. Foreign powers do not have the same success as domestic totalitarian regimes with strong-arm tactics. Modern history has been very clear about this. The British were not cowered when bombed by Germany in World War II, nor did the Allied fire bombing of Dresden cause the Germans to surrender. The Japanese attack on Pearl Harbor did not cause Americans to withdraw into a shell, nor did the 9/11 attacks. Millions of

---

3 From *Electing to Fight* (2005).
4 From *Never at War* (1998).

Vietnamese being napalmed and killed did not break their resistance.

History has demonstrated repeatedly that acts of aggression prevent a foreign opponent from doing future harm only if total conquest can be achieved, or after long engagements with wearying attrition on both sides causes the opponent to acquiesce. Otherwise, acts of aggression have the same effect as swatting a hornet's nest. In effect, we have swatted at so many terrorist hornet's nests around the world that eliminating all the hives through total conquest is impossible. That leaves a long engagement of wearying attrition on both sides as the only feasible alternative for getting terrorists to acquiesce.

"Fighting the terrorists over there so that we do not fight them here," a quote by the notable neoconservative William Kristol, editor of the *Weekly Standard*, is a tactic that fits with the goal of engaging terrorists indefinitely. Yet this tactic just takes confused security a step further. First, this boosts terrorist recruitment across the globe to counteract the attrition on their side. Second, citizens who are not soldiers have to be turned into cowards that believe their lives are more valuable than both our own soldiers and innocent citizens abroad. This culture of cowardice hurts the effort to recruit more expendable soldiers to counteract the attrition on our end of a long engagement.

Why do we emphasize homeland security, if neoconservatives genuinely think that fighting terrorists somewhere else works? The neoconservative might offer the explanation that there are lots of potential terrorists, but fighting terrorists elsewhere siphons off some that might have otherwise tried an attack on our soil. Preventing attacks thus becomes a more manageable goal from a numbers perspective. This rationale reveals yet another confused approach to security: one that treats as one and the same the type of terrorist that patiently plans a sophisticated, diabolical attack and the type that plunges zealously into a war zone. Stopping patient, sophisticated, diabolical terrorists requires covert methods of attack to accompany effective homeland measures. Kristol's logic, echoed by Bush II, implies we need to provide a diversion or else terrorists worldwide will form a cohesive army, command a large fleet of ships and invade our shores en masse. Now there's some confused thinking, brought about by the urgent apprehensions of neoconservatives.

Confused Morality

War may be waged to claim another nation's territory or resources. War may be waged to halt the aggression from another nation, or to impose specific beliefs on that nation. The end results of war are either conquest or negotiated treaties. An overt "War on Terror" literally cannot achieve any of the goals of war, there is no entity that can capitulate or negotiate. Fighting terrorism constitutes a war only in rhetoric, not in reality.

An act of violence not sponsored by a nation state literally constitutes a crime, such as the crime Timothy McVeigh committed with the Oklahoma City bombing, or the 1993 bombing of the World Trade Center. Terrorists usually do not act on behalf of a nation that can be changed or conquered; they are criminals who we wish to prosecute and, in some means, eliminate. In this country the punishment for crimes can be of the most severe nature, such as the death penalty for McVeigh. In fact, committing acts of violence as a criminal generally draws more severe punishment than violence committed by prisoners of war. However, crimes must be processed through the rule of law. Solving and prosecuting crimes through the legal system will never do for urgent people filled with cowardice.

Declaring "war" on terror allows greater latitude for rounding up suspected combatants and interrogating them. The resources of the military can be used to sweep an area we designate as a war zone and take large numbers of prisoners, whether or not any are actually terrorists. Since a war on terror must be waged indefinitely, these prisoners of war can be held indefinitely. Yet the military is bound by rules as well, including international treaties such as the Geneva Convention. The Geneva Convention is an application of the Golden Rule, the granddaddy of all morality codes. You agree to treat prisoners of war in certain ways because that is how you want your captured soldiers treated.

Suspected terrorists are considered not to be prisoners of war since they do not represent nation states. The military can thus hand them off to institutions—and detention centers in other countries—not tightly bound by troublesome Golden Rules. They still can be held indefinitely while subjected to secret interrogation methods, or at least until the "war" (wink, wink) is over; yet in the neoconservative's confused mind this little trick does not break any morality code.

Such a system ensnares many innocents. They may not even be suspicious under normal conditions, but happen to be in a designated war zone at the wrong time. Sending innocents off to detention centers in foreign countries where … stuff happens … is immoral. Even applying this method to guilty terrorists is immoral, since we still declare with our methods that we are above the Golden Rule of civilization. Neoconservatives may counter that we do this to morally defend ourselves, which only confirms their moral confusion. Ignoring the Golden Rules that you actually helped to establish may be judged a practical course of action at best, but not a moral one.

Murray emanates the moral confusion of the neoconservative perfectly when he declares:

"All societies have their enemies, but the

pervasive methods of political correctness, equivalence, and relativism have allowed these opponents of our society to become absorbed into the status quo and cosseted within our midst. Whether it is in the House of Representatives, the networks, the press, or in society at large, neoconservatives should lead the way in pointing the finger and isolating those who have, for too long, been allowed to get away with being traitors and opponents of the very country which gives them sanctuary." (pgs. 153-154).

The chances are good you already find that statement morally confused without much further discussion. Before I pick this apart, however, let us recall once again that Murray was a young man when he wrote this, perhaps not quite capable yet of understanding morals, and that his writing ability (though not his positions) has been faulted by other neoconservatives. Perhaps Murray does not mean what he declares, but we will take his declaration at face value.

What Murray endorses with this declaration is the moral authority to brand critics of American policy as "traitors and opponents." Who should hold such moral authority? "Neoconservatives should lead the way." Why should neoconservatives be considered moral authorities? Neoconservatives believe in moral clarity and are against relativism. What are the absolute morals that these moral authorities have clarified? Now that is where things get a little confused.

Murray treats both patriotism and organized religion as inherent goods for society. He makes no moral distinction between false and true patriotism, as was done in Essay 19. He makes no moral distinction between false and true evangelism, as was done in Essay 20. Without making any such distinctions he implies that any kind of patriotism, or any kind of organized religion, satisfies moral criteria. The nationalism of pre-war Germany and the Church sanctioned Inquisition would fall within the scope of being moral. Obviously, a little more clarity is needed than blanket references to patriotism and organized religion.

Neoconservatives treat natural rights and natural law, as handed down to us in scholastic fashion from historical philosophers, as moral absolutes. Yet how these doctrines translate to moral absolutes in domestic or foreign policy is never clarified. We are, instead, to simply trust in the moral judgment of neoconservatives, the self-designated representatives of the unquestioned moral authority of the United States.

We all make mistakes. True moral authorities accept the responsibilities for mistakes and will be their own severest critics. The torture that occurred at Abu Gharaib was a mistake; at least one would hope that would be the judgment of a moral authority. Murray refers to Abu Gharaib and other "mistakes," but always in the defensive, never in critical self-censure. Complaints about torture, preemptive strikes and "noble lies" are examples of "traitors and opponents" using "pervasive methods of political correctness, equivalence, and relativism" to bring down the "very country which gives them sanctuary."

Tortured Confusion

Torture has not been officially endorsed by the neoconservatives in the administration, but torture indeed has been their intent. The book *Administration of Torture* (2007), by Jameel Jaffer and Amrit Singh, details the Bush II administration's endorsement of torture, based on hundreds of government documents obtained through the Freedom of Information Act. This inclination for torture culminated in the Military Commissions Act of 2006, promoted by Dick Cheney, which loosens the interpretation of torture. The Act prompted thirty-eight retired generals to send a letter on September 12, 2006 to the Senate Armed Services Committee denouncing the use of torture.

The retired generals acted on military principle. The Army Field Manual No. 34-52, 1-7, states: "Use of torture and other illegal methods is a poor technique that yields unreliable results, may damage subsequent collection efforts, and can induce the source to say what he thinks the interrogator wants to hear." Yet no active generals had the courage of retired generals to sign on to the letter; perhaps fearing that would not be a good career move with the current administration. Or maybe active generals feared that neoconservatives could charge them with being cowardly, not wanting to torture out of fear that our own soldiers will be tortured. Neoconservative policy wonks are quite the source for inspirational courage as they posture from their armchairs.

Suskind documents in the *One Percent Doctrine* that the FBI sides with the military in forsaking the use of torture for information gathering. They judged that the CIA's interrogation techniques thwart that very stated purpose. The FBI is in the business of getting reliable evidence in order to solve and prosecute crimes. Torture, as made famous in a few East Asian countries, succeeds mainly at getting confessions void of reliability. As Suskind also documents, the FBI's view of ineffective torture was verified in the administration's response to 9/11. Little has been gained to date by the CIA/Cheney method of information gathering, though much liberty has been lost.

Neoconservatives presume that citizens rhetorically encouraged by a "moral authority" to be cowardly want to prevent death at all costs. Protecting us by any means becomes the moral absolute of which neoconservatives speak. We have established that prioritizing security over morality jeopardizes both. The neoconservative's "tortured" solution is to declare that security IS morality.

Please allow me to interject some more "faked outrage" at this point. In case there are a few of you who do not agree, I will express this in the first person. No spineless CIA agent or soldier tortures on my behalf. I would rather die in a terrorist attack than be associated with the utter cowardice of these morally bankrupt human beings. I realize these creatures act on the orders of those even more cowardly than themselves, with the point of origin traceable back to some confused and gutless neoconservative applying something like the one-percent doctrine, but that does not release from moral responsibility an act that everyone should quite simply refuse to do.

This counter declaration amounts to a good deal of rhetorical flourish on my own part; I am well aware that the likelihood of me dieing in a terrorist attack actually decreases if the United States refrains from torture. Even if torture could uncover an immediate terrorist threat, the motivation for future terrorist threats increases tenfold if the most powerful nation on earth brands itself as gutless torturers. Yet, as mentioned in previous essays, torture takes too much time to prevent immediate terrorist threats. This is a lesson learned by the military and the FBI; but why should we take their word over the actions of fictional Jack Bauer, as cited by wise Supreme Court justices such as Antonin Scalia?

Thanks, but no thanks. Perhaps I speak for too few middle class Americans at this point, with neoconservative leaders doing their best to make us all tremble for our security. Yet at least my position far surpasses neoconservatives in moral clarity. Spineless CIA agents, soldiers or neoconservative leaders who condone waterboarding, sleep deprivation, electric shock, undetectable physical harm, emotional duress, etc., do so only on their own apprehensive and urgent cowardice, not for the sake of making this middle class citizen protected or free.

Zealotry

False neoconservatives are allies with false patriots and false evangelists. Spreading American democracy as the authoritative leader of the world plays well to the vain pride of false patriots. Charging others of moral failure engages the cynical anger of false evangelists. This alliance is critical for the neoconservative, since their cowardice in the face of uncertainty, truth and responsibility would not play well if that was all they were peddling to the middle class. We do not handle our daily lives well when infused with the type of confused cowardice possessed by neoconservatives. Mixing in a little vanity for country and a little cynicism derived from an "angry God" helps to swell their ranks. Let us lump these three groups together as zealots, distinguishable from each other only by the dogma they respectively idolize.

Together these different zealots pose grave threats to harmony and our quality of life. We now wage war in the Middle East for the combined urgency of enhancing our security, spreading democracy and preparing the predestined conditions of the Apocalypse. The most empirically and logically sound reason for such a war—OIL—never needs to be mentioned by leaders. We support a more authoritarian government where secrecy and distortion apprehensively prevails, distinctions between Church and State are cynically eroded, and citizens are vainly stroked by corporate media and political parties to do nothing more substantial than vote for the right issues and candidates. We support *laissez faire* economics where resources can be concentrated for the wealth, power and dogma elites that rule an authoritarian nation.

Zealots manipulate public debate to establish a false dichotomy of tolerance and intolerance. Zealots stand for something, and thus are intolerant of beliefs and behaviors that threaten their ideals. The rest of us are painted as tolerant of anything and everything, alleging that we have no ideals. We play into this trap by touting the virtues of tolerance, and faulting zealots precisely for being intolerant. In truth, we all are intolerant of something, even if we profess to only being intolerant of intolerance. Thus the hypocrisy appears to be on the type of folks that promote tolerance, rather than the type of folks whose zealotry tolerates torture as a justifiable means to an end.

To reiterate what was expressed in the previous essay, the real dichotomy for cultural beliefs is not one of intolerance versus tolerance, but idolatry versus harmony. Zealots idolize dogma. What zealots deem should be tolerated or not is relative to their dogma, ungrounded in normative, natural standards or real experience. They heed not the caution of John Stuart Mill that treating beliefs as infallible risks eliminating important elements of the truth, being trapped by dogma and eroding real understanding of the very things one professes to believe. Sometimes their dogma can be devastatingly wrong, resulting in consequences that the rest of us simply should not tolerate.

Advocates of harmony want to remove our separations from others, a higher order or our selves. We are intolerant of cultural systems of beliefs and behaviors that induce separation; but tolerate diverse beliefs that commonly promote our sense of belonging in myriad ways. Our patriotism is rooted in the experience of loving people and places, rather than in nationalist propaganda. Our evangelism is rooted in personal experiences of peace, love and joy, rather than in infallible beliefs of an "angry God." Our neoconservatism is rooted in the real experience that morals promote security, rather than in dogma that security promotes morals.

Without empirical experiences from which to induce the logic of their dogma, zealots instead wield rhetoric to deduce fantastic claims. They promote patriotism with vain rhetorical flourishes about greatness. They promote evangelism with cynical rhetorical flourishes about an angry God and the Apocalypse. They promote neoconservatism with cowardly rhetorical flourishes about the primary role of security. With the weight of corporate media, authoritarian leadership and special interest groups supporting these zealots, the rhetoric of their dogma trumps the inductive logic and real experiences of empirical evidence in our public discourse.

With so much in common between these various zealots, we must consider the possibility of a common influence. Something rooted in our history has culturally evolved to cause this varying yet similar zealotry. The most notable period of western history in regards to the impact on our current beliefs and behaviors was the Enlightenment. At first glance the Enlightenment would appear to stand out as a tonic to withstand the ills of authoritarianism and idolatry. Indeed, one of the major movements of the Enlightenment was to promote empiricism over scholasticism. But perhaps something lurked within the Enlightenment period that compromised the message. Perhaps planted within the Enlightenment were the very seeds for our UnEnlightenment.

ESSAY 22 – THE UNENLIGHTENMENT

The Delight Song of Tsoai-Talee
> "...You see, I am alive.
> You see, I stand in good relation to the earth.
> You see, I stand in good relation to the gods.
> You see, I stand in good relation to all that is beautiful.
> You see, I stand in good relation to you.
> You see, I am alive, I am alive."
> - Kiowa Native American Poem

"Savages pride themselves in being hospitable to strangers."
- Daniel Williams Harmon, *Early Pioneer*[1]

Overview

- The Enlightenment was misanthropic about our natural condition.
- Early cultures provide baseline data regarding our natural condition.
- Scholastic dogma concludes that natural humans were "solitary."
- False objectivity concludes that early cultures were "poor."
- False deduction concludes that early cultures were "nasty."
- Circular reasoning concludes that early cultures were "brutish."
- Invalid and unreliable data concludes that the life of natural humans was "short."
- Early cultures had greater longevity than civilized empires.
- UnEnlightenment economics substitutes colonialism for domestic production.
- UnEnlightenment politics substitutes contracts for generosity and respect.
- UnEnlightenment culture substitutes idolized beliefs for people and places.
- Misguided adolescence reflects the misguided UnEnlightenment.
- Our current culture forsakes the enlightenment of traditional rites of passages.

---

1 As quoted by Marshall Sahlins in *Stone Age Economics* (1972, p. 217).

A Penny Well Spent

Because I had an aptitude for math during the time of Sputnik I was pushed towards science. But science as an academic pursuit, and later a vocation, never shaped my cultural or religious beliefs. I was agnostic early on thanks to an eleventh grade English vocabulary word that initiated the most unenlightened period of my life. The word was "misanthrope," defined on the vocabulary handout as "a cynical belief that all human behavior is self-motivated." The more I reflected on this definition the more I agreed with its apparent truth. I convinced myself that even when we do good deeds, we do so for our own selfish motives of self-esteem. A bit of darkness invaded my soul that, given my aptitude for math, could have paved the way for me to become a *laissez faire* economist. That lasted until the incident with the penny.

After high school I took a year off away from school with the intent of growing up (some goals are never achieved). I lived with my oldest brother, one of the charter professors for Evergreen State College, and worked at a McDonald's for $1.60 an hour. One day I went to the Tacoma Mall to go Christmas shopping for my brother's family. During a break from shopping I waited in line at an ice cream parlor behind a disheveled, elderly woman buying a 15 cent ice cream cone. When the woman put her money down the clerk stated, a bit coolly, that there was a penny tax. The woman hesitated and during that moment I reflexively reached into my pocket and slapped a penny down on the counter.

You may think this silly, but slapping that penny down was a key moment in my life. To my mind there was no real reason why I did that, which was precisely the point. A cultural ethnographer might hypothesize that some type of general reciprocity was at work, but I think not. I certainly did not expect that woman to repay me some time in the future, nor could my reflex be explained by a subconscious expectation that anyone else might pay a penny sales tax for me some day. A penny is simply too trivial an amount to justify any self-motivation as an explanation. I gave out of some instinct that only much later in life I could define as a sense of belonging to others.

After purchasing my own ice cream cone I practically was skipping along the corridors of the mall. I went up the down escalator and down the up escalator. Observers might have described me as giddy, perhaps even daft. But I had a brief insight into the real nature of things, and a burden of cynicism was lifted from my shoulders. I had become enlightened.

To become enlightened is, literally, to emerge from existing darkness. The period of western civilization named the Enlightenment implies that we emerged from previous eras of darkness. In contrast, to become unenlightened is plunging into darkness by turning off the existing light. The Enlightenment, despite its reputation as leading us out of darkness, had some misanthropic elements that plunged us further down a dark tunnel. These elements resulted from misconceptions about early cultures and natural humans, which led to misdirection for the future. Our endeavor now is to shed some light where there has been darkness, a darkness augmented by the Enlightenment.

Early Cultures as Baseline Data

From the viewpoint of economic production, the agricultural age of civilization ushered in production surpluses; the industrial age ushered in production efficiencies; and the current information age now ushers in energy efficiencies for the production of both goods and labor. When our colleague Hans, a modern day man, considers the scope of these three ages together he concludes how wonderfully advanced we have become. He readily accepts the conclusion drawn by the Enlightenment thinker, Thomas Hobbes, that in our natural condition: "the life of man was solitary, poor, nasty, brutish and short."[2]

An argument could be made that Hobbes was the consummate misanthrope, but he was not alone among his Enlightenment peers in his dim assessment of "primitive" man. John Stuart Mill was known for his enlightened attitude towards women but he had a paternalistic attitude towards other races, exempting them from his rule that government should not interfere with the liberty to do harm to ourselves. Even the Enlightenment champion of early cultures, Rousseau, thought of them as "noble savages" whose main attribute was avoiding urbanization.

This Enlightenment dogma has been echoed by the most esteemed scholars of the present age. I was channel surfing the other day when a quote from Stephen Hawking flashed on the screen. In his opinion our only chance for planetary survival is to enable our reason to overcome our instinct. Hawking ironically bases his high esteem for reason on reason alone. He personally has not had the natural experiences to back up his reasoning about our natural instincts. He has not dabbled in cultural anthropology to observe what other early cultures experienced. He apparently has not even paid much attention to the science of ecology, which would characterize our natural instinct as that of an altruistic species.

Hawking merely echoes the dogma of scholars before him, in the fashion of *laissez faire* economists and Supreme Court justices. None of these scholars based their "reasoning" on their own natural experiences or even the trained observations of cultural anthropologists. Like Thomas Hobbes they ruminated from their armchairs. At best they observed the experiences of individuals suffering at the bottom of their respective cultural systems and concluded that must be natural.

Given this shortcoming of great scholars, we cannot blame our friend Hans for being misinformed. During the bicentennial celebration of Lewis and Clark, he no doubt heard much about the trading and lending of Native American wives like Sacagawea. Small chance, though, Hans knows that Iroquois women

---

2 From *Leviathan* (1651).

had more freedom and responsibility than any European counterpart of that era. This, in fact, was true for many Native American tribes, though taken all together their cultures are quite diverse.[3] There is virtually no chance that the modern Hans knows of the near equal status of women in band level foragers such as the Ju/'hoansi, influenced in his thinking instead by movies about early humans like *The Quest for Fire* and cartoons of cave men dragging women by their hair.

Early cultures provide empirical baseline data for comparing economic production, gender roles and other economic, political and cultural attributes. With this baseline understanding we can identify and qualify the changes cultural evolution has imposed, for both good and bad, on our natural condition. Unfortunately, we waste this baseline data when we make a tautological assumption that civilizations advance as a natural function of time. Many have concluded along with Hans that early cultures represents a "darkened" state of humanity, while "enlightened" beliefs and technologies have enabled civilizations to shine increasingly bright ever since. Misconceiving the baseline data corrupts not only our understanding of early cultures, but distorts our view of the progress of later cultures as well.

Let us examine the claim by Hobbes that the life of natural man was "solitary, poor, nasty, brutish and short" with a bit more scientific empiricism than exhibited by scholars from Hobbes to Hawking.

"Solitary" Early Cultures

If modern culture permits one favorable opinion Hans may have about natural humans, it is likely the privacy we must have enjoyed once as "solitary" creatures. In reality, the least private cultures in human existence were probably the earliest bands of foragers. Speaking from personal experience, you cannot keep secrets from a band of people you are living closely with in a natural setting. Once two or more people are gathered together in close proximity only cultural contraptions such as walls and computers provide privacy. Aside from the impracticality, band members of early cultures did not wish to be private; this created the need for strong social mores.

Many foragers create a social contract with each other through a series of gift-giving, referred to by cultural anthropologists as general reciprocity. The material value of these gifts means little; the real purpose of the gift-giving is to cement social bonds. The "general reciprocity" involves giving a gift one year and not receiving anything back until much later. The uncertainty of the timing and value of the gifts are to reinforce the purpose of social bonding rather than economic exchange.

Humility is the key for a sense of belonging among others. Foragers understand the need to keep each other humble. If one of the Ju/'hoansi happens

3 The publication *The World of the American Indian* (1989), produced by the National Geographic Society, documents a wide variety of Native American tribes.

to be a great hunter, all the band members will insult the game he brings back. The elderly follow a custom of complaining about how the young do not care for them; even though, by the standards of any "advanced" culture, the foragers pay great respect to their elderly. The men do not lord over women because, frankly, the women have the more important "job" of foraging the higher caloric foods.

Early cultures like those of the Native Americans were keen on relationships—of all kinds, as the Kiowa poem at the start of this essay expressed succinctly. Of course, American pioneers may have viewed the Native American reverence for good relations a little differently, like the one who observed that "savages pride themselves in being hospitable to strangers." Had Native American cultures been allowed to coexist with ours with their emphasis on seeking relationships we might have gained some insight into harmonizing diverse systems of beliefs and behaviors, the mark of an advanced civilization.

No one possibly could induce that natural man is solitary based on empirical evidence. Perhaps we could forgive Hobbes for not having access to such evidence, yet we still must conclude that in an age that championed empiricism Hobbes basically just spouted off dogma backed by no experience at all. Joined by other Enlightenment philosophers in this outlook on natural man, together they exhibited an authoritarian scholasticism that betrayed the main alleged characteristic of the Enlightenment. Modern day scholars, and even some esteemed scientists, adopt these uninformed and idolized beliefs as enlightened.

"Poor" Early Cultures

OK, so early cultures had accorded greater status to women than occurred during the Enlightenment and were not solitary. Hans still would infer from Hobbes that they were "poor." Good Lord, they walked around in loin cloths! However, early cultures perceive material possessions differently from westerners, as the following quotes compiled by Sahlins in *Stone Age Economics* (1972) reveals.

> *About the Native South American:*
> "Expensive things that are given them are treasured for a few hours, out of curiosity; after that they thoughtlessly let everything deteriorate in the mud and wet. The less they own, the more comfortable they can travel, and what is ruined they occasionally replace. Hence, they are completely indifferent to any material possession."[4]

---

4   From Martin Gusinde's The Yamana (1961, p. 87), cited by Sahlins.

About the Native Kalahari African:
"They themselves had practically no possessions:
a loin strap, a skin blanket and a leather satchel.
There was nothing that they could not assemble
in one minute, wrap up in their blankets and carry
on their shoulders for a journey of a thousand
miles."[5]

We can see from these quotes, particularly the one about the Native South American, that perception is everything. Being "completely indifferent to any material possession" is irresponsible and perhaps lazy to the "civilized" westerner; however, there is no indication that the Yamanas themselves are particularly bothered by this scarcity. The lightweight gear and long travels of the !Kung may seem the very essence of poverty and burden to the middle class Hans, but would not trouble such contented folks as Jesus, Gandhi or a good many long-distance backpackers of my personal acquaintance.

This highlights what has been an epistemological thorn to empiricism. Some empiricists of all eras confuse the meaning of empirical with objective. An objective criterion is independent of subjective cultural standards; the meaning is embedded in the object. Numbers and statistics are objective measures, yet they are employed to describe subjective phenomena. The meaning of "poor" cannot escape from the subjective context of different cultures. The best we can hope for in determining "poor" is an empirical standard, with meaning embedded in cultural experiences. To observe what is "poor" about natural man or early cultures, both the Enlightenment Hobbes and the modern day Hans would need to know the context of cultural experiences. Otherwise they are, once again, just spouting idolized beliefs.

"Nasty" Early Cultures

The evolutionary axiom "survival of the fittest" provides a nasty image of all organisms, humans included. This axiom has acquired a status of infallibility, particularly with *laissez faire* scholars from Herbert Spencer to Milton Friedman. To survive we must compete better, to compete better we must work harder. Any slackers in the natural world of survival would have been weeded out and discarded. The nasty burden of a primitive quest for survival is reinforced by a corporate culture that wants to convince us how much leisure we have in a modern *laissez faire* economy. Hans believes this without reservation, since he knows early humans did not have access to television, automobiles or other leisure-enhancing technologies.

The alleged gain in leisure from our cultural evolution has proven to

5 From Laurens van der Post's The Lost World of the Kalahari, (1958, p. 276), cited by Sahlins.

be more fallacy than fact. Conserving energy drives the behavior of all natural organisms. Lions lie around for a good portion of the day in wise management of their energy budgets, while bears hibernate for a good portion of the year. For Hans to believe that "survival of the fittest" created a burdensome struggle to exist for early cultures, he must also believe that natural humans refute other laws of nature. He must believe that we are dumber and grossly more incompetent than lions. Humans include more caloric rich foods in their diet than lions and other carnivores, yet Hans uncritically accepts the implication that humans have not the wit to use this to their advantage for conserving energy. Thankfully, the baseline data from early cultures provide no support for such a self-debasing assumption of natural human ineptitude and inferiority to other species.

All studies of the production (foraging) time spent by early cultures put them around the 20 hour a week category, part-timers at best.[6] A study of the Ju/'hoansi in Botswana revealed that the men worked 21.7 hours a week at the foraging culture's version of a job, and the women worked 12.6 hours.[7] What makes this striking is that the women, as the main gatherers of mongongo nuts, are the more prolific producers of calories. This means that the foragers of the Ju/'hoansi could have even more idle time if they did not choose to supplement their diets with game. As with modern civilizations, the hunt just might be more of a leisurely diversion than real work to the Ju/'hoansi and, just as with modern corporate executive culture, the males protest how hard they are working while out having a good time with the boys.

The production surpluses of the agricultural age were not due to increased work efficiency, getting more food from the same amount of work. Comparisons of the work hours versus the calories produced reveal early cultivators to be no more efficient than foragers. The production surpluses of agriculture were a function of land efficiency, extracting more food from a smaller area, thus enabling humans to settle down and congregate. Early farmers actually worked longer hours than foragers, though they worked less than the modern day farmer.[8] A nasty existence of sixty hour work weeks or more for a family unit occurs only in "civilized" cultures.

The trouble with all "infallible" axioms is that none are based on infinite experience. Without the benefit of infinite experience to draw from all axioms are vulnerable to being proved fallible at some point. Sometimes an "infallible" axiom is refuted just by the limited experiences provided by getting away from one's armchair. But that would prove to be too much of a struggle for some scholars spouting their idolized beliefs.

---

6 In the chapter "The Original Affluent Society," in Stone Age Economics (1972), Marshall Sahlins provides an overview of these studies.

7 From The Dobe Ju/'hoansi (2001), by Richard B. Lee.

8 Based on comparing data for cultivators in Sahlins with Lee's Ju/'hoansi.

"Brutish" Early Cultures

No one wants to sign on the dotted line for a "brutish" life, whether short or long. Hans believes that survival of the fittest not only implies working harder, but under the natural conditions of "man's inhumanity towards man." This reveals a tautology about the way we think about early cultures. What is brutish? The natural, primitive condition. What are we to conclude about early cultures, not far removed from the primitive condition? They are brutish.

Defining what is brutish is arbitrary at the individual level of experience. Climbing a mountain may be brutal to one, exhilaration to another. In contrast, living a life of luxury may be heavenly for some, while others are mindful of the saying: "that which you would possess, possesses you." To judge when conditions are "brutish" we need a criterion that applies to the entire culture without being tautological. We can borrow from ecologists for this task.

From the early discussion in Essay 2 regarding k-species and r-species please recall that these two fundamental types of population growth relate to the carrying capacity of the environment. K-species moderate their growth and use of resources to stay within this maximum level of sustainability. R-species multiply and use up resources quickly, like the bacteria in a Petri dish. This shoots them beyond the carrying capacity of their environment and they crash. Populations crash from some combination of famine, disease and/or aggression. An empirical description of "brutish" would be population crashes that occur in any of these ways.

Early human foragers fit the k-species stereotype; they managed their own population growth and resource use at sustainable levels, thus avoiding "brutish" conditions. The demands of early agriculture and industry encouraged greater population growth rates because: 1) more family members and labor hours were needed for economic production in these "advanced" civilizations and 2) early farmers and industrial workers died younger than early foragers. With greater birth rates and concentrations of populations came a shift towards r-species resource use and behaviors, and a shift towards "brutish" conditions for those being exploited by such behaviors.

Early cultures avoided "brutish" conditions in another typical manner of k-species, they dispersed into different areas. From a limited area of origin early humans dispersed over the entire globe, except for Antarctica. In each new location they adopted a different culture in accordance with their environment. The Jo/'hansi of the desert, Yamana of the tropics and Inuit of the tundra adopted different foraging cultures to go after different food sources. Though aggression occurred between neighboring cultures and even within tribes, they avoided the "brutish" population crashes from aggression, typical of both r-species and nation states involved in world war.

Tautologies, like objectivity, have been another thorn to empiricism. In our eagerness to attach something observable to abstract concepts, we occasionally define abstract concepts biased by what we expect to observe. Tautologies, such as the one affecting Hobbes and Hans (and Hawking), derive from the conventional wisdom of authoritarian dogma, rather than the collective wisdom born out of experience. Rather than a product of empiricism, tautologies are yet another vehicle for spouting idolized beliefs.

"Short" Early Cultures

Perhaps the most pervasive bit of conventional wisdom about natural man and early cultures is that their lives were short. Keys to longevity must be unlearned in order to uncritically accept this conventional wisdom. There was no excuse for Hobbes in this matter. Health care in sixteenth century Europe was not much different from prehistoric levels. Indeed, the life span of humans had decreased during the time of Hobbes from earlier eras.[9] A great thinker like Hobbes should have at least suspected the impact of culturally induced stresses on health.

We can allow the modern day Hans considerable more latitude for his belief in the conventional wisdom spouted by Hobbes. Compared to our age of significantly reduced infant mortality and excellent health care, early cultures do have short lives. Hans even knows of empirical evidence that backs up this conventional wisdom. Like Temperance Brennan, we have come to trust in the evidence of bones.[10]

Much of the empirical evidence echoed about the short lives of early cultures stem from determining the age of Paleolithic bones. Paleolithic bones have been discovered for cultures engaged in early agriculture as well as foraging. The average age of bones for one early cultivator, the Dickson Mounds Indians, was determined to be 19 years.[11] Apparently the early farmer had but 19 years to grow up, have kids and raise them to be future farmers. Anthropologists confirm that the children of early farmers work earlier in life than the children of foragers, but a 19 year lifespan to perpetuate the cycle assaults basic common sense. You do not need Temperance Brennan to detect a serious problem with this interpretation from Paleolithic bones.

The technology for dating artifacts is marvelously reliable. We can date bones to the Paleolithic era with certainty. However, the technology is much less certain for aging prehistoric bones. A scholarly compilation of articles on longevity, authorized by the National Research Council, provided this criticism:

---

9 A few examples of how the Middle Ages were better off than the ensuing Renaissance and early Enlightenment are provided in the course on CD by the Teaching Company, *The Foundations of Western Civilization* (2002), taught by Professor Thomas F. X. Noble.

10 Temperance Brennan is the main character in *Bones*, a TV series about a forensic anthropologist

11 Reported in "The Worst Mistake in the History of the Human Race," a PowerPoint document by Jared Diamond available for download from the Internet.

> "These estimates have well-known weaknesses that arise from differences by age in the probability that a dead person will be represented by bones in the collection, difficulty in ascribing an age at death to the bones, distortions due to nonstationarity of the age distribution of the population giving rise to the specimens, etc."[12]

Ethnographic studies of contemporary foraging cultures were given more credence by this scholarly publication, such as Lee's study of the Ju/'hoansi. When Richard Lee made his first contact with the Ju/'hoansi the matriarch he first met was 70 years old. What are the odds?! These early foragers are supposed to have an average lifespan of 30 years yet Lee meets one right off the bat that is 70. Furthermore, Lee describes her as "spry."

Perhaps just the mere incidental contact with Europeans in the nineteenth century increased the life spans of these foragers, even though their culture was not impacted until later in the twentieth century. This explanation does not work with the early Amazonian cultures which were undiscovered until the twentieth century. The opportunity to study these cultures immediately followed the contact and, lo and behold, these humans live into their 60s and even 80s. Studies have shown that once they reach adolescence, these aboriginals have a long life expectancy that might mistake them for actually being modern.[13]

The one thing that does make sense about the data from old bones is that early foragers apparently lived longer than cultivators from the same era. This might result in part from a more leisurely lifestyle, but is supported as well by findings that the early cultivators had more limited diets and suffered from diseases not found among hunters and gatherers. This comes as no real surprise. We naturally evolved over hundreds of thousands of years for our bodies to work best on the varied diet, band level relationships and leisurely lifestyle of a forager. The males of the Ju/'hoansi may be having a good time with the hunt, but the varied diet they help provide serves an important function as well.

This seeming contradiction in the usefulness of bones highlights one of the chief concerns for empiricism. How do we know when a method for obtaining observable data is both valid and reliable? The method is valid if the empirical evidence reflects the meaning we seek. The method is reliable if using the method in similar situations provides similar meaning. Difficulty in "ascribing an age at death" hurts the reliability of dating old bones. Problems with the probability that

---

12 From the chapter "The Evolution of the Human Life Course," by Ronald Lee, in *Between Zeus and the Salmon: The Biodemography of Longevity* (1997), edited by Kenneth W. Wachter and Caleb E. Finch.

13 From a paper available from the Internet, "Longevity among hunter-gatherers: a cross-cultural examination," (2006), by Michael Gurven and Hillard Kaplan. Much of this research is also in *Between Zeus and the Salmon*.

dead people of all ages are represented in a bones collection make the method invalid for determining average age. Yet the biases that might affect misrepresenting the ages of early foragers in the bones collection should also affect early cultivators. While the method is invalid for determining absolute ages, the method should be valid for determining relative differences in age.

Problems of validity and reliability exist for ethnographic studies as well. Once contact has been made by an advanced civilization the possibility exists for the evidence about early cultures to be distorted. Perhaps some support has been provided that biases the evidence. Yet ethnographic studies have been done shortly after first contact, minimizing the impact of this on the validity and reliability of the evidence. Simple and direct methods, when valid and reliable, are preferable to complicated ones. This hearkens back to Essay 4, when the Federal Reserve Board used extremely complicated methods to prove to us all we are having more leisure these days, instead of using something much simpler like trends in day care. Attaching greater significance to the age of old bones rather than the age of live humans would satisfy only those just spouting idolized beliefs.

Running out of Time

The conclusions that the modern day Hans makes about the longevity of early cultures are as problematic as his conclusions about the longevity of early humans. Westerners tend to think of the Roman Empire as the civilization with the greatest longevity, which neoconservatives hope to surpass with the Pax Americana. In reality, the Greek and Roman era combined are but adolescents to the Chinese Empire that predated both and lasted until at least the eighteenth century, with but a brief incursion by the Mongols. Only in the nineteenth century did technology and the balance of trade with other civilizations no longer tip in the Chinese Empire's favor. But even the Chinese are mere toddlers in swaddling clothes compared to the Ju/'hoansi and other aboriginal cultures. Up until European contact in the nineteenth century, the Ju/'hoansi used the same cultural style of bone-tipped arrows for their hunts that they used in 20,000 BC. Now that's longevity!

Early cultures modified their internal behaviors to maintain a balance with their environments. External disturbances could upset this balance. The external disturbance could be natural, such as an exploding volcano, or from a different culture, such as colonialism. An "r-species" culture that rapidly exploits and colonizes environments has an advantage over a "k-species" culture that lives in balance with their environment. The "r-species" culture uses up the resources of their original environment and then seeks to colonize and exploit the environments inhabited by "k-species" cultures. In this manner the "r-species" can shift the "brutish" nature of population crashes to the exploited "k-species," at least for awhile.

Cultural evolution has created both k-species and r-species variants of humans. In regards to external environmental conditions, the k-species variant lasts the longer of the two. Great empires have evolved, dominated their age and expired, while a few remaining foraging cultures continued uninterrupted throughout human history and prehistory. But even these few remaining cultures could disappear as r-species variants of the human population continue to exploit resources outside the boundaries of their own environments.

As might be defined by an ecologist, western civilization became an r-species variant of the human population. Western colonialism was a process of imperial nation states spilling over their uncontrolled use of resources to new environments. Growth patterns in colonies responded with higher birth rates and concentrated populations, a boon for the exploitive agricultural or industrial activity favored by the colonizers. Thus, "brutish" conditions result from both external and internal pressures ultimately caused by the colonization of the "r-species" variant of humans.

Historically, "backward" civilizations choose to emulate their "forward" neighbors. Thus during the post-classical period the Japanese chose to adopt those technology and beliefs from the Chinese Empire that they thought would make them more advanced. Also during this period western civilization chose to emulate the more advanced Ottoman and Chinese Empires in ways that contributed to our own advancement perhaps as much as did our own Enlightenment. Western civilization has closed the door on this path towards advancement. Developed countries now dictate the terms and pace of advancement for underdeveloped countries, with frequent "brutish" results.[14]

Africa has been the continent most colonized by imperial cultures, and consequently experience some of the most "brutish" conditions on the planet. We can broaden the term "colonialism" to include seemingly independent governments that yet are forced by some means to abide by the uncontrolled resource use of other countries. Much of the Latin American countries that were entrapped by the Washington Consensus of big loans for big obligations to multinational corporations fit this description of "colonialism." Thus the "brutish" conditions found in both Africa and parts of South America are brought about by colonizing variants of the human species that pride themselves as being products of the Enlightenment.

There may be no more early cultures out there that have not had their first contact with "advanced" civilizations. Given the rapid colonization now possible, the time may come sooner rather than later when no early cultures are left as contemporaries. This sad prospect has a few depressing implications. First, we will witness our longest continuous cultures come to an end. This is a bit more ominous than something like Cal Ripken retiring. Second, in coming to an end they likely will shift from what Wasserstein would label an external economy, operating

---

14 This quick overview of civilizations imitating others was abstracted from a course on CD by the Teaching Company, *A Brief History of the World* (2007), by Professor Peter N. Stearns.

independently of global economics, to a periphery economy that is exploited by the core developed countries of the world. As part of the economic relationship with the core countries, they will be on the low end of the wealth disparity continuum, where having very few material possessions will now indeed be an indicator of "poor."

Finally, when we lose all early cultures as contemporaries, we will lose a source of valid and reliable data for the baseline of who we naturally are and what real impacts cultural evolution has had on our species. We will have less empirical evidence to combat the idolized belief that the life of natural man is "solitary, poor, nasty, brutish and short." Those who have the most to gain from this myth, namely colonizers, will continue their mission aided by greater gullibility. The time is now, then, to set the record straight about some of the authoritarian beliefs that sprang from the Enlightenment; beliefs that evolved western civilization into the greatest colonizing variant of the human species ever to exist.

UnEnlightenment Economics

So far, we have criticized Thomas Hobbes only. Thomas Hobbes was not the only Enlightenment philosopher to scholastically reflect on the natural condition of humans from his comfy armchair, only to remain clueless about natural man. The Enlightenment was a broad movement, covering the full span of economic, political and cultural systems. Yet all the enlightened ideas that came out of these philosophers were built on a similar misconception of early cultures being "solitary, poor, nasty, brutish and short." Great philosophers such as Adam Smith, John Locke and even John Stuart Mill turned off the light of understanding for our early cultures and natural condition, advocating beliefs without empirical evidence, constructing their ideas for civilization from a vantage point of relative darkness. We could just as well call this critical period of western civilization, when even sympathizers such as Jacque Rousseau viewed the noble foragers he championed as savage, The UnEnlightenment.

At the heart of The UnEnlightenment is a failure of the sense of belonging. The great thinkers of that age separated themselves from what they saw as our primitive natural condition. Thus an abolitionist such as David Hume can nevertheless write in his essay "Of the Populousness of Ancient Nations" (1758): "There never was a civilized nation of any other complexion than white, nor even any individual eminent either in action or speculation." The failure to connect with early cultures at this level prevented these unenlightened philosophers from understanding the deeper meanings of how our sense of belonging determines human systems.

The economic system formed by foragers was based on what Sahlins termed, in *Stone Age Economics*, the Domestic Mode of Production (DMP). The "domestic mode" is the communal unit formed by early cultures through a sense of belonging, called a band. As Lee describes for the Ju/'hoansi the kinship lines that form these bands can be extensive and flexible. People move from one band to another based on their sense of belonging. If unresolved tensions occur between the kin of a Ju/'hoansi band, one of the parties simply moves on to another band.

The "production" of foragers is for the internal use of the band, and many times just for the nuclear family units within the bands. Only a limited amount of goods might be produced for exchange outside of the unit, such as an exchange of marriage gifts. Within the band everything is shared. Meat mainly gathered by males and vegetables mainly gathered by females are shared, sometimes with elaborate rules to guarantee fairness. Healthy adults produce goods on behalf of their children and elderly. Thus the sense of belonging that develops among foragers not only determines their cultural system but also their economic system of resource distribution, their DMP. Something like the DMP happens to be the *modus operandi* of k-species throughout all of nature.

DMP economics falls significantly short of the carrying capacity of the environment. This holds true even for early agriculture. Slash and burn agriculture gets a bad reputation these days for good reason, because farmers are forced to extract huge surpluses of raw goods for the sake of developed countries. When part of a DMP economic system, studies have shown slash and burn agriculture to remain below the carrying capacity of poor tropical soils.[15] The patches are small enough and the rotation cycles long enough to be permanently sustained, which is why those slash and burn agricultures could be discovered in tact and thriving still in the twentieth century.

Enlightened philosophers such as Adam Smith, the father of economics, claimed that market economies are best driven by the self-interest of greed. A disclaimer should be made that Smith was, by no means, a greedy person. Had modern day *laissez faire* economists truly followed the ideas of Smith, rather than idolize those parts that prove most beneficial to corporations, the middle class would not be on a downward spiral of debt. Still, some blame must be attributed to Smith for contributing to our emulsion into darkness with his "enlightened" vision for economics that discounted either merit or a sense of belonging as a factor in markets.

Herbert Spencer took this economic "enlightenment" a step further with his reflections on the economic "survival of the fittest." Spencer was the earliest proof that would-be economists do not know what the hell they are doing when they borrow from ecology. As discussed in the first essay on economics, natural competition in an environment of abundant resources leads to increased diversity, not the survival of either fewer superspecies or multinational corporations. Only cultural institutions such as government can provide the means for something like

15 Table 2.1, pages 44-45, of *Stone Age Economics* provides a summary of such studies done by a variety of anthropologists.

a multinational corporation to concentrate capital and thrive to the competitive disadvantage of proprietorships.

Dog-eat-dog survival of the fittest also implies that resources barely meet subsistence levels. For early foragers, and even early agriculture, this simply was not true. The cultures dispersed and diversified, in accordance with an ecologist's understanding of competition, and they used resources at a rate that remained below the carrying capacity of the environment, in accordance with typical k-species behavior. The UnEnlightenment provided the cultural beliefs and behaviors that turned us more towards r-species economics, where the point of competition is not to subsist but to colonize and use as many resources as possible, including the resources of other cultures. Without The UnEnlightenment, modern day *laissez faire* economists and puppet libertarians would be derided and laughed at for seeking to degrade two of the most important components of any system, diversity and sustainability. Modern day cult economists like Milton Friedman stand on the shoulders of unenlightened giants in regards to denying the true normative altruism of our natural being.

UnEnlightenment Politics

The simple sharing of resources within a band involves egalitarian politics. Rules of sharing are followed, but these are so well understood and accepted by the band that no formal system of law or contract is required. Consequently, there is not much basis for comparing our current political systems to the earliest forms of band level culture. The stationary tribes that evolved from foraging bands provide the baseline data for a distribution of resources not based directly on sharing. The DMP is replaced by a more political redistribution of resources involving a tribal chief.[16]

A portion of the resources earned by the merit of the tribe's labors is redistributed upwards to the chief, much like what occurs with corporations and shareholders. The analogy breaks down miserably at that point. Many tribal cultures have this quaint notion that respect is earned through generosity. Through the respect of the tribe comes the authority that the chief can wield. Thus the most authoritative man in a tribe, also controlling the most resources, is often the poorest. The chief redistributes the resources back to the tribe to complete, in essence, a politics founded on humility.

Though we may judge chiefs to be complete fools from the corporate or shareholder perspective, we should not think this totally strange from the point of view of culture or politics. One of the foundational beliefs of Christianity is that "the first shall be last." In the United States we still on occasion use the term

---

16 Tribal politics information was gleaned from *Stone Age Economics* (1972) by Marshall Sahlins and from *Peoples and Cultures of the World* (2004), a Course on CD by the Teaching Company, taught by Professor Edward Fischer.

"public servant" to describe the officials we elect to run our governments, though perhaps we have lost the original meaning of the term. Many might consider the principle of ruling through the authority granted by generosity as the epitome of wisdom. Pork barrel politics, though part of a corrupted system that enriches politicians, nevertheless is based on this principle of retaining authority through generosity. The analogy breaks down because the "pork barrel" is used to empower politicians at the ultimate expense of constituents.

The wisdom of generosity derives from our sense of belonging being the foundation of a political system. Generosity and respect result from the sense of belonging people in a tribe hold for each other. Through this respect comes authority, whether in a tribe or in local communities from western culture. There is even some corollary for the politics of a sense of belonging at the scale of a large civilization. The Chinese Empire was based on the cultural foundation of Confucianism, which insisted on a paternal obligation to the people. The early Chinese dynasties were obliged by a cultural code to look after and care for those they ruled.

In contrast to our sense of belonging, the UnEnlightenment established contracts and laws as the foundation of a political system. The terms of contracts, not the generosity of people, became the ultimate sources of authority and respect. While unavoidable at this point of our cultural evolution, we must be mindful that contracts and laws now facilitate exploitation. Considering the lofty esteem placed in contracts and laws, this assertion requires some justification.

The cause for the "enlightened" view of contract was obvious. Western civilization had gone through a period where the individual was subjugated to the capricious whims of monarchies, papal authorities and feudal lords. Even before the Middle Ages the abundant use of slavery by the Roman Empire, in contrast to the sparser use of slavery by the Chinese Empire, foreshadowed that we were a civilization destined to be culturally challenged with nurturing our sense of belonging. Contracts were a political means of instituting civility between the State and the individual where the attrition of our sense of belonging encouraged exploitation.

We can therefore sympathize with Hobbes a little bit in his view that our natural condition was "solitary, poor, nasty, brutish and short." From the Roman Empire onward what else could he conclude about western civilization? Hobbes was an early advocate of the contract as a means of saving us from ourselves. We needed the contract more to prevent the consequences of our base natures than to promote the cultural good.

John Locke was another early pioneer for contracts during The UnEnlightenment, but took a more optimistic view for our natural condition than Hobbes.[17] Hobbes condemned social protest and revolution, since the sovereign

---

17 *Two Treatises of Government* (1689) conveyed Locke's beliefs on natural rights, property and contracts.

contract was saving us from ourselves, but Locke championed the notion that the individual actually had an obligation to ignore and rebel against contracts, laws or government if principles of "life, liberty and property" were being abused. Locke even acknowledged that Native Americans used something similar to contracts.

The protection of life, liberty and property constitute what Locke viewed to be natural law. There are flaws with all of these, the result of Locke himself never having empirically examined the natural condition. Liberty and property have no meaning save in a cultural context. Locke normatively stipulates that property is based on the merits of labor (we can forgive him for not foreseeing *laissez faire* economics or puppet libertarians actually seeking to compromise merit through the status of property). But by choosing property rather than labor as the determinant of economic worth, Locke effectively endorses the contract as the ultimate judge and authority. Unfortunately, a contract imposes no inherent judgments between the honest merits of labor and unmerited greed.

Liberty sounds like a nice political goal, but if the contracts or laws intended to secure liberty do not forbid distortion and secrecy, we have lost the real freedom of natural thought. A free market, unless you think like a "free market" libertarian, must be driven by open and honest information about the goods being exchanged, allowing the natural thoughts of consumers to determine their economics. A free government, unless you are a neoconservative, must be driven by openness and honesty, allowing the natural thoughts of citizens to determine their politics. There are no inherent political virtues of contracts and laws that require openness and honesty. They could just as well be driven by a political authoritarian principle of money being an expression of free speech, as alien as that principle is to any real understanding of liberty.

Protecting life is indeed a natural instinct, but that does not make prolonged life a natural right. Yet just as we have instincts to protect our lives we, as do other k-species in nature, have opposing instincts to risk our lives for proper causes, such as to protect our young or our community. Our natural sense of belonging determines our cultural altruism, including when to protect and when to risk life. Contracts and laws, to repeat once more, have no inherent ability to make such cultural judgments.

To sum up, contracts and laws have no inherent political wisdom. They have no natural inclination towards economic merit; they have no natural inclination towards political openness and honesty; they have no natural inclination towards cultural altruism. Contracts and laws are simply tools, nothing more or less. How they are to be used as tools ultimately depends on our sense of belonging, and whether we strive to idolize or harmonize our beliefs and behaviors. That contracts and laws are necessary to prevent the barbarism generic to r-species colonization now appears irrefutable, but they carry with them their own dangers.

The same resolute defenders of contracts will also recommend that contracts be negotiated from a position of strength. The same advice holds true for laws. The demands for labor do not grant a position of strength over the resources of corporations to weather brief storms when negotiating contracts. The demands of a democracy cannot ensure a position of strength over the resources of wealth and power elites when passing laws. While the tools of contracts and laws are not the root of the greed and special interests driving our political system, they do not provide a cure. Contracts negotiated from a position of strength will redistribute the overall balance of resources to the side holding the advantage, generally in contradiction to merit, wisdom and harmony.

At the stage of international law and contracts, being in a position of strength is a license to exploit and/or colonize. Contracts and laws then become the tools by which we pursue an r-species approach to life. The justifications we provide for the politics of contracts still take us back to Locke and Hobbes and other great thinkers of the UnEnlightenment.

UnEnlightenment Culture

There are no political boundaries to a band or tribe. In the case of foragers the "boundaries" move along with the band. Their "nation" consists of a group of people bonded by a sense of belonging and the geographic area they need for food and shelter during any particular season. They identify themselves primarily with the people and places of their living conditions, not with abstract beliefs and behaviors that align with political boundaries.

Nation forming and building are phenomena of western civilization. War has been the main impetus over the years for forming nations internally; colonization has been the main impetus for building nations elsewhere. An example of nation forming is the 100 Year War. William of Normandy conquered Britain and became king. Since William retained land in Normandy over the years the English royalty felt an entitlement to these original lands and other lands even farther south. A series of battles were launched, and mainly won, by England. Yet they were trying to occupy foreign lands that did not want to be occupied and the war was ultimately lost. The nations of England and France formed and coalesced through the course of this war. Incidentally, the ability of a superior invading foreign power to win most of the battles and still lose the ultimate war would become a familiar theme in western civilization.

War costs money; authorities seek to cover the costs of war through taxes. Collecting taxes necessitates boundaries that delineate those to be taxed, apart from their natural sense of place or belonging. War also requires manpower from within these same boundaries. Gathering the support needed for manpower took the form of nationalism, a mindset that championed abstract nation states over concrete communities. Many European countries formed during the UnEnlightenment in conjunction with war and nationalism.

Nation building became an extension of colonization. To colonize is to tap the resources of other cultures to use in markets. The best tool for this is the corporation, which came into existence mainly for the purpose of market expansion. Corporations cannot exist without the type of government intervention that nations provide. The governments of core countries can suffice for creating and backing corporations, and only the intervention of core country governments fueled the initial periods of colonization.

A transition from colonies towards nation building provided benefits to corporations. More nations in the world mean more governments that multinational corporations can play against each other for the sake of bargaining strength. International development organizations such as the World Bank and International Monetary Fund enhance the bargaining strength of multinational corporations further through financial "aid" with strings attached to nation states.

Corporate sales and shareholders benefit from the government interventions of a developed country, while a box office (for tax purposes) and exploited labor can be sanctioned through developing countries providing a "bargain." Now nation building accomplishes the neat trick of political democratization and economic colonization in the same process. Neoconservatives can trace the lineage of their manifesto back to the colonial seeds planted by the UnEnlightenment.

Ontogeny Recapitulates Phylogeny

There is a theory in developmental biology that ontogeny recapitulates phylogeny. Translated into English, the development of an organism resembles the evolution of that species. The journey from embryonic to adult form resembles the journey from simple to complex organisms. The theory does not fit the empirical data entirely, but still has some merit.

We have explained how modern western civilization is a product of the UnEnlightenment. The problems we have cited, such as nationalism and colonialism, result from character flaws that infect adults more than children. Children are committed to people and places. As a group they lack the potential vanity of adults to wrap their self-esteem in abstract ideals; certainly they are more humble than the vain endeavors of interest groups like the American Legion. Children have faith. As a group they lack the potential cynicism of adults that commits them to materialism; certainly they are less cynical than interest groups like the Christian Coalition who are devoted to power and wealth. Children also have great courage. Children may be afraid of things such as the dark, but they will accept the unknown and the truth straight up with less apprehension than adults. They seek responsibility they are not yet ready to handle, rather than avoid responsibility that should be their duty to face. Children are a good deal less apprehensive than interest groups such as PNAC.

All of this stems from the reality that children have a much greater sense of belonging than adults. Neither their physical nor their mental abilities are fully developed, they cannot compare with adults in regards to the merits of our labors or the freedom of our thoughts. Yet we know instinctively that the sense to belong starts out strong at the beginning of life. The developmental atrophy of this belonging from child to adult resembles the cultural atrophy of belonging from early cultures to modern western civilization. Perhaps something about our adolescent period of development "recapitulates" the cultural evolution of the UnEnlightenment, at least for those who become our economic, political and cultural leaders.

We have a tendency to brand any culture as primitive that engages in rituals bizarre to us. This may be imperial arrogance on our part typically, but occasionally you have to forego political correctness and call things as you see them. Neoconservatives should appreciate the moral clarity of this stance. There is one particular culture that engages in a series of bizarre and degrading rituals that clearly makes them primitive barbarians. Allegedly, they lie in burial artifacts and masturbate; they wrestle each other in mud; they urinate on each other; they scream at bones. Once they have established a social contract through these rituals they then hold each other in the highest esteem. They idolize their beliefs to an extreme, yet they cloak their behaviors in secrecy. We must describe their behaviors as "allegedly" because we must rely on the testimony of third party accounts not sworn to such grave secrecy.

The members of this culture think they are special; to that extent they are vain. They cynically degrade each other in ritual even as they assume superiority to people outside their culture. Finally, they are filled with apprehension for openness and honesty about their behaviors. This primitive culture does not exist from long ago or far away; unfortunately, they are right across the state from me. The Skull and Bones secret fraternity of Yale University has spawned captains of multinational corporations and world leaders. These vain, apprehensive and cynical primates were, in fact, instrumental in establishing the CIA.[18]

A period of transition that prepares children to become adults is known as a coming of age or rites of passage. In some cultures this period has a set structure and purpose, such as the walkabout for Australian aborigines or the vision quest for Inuits. The structure involves going into the wilderness during that period and leaving culture behind. The purpose is to reenter culture with a better sense of who you are and what your role in the culture should be. Alone in the wilderness, a sense of belonging is developed for others uninfluenced by social cliques. A sense of belonging to a higher order forms independently of fundamental beliefs. A sense of belonging to one's self does not get confused by the complexities of

---

18 You can read about their alleged behaviors at http://skullandcrossbones.org/articles/skulland-bones.htm and http://skullandcrossbones.org/articles/skullandbones-esquire.htm.

social temptations.

In our country most adolescents "come of age" in school. Rather than nurture their sense of belonging through introspection, students typically become inundated with social pressures for which they have little perspective or little guidance to navigate. The Internet has exacerbated this inundation. They are greeted by a plethora of beliefs, virtually all of which are idolized by those who hold them. They must adapt to these social complexities without an anchor in first knowing who they are. They may get involved with a "good" or "bad" crowd, but in neither case do they establish a natural perspective for understanding the normative role of our sense of belonging in culture.

Thus the developmental impacts of schools are much like the evolutionary impacts of the UnEnlightenment. Schools offer terrific avenues for intellectual and cultural stimulation, but no better insight into our natural condition or sense of belonging than does Thomas Hobbes. Secret societies within a school, or within the broader culture, then become a perverted caricature of what our "coming of age" should involve. Members not only have lost any natural perspective, they insulate their own cultural beliefs and behaviors against the influence of others. Harmony or a genuine sense of belonging to the broader culture becomes virtually impossible to achieve. As the Skull and Bones members demonstrate, they insidiously network themselves into positions of authority based on their shared idolatries.

My Own Rites of Passage

My own rites of passage consisted of backpacking thousands of miles, spread out over a number of years. Yet I can point to one specific moment in the wilderness, in 1977, when I gained the essential wisdom needed to become an adult. I was on the Pacific Crest Trail in the Sierra Nevada, heading south for the Mexican border. I stood alone at a trail junction, peering through a gap in the mountains to the expansive desert east.

I arrived at that trail junction having first completed the Appalachian Trail, a challenge set and met. Now the goal of completing the Pacific Crest Trail seemingly was assured. I had carried heavy packs, hiked long miles and endured many discomforts without being deterred. Our guidebook warned that people got lost for an average of 200-300 miles on the PCT (an unfinished trail in 1977), a number our Expedition at least equaled, yet we always managed to find our way in the end. The previous night I made camp soaked by wet snow, yet addressed that situation with absolute confidence that I would prevent hypothermia. Wilderness no longer posed a serious physical or mental challenge to me.

A cold drizzle sprayed my pack and parka as I stood at that trail junction, watching wisps of smoke rise from chimneys in a beckoning village. I confronted myself as to why I should not take the side trail down out of the mountains to warmth and civilization. What was there left for me to prove? The goal was not finished, but I previously completed a similar journey and everything this goal represented—strength of body, independence of spirit and resourcefulness of mind—I already achieved. The Mexican border was no more a meaningful end for me than heading for the immediate comfort of a village.

There really are only three ends that matter for civilization: to enjoy and share the merits of our specialized labors without exploitation; to collect the wisdom of our diverse, independent and decentralized thoughts; and to achieve harmony despite diverse belongings. Everything else becomes only the props for the journey. Capitalism or communism, monarchies or federations, interest groups or neighborhoods, are good or bad only in the context of how they augment our natural rights to the free merits of our labor, free thought and free will.

We can be sidetracked into longing for "wisps of smoke." We can abandon a quest for civilized advancement when we think a false patriotism, evangelism or neoconservatism might satisfy more urgent goals. We can fool ourselves into thinking that the end of history is near, changing our patient journey into an urgent dash for the finish. We can evolve culturally into something we naturally are not, and even declare such evolution to be the Enlightenment.

As I stood gazing longingly at the cozy village, a flood of thoughts and memories swept through me. A vision of an old woman needing a penny came to mind. I recalled a moment standing on top of an overlook along the Appalachian Trail when I was overwhelmed by the calm sunset after a storm, and I sensed that I belonged to something tremendously greater than myself. I knew that the cozy village below me now was just a mirage. There would be no end to my journey any more than we have ever witnessed an "end to history." As long as I live, as long as we live, we are constant sojourners.

Though I stood alone I was far from being "solitary." Most people would have concluded from the sum of the possessions on my back that I was "poor," but richness surrounded me in ways that mattered most. Granted, I might have smelled "nasty, brutish," but that merely was the cost of being in the best condition of my life. Would life be "short?" How was I to know? Only fools and cowards sacrifice the quality of life for the sake of speculative security. The point was not where or when the destination of a secure life was reached but the quality of my life's journey along the way. That quality depended only on the company I kept, the senses of belonging I nurtured along the way.

I tightened my pack straps and turned away to catch up with Dave, Ken and Dan, the people I belonged to for this part of my journey. There would be no urgency to reach a destination. That was the moment I became an adult. As I headed south towards Mexico one other memory came back to me. When I had neared the end of my first Appalachian Trail thru-hike I encountered a former coal miner also thru-hiking and also near the end of the trail. He recounted how he discovered he had black lung and determined that he would spend his last days pursuing his dream of hiking the AT. He never expected to live long enough to actually reach Katahdin. I asked him what he would do now that he was about to reach his destination after all.

"Just keep on goin' I s'pose," was his reply.

And so the wisdom of a West Virginia coal-miner was transferred to a college student from Connecticut, without having gone through a Skull and Bones initiation. Meanwhile, three thousand miles away from the trail junction where I stood amidst the majesty of the Sierra Nevada, at that same time some of our country's current wealth and power elites were then in a secret society shouting demonically at old bones. Only the elite can get away with such primitive behavior without being castigated for their blatant barbarism; just one of many unfortunate consequences from The UnEnlightenment.

ESSAY 23 – BALANCING CULTURAL "ISMS"

When Life Was Full There Was No History

> "In the age when life on earth was full,
> no one paid any special attention to worthy men,
> nor did they single out the man of ability. Rulers
> were simply the highest branches on the tree, and
> the people were like deer in the woods. They were
> honest and righteous without realizing that they
> were 'doing their duty.' They loved each other
> and did not know that this was 'love of neighbor.'
> They deceived no one yet they did not know that
> they were 'men to be trusted.' They were reliable
> and did not know that this was 'good faith.' They
> lived freely together giving and taking and did
> not know that they were generous. For this reason
> their deeds have not been narrated. They made
> no history."

- Chuang Tzu, as compiled and translated by Thomas Merton,
Way of Chuang Tzu (1969)

Overview

- The sense of belonging displayed by early cultures can be found in middle class communities.
- We naturally evolved as an altruistic k-species with a strong sense of belonging.
- Our cultural evolution as a colonizing r-species has had severe drawbacks.
- Civilized beliefs need to be harmonized with natural rights and conditions.
- Materialism corrupts belonging, but encourages specialization and diversity that can contribute to harmony.
- Individualism threatens community, but can reveal to us our natural condition and insights about why we live in community.
- Communalism threatens free will, but provides a foundation for federation.
- Utilitarianism ignores our natural condition, but promotes empiricism.
- Scholasticism induces idolatry, but provides support for effective leaders.
- A full life is one without idolatry or idols.

Middle Class Community

In the previous essay I gave a seemingly rosy portrait of early cultures. This was not done to encourage us all to become nomadic foragers. In order to use early cultures for the sake of baseline comparisons of current cultural systems I needed to debunk some myths. Since these myths provided a naive pessimistic outlook about our natural condition, debunking them necessarily provided an optimistic view in comparison. In reality, idolizing the beliefs and behaviors of early cultures gets us no closer to harmony than idolizing our own. In this essay we will construct a cultural system of belonging by harmonizing current beliefs and behaviors with our natural condition and rights.

Every December Cindy and I engage in general reciprocity, defined in the previous essay as a system of gift-giving for the purpose of cementing social bonds. Cindy and I work out our gift-giving in what I consider to be a fair and balanced way. She spends at least a hundred hours baking her famous cinnamon and maple walnut breads. Then on the day before Christmas the kids and I go out for a few hours in the afternoon giving the bread to friends and neighbors, gladly accepting any of the hospitality and good cheer that might be reciprocated. Hey! If *Fox News* can consider what they do to be fair and balanced I see no problem with this arrangement between Cindy and the rest of the family.

We are not alone in the giving of baked goods before Christmas. Nor is the giving of baked goods the only way in which middle class neighbors and friends cement social bonds. We help each other with pet-sitting, shoveling snow, running errands, driving kids to their activities and many other daily needs typical of middle class culture. The mutual support is nice, but the mutual belonging is even better.

Middle class communities such as the one on Emerson Street have a good deal more in common with the foragers of the Ju/'hoansi than with the fraternal members of the secret Skull and Bones society. But, again, let us not be guilty of romanticizing. There were beliefs and behaviors of early cultures that we justifiably would find abhorrent in modern times. Infant mortality was high, with some of that mortality intentionally arranged to keep down population growth. The elderly had to be abandoned when the demands of a nomadic lifestyle precluded their adequate care. Though mass aggression is more typical of modern cultures, some evidence suggests that early cultures had higher rates of individual aggression. Without the State providing medical technology or security services disease and aggression would cut the lives of some short; even though their healthy lifestyles enabled long lives to most of those that survived adolescence.

Our middle class community strikes a harmonic balance between the natural sense of belonging typical of early cultures with modern beliefs and behaviors. Unfortunately, much of modern culture outside the community places a higher priority on materialism over our sense of belonging. The community is being replaced by the interest group. Individual free will has succumbed to authoritarian appeals for destiny. The patience of everyday life has been replaced by the urgency to do or support great things on national or global stages. We are, ultimately, a culture of idolatry rather than harmony.

The task, then, is to sort out the good from the bad. Let us identify important elements of modern culture that do not compromise our natural sense of belonging, and condemn that which reinforces idolatry. To do this let us review again our empirical natural condition as an ecological k-species.

K-Species Supreme

Throughout these essays we have treated k-species and r-species as natural stereotypes. Most organisms have a mixture of these traits. That makes our own k-species heritage all the more remarkable. Humans are as close to the natural stereotype of a k-species as any species can be. Consider the remarkable adaptations of our opposable thumbs, large brains, long gestation periods and sense of belonging.

Most r-species evolve to be efficient colonizers of specific environments. Together, our opposable thumbs and our large brains make us a highly adaptable organism that survives all environments. We do not have to frequently colonize as a survival strategy for the species, we have the brains and tools to adapt and persist in any given environment. While we also use our extreme adaptability to colonize, our life cycle and sense of belonging are further adaptations for moderating the demands we place on resources in order to achieve sustainability over long periods.

Other k-species are distinguished similarly by these traits. Whales and dolphins may be as intelligent as we are. Other primates also make tools. Elephants have strong kinship ties. However, none of them combine all these adaptations to achieve sustainability in all environments as effectively as the human species. The long process of natural evolution, whether through randomness or intent, has made humans the k-species supreme. Through this natural evolution we have the potential to be one of the last species remaining when cosmic forces put an end to the planet.

Out of these k-species adaptations, the one that most sets us apart is our sense of belonging. We marvel at the social organization of bees and ants, but there is no free will and diversity in this matter. Whales and dolphins, not to mention a host of other k-species, have a similar sense of belonging as ours in regards to family and communal units. There is no evidence that their sense of belonging can be federated, harmonizing the sense of belonging across communal units up to advanced levels such as the State. There is no evidence that their sense of belonging extends to a higher order of life. Our sense of belonging can be used for conventions of altruism, resource sharing and sustainability that, once again, make us the k-species supreme.

What natural evolution accomplishes over eons, we can change through culture in an evolutionary moment. Cultural evolution cannot effect significant physical change over a few thousand years to our intelligence, our life cycles or our anatomy. Cultural evolution can change our sense of belonging over the short period of human history. Cultures with less of a sense of belonging will have more of an attachment to material resources. They will adapt to compete for these resources more effectively, to the point of uncontrolled resource use and colonizing the environments of other cultures.

Foraging cultures, the earliest and longest lasting of all human cultures, now face extinction. If the land that they forage can be taken and owned, then foragers can be restricted to smaller amounts of land. They can be rounded up and constrained to a specific area, keeping them on something like a reservation. At this point their former culture is no longer viable. The remaining few can be exterminated or assimilated. All these methods were used to conquer and colonize Native American land.

R-Species Drawbacks

Why not just "go with the flow?" Several lines of reasoning suggest we should welcome our transformation into an r-species. Scientists are fond of predicting that bacteria, the r-species supreme, will outlast all other organisms. Though k-species cultures have lasted well over the ages, now that humans have evolved into an r-species our exploitation of resources has ended or threatens their existence. Within our own species the r-species variant appears headed to become the ultimate winner. Why should we not welcome this shift to the winning side of the evolutionary game? The ecologist's caution to this would be that humans naturally evolved to be k-species. There are expected costs to culturally supplant what Nature intended. Let us examine a few of the empirical costs that accompany the r-species gains of uncontrolled resource use.

R-species cultures lack sustainability – The longest running cultures, though they finally face extinction in the twenty-first century, are early k-species bands and tribes. The longest running empire to date, the Chinese Empire (with no close competitor for second place in terms of longevity), showed the least inclination of all empires to colonize distant places.

R-species cultures have suboptimal utility – Exploitation of goods to gain a surplus leads to suboptimal indulgence, waste and/or neglect of resources. Exploitation of labor leads to suboptimal performance, such as occurs with slavery. Wall Street claimed Henry Ford to be a fool for giving high wages to factory workers, until his "generosity" proved to spur high production from labor. The utility of greed also has been refuted by game theory (see Essay 3).

R-species cultures do not promote happiness – Despite a media culture that defines happiness for us as having wealth, and despite our unparalleled success at accumulating and concentrating such wealth, our happiness has not increased. Our inherent nature rejects what mass culture is peddling.

R-species cultures increase stress and decrease health – Granted, medical technology can overcome the detrimental health factors created by an overworked, urgent culture, but the technology of urgent cultures driven by greed benefits a decreased percentage of the population. A better approach would be to pursue medical technology without the unhealthy urgency induced by greed, power or idolatry.

R-species cultures experience mass mortalities – This is a law of nature for all r-species, and we are not exempt. The crashes come from famine, disease or aggression, brought on through resource exploitation. We have evolved to colonize and exploit the resources of far-off lands, shifting the population crashes to these areas. Yet the World Wars of the last century prove that not even the core countries of the world can escape the mass mortality brought on by our conversion to r-species behavior.

R-species beliefs and behaviors must be enforced culturally – Without exploitation, the suboptimal use of resources by r-species cultures would put them at a competitive disadvantage. At an individual level we naturally tend to resent and resist the exploitation necessary for r-species cultures to successfully compete. Our instincts for a communal sense of belonging and a high quality of life must be thwarted by enculturation. This enculturation steers us towards an economics of greed, a politics of authoritarianism and a culture of idolatry.

Cultural Evolution

Ecologists would infer from the baseline data that our cultural evolution as a colonialist, corporatist r-species has undermined our natural evolution; but let's not trust ecologists. They are the same alarmists that have been trying to warn us over the past two decades about the cultural warming of the earth. Fortunately, over those same two decades we had corporate media providing "balance" by echoing the counterclaims of corporate funded research. News talk hosts provide the same type of "balance" when echoing their support for the greed of corporations, the authoritarianism of our administrations and the idolatry of cult heroes.

The cultural evolution of western civilization to produce the r-species variants of humans has been a history of fitting the proverbial square peg in a round hole. Even the colonialist Spaniards and British have the natural k-species adaptations of long gestation periods, opposable thumbs, intelligence and a strong sense of belonging. You need to apply a whole lot of force, and a dearth of wisdom, to overcome these natural adaptations for social survival in order to manifest cultural greed. Forcing that "square peg" involves shaving off slivers of sustainability, economic optimization, happiness, natural health and the quality of life that hinges on community. There ought to be a better way for us to culturally evolve.

What ought to be can be based on natural, normative and/or moral criteria. These three "ought to be" criteria can be combined into one. The counterexample to natural beliefs and behaviors are those that are forced, or are artificial to our character. In the absence of enculturation, mass media, political brainwashing and other forms of culturally induced conformity the natural experiences of humans would vary; but some types of natural beliefs and behaviors would emerge as most typical, or normative. The process of enculturation includes fixed beliefs that we call morals for what we ought to belief and how to behave. These morals are relative to the culture that produces them, such as the relativistic morals of neoconservatives and fundamentalists. Morals that are absolute must be independent of the idolatrous beliefs developed through enculturation. Absolute morality derives instead from the natural and normative human experience.

We have an absolute natural, normative and moral right to the merits of independent labor. A free market exchange of the merits of our labors is natural and moral; cultural redistribution of productive labor to concentrate the benefits for a few is unnatural and immoral. We have an absolute natural, normative and moral right to the wisdom of independent thought. Open and honest information fuels this natural and moral right; secrecy and dishonesty are unnatural and immoral obstacles. We have an absolute natural, normative and moral right to the harmony of independent belonging. Humility, faith and courage strengthen this natural and moral right to belong; vanity, cynicism and cowardice are unnatural and immoral character flaws that cause separation.

A cultural system of beliefs and behaviors based on absolute natural, normal and moral rights would strive for harmony. Though early cultures had a strong sense of belonging, their dispersed situations required little need for harmony between cultures. Like the Ju/'hoansi, early cultures often thought of themselves as the "real people," significantly different from all other people outside their own culture. Since the planet was a large place and the diverse bands of early cultures small, learning to live in harmony with each other simply was not an issue thousands of years ago. We have the opportunity now to achieve real harmony among diverse cultures; we simultaneously face the alternative danger of culturally evolving further away from what is natural and moral.

If we accept the natural and moral right to our belonging, if we commit to harmony, there are a few other choices we need to make for a cultural system of quality living. Community should trump interest groups. Free will should trump destiny. Patience should trump urgency. The meaning of experiences should trump dogma. Loving people and places should trump zealotry. Let us now harmonize the early with the modern using these requirements as our guide. Let us harmonize some of the most important "isms" affecting our culture today with what we need to hold onto from the natural rights and conditions of our natural, normative existence.

Materialism and Specialization

Of all the cultural "isms" that evolved us away from our k-species heritage, materialism has the most obvious impact. One either prefers to bond with people or with things. Let us start with this duality to prove that one can achieve harmony between any cultural "ism" and our natural selves, as long as we preserve our natural belonging.

There are two things to keep in mind about wealth. First, having wealth does not interfere with belonging to others; that is the consequence of desiring wealth. The emotional want, not the material possession, drives wedges between people. Second, wealth does not require greed. The essence of wealth is trade, and trade requires only specialization as a necessary and sufficient condition. Therefore, we do not have to want wealth to enhance our material condition; we have to want and pursue specialization, in which case wealth will follow.

Of course, the Powell Cabal would like us to believe that only greed provides the necessary and sufficient motivation for everyone to become specialized. To believe that we also must believe that only greed motivates one to learn or become well-educated, for with increasing education comes increasing specialization. With all other things equal, increased education means increased wealth. Greed is necessary and sufficient only for wealth concentration apart from specialization, not for wealth generation.

If people want to become better educated or more specialized for other reasons than greed, then this becomes good news for our quality of life. Increased specialization not only means increased wealth, but increased cultural diversity as well. The diversity is not limited just to labor. You would not expect a farmer and a lawyer to extract the same wisdom from their experiences, nor develop the same sense of belonging to others. According to my definition of advanced civilization, increased cultural diversity provides the potential for civilizations to advance through a greater achievement in harmony, as long as the primary motivation for specialization is not greed.

One economic tool for materialism is capitalism. What we do with capital determines the nature of our materialism. Concentrating capital responds to an emphasis on greed; diffusing capital responds to an emphasis on specialization and diversity. Corporations are another economic tool for materialism. Business corporations exist to expand and/or combine markets, enabled only through the support of government. If the "bottom line" of market expansion is to provide wealth to shareholders in exchange for no productive labor, then corporations serve greed and fuel the cultural materialism that reduces our quality of life. If the "bottom line" of shareholders were similar to those of non-profit corporations, if only a meager return from their investment was expected because the corporation was chartered by government with the direct intent of enhancing the public good, or merely to specialize in something new, then we would expect limitations in the size of corporations and greater specialization as the alternative result.

In theory, government could structure capitalism and corporations to facilitate specialization rather than greed. That would require acknowledging there is a fundamental "Why?" question to economics, and the correct answer is not "selfish self-interest." We cannot expect *laissez faire* economists, puppet libertarians or the Powell Cabal to acknowledge that normative "Why?" question. We certainly cannot hope for the collusion of corporations, politicians and special interest groups to do this. Demanding that we address that question needs to be done by the middle class.

Individualism and the Natural Condition

Please forgive me as I let slip a tiny bit of arrogance. I have backpacked thousands of miles, on journeys of up to seven months. I have gone into the wilderness alone for over a week to survive with only what could be carried in a daypack. I have traveled as much as eighty miles in one day in the wilderness, by my own independent labors. My entire life I have been a maverick that fiercely resists allegiance to any party or ideology. I belong to no interest group outside of local organizations addressing local issues.[1] My friends at times make fun of what appears to them to be my extreme independence. If there was anyone that qualifies as pursuing individualism in modern culture, I no doubt meet those qualifications.

Yet I am far from pursuing individualism. Indeed, those "solitary" early cultures were far from pursuing individualism as well. Their total culture revolved around the communal unit. I have done things independently from others in stretches, similar to the walkabouts or vision quests of early cultures, but I then returned to the communal units that determined the quality of my life.

---

1 Actually, I am a life member of two organizations of long-distance backpackers; for one of them that status simply was granted to me for having completed the Triple Crown of backpacking in 1985.

The puppet libertarians and think tanks that ascribe to a rugged individualism as part of the American identity are laughable. They would be cute in their naiveté if not for their impact on our sense of belonging. As usual, those that protest too loud are the ones most suspect. In an ironic twist, the loudest calls for individualism are generated by the special interest groups formed by the Powell Cabal. As individualism requires independence from others, let us explore what independence a puppet libertarian must have to avoid rank hypocrisy in their calls for individualism.

The puppet libertarian must be independent of formal education and security services. The former could be accomplished through home schooling and no college, but no puppet libertarians are likely to fit that requirement. Independence from the security would be forfeiting one of the cultural entitlements puppet libertarians ardently promote. No puppet libertarian wants to be independent of the police, fire departments, judicial system, homeland security and military services. Puppet libertarians would need to be independent from corporations, since corporations perhaps are the most dependent on government policies out of any culturally contrived, government-backed entity. By extension, we should expect that a sincere puppet libertarian would divest themselves entirely of stocks, since individualism cannot be pursued when one receives income without productive labor, based on a system only made possible through corporations and government.

The proponents of individualism provide ironic entertainment, like watching children at serious play-acting. But their "individualism" is really a pursuit of indulgent self-interested entitlements. This pursuit often leads them to join those interest groups, particularly think tanks, they feel respond to their indulgent needs. Their increasing commitment to interest groups means a decreasing commitment to community. They undermine the arena that provides the best hope for achieving harmony, while selling out their individualism for the sake of special interest groups like the U. S. Chamber of Commerce, Cato Institute or the Heritage Foundation.

Unless you are a hermit, individualism for sustained periods is less possible for modern cultures than early cultures, yet early cultures would not be so foolish as to think sustained individualism desirable. Only individualism for short periods is both possible and desirable. If for brief periods of your life you can abandon all connections to culture (all connections, forget about those investments), you can obtain a glimpse into our natural condition. Only through this glimpse into what is truly natural, a quick assessment of the "baseline data," can you compare and know what is either good or bad about what is cultural.

Without empirical baseline information on what is natural you could be as mistaken as John Locke, unaware of the natural conditions for the merits of independent labor and determining from your armchair that property is a natural right. You could be as mistaken as our Supreme Court justices, unaware of the natural conditions of openness and honesty and determining from your armchair that money is an expression of free speech. You could be as mistaken as John Calvin, unaware of the natural condition of our free will to belong and determining from your armchair that there is absolute predestination. As much as this pains me to admit, you could be as mistaken as John Stuart Mill, unaware of the true conditions of early cultures and determining from your armchair that inferior people from inferior cultures require paternalistic intervention on their own behalf. You could become a disciple of Thomas Hobbes, concluding that left to our natural condition life would be "solitary, poor, nasty, brutish, and short."

With the empirical knowledge of our natural condition we can appreciate what culture truly has to offer. At the least you gain an empirical understanding of our natural compulsion to belong, and the necessity of social groups for that fulfillment. You gain an empirical understanding that humility, faith and courage not only reinforce belonging but, by extension, contribute to making us naturally and socially whole. You gain an empirical understanding that while the merits of your independent labors are natural and good, the merits of diverse labors in the context of culture are even better. You gain an empirical understanding that while your independent thoughts are natural and true, the aggregation of those independent thoughts in the context of culture provides wisdom. You gain an empirical understanding that while independent belonging is natural and moral, the free will of diverse belongings in the context of culture provides the key for advancing civilizations.

Communalism and Federation

As counterintuitive as individualism may seem to nurturing our sense of belonging, insight into our natural condition leads us to appreciate the very purpose of civilization. This demonstrates that, as with materialism, we can work towards achieving harmony with major cultural "isms" if we have the free will to do so. The importance of free will hints at a different type of problem with harmonizing cultural "isms." Some cultural systems of beliefs and behaviors may seem to nurture our sense of belonging and achieve harmony, except that they constrain free will.

Communism at a national scale has not succeeded. Communalism applied to a more local scale still thrives. At this level communalism would seem to be ideal for a cultural system of beliefs and behaviors that promote belonging and community. In many respects this is true, but the biggest problem with communism at the national scale also surfaces with some forms of communalism at the local scale.

Laissez faire economists like Milton Friedman are eager for us to condemn communism for economic reasons. They fault communism as a tool used by government to circumvent the free market. That is true, but that exact same description applies to business corporations, the idols worshiped by *laissez faire* economists. What *laissez faire* economists really object to with communism are the constraints on indulgent wealth disparity; which corporations can nurture better than any other cultural entity by sabotaging free markets.

Nevertheless, we should condemn communism for reasons similar to the pretense adopted by *laissez faire* economists. Communism constrains freedom in all forms: the economic free market, political free thought and cultural free will. Communalism also poses the danger of constraining cultural free will. In the alienated age of urbanization and suburbs most communalism is religious based. We described in Essay 20 how fundamentalist Christians, in their fervor for destiny and apocalyptic visions, constrain free will. Yet there are religious movements that acknowledge free will instead. The free will to belong to others within a community can extend to belonging between communities. In that case communalism provides the foundation for federation.

Somewhat embarrassingly, the Christian lineage of my Church traces back to Calvinism (in case there are Lutherans out there feeling smug, your founder had his own issues with free will). Calvinism started out as a grassroots communal approach in strict accordance to fundamental beliefs. Anyone who might empirically have sensed belonging to a peaceful, loving and joyful higher order would not have fit in with these communities. They would have been informed that their free will to belong to this wonderful higher order was a figment of their imagination. Either God predestined that they belonged to Him or they were out of luck. Of course, being part of a Calvinist community did prove as a sign that you just might be predestined to belong.

Fortunately, the particular branch of the Calvinist tree where my Church resides is Congregationalism. Our particular spin on things was to pick up on the importance of the Bible stressed by Calvinism, and declare that each community of believers needed to be able to read and interpret the Bible for themselves. My embarrassment at having Calvinism in my Church's past is tempered by the fact that Congregationalism was the main impetus for public education in this country. Deciding things as congregations led to the first female and first black ministers. We also were the preeminent witch burners and were fixed still on the notion of an angry God but, um, let us skip over that for now.

In 1957, Congregationalists joined with three other Churches to become the United Church of Christ (UCC). In so doing we have become, in essence, a grand federation. Each Congregational Church previously federated with others to provide some common structure and purpose, even as each Church was allowed to be governed by their own congregation. Now the federation of Congregational Churches is in turn federated with the German Reformed Church, Evangelical

Synod and Christian Churches.

The UCC grants me further redemption from my Calvinist heritage. One of the earliest battles taken up by the UCC was to fight media consolidation during a time when minorities were being victimized further by a lack of voice. The concern for the poor by the UCC is more closely aligned with Joel Hunter, the short term Director for the Christian Coalition who had to resign, than with that special interest group's founder, Pat Robertson. Yet there is a cautionary tale to be told here as well.

That a religious organization like the UCC shows some concern for the poor is not surprising. Even the Christian Coalition would profess to have some concern, though they also are likely to put all of the blame on the poor themselves. Yet the UCC has little direct representation by the poor in their centralized political structure. The UCC cannot be blamed for this; the poor are incapable of assuming positions of authority in any organization. The poor become visible only in the context of local community. This means that there are times when the priority of helping the poor has been compromised by interest groups embedded in the UCC political structure that have other higher priorities. The late nineties and early millennium reflect some of the most troubling times ever for the poor in this country, but there were some other issues that drew more resolutions and greater attention from the UCC during this same time period.[2] If marginalization of the poor can be compromised in a socially conscious yet centralized structure such as the UCC, just imagine the lack of representative interest in the federated entity known as Congress.

This is not to chastise the UCC; they have my sincere thanks for rescuing my Christian lineage from Calvinism. The point is that federation in any form comes with some challenges. The federation of neighborhood communities, religious based or otherwise, promotes the free will to achieve harmony across different communal units, but increases the potential for corporations, politicians and special interest groups to corrupt the federation through authoritarianism. In that case the wisdom and harmony that can be produced by a federation of communal units is lost.

Social Capital

Let us take a back door approach to the next cultural "ism" by first exploring one of the conceptual consequences. Economic concepts sometimes are adapted for cultural use. The concept of social capital was introduced early in the twentieth century, on the heels of *laissez faire* economics, and used sporadically by social researchers since then. Economic capital is created through economic production (except in our system) and subsequently redistributed either to enhance future

---

2 I do not wish to elaborate any further on this, choosing instead the fidelity of belonging, but you could scope out the UCC web site to review their resolutions around the turn of the millennium.

economic production or to concentrate wealth. Social capital is created through social involvement and can be "redistributed" to enhance society in various ways, from reducing crime to increasing productivity.

At the turn of the millennium the concept of social capital gained wider recognition from *Bowling Alone* (2000), a book by Robert Pullman reporting his thorough research on social involvement. One type of social involvement described by Pullman is the sense of belonging among tight groups, which he calls bonding. The emotional and health benefits Pullman attributes to bonding are similar to the quality of life benefits I attribute to belonging.

In Pullman's view bonding is a means towards the end of building social capital. Consequently, bonding for Pullman could be negative if detrimental to social capital, such as with xenophobia. In contrast to Pullman's bonding, the sense of belonging discussed in these essays involves only the normative experience of attachment. We belong because that is what our species has evolved to do and what our species needs to do as a natural condition for our quality of life.

Remember the empirical criterion to reliably interpret evidence. To satisfy a criterion of reliability, cultural beliefs cannot be allowed to alter the meaning of the experience. Xenophobia is an example of an unreliable interpretation made from the experience of belonging. Idolatrous beliefs in general are unreliable interpretations to make from the belonging experience; others will not reliably come to the same idolatrous conclusions from their own independent belonging. Idolatrous beliefs such as xenophobia must either be derived from other idolatrous beliefs or from additional experiences other than normative belonging.

Pullman describes one other type of social involvement as bridging. "Bridging" together people from diverse cultural backgrounds becomes a cultural means for promoting a cause, in addition to building social capital for other causes. Despite the common emphasis on diverse cultural backgrounds, bridging is different than the goal of harmony for civilization. When we consider that a "cause" can be an "idolatrous belief," we see the conflict. The members of interest groups bridge together to promote common causes; the members of diverse communities learn to negotiate their causes. Pullman would caution that the causes promoted through bridging should be good, though he seems less concerned about harmful bridging than about harmful bonding. But even good causes can disrupt harmony if people are idolatrous in their attitudes, with special interest groups facilitating concentrations of wealth and power to impose dogma.

As an illustrative exercise, let us pretend to form a special interest group for the noble cause of stamping out zealotry. We wish to combat zealots such as the vain false patriots of the American Legion, the cynical false evangelists of the Christian Coalition or the cowardly neoconservatives of PNAC. What chance of success would we have? These three special interest groups are motivated, at least in part, by the concentration of wealth and power through materialism. We would lose battles with these types of special interest groups if we did not succumb likewise to materialism; yet we would lose our own souls if we did. Our best chance to effect change while preserving morals would be to concede the interest group strategy and instead invite zealots into communal units.

For example, we could entice American Legion members to serve an actual support group function that negotiated with different levels of federated government. We certainly could use their undivided attention and resources for restoring lost education and health benefits to veterans, benefits that were eroded while the American Legion focused on imposing dogma such as flag idolatry. At the same time we could encourage American Legion members to participate in community negotiations about the quality of life, rather than concentrate wealth and power away from supporting veterans to impose dogma in their "Mentoring Youth" initiatives. To function in community American Legion members eventually would acquire the humility, faith and courage to negotiate their causes for the sake of harmony, rather than conclude they must vainly impose their dogma without compromise.

There is another significant distinctions between Pullman's advocacy of social capital and the harmony achieved through belonging. Pullman promotes volunteerism, asserting that volunteerism would increase if there was less cocooning and our awareness of societal problems increased. He points to external forces such as wars and urbanization as ultimate causes affecting our rates of volunteerism. All of this is true enough but overlooks one important fact. The cultural quality of life depends on the belonging to social groups that reduces the need for volunteerism or social capital.

Pullman's position on volunteerism as social capital resembles the use of economic capital as the source of charitable donations. Puppet libertarians defend our greed-based economic system in part by the Pullman paradigm of increasing capital that can be used for good works. Rather than generating a lot of concentrated capital, much of which is welfare for no return in labor, a better ideal would be a world not so much in need of charity. How do you reduce the need for charity? Do not redistribute capital welfare away from the productive labor that generated the wealth.

The Taoist poem that begins this essay contains the line: "They were honest and righteous without realizing that they were 'doing their duty.'" The poem repeats this message in different forms. A full life involves people living in community where doing the right thing is nothing extraordinary. We could also change the title of the Taoist poem to confront Pullman's thesis directly: "When life was full there was no social capital." Being "honest and righteous" and "reliable" are not the means to an end, like social capital; they are the end that results from a sense of belonging.

Another line of the Taoist poem states: "They lived freely together giving and taking and did not know that they were generous." This resembles the general reciprocity among early cultures, and by many middle class communities. The purpose of giving and taking in a full life was for no other purpose than belonging to each other in community. Charitable organizations like the Bill and Melinda Gates Foundation would be viewed as strange at best, and at worst the guilt-driven endeavor of the greedy. Focusing on the utility of social capital for charitable ends—rather than eliminating the need for charity—ultimately stems from the same source of "wisdom" that was clueless about early cultures: the Enlightenment.

Utilitarianism and Empiricism

The belief in the utility of social capital reflects one of the most pervasive yet largely unidentified cultural "isms." Utilitarianism seeks to achieve the greatest good for the greatest number in society, identified as the greatest average utility. Utilitarianism is a product of the emphasis on empiricism that came out of the Enlightenment along with the unfortunate ignorance by armchair philosophers about natural rights and conditions.

Before the Enlightenment knowledge was based on authoritarian claims made according to infallible beliefs, or dogma. Universities and schools of thought focused on this type of knowledge, often religious based. Empiricism changed the basis for knowledge by requiring beliefs (theories) to be flexible, subject to alteration based on empirical tests of experience, called experiments. The claim that there is no free will can be made from the infallible belief that an omnipotent God would have everything figured out and determined ahead of time. Yet everything in our experience with a higher order suggests we have the free will to independent belonging. The normative claim that free markets are driven by selfish self-interest can be made from the infallible belief that economics should be void of normative claims (though only *laissez faire* economists have the cleverness to make such a logically challenged claim). Yet everything in our experience with greed suggests that selfish self-interest would coerce markets if granted a position of strength. These examples reveal that normative claims deduced from infallible beliefs are seldom verified by either experience or inductive logic, and that the Enlightenment did not eliminate this approach to knowledge.

We could make normative claims and empirically test them based on experiences of our natural condition. Claims that culture should preserve the natural and moral rights to independent labor, thoughts and belonging are normative based on the natural human experience. Such claims could not be made by Enlightenment philosophers, since their armchairs failed to let them know what was natural. In the absence of viable natural experience for normative guides to empiricism, utilitarianism substitutes objective economic measurements. This reverses the normative role of culture. The natural sense of belonging of early cultures formed communal units that dictated economic production. With utilitarianism economic cost-benefit analyses dictate cultural beliefs.

Cost-benefit analyses serve the utilitarian goal of determining the greatest good for the greatest number based on objective measurements. These analyses assume the main purpose of human activity to be economic production and that objective numbers capture all the costs and benefits to this activity. Other self-interests of labor such as political involvement, community service, family obligations and personal growth are either ignored or suffer in the conversion to economic measurements.

The authoritative application of empirical cost-benefit analyses creates quite a stir in the field of natural resources. Many people would attribute some value to wilderness. Yet this value does not translate directly to an economic benefit any more readily than meeting family obligations. This forces the defenders of wilderness to devise complex assumptions and measurements if they wish to abide by a utilitarian approach. Only wilderness as something you pay for with hunting permits or park fees has direct value in a cost-benefit analysis, much like the value of an amusement park. The important values of wilderness you would not pay for—like the value of air, serenity or the self-exploration of real individualism—cannot be objectively captured without the same complexity of assumptions *laissez faire* economists make about leisure. We are no more likely to best *laissez faire* economists at the game of cost-benefit analyses than we can neutralize zealotry with special interest groups.

An alternative for frustrated wilderness advocates would be to refute empiricism and rely on rhetorical persuasion. A long-distance backpacker or avid hunter might find some of the resulting arguments persuasive, but not most middle class citizens who have had insufficient empirical experience with wilderness. Beyond the problems with reaching the "audience," wilderness advocates attempt persuasion at a severe disadvantage. If you were to choose your "fantasy rhetorical persuasion team," would you pick wilderness advocates or the large network of the Powell Cabal? Overcoming the inadequacies of utilitarian cost-benefit analyses will not be accomplished by shunning empiricism for the use of rhetoric, but by changing the objective standards guiding utilitarian approaches.

Utilitarianism can be based on either one of two contrasting standards. Greatest average utility is the standard typically endorsed by western civilization. The goal of this standard is to increase the mean (average) as much as possible: mean standard of living, mean family income, mean level of education, etc. The assumption is made that the distribution around the mean increases in similar manner, thus increasing the utility for everyone. This assumption simply does not hold true. A strict emphasis on maximizing the mean tends to do so in ways that increases the good for those above the mean much more than for those below the mean. The reason for this is greed.

Through our greed based commitment to greatest average utility we have increased our economic means by taking from other cultures, taking from the future children of our own culture, and increasing monetary flow to cover the capital investment returns that exceed productivity. All these methods circumvent the merits of our own production. All these methods concentrate the capital and benefits from greed for the wealthy more than for the middle class. The empirical data presented in Essay 7 reveals a staunch commitment for over thirty years to this greed based utilitarian standard.

The alternative utilitarian standard is known as the maximin, or the maximization of a minimum objective standard. Minimum standards such as eliminating hunger, or basic health care for all, are maximin pursuits. Greed does not abide by such standards. Greed fuels the feelings of entitlement that begrudges any redistributed and concentrated capital be returned back to productive labor in order to meet minimum standards. Greed prefers instead to hold on to redistributed and concentrated capital, thus having "too many dollars chase too few goods" and inflating the costs of some essential and expensive items that we would wish to include with maximin pursuits. The maximin standard has become all but obsolete in a global economy that champions comparative advantages and isolates the goods from the labor markets, which are both tricks of economic trade to divert capital from the producers to the consumers. We now would have to study early cultures with their communal units and domestic modes of production to understand how the maximin standard once operated.

Viewed in this light, Pullman's social capital is an empirical improvement over the utilitarian standard of cost-benefit analyses. Pullman's focus on culture over economics is true to the real causal nature of human experience. The political, communal, family, and personal components of our labor become as important as the economic. The maximin standard for utility is revived as the ends for which social capital can be applied. Most importantly, empirical evidence for cultural phenomena has been granted a utilitarian platform. Yet let us depart from Pullman by considering that his means of social capital serves a different utility than the ends of belonging and harmony that derive from our natural rights and condition.

The Most Pervasive "Ism"

There is one cultural "ism" that, in effect, reigns supreme in our idolatrous culture. This "ism" is immune to criticism because very few people realize it even exists. Many of those who know about this "ism" claim that the Enlightenment replaced it with utilitarianism. I am speaking about the way of knowing called scholasticism.

We have touched on scholasticism throughout these essays. For one example we discussed in Essay 9 the support of the death penalty by Marilyn vos Savant, by one standard the person with the highest IQ in the world. She offered only one reason for the death penalty, deterrence, but offered absolutely no empirical evidence that deterrence works, or that deterrence trumps the other reasons vos Savant admitted works against the death penalty. There is a good reason for that, the supporting evidence that the death penalty deters crime in a democratic society lacks validity and reliability. In lieu of valid and reliable evidence, vos Savant offered only rhetoric aimed at shaming people for being emotional if they disagreed with her. No doubt her rhetoric was an effective tool of persuasion because: 1) her status of having the highest IQ grants her great authority and 2) scholasticism as our way of knowing reigns supreme.

Empiricism furthers knowledge by allowing our experiences to challenge our beliefs. The utilitarianism endorsed by the Enlightenment supposedly steered culture towards this way of knowing. Scholasticism is the opposite of empiricism, basing knowledge on the process of dogma determining the meaning of our experiences. The complete disregard for empirical data by vos Savant resembles the most blatant form of scholasticism in our society, similar to the politician's practice of rhetorical persuasion without any empirical evidence. Vos Savant also illustrates that this dogmatic route to knowledge can be wielded by those with the greatest intellect.

What is accepted as the legitimate way of knowing affects all beliefs and behaviors. Scholasticism pervades culture with idolatry, because of the primacy of beliefs over experience. The idolatry can be both for the beliefs and for those who champion the beliefs. False patriots idolize materialism and champion jingoistic leaders. False evangelists idolize materialism and champion televangelists. Neoconservatives idolize materialism and champion chicken hawks.

When scholasticism infects culture with idolatry, politics is infected with authoritarianism. Party politicians use only rhetoric to promote their beliefs, and the rank and file members respond by pulling the party lever. Corporate media chart a pro-authoritarian course through their echo chambers and news talk hosts while viewers quibble over whether the authoritarian noise is liberal or conservative. Supreme Court justices are granted life tenure via authoritarian appointment, and people consider our rule of law to be in the care of wise old men with no elite biases. Executive leaders establish policy without evidence to support their beliefs, or without even revealing their true beliefs, and we trust in the authority of our leadership.

Scholasticism and the primacy of beliefs benefit not only a politics of authoritarianism, but an economics of greed. Thus where scholasticism pervades culture you might find an economic system where authoritarians have decided that money is an expression of free speech; where even ACLU lawyers accept this concept with a gullibility that makes our lovable Hans a hardened skeptic in comparison. Taking full advantage of this system are the think tanks, public relation firms, endowed academic chairs, corporate media and lobbyists of the Powell Cabal.

In paying homage to the Enlightenment, scholasticism occasionally incorporates empirical evidence rather than rely on rhetorical persuasion alone. We must distinguish whether empirical evidence is allowed to challenge theoretical beliefs, or if dogmatic beliefs dictate the meaning of the empirical evidence. We must apply rudimentary empirical tests of validity or reliability. Scholars often choose their definitions and relationships carefully, to be fulfilled by circular, tautological reasoning. They will discredit counter evidence that does have validity and reliability, attributing claims made from true empiricism to be the work of scholars that cannot be trusted. This is the pot calling a sterling silver kettle black.

In the previous essay I cited a few ways that empirical evidence was used to disguise scholasticism. False objectivity was used to conclude that early cultures were "poor." A false axiom was induced from limited experiences to conclude that early cultures were "nasty." Circular reasoning was used to determine that early cultures were "brutish." Unreliable old bones were used to claim that life in early cultures was "short." Let us recap other examples from these essays of scholasticism disguised by empirical evidence. These include:

- A research foundation manipulating the aggregation of data to promote a belief about wealth and happiness.
- A think tank compiling fifty economic indicators, none of them corresponding to private coercion of markets, to promote a belief about the liberating economics of greed.
- A government agency using a plethora of assumptions, forsaking simpler methods that would gather more valid data, to promote a belief about the abundance of leisure.
- A university scholar claiming correlation exists with scattered points on a graph to promote a belief about the morality of economic growth.
- Executive leaders distorting intelligence to promote a belief about the need for war.
- Supreme Court justices using flexible doctrine and philosophies of judicial interpretation to promote the dogma for which they were appointed.
- Corporate media using bizarre operational definitions of market share to support media consolidation.
- Politicians cherry-picking evidence to promote their party's platform.

Our dominant way of knowing, allowing dogma to determine the meaning of empirical experience, is the common thread that weaves idolatry, authoritarianism and greed together. Scholasticism empowers the Powell Cabal to promote causes supported by special interest groups, as codified by wealth and power elites fulfilling life time political appointments, and echoed by corporate media. Up until now we have found the natural good that could be extracted from every cultural "ism." Materialism offers the specialization that brings us diversity; individualism offers the exposure to a natural condition by which we can evaluate culture; communalism offers the federation by which we can harmonize diverse belief systems; and utilitarianism offers the empiricism that contributes to harmony, wisdom and merit. The remaining challenge is to harmonize scholasticism with our natural condition.

Leadership

We opened Essay 9 with the evidence that there is a natural trust in authority. This bolsters authoritarianism, but we must accept that trusting our leaders is natural. All species strive to conserve their energy budgets through efficiency, following the alpha male of a pack or the president of a country is an efficient way to live. Place your trust in good, strong national leaders and you can conserve your energy for the local needs of your "communal unit."

The Taoist poem we have been referencing acknowledges the existence of leaders, but they do not receive any acclaim. "Rulers were simply the highest branches on the tree" and "no one paid any special attention to worthy men, nor did they single out the man of ability." Whether Chuang Tzu knew this or not, his characterization of leaders from an earlier "age" was not far off the mark.

Early foragers were egalitarian in political structure, but they did have lead hunters. The lead hunter earned that position through merit, perhaps a strange concept in modern times of large inheritances and political campaigns driven by corporate media. The collective wisdom of the foraging band determined who had the best merit. No self-promotion was involved. In fact, Richard Lee reports on the Ju/'hoansi that the successful hunter could expect to be insulted.[3] The better the game he brought back, the more likely the others would find some fault with the meat. In an attempt to maintain harmony in the communal unit, leaders were kept humble. As mentioned in the previous essay, the tribal practice of leaders being generous to the point of depravation, in order to gain authority through respect, fulfills this same harmonic basis for leadership.

In the era of nation states citizens are not capable of accurately assessing the true merits of their leaders. We cannot be privy to all their policy decisions and offer our collective wisdom. The focus of policy often shifts from domestic to foreign matters, eliminating harmony as a priority. In this context we still need leaders. Since empirical ways of knowing fail to deliver the information we need to choose and follow our leaders, we turn to scholasticism instead. Scholasticism,

---

3 We discussed this in the previous essay. The source is The Dobe Ju/'hoansi (2003) by Richard B. Lee.

like any cultural phenomenon, seeks to reinforce itself. The orientation of cultures turns more towards idolatry, authoritarianism and greed as we depend on dogma in party platforms to dictate the meaning of who should lead.

The problem with leadership is idolatry. The advisors to the Bush and Clinton dynasties do not offer a barrage of insults to keep their bosses humble. The urge to idolize our leaders compel us to pardon or make excuses for their mistakes even after they are long gone. When President Ford pardoned President Nixon that was politics as usual. Eulogizing the late President Ford for giving the pardon was promoting a fixed, vain belief in the sanctimonious experience of our democracy. A more drastic example of this scholastic idolatry surrounds the decision and subsequent responses to dropping the atom bomb; a focus for the next essay.

Leadership does not have to be in the form that party politics assumes. In Essay 9 I reported on John J. Curtiss, the leader of our small town for forty-two years. Town commissions decided and he executed in good faith. Democrats and Republicans alike have the natural urge to trust in a good leader when they have the empirical basis for identifying one, and both parties shunned their politics to continue endorsing Mr. Curtiss throughout his tenure. This more closely resembles the type of democracy our founding fathers intended than what occurs now on our national stage. The only caveat is that our founding fathers never intended "public service" to become a career. Mr. Curtiss was first selectman only part time in addition to being a farmer.

The intent of our founders was for the direction of the country to be determined by a legislative branch, and then trust in the executive branch to provide good leadership. There would be short tenure and constant turnover in the legislative branch, particularly in the House, which would increase their response to wise democracy. Citizens would do their part through active political involvement within the context of their communities, not through special interest groups (including political parties). Our "rulers" were meant to be "simply the highest branches on a tree" and not worshipped for their "service." The scholastic tendency to trust in the beliefs of authorities might yet prove adaptive if we emulated our ancestors by insulting leaders whenever they did something meritorious.

"When Life Was Full There Were No Heroes"

May I share a personal account that illustrates a democratic form of leadership? Upon my arrival as a new teacher at a high school, I was told early on that I might get into clashes with the principal. I was told that I had too many new ideas and some of them were bound to get me into trouble with someone who was a strong leader. At the time, and to this day, I respected and supported his strong leadership. He was a former teacher who was grounded in the empirical realities of high school and he commanded respect from the faculty.

The Director of Instruction for the school district approached me before my second year at the school and charged me to organize a twentieth anniversary Earth Day celebration, to be held in April of 1990. He wanted the celebration to include not just the high school, but the 7th and 8th graders of the district's elementary schools as well. My backgrounds in both natural sciences and wilderness travel made me a logical choice to lead this effort, but I was a mere tenderfoot as a high school teacher. My first task was to overcome my inexperience by meeting with every department in the high school and ask every teacher what they would like to do. They sculpted a vision that was a bit ambitious, but they became enthused about their vision.

The vision had to be officially approved at the executive council of the faculty, led by the principal. The outcomes of the council generally go the way that their strong leader recommends, yet this would be different. The principal offered an alternative plan for Earth Day, but the executive council voted in favor of the plan I presented. There was good reason for this; my plan was their plan. The principal then responded by appointing someone else to be chairperson of the project. The executive council countered by approving a motion to make me co-chair. Earth Day 1990, enthusiastically supported and administrated by the high school faculty, was a great success. My leadership involved nothing more than executing the collective wisdom of an experienced faculty. Ultimately, our Earth Day 1990 celebration was not a testimony to good leadership so much as good democracy.

At the national level we always will need to place some trust in authority without the type of empirical evidence that early cultures used in choosing their leaders. This trust enables our leaders to be more efficient, and our country to run more smoothly. Yet the dangers of this trust are great. A gullibility that allows the dogma of others to dictate the meaning of our experiences heads us towards idolatry, authoritarianism and greed. To avoid these dangers we must provide our trust without treating our leaders as heroes. We must ensure that the conditions for leadership are to execute the collective wisdom of democracy.

The concluding lines of the Taoist poem are: "For this reason their deeds have not been narrated. They made no history." The poem could have been titled: "When life was full there were no heroes." Even volunteers would be a strange concept when everyone "does their duty." If we view a full life as being of high quality, and if we view heroes as idols, then we touch upon the main theme throughout these cultural essays. We could have paraphrased the Taoist poem and titled Part Three: "When the quality of life was high there was no idolatry."

Before we start on a path to shed the idolatry currently infecting our country we need to face some truths long disguised by misinformation. We will need to bring to light certain things that our culture has considered unspeakable.

ESSAY 24 – UNSPEAK AND UNSPEAKABLE

A Letter to the Editor of *National Geographic*

> "An 'empire'? They were barely a hunter-gatherer tribe. Once again, an eco-freak takes us on a flight of fancy to undermine American pride and depict generations of immigrants in this land as the big, bad invaders. Did we change the landscape? Yes! And hooray, to become the breadbasket of the world.
> - Deborah Dee Volluz

Overview

- Pride can lead one to either feeling satisfied or superior.
- Native American culture confirmed that culture naturally determines economics, and that our natural condition focused on harmony rather than greed or utility.
- Freedom as unspeak is based on property and law instead of our free will.
- Free speech as unspeak is based on money instead of open and honest thoughts.
- Free markets as unspeak is based on corporations instead of free exchange.
- Our economic system experiences unspeakable failures as a meritocracy.
- Our political system experiences unspeakable failures as a democracy.
- Our cultural system experiences unspeakable failures with morality.
- Our way of knowing for citizens has been an unspeakable failure at empiricism.
- Our social systems need to undergo a paradigm shift in order to restore balance to the functions of merit, wisdom and harmony.

Satisfied Pride

The letter to the editor above was a response to a National Geographic article about the early Jamestown settlement.[1] I like to read letters to the editor because they represent a diversity of opinions from readers. However, this letter reveals that the respondent, presumably middle class, has succumbed to both unspeak and

---

1 The letter was in the September 2007 issue of *National Geographic*.

the unspeakable. These represent grave threats to the homeostasis for our cultural system of beliefs and behaviors, the focus of this last essay on culture.

We can assume that the author to whom Ms. Volluz refers is not a "freak" in the literal meaning of the word. Without knowing anything about the author that draws her ire, or even what he wrote, we can assume he probably does not have two noses or anything else particularly freakish about him. If we extend the figurative meaning of "freak" to include freakish opinions we still cannot condemn the author. He did not write something freakish like suggesting we eat our babies as a means of population control. The main thesis of the National Geographic article was that European colonizers changed the ecology of the American landscape when they arrived. While this may be an unpopular opinion, there is nothing freakish about it.

The middle class writer used the term "freak" as a means of pejorative branding, independent of the real meaning of the word. This phenomenon was covered in Steven Poole's delightful book *Unspeak* (2006), first introduced in Essay 17. The impact of unspeak in our culture is the same as the "black is white" economics practiced by the Powell Cabal, or the "black is white" waggle dance of politicians. Unspeak facilitates the scholastic imposition of authoritarian beliefs, but distorts the meaning of empirical experience.

In this essay I will focus on unspeak in our culture that accompanies the word "free." We have developed serious misconceptions about the structure and function of free markets, free speech and freedom in general. I have alluded to some of these misconceptions throughout the essays and chastised the authoritarian perpetrators. Let us focus now on the consequences of the middle class adopting these misconceptions as a source of "American pride."

From the point of view of Ms. Volluz, to "undermine American pride" is to broach topics that should remain unspeakable. The meaning of pride differs among the middle class. Some of us think about pride as satisfaction in something well done. People usually are open to improvement when our satisfaction comes from what we do. Perhaps we think our impact on land has been good; but we are open to improvement by learning from the experiences of other cultures to become even more satisfied.

Others derive feelings of superiority from something well done. If we take our impact on land as a byproduct of our cultural superiority then undermining such pride is an unspeakable blow to our authoritarian ego. That our land use practices degrade soil productivity in comparison to Native Americans matters not. No one should dare undermine our pride in being the breadbasket of the world.

Unspeakable cultural topics have the same consequences as "black box" economics and "black box" waggle dances. When certain experiences become unspeakable we can only make invalid generalizations from the limited experiences we are allowed to consider. Satisfaction in our impact on land has little empirical validity if we are not to consider all the possible alternatives. Hiding experiences that should be considered serves the purpose instead of validating scholastic beliefs that authoritarians wish the middle class to adopt for our feelings of superiority.

If I have retained your good will up until this point I beg your further tolerance at this point. These essays have maintained that greed corrupts our economic system; authoritarianism corrupts our political system; and idolatry corrupts our cultural system. Most middle class folks will neither be surprised nor offended by such claims. However, to prove these points we now will draw upon empirical experiences that have been declared unspeakable in our culture. This might engage the wrath of middle class folks like Ms. Volluz.

Here is a disclaimer for what is to come. I have sensed unconditional love from both my parents and from a higher order. This shapes my patriotism. This country does not need to be superior at anything to retain my love, in contrast to the false patriots that infiltrate special interest groups like the American Legion. Satisfaction in things well done fuels my pride in the country I love, as I hope is true for you. But there are "unspeakable" experiences that should undermine this type of pride in every single middle class patriot, if we choose not to let vanity, cynicism or apprehension get in the way of the empirical evidence. With this in mind let us broach unspeak and the unspeakable.

Culture Determines Economics

The article that draws the ire of Ms. Volluz, titled "America Found and Lost" in the May 2007 National Geographic, written by Charles C. Mann, provides an empirical base of reference for examining our culture. The "empire" to which Ms. Volluz refers was Mann's term for a federation of different Native American tribes that were united under a chief called Powhatan. The reference to "barely a hunter-gatherer tribe" probably was intended to mean "barely more than" from the perspective of Ms. Volluz. The Powhatan tribes hunted and gathered, but they were also agrarian. A family would farm a small area for awhile, and then let the area revert back to a commons for hunting and gathering.

While the land use practices of European colonizers also included the commons, the land devoted to the commons remained fixed (like dogma), while other land became fixed for private property instead. Native Americans had greater success at farming than the European colonizers because our ancestors would tap out the soil productivity of their inflexible private properties. Yet from one crucial perspective European land use had a distinct advantage. European colonizers delineated and defended the land they privatized. By such means they gradually expanded the land they controlled while constraining the commons of the Powhatan tribes. Eliminate land as a commons and for most Native American tribes you eliminate their culture, without even going through the pesky troubles of ethnic cleansing.

"America Found and Lost" addresses two thorny natural resource issues I have alluded to already in these essays. In Essay 4, which covered economic self-interest, we discussed "The Tragedy of the Commons," a famous article in the natural resource field written by Garret Hardin. In the last essay, which analyzed our cultural system from our normative natural condition, we discussed utilitarian cost-benefit analyses. Both topics have generated much controversy among natural resource professionals; the land use practices of the Powhatan tribes provide a resolution to both.

The commons invokes the tragedy of depleted resources, as described by Hardin, when numerous individuals exploit the commons for their own selfish gain. The solution to this dilemma according to Hardin is regulating the commons to prevent such exploitation. Hardin's perspective fits that of the cynical misanthrope Thomas Hobbes. The presumption that we humans are naturally greedy bastards fits with what *laissez faire* economists and virtually all authoritarians want us to think. Puppet libertarians may take exception to Hardin's proposed solution of regulation, but they agree whole-heartedly with his assessment of our greedy condition. Even the view of volunteerism as social capital, advocated by the well-intentioned and well-informed Robert Pullman, ultimately assumes such an orientation that volunteerism can help remedy.

The alternative solution practiced by the Powhatan tribes was to make everything a commons. While a family was producing food from the merit of their independent cultivation labors the land was "theirs;" otherwise the land became available for the merits of all independent hunting and gathering labor. This "primitive" practice confirms that private property and individual greed are not natural rights or conditions but cultural entitlements and artifacts. Property originally was not a private good that could be greedily obtained, hoarded and passed along independently of any merited labor. Property in original and natural form only had meaning in terms of the transient usage that could be employed through the merits of independent labor.

Suggesting that our culture convert everything to a commons would indeed be a "freak" opinion. That will not happen. The more important empirical base of reference to draw from Mann's article is that we are not naturally "wired" for selfish self-interest as corporations so desperately want us to believe. All the evidence of our natural condition suggests that we are "wired" for the communal support system demonstrated by advanced k-species. This empirical evidence provides us better insight for addressing the consequences of greed perpetrated by a corporate culture. For example, while private property always will be held in high regard, we yet might legitimize property rights only as a placeholder for the merits of independent labors rather than a reward for unbridled greed. No doubt there would be less need for regulation with this economic orientation, though this likely would not placate puppet libertarians and the Powell Cabal. A culture that removes greed as an incentive would prove upsetting to those who dance for their corporate puppet masters.

A utilitarian cost-benefit analysis on the land use practices of the Powhatan tribes would be utterly pointless. The empirical standard used for cost-benefit analyses is greatest average utility, as reflected in overall consumption. If the "greatest good for the greatest number" cannot be determined directly by economic measurements, then clever assumptions are made to convert those values into quantifiable numbers. This would not work with the Powhatan tribes because the empirical base of reference for their well-being was good relationships with land and people. Or, in the jargon we have been using for these essays, their well-being depended on overall harmony in regards to their belongings, not overall consumption that can be quantified.

The Powell Cabal convinces us that economics determines our nature. That is a cultural artifact that authoritarians and televangelists also wish us to believe. In contrast, how we naturally evolved as a k-species normatively determined how we distributed resources. K-species do not maximize their consumption. They "relate" their behavior to the conditions of their environment and of their social group, enabled by their supreme abilities to adapt. An empirical reference based on our natural condition would be intended for evaluating harmony, not utility. The conversions of measurement needed would be for how economic consumption or productivity, say with new medical technologies, translated into harmonic relationships.

Maximizing consumption versus maximizing harmony is as mutually exclusive as the stereotypic behaviors of r-species and k-species. A utilitarian cost-benefit approach necessarily means that harmony will be undervalued in deference to greed. This was not how we naturally evolved. As much as *laissez faire* economists may want us to believe otherwise, we evolved to be more like whales, wolves and elephants than like bacteria, weeds and vermin. Thus a cost-benefit analysis can serve only the scholasticism of imposing authoritarian beliefs, rather than the empiricism of fueling wisdom based on our natural conditions and rights.

This final analysis on unspeak and the unspeakable will once again empirically draw on our natural condition and rights as a base of reference. The analysis assumes that cultural beliefs and behaviors determine our economics, not vice-versa. It assumes that harmonizing beliefs and behaviors represents the natural norm, not maximizing wealth through greed. With this understanding let us now examine some unspeak and unspeakable beliefs and behaviors of our culture.

Freedom Unspeak

Freedom was one of the unspeak words featured in Steven Poole's book. Poole describes how the term freedom has been manipulated to serve market economies. We are free when our corporate economic system can operate unfettered. This reflects the problematic view that economics determines our culture. Poole disagrees, asserting that actual freedom is embedded in the rule of law, and citing John Locke as confirmation. Poole then documents that freedom as unspeak has been used to defend lawless behavior when imposing democracy on others.

The rule of law in western civilization was meant to serve private property, as Locke himself would maintain. Hence, we are no better off if we ground freedom with the rule of law rather than economics. The rule of law is a necessary byproduct of shifting land use from the commons to private property, but there is no valid and reliable empirical evidence for equating political law with natural freedom. We have been relying instead on the declarations of Enlightenment scholars weaned on colonialism and ignorant of our natural condition.

Individualism is no better than the rule of law for determining what freedom means. The puppet libertarians that work for the Powell Cabal fancy themselves as individualists, even as they cash in their stock dividends. In their view freedom means government leaving individuals alone, but government is only one of several cultural institutions that intervene in the lives of individuals. Thanks to the rule of law, corporations are included as individuals that puppet libertarians want government to leave alone. This is a bit of chicanery, since corporations exist by virtue of government. Government leaving corporations alone in puppet libertarian parlance means that government interferes with the lives of individuals through the infrastructure they provide to benefit chartered corporations. When the economic freedom of individuals known as people conflict with the freedom of individuals known as corporations the rule of law, interpreted in significant part by corporate lawyers, favors the corporations.

Our natural freedom amounts to the package of natural rights we first detailed in Essay 15. Nature has granted us the natural rights of independent labor, thoughts and belonging. Of these three rights the most basic and essential freedom, the one that influences the others, is independent belonging. Once we choose to belong our lives are constrained by the objects of our belonging. As rooted in the free will to belong, freedom does not involve being left alone as individuals, nor derives from the cultural artifacts of property or law.

Basing the meaning of freedom on markets, the rule of law or individualism, instead of free will, directly or indirectly serves the self-interests of wealth, power and dogmatic elites. They weave greed and self-indulgence into freedom as unspeak. Like Thomas Hobbes, they persuade us that "the life of (natural) man was solitary, poor, nasty, brutish and short" and to trust in authoritarian institutions to channel our greed in positive ways. Considering freedom to actually be based on free will, coupled with an accurate portrayal of our natural condition, runs a risk to elites that we might constrain what we believe and how we behave independently of their self-interests.

Free Speech Unspeak

Since the Supreme Court ruling in *Buckley v. Valeo* (1976), money has been equated with free speech. This bit of unspeak turns free speech into a quantifiable economic commodity. The more money invested into packaging information the greater the value of that information, regardless of empirical validity or reliability. The middle class can increase the quantity and value of the free speech they favor by pooling their money and supporting the right kind of special interest group.

Special interest groups support using money as an expression of free speech for obvious reasons of self-interest. The special interest groups of the Powell Cabal benefit the most, as the middle class is no match for corporations in the pooling of money to quantify free speech. Corporate media receive the direct benefits from special interest groups and corporations quantifying free speech. Consequently, we will never receive much critical news about this topic of unspeak from the echo chambers and news talk hosts. At best, corporate media provides limited coverage of one of the dangerous consequences of the money as free speech ruling, campaign finance. The support that matters most in quantifying free speech with money comes from the Supreme Court justices, considered to be the wisest of old men.

Empiricism generates wisdom. From a foundation of multiple experiences we seek those most valid and reliable to shape what we belief. Wise old men sitting in judgment should rely on empiricism to establish wise judicial doctrine. Those wise old men favoring judicial restraint would rely on a doctrine of textualism, arbitrating court cases in terms of what the Constitution literally says. If the Constitution appears to be missing something, the empirical wise old judge would use textualism as a means of forcing legislature's to deal with the issue, where the collective experiences of a democracy can be brought to bear through the legislative process.

Those wise old men favoring judicial activism would wield a doctrine of structuralism, intended to allow judges to interpret the Constitution in response to new and accumulated experiences. Structuralism can implement the wisdom of a democracy faster, but puts such wisdom on tenuous ground. Experiences are not infallible, including those of a democracy. Errors can occur in prioritizing which experiences are the most valid and reliable reflection of truth and justice. Yet a commitment to empiricism means having faith that over time enough experiences will occur to focus on what is valid and reliable.

Neither textualism nor structuralism is an inherently better approach to empiricism for wise old men to employ. Both empirical doctrines require time and patience in different ways to eventually get things right, attributes we normally attribute to wise old men. Currently, structuralism is the only available empirical option for Supreme Court justices. Textualism at this point is merely a charade, unless our wise old men were to first and foremost overturn *Marbury v. Madison*, which gave the Supreme Court the final say on interpreting the Constitution, without the Constitution granting this power. From that point on all our justices became activists, despite a few shameless or naive claims to the contrary. From that point on our justices used a mix and match approach of judicial doctrine to scholastically justify authoritarian beliefs.

No Supreme Court justice now, or ever, adhered strictly to either textualism or structuralism. Real structuralism is limited because of an overall allegiance to precedence. We have good ol' boys, not wise old men, sitting on the bench. These good ol' boys are dedicated members of the wealth, power and dogmatic clubs of elites that support authoritarian government. Judicial authoritarians use their scholastic beliefs to dictate the meaning of experience. In *Buckley v. Valeo* our esteemed good ol' boys altered the meaning of free speech to accommodate the expressions of special interest groups, corporations and political parties. Overturning this decision will now be problematic because the influence of elites and the precedence that commands the allegiance of good ol' justices.

The value of free speech to a true democracy is solely in the representation of free thought. To claim that saying whatever we like is a valid definition of free speech, even when contradicting what we truly think or know, is similar to claiming that doing whatever we like is a valid definition of freedom, independent of our free will to belong. Through expressing our collective independent thoughts we contribute to the wise functioning of democracy. Free speech is reliable only when we honestly translate our independent thoughts; free speech is valid only when we hide nothing to disguise what we really know. The only quantitative element to free speech in a true democracy is giving the open and honest thought of each separate person equal weight.

Placing money as the crucial element in free speech derives from the orientation that economics should determine our culture. Since money is not equally distributed neither is the weight of individual thoughts that money represents, but this is not a problem when greed is viewed as the overarching cultural norm dictated by economics. The importance of using money for speech increases with the desire to hide or distort free thought. As a general rule the larger the gap between reality and misinformation, the more money required for persuasion. Without unspeak (and the good ol' boys on the Supreme Court) we would conclude from a plethora of experiences that large sums of money is a liberator of false speech. Equating false speech with free speech through the use of money is a gross distortion of our natural normative experience.

Free Markets Unspeak

The belief that economics determines our culture fuels a pattern of unspeak where the meaning of "free" implies no constraints on cultural beliefs or behaviors. We begin with free markets as our base of reference for how life was meant to be and within that absolute economic context we can do or say whatever we like. This belief defies simple logic. Once you choose some beliefs, you are constrained from adopting other beliefs. What you believe in turn constrains how you can behave. From a normative, natural point of view being "free" means to have the free will to belong; but the exercise of free will in turn initiates a chain of constraints on beliefs and behaviors.

Pursuing a free market economy could be consistent with a natural meaning of free. This is not the meaning the Powell Cabal supports, and this has shaped other terms of unspeak treasured by "free market" (puppet) libertarians. As members of an economic club that features impressive academic credentials these people might maintain that they speak the real truth of the matter, backed by scholarly endeavors to shape the "correct" meaning of important economic terms. Us ordinary folk must rely on empirical tests of validity and reliability, however, and assume that the meaning of words corresponds to their actual definitions. Let us now detail a free market economic system where we take the slogans of puppet libertarians at their literal meanings.

We would have to get rid of welfare with the puppet libertarian's view of free markets. Since the empirical meaning of welfare is to receive benefits without the bothersome trouble of productive labor, we would need to get rid of stocks, inheritances and many of the uses for capital. We would need to rely on savings rather than lucrative retirement plans that give a greater return than the rate of inflation. Our government would be constrained to print money only at a rate that reflects actual economic productivity, rather than provide the backing for some of the inflationary shenanigans of capital markets. Perhaps the Powell Cabal and puppet libertarians would accept a compromise to their literal call to end welfare. If we merely indexed the amount of welfare the wealthy receives through government policies to be no more than that which the poor receives, we would reduce the size of our welfare state greatly.

We would have to adopt free trade practices to heed the literal call of puppet libertarians. This means going a bit further than our duplicitous reneging on trade agreements for German steel and Canadian lumber. Every economist or business person will tell you that you want to bargain from a position of strength. Why? You can coerce the terms of the bargain to give yourself an unfair advantage. No country can bargain from a position of strength with the world quite like the United States. Colonialism, comparative advantages, regime change and international loan practices are all coercive tricks of the economic trade that have been employed by the United States. The objective for all these practices has been to expand corporate markets where they would not be wanted by the general population of countries exercising their own collective free will. In order to abide by the literal word of puppet libertarians we must stop all these practices, and consequently stop siphoning capital from other countries to supply our numerous welfare programs for the wealthy.

For that matter, what puppet libertarian could argue with abolishing the free market interference of minimum wages and substituting that with the market neutral application of maximum compensation ratios? Maximum ratios escape the problem of free market interference; since the consumer is not affected by how his dollar for purchasing goods is distributed throughout the corporation. If we hold to a maximum salary ratio standard of 25:1, met in the sixties, either the wages of oversea workers will increase quite nicely, the salary of CEOs and other corporate executives will plummet, or some compromise of the two will occur. Free trade would then take on a much different, more accurate meaning.

Most importantly, if we are to abide by free markets so vigorously advocated by "free market" (puppet) libertarians, we need to abolish business corporations. Business corporations exist only through government intervention in market economies. Without government charter the structure and function of a corporation to concentrate capital in the pockets of shareholders would not exist. There would be no protection of assets when something goes wrong for the corporation in the marketplace. Furthermore, the main objective of this government intervention is to support the private coercion of markets. The function of business corporations in an economic system is to expand markets and, through this expansion, to increase wealth. When the structure of a business corporation allows greed to be the bottom line for people not involved with the labor of production you practically beg those corporations to coerce markets to their advantage. False hype, no-bid contracts, indebted politicians and good ol' boys on the Supreme Court are all part of this coercive package.

The Powell Cabal would be in danger if we start taking puppet libertarians at their literal word. Withdrawing the government charters of business corporations would force businesses to compete only on the merits of what they produced, and forego the greed that serves shareholders. Under a system of competitive productive merit businesses could not afford the extra expense of diverting capital to the Powell Cabal for coercing public opinion. Special interest groups like the Cato Institute, American Enterprise Institute, Heritage Foundation and the U. S. Chamber of Commerce would shrivel up and disappear. Out of compassion for their sense of entitlement perhaps government could charter these special interest groups to operate a few casinos instead.

Unspeakable Economics

When merit is our ideal, we expect to earn what we extract from other people and lands without having to resort to exploitation. The great academic thinkers in the Powell Cabal might counter that being able to successfully exploit others is a reflection of greed-based merit, but we must consider that they are called upon to make this argument to justify corporate sugar daddies. Until our economic productivity can succeed on our own merit, including the merit of free and equal exchange, the logical generalization to make from our experiences is that we have failed miserably as a meritocracy. We have demonstrated no more productive merit with our economic system than a fetus in a womb. Them's unspeakable fightin' words, so here's the evidence to back them up.

The Jamestown settlement is a capsule of how our unmerited system of economics began, by stealing the land needed for production from other cultures, converting the land to unmerited private property, and exploiting natural resources until they were tapped out. But that example alone just means we started out on the wrong foot. Unfortunately, the subsequent causes of our economic wealth were no more meritorious.

A significant portion of our early economic production was done by slaves or indentured servants. Southern slaveholders revealed they had not the courage to succeed on their own merited labor. Northerners may feel smug about this, but our lineage exploited indentured servants and cheap immigrant labor to work at wages far below what their productive labor merited. We pride ourselves in our Industrial Revolution throughout the nineteenth century; but we showed no ability to make that economic system work with labor that was not exploited.

The year 1893 marks a watershed moment in the transformation from our nineteenth century to our twentieth century economy. Like our colonial forefathers before us, we went global with our exploitation by our first overthrow of a foreign government. Hawaii's new monarch was about to decree that Hawaiian natives would embark on their own self-governance, displacing the few foreign landowners that were controlling the resources and government policy. American diplomats arranged for an alternative government to be declared. The United States recognized this largely fictitious alternative government formed by a few ambitious diplomats and foreign landowners. We invaded the island with a few troops to ensure the transition to the new government, which would maintain authority concentrated in a few American landowners. The real cause for this first bold regime change was to control the natural resources, particularly sugar.[2]

Once we got things started, overthrowing governments to gain or maintain access to natural resources became an acceptable thing for us to do. Cuba, Puerto Rico, Panama, Nicaragua, Honduras and Guatemala all witnessed a colonial-style

---

2 *Overthrow: America's Century of Regime Change from Hawaii to Iraq* (2006), by Stephen Kinzer, provides fourteen accounts of American-backed regime changes.

invasion of American troops or mercenaries as a prelude to setting up governments that knew how to be friendly to American corporations. The Powell Cabal might take pride in these early initiatives to control foreign governments for the sake of our economy, but no one can claim honestly that the results reflect the courage, humility and faith to earn your own keep based on productive merit.

The two World Wars were catastrophic in many respects, but provided some rescue and relief to our economy. In between the World Wars were the Roaring Twenties, a time of great wealth disparity, and the Great Depression. These were products of our *laissez faire* economics that allowed corporations to exploit their way into any contract agreement from an unassailable position of "bargaining" strength, granted to them by the good ol' boys on the Supreme Court in *Lochner v. New York* (1905). The World Wars provided Keynesian-type relief to this *laissez faire* exploitation. Through destruction on foreign lands the wars created foreign demand for American corporations to rebuild infrastructure. The wars put American citizens to work overseas as soldiers, creating an additional demand for domestic labor at home. In essence, foreign wars rescued the middle class from a meritoriously bankrupt economic system that had the middle class at a severe disadvantage.

In the fifties and sixties resistance developed to *laissez faire* economics. Our fiscal policy, with higher taxes on capital gains and large wages, provided a disincentive for greed. The GI Bill provided upward mobility for those who would choose merit. Regulations were passed to limit some of the unmerited exploitation caused by corporations. Together with continued Keynesian stimuli from a couple more foreign wars, and the Interstate Highway System, this became the golden era of economic prosperity for the middle class. Yet even then some of our economic productivity continued to be fueled by the demands of foreign wars.

The seventies reversed these trends, ushered in by the propaganda efforts of the Powell Cabal to convince us all just how marvelous corporations and *laissez faire* economics were. The good ol' boys on the Supreme Court assisted the Powell Cabal efforts with their money as free speech doctrine of the seventies; corporate media assisted with the blossoming of entertainment news and echo chambers in the eighties; Congress assisted by legislating corporate deregulation and the consolidation of media and financial institutions in the nineties; and the Bush II administration assisted by letting the corporate foxes into the regulatory henhouse in the new millenium.

After the World Wars we resumed our colonialism with a diplomatic twist. The World Bank and International Monetary Fund, created in 1944, coordinated their efforts to create lending practices for developing countries that would make a loan shark envious. The conditions of loans forced multinational corporations into these countries, providing a means of siphoning wealth away from the workers of developing countries to the shareholders of developed countries. The autonomy for these countries to develop their own independent corporations or develop an alternative economic system of their own choosing was not an option our diplomatic colonialism—oops, free trade—tolerated.

For the developing countries that could not be persuaded by normal diplomatic channels a special type of loan shark, an economic hit man, would be sent in for some extra persuadin'.[3] If even the hit men for the loan sharks could not succeed, then the CIA arranged for destabilizing events that would lead to regime change.[4] The result has been a string of democracies undermined and replaced by military dictators with a fondness for corruption and American corporations.[5][6]

When our economic system runs without merit at the macro level, we become numb to how we exploit others at the micro level. We assume that the income from stocks, inheritances and lucrative investment plans are meritorious entitlements from previously earned money. We can buy land that ultimately was once a commons, create subdivided lots and sell the land to others for a large profit that far exceeds the merits of our labors. We can exchange money earned by our labor for goods produced by foreign labor and assume that to be an equal exchange of merit through free trade.

We the middle class have been duped into becoming willing supporters of a greed-based economic system totally divorced from free market principles, through appeals to our vain desires. Corporate media informs us that our self-esteem equates with the vain accumulation of wealth, power and/or status. Our vanity cannot accept that our economic system of exploitation causes the conditions for famine, disease and/or aggression elsewhere, and even in our own country. We focus instead on being the "breadbasket" of the world that comes to the rescue when these "nasty, brutish" consequences of intemperate demand and wealth disparity occur. The false patriots among us turn this vanity into a feeling of superiority, and chastise those who wish to steer us on a more humble path.

We are not to question for a moment whether or not the empirical data of early human cultures supports that greed is natural and normative. Hiding and distorting the evidence that reveals greed to be unnatural provides a tautological basis for concluding that greed is desirable. From Thomas Hobbes to Milton Friedman our natural greed is a scholastic dictum we have received from on high, with the Powell Cabal providing ample rhetoric in support. If we believe that greed is only natural, we must trust in the learned scholars that have decreed greed is good and market economies run on selfish self-interest. The question of "Why?" an economic system should function is rendered unspeakable, particularly

---

3 *Confessions of an Economic Hit Man* (2004), by John Perkins, relates his experiences as such.

4 *Overthrow* reports on CIA shenanigans undermining democracies abroad.

5 Jubilee Research documents the billions in aid dollars and subsequent corporate indebtedness that typify American backed dictatorships, http://www.jubileeresearch.org/analysis/reports/dictatorsre-port.htm

6 The Condor Years (2005), by John Dinges, reports on Operation Condor, a brutal collusion of South American military dictators operating with partial U. S. blessings.

in economic textbooks, not to be answered, not even to be asked.

Anthropological and ecological evidence indicates that human altruism is natural, adaptive and at one time a major factor in shaping our social systems. We now have an economic system that not only shuns altruism, but even merit. Our economic system has generated great wealth for us, but only because we have relied on exploitation to make it work since our very beginning. That may be an unspeakable truth for hard working middle class folks but eliminating misinformation is essential for achieving balance. We face political barriers to eliminating misinformation that rival the economic challenges.

Unspeakable Politics

The book *Hiroshima's Shadow* (1998) is a collection of documents, edited by Kai Bird and Lawrence Lifschultz, about our use of the atomic bomb in World War II. The subtitle reveals what truly prompted the book: *Writings on the Denial of History and the Smithsonian Controversy*. The "Smithsonian Controversy" was the canceling of a Smithsonian exhibit on the *Enola Gay*. Many Americans know that the *Enola Gay*, an airplane, helped us become the first and only nation to use atomic weapons on civilian targets. Few of us realize that the Smithsonian exhibit was canceled because certain corporations, politicians and interest groups have rendered discussion about our use of state-sanctioned terrorism unspeakable.

World War II was our initiation with the firebombing of cities. Prior to that time there was a code to which the United States paid lip service that you did not attack civilian targets. In contrast, firebombing was a method of dropping bombs that created an indiscriminately raging inferno. The Allies used firebombing on cities composed mainly of civilians, such as Dresden and Tokyo, to demoralize civilian populations. In other words, firebombing was unspeakable state-sanctioned terrorism, by any valid and reliable definition of the term. You may or may not feel you can defend the use of firebombing to attain our goals, but to deny that it precisely fits the definition of terrorism is simply ignorance. Our use of nuclear weapons on cities in Japan represented an extension of state-sanctioned terrorism that actually began with firebombing. Indeed, less people were killed initially in Hiroshima than in Dresden; the atom bomb merely represented a more efficient means of inflicting terror.

There were alternatives to ending World War II left largely unspoken, because ending the war was not the main intent of dropping the atomic bomb. There were very few cities left in Japan that had not been destroyed already, and documents in *Hiroshima's Shadow* reveal that the Emperor was looking for a way to end the war while saving face with the Japanese people. The alleged reasons of avoiding prolonged battle and saving the lives of American soldiers were bogus, not even supported by our military leaders such as General Dwight Eisenhower and Fleet Admiral William Leahy. The surrender terms for Japan were reported to be much like the terms the Emperor was looking for before we dropped the bomb (mainly, to preserve his own neck and title), but those terms were unacceptable to us until after we destroyed Hiroshima and Nagasaki.

Sir Arthur Conan Doyle's fictional character, Sherlock Holmes, premised that once you rule out the impossible you are left with the probable. If dropping an atomic bomb was completely unnecessary to end the war with Japan, or even to save one single American life, we are left with reasons that really do not have to do with Japan. There is much evidence in the *Hiroshima's Shadow* documents that we were concerned primarily about Russia. The atom bomb was actually a warning signal at the start of the Cold War. If true, then there were better means of providing a warning signal than demonstrating a new efficient means of state-sanctioned terrorism. The bomb could have been dropped on top of Mt. Fuji, or any number of noncivilian targets, to get the message across. Granted, there are plenty of reasons why we should not blow the top off of another country's national treasure; for that matter, there are plenty of reasons never to have used a nuclear weapon at all. The main unspeakable point is that our political system has produced executive leaders for whom avoiding civilian targets (terrorism) is not a major concern in the pursuit of their objectives, even when this runs counter to advice from our military, nor is it a major concern in this country's evaluation of our executive leaders.

Few of us favor terrorism, certainly not a majority of us in the middle class. Yet we have a political system that not only failed to democratically respect the wishes of the majority regarding terrorism, but seeks to hide that failure from us. The usual suspects collaborated to prevent the Smithsonian exhibit of the *Enola Gay* from fulfilling a democratic function. Lobbyists, corporate media, and special interest groups form a censorship triumvirate dedicated to hiding empirical evidence from American citizens.

The Air Force Association was a lobbying group pressuring the Smithsonian to cancel their exhibit. They represent the portion of the military industrial complex responsible for making nuclear weapons. Bringing to light a horrible episode in our history would be bad for business with this industry sector, and we know how touchy corporations can be about our government maintaining the feeding trough for them. Of course, greed alone does not make a compelling message, even in our corporate culture. The AFA incorporated fear into their message. Our safety and security depends on our pursuit of nuclear weapons without academic exhibits undermining our resolve. They speak for a democratic citizenry as if we are all cowards, willing to allow anything to be done for the primary sake of protection.

The empirical evidence surrounding our decision to drop the bomb makes us look bad. That would never do for a collection of false patriots such as the American Legion, who apparently can only love the people and places of this country if they belief we fit certain ideals regardless of the empirical evidence. The American Legion claimed the Smithsonian exhibit to be revisionist history. Among the "revisionist" documents were those written by General Eisenhower and Fleet Admiral Leahy, but perhaps the American Legion does not place much stock in the opinions of the military in matters of war, at least not when vain feelings of superiority are being threatened. Clearly, the American Legion does not hold the type of love for our country that resembles family members acknowledging and proceeding to help a functioning alcoholic. Some things are just too embarrassing for some types of "patriots" to face.

With powerful corporations and influential special interest groups against the exhibit, politicians were bound to jump on board. Unfortunately, just as predictable was the eagerness of the fourth estate to echo the beliefs of corporations, politicians and special interest groups condemning an exhibit of empirical evidence. The Wall Street Journal and the Washington Post wrote scathing opinions about academic ideologues and zealots, with the assertion that they were unpatriotic. An industry dedicated to providing information instead condemned information in the case of simply allowing historical documents to be on display. The Wall Street Journal and Washington Post could not have been more cynical than if they suddenly endorsed totalitarian government in their editorial pages.

The chilling effect of these combined efforts has been to shut off open and honest debate about the single most destructive terrorist act in history, a terrorist act that was state-sanctioned. Instead, middle class America considers Harry Truman an admirable president for going against the advice of military leaders to nuke civilian targets. This represents a total failure in democracy. As bad as that has been for our political system, the consequences spilled into our culture as well. We have not the cultural patience for a political system geared towards wisdom; not when vain pride, fear of security, and cynicism for empirical evidence rules our hearts. When patience runs short, so do morals.

Unspeakable Culture

Neoconservatives have not been treated well in these essays. In Essay 21 we outlined the basic neoconservative mission, spreading democracy to enhance security and morality at home and abroad. The mission appears well-intentioned, but deserves our scorn because neoconservatives butcher the meanings of democracy, security and morality; consequently, they have butchered their overall mission of spreading democracy as well. What has become unspeakable about American culture is that we are all neoconservatives that have contributed to this folly.

We currently are "spreading democracy" in Iraq for the sake of "security" in the fight—oops, I mean war—against terror and the "morality" of eliminating radical Islamists. "Democracy" in Iraq has been imposed, shaped and manipulated by the United States to ensure protection of our interests. Our "security" efforts have enhanced recruitment for Al Qaeda and involve more deaths of American citizens than the sum of all the foreign war and terror casualties since the Vietnam War. Our "morality" allows for preemptive strikes against vastly inferior foes and state-sanctioned torture that accomplishes little (though it works well in the fictional realms of Jack Bauer and Antonin Scalia's scholarly mind).

Our regime change in Iraq is only the latest in a string of neoconservative campaigns in the Middle East that started with the CIA backed coup of a democratic Iranian government in 1953. The Middle East was only a shift in geographic focus for neoconservative campaigns that began with the overthrow of the Hawaiian monarchy in 1893. Throughout the twentieth century the regime changes we brought about were either done in secret, such as the string of coups we sponsored after World War II, or with full blessing from media and the public. We cannot blame our habitual overthrow of governments in developing countries on just a few urgent "piffle" folks in the executive branch. We cannot cathartically point to President Clinton for stimulating our neoconservative lust or to President Bush II for delivering the climax. Once again, the unspeakable part of this is we all have woven neoconservative immorality into the fabric of American culture.

Our early neoconservative campaigns occurred in the Pacific islands, Central America and the Caribbean. In each campaign governments were overthrown that had more democratic leanings than the alternatives imposed by the United States. Stephen Kinzer, in his book *Overthrow* (2006), describes two other common traits of these campaigns.

> "Why did Americans support policies that brought suffering to people in foreign lands? There are two reasons, so intertwined that they became one. The essential reason is that American control of faraway places came to be seen as vital to the material prosperity of the United States. This explanation, however, is wrapped inside another one: the deep-seated belief of most Americans that their country is a force for good in the world."
> (pg. 107)

Many people in a greed-based economic system, particularly neoconservatives, link security to apprehensions about "material prosperity." At the turn of the previous century these apprehensions hinged on protecting the access of American corporations to natural resources such as fruit and sugar. At the turn of this millennium the apprehension hinges on protecting access to oil. In both cases we vainly convinced our egos that we were overthrowing foreign governments for their own good. Mainstream media helped to fuel this deception. As Kinzer continues to write in *Overthrow*:

> "They (Americans) believed Latin Americans and Asians to be as they were portrayed in editorial cartoons: ragged children, usually nonwhite; who had no more idea of what was good for them than a block of stone." (pg. 108)

Such paternalism emulates Mill and other UnEnlightenment philosophers who were brainwashed by the western colonialism of their day. Our colonialist heritage aside, the most striking yet unspeakable feature about our neoconservative campaigns has been our cynical disregard for moral outcomes. In every case of American intervention we replaced governments that were more democratic than the new regimes we helped to usher in. All of the Central America countries that were victims of our neoconservative campaigns have been burdened with great wealth disparity ever since, an inevitable consequence of our *laissez faire* economic imposition. In some cases, such as Chile and Guatemala, governments that were fond of mass murders resulted from our efforts at regime change. Indeed, the citizens of countries where regime change fails, such as Cuba and Vietnam, ultimately fare better than in countries such as Nicaragua, Guatemala, Honduras and Haiti where regime change succeeded.

The Condor Years (2004), by John Dinges, describes the alliance of Argentina, Bolivia, Brazil, Chile, Paraguay and Uruguay to combat socialist movements in South America. Their efforts took on a totalitarian fanaticism to crush any dissent anywhere, even if they had to arrange for assassinations in foreign countries. Dinges rigorously documents what he asserts at the beginning of the book:

> "The political tragedy of this story is that the military leaders who carried out the assassinations and mass murders looked to the United States for technical assistance and strategic leadership. The U.S. government was the ally of the military regimes. The tragedy is the United States acted not to promote and nurture democracy, but to encourage and justify its overthrow. Even more tragic, and arguably criminal, were the cases in which the U.S. officials were directly involved in plots and liaison relationships with those engaged in political assassination and mass murder." (pg. 2)

Much of the American public either knows nothing about our dubious foreign policy of overthrow, or has adopted the urgent apprehensions of neoconservatives that security trumps everything. Admittedly, security does not trump everything for the soldier, the only type of American citizen expected to have courage and whose deaths don't count against our security efforts. Security does not trump everything for those who must rely on hazardous occupations in order to make a living. Security does not trump everything for the wilderness adventurer looking for excitement. Security does not trump everything for parents that would sacrifice their lives to protect their children. In many ways we have the k-species courage that Nature bestowed us with to survive and enjoy our environments.

Yet the security of material prosperity does appear to trump everything when we cash our stock dividends from exploitive multinational corporations. Security does appear to trump everything when we become incurious about why we are the only country to drop the atomic bomb. Security does appear to trump everything when we collectively condone the overthrow of democratic governments, to be replaced by corporate friendly dictatorships. Security does appear to trump everything when torture and preemption become normal foreign policy. Security does appear to trump everything when we condone preemptive policy for the most powerful nation on earth. Such assent to the ends justifying the means for our security, even unwittingly, associates all of us—middle class included—with the urgent "piffle" folks who have proven to be unspeakable cowards with unspeakable immorality.

Unspeakable Ways of Knowing

There is nothing extraordinary about the American Legion and the AFA advocating their beliefs. In a true democracy there will exist a wide variety of beliefs, including those that support torture, preemptive strikes and the state-sanctioned terrorist use of atomic weapons. Nor is there anything extraordinary in attacking the Smithsonian and the people behind the *Enola Gay* exhibit for being revisionists, leftists and academics. Attacking the messenger instead of the message, particularly when your own beliefs are indefensible, has become commonplace. The most extraordinary aspect of canceling the *Enola Gay* exhibit was that empirical evidence became unspeakable; even to the point that a special interest group that used to be supportive of the military wanted no part of empirical evidence that came from military leaders.

Public discourse always will involve a "battle of beliefs" rather than an in depth examination of empirical evidence. Public discourse, to be most effective, must be concise, which leaves out empirical details. Corporate media insists that they only give the public what they want, and are not to blame for "news" that is either more fluff or opinions than real events. But anything can be made entertaining with the right packaging. Consider the following "press release:"

> For the past thirty years there has been a steady increase in the proportion of wealth concentrated in the richest 1%. Much of this concentration of wealth has come from investment capital that does not reward productive labor. At the same time there has been a steady increase in the proportion of housing costs, health care costs and education costs to median family income. This verifies the economic principle of what happens when "too many dollars," concentrated in the pockets of the wealthiest, chase "too few goods" that happen to be the most essential and expensive for the middle class to own. Increasing wealth disparity is unfair, inflationary and goes against the very principles of our democracy.

That little clip of news could provide hours of "entertainment" with the news talk hosts, echo chambers, and other entertainment enhancers available to corporate media. The trouble lies not with the newsworthiness of such clips, but the corporate media infrastructure. For corporations do not fund academic endowments or fellowships for journalism to point out the greed of corporations. Think tanks full of pundits on loan to echo chambers do not exist through contributions from the poor. The self-proclaimed champions of the middle class on corporate media do not get rich by reporting on the empirical data that matters most to our pocketbooks.

We must also face the reality that empirical evidence is not always valid and reliable, even as wielded by scientists. For example there still are scientists, funded by large corporations, claiming that global warming is no big deal. They can provide abundant empirical evidence that the amount of global warming has been higher in the past and will be higher in the future regardless of what humans do. Evidence about the *amount* of global warming is not valid for a discussion about the *rate* of global warming, which is what human activity is affecting. Natural systems have had to evolve both slowly, such as with natural climate change, and catastrophically, such as in response to a traumatic meteor strike. Most folks would agree, if presented with the valid and reliable empirical evidence, that slow change is the preferred way for systems to adapt. Certainly most scientists agree to this, as most scientists are committed to the empiricism that was reintroduced by the Enlightenment.

Yet the Enlightenment is precisely the reason why empirical ways of knowing has become unspeakable outside the realm of science. Along with the Scientific Revolution, the Enlightenment reintroduced to the world the ideals of free markets and democracy. Free market exchange in theory is based on the experiences of what people value when not coerced or paternalistically guided. Democracy in theory is based on the collective experiences of citizens producing wisdom. Unfortunately, these theories consistent with experiences that extend back to prehistoric times had to be made consistent with the dogma of western colonialism. No valid and reliable evidence, by definition, can confirm that exploitation is good for either free markets or democracy. Ever since the Enlightenment our culture, politics and economics have had to be justified through scholasticism, distorting natural experience to idolize scholarly beliefs focused on greed and authoritarianism.

Distorting the feedback of natural experience disrupts the homeostasis of a system. Negative feedback loops are transformed into positive feedback loops. Unreliable information is invented to claim that "black is white" with the aid of unspeak. Invalid indicators and assumptions are cooked within the shrouded conditions of the "black box" and insulated by the unspeakable. These misinformation tools assist corporations, political parties and special interest groups in changing the function of our economic, political and cultural systems to their advantage. Consolidated corporate media and think tanks apply these tools, increasing the centralization and dependence of the middle class on this misinformation, and constraining the diversity that contributes to civilizations being advanced.

A New Paradigm Shift

Paradigm shifts, introduced in the first essay, involve a radical change in a belief system brought about by the contradictions and anomalies of experience. We poked fun at *laissez faire* economics as an exception to the rule of paradigm shifts, as their belief system increases the anomalies between whom we really are as an altruistic species and how we are supposed to behave as greedy bastards to make markets work. Yet their belief system did provide a useful shift from feudal lords to business corporations as the entities for concentrating wealth. Feudal lords no doubt felt as entitled to wealth from the labors of others as do our current shareholders. They simply provided land instead of investments to "earn" their entitlements.

Business corporations represent a distinct improvement over feudal lords for the concentration of wealth. They are less arbitrary and can be more democratic in theory; though the Supreme Court considers them to be individuals just as much as feudal lords. If free markets and democracy are to be avoided anyways, then we are better off doing so with a system based on property and contracts than one without. Yet the utility of the *laissez faire* dogma to excuse current economic problems is starting to wear thin. Indeed, the belief in economic utility as a foundation for all our belief systems presents too many moral dilemmas. The time has come for a new paradigm shift.

We need to shift our beliefs away from being indulged by cultural entitlements to the true liberty of our natural rights and conditions. We need to discard the fixed dogma thought up by great thinkers sitting in their armchairs and build flexible theories based on the ongoing experiences of what is natural. We need to experience the natural primacy of our independent belonging; through this experience we can understand the normative and moral good of humility, faith and courage. We need to experience the natural primacy of our independent thought; through this experience we can understand the normative and moral good of open and honest information. We need to experience the natural primacy of our independent labors; through this experience we can understand the normative and moral good of diversity.

We are fooling ourselves if we think the paradigm shift needed can be accomplished through the same system of corporations, political parties and special interest groups. These are structured to best accomplish their original functions of greed, authoritarianism and idolatry. Changing the function necessitates a drastic shift for the agencies of change. Nor can we rely on consolidated corporate media to echo a significant counter message to the established cultural institutions. If we wish to reinforce messages of merit, wisdom and harmony we will need a different infrastructure for obtaining information that will guide our systems.

Along with a shift in cultural agencies for change there will need to be a shift in the cultural agents. We cannot rely on wealth and power elites to lead a charge towards merit and wisdom. We cannot rely on dogmatic elites, including religious icons, to lead a charge towards humility, faith and courage. We cannot rely on academic scholars whose reputations were built on entrenched dogma to lead a charge towards learning and improving from experience.

The middle class needs to step up to bring about this paradigm shift. We must call upon Hans to shed his gullibility. We have played both the victim and the villain in our cultural evolution from moderate k-species to exploitive r-species. The time has come for the middle class to now be the vanguard for advancing civilization towards the functions of merit, wisdom and harmony.

I happen to have a few specifics on how we can proceed.

RESTORING BALANCE

Our Natural Condition

These essays first explored the economic pursuit of happiness and then peeled back layers to arrive at our cultural quality of life. *Laissez faire* economists advocate that such a sequence follows the chain of causality in our social systems. Our economic self, governed by individual self-interest and greed, determines our political self for pursuing policies and plans to fulfill that greed, which in turn determines our cultural self of beliefs and behaviors to legitimize that greed. But throughout the essays there has been an undercurrent that the chain of causality really runs in the opposite direction. Our social system of beliefs and behaviors determines our social system of governance, which in turn legitimizes our social system of economics. Regardless of which direction the chain of causality flow, the worship of greed by *laissez faire* economists runs counter to what evolved as our inherent nature over hundreds of thousands of years. As we act to restore balance to our social systems this is where we must start, with our natural condition.

These essays triangulated three types of information in detailing our natural condition. One source was my own experiences with wilderness travel. I am but one person and we should not make too much out of one set of experiences; seeking instead the wisdom of collective experiences. Yet neither should we be persuaded by the trite arguments of scholars chastising us ordinary folk for being so bold as to question the "wisdom" of great thinkers who came before us. Our ability to reason may not be comparable to Hume or Locke, but when our personal experiences seem to contradict the conventional wisdom (not the same as collective wisdom) we should not be too intimidated to ask why that should be so. My understanding of our natural selves, gained from thousands of miles and quite a few years spent in the wilderness, could not be more opposed to that contrived by Thomas Hobbes, or of *laissez faire* economists. In this particular matter these armchair thinkers should not be considered adequate scholars.

I have enough training in ecology to draw upon that as another source of information for triangulating our natural condition. Ecologists might caution anyone not to make too much of the r-species and k-species duality as a general principle; real organisms deviate from these stereotypical models in a variety of ways. Yet the traits of natural human beings come as close to the altruistic k-species stereotype as any organism that ever existed on the face of this planet. We can think and we have opposable thumbs, handy traits to have if you want to adapt to whatever the environment throws at you, or to migrate away from other humans to another environment and diversify as a "competitive" response. We naturally evolved as a "pack" animal with long gestation periods and long periods of caring for our young. We simply did not evolve to be rapid or voracious colonizers like bacteria or vermin; that is an artifact of western "civilization."

This does not mean we were a uniform species in prehistoric times, far from it. As we migrated and adapted to different environments we adopted different beliefs and behaviors. Even apart from cultural differences, our proclivity for diversity is manifested in our natural diets. Few organisms get their nourishment from as wide a variety of food sources as good old *Homo sapiens*. If nothing else, this variety helped our natural ancestors to maintain a leisurely lifestyle, conserving our energy budget as is the natural objective of all organisms. Only culture turns us into workaholics that defy our naturally adaptive preferences for leisure.

Early cultures moderated their population growth as an environmental response; though we now have better ways of doing this with our modern culture and technology. The evidence for this comes from the third source of information for triangulation, cultural anthropology. The primitive cultures discovered and studied by cultural anthropologists who ventured into the field do not fit the image conjured up by armchair thinkers from the Enlightenment. They are not even as short lived as paleontologists who study old bones would have us believe, though life expectancy is one of many areas in which the technology of modern culture has brought civilized improvements.

Perhaps the best compilation on early cultures is *Stone Age Economics* (1972) by Marshall Sahlins. The most telling information of all, in my opinion, is the quote from a pioneer shared at the beginning of Essay 22: "savages pride themselves on being hospitable to strangers." What more can be revealed about the key difference between Western and Native American cultures, and how the former perceives the latter? Yet as primitive as hospitality may seem to be to western civilization, Native Americans manifested an altruism that has been hot-wired into us from our natural beginnings. No doubt there were plenty of greedy individuals among the earliest cultures, including Native Americans. But a greedy person would have been ill-suited for survival among early bands and tribes of humans who had to survive communally; only culture has turned unnatural greed into a social advantage for individuals.

This is a brief review of our natural condition, but provides almost enough base data for us to move forward with a plan for restoring balance to our economic, political and cultural systems. One more natural trait needs to be mentioned; a trait as natural as conserving our energy budgets. Humans, along with all other organisms, survive by being empirical. We learn from experience. Seeing is believing. Only culture seeks to distort or obscure the meaning of experiences to keep our social systems out of balance.

Knowing

The ways in which we come to know things was an important theme in these essays. Changing our beliefs (theories) based on valid and reliable experiences is empiricism. Changing the meaning of experiences based on scholarly beliefs (dogmas) is scholasticism. Empiricism as a way of knowing, besides being the preferred epistemology of science, benefits the middle class. With empiricism the collective experiences of the many would outweigh the "scholarship" of much fewer corporations, politicians and special interest groups. With empiricism we must be granted the liberty of decentralized independence to be able to form diverse thoughts, rather than conform to the dictates of a political party or corporate media. With empiricism we depend on our collective experiences to get at the real meaning of our cultural quality of life; our political liberty; and our economic pursuit of happiness. The wisdom of our collective cultural experiences would form our economic beliefs, rather than allow the authoritative imposition of economic beliefs to form the meaning of our cultural experiences.

We were not born with fixed beliefs, nor did we naturally evolve to have dogmas determine the meaning of our experiences. Our species did not evolve the traits that would make us adapt to environments by mutations or rapid colonization. We developed the k-species ability to adapt by assessing environmental conditions and changing our beliefs and behaviors accordingly. We evolved to be the most sophisticated empiricists on the planet. Cultural evolution has changed this; bestowing an advantage to those who could combine wealth, power and dogma to both rapidly colonize and to dictate the meaning of what we experience, at times using secrecy and distortion, at times using "superior" scholarship. In reintroducing our natural empiricism, the Enlightenment unfortunately bungled the job by limiting the empirical approach only to the Scientific Revolution. Science and technology have blossomed ever since, with contributions from the many. Disciplines such as economics and political science progress slowly in their beliefs, if at all, with contributions from chosen icons in chosen areas, generally supported by wealth, power and/or dogmatic elites.

The middle class faces the problem that much of what we wish to know cannot be experienced by us directly; we rely on information provided by others. This leaves us vulnerable to "black box" economics and politics that hide the real meaning of experiences. Indexes of Economic Freedom that do not account for private coercion and secret meetings to discuss our energy policy are examples of this assault on experienced-based merit and wisdom. Complexity is another "black box" tactic designed to promote beliefs over experience. The quest for complexity results from either an intent to deceive, or from Herculean efforts to prove a point when the simple truth based on empirical evidence will not cooperate.

The middle class needs to trust in the validity behind our own experiences. The Federal Reserve Banks sponsored an exceedingly complex study to prove their point that leisure for the working class has increased, when the empirical evidence based on our everyday experiences reveal the increasing necessity of day care. Housing is arguably the most essential good, and unarguably the most expensive portion of our budgets. Steadily increasing housing costs as a proportion of income head us away from our empirical roots that acquired comparable shelter for all, and in the direction of the imposed serfdom that infected the scholastic middle ages. If complex standard of living indicators, consumer price indexes and NASDAQ all imply something different from the simple ratio of ownership housing costs to median family income, we must ignore those scholarly black box indicators and focus on what our experiences are telling us.

"Black is white" economics and politics distort the meaning of empirical experiences to fit authoritarian and idolatrous beliefs. Economic data that lacks validity and reliability, such as data that supports the morality of greed, can deceive untrained citizens. Bait and switch tactics can fool the middle class into trusting the legitimacy of politically manipulated evidence on everything from WMDs to climate change. These threats require more than what we know from our own simple experiences to remedy. Obtaining valid and reliable information will require deliberate actions by the middle class that go beyond our normal everyday routines. But before we act we must care.

Caring

Think tank pundits and news talk hosts undeniably are in great demand, as are authoritarian leaders. Our friend Hans from the fable was perfectly happy as he was being swindled. Corporations, politicians and special interest groups appear to have convinced the middle class majority to accept greed as the norm of economics, authoritarianism as the norm of politics and idolatry as the norm of culture. Why should we care about "black box" and "black is white" economics, the waggle dances of politicians or the role of unspeak and the unspeakable in our culture? There are five important reasons to care.

First, there is a strong component of our human make-up that detests hypocrisy. Perhaps this is a carry over from our empirical roots, when trusting what we experienced was of utmost importance to our well-being. As cynical as we may have become about much of our culture, we desperately want to be able to trust what others are telling us, as that is how we once survived. When such trust is betrayed through hypocrisy we want to know and we want to react accordingly.

Second, there are intimate connections between greed, authoritarianism and idolatry. We cannot conveniently choose to be for an economics of greed without endorsing a politics of authoritarianism and a culture of idolatry. Corporations, political parties and interest groups work in tandem. Conversely, should our ethics lead us to care about one of the virtues of merit, wisdom or harmony; we need to care about all three. There is no escaping the holistic relationship of economics, politics and culture.

Third, we do not come to endorse greed, authoritarianism or idolatry except through the personal traits of vanity, cynicism and cowardice. Our sense of belonging steers us towards merit, wisdom and harmony; that which corrupts our belonging corrupts those social goals. Thus there are severe personal costs for even the wealthy, the powerful and the zealot who seem to be accommodated by our r-species behaviors. Vanity corrupts all of us socially; cynicism corrupts all of us spiritually; and cowardice corrupts all of us emotionally. These costs ultimately impact our health and happiness even as we fool ourselves with Hans-like gullibility into thinking all is fine on the surface.

Fourth, the damage done by vanity, cynicism and cowardice are not limited to the health and happiness costs to our own lives. The urgency induced by these traits causes us to forsake patience and peace. For example, our urgency considers the lives of soldiers more expendable than citizens. If we were to consider the soldier's life as equal to the normal citizen's, then we have lost more lives in our response to 9/11 than was caused by that tragedy. The additional lives of innocents abroad destroyed literally and figuratively by our urgent response to the Iraq War and our other regime changes are incalculable. All because the citizens at home, unlike the soldiers abroad, are to be cowards that refute our natural heritage and consider security the primary goal of life and government.

Fifth, by becoming more of an r-species than a k-species we fall victim to the biggest liability that r-species share. Their populations go through periods of boom and bust. Widespread famine, disease and aggression do not happen to people that moderate their behavior in accordance with their environment. This "brutish" consequence of our cultural evolution was accelerated by western colonialism, in spite of, or perhaps because of, the ruminations of great Enlightenment thinkers sitting in their armchairs.

Knowing and caring about the hypocrisies of corporations, politicians and special interest groups does not suffice. The middle class needs to change our social systems holistically to promote merit, wisdom and harmony. We need to rid the infections of vanity, cynicism and cowardice from our souls. We need to temper our urgency for the sake of patience and peace throughout the world. Such causes are worth whatever any of us can contribute. We have two possible courses of action to pursue.

Acting

The easier of the two courses of action would be for the middle class to effect change within the structures of our current systems. We would need to identify and empower those leaders and scholars in corporations, political parties and special interest groups whose beliefs have the best interests of the middle class at heart. I have touched upon the dangers of this scholastic approach throughout these essays, but let us return our focus on Benjamin Friedman, the well-meaning Harvard scholar who advocated maximizing economic growth for the sake of moral consequences.

We will ignore the peculiarities of his logic, which if taken seriously we must conclude there is such a thing as a "free lunch," and greed is ultimately a moral stimulus. In his well-meaning advocacy for the middle class B. Friedman suggested that government needs to make sure that economic booms are equitably distributed. OK. The middle class will not complain about that. But who will pressure government to effect such change? Special interest groups wield significant influence; perhaps the middle class can rely on them. But what empowers the most influential special interest groups? The answer: corporations that thrive on greed because of how our economic system is structured. The U. S. Chamber of Commerce is the extreme heavyweight in lobbying dollars; they lobby for the benefit of business corporations, not the middle class. The circularity to effecting change within our social systems as structured dooms us to failure. Even if B. Friedman was correct about his thesis, he is naive about his solution for corrective measures.

Late in the process of writing these essays I read another collection of essays called *Inequality Matters: The Growing Economic Divide in America and Its Poisonous Consequences* (2005). I learned with a tiny bit of chagrin that many of the themes I present in this book already were covered by these essays; I was not as original about some of "my" ideas as I thought. To their credit, these essayists relied on better empirical evidence and inductive reasoning than B. Friedman. The economic report card I presented in Essay 7, admittedly with some pride, could have been substituted with a bit of crafting and abundant citations to the essays of *Inequality Matters*. Nonetheless, many of these essayists were scholars convinced in their beliefs. They thought that they could work through the typical authoritarian structures of interest groups, political parties and even corporations to convince the public to adopt the specific beliefs and behaviors they prescribe.

A true empiricist would be skeptical of this scholastic course of action. The empirical evidence strongly suggests that business corporations, political parties and special interest groups coevolved. Furthermore, they continue to coevolve now along with consolidated corporate media. Expecting to impose new functions on our cultural, political and economic systems using the same components adapted for our existing functions defies logic. The middle class will need to rely on our own collective experiences, operating independently of current social system components, to build up the components for an economics of merit, a politics of wisdom and a culture of harmony.

Our experiences fall into five categories. I alluded to these in the economic essay on the self-interests of labor, and again in the cultural essay on false patriotism. These categories are:

- Natural Well-being,
- Family Devotion,
- Community Service,
- Political Involvement,
- Economic Productivity.

A rough course of action for restoring balance taps into each of these five categories of experience. They will be presented in the recommended sequence that they should be pursued. In the end, they are not meant to be considered in isolation, but as holistic parts of our overall social systems.

Natural Well-being

For the middle class to make social changes we need to start with a strong individual foundation. Should all else prove too daunting, we at least need to strengthen and fortify our own well-being. Most pertinent to our natural well-being is the free will to our independent belonging and the quality of life that brings. Humility, faith and courage stimulate our free will to belong, but modern culture has compromised all three of these individual traits.

Culture has instilled a vanity in humans at a level that did not exist for altruistic foraging bands. No doubt there were individual exceptions; that is to be assumed. Yet only culture has taken individual vanity and turned it into a social adaptation, rather than an individual trait that risks being ostracized by the tribe. Vanity is expressed in a variety of ways. The hypocrisy of feeling entitled while at the same time condemning the entitlement of others—such as occurs with shareholders—is induced by the blinders of vanity. The desire to be "better" or the "best"—such as experienced by false patriots—is another expression of vanity. Our belonging to others calls for a return to humility.

Culture has instilled a cynical materialism in humans that did not exist in our inherent natures. Early foraging bands, not to mention modern-day wilderness travelers, acquire awe for things that go beyond the self. This awe can still be cultivated through culture, such as when one feels awe for democracy or other social systems that transcend the individual. Yet some cultural systems nurture an absorption in the self and the self-centered materialism this includes. We are willing to sacrifice our natural rights to be indulged with cultural entitlements. Our well-being calls for a return to faith in things that transcend the self.

Culture has instilled cowardice in humans that would have led to severe neurosis in early humans. Early foraging bands lived with uncertain conditions.

They had to be prepared for whatever occurred and adapt to make the best of the situation. Fortunately, we were given powerful brains and opposable thumbs that helped us to adapt quite well. Culture alone introduced the expectation of a strong government controlling the conditions we face and placing security as the utmost priority in our individual and social behaviors. But along with these expectations of control and security comes heightened apprehensions for when they might fail; apprehensions that authoritarian leaders are all too eager to exploit. Our well-being calls for a return to the courage that handles uncertainty and resists exploitation.

Early humans experienced individual rites of passages in temporary isolation from their bands, like the aboriginal walkabouts, which nurtured humility, faith and courage. My own rites of passage involved thousands of miles of long-distance backpacking, but this is not an option for most of the middle class. Thirty years ago I could go through college without burdening myself with large debts; that is an unrealistic goal now for most middle class students. Once we are in the work force, health care plans and pensions too often bind us to our employer, regardless of how unsatisfactory our terms of employment may come to be. By the time we have the economic freedom for something like an individual rites of passage, too much lost time has passed in our lives before we can start to identify and nurture our natural rights.

Schooling has replaced individual rites of passages for coming to terms with who we are before joining the "real world." Schooling can do many wonderful things, particularly in this country where our higher education is the best in the world. Alas, returning us to our inherent natures of humility, faith and courage are not among the wonderful things delivered by our educational system. "Schooling" too often involves the mission of "schools of thought:" promoting fixed dogma at the expense of learning from experience.

Let us distill from long-distance backpacking those necessary conditions for nurturing our free will that we could pursue at any point in our lives. The most essential ingredient is being alone. Business corporations, political parties and special interest groups all attempt to manipulate what we believe and how to behave. Much of this manipulation occurs anonymously, through talking heads on television or over the Internet. The belonging that results from these pressures typically involves saying and doing the "right" things. Nurturing free will means turning away from these groups with set norms of beliefs and behaviors to tune into our basic natural rights.

Another necessary condition for strengthening our free will is to heighten our awareness. The constant exertion of long-distance backpacking stimulates beta-endorphins, hormones that heighten awareness. This has been called runner's high, but you do not need to be a backpacker or a runner to unleash these beta-endorphins. Swimming, cycling, yoga or other aerobic activities can do this as well. Some people have trained themselves to achieve heightened awareness through the inactive means of prayer and meditation as well. "Practice makes perfect," which leads to our third necessary condition.

Our heightened awareness alone must occur on a regular basis. For long-distance backpacking this condition is built in, but after such long journeys are over our own free will can weaken to the pressures of those people and groups who would impose their will and dogma. To resist these pressures we need to build in solitary time with heightened awareness into our daily schedule. If that proves too difficult, despite all that "leisure" time puppet libertarians tell us we are getting these days, then a weekly slot of solitary heightened awareness is a minimum standard.

The target of our awareness should be something of beauty, which can be defined broadly. Beauty helps transcend us out of our self-absorbed reality into cosmic reality. For the long-distance backpacker the wonders of the natural world provide a constant input. Music and art can provide the same stimulus of beauty. The written word can be powerfully beautiful, though for nurturing our free will the beautiful poem or passage should not be one intended to promote dogma. The most striking beauty of all, in my opinion, are the images of tenderness, loyalty and love extended by one human being to another. These beautiful images are waiting everywhere to transform and transcend us.

Along with images and other forms of beauty, you might insert a mantra into your routine of solitary awareness. Mantras are common for those who practice prayer or meditation. Keeping in mind that our goal is to strengthen our free will, the mantra might take the form of something like: "I will have courage; I will have faith; I will have humility." Repeating this at the beginning and end of our routines for solitary heightened awareness will help to keep the focus on the natural attributes that compose our free will.

Strengthening our free will to independent belonging is just a start. We have additional natural rights that we must cultivate as well. Our natural right to independent thought is in great jeopardy, given the cultural and political climate that justifies money as free speech. Selling hype and distortion requires more money than selling actual information; and the necessary extra expenditures to sell hype and distortion are concentrated in the coffers of glitzy, corporate media rather than localized media. By equating money with free speech we have doomed ourselves to spiral down the path of consolidated media and misinformation networks in our public discourse. We cannot change this jurisprudence on our own and overnight. In the meantime we simply must resist the tools of hype and distortion wielded by consolidated corporate media. We should not be getting important news about current events from twenty-four hour news networks, news talk shows that entertain with incivility, or the echo chambers of corporate-sanctioned opinions.

Along with distortion we must be immensely skeptical of secrecy and complexity. If something is too complex for us to understand, involving myriad indicators and assumptions, there is a chance that someone is trying too hard to combat the simple truth. If we are told decisions must be kept in secret we must be skeptical of the motivations. There is very little that must be kept secret in order to work, particularly when we are the wealthiest and most powerful nation. Fidel Castro knew the CIA wanted to assassinate him even when this was a secret to be kept from U.S. citizens. The only thing secrecy accomplished then, and now, is warding off the disapproval of a democracy.

To be skeptical of the sources of distortion and secrecy is different than being cynical. The great Skeptic Pierre Bayle was also a man of great faith. You can have great faith in the virtues of openness and honesty while being skeptical of how those virtues fare in current social systems. To protect our faith in the natural right to independent thought we must become skeptics of even the interest groups and political parties to which we belong. The time may come when *Buckley v. Valeo* goes the way of *Lockner v. New York*, and *Dred Scott v. Sanford*. One specific goal of ours should be to bring about that change, but until such time we must view all information about current events from corporate media and political parties with a skeptical eye.

Few people retire to become inactive. Some dedicate themselves to new or old productive hobbies when they retire. Some work part time somewhere else, or in a different capacity at their old job. Some people, like my self-employed father, simply choose not to retire. The prime motivator for retirement is not inactivity but avoiding the "same ol', same ol'" dictating how they are to be productive with their independent labors.

Diversity is one of the major ingredients of an advanced civilization. We should strive for the productivity of our independent labors to be rewarded by this opportunity for diversity, or else we have forfeited one of the advantages of being civilized. Long term indenture to a large corporation through health care and pension plans constrains this opportunity, no matter how lucrative the financial trap. I have witnessed teachers absolutely miserable and unproductive in their employment, but they continue on for thirty years or more for the sake of their pensions.

This is not all civilization has to offer. We should not have to do the same work all our lives, like the unfortunate lot of early foragers or agrarians. If we choose to, fine. Feeling compelled to because of economic incentives: 1) concentrates capital for financial institutions; and 2) grants to the employer the bargaining strength to manipulate other terms of the contract. The good ol' boys on the Supreme Court demonstrate a fondness for protecting the bargaining strength of corporations; we must counter by valuing our independent labors in additional areas to economic productivity. Our labors in all facets of our long lives will determine our well-being more than the amount of capital we hoarded for a grand time at the end.

These recommendations are directed at the middle class, but the wealthy may take heed for the advice provided here as well. The wealthy may claim they are happy because all the media news and entertainment inform us that wealth makes us so. But there have been too many experiences indicating that the wealthy are trapped more by vanity, cynicism and cowardice than we are. There is too much evidence that the wealthy weave themselves in webs of distortion and secrecy more than we do. Their labors are less constrained by economic entrapments than ours to be sure, but the grand times they plan with their concentrated capital sometimes come at the expense of depriving themselves of a loving community.

We all have an inclination to evangelize. When we find something that works for our lives we like to share that with others. As the foundation of our well-being is strengthened and fortified, we should wish to share the tips presented here…or better tips that your own experiences uncover. To be most effective with our evangelism we could use the pyramid approach; we might share this approach with five others and, after they embark on this path encourage them to evangelize to five more. In so doing we lay the foundation for building community.

Family Devotion

Families and communities have much in common. For some people they are one and the same. In some cases a large family might serve the same extended functions of a small community. In some communes everyone is treated as a member of the same family. I will maintain one important distinction between the two. A family requires devotion while a community thrives on service.

Family devotion involves those labors that the people we live with require from us. Parenting tops this list. Once we become secure in our own humility, faith and courage we can be devoted to spreading that throughout the family, and particularly with our children. The place to start is simply to treasure being middle class.

We identify with the middle class when we think about ordinary folk getting along with each other in a tight-knit community. We identify with the middle class when we think about the merits of earning our way through life through our own labors. We identify with the middle class when we think about a democracy collecting the voices of the many. When we solidify our foundation of humility, faith and courage we are drawn to such middle class goals.

Treasuring these middle class goals means changing many things we typically wish for our children. We often wish our children to be wealthy; but a commitment to wealth generally requires a commitment to greed, which in turn means concentrating wealth independently of merit. We sometimes wish our children to wield great influence, power or authority; but a thirst for power seeks authoritarianism, which invariably means thwarting democratic efforts. We often wish our children to "make a name for themselves;" but this leads to idolatry, with your children not quite sure of the intentions of their "friends."

The main problems with wealth, power and status lies not in having them or wielding them effectively, but with wanting them. If we show ourselves to be content with our own middle class goals and way of living, we help our kids to emulate this as well. Should their merits or fate then lead them to wealth, power or status they are equipped better to control these furies, rather than being controlled by them.

There was a time when the advice to treasure being middle class would be treated as common sense. Coming out of World War II people identified themselves with the middle class whether or not their incomes warranted such a classification. Now, after close to forty years influence by corporate media and the Powell Cabal, we overestimate our wealth standing (Essay 1). Part of this is due to people slightly well off not being aware of just how obscenely rich the wealthiest people are, but this would be mitigated if we still had the urge to identify ourselves in this country as being middle class.

We have been convinced by forces such as the Powell Cabal that economics dictates culture. Consequently, our choice of jobs typically dictates what type of community we need to live in. Part of our family devotion should be convincing our children that who we are begins with family devotion. That is to say, culture dictates economics. Letting our job determine the community we live in, or letting the community we desire determine what job we have, both boil down to cultural decisions. Our beliefs determine our behaviors, whether we believe in corporate greed or harmonic communities. We need to convince our children that cultural aspirations are the starting point of what to do and where to go; hence, they need to be aware of their cultural aspirations and choose them carefully.

I am not here to tell you to do the same things I did as a parent. Frankly, I did many things wrong, falling victim to the common parental complaint that my children did not come with a manual. However, there are two types of actions that I am convinced Cindy and I got right and now recommend to you as requirements for family devotion. First, we read profusely to our children. Second, we demonstrated devotion through quantity time, not quality time.

Reading to our children models for them our basic natural rights. Reading is the most basic and essential skill that our independent labors through life will require. Reading opens up a realm of creative fantasies that stimulate our independent thinking. Most importantly, reading is a nurturing activity that reinforces our belonging. There is nothing quite as special as your child curled up on your lap reading Dr. Seuss along with you.

Cindy and I were fortunate. Our early years with our family were spent in an apartment with no electronic entertainment. We had to read profusely to our children whether we would have been inclined to do so or not. Our official economic status at the time, as viewed from the perspective of the State, was poverty. From the perspective of what really counts we were blessed.

Quality time is great; obviously, we all wish to have nice quality times with our children. Yet quality time requires little in the way of devotion. What sacrifice is there in having good, quality time? Perhaps our children can get warm and fuzzy feelings through quality time, but do they learn that they are our first priority? When we are free to choose, the bulk of our time and effort go to where our heart lies. If our kids are to treasure being middle class and to choose their cultural aspirations carefully, if they are to be devoted to their own families, we need to model for them this behavior.

The principle of quantity should be applied to interacting with your extended family. There are good reasons for some people not to interact with your extended family, but there are bad reasons as well. The point of family devotion is to not let the bad reasons take over. We should not let vanity cause us to be unwilling to share or compromise with others. We should not let cynicism harden our hearts to the value of devotion to a broad circle of family members. We should not let cowardice force us to preempt hassles we foresee in the future with our extended family. Vanity, cynicism and cowardice cause us to forego an extended family allegedly for our own sakes, but in reality we do the greatest harm to ourselves when we let these culturally cultivated sins rule us.

Community Service

Caring for our family of loved ones can be tough work. From the earliest of our prehistoric existence one resource we relied on for help was the community. But now the community is being eroded by other options. Community fellowship is being supplanted by the work place and the interest group. Community activities are being replaced by electronic entertainment. Instead of seeking to harmonize diverse beliefs and backgrounds in the context of community we have turned to political, ideological or entertainment heroes and their dogmas.

We have instituted external incentives to actually draw us away from community. Most striking of these is the home as an investment rather than a castle. Goods and services are supposed to depreciate over time. Homes are the one exception, creating an incentive not to stay in the same community but to have greater allegiance to increasing capital. In some cases homeowners apply productive labor to enhance the value of their homes through additions or repair. But homes increase in value faster than inflation even without productive labor, which either exploits economic production from other sources or inflates and destabilizes our economy. Ironically, the appreciation of homes proves not to be much of an investment after all. On balance the "home as investment" strategy has led to an increasing portion of our incomes devoted to covering housing costs (see Essay 7). Home investment as an external incentive to devalue community has done both economic and cultural damage.

If home investments are the external push away from community, labor entrapments are the external pull. Retirement and health insurance costs rise faster than inflation, faster even than housing costs. Since the seventies these costs also have shifted more to the private sector, the inefficiency of which contributes to the inflated costs. When corporations apparently subsidize these costs our primary allegiance is pulled towards our employers. Another powerful incentive has formed to forsake community.

Our transient lifestyles increase the demand for loans. When we were predominantly a rural agrarian culture the community functioned as a financial institution. Loans were consummated with a handshake and bankruptcy did not exist. If capital could not be used to repay a loan, barter or labor would suffice. If hardship struck, neighbors would come to the rescue. The loan and insurance functions of community have been replaced by financial institutions adept at concentrating capital away from the merits of production or community. Had financial institutions remained small—on a neighborly scale—that would be one thing. But during the Clinton administration the consolidation of financial institutions rivaled that of corporate media. In 2008, months after I wrote the last essays, we are witnessing the degradation of system diversity, adaptability and stability due to this consolidation.

As long as the capital can be repaid a loan is better than a handshake, providing a government backed contract arrangement for acquiring something on the speculation of your future labor. A loan, in theory, stimulates the economic productivity to pay back that loan. Yet by enlarging the scope of capital markets, where capital serves capital, we tread precariously with shifting our economy further away from being fully covered by productive labor. We take out increasing loan amounts with the inevitable but unrealized impact that we inflate the economy that much more, which in turn fuels further need for loans.

Our transient lifestyle also devalues the community as an important source of news. Corporate media, echo chambers and news talk shows have filled in the gap. The meaning behind the news is not being placed in the context of community but in the context of special interests as represented by pundits from think tanks. Through community we gather the wisdom of our collective experiences; but we forsake that wisdom when we devote our allegiance to special interests. By turning to consolidated and centralized media we lose both community and democracy.

The community functions we have been losing, taken all together, are too overwhelming for us to recapture all at once through renewed commitment to community service. Fortunately, community is its own reward. As the k-species supreme we evolved to live in community. Our community service at this point should be dedicated primarily to simply reforming communities, independently of the functions we might wish to recapture. Just as we need to schedule solitary heightened awareness in our lives, our most valuable community service at this point is to schedule time to gather with others who share the same sense of place. Scheduling time for community requires reciprocity, of course. The best time to gather should be determined by each decentralized community, but let us use Friday evenings as an example.

Community gatherings could be done through different venues. Neighborhood gatherings would be the most appropriate choice, in whatever manner the neighborhood might be delineated in an urban or rural setting. The community gathering could be geared around a community activity, such as beautifying the neighborhood. Community gatherings could piggy-back off of other community events, such as the Friday night high school football game. In either case the primary goal is fellowship.

Religious organizations could host Friday evening ecumenical gatherings, where the emphasis is on experiencing harmony rather than the fundamental beliefs of any particular faith. People of different faiths within the same geographic area could join together over common moral ground, nurturing humility, faith and courage. Retreats could nurture the empirical soul, seeking a transcendent experience rather than memorizing and espousing fixed dogma.

Colleges could host Friday evening forums for sharing both ideas and fellowship. There is a movement within academic institutions towards greater interdisciplinary and holistic approaches to knowledge. What can be more interdisciplinary than the integration of culture, politics and economics in relation to the middle class? Curricula could be devised along this theme as part of the course offerings from the university. The duality of empiricism versus scholasticism is an example of a unifying theme that could link the interdisciplinary content together.

Just as we might begin our sessions for solitary awareness with a mantra, our community gatherings might benefit if we start by reminding each other of our basic purpose for coming together. We might open with a pledge along the lines of:

> We will have the humility to love and belong to
> others rather than ideals; we will have faith that
> there is more to life than materialism; we will
> have the courage to resist authoritarianism.

Through their structures we can broaden the appeal of our Friday evening gatherings. Just as the kitchen often becomes the place where people congregate, a potluck dinner is a good place to start for bringing neighbors together. An entertainment component could follow, tailored to the venue of the gathering. Coffeehouses, games night, travelogues, and even strategic electronic entertainment are but a few of the possibilities. The wisdom of the community should be engaged to determine what entertainment activities will best bring people together in fellowship, and we need the humility to respect that wisdom if growing consensus runs counter to our wishes.

The gatherings should include an opportunity for economic exchange. A potluck is an exchange of food, and there are additional ways our lives can be enhanced if we open up the avenues of neighborly exchange, rather than rely solely on corporate-based markets. Carpooling is a form of community exchange, as are many cooperatives. Our first essay began with a reference to "keeping up with the Joneses." The point of a community exchange system, fostered by the Friday evening gatherings, is to escape this trap. Why compete for each of us to have it all, when exchanging and sharing in the community context serves the dual purpose of harmony and affluence? The possibilities of enhancing our happiness through community exchange are wide open.

We should strive to revive natural communal support functions. The provisions for our health and old age should not be a function of corporations. Such provisions subvert the free market to begin with, substituting speculative future compensation for real wages, trapping laborers in contradiction to how the supply and demand for corporate jobs might otherwise work. They also remove the "love" from "loving care." Our community gatherings should provide forums to discuss economic solutions for returning the "love" to loving health care once again.

We also should set aside a small portion of time at each of these community gatherings to share news. Sharing news does not mean focusing on differences in opinions. The focus on news, particularly early on, should be on the quality of the information being doled out to the middle class, not on the differing conclusions we might make.

Corporate media focuses on cyclical indicators like unemployment, faulty indicators like the Consumer Price Index, or indicators that rise independently of what is happening to the middle class, like the stock market. In May of 2008 the *Wall Street Journal* featured an opinion piece that people should not be so pessimistic about housing and unemployment because those indicators have proven to be cyclical over the past half century. It's too easy now to point out just how wrong that *WSJ* article was based on what happen in the fall of 2008. In reality, that article was wrong based on the noncyclical, long term trends that have occurred since the 1970s. But, then again, it's not unusual for the *WSJ* to be wrong about middle class issues.

We need to be informed about economic indicators that reveal long term trends, are transparent, and are most pertinent to the middle class. Examples would be the ratio of home sales prices, health care costs, education costs, debt burden and savings to median household income. How often do you see any of these indicators become the focus of the *Wall Street Journal*? Our community gatherings do not have to get bogged down about what to do about these negative long-term trends, at least not at the beginning; we just need a source of news outside of corporate media to make us aware.

In the political realm the quest for open and honest information could lead to discussing what types of indicators truly meet certain political objectives. For example, quantifying the number of deaths to American citizens could serve as an indicator for our effectiveness in combating terror. A debate might ensue about the validity and reliability of considering soldiers as citizens whose loss of life should be given equal weight in the equation. Once again, the gatherings do not have to get bogged down debating how to best proceed given the information. That might be accomplished during times of solitary heightened awareness.

Perhaps you see where I'm going with this. If we commit ourselves to these community gatherings and all the wonderful things that can come out of them our communities become family and our service becomes devotion. The community gatherings do not become our social capital but our lifeblood. There is a flip side to this equation. As we devote ourselves more to community we must be willing to wean ourselves from special interest groups. As a general rule, we should forsake the largest, most powerful groups that idolize dogma at the neglect of providing support or service, such as the American Legion.

Over time, we need to replace the external incentives for drawing us away from community to more attractive community alternatives. For example, health care costs could be insured by communities instead of corporations in proportion to length of time residing in the community. There are many political and economic hurdles to solutions such as these. Changes in regards to our political involvement and economic productivity will need to occur to facilitate abolishing the external incentives that draw us away from community.

Political Involvement

We empower leaders because trusting them saves us time and energy, a natural adaptation for all organisms. Good leadership serves all cultures well, yet cultures differ in how they treat their good leaders. As recounted previously many early cultures, cultures that lasted far longer than the Roman Empire, kept their good leaders humble. The best hunters were insulted for the game they brought back. Tribal leaders that controlled the tribe's resources were sometimes the poorest members; they earned their authority through generosity and respect. Merit-based leadership needed to be proven daily to those who were to be led. The following observation of cultural anthropologist Claude Levi-Straus, as recorded by Marshall Sahlins in *Stone Age Economics* (1972), reveals how leaders were utilized by a tribal culture:

"The chiefs were my best informers, and as I knew the difficulties of their position I liked to reward them liberally. Rarely, however, did any of my presents remain in their hands for more than a day or two. And when I moved on, after sharing for weeks the life of any particular band, its members rejoiced in the acquisition of axes, knives, pearls, and so forth from my stores. The chief, by contrast, was generally as poor, in material terms, as he had been when I arrived." (pgs. 133-134)

In contrast to this "primitive" method of dealing with leaders, our western civilization chooses to either idolize or demonize leaders, flip sides of the same coin. Our selection criterion for merit in this country is to make politics a lucrative venture and assume that this necessarily attracts "the best and the brightest." We have lost sight that willingness to selflessly serve is, surprisingly enough, the most important ingredient for service.

This is not to suggest that we should have low standards for our presidents. There were a few of our past Presidents that I held out the hope of having fulfilled high standards, only to come away disappointed upon closer inspection. Teddy Roosevelt was one such prospect, and he still makes my top five. Roosevelt stood up for the middle class. Born of wealth and entitlement, he yet had compassion for those who earned wages through labor. Yet the man was a bigot, and could be considered the founding father of present day neoconservatism.

There remains one past President that fulfilled the highest standards of what we should want in a candidate. The man was an exception in many ways. Though he belonged to a party in the end, he was the only President elected independently of party politics. He was the only President who did not have the ambition to be President, but rather was drafted into serving as he had done repeatedly in the past. He refused the compensation due to him for being President. His most important contribution, indeed the most important contribution to our political system that any of our Presidents have made, was simply to step down. He said "No more!" to power and being made an idol, when the whole nation would have empowered and idolized him indefinitely. I am speaking about George Washington, of course, the only man who became President before political parties could consolidate wealth, power and dogma to influence elections.

I get nostalgic just thinking about the prospect of another George Washington. Imagine once again a President who never really wanted to be President, but merely consented to serve as called upon by his fellow citizens. Imagine such a President getting elected without needing connections to wealth or power, only to the citizenry that drafted him/her. Imagine corporate media being rendered completely ineffective in the election process. Imagine a Presidential election with no negative campaigning from one of the candidates, aside from negatively pointing out flaws in the political system.

Idolizing leaders divorces them from our middle class experience as we practically beg them to treat us like the gullible Hans. Our political system has become a breeding ground for authoritarianism. We are past the point of being able to save our energy by trusting leaders to restore balance to the system. We can restore balance at this point only through our own political involvement.

A common lament in newspaper editorials throughout the country runs along the lines of: "Americans should be united in their disgust of squalid housing conditions for wounded soldiers." The sentiment is spot on, except that it begs the question of why should we not be disgusted about squalid housing conditions for all citizens. Part of the reason lies in the assumption that anyone with squalid housing conditions must not be doing their part in contributing to our economic productivity, a false assumption for most citizens living in these conditions.

Another reason for focusing on the ill treatment of wounded soldiers is the assumption that only they have provided heroic service to their country. This is precisely the attitude authoritarians want us to have. Soldiers serve, the rest of us are merely to vote for the incumbent authoritarians who dictate the terms of service for soldiers. The less real service us ordinary citizens provide, particularly in terms of real political involvement, the greater the opportunity for authoritarians to use this as a weapon for shaming us into supporting their policies.

My academic and personal experiences taught me two important lessons for citizenship. First, the willingness to die should not be such a big deal; it is hot-wired into our nature as it is for many altruistic k-species. Only authoritarians and their support network of special interest groups persuade us otherwise, that the natural sacrifice of dieing for others in our communal unit is the "ultimate sacrifice" if done by the American citizen known as a soldier, at the behest of authoritarian leaders. We should not be a society where only soldiers have courage.

Second, serving the people and place that we love enhances well-being. We need not be a society where only soldiers fulfill duties beyond voting and economic productivity. We the middle class can and should all become soldiers in our own way. Through our political involvement do we not only increase our chance of selecting responsible leadership, we increase our ability to stand up to them when they fail their responsibilities.

A true democracy requires the political involvement of citizens that transcends pulling the party lever or giving complete allegiance to any special interest group (these are both precisely the same phenomena). "Love it or leave it" should mean that if you do not "love" democracy enough to exercise your liberty to think independently of a political party, you should "leave" for the totalitarian regime that suits you best. Our government provides support to a wide selection of military regimes for party loyalists to choose from.

The extent of political involvement needed from us begs the question of whether the middle class will ever choose this course of action, rather than merely hope for the right leaders to come along. There is a strong, paternalistic tendency even for those who would be advocates for the middle class. I had a conversation with a well-known author who writes about how much the middle class has been wronged, yet expressed to me a lack of faith that certain geographic segments of the middle class could remedy their plight on their own. Advocates such as this witness groupthink among the masses and deem this a cause, rather than an effect, of how our political system is structured to reinforce authoritarianism.

If you are willing to get politically involved enough to discover that the best person for an elected office does not always come from the same party, as mere logic and probability would suggest, we still have a dilemma. The real choice between candidates from the major parties is limited. Candidates from both sides are supported by a party structure that merges wealth, power and dogma in a way that seeks to maximize the influence of each. Parties are not structured to collect wisdom from a diverse democratic citizenry; they are structured to wield authority and impose a conventional "wisdom" on their dedicated followers. We must come up with an alternative to party politics if we are to maximize our involvement and collective wisdom.

Community Politics

Many people consider democracy to be our greatest political initiative, but democracy was present in the earliest of cultures. Only culture deprives us of our natural democratic impulse. On the other hand, federation could only be introduced once civilizations became advanced enough to blend different cultures from different regions. Rather than democracy, our country's most wonderful political innovation has been constitutional federalism. We should use this greatest political achievement of the founding fathers to reform their greatest political blunder, political parties.

Our practice of federalism requires the politics of the nation to be influenced in part by the collective wisdom of the states. To accomplish this, the basic ingredients for collecting wisdom must be in place. States must be diverse, independent and decentralized, with the autonomy to come up with their own political solutions. Yet there also must be means of aggregating these diverse political solutions and applying the best ones to all the states of the nation when the need arises. The ratification and amendment processes of the Constitution provide this means

In addition to a federation of states, we have federations of counties and towns, though they are not formally called as such. At each descending level of federation our ability to collect the wisdom of the democratic experience increases, with the participatory town meeting representing the apex. Federation at its heart is community politics instead of the interest group politics of political parties. Why not use this wonderful tool to infuse wisdom in how we elect public servants? Why not use federation to change our political system away from authoritarianism?

Elections in Congressional districts occur every two years. While the weekly activities of community gatherings would serve their own ends for cultural belonging, we could add a federated element that empowers us politically to influence the biannual elections. During the off year from the Congressional elections a handful of community gatherings could be devoted to developing a community platform. Our strategy should be to divide and conquer. We aim to divide the alliances of business corporations, politicians and special interest groups that govern political parties. Doing so will enable us to conquer their attempts at imposing a conventional "wisdom" that preempts the collective wisdom produced by a true democracy.

The focus of our community platforms should be on reforming the system, rather than resolving divisive opinions on traditional issues. We must prevent ourselves from dividing "us" rather than "them." Towards the end of the off year each community would designate a member that would represent them in a federation of other communities. This will require some coordination. By the time you read this essay a web site titled "The Middle Class Forum" has been set up that could assist by reporting on the formation of community federations.

Early on in an election year the community representatives of a federation would meet to produce one united platform. The federated platform may differ in significant ways from many of the community originals, but each community would need to have the humility, faith and courage to trust in the wisdom of the federated process. What should help us all to compromise is the common focus of changing a system currently geared towards authoritarianism, rather than attempting to blend divergent views on taxes, defense, education, etc. The community federation also chooses one representative willing to serve in Congress, just in case.

The platforms between community federations may vary greatly in the detail, but the key components to "divide and conquer" wealth and power would form the common backbone. One of the most important changes to the system we need to make would be a limit to the terms for public servants serving the public. We can point to business corporations, politicians and special interest groups all we want for laying blame, but the term limit issue illustrates why, in the end, the real blame lies with us in the middle class. A moving target is harder to hit; an old adage we instinctively understand. Term limits would make our public servants harder to "hit up" by wealth, power and dogmatic elites. The electorate supports term limits; yet the electorate reelects incumbents about 90% of the time. Term limit advocates will nevertheless vote for the same politician in four or more consecutive elections. We thus have only our own hypocrisy to blame when our political system is infected by self-interest and corruption.

Through a bit of planning and nationwide solidarity we can enhance the power of community federations further. If we purposefully target incumbents that meet certain criteria, and proceed to defeat them regardless of gerrymandering or other political maneuvers, then we provide a disincentive for politicians to extort the political system. We might want to target those that receive the most campaign contributions from the oil industry, or the longest tenure as chairman of a committee. The number of people in Congress elected through the work of community federations could be quite small yet quite effective if there was a level of certainty to a politician committed to self-interest being dethroned.

No servant of the public, by definition, should expect a perk not enjoyed by all citizens. Conversely, if a perk is deemed absolutely necessary for a public servant, such as perhaps health care, then we must conclude that perk must be necessary for all other citizens as well. Private health care and pensions provide coercive bargaining leverages for corporations over proprietorships, and help cement the marriage between wealth and power further. Our platforms will need to address these combined labor entrapments and political perks for the sake of both economic merit and political wisdom.

Other financial perks, the ones that cannot and should not be enjoyed by every citizen, should be kept close to nothing. Representatives from community federations will need to pledge they will refuse any wining and dining by lobbyists beyond a hamburger and fries at Wendy's. Public servants could be well-compensated for their short tenure in office, but such compensation should be indexed to a fixed ratio in relation to the median household income, and the compensation should not be so generous as to tempt a politician to embark on a career. Limits should be imposed on committee chairs as well; the more frequently a chair is rotated the harder it becomes for any one chair to game the system for personal gain.

Halfway through the election year community federations present their joint platform to the candidates for their respective Congressional districts. Three outcomes are possible. All the candidates could adopt the platform, in which case the federation recommends voting for either candidate according to our diverse preferences. If only one candidate is willing to adopt the platform, then the federation backs that candidate regardless of party affiliation or position on the issues. This will require courage on the part of some folks to deny the party or issues they favor in the short term to strive for a permanent remedy to authoritarian government.

The third possibility is that neither candidate adopts the platform, in which case the representative chosen by the community federation proceeds to run for office. For the most part, middle class communities would want to avoid this option. Few decent middle class candidates would want to subject themselves to political campaigning. The very platforms federation candidates would be promoting would seek to deny the perks to politicians that make negative campaigning profitable and turns their "public service" into a lucrative career move. Because of this, the communities that make up a federation would need to do the actual political campaigning on behalf of their chosen representative. If humble middle class citizens show the willingness to serve without the perks commonly enjoyed by politicians, doing the bulk of campaigning on their behalf is the least that community federations should do.

The people involved in the community gatherings would need to talk to everyone they know, employing a pyramid scheme if need be, and communicate the platform their candidate would be running on. If asked what specific issues a community federation candidate supports the response should be a shrug of the shoulders and an explanation of why that is not the point. The candidate is running to change a system, so that in the future the most important issues may be tackled in the wisest way possible.

With the support of the community federation and community gatherings, one objective of a federation candidate will be to win an election while spending next to nothing on campaigning. If this can occur just once, if a community federation should win an election through "manpower" rather than "money power," then we have destroyed the tortured rationale of Justice Breyer that overturned campaign finance limits because they allegedly impose a hardship on challengers. We also demonstrate the independence of free speech from money, emphasizing instead how most political candidates need money to embellish false speech. This can become our foundation for empirical politics.

Empirical Politics

Since homeostasis is the key ingredient to keeping our systems in balance, our community platforms must address the fourth estate and the information network. Those who have become the wealthiest and most influential at their job of providing information must be scrutinized closely and held to the highest standards. The details will differ between platforms, but we must call for something like automatic audits of the top three public relation firms, think tanks, lobbyists, columnists, endowed academic chairs and, of course, corporate media firms. We need the ability to distinguish and penalize the "black box" and "black is white" treatment of information. The top information handlers must be reviewed, audited and penalized for the most minor of transgressions. In the process we provide a disincentive for becoming the wealthiest and most powerful at dispensing information, leaving as an alternative incentive the actual desire to provide information with integrity.

Our community platforms should have provisions for making the political process less complex and more transparent to those who want to be politically involved. The length and complexity of bills should be minimized to enable the average citizen from the middle class to obtain the information in them. In a similar vein, bills should not be a hodge-podge of legislation that would confuse constituents as to the voting priorities of their elected officials. In particular, no bill should have appropriations attached that benefit only a particular district. If something in Kansas needs to have federal funding, then a Congressman from Washington should be willing to sign on without also having to approve something of national importance. Needless to say, simplification and transparency needs to be applied particularly to the tax code.

Our authoritarian politicians and idolatrous special interest groups are reinforcing the idea that citizens have only the obligations to pay taxes and vote. They offer us cultural entitlements such as security with the intent that we will relinquish our natural right to independent thought. We need not empirically investigate the issues beyond listening to the entertaining news talk show hosts and the echo chambers of corporate media. We need only apply to matters of citizenship what all organisms seek to do in Nature, conserve our energy budgets.

I started with a plan for personal growth, with the understanding that even if we went no farther with that plan we have accomplished something for ourselves. Taking the next steps for meeting our family obligations and serving our communities also provide immediate personal benefits. Yet there is no immediate personal benefit to political involvement. If we endeavor to grow in our humility, faith and courage; if we fulfill our duty to our families and serve our communities; that is a good sign that we have prepared ourselves to take the next step. But many of us would still need further motivation that compels us to overcome the natural adaptation for saving energy.

That motivation could be the same one that compelled me to write these essays. We have now lost more American citizens in Iraq than the total amount of citizens lost to terrorism since 1993, whether soldiers or otherwise, in all other places outside of Iraq. The additional costs of innocent Iraqi lives has been staggering, beyond our comprehension if the same proportional loss of innocent lives occurred in our country. Their infrastructure has been destroyed and we are rebuilding it through no-bid contracts to American business corporations structured for greed, and with projects such as a U. S. embassy that will be the most expensive one ever built. All the while none of our "democratic" leaders, not even the recent crop of presidential candidates, shared insider information that oil was a major cause for why we are there.

You may be for or against our invasion of Iraq; but that is not really the point. The point is the citizens of a democracy were never provided pertinent information as to why we invaded a third world country. Leaders either thought we were too dumb to handle the truth, or we would refuse to go along with it. Neither reason for avoiding the wisdom of our collective experiences should be acceptable to the middle class. Had the truth about oil been shared from the beginning, and we still condoned the invasion, then you can bet we would have done things differently. We would have met our real objectives efficiently instead of attempting to maintain a duplicitous strategy. On the other hand, our democracy might not have condoned the invasion and we would have concentrated our resources on other means of fighting terrorism, and on developing energy sources other than oil. The employers and employees of Halliburton would have suffered from an appeal to real democracy and economic merit, but we must have the courage to allow large business corporations connected to oil and the military industrial complex to fail when they do not have the merit to succeed without government nurturing.

We could blame some loose cannons at the top for this breakdown in homeostasis, for preventing pertinent information from reaching the citizens of an alleged democracy. Or we could blame the incurious nature of Democrats in Congress. Or we could blame the allegiance of Republicans in Congress. Or we could blame the corporate media that reduces the staff of investigative reporters and promotes belligerent but entertaining news talk hosts wrapping themselves up in the flag. ... Or we could blame ourselves.

Yes, there were millions of informed demonstrators against the invasion of Iraq beforehand. But in the end there was 80% support for an invasion in an oil-rich nation, championed by oil-rich leaders, without the reason of oil ever needing to be provided to an incurious citizenry. Every single one of us in the middle class had sufficient wisdom from past experiences to know there was something wrong about that. A fast one was being pulled on us and 80% were content to save our energy budget. Once again, the point is not that we should have been overwhelmingly against the invasion from the start; that is up to you to decide based on your own opinion, independently from what politicians, corporate media and think tanks are telling you. The point is we should have been overwhelmingly against the invasion unless we were provided pertinent information that we knew from experience had to be part of the reason for our actions.

The past one hundred years of western intervention in the Middle East has been nothing but disastrous from a moral viewpoint, though we do have cheaper gas and greater military strength as a result. We absolutely cannot take the word of politicians, think tanks and corporate media that a future one hundred years of western intervention in the Middle East will produce different types of results from the past one hundred years. There is no previous experience supporting the dogmatic belief that having us call the shots for Middle East countries is for their own good. We need to become politically involved by being seekers of good information.

When something reeks, like not being told oil is at least a partial cause for invasion when all our past experience suggests this is so, then we need to discover and eliminate the rotting corpse. If you want to save your energy budget while a soldier dies in Iraq, or an innocent Iraqi girl gets raped, or an innocent Iraqi businessman gets murdered, or we build a foreign embassy for close to a trillion dollars, or we protect the oil ministry while weapon dumps get looted, you are distinctly part of the ultimate problem that faces us. If getting information apart from political parties, corporate media or your favorite special interest groups and think tanks is too much of a bother, please consider voting to be too much of a bother as well. Or leave for the totalitarian regime of your choice.

Otherwise, the time has come for all of us to pursue a dream. The time has come for political campaigns without negativity. The time has come for marginalizing corporate media echo chambers and belligerent news talk hosts. The time has come for elected officials that were drafted by their constituents to serve. The time has come to divorce wealth and dogma from power. The time has come to overturn the dangerous and false belief in money as free speech. The time has come to chart our political system on a path towards wisdom.

Economic Productivity

I now have arrived full circle to the starting point for *Systems out of Balance*. We, the middle class, view ourselves as the bulwark of a meritocracy. The financial compensation and perks we receive are in exchange for our economic productivity, upon which the existence of any nation depends. There are people who merit greater compensation than us; there are people who merit less. We begrudge not those richer than us, as long as their wealth is due to the labor and specialty of their production and not due to capital inflated by serving capital.

Specialization is the driving force behind markets and trade. Our economic productivity begins with specialization of the goods and services the middle class can provide each other. This specialization and economic productivity is threatened by the escalation of corporate mergers through deregulation. Within either ecosystems or economic systems consolidated resources means reduced diversity, reduced adaptability and reduced stability. When merging corporations become multinational corporations the threat to middle class productivity and economic systems becomes all the greater.

The economic productivity of the middle class is undermined when goods are being sold to us here at one market equilibrium, while labor is being compensated at different market equilibriums in other countries. The excess capital generated from separating the goods and labor markets is not going to the producing countries, which would be consistent with both fairness and a free market system. We should either be paying the same price for their goods as would the laborers who produced them, or they should be receiving the extra capital being generated. Instead, shareholders in the consumption countries get capital for which they provided no productivity while laborers both home and abroad get shafted. That is a system of exploitation.

Our economic compensation is being undermined when large amounts of capital are redistributed away from labor. Redistributing what is exchanged in the goods and labor markets for capital improvements is a concession laborers are willing to make in order to enhance future production. The redistribution becomes excessive when corporations are encouraged to maximize the gain in capital markets for the sake of shareholders. The excessive redistribution goes two steps further when government employs supply side economics to concentrate capital for corporations and levies taxes that shift the fiscal burden away from capital gains to wages. The Powell Cabal warns us against such massive welfare entitlements discouraging the incentive to produce, though they do not wish to apply this principle to discourage welfare entitlements to the wealthy.

Our economic labor becomes exploited when business corporations, in essence licensed wards of the State, bargain from a position of incredible strength as self-interested "individuals" in negotiating contracts. Not only do they use that strength to keep current wages down in exchange for labor, but they substitute the speculative compensation of health care plans and pensions to perpetuate an entrapment of labor. A free market would determine the equilibrium for exchanging current wages with current labor straight up; but free markets were never the desire of business corporations, *laissez faire* economists or puppet libertarians. They instead would have us lose sight that the same corporate management objective that maximizes capital gains for our speculative retirement plans also minimizes current wage compensation.

Ratios often make the best indicators, precisely because they are relating two different variables. One particular ratio could provide a second tier solution for changing our economic system towards a free market and merit. Few people think that one person's labor is worth one thousand times another. A few CEOs and hedge fund managers may have different opinions on this, but these people do not want free markets. Most people understand that the labor contract is flawed because the corporation has far greater bargaining strength than the laborer. Minimum wages result from our compassion over this injustice, but we need to recognize that wage and price controls interfere with reaching free market equilibriums for supply and demand. Nor have they been effective in neutralizing the corporate coercion of labor contracts.

The same charge cannot be levied against a maximum compensation ratio. The equilibrium price determined in a free market exchange cares not how the consumer's dollar gets distributed among the producer's payroll. If anything, the consumer might be favorably inclined towards a business that offers a good maximum compensation ratio, such as Ben and Jerry's. The impact of a maximum compensation ratio on the free market is less than government enforcing a minimum wage. The impact on free market exchange is also far less than granting corporations both a State-sanctioned license to divert profits to shareholders and a coercive advantage as an "individual" in the bargaining of contracts. Yet the maximum compensation ratio would have a revolutionary impact on markets in a few beneficial ways.

A maximum compensation ratio would temper the mission of greed forced upon our economic system. Shareholders would still expect CEOs to maximize capital gains, but their own compensation would now be tied in strictly to the performance of the company. A CEO could not increase their compensation by jumping from two hundred to four hundred times that of their blue collar workers. They could only increase their own compensation by increasing company performance well enough to increase the compensation of laborers on the lowest rungs. Shareholders would have to fall in line with a skilled entrepreneur's desire to raise the compensation of workers across the payroll, or lose the skilled entrepreneur to another corporation. Granted, some current CEOs, not to mention some libertarian think tanks, will whine aplenty over the prospect of companies actually having to earn large increases in executive pay. The true entrepreneurs, like Henry Ford, will rise to the challenge.

The combined effects of a maximum compensation ratio, plus shareholders that must support overall raises in payrolls in order to compete for skilled entrepreneurs, are far reaching. Wealth disparity will go down, as will the supply of capital gains flooding markets. Moderating the supply of capital will moderate the costs of essential but expensive items. Moderating these prices will help to limit debt and the amount of hours a family unit has to work. Reducing the amount of hours a family unit has to work in order to just get by allows laborers to be less desperate when negotiating with corporate "individuals" for contracts. In other words, substituting a maximum compensation ratio for a minimum wage would help reverse all the noncyclical economic trends that have hurt the middle class since the Powell Cabal came into existence in the seventies. For that reason you could expect staunch resistance from that very same misinformation network.

The biggest impact of a maximum compensation ratio might be felt overseas. Can you imagine restricting an American CEO's salary to just twenty-five times that made by one of their laborers employed in a developing country? One or both of two trends would develop. There would be greater demand for American laborers, or at least American wages, to bolster the compensation of executives. In addition, capital would be aligned more with the countries of production, rather than countries of consumption. These trends resulting from the prices for goods and labor being determined by the same market equilibriums should be welcomed by the middle class as not only a triumph in fairness, but also for free markets. This would reduce the need for "Christmas bonuses" of foreign aid in lieu for comparative advantages that keep the feeding trough flowing for multinational corporations. Local corporations formed in developing countries would be able to better compete. Developing countries would no doubt be all too glad about this liberating development. "Free trade" might actually resemble the meaning of the term if overseas labor could not be exploited by multinational corporations with obscene bargaining strength bolstered by governments and global trade organizations.

One test for the foolishness of government intrusion into markets, at least as hypothesized by "free market" think tanks, is the proliferation of a black market. Unbearable regulations for an economic system will induce businesses to form and operate outside that system. Can you imagine a black market of businesses forming just so they can pay their top executives umpteen times more than the bottom line employees? No? I thought not. Then why have neither "free market" think tanks nor corporate media ever trumpeted the maximum compensation ratio, trumpeted first by none other than that capitalist's capitalist, J. P. Morgan? The answer is that a maximum compensation ratio is really too good of a free market solution for the corporate masters that these shills really serve.

One possible argument that puppet libertarians and the Powell Cabal might make against a compensation ratio would be similar to their rants on socialism. Reducing the potential for disparity in compensation reduces the motivation to produce, since greed is what motivates us all. Supposedly, CEOs would be just as content to be a janitor unless they could be compensated one thousand times as much.

The Powell Cabal also applies such reasoning to discredit universal health care. We evolved to treat health as a communal concern; something that we would treat economically as part of the commons. But the "commons" sounds much like "communism" to puppet libertarians. They maintain that humans should not feel entitled to anything arranged by government (except capital gains and property, of course) or we would degrade into slothful communists by equal measure. Our economic productivity would come to a grinding halt if we treated anything but the air we breathe as part of the commons that did not require enough hard work to generate large capital gains for shareholders.

This attack would be false, of course, as most people in the middle class readily understand. There are many reasons why people work, and work hard, with greed and/or desperation being merely the only official motivations endorsed by business corporations and the Powell Cabal. Some people work because they enjoy what they do; some people work to prevent boredom; some people work for a sense of purpose; some people work to contribute something to society; some people work as part of their self-esteem; some people work to help others. To think that economic productivity would be severely constrained because people became entitled to good health is beyond absurd. Heck, even some people who receive large inheritances and capital gains from investments still choose to work!

Empirical Economics

Changing our economic system will be difficult. The linkages between power and wealth need to be weakened first for us to have much success. We will be fighting corporate media and the rest of the misinformation network the entire way. I do not pretend that I, just one empirical middle class citizen, have the wisdom needed to suggest specific solutions for returning our economic system towards merit. Yet empiricism and a systems approach provide us a general outline.

Above all we need the information that will help us keep our economic system in balance. Proper economic indicators become the first tier solution for our return to merit. We will not take the same approach to indicators used by The Heritage Foundation. We will not lump a bunch together to obscure the effects of each. We will not throw out ones proven to have the most effect, like The Heritage Foundation did with their informal market indicators. Nor will we devise additional analyses to justify weak indicators we fancy; once again, a practice of the good scholars over at The Heritage Foundation (Essay 5).

When looking to keep a system in balance the most important indicators to watch out for are those revealing long term harmful trends. Instead, corporate media feeds us indicators about unemployment and the stock market. Unemployment indicators hit a nerve, but have been cyclical during my lifetime. There also are a myriad of conditions, both good and bad, for causing employment to cycle back and forth. The causes and effects surrounding unemployment can be interpreted many ways. With corporate media providing the filter, they are used to influence economic policy that benefits business corporations, not the middle class. Meanwhile, the long term success of the stock market may be, in reality, a reflection on the harm done to a meritocracy.

Simpler is better. The "basket of goods" used for determining the Consumer Price Index, which in turn determines the poverty level indicator, is a muddled mess, perhaps intentionally so. Only economic scholars can come up with such a mess, and the result does not track with the most essential and expensive items for the middle class. The simple indicators we need must be grounded in the most important elements of the middle class experience. Increases in housing sales prices have greater meaning to developers; increases in ownership housing costs relative to median family income have greater meaning to the middle class. Would you, a middle class citizen, rather be kept informed as to how complex indicators determined by economic scholarship change over time, or simply how your empirical health care costs have gone up in relation to your wages?

There are other ratios worth exploring to help change our economic system towards merit. Assuming we want to provide incentives for individuals to actually produce something for a market economy, a ratio limiting capital gains in proportion to wages would be helpful. A variation of this might be to limit the welfare from capital gains protected by government to be no more than the welfare provided to the poor provided by government. What the poor should be provided is a matter of great debate, some of it even sincere. We could have confidence in economists coming up with the right balance of government assistance if the wealthy could receive no greater amount in welfare than the poor. There are far fewer people of wealth than in poverty, of course, but we might as well allow them the greater concentration from distributing the same amount of welfare dollars as to the poor, a consolation for reducing their entitlements. Ironically, if we were to index the amount of welfare the wealthy can get without productive labor to what the poor can receive, we may have puppet libertarians and the Powell Cabal lobbying for a veritable welfare state.

Appropriate ratios and indicators could fuel an empirical economics if not derailed by the propaganda of puppet libertarians and the Powell Cabal. Most pervasive and harmful is the propaganda that business corporations operate best in free markets. In reality business corporations could not operate at all in a free market, as they require a large amount of government intervention to exist and succeed. Believing this propaganda causes us to equate free markets with greed rather than merit, and to prevent government from tempering the greed of business corporations. In every existing nation state government unavoidably intervenes in the economy in some way. Understanding this simple empirical truth empowers us to best shape our economic system and government's unavoidable role.

Political Economics

In most economic systems, including our own, there are some resources that could be considered as part of the commons. The commons are important resources that belong to all in the same community or nation. In the earliest cultures most resources were part of the commons: health care, water, air, food, energy, land and even tools. The early commodities being traded were nonessential items. Almost all of the commons has disappeared from our economic system, converting virtually everything but air and some public lands into "nonessential" commodities. There is an obvious reason for this: the commons is not profitable for business corporations. An economic system that allows for profit on everything generates more wealth.

More wealth is what it is all about, right? Wealth grants us the "liberty" of greater choice, doth claim the puppet libertarian. But the real choice boils down to this. Resources converted from the commons to commodities enables more people to have their own home entertainment centers and swimming pools, but more people are deprived of having essential resources. More resources in the commons will lead to more home entertainment centers and swimming pools being shared in the context of community. If the importance of "liberty" is being indulged by our government-protected economic system, then we want as many resources converted to commodities as possible. If the importance of "liberty" is the independence of our natural rights, then the resources most essential for our well-being must remain in the commons for all.

Treasuring liberty for the sake of independence and overall well-being, rather than indulgences and individual wealth, requires the removal of some pretty important "commodities" from the entitled realm of business corporations. Can you imagine the howl from the Powell Cabal if they got a whiff of such heresy? Corporate lobbyists would influence legislators to resist any such changes to their corporate sugar daddies. Corporate backed think tanks will provide contrary "analysis" to "prove" that negative trends for the middle class and positive trends for business corporations have nothing to do with each other. Corporate backed public relation firms will work overtime to promote the "altruistic" mission of corporations. Academic positions endowed by corporations will be charged to subjectively "educate" other academics about the objective merits of greed. And corporate media will work tirelessly to filter the information from this misinformation network and "educate" Hans and the rest of the middle class. In other words, the misinformation network will continue to do what they have been doing, but redouble their efforts.

One of the claims by the Powell Cabal would be that you cannot trust government to be in charge of anything, the important resources of the commons least of all. Fine. Government's role in commanding or managing the economy can be limited. We mainly want to reverse long-term negative trends that have harmed the middle class, with the greed of capital markets imposing extra costs on the necessities of life. Business corporations function to expand markets, but this is hardly necessary for the goods and services that might fit the criteria of the commons. If you want to make money by exchanging something necessary for your neighbor's survival, then your compensation should be limited to what your entrepreneurial skills and your labor can earn. An additional amount for capital improvements is understandable, but not the extra welfare entitlements of capital gains. There are other means to stimulate markets than by investments that return capital at a greater rate than inflation. If puppet libertarians want to hold fast to the principle of no entitlements then, by golly, let us hold fast.

We have been all through the empirical evidence and the logic by now; though of course there will be some economic scholars never to be persuaded by empiricism. The business corporation is not essential for either progress or productivity. The business corporation, as a producer, is crucial only for expanding markets by whatever means, indulging folks as much as possible, and providing some welfare to entitled shareholders in the process. Being able to expand markets is not a concern when producing essential goods and services, and the inflated costs from injecting a little welfare greed into the commons should be forsaken when the well-being of humans is at stake.

One candidate for the commons would be energy. Energy has become essential to our everyday lives. In a sense, government already has treated this commodity as a commons, at least in regards to oil. In an article titled "Oil subsidies for dummies" (January 5, 2007), the Cleantech Forum provides a laundry list of ways that government has commanded advantages in the energy market to oil corporations. I have cut and pasted them here from media.cleantech.com/node/554.

- Construction bonds at low interest rates or tax-free
- Research-and-development programs at low or no cost
- Assuming the legal risks of exploration and development in a company's stead
- Below-cost loans with lenient repayment conditions
- Income tax breaks, especially featuring obscure provisions in tax laws designed to receive little congressional oversight when they expire
- Sales tax breaks - taxes on petroleum products are lower than average sales tax rates for other goods
- Giving money to international financial institutions (the U.S. has given tens of billions of dollars to the World Bank and U.S. Export-Import Bank to encourage oil production internationally, according to Friends of the Earth)
- The U.S. Strategic Petroleum Reserve
- Construction and protection of the nation's highway system
- Allowing the industry to pollute - what would oil cost if the industry had to pay to protect its shipments, and clean up its spills? If the environmental impact of burning petroleum were considered a cost? Or if it were held responsible for the particulate matter in people's lungs, in liability similar to that being asserted in the tobacco industry?
- Relaxing the amount of royalties to be paid (*explained in the article*)

Confronted with all the ways in which oil corporations have been pampered and coddled, one would think that puppet libertarians would be in an uproar. Taken all together, these incentives and protections by government effectively command capital investments to target one particular energy sector at the expense of others. Though government imposes environmental regulations that limits drilling, this disincentive does not overcome being allowed to store energy "goods" in reserve for maximum market gain; a government-funded transportation system that selectively favors the oil industry; the use of government resources for free or below market costs; and limits the investment risk that otherwise would prove to be a deterrent for the oil industry. If you were an investor whose only interest was maximizing profit how would you react to these commands from government?

Yet the Powell Cabal calls for removal of the one disincentive, environmental regulations, thus strengthening government command for oil further.

There is nothing more disruptive of a free market than commanding the economy. General taxation and regulation may be disincentives to investment, but if applied fairly do not cause markets to favor certain goods over others. A command economy is the definition of socialism, faulted because of the severe constraint imposed on entrepreneurial freedom. This is the basis for the Cato Institute, recognized as one of the most "faithful" libertarian think tanks, to condemn all future government subsidies. Their position is disingenuous in regards to energy. If government were to once command the economy to favor cocaine over other drugs, it matters not that the government later refuses to subsidize all drugs; the addiction has been put in place. Drug dealers work on the same principle.

The Cato Institute and other members of the Powell Cabal actually want the addiction to be nurtured further and the command of oil to continue. This is not hard to understand when you learn that the Cato Institute was started by an oil family with oil money. Yet the general public does not know about the lineages for the Cato Institute and other think tanks. Corporate media introduces talking heads from these advocacy think tanks as experts to educate us about free markets. They do not include disclaimers as to who ultimately funds their paychecks. There are severe consequences to this misinformation network, as nothing has demonstrated quite as well as the oil industry.

The consequences of our government's command for oil includes the CIA coup that halted Iranian democracy in 1953; the subsequent backing of a brutal Iranian shah; the political and weapons support provided to Saddam Hussein in the eighties; the terrorist responses to our growing Middle East influence throughout the nineties; and the invasion of a third world country on false pretenses in the new millennium. To this very day oil does not get mentioned by administrations as a reason for that invasion, just as our command economy for oil never gets mentioned by corporate media or the puppet libertarians from the Powell Cabal.

Our energy policy has impacted all our systems greatly, sometimes severely. For this reason we should recognize energy as part of the commons as soon as possible, independently of any sequential steps proposed in this essay. Rather than commanding the economy for oil through maximizing the potential of capital gains, that greed-based incentive should be removed. Perhaps we can continue trusting government, with the stipulation that they now command the economy away from oil. Perhaps we leave government out of direct influence, except for refusing and revoking business corporation licenses related to energy. Entrepreneurial nonprofit corporations and proprietorships would pursue the opportunities that become available. Perhaps we still allow capital gains to be generated, but capped so that hoarding a finite resource like oil becomes no more profitable than investing in infinite resources like solar and wind.

Perhaps there are totally new business approaches out there that would work even better for the commons. Perhaps all we need to do is encourage economics to be driven by empiricism rather than scholasticism and a wave of experimentation will help us find this best solution. In the meantime, I have one suggestion for a new business model to try.

The Closing Case against Business Corporations

Hopefully, I have convinced you by now that the business corporation model assaults free markets, but let us do a final review. For a business corporation to even exist you need government. The same can be said for proprietorships, but a proprietor could do "under the table" business illegally while otherwise meeting the criteria of a proprietorship model. While there may be plenty of illegal activity associated with capital markets, the only illegal version that can exist independently of government is called loan sharking.

Business corporations have limited liability in comparison with proprietorships. In theory they face greater regulation and taxation for this protection, but over the past thirty years the tax burden has been shifted away from capital gains to the point where all capital gains are taxed less than the highest wage tax bracket. Some capital gains are taxed less than middle class wages, such as has been historically true for oil corporations that sang us such a piteous song of free market woe in the spring and summer of 2008. If you want to play you oughta pay, and business corporations ought to be paying what's due for playing their games with limited liability. But even if they pay their due this is a system totally dependent on government to work.

Business corporations depend on governments providing the infrastructure for long-distance commerce. This is much more involved than is first apparent. A business that extracts and refines oil only within our borders would have no need for governments to interfere in the Middle East; only multinational corporations lay that burden on us. Perhaps you support that involvement by governments, but a free market it's not.

Only government can define business corporations as individuals and then legitimize contracts where one of the bargaining agents has protections as both an individual and licensed ward of the State. A proprietor, at least, really is an individual. But a proprietor in general cannot offer speculative labor entrapments as lucrative as those provided by business corporations, entrapments that provide a little extra binding to those contracts that could not exist without government. This presents the dual problem to free markets of intervention by government and exploitation of independent labors.

There are further exploitations of independent labors. Comparative advantages and segmented markets imposed with the carrot of foreign aid or the stick of debt from foreign aid exploit foreign labor. Stagnating wages exploit labor at home. Finally, business corporations have much greater means to turn "money as free speech" into "money as false speech" and all the repercussions that has economically, politically and culturally. This is an assault on our right to independent thought as well as free markets.

OK. If I have not convinced you that business corporations subvert free markets by now, I never will. But before I suggest an alternative to the business corporation model allow me to next present the case of why business corporations subvert capitalism. I am neither an advocate nor an opponent of capitalism. Free markets, to me, are an inherent good, an end to which we should aspire. Capitalism is instead a tool for facilitating free markets, or not. The essence of capitalism is private production generating profits. The essential systems advantage of capitalism is greater economic flexibility.

Business corporations subvert capitalism when generating profits without production. Capital then becomes like fantasy money that grows on trees, or counterfeiting, or government printing money that surpasses the increased productivity of an economy, with the end result of inflating and/or destabilizing an economic system. All forms of futures trading subvert capitalism in this manner, as does sitting on oil reserves to maximize profit.

Admittedly, this is not an affliction confined to just business corporations. If you own one hundred acres of land you have never used, subdivide forty lots out of that acreage, and then make a profit of one million dollars, you have impacted the economy the same way as a hedge fund or a counterfeiter. Yet you would no doubt feel just as entitled to that profit as would a hedge fund manager. Entitled or not, that is not the essence of production-based capitalism. The entire real estate industry is prone to this generation of capital without productivity, and they are not the only ones.

Just as *laissez faire* economists would fool us into thinking that capitalism equates with free markets, the same folks would have us believe that financial institutions equate with capitalism. Financial institutions can facilitate capitalism, no doubt, just as capitalism can facilitate free markets, but blurring the distinctions has been to the end of ultimately having both financial institutions and capitalism serve greed. After all, one offshoot of financial institutions, the insurance industry, has more in common with casinos than with productive manufacturing.

Business corporations subvert the flexibility of capitalism when they dogmatically entrench what is to be done with capital. Capitalism could open the doors to the type of experimentation that characterized empiricism and the Scientific Revolution. There is some tinkering done with the business corporation model in terms of what regulations and taxation there should be in return for government licensing and protections (and the privilege of being considered an individual). There is virtually no tinkering with the current objective of profits:

satisfy the greed of investors.

Consequently, the business corporation model has changed hardly at all since stock was first issued over four hundred years ago. There are a variety of ways that the "capital" in capitalism can be used, though you would not know that from listening to *laissez faire* economists and various economic schools of thought. Capital improvements, market expansion, bonuses for the labor of production, further investments, taxes, charity and dividends are all possible ends for the profits generated by privately controlled production.

An empirical approach would tinker with formulas for how these capital ends are divvied up, with experimentation bringing us closer to a preferred formula over time, a formula that probably should differ for different cultures at different times. That is, after all, what the essential advantage of capitalism is all about, introducing greater economic flexibility than allowed by simply exchanging goods and services. But business corporations never got the memo on this, nor did many prestigious academic institutions, well-endowed by the corporate sector. Certainly, you will not hear suggestions for this type of tinkering from puppet libertarians and the Powell Cabal.

There is an obvious reason to why business corporations are dogmatic about their approach to capitalism, and why they are terribly confused about free markets. Business corporations are a greed-based model. As such, those who rise to the top in this model are going to be among the greediest folk in any culture. I can point to no concrete studies to support my next claim, but I ask everyone to draw upon their own observations and experiences to refute or support the assertion. Greedy people tend to be dogmatic people. They are set in their ways, the ways that they think will maximize wealth, and they have no interest in alternatives or experimentation that they fear might threaten their wealth. Since the dogmatists in charge of the corporate world will discourage any experimentation with the normative ends of the capital in capitalism, please allow me to suggest my own "experiment."

Community Economics

There are some "commodities" for which the business corporation norm of "greed is good" simply does more harm than good. The most obvious example of this is with health care insurance. Advocates of our privatize health care system point out that we have the most advanced care and less waiting for certain types of health problems. What they neglect to mention, or fail to realize, is the disparity in providing this care. Our growing health care disparity mirrors our growing wealth disparity. If we were to look at the greatest good for the greatest number, a utilitarian ideal that economists usually support, our health care system is pitiful in comparison to nationalized alternatives that provide essential and mainstream care for all.

We pay more for health care per capita and receive less than other developed countries with universal health care. This is the expected market result from partitioning a joint commodity. The partitioning allows for competition, but business corporations compete specifically to expand markets, improving products is just an occasional means towards that primary end. Expanding markets neither practically nor morally applies to health care. When we go in for a health cure, we hope to avoid renewable demand for the same cure. Not even the exorbitant marketing and lobbying budget of business corporations could persuade consumers that we should get sick more often. This helps to explain why nonprofit corporations perform better than business corporations in the realm of hospital care in this country (see Essay 5). In comparison to nonprofit corporations business corporations have the extra costs of providing capital gains to shareholders, without marketing for renewable demands or exploiting consumers.

These observations collectively point to the wisdom of excluding business corporations from joint markets. Shareholders should not receive the welfare of capital gains in addition to the economic inefficiencies of privatizing joint commodities. Whether proprietorships, nonprofit corporations or government might be a better alternative could be discussed and resolved according to the particular industry. When the joint commodity must be commanded and paid for by government, such as with national defense, deciding in favor of government control should be easy. No matter what the alternative decision, both economic efficiency and fairness would increase in joint markets by the exclusion of the business corporation model. But it's easy being a naysayer. News talk show hosts make a living out of this. What would be the alternative?

The niche of nonprofit corporations could be expanded to cover joint commodities such as health care, but please allow me to suggest something new. I propose a community corporation model for both joint and market commodities. This tinkers with capitalism by throwing away the "greed is good" bottom line and substituting "community is good."

Business corporations are licensed by states and maximize profits to benefit investors. A community corporation would be licensed by municipalities and use profits to benefit citizens of the same municipality. A community corporation also would differ in terms of the protections granted, taxes levied and regulations applied.

Some federal and state regulations would apply the same to either business or community corporations. Other regulations would default to those set by the licensing municipality. Towns may wish to set stricter regulations than the state or federal governments, as sometimes occurs with development zoning, and that should be their privilege. They weigh whatever benefits they judge comes from stricter regulations with the costs of not attracting businesses. In some areas the town might be deferred to for more relaxed regulations, if the community setting naturally compensates for potential corporate malfeasance. For example, some types of paperwork and accounting practices might be relaxed when the bottom line is "community" instead of "greed."

Taxes would be levied on the community corporation by the town instead of the state. The loss of taxes for the state would be compensated by a comparable reduction in state aid to the community. This would be a zero-sum game for the municipality if corporate taxes usurped the total profits made by the community corporation. If corporate taxes are a fraction of corporate profits, as occurs with business corporations, the excess can be used to benefit community "investors."

The shareholders of a community corporation would be, in essence, the taxpayers of a community. Instead of paying property taxes to a town, an "investor" could choose to apply that as an investment into the community corporation. The return on the investment would go to the town, including the excess profit. People may refuse to "invest" their property taxes in the community corporation, paying them directly to the town in traditional manner, but they lose any voting privilege as to how a community corporation's excess profits may be applied to benefit the town.

A community corporation would at times need more investment capital than provided by community shareholders, just as is the case with business corporations and their typical shareholders. This is where the crux of the matter comes in. How government "stacks the deck" in terms of rewarding investment capital is how the economy will be commanded. For example, if capital gains are allowed to be maximized for investors, then finite oil reserves invariably holds greater attraction than infinite renewables, despite all other costs and benefits involved. Government will have to "stack the deck" for investment capital to favor community corporations, or for any other experimentation of what to do with the capital in capitalism, in order for these experiments to succeed; just as business corporations always have needed government to "stack the deck" for their own success. Thus in suggesting community corporations or any other alternative we will need to anticipate and be full aware of the hypocrisy puppet libertarians and the Powell Cabal will employ when they level the charge of "socialism" to thwart our empirical testing.

By avoiding being a slave to greed the community corporation has the economic flexibility that capitalism can provide. Capital gains can be used to create a self-insured corporation for health care, eliminating insurance as a nonproductive profiting entity. The health care network could be extended to the community "investors" as well as the laborers, and perhaps even for the community at large. All manner of public parks or works might be funded when the bottom line for capitalism is "community" instead of "greed."

Of course, puppet libertarians and the Powell Cabal will apply the same argument to investors as they would for laborers. Who would want to invest money in a corporation where they cannot maximize a return to their own pocketbooks? They think greed motivates us all, but what do you say? Would you be willing to divert property taxes to a corporation that might provide a greater return to your town than just your taxes could? I suppose you would have to value your community to answer "yes" to that question, but that is precisely my sincere hope.

Final Independent Thoughts

I began the *Systems out of Balance* journey four years ago. "Essay 3 – The Supply of Capital" and "Essay 7 – An Economic Report Card" were written in 2006, more than two years before the economic collapse that they essentially predicted (though Essay 7 was updated with 2008 data). I do not take credit for being an astute economist; I do not take credit for being any kind of economist. I merely take credit for looking at different types of information than covered by the *Wall Street Journal* or *laissez faire* economists, information more important to the real experiences of the middle class.

The final push to start this journey came when the Bush II administration started to make threatening overtures towards Iran. Everyone has their breaking point; enough was enough. After having witnessed the administration manipulate information about Iraq and the economy, supported by a misinformation network and corporate media, I felt compelled to do something. Writing from the perspective of a person who lives in the same middle class house, in the same middle class neighborhood, in the same rural town seemed like a good place for starting the journey.

My objective as an empirical scientist was to organize the economic, political and cultural parts around a holistic systems analysis, with the purpose of challenging the scholarship promoted by the misinformation network. I did not know when I started that my experiences as a "mountain man" might prove to be the most valuable perspective of all. I have spent more time in natural wilderness settings with "bands" of humans than Enlightenment scholars encountered from the luxury of their armchairs. I knew from empirical experience how faulty their syllogistic scholarship was in this matter, built on "infallible" axioms of our natural rights and conditions that were uninformed and simply wrong. Build a foundation with as many cracks as Enlightenment axioms about our natural rights and conditions and whole systems lose their integrity.

The Scientific Revolution was a product of the Enlightenment. The pace of science and technology, embedded in empiricism, has both diversified and accelerated ever since. Empiricism belongs to the common man. We are all empirical scientists in our own way. The process of migrating as a species from one location to all over the globe is a scientific process undertaken by the masses, constantly learning from experience in order to adapt. So, too, does the responsibility for the Scientific Revolution range far and wide.

The Enlightenment also spawned nation states and capitalism. Fundamentalist scholarship predates the Enlightenment, but experienced new outlets during that time. The pace of economics, politics and civilization, which remain anchored still in scholasticism, lags far behind the pace of science and technology. Scholasticism belongs to the elites who think great thoughts from their armchairs…and receive great perks from those with wealth and power. Thus the responsibility for the slow pace of economics and politics lies ultimately with just a few "great" thinkers operating within stagnant systems.

One could argue that we need no further empirical experimentation with economic, political and cultural systems; that nation states and capitalism pretty much represent the pinnacle of civilization in these matters. That is hard to accept when considering that politically induced wars and economically induced famines have increased in severity of impacts to civilizations since the time of the Enlightenment. You need an impressive misinformation network like the Powell Cabal to argue that the advent of nation states and capitalism, each related to the other, had nothing to do with this. The scholars from that network might assert that we have yet to realize the true nation state or true capitalism. Yet nation states and capitalism have not evolved much in the past few hundred years, and are not likely to evolve further if we continue to trust in the political authoritarians and economic scholars that drive our systems.

Attempting to divorce one system from the other, as libertarian think tanks are inclined to do, has no empirical basis. Many a "free market libertarian" might claim that capitalism is the perfect expression of a free market, as long as you get the nation state out of the picture. Where is the evidence for that? Perhaps we have been getting the "wrong" form of capitalism with nation states, but any form of capitalism has only proved possible with the existence of nation states. Suggesting that the algae in lichen would produce better without being associated with the fungi providing protection is a bit beside the point. The two coevolved, just as nation states and capitalism coevolved. To suggest one would do well without the other is nothing more than scholastic ruminating from armchairs.

Before the Enlightenment civilizations evolved at their own pace, imitating other civilizations as their need required. All that was needed for this means of advancing civilizations were open trade networks where information flowed freely along with commerce. Since the Enlightenment the colonial powers of western civilization dictated when and how other civilizations should evolve; whether they were ready for it or not; whether they liked it or not. We are still witnesses to how well this approach works even now in the Middle East. When the wealth gets too disparate from comparative advantages and segmented markets we toss in a nice "Christmas bonus" of foreign aid ... with the condition that multinational corporations still get the business, of course.

By focusing only on the empirical evidence, and ignoring the scholarship that comes from corporate-funded endowed positions, one would conclude that nation states must not be the pinnacle of governance, and corporate capitalism must not be the pinnacle of resource distribution. In fact by this very litmus test we must conclude that the scholarship produced in economics and politics has amounted to no more than dogma. No empirical observations of history verify the ability of nation states or capitalism to provide the greatest good for the greatest number. Our form of capitalism has "worked" only if we ignore the few billion people in periphery countries that are malnourished, and just apply the standard to the core countries siphoning resources away from them. That is, in fact, the traditional method of scholasticism, adjust or constrain the meaning of experience to accommodate fixed beliefs. The scholars employing this method are bolstered by the fact that the malnourished of other countries have little voice, though their actual experiences might not matter to the lofty scholar regardless.

I do not profess to be a gifted scholar capable of declaring what should be the pinnacle of economics, politics or culture; I am but a humble empiricist, content with learning from experience as did my prehistoric ancestors. Yet together with enough humble empiricists—i.e., everyday people—allowed the decentralized independence to come up with their own solutions for how resources should be distributed and lives governed, with a means of aggregating our varied and collective experiences, we could propel ourselves forward with economic and political wisdom at a similar pace as science and technology. The means justify the ends when advancing civilizations.

That is as it should be. Changing our human systems should not be the province of authoritarians, scholars, heroes or even good leaders imposing their solutions. All we need for the task is true freedom: the free exchange of goods and independent labor without exploiting or being exploited; the free expression of independent thoughts instead of falsehoods cloaked in free speech; and the free will to independently belong to communities rather than be enslaved to corporations, political parties or special interest groups. The conditions of true independence will foster diversity and homeostasis, bringing our social systems into balance over time. Allowing these conditions to thrive may mean abandoning some sacred cows along the way, like nation states and capitalism, but the merit, wisdom and harmony we achieve would be worth the sacrifice.

We are, in fact, a nation supremely suited for empiricism. We have the best system of higher education in the world. The entrepreneurial experimentation of proprietors still thrives, albeit handicapped by our favoritism to business corporations and their enabling deregulation and mergers. We have federated governance, with fifty states performing diverse political "experiments" that can be sorted through and prioritized at the federal level. We are a nation of immigrants, with an amazing assortment of decentralized experiences to draw knowledge from. The diverse, experimental impacts of education, entrepreneurs, federation and pluralism provide whatever adaptability, stability and resiliency we have enjoyed as a nation. The conforming, dogmatic influence of business corporations, political parties and special interest groups serve only to get in the way of balanced systems.

Thank you, dear reader, for joining me in this journey. I can promise you that I have not reached the end. By the time you read this a web site has been created to further discussion about the middle class experience.[1] The web site will include an annotated bibliography for these essays. I will be performing music that delivers the message in *Systems out of Balance* to middle class communities. I will be devising college curriculum for analyzing human systems. I will help organize at least one ecumenical retreat for nurturing humility, faith and courage. Perhaps more ideas will come to me as I go along, as long as I maintain my independent thoughts.

Your help is desperately needed with this. The ultimate success of the middle class depends on the middle class as a whole, not on individual heroes or even good leaders. So please, dear reader, please continue along in this journey with me. If we are persistent and united we can reach a time when life will be full and there will be no history.

---

1 Go to www.middleclassforum.org and bookmark it .... Please!

EPILOGUE: HANS IN LUCK
A Modern Adaptation of the Brothers Grimm Fable

Hans worked for a community corporation for seven years, a corporation whose bottom line was "community" instead of "greed." At the end of his seven years he decided to return to his native home. He said to the CEO of the corporation, whom he knew well: "I have felt like one of the family working for this community corporation, but the economic times are tough and I must return to my childhood home to help my parents."

The CEO knew Hans well and was appreciative of his work. He provided to Hans a generous severance package, which in addition to unused vacation days and his savings in the bank provided Hans a considerable sum of money. That evening Hans was packing up to leave his apartment, still thinking about what he should do when he returns home with his savings. He took a break from packing to relax and turned on his 21" television—in his modest apartment he needed nothing larger.

Hans first came to a news clip of a Barack Obama campaign speech, giving some straight talk that times would be tough and the middle class would need to be part of the solution. "OK." Hans thought, "I can understand that; I'm on board. I wonder what he is going to require of us." But throughout the remainder of the inspiring speech no details were provided for what the middle class should do specifically, a common occurrence with campaign speeches from both political parties. Hans then began to channel surf.

Hans next came to an infomercial about a fitness machine that would get him into the best shape of his life and turn him into a sexy man. Yet a man who works hard and saves well is not the vain type of man compelled into buying something to stay in shape. Besides, buying a fitness machine would not help the country in tough times.

Or would it? Hans surfed to a corporate media news station. Their financial reporter was on, telling America we needed to be ardent consumers to help the economy. Hans briefly wondered if all his savings was a bad thing, contributing to the tough times of the economy. But he was aware that savings as a whole for America had gone way down to virtually zero. If spending more and saving less was a solution, it certainly had not worked well so far. Besides, Hans felt there must be some grander purpose for his savings than to vainly indulge himself.

Hans surfed to C-Span where a politician was giving a speech about how government needed to take less of taxpayers' hard earned money. He added that government needed to reduce spending by slashing welfare benefits and socialized health costs. Hans was puzzled by this. For thirty years welfare benefits have been reduced proportionally to gross domestic productivity, while the proportion of privatized to socialized health costs has increased. Hans concluded that if slashing these government costs was a solution, we were a country still waiting for such a solution to work. Besides, this was not advice for what he should do for his country, but a cynical message about what government should do for him.

Hans surfed to a corporate media news talk show where they were discussing the stock market. A pundit from a think tank discussed how the market was bad, no doubt, but that was all the more reason for a person with savings to invest now and ride the upswing. Hans currently was earning a small one-percent interest on his savings, but that was better than losing money. When the economy rebounded he knew the interest he earned would as well. True, he would not receive as great a return on savings as investing in successful stocks, but he remembered the politician's speech against welfare. What was receiving a return that exceeded the pace of economic growth but a cynical form of welfare? Cynical people do not commit income to savings in the first place and Hans resisted turning those savings into stocks. Besides, he was not sure how getting capital for nothing was going to help an economy that was hurt by generating more capital than productivity to begin with.

Hans surfed again and came upon a commercial for investing in a retirement account, featuring elderly people lounging on a Caribbean beach. One of the premises for the retirement account was the same for the stocks: through investment a person can get more than by producing and saving. There was also an additional element of apprehension in the commercial. If Hans did not invest in a retirement account, all manner of catastrophe could befall him and his loved ones in their advancing age. But Hans was only in his late twenties and unmarried, too young to be cowardly about how he might provide for retirement by the responsible means of producing and saving. Besides, this was yet another form of receiving capital for nothing, in an economy that suffered precisely from that.

Hans surfed again and came upon local news featuring a story on people's opinion of the economy. A blue collar worker was being interviewed about raising taxes on the wealthy. The worker stated: "Why tax the wealthy? They create the jobs."

Something about that interview struck Hans all wrong. For the wealthy to claim they are indispensable would come as no big surprise, but middle class workers claiming their salvation depends on the wealthy seems like a very dangerous sentiment indeed. Besides, this would render President Obama's call for the middle class to be part of the solution to be meaningless. The best Hans could do for his country would vote for the politicians that favor shifting even more of the tax burden away from capital gains to wages. Of course, corporate media would keep Hans aware who those politicians were.

Hans had heard enough from corporate media. He turned off his television and turned to his own independent thoughts, his own natural instincts for what he should do to help both himself and his country. If the middle class is not to rely on the wealthy for jobs then they must rely on themselves. The entrepreneurial spirit had called out to Hans in the past, offering independence to those with humility, faith and courage. Corporate media conveyed that the entrepreneurial spirit mainly applied to the rarified climate of mergers and takeovers, but Hans felt there might be entrepreneurial niches for those in the middle class, for those who would not rely on government or corporations to indulge their needs or excuse their responsibilities.

Hans returned to his native home, bringing with him the knowledge he accumulated from his old job. He used some of his savings to start his own proprietorship, with the intention that this may also become a corporation whose profits were devoted to serving "community" rather than "greed" some day. He used some of his savings to fix up the home of his parents to become resource efficient to the point of being almost resource independent, and to build an add-on after he got married.

Sharing the resource efficient house with his parents allowed Hans to build his savings up quickly again. When he eventually bought the house from his parents, they did not try to make a huge profit on the sales. After all, that would be just another case of trying to get extra value not backed by productivity. They received enough for them to remain autonomous in their golden years; though Hans let them know he would take care of them if the need arose. Meanwhile, the reasonable price Hans paid for the house, while homes around him inflated independently of their real value, minimized his mortgage and contributed further to his ability to produce and save.

Hans never did invest in stocks or retirement accounts. Between Social Security and his own savings he was able to retire comfortably. True, he could not indulge himself with vacations to Caribbean beaches on a yearly basis, but he chalked this up as part of the "sacrifice" he made for the sake of what ultimately was in the best interest of both himself and his country. Throughout his life Hans considered himself to be a very lucky man.

AUTHOR'S BIOGRAPHY

Kirk Sinclair earned a Bachelors of Arts in Mathematics from the University of Connecticut; a Bachelors of Science in Biology from Eastern Connecticut State University; a Masters in Science Education from Cornell University; and a Doctorate in Natural Resources from Cornell University. During that time he also accumulated minor concentrations of credits in Sociology, English, Statistics, Chemistry, Urban Studies, Ecology and Environmental Information Technologies. Kirk has been a teacher in both traditional and alternative education settings at the elementary, high school, college and university settings. On his last day as a high school teacher the student body gave Kirk a standing ovation during an awards assembly, though whether this was out of gratitude or relief he never knew. Trained as a Geographic Information Systems (GIS) specialist, Kirk created and managed the GIS Department for the Housatonic Valley Association, a nonprofit conservation organization. He has presented at international, national, regional and local forums regarding GIS applications and natural resource issues. Kirk has received awards for teaching, research, singing, writing and long-distance backpacking. In 1985 Kirk was the third person to achieve the Triple Crown of long-distance backpacking, having organized the first successful expeditions to backpack the Pacific Crest Trail and Continental Divide Trails, in addition to having backpacked the Appalachian Trail three times. Kirk's then fiancée Cindy Galvin hiked the Continental Divide with him and they still married afterwards, perhaps Kirk's greatest accomplishment to date. Kirk and Cindy have three children. Noah, Charissa and Serena get their good looks and charisma from their Mom. They refuse to comment on what they got from Dad.

ACKNOWLEDGEMENTS

I am grateful for those who reviewed the material in my book. Nels White in particular was thorough in his review and comments; most of the rewrites that occurred were due to his input. Mark Brown reviewed and commented on the economic essays, in addition to providing hours of stimulating conversation that factored into the writing and rewriting of those essays. Teri Padua provided editorial feedback while Nancy Pfaff and Bill Esborn provided comments on content. My wife, Cindy, provided large measures of encouragement throughout the four-year process.

I would like to thank the people at Mill City Press for their assistance in getting my first book published. In particular, Michelle Brown served as my liaison with the publication process; Jenni Wheeler coordinated the production process; Kristeen Wegner formatted the interior layout; Wes Moore designed the cover; and Sarah Kolb was the back cover copy editor. Sara Tonko and Rosey Cashman coordinated the book's web site publication, and marketing.

Printed in the United States
219421BV00001B/2/P